The Mighty Eight..
WAR MANUAL

The Mighty Eighth

WAR MANUAL

ROGER A. FREEMAN

with drawings by Norman Ottaway

CASSELL

Cassell
Wellington House, 125 Strand
London WC2R 0BB

First published by Jane's Publishing Company 1984
This corrected edition 2001
Reprinted 2002

British Library Cataloguing-in-Publication Data
A catalogue record for this book is available from the
British Library

ISBN 0-304-35846-0

Distributed in the USA by
Sterling Publishing Co. Inc.
387 Park Avenue South
New York
NY 10016-8810

Printed and bound in Great Britain by
The Bath Press, Bath

Acknowledgements

The compilation of material for this book owes much to the
contributions and help of many individuals. In addition to his
excellent draughtsmanship, Norman Ottaway advised on matters relating to airfields. Patricia Keen spent many hours seeking obscure details in US archives, while Alan Crouchman
extracted large amounts of information from microfilms. Rowley
Andrews, John Archer, Mike Bailey, Roy Baker, Dana Bell, Cliff
Bishop, Stan Bishop, Al Blue, David Carpenter, Pat Carty, Peter
Corbell, David Crow, Stewart Evans, Peter Frost, Garry Fry, Mick
Gibson, Chris Gotts, Steve Gotts, Charlie Gallagher, Roy Hand-
forth, Ken Harbour, Harry Holmes, Martin Jeffrey, Bill Larkins,
Ron Mackay, Vic Maslen, Danny Morris, Tony North, Malcolm
Osborn, Dave Osborne, Gordon Richards, Kenn Rust, Graham
Simons, Martin Streetly, Geoff Word and the 100th Bomb Group
Association officers were among others who assisted. Many 8th
Air Force veterans responded to my requests, including Edward
Anderson, James Coffey, Willis Cude, Clyde Christian, Phillip
Day, Francis DiMola, Bobby Dodd, John Driscoll, George Dup-
ont, Charles Freudenthal, Arthur Gulliver, Leon Hendrickson,
Pete Henry, Dick Hairston, Joe Hollywood, Don Hyde, Ed Hunt-
zinger, William Jameson, Sheldon Kirsher, Fred Krueger,
Tommy Land, Will Lundy, Howard Moore, Claude Muvoay, Willy
Noble, Merle Olmsted, George Parks, Louis Pennow, Robert
Powell, Fred Rabo, Larry Redman, Paul Reeves, Ed Richie, Bill
Robertie, Rick Rokicki, Russell Ross, Joe Soder, William San-
ders, Glesner Weckbacker, K. C. Winslow, John Woolnough
and Earl Zimmerman.

The staffs of the Imperial War Museum, RAF Museum and
Public Record Office in the UK, and those of the National
Archives and USAF Historical Research Center in the USA
were ever helpful.

Major General John W. Huston, USAF(Ret), gave pertinent
advice that was much appreciated, Bruce Robertson provided
extensive editorial assistance, Jean Freeman undertook the
marathon manuscript typing task, Ken Ranson proofed the copy
and John Archer the galleys. John Rabbets once again produced an attractive jacket painting and Alex Vanags-Baginskis,
the publisher's editor, patiently accommodated my foibles.

To all I extend my most sincere thanks.

Roger A. Freeman
Dedham, England

April 1984

Contents

Introduction

This is the final volume in a trilogy concerning the United States Eighth Air Force in the Second World War. First of the three, *The Mighty Eighth*, is a general history of the organisation with emphasis on the units, men and aircraft, while the following *Mighty Eighth War Diary* features a daily record of operations. This present volume covers the operational techniques and the equipment employed by this Force, together with a study of its special projects and support facilities. While complementary and a companion to the other *Mighty Eighth* volumes, this is, nevertheless, a completely self-contained book, and in no way dependant on the earlier works.

In terms of men and machines, the Eighth Air Force was the largest air striking force ever committed to battle. The complexities of putting two thousand bombers and fighters *in a single day* over Hitler's Reich were extraordinary and might involve, directly and indirectly, one hundred and fifty thousand men and women. The daily logistical requirements could be enormous: some three million gallons of fuel, four thousand tons of bombs and four and a half million rounds of ammunition to give just the major items. And such efforts were often repeated for several days in succession. This book tells how and with what it was done.

A further Mighty Eighth volume, companion to the three books in the trilogy, is also published by Cassell. Featuring the men and machines of the Eighth Air Force in full colour, *The Mighty Eighth: The Colour Record* is a much expanded version of Roger Freeman's earlier book *The Mighty Eighth in Colour* and presents an unparalled collection of contemporary colour photographs of the Mighty Eighth in action.

PART 1 OPERATIONAL TECHNIQUE AND PROCEDURE

Bombers

Heavy Bomber Mission Procedure

Bombing operations against strategic targets was the primary mission of the 8th Air Force. During the 983 days of its campaign the fundamental technique of these operations remained the same – daylight high-altitude precision bombing employing large formations of heavy bombers. Detail changes to improve performance and meet enemy counteraction were frequently introduced as operations progressed, but there was no departure from the basic tactical doctrine established in the first few months of combat.

The following description of the procedures involved in mounting and executing a heavy bomber operation is typical of the winter of 1943–44.

Variations of this form did occur within individual units, but these, and changes made during the remainder of hostilities, were minor and did not affect the overall scheme. Studies of individual facets of heavy bomber operations are detailed in following chapters.

Unless requested by a higher command, all bomber operations were initiated by VIII Bomber Command in compliance with the priority listing of objectives in the Combined Bomber Offensive directives. Headquarters, 8th Air Force at Bushey Park, Teddington, was concerned mainly with operational policy and administration. However, in February 1944, when this Headquarters (Hq) was utilised for an over-all headquarters for the direction of both 8th and 15th Air Forces and renamed Hq, United States Strategic Air Forces in Europe, the VIII Bomber Command at High Wycombe (code name *Pinetree*) became the new Hq, 8th Air Force, combining most functions of the old Hq 8th AF and Hq VIII BC – the latter then being defunct. This reorganisation had little effect on operational procedures.

The principal controlling factor for operations was weather. Every day at 1015, 1600 and 2200 hours weather briefings were held at High Wycombe from which senior operations officers obtained the forecasts of conditions in prospective target areas and for the bomber bases. With the advent and availability of radar 'blind bombing' devices, weather forecast for the target area was no longer the make or break point for operating as in earlier days; some targets with distinctive topography could be attacked with a high chance of success using the new technology. Prior to radar aids, adverse next-day weather forecasts at 1600 hours would generally prohibit operations. Even if the target forecast was favourable, a mission would not be considered if bad weather was predicted for base areas. A large force of bombers could not formate in severely restricted visibility or other dangerous conditions.

With the elements forecast as favourable, the Deputy Commander of Operations, or his assistant, would be notified while the Operations staff selected suitable targets from the priority list. The scale of an operation would also be influenced by weather. A stable high pressure situation with clear skies promising good visibility to allow visual bombing were the conditions sought to make a concentrated attack on one of the most important targets in the priority list. Where some cloud was likely to be present, and accurate attack less certain, the bombers might be split between two or among three primary targets to spread their chances of success. Frequently only part of enemy territory could be given a suitable weather forecast, thus restricting the selection of targets to that area.

Many factors other than weather were instrumental in target decisions, not least the availability of crews and aircraft. Deep penetrations of hostile airspace could only be prudently undertaken by a very large force of bombers.

Having considered the advice of experts on his staff, the Deputy Commander of Operations (Chief of Operations) would make the final decision at an operational conference held during the early evening. Another operational conference followed at 2220 hours to review an up-dated weather forecast and any further pertinent information available. Changes might be made, or the proposed operations cancelled, if there were signs of a deterioration in weather prospects. However, all crucial decisions had usually been taken by this time and subordinate headquarters in the chain of command informed. The decisions made at *Pinetree* involved targets, the force required to destroy them, plus a co-ordinated plan for the participating divisions.

While this information would be incorporated in a formal Field Order directing the Force into action, its final form could not be compiled at that stage. As the maximum possible warning time was needed by participating units to prepare aircraft and brief personnel, most of the operational directives reached units as an advance to a Field Order.

The three Bomb Division headquarters would receive advance warning of an impending operation soon after the first conference decision at High Wycombe; they then alerted the Combat Wings who in turn gave notice to the individual groups. Once Division received the target and ordnance requirements they could be planned in detail. Their specialists studied target identifications, established Mean Points of Impact (MPI) for bomb strikes, calculated bomb tonnages and prescribed the types – demolition, incendiary, etc – assessed the force of aircraft needed, plotted routes and times, specified altitudes and, in consultation with VIII Fighter Command, arranged fighter support. This information was passed by teleprinter to combat wing headquarters as it became available. This advance information to the Field Order gave the essential details for both combat wing and group to initiate preparations – target (by coded reference), order of combat wings and the number of squadrons in each, together with a tentative route and times.

The combat wing headquarters was concerned almost exclusively with operational matters, its prime function being to produce a co-ordinated plan for its groups – normally three – for all stages of a combat mission and to act as the controlling agency during its execution. A succession of annexes to teletype mes-

Teleprinter operators send out Field Orders. Pfc William Archer using a British machine at Brampton Grange.

crews and aircraft available from the other three squadrons. Likewise, lead crew commitment followed a prescribed rota. A schedule of crews to be called in the event of a mission was posted at squadron sites at a set hour the previous evening in some bases.

With the arrival of the advance to the Field Order, the selected aircraft and crews for the mission were chalked up on a blackboard using a schematic formation plan. Each aircraft was represented by a T-shaped device with the pilot's name above the head, identifying the crew. The last three digits of the aircraft serial number, plus squadron call-letter and, at times, the number of the hardstanding where it was parked, were marked around the tail of the T. These details being posted as quickly as possible after the advance to the Field Order had been received, duty clerks from equipment, engineering, armament and other sections involved went to Operations to obtain pertinent information. Formation plans and relevant data were duplicated on paper forms by Group Operations staff for distribution to pilots and briefing officers.

A copy of the initial teletype message from Operations gave the S-2 duty officer the target, by coded number. The S-2 Intelligence Office, sometimes housed in the same building as S-3 Operations, was more usually in a large adjacent Nissen type structure. The hub of S-2 Intelligence was the War Room, most secret establishment on the base. Adjoining this was the cipher office kept under lock and key, where the duty officer obtained the cipher book to decode the target reference. He then withdrew the appropriate target folder from the large stock filed – approximately 1500 had been amassed in most bomber group intelligence sections by the end of hostilities.

Each target folder contained a clear vertical photograph of the target to a standard size. A transparency with numbered grid lines was placed over the print and by reference to a number code in the teletype order, the required MPI – centre of desired bomb pattern on target – was established. Target information from S-2 files was then dispensed to Group Operations and the Bombardier and Navigator offices which were usually in the same headquarters building. The principal function of S-2 was to provide all necessary intelligence data for briefing officers and combat personnel from the continually up-dated target files, concerning all forms of enemy defences.

In another part of the Intelligence building staff began to assemble the maps, photographs and other relevant material

sages followed back and forth along the chain of command, notifying corrections and adding new information. Division teleprinter messages to combat wings were also transmitted to combat groups.

The Group, the principal combat unit, received a first warning of an impending mission in the form of a telephone message on the secret 'scrambler' line in Group Operations' Message Center. This usually came in late afternoon or early evening if a major mission was scheduled for the following day. Short-range or small force missions might first be advised in the early hours of the morning of the operation. The Watch Officer in the windowless, gas-proof, constantly manned Group Operations building immediately instructed his duty clerk to notify all services on the base that would become involved. The list commenced with the Group CO or his stand-in, the Air Executive, S-3 Group Operations Officer, S-2 Intelligence Section, Group Navigator and Bombardier Officers, Weather Office, Flying Control, ordnance and armament sections, engineering office, the signals and photographic units, mess hall, transportation (motor pool) and the Charge of Quarters (CQ) on each squadron living site. This telephoned message would be no more than a simple 'Mission Alert' message to prepare each section for the receipt of a field order. If this occurred in the afternoon or early evening, an hour or two might elapse before the first advance information stuttered out of the teleprinter machine in Group Operations. Meanwhile the duty officer informed the guard room, told the base telephone exchange to restrict calls and requested the Military Police detachment to post MPs at the doors of Operations and the War Room – the main office of the Intelligence Section. On the living sites CQs raised the red flag, restricting personnel to the camp. At some stations a red light was lit over the bars at officer's and NCO's clubs – which theoretically shut off the supply of spirits to flying personnel.

The advance information to a Field Order usually gave the numbers of aircraft the group was to prepare, with bomb and fuel loads. Following the alert squadron operations officers would proceed to the Group Operations building to obtain this information. Their immediate task was to make any last minute amendments to crew and aircraft status boards on the walls of the operations room. From these a tentative availability list was drawn up. It was general practice for one squadron to stand down on every fourth mission unless there were special circumstances such as a 'maximum effort' requirement or insufficient

S/Sgt Lloyd Baskerville 'pulling' target files in 385th BG Operations, October 1943.

for navigators and bombardiers while the photographic laboratory copied 'flak charts' and 'Mission flimsies' prepared in the war room. In Operations the route to the target was plotted on a wall map using different colour cotton thread or, if the map had a protecting transparent sheet, with a red grease pencil. The Group navigator's office plotted courses and distances and times for assembly. On receipt of weather information giving temperatures and wind data expected on route, the air speeds, ground speeds and drift on various legs to be flown were calculated and checked against times given in the Division figures received. The Group bombardier's office obtained information from Intelligence, Navigators, and the Weather Officer to assess target conditions and with speeds, drift and heading data computed bombsight settings for the attack altitude.

Information in the advance to the Field Order varied and many sections of a group were often kept in suspense for several hours before the pertinent information they required chattered out of the Operations teleprinter. The actual Field Order from Division might be delayed for some hours, while details were worked out and checked at that command – in some cases seven or eight hours could pass. More usually it would come late in the evening or around midnight, taking the teleprinter several minutes to disgorge on a strip of yellow paper, frequently running to three or four feet in length. Bomb load was often not available until now, and sometimes the all important 'zero hour'.

Zero hour was a planning reference point for the launch of the mission, common to all participating units. The actual time would be identified in an annex to the Field Order. In the meantime it allowed a group to set up a time schedule based on

Windowless Operations Block building had wall boards on which current status of crews and aircraft were maintained to provide operations staff with a ready up-to-date reference for use in scheduling missions. At Bury St Edmunds crews and aircraft available for combat were divided into 'A' and 'B' groups when the 'double group' procedure was introduced in December 1943. Staff are (l. to r.): Capt James Ainsworth, Lt David Vinson, Lt Mathew Murray, Sgt M. D. Horn, Lt Col Louis Thorup, (Air Executive) and S/Sgt Joe Haddonfield. The 457th BG status board at Glatton followed the more usual form of listing under squadrons. Photograph taken in May 1945 when combat operations had finished.

Above: **In the early morning mists, the ground crew still toils on 303rd's *Green Hornet*, January 1943.**

Right: **Two hours before sunrise Corporals Jacob Orth, Virgil Comer (centre, almost hidden from view) and Albert Scherzinger commence to load the bay of a 94th BG Fortress with 500 pounders; a slow laborious job, December 1943.**

intervals removed from Zero Hour. These considerations were an hour, at a minimum, for formation assembly from the time of first take-off – more in adverse conditions; 10 or 15 minutes for marshalling and taxiing, 10 or 15 minutes for engine starting, 10 minutes for 'stations' – crew in aircraft. Then 'readiness' – crews at their aircraft a minimum hour before engine start, main briefings for crews a minimum hour before going to the bombers, breakfast an hour before briefing and crews awakened a half-hour before that. As Group Operations made out the schedule more annexes to teletype messages would come in, correcting or adding new information. A Field Order from the combat wing followed that from Division, generally within an hour. It covered, in detail, the order and formations to be flown by groups within the combat wing, assembly instructions, order of bombing at the target and post-target rally. Annexes might also be received to this Field Order.

As soon as the bomb load was known the information was passed to Ordnance who already had a list of the aircraft scheduled for the mission. Bomb loading crews, already alerted, were on hand at the bomb dump office. Most tried to get some sleep until the telephone rang, invariably in the middle of the night. Ordnance's job was to load the required bombs onto the special bomb trailers at the dump and convey them to the aircraft.

Armament's task was to place the bombs in aircraft bays. In practice both Ordnance and Armament men worked together on hauling and loading, the line of demarcation being arbitrary. The vehicles commonly used by Ordnance were Dodge trucks fitted with a hoist over the rear axle. A tricycle low-loading trolley pulled behind this vehicle could be loaded by the hoist. Loading was a slow operation; Ordnance men preferred to roll bombs from the piled rows in the dump across two wood beams onto the trailer bed. A trailer could hold a maximum of 6000 lb, a load for one bomber. With B-17s the trailer could be backed right under the bomb-bay, but for B-24s it was necessary to off-load the bombs onto special steel cradles. These were them picked up on a hand jack-trolley and manoeuvred under the low bomb-bay. Bomb fins were fitted at the hardstandings before the bombs were winched into the bays.

The armourer in each bomber ground crew had previously started the 'putt-putt' (auxiliary power plant), a two-stroke petrol engine generator, to boost the aircraft's electrical supply. He tested all the release mechanisms for the racks to ensure they were functioning properly prior to bomb loading. Squadron armament men on each bomb loading vehicle crew – usually four – loaded the bombs by hand, later electric, cable winch in the bay. Stainless steel shackles were first fitted to the two lugs on the bomb and the two-cable hoist used to elevate it to the desired position on the vertical rack where the shackle was attached to the rack. Once all were in place an Ordnance man screwed in the nose or tail fuses and safetied them with a pin and wire to prevent the arming vane spinning and arming the bomb while the aircraft was still on the ground. With some groups, fuses were fitted before loading as this made the task easier. This practice was, however, considered dangerous. Working in bomb-bays was difficult, being fairly confined spaces with poor lighting. The work was arduous and it was easy to sustain an injury working with such heavy objects in semi-darkness. Moreover, if a mission was 'scrubbed' (cancelled), armament and ordnance men would have the equally tiresome job of removing all bombs and transporting them back to the bomb dump.

Other ordnance men collected ammunition from the sheds adjacent to the bomb dump, using flat surface trolleys to convey them to the bombers. The rounds had previously been belted by the armament section and then stored in wooden boxes. These were placed in the aircraft at prescribed locations ready for gunners to set up when they arrived. The quantity of ammunition specified for each attack depended on the opposition expected and depth of penetration into hostile airspace, although it was usually not less than 5000 rounds. The .50-calibre guns, always removed from aircraft after a mission for cleaning, were usually stored in squadron armouries on the technical site. Another armament team vehicle collected and dispensed these weapons. To protect them from the elements they were placed inside the aircraft or in the ground crew's tent beside each dispersal point.

Above: **M103 nose fuses being delivered and fitted to RDX-filled M-64s prior to loading in 'M Plus' at Hethel, May 1944. An armed guard patrolled outlying dispersal points during darkness and preparations for launch of a mission. Note yellow stripes along edge of bomb-bay doors to enable their position to be checked from other aircraft in a formation.**

Left: **Armourers preparing to hoist an M-43 into a 93rd BG B-24D, November 1943. Note narrow central catwalk which was only 10 ins wide.**

The first combat personnel to be awakened were the lead crew officers, the specially trained men who would lead the group formation. They rose at least a half-hour before the main body of fliers and four hours before take-off, to attend a series of pre-briefings at Operations or the War Room. Lead navigators and bombardiers were given target and route details and on a 1/25,000 scale map picked out check points and numbered them. Command pilots received similar pertinent information. All these key men then received a general briefing together in one of the buildings, aimed at ensuring that they were conversant with the task ahead. The lead crews would then be driven to breakfast, although at some bases they would eat before any briefing.

Meanwhile the rest of the men to be involved in the day's operations were wakened. For many combatants there may have been only fitful sleep, the mission alert putting them in an apprehensive state of mind. The CQ, the duty sergeant on each living site, entered each hut and called the names of men scheduled to fly. Although enlisted men and officers were billeted separately, those on the same crew usually shared the same living quarters, so the CQ had only to call the crew name –

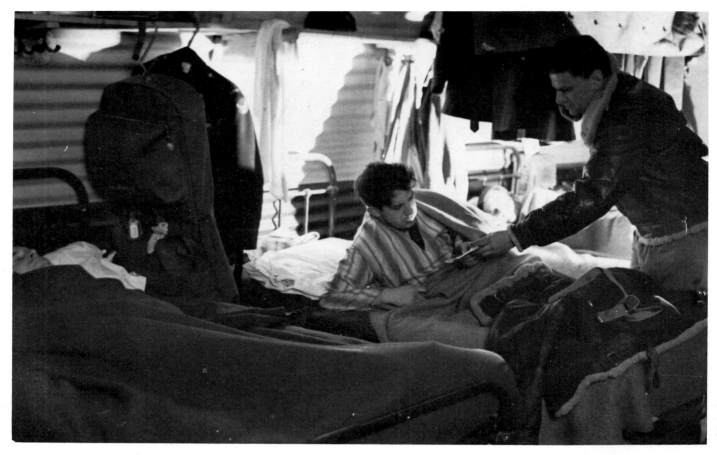

Above: **The CQ – Sgt Jack Gordon – wakes aircrew at Bury St Edmunds, December 1943. Lt Russ Laubaugh is being shaken from his slumbers to go to war.**

Right: **Lt John McMickling and Sgt Jerome Gans marking the planned route with pinned red ribbon on the Briefing Room map at Great Ashfield, October 1943.**

Below right: **Capt Pollock handing out data sheets to aircrew in the 385th BG Briefing Room, October 1943.**

Far right: **Col Irvine Rendle, CO 392nd BG gives bombardiers a time 'hack' for synchronisation of their watches at the termination of briefing, June 1944. Group Bombardier, Capt Harold Weiland (left) sports a .45 pistol. The carrying of such individual weapons on missions was not encouraged although policy differed from group to group.**

that of the first pilot. To crews being awakened at 2 or 3 o'clock in the morning to go to war was a most objectionable feature of this form of warfare. Thirty minutes were allowed for dressing, a wash and shave, visit to the latrine and getting to the Mess Hall. Shaving was essential to prevent discomfort in an oxygen mask. Some living sites were half a mile from the mess halls and transportation was made available. Men billeted nearby were expected to walk or use bicycles.

Cooks and kitchen staff were awakened an hour before the combatants to prepare breakfast of non-flatulent foods. For those on the mission this consisted of grapefruit juice, cereal (oatmeal or post toasties), toast and coffee with either eggs or flapjacks as the main dish. The eggs were the much detested powdered form. However, as organisation prospered, fresh eggs became available for combat crews only. The Combat Mess on the communal site consisted of a central cookhouse connected to two large dining halls, one each side. There was ample capacity to feed the 200 to 400 men, the Group's combatants for a mission. Transport to convey the men from the Mess Halls to the Briefing Rooms was on hand a half-hour after breakfast began. The six-wheel 2½-ton GMC covered truck was general transport around the base; each could squeeze in two or three bomber crews. Briefing was normally planned for an hour and a half after the crews were awakened.

The large briefing room complexes were usually situated close to the flying field near the technical site. Each of the two rooms could seat 200 men and they were joined by linking corridors. At some stations officers and enlisted men were briefed together, at others separately in different rooms or buildings. Generally a large Nissen, the Briefing Room had a raised podium at one end above which, on the wall, was suspended a large-scale map of western Europe. Prior to briefing a duty clerk from Operations had marked out the mission route, target and fighter rendezvous points on the map, using coloured ribbons and pins. The map was then hidden by curtains so that its implications were not known to those entering for briefing.

The main briefing was not without a touch of staged drama as the Briefing Officer, or Group Commander, entered and marched down between the rows of seated airmen to the dais and drew back the curtains. If the target was particularly important or involved special circumstances the Group CO would open or close the proceedings with encouraging words. The briefing officer had to be articulate, concise and accurate in his delivery. As his audience would be tense he was expected to provide some light relief to alleviate tensions. A good briefing officer could regularly lift morale.

Inevitably there was audience reaction when the curtains were drawn back. The target name and depth of penetration involved would signify whether or not the impending mission was particularly perilous. The exclamations and wisecracks

following this exposure were means of relieving tension. The Operations Officer, or his delegate, then briefed on the importance of the target, route, check points and mission procedure. He was followed by an Intelligence Officer who dealt with target detail and enemy defences. Using an epidiascope or projector, target photos were presented on a screen. Finally, the staff weather officer went over known and forecast conditions for the flight. Prior to closing the session the principal briefing officer invited questions and then called for a 'time hack', calling a count-down so that all crewmen could synchronise their watches. The main briefing averaged about 40 minutes, following which bombardiers and navigators moved to an adjacent room or rooms to make their individual preparations with Operations and Intelligence staff on hand to help and advise.

Navigators collected maps and 'flimsies' (special destructible information sheets) from the distribution point in the room and sat at tables to draw up their flight plans. Although the Group would fly as a formation each individual navigator had to ply his trade as if his bomber was making a solitary sortie. Bombardiers studied target data and photographs, noting prominent features that were to be used as check points. Meanwhile pilots sat around in the same room going over engine control data while waiting for any last minute instructions. After briefing, co-pilots went to the personal equipment store nearby to obtain the whole crew's evasion kits.

The gunners' briefing usually took place in an adjacent room or building. In early 8th Air Force operations, when the group force despatched was smaller, all crewmen had attended the same briefing, gunners sitting at the back. By winter 1943–44 another Intelligence Officer usually conducted the separate gunners' session, covering general details of the missions, concentrating on enemy defences, particularly the latest known deployment of fighter forces and where interceptions were most likely to be encountered. He was followed by an Operations

Above: **Col Fred Castle, CO 94th BG, concludes a briefing in December 1943 with a personal 'Godspeed' and 'good luck' to crews about to fly a mission to Emden, 11 Dec 1943. Formation diagram has been hung over target wall map to conceal target from photograph.**

Left: **During the Frantic shuttle missions of summer 1944 briefing for the second leg – Soviet Union to Italy – often had to be conducted in the open. The wall of a bombed-out railway building and rough wooden bench served the briefing officer on this occasion at Poltava. Crews are from 96th and 452nd BGs.** (Via M. Gibson)

Below left: **In the inaptly named Peace Room at Hethel, 389th BG navigators draw up their flight plans following the main briefing, May 1944.**

Officer who briefed on altitudes, weather, escort fighter types and rendezvous. A senior group officer also put in an appearance and gave words of encouragement. The gunners' briefing, shorter than the officers', averaged about 20 minutes. Gunners then walked to the personal equipment store attached to the briefing room complex to collect flight rations, electrical flying suits or heavy clothing, harness and parachutes, oxygen masks and Mae Wests (inflatable life jackets), at the same time handing in personal belongings from pockets for safe keeping.

Gunners then dressed in the Flight Equipment Room (Locker Room) and moved out to the waiting trucks. Radio Operators, however, stayed behind after briefing to receive signals information and any special radio and wireless procedures. Before going to collect their equipment and dress they would each receive the day's wireless codes, radio call signs and frequencies on a sheet of rice paper anchored between two pieces of celluloid – to prevent the precious document from being sucked or blown out of the aircraft. With the increasing availability of electrically-heated flying suits, airmen were supplied with large carrying bags in which all personal equipment could be carried from the Locker Room to the aircraft where flying clothes were then put on. Apart from protection from the elements, the bag aided in preventing individual items being misplaced.

The gunners were joined by their officers in the trucks. The co-pilot would be on hand first to see all his crew's gunners were present with correct equipment and to give out escape packs. Sometimes bombardiers or navigators might be delayed because of last minute changes or corrections and the crew trucks would leave for the aircraft dispersals without them. As it was essential that gunners arrived at the bomber in good time to prepare their weapons, at some stations gunners were transported separately.

Group Engineering roused aircraft mechanics to pre-flight the bombers at least three hours before take-off. Those ground crew chiefs whose aircraft were scheduled, often went to their charges soon after the mission alert was received and got what sleep they could in the hardstand tent. Each bomber had two ground mechanics assigned, a Crew Chief and an Assistant Crew Chief. These two administered the same aircraft and it became 'their plane' far more than the aircrew's who flew it. In any case, the policy of assigning a particular aircraft to a particular flight crew proved impractical and was generally discontinued during the later stages of the war. The armourer was the third member of the ground crew team, usually assigned to one aircraft but sometimes having to serve two. He was the first member of the ground crew at the aircraft, and most armourers tried to steal some sleep in the tent before the crew chief arrived by cycle to carry out pre-flight checks.

The two mechanics would begin by 'pulling through the props', the laborious job of pulling on each propeller blade to turn the engine and remove any fuel that had accumulated in the cylinders overnight. The crew chief then climbed into the cockpit and went through the engine priming procedure. After starting the 'putt-putt' to boost battery power, his assistant, with fire extinguisher at the ready, positioned himself where he could see hand signs from the cockpit. The first engine started was that which drove the electrical generators. Each engine was then run up and held at maximum revolutions to check oil pressure, turbo-supercharger and magneto performance. Propeller feathering mechanism was also tested and all electrical and hydraulic functions that could be safely carried out while the aircraft was parked. With everything satisfactory the engines would be shut down to await the 'gas wagon' which visited every aircraft scheduled for the mission to top fuel tanks.

Unless the mission was of very limited duration tanks were topped off to allow a large reserve in case of emergencies. A full load for both B-17 and B-24 was approximately 2800 US gallons, representing nearly one quarter of the gross weight at take-off. The 100 octane gasoline was power-pumped from the

Below: **Ice and snow made the ground crew's lot particularly unpleasant and in January 1945 there were many days when such conditions occurred. This 'on the line' scene was photographed at Nuthamstead.** (M. Osborn)

Bottom: **Topping up the tanks of an H2X pathfinder at Bury St Edmunds, June 1944. Although assigned to the 333rd BS, 94th BG at this base, the aircraft served as a pathfinder for 385th BG and its specially trained crew were from that unit.**

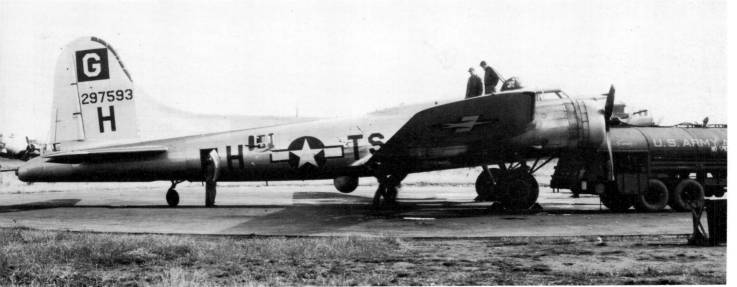

tanker vehicle, a member of the 'gas crew' going out onto the upper surface of the wings to the filling points while the others manhandled up the fuel hose and worked the controls. The oxygen truck also visited each scheduled bomber to conduct an oxygen check and replenish any bottles not registering full.

On those aircraft scheduled to carry strike cameras – which operated automatically at pre-set intervals to record bomb strikes on the target – the 'photo man' arrived with a K-21 type to install. The camera well in a B-17 was beneath the radio room floor, accessible through a door in that compartment. In the B-24 it was situated to the rear of the fuselage floor hatch. After securing the camera the photo mechanic set the shutter speed, aperture opening and the heater switch to prevent the mechanism freezing at altitude.

Flight crews arrived at their bomber at least an hour before the scheduled take-off time. This gave gunners time to carefully inspect their weapons, clean them again if necessary, and remove surplus oil which might freeze at altitude, before installing each gun on its mount. Assistance from the ground crew armourer was necessary when installing turret guns. To avoid accidental firing, guns were not charged with ammunition until after leaving the English coast.

Gunners of 379th BG's *Pistol Packin' Mama* putting on flight equipment before entering the aircraft for a mission to France, February 1944. Left to right they are: **Sgts Leonard Walter, Ernest Davis, Arthur Murrey** (in doorway), **Joe Martin and Eugene House** (in waist window).

While gunners were busy the pilot filled out the crew Loading List and the Form 1A for the ground crew chief and went over details with him. This form gave the current engineering status of the aircraft and was used by the crew chief to record servicing and repair work. Pilot and crew chief then walked round the aircraft together, inspecting tyres, movable flying surfaces, fuel vents, propellers, wing de-icing boots and undercarriage struts as a final visual check to ensure everything was satisfactory. Flak suits (body armour) and steel helmets had earlier been delivered to the dispersal point, being placed in either the bomber or the nearby tent. In the latter case these were now taken to the aircraft with other personal gear. Often officers, pilots and navigators in particular, did not have time to don flying suits before coming out to the aircraft. There was usually time to spare at the hardstand and the flight crew could lounge in the tent having a last cigarette.

Ten minutes before 'start engines' each crew member checked out one another's safety harness (parachutes straps and Mae West) before climbing aboard the bomber to man 'stations'. Most men chose to enter a B-17 by the rear fuselage door and walk forward through the bomb-bay. Athletic bombardiers and navigators pulled themselves up through the nose hatch door but it was difficult in heavy flying clothes. On B-24s the rear fuselage could be reached via a ladder through the floor hatch. Most men, however, chose to stoop down under the open bomb-bay and get onto the narrow catwalk to go forward to the flight deck. Navigator and bombardier could gain access through the nose wheel hatch. However, for safety they took up positions on the flight deck behind the pilots during take-off. The roll-up Liberator bomb doors were kept open while the aircraft

was parked or taxiing to dispel any fuel fumes which might collect from the fuel transfer system at the forward end of the bay.

Engines were started 25 minutes before scheduled take-off and ten minutes before taxiing time. A green flare fired from flying control was the start signal. This allowed the pilots to run up engines, repeating those checks carried out by the crew chief two or three hours earlier. The flight engineer – who also served as top turret gunner – stood behind the pilots and monitored instruments and gauges. To conserve fuel it became practice for the high squadron to wait five minutes and the low ten minutes after the lead before starting engines. At the appointed time to move, the pilot signalled the ground crew man who was watching the cockpit to remove the wheel chocks. If there was a long access track from the dispersal point to the perimeter track the bomber taxied to a safe distance from the track, then halted – a misjudgement of distance could result in the nose or a propeller fouling the wingtip of a passing bomber. Pilots knowing their take-off order from the flight plan, watched for an aircraft with the tail call-letter that should precede them to pass their dispersal before turning out onto the perimeter track. Taxiing demanded much more skill in a B-17 than in a B-24, as it was not possible to see directly ahead over the nose. Caution was essential, particularly in winter, for once a main wheel ran off the concrete the bomber could bog down, making it necessary for following aircraft to take a longer and more tortuous route to the head of the runway.

The runway in use would be dictated by the direction and force of the wind but the main, long runway was preferred and used whenever possible. The leadplane – often the two wing aircraft of the lead element as well – pulled squarely onto the head of the runway, and the tail or nose wheel leg was locked. Following bombers held 'cab rank' on a perimeter, spaced about a bomber's length apart. Usually squadrons approached from the side of the runway head nearest their dispersal area. Marshalling and taxiing was a noisy business with between 100 and 160 powerful open-exhaust engines running and the frequent squeal of brakes. Each bomber would consume about 60 gallons of fuel during this period. Order of taxiing was lead, high and low formation position squadrons.

Right: Ground crews who had been up since the small hours could at last go for breakfast. Molesworth 'chow' was reckoned to be good.

Below: Slightly angled across the perimeter track so that pilots' forward view is not obstructed by the nose turret, Liberators of 445th BG wait 'cab rank' at Tibenham for take-off, D-Day, 1944. (J. Archer)

Meanwhile the Group Operations Officer was in the control tower where he arrived by Jeep prior to 'start engines'. His duty there was to supervise the take-off and deal with any problems that might arise. If a bomber blew a tyre and obstructed the runway, or some other emergency occurred, it was his responsibility to assign another runway for use or take whatever action was necessary to launch the mission. Delay had to be avoided at all costs. He could contact pilots via their Command radios, but this only in a case of dire necessity as it was feared too frequent use of radio would forewarn the enemy radio listening service of an impending mission. With the vast increase in air activity over south-east England during early 1944, the use of radio for tower-to-aircraft communication was relaxed.

Take-off commenced when a green light was flashed from the checkered flying control van parked off to the left of the runway head. The operator had previously been given the take-off time schedule. Pilot of the leadplane immediately released brakes, heading the aircraft centrally down the runway while the co-pilot advanced all throttles for maximum power and the flight engineer monitored instruments. Depending on gross weight, a battle-bound B-17 or B-24 became airborne in about 3000 feet but it was practice to keep the main wheels on the ground until near the end of the runway in order to gain the maximum airspeed possible for sustained lift-off. At this point the bomber would have attained 110–120 mph if all was well, and while the undercarriage retracted it began a shallow climb away from base. The control van Aldis lamp would flash other bombers off at 30 or 45 second intervals as required, each having taxied onto the runway head and run up engines to full power against the brakes while awaiting the signal. Alternatively, each pilot

Top: **Staggered across the head of Chelveston runway, the lead Fortress and its two wing aircraft await the 'go' flare from the tower, June 1943.**

Above: **Off Duty ground personnel often assembled to watch a mission depart. This occasion was a mission to Berlin in March 1944. Clearing the runway is B-17G 42-38112, JD:J, with a gross weight of over 30 tons.**

would time the start of this take-off and no signals were given.

Sometimes visibility was down to less than 1500 feet adding to the danger inherent in every launch. In order to maximise striking power the bombers regularly hauled a 'war emergency load' which in plain language was a considerable overload. While both types had sufficient engine power to raise and sus-tain a gross of 65,000 lb, the failure of an outboard engine at the moment of lift-off, or shortly thereafter, could cause a wing to drop and precipitate a crash. A faltering inboard engine did not affect directional stability so severely, but could produce a critical situation resulting in aircraft and crew 'buying the farm'. In B-17s, turret gunners rode in the radio room during take-off for safety in case of a crash or undercarriage failure. The ball gunner did not usually enter his cramped quarters until several thousand feet had been reached.

After take-off each bomber normally kept a straight course for at least two minutes and then proceeded to the group assembly area, climbing at a predetermined rate – usually 300 feet per minute at 150 mph Indicated Air Speed (IAS). The assembly area originally involved a five mile radius left-hand orbit of home base. When the participant groups grew to sizable numbers, assembly areas were more positively specified both in location and height. However, the height at which assembly was made depended on cloud conditions. If the weather was clear assembly would generally take place from between 5000 and 10,000 feet. With extensive cloud, assembly sometimes had to be made as high as 20,000 feet with climbs of up to 90 minutes through overcast. Pilots having exact headings, speeds and timed legs to fly, attempted to follow these faithfully as the risk of collision was a very real one in bad weather. To minimise the risk when conditions dictated instrument procedure, each group had a designated assembly area separated by at least five miles from the next, and in some cases as much as 25 miles from home base.

Having reached assembly altitude the bombers first formed elements of three by the trailing aircraft turning inside the leader to catch up – cutting corners. In the same way each three-plane element turned inside the leading element to obtain its correct position and so built up squadron and group formations. Squadron formations were separated by 400 to 500 feet – the high squadron 400 to 500 feet above the lead squadron and the low 400 to 500 feet below the lead. A basic squadron formation was two, three or four three-plane elements and the basic group formation three squadrons flown as an inclined wedge, the high squadron on the right and trailing the lead, the low squadron on the left and trailing the lead. During the course of the 8th's campaign formations were changed many times to meet enemy countermeasures and improve formation bombing.

To aid aircraft in joining the correct formation, the group leadplane periodically fired a specified colour combination of two flares or flashed in morse the group identification letter by Aldis lamp from the tail position. An alternative was flying with undercarriage lowered or trailing a cable flare. 2nd Bomb Division developed a system whereby time-expired combat B-24s were fitted out specifically for leading assemblies. Each group painted its example in bright distinctive markings, installed an array of electric lights in the fuselage sides to flash the group identification letter, and made special flare dispensing arrangements. These 'assembly ships' returned to base once a group formation had been gathered.

From the summer of 1943 radio beacons were used increasingly for mission assembly and eventually became a regular feature of the process, regardless of visibility. Initially RAF medium frequency beacons called Splashers were used while a system of special low-powered radio transmitters, specifically for group assembly, was developed. Known as Bunchers, these were mostly positioned close to an airfield boundary, the transmitter being located in a hut or trailer. Each site pulsed a distinctive morse signal which could be picked up by a receiving set in a bomber over a range of 15 miles. The beacon was used as a fixed point in the assembly orbit, the strength of the signal indicating when the receiving aircraft was overhead. In poor weather Bunchers were particularly advantageous enabling assembly to be successfully accomplished in conditions which would otherwise have caused a mission to be abandoned.

Depending on the briefed altitude and conditions, between 30 and 60 minutes was normally allowed for group assembly, the larger the formation and the higher the altitude the more time allocated. Lead navigators kept a constant check on their position by Gee (navigational radio beacon) fixes or radio, or if visual, on check points during assembly. A pilot or co-pilot in the lead aircraft sat in the tail gun position to watch the formation and report to the Command Pilot or senior member of group staff who had taken his place in the cockpit. The group CO, air executive or a senior officer from combat wing often flew in the

leadplane as Task Force Commander if this was also to be in the van of the combat wing or division formation. He was responsible for decisions and control affecting his command during the mission.

At the specified time the group departed on course for the combat wing assembly point, flying directly across the Buncher. The route was mostly planned as a dog-leg, using a prominent English town as the turn point. Apart from allowing trailing elements or squadrons of the group to catch up by shortening the turn at the dog-leg, it enabled the group to lose or make up time for the rendezvous with the other groups of the combat wing at the precise time and location. Alternatively, combat wing assembly was affected by a large orbit of 12 minutes around one of the group Bunchers. A rigid schedule had to be adhered to for if a group was a few minutes late or early at a control point the complete divisional bomber stream could become disorganised.

Manoeuvring a formation of heavy bombers was extremely difficult and it could easily become scattered and disorganised by abrupt changes of course and air speed. Groups of the combat wing would be scheduled to arrive at the assembly point at precise times and altitudes so as to place them in their designated positions of lead, high and low, making up an inclined wedge in the same fashion that squadrons did within each individual group. The combat wing then set out on a dog-leg course for the division rendezvous with the turn point again enabling groups to improve their positions and the wing leader to marshal the formations so that they would arrive at the division meeting point on time. The turn in the dog-leg was again a prominent town or landmark, but if visibility was poor a Gee fix was taken to ensure the location of the turn.

When 10,000 feet was reached during the later stages of mission assembly, the navigator or co-pilot called the rest of the crew via the interphone system to 'go on oxygen'. Following this instruction every man adjusted his mask and checked his oxygen flow regulator. Every 15 minutes throughout the mission while at altitude the bombardier, or sometimes a pilot, called each member of the crew for an acknowledgement. Faulty supply equipment of a disconnected line could lead to uncon-

Above: **Waist gunner's view from the 303rd BG's low squadron. Two B-17s straggle in the last squadron, September 1943.**

Right: **Contrails begin to form as a 45th CBW B-17 formation heads out over storm clouds above the North Sea.**

sciousness in a few minutes and death in as little as 20 minutes. Thus it was imperative that crew members were continually alert to this possibility, because a victim was usually unaware what was happening to him as drowsiness took over.

Prior to going on oxygen, the bombardier or someone delegated by him, went to the bomb-bay and removed the safety pins from the bombs. Left until a higher altitude the pins might prove difficult to draw because of icing and it was also easier to carry out this work before going on oxygen. If heated flying suits were worn these were plugged in and switched on and the rheostats set to effect the desired temperatures. The ball gunner entered his turret from inside the rear fuselage and settled down to some uncomfortable hours. In the B-24, with its retractable turret, the gunner did not enter until approach to enemy territory. Also in B-24s fuel transfer between auxiliary and main fuel tanks was carried out not later than one hour after take-off.

Division assembly was made approximately 20 minutes after wing assembly, usually over a coastal town adjacent to a Splasher beacon in case there was an undercast preventing visual reference. Flares were fired by each combat wing as it reached the Divisional assembly line. The Division column would be formed at altitudes between 15,000 and 20,000 feet, depending on the distance to the point of penetration of hostile airspace where it was desirable to be high enough to minimise the effects of anti-aircraft fire.

Originally, throughout assembly and mission despatch, radio silence was strictly observed, but by spring 1944 group and combat wing leaders were permitted to call out positions over 'A' Channel for a time check. It was, however, not infrequently broken when difficulties arose and in order to confuse enemy listening stations as to the nature and objective of the aircraft mass by then indicated on his radar, 'spoof' information was broadcast by selected aircrews. Spoof was the term used for deliberately misleading activities and might involve exclamations or altercations embodying subtle pieces of false information that might be picked up by the enemy's listening service.

If all divisions were briefed for the same target or target area, they were often brought into a single bomber stream on crossing the enemy coastline to facilitate fighter escort. On entering hostile airspace the bombers were normally at altitudes of over 20,000 feet. Altitudes maintained over enemy territory were mostly between 24,000 and 27,000 feet for B-17s and 20,000 and 24,000 feet for B-24s which, when heavily loaded, were more difficult to control at the greater heights. Lower altitudes were used on special occasions, particularly when there was an opportuniity for improved bombing accuracy without compromising safety.

Until late April 1944 it was policy for each group to despatch three or four 'spares' – bombers which took off and assembled as a high element to the high squadron and filled in any places in the group formation vacated by aircraft forced to 'abort' by mechanical or other failures. If at the English coast there was no requirement for a spare, the aircraft concerned returned to home base. From late April 1944 a change of policy required all aircraft taking off for a mission to complete it, thus eliminating the spares status. Crews of any aborting aircraft – and there were usually several that returned to base early – were interrogated by an Operations Officer. Deliberately contrived abortives were rare. Nevertheless, all early returners came under a thorough scrutiny to ensure that there was a legitimate reason.

When at least ten miles out from the English coast, the navigator instructed the radio-operator to switch off the IFF (Identification Friend or Foe). This device could be triggered to pulse a signal that identified an aircraft as friendly to British radar defences. In mid-Channel or some 25 miles out from England the bombardier called the gunners to test-fire their guns. A short burst aimed at the sea or a clear patch of sky revealed if the weapons were functioning correctly.

Throughout the mission radio operators listened on division Headquarters frequency on the hour and half hour for any recall, diversion or other coded morse message that might be broadcast. To ensure undivided attention, the radio operator of the lead plane had no gun and his gun hatch was kept closed. Verbal radio transmissions were received by the pilot and co-pilot of all bombers and one or other maintained a listening watch on the channels assigned for the mission.

The Liaison Set was used for W/T (Wireless Telegraphy in Morse signals) and had a range of up to 600 miles at combat altitude. The Command and VHF sets were for R/T (Radio Telephone – verbal) having maximum ranges of 30 and 150 miles respectively. Both could be used for bomber-to-bomber communication but in practice the more reliable and easily oper-

Above: The strange world of vapour trails five miles above the earth as B-17s and B24s fly to their targets. Vapour trails helped enemy interceptors locate bomber formations. A few hundred feet change in altitude was sometimes all that was necessary to escape from the contrail belt but it was not practical to do so with large formations.

ated VHF set was employed for air-to-air communication and the command set for contact with home base when over friendly territory. Radio silence was rigorously maintained on penetration; the only urgent calls permitted were from the bomber leader for bombing changes or to the fighter escort if under attack. A practice was adopted whereby the lead aircraft of combat wing or division had two navigators on board, one concentrating on 'pilotage' – pin-pointing landmarks on his maps – if conditions were favourable; the other on DR. Navigators could make use of enemy radio beacons for navigational purposes in addition to the Gee chain in England which provided a fix for up to 200 miles. The prime source of navigation was DR (Dead Reckoning) based on calculations con-

ducted before take-off and amended to incorporate any changes necessary if wind direction and velocity differed from that given at briefing. Throughout the mission the navigator called out times and headings to the pilots over the interphone. When H2X radar became a regular feature of missions, the radar navigator used his equipment to supplement the DR navigator's plot.

Mission routes were rarely straight to the Initial Point (IP), the point where the bomb run on target commenced. While enemy fighter interception was a major threat, routes were designated to deceive the enemy as to the intended objective by a number of changes of course. The endurance of Luftwaffe single-engine fighters, even with an auxiliary fuel tank, being under two hours, such changes in course often resulted in deflecting interceptions.

The tactics employed by enemy fighters in attacking US heavy bombers varied considerably even on the same mission and were influenced by the type of aircraft, weapons employed and the preference of different units. Nevertheless, because the bomber formations presented massed defensive firepower, Luftwaffe interceptions were characterised by hit and away passes. Bomber crewmen made a practice of calling out fighter approaches over the interphone, using the clock position method. For example, an attack from the rear would be 'six o'clock high, low or level' according to its relative altitude. This enabled gunners who could not see the enemy from their position to anticipate its flight path and be prepared to fire when it came into view. Only limited evasive action by bombers was possible – chiefly an up and down oscillation – due to the danger of collisions within the formation. In some groups it was considered a better policy to hold a steady course and give gunners a greater chance of hitting the enemy.

Because body armour was weighty and uncomfortable some individuals did not put on their flak jackets and steel helmets until approaching flak areas or starting the bomb run. If spare flak jackets were available these were positioned to give additional protection.

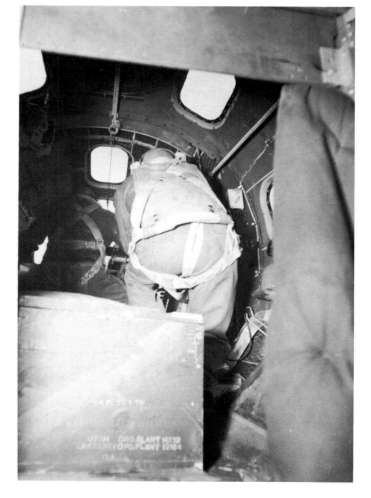

The Initial Point was a prominent landmark that also had a good radar image. A turn towards the target was made at the IP, ideally at 30 degrees, but not more than 45 degrees as this would cause groups to become scattered. The purpose of the turn was to allow combat wing and group formations to position for the run on the target in line astern. To effect the necessary separation of formations so that they were spaced for individual runs on the target, the high group could not make its turn until sufficiently separated from the lead group which turned directly over the IP. Likewise the low group did not turn until the high group was clear. This placed each of the three groups approximately two miles apart on slightly different courses which converged at the target. If the bombing was to be by squadrons then they uncovered in similar fashion. This was the usual procedure at the IP until March 1944 when manoeuvres were introduced that placed all three groups directly in trail on the briefed target

course. An analysis of bombing results during preceeding months had shown a distinct tendency for the lead group to achieve a more accurate strike than those following. The principal cause was adjudged to be confusion with target identification through making approaches other than on the briefed line. The new procedure involved the high and low groups fanning out not less than five miles from the IP and assuming the required order and separation so that each should turn over the IP and follow in train to the target. The distance between groups on a bomb run was planned as two miles but on average was double this. A check in September 1944 found the average to be five miles apart.

The turn at the IP was originally indicated by the lead aircraft opening bomb-bay doors and then supplemented by firing a flare signal – red for attacking the primary target, red and yellow for the secondary. In later months a change of target or bombing altitude was more usually accomplished by a coded radio message. In B-24 units bomb doors were opened five minutes before the scheduled drop as a matter of course in the later stages of hostilities.

At specified times before and over the target a waist gunner might be required to feed bundles of foil strips called Chaff down a chute. Once released, these strips created spurious images on enemy radar, reducing the accuracy of anti-aircraft fire and obscuring the size of the formation. During the run the lead plane of each formation was directed by the bombardier. Whether the bombing was to be by groups or squadrons, the lead bombardier sighted on the target for range and deflection while the lead aircraft of elements in a squadron or squadrons in a group sighted for range only. Range involved the distance

Left: The initial point and bomb doors are opened for the target run. B-17G in foreground, *El Lobo* of 749th BS, 457th BG survived hostilities and 113 combat missions.

Below left: A 305th BG bombardier bends over his Norden while the navigator mans the right cheek gun.   (Q. Bland)

Below: Opened bomb-bay doors reveal the load of M-47 incendiaries in a 452nd BG B-17G.

between aircraft and target, deflection concerned adjustments to ensure the bombs did not fall to one side or the other of the target. Manipulation of the controls of the bombsight actuated an instrument in the cockpit known as the Pilot's Directional Indicator (PDI), the dial needle showing desired lateral flight attitudes with which the pilot complied. The PDI was less used after the spring of 1943 when Automatic Flight Control Equipment (AFCE) proved successful. AFCE was simply an electrical transfer system which coupled the bombsight to the automatic pilot, allowing the bombardier's manipulation of the sight controls to actually fly the aircraft. The bomb release point was predetermined by formula and data calculated prior to briefing and this was set up in the bombsight. The sight was put in motion when the bombardier had centred the target in the telescope of the sight and it computed the precise moment to release the bombs, triggering them automatically.

In those aircraft without bombsights the bombardier opened the bomb doors when the leadplane did, set up the desired drop pattern, and watched the bomb-bay of his element or squadron leader. The instant the leader's bombs began to leave their bay the watching bombardiers pressed and held the toggle switch which released his bombs. The time lag between the leader's and the other releases was allowed for in the data fed into the bombsight. The toggle switch could also be used to by-pass the automatic work of the bombsight in an emergency and there was also a manual release for jettisoning all bombs at once. The electrical bomb release controls incorporated an intervalometer. This device allowed the pre-selection of the desired number and time spacing of bombs. Alternatively bombs could be 'salvoed' – part or the whole load released together. A display panel at the bombardier's position registered the release by extinguishing a red light for each departing bomb. In aircraft that flew without a bombsight, there was often no bombardier and the bomb release duties were assumed by a navigator or gunner. He watched for the leadplane release and operated the toggle switch and for this reason became known as a 'Togglier'.

When the bombsight was set up the bombardier instructed the radio operator to switch on the strike camera. Operating automatically, it took five or six pictures of the bomb strikes on target at six to ten second intervals.

The selection of the bombing run briefed was usually a compromise between avoiding the heaviest anti-aircraft concentrations and direction of wind and sunlight. Ideally the wind should carry smoke from first strikes, or smoke screens, away from approach landmarks. Down-wind bombing had been found to reduce accuracy. During early missions, when anti-aircraft fire was anticipated on the bomb run, the lead pilot would engage in irregular evasive action – slight changes of course until a specified time from the bomb release line, generally 45 seconds. This activity was largely abandoned with the introduction of AFCE and straight runs became the general order with the object of improving bombing accuracy.

Above: *Wiskey Jingles*, B-24J 42-51114 of 453rd BG, salvoes ten 500 pounders and a target marker over Karlsruhe, September 1944.

Left: The 100th BG unloads on lead's smoke markers. Distorted trails from earlier drops still hang in the sky. (100 BG Memorial Museum)

Right: B-17G 44-8329 of 407th BS, 92nd BG releases 500 pounders in train. Smoke plume is from target markers. (AFM R. Cavanagh)

Should the lead bomber fall to enemy attack on the bombing run, a deputy flying as a wing aircraft in the lead element, or the lead of the high squadron, took over. When the bomb run was made on instruments the Pathfinder – radar-guided bomber – flew in the van of the combat wing. Skymarker bombs were included in its load and these produced thick white smoke trails soon after release. A further signal was the discharge of coloured star shells from the Pathfinder. Following formation that did not have their own radar lead-sighted on the smoke marker trails. Use of smoke marker bombs was eventually adopted for all bombing.

After bombing the lead aircraft continued straight ahead for ten seconds to allow trailing bombers of the formation to complete their drop and close bomb doors, then turned and made for the Rally Point. The rally point, selected to be out of range of known flak batteries, was the briefed location for groups or squadrons to re-form into defensive combat wing formations. At the rally point the high and low groups shortened the turn to regain their original positions relative to the lead. Once clear of the target the combat wing leader instructed his radio operator to send a 'target bombed' signal to headquarters.

Devoid of bomb and half fuel load, air speed was increased from 130–150 mph to 160–180 mph IAS. At the enemy coast going out, radio communication was relaxed. When 100 miles from England damaged aircraft in distress could call direction finding stations for a course to steer to the nearest airfield. At mid-Channel or 100 miles from friendly territory the IFF was switched on. Throughout the mission after leaving England, aircraft separated could identify themselves to fighters or other bombers as friendly by the 'colors of the day' flares, or flashing a

code letter by Aldis lamp. To avoid their use by the enemy, each set of two colours and letters was only in use for set periods.

After leaving hostile airspace the bomber stream separated into divisions, each with its own briefed point of landfall. Letdown was made at 500 feet per minute – 170 to 175 mph IAS. When altitude was reduced past 10,000 feet the crew came off oxygen and could have a smoke. The combat wing leader informed division home station of the time anticipated for landfall. By the time the English coast was reached, altitudes were reduced to only a few thousand feet. After crossing the coast each division would separate and individual groups made for their bases. The 1st Division, being based further inland, avoided the airfield areas of the other divisions before dispersing.

At home base reception activity was based on the estimated time of arrival (ETA). The first intimation of the approaching formation came when flying control picked up radio talk on the VHF receiver. Operations was immediately notified and the delegated Operations Officer went to the tower to supervise

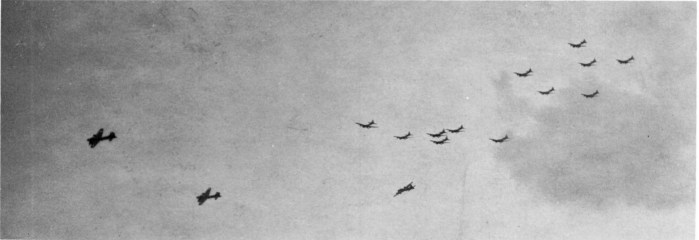

landing. The duty clerk in Operations also alerted other sections on the base that would be involved with the homecoming. MPs were posted at the briefing room. Ambulance and fire tender crews went to their vehicles.

On arrival over home airfield at a few hundred feet the group formation was loose and more widely spaced for safety. Aircraft with casualties aboard or suffering severe damage had priority in landing, signifying their distress by firing two red flares. When these bombers were down or if there were no other priorities, the order of landing was lowest elements first. In the initial run over the airfield flown in the direction of landing, the left placed aircraft of the lowest left-most element of the low squadron peeled off, followed by its element leader and the third aircraft of that element. The second lowest element of the lead squadron peeled off in similar fashion on this first pass so that six bombers were curving round to position to land. Remaining elements of the low squadron separated from the rest of the group and made an orbit above the landing aircraft, taking their turn to separate and to lower undercarriages on the second run across the airfield. Meanwhile the lead and high squadrons made a wide left-hand orbit of the base, the lead squadron then following the low and breaking formation in the same way. The high squadron landed last with the right aircraft of the highest

Top: **Coming home. Contrail shadows on the undercast below an 18th BS 34th BG Fortress.** (Via S. Evans)

Above: **The 92nd BG arrives over home base and the lead elements peel off to land.**

Above right: **Flaps lowered, a 486th BG Fortress comes in on its 'final' at Sudbury. Truck waits to cross runway head and pick up crews.** (R. Andrews)

Right: *Thundermug* **42-38205, leadship of the 305th BG on a mission to Berlin taxies in at Chelveston while ground men wait anxiously to learn 'How d'it go?'**

element making the final approach. Normally bombers landed 10 to 20 seconds apart, sufficient to give the plane ahead time to clear the runway. In some units it was policy to keep the top turret gunner in his turret to watch the rear for other aircraft.

In the final months of operations B-24 groups of 2nd Division favoured a different order of landing. Either during the descent to the English coast or as the group formation made its initial turn over the home airfield, the low left element slid under its squadron formation and positioned on the high right element. In some groups only the lead squadron low element changed position in this way. On reaching home base at 2000 feet the group formation turned to fly down wind by the runway in use and continued on this course for one minute after passing the airfield boundary. The whole group then made a 180 degree turn during which the high right and low left squadrons went into trail behind the lead with any changes in position of elements as previously described, made at this time. When the lead squadron reached the approach end of the runway the leader dipped his left wing to signal a 'peel off' which would be started by his left wing aircraft (No 3). The two left-most elements were involved in this first peel-off, the remainder of the squadron reducing height as it circled once more before a final approach. The other two squadrons retained altitude, the second (high) orbiting once more over the original course and the third squadron twice.

Bombers with wounded aboard turned off the runway as soon as possible, halting on the taxiway or in the nearest hardstand where an ambulance would be waiting. Other bombers taxied directly to their dispersal points, on B-17s the two inboard engines having been shut down to allow easier control. B-24s opened bomb-bay doors once back on the ground to allow fuel fumes to escape. If the bomber that led the mission was routed past the briefing room area it would sometimes be halted to let any command staff officers get out. On reaching the dispersal the ground crew were on hand to give signals in parking the aircraft in the required position. Care had to be exercised in pivoting the bomber so as not to run off the concrete.

Crew disembarked from the most convenient exits, bringing out personal equipment. Electrically heated flying suits and other flight garb were usually removed on the hardstand and put into carrying bags. Gunners removed and cleaned their guns and placed them for collection by an ammunition crew truck. Alternatively, guns were cleaned at the squadron armament hut after interrogation. In some groups navigators had to clean their own guns; in others gunners did it for them. Flight engineer and pilot completed the Form 1A on which the pilot reported any mechanical problems or known damage. Both air and ground crews inspected their bomber for battle damage while the former awaited transportation.

A truck collected combat crews and took them to the briefing room complex. Here each crew was first checked in by a clerk. The men entered the large locker room to hand in personal equipment – parachutes, flying suits, Mae Wests, escape kits, oxygen masks – and to obtain refreshments, which were available from Red Cross girls serving at tables placed at one end of the room. The fare varied from coffee and doughnuts to more substantial powdered egg and corned beef sandwiches with grapefruit juice. There was also 'two slugs' of whisky. At another

27

Top: **A crowd gathers to view the flak damage on a 94th BG Fortress just back from Bremen, December 1943. Truck waits to convey crew to interrogation.**

Left: Guns had to be removed before crews left their aircraft. A **445th BG waist gunner gets a helping hand, March 1944.**

Above: **Some wait in vain: Ground crew of a missing 91st BG Fortress. Plexiglas cover is that removed from radio room hatch before the mission.**

Right: **Sgt McManus, top turret gunner on** *Hard To Get*, **B-17G 42-39788, being lifted from waist window to ambulance in splint stretcher, Bury St Edmunds, December 1943.**

Left: 1/Lt Sam Dixon, pilot of *Lady Susie II*, 42-5912, completes Form 1A after return from Stuttgart, 6 September 1943. On left is 385th BG CO, Lt Col Elliott Vandevanter who flew as Command Pilot. T/Sgt Alford Peterson, crew chief has back to camera and co-pilot, 2/Lt Warren Bock, is on right.

Below: Wounded crewman is conveyed to a waiting ambulance from 379th BG's veteran B-17F *Stump Jumper* which at this date, June 1944, had over 70 missions to its credit.

table an operations officer collected 'Hot News'. This referred to information deemed essential for transmission to the concerned authorities as soon as possible, such as enemy convoys, shipping or activity that might affect other operations, aircraft seen in distress, crashes and ditchings. Meanwhile command pilots reported to the operations officer in the briefing room, giving a brief rundown on the Group's performance during the mission which would form the basis of a 'flash' report telephoned to Wing.

As soon as crews had deposited their equipment and taken refreshment, they were called into the briefing room for interrogations. In their absence the room had been rearranged so that sufficient chairs for a crew and an interrogating officer were placed round each table. As the number of tables was limited, crews were called in batches. Each interrogating officer was provided with a standard set of questions covering target observations, flak and fighter opposition where encountered, tactics, fighter claims, weather, fighter support, aircraft in distress, plus other pertinent observations and suggestions. The last often brought complaints about matters not really related to the mission, but might be accepted.

Gunners' claims were then reviewed by an intelligence officer with a special brief to compare the claims of various crews in an effort to eliminate duplication. Navigators and bombardiers were required to give separate reports on their part, navigators handing in their logs and bombardiers filling out bombing forms. Interrogation of lead crews was more searching, particularly if there had been some tactical error. This debriefing might take up to an hour and a half before all crews were processed.

On tactical missions (support of ground forces) flown during

Top: **Red Cross Club girls were usually on hand to distribute coffee, sandwiches and doughnuts, here enjoyed by 351st BG crews waiting to be interrogated.**

Above: **Members of one crew were interrogated together. While the S-2 officer fills out a report, the bottle of *Johnny Walker* helped relieve tensions. 401st BG, April 1944.**

Left: **Mission leaders relax over a meal. Col 'Mo' Preston, 379th BG CO and one of 8th Air Force's most distinguished commanders, chats with Major Otis Parks, leader of the low group in the** *Stump Jumper* **for the raid on Kiel, 4 January 1944. On left is Lt Lester Gibson who flew as tail gunner/observer in** *Ragin Red II* **the leadship in which Col Preston flew as Task Force Commander.**

Below: **Some battle damaged aircraft sought sanctuary in neutral countries and towards the end of the war a few made it to Soviet-held territory. Lt King of the 401st BG took 44-6508 to Poltava but the Russians would not let him leave after they discovered he was trying to fly out a Pole who wanted to reach the west.**

Bottom: **Chaplain Biggs of 91st BG writes a letter to next-of-kin of a man known to have been killed in action.**

the last 18 months of the war, interrogating officers met crews on hardstands as they returned to carry out interrogations. Tactical missions usually only entailed brief trespass into hostile airspace and if no opposition was encountered there was little point in interviewing all crewmen. In some groups it was the practice to only interrogate lead crews after tactical missions.

Following interrogation, flight crews were released to go to their barracks or the mess hall. Trucks ran a shuttle service to the living sites and the communal area. Most men were exhausted after a mission and sought sleep. Some would not trouble with a main meal, preferring to 'hit the sack' right away. The more resilient showered and dined before going to bed. It might be that another mission was already being organised and that within a few hours they would be called upon to fly again.

Group Operations and Intelligence offices continued to be a hive of activity. The strike cameras had been collected from those bombers carrying them, the films removed and processed. As soon as prints were available they were scrutinised by Intelligence officers to plot the group strike pattern on target. A more detailed report of the group's effort, losses and claims was prepared and sent via teleprinter to both wing and division as soon as possible after interrogation, generally within an hour. Missing In Action (MIA) forms had to be completed for crews and individuals, aircraft damage reports compiled and all such major damage photographed. Enemy aircraft claims and the location and strength of flak were detailed in other reports. Additional teletype messages might be necessary and there would be telephone enquiries from combat wing and division on aspects of their particular interest.

For the ground crews work began again with the return of a

mission. Most of these men caught up on their sleep while the bombers were absent, for later there might be heavy battle damage or a major engineering problem to keep them working all through the night. Routine maintenance was carried out on each bomber when it returned – in line with engineering requirements. If shrapnel or bullets had caused minor skin damage, the metal shop repair team were called to rivet patches. However, when a bomber was punctured in hundreds of places it became a major undertaking. The line chief, who was responsible for overseeing the mechanics, would notify his squadron engineering officer of major problems and, in consultation, they would decide which bombers could not be readied in time for a mission on the morrow. Fuel tanks and oxygen were replenished by the sections responsible and the bomber brought to serviceable standard as quickly as possible.

A preliminary assessment of bombing results from the reports and strike photos received from groups occupied the attention of intelligence staff at division headquarters during the immediate post-mission hours. After refinement a report was transmitted by teleprinter to *Pinetree*. Annexes to this would follow as division staff had more time to examine the input from its groups and wings. At *Pinetree* analysts established the degree of target destruction, the resulting loss to the enemy and, if necessary, a priority for future attack on the same target. Information received on enemy defences was also carefully examined and used to up-date intelligence data. This work would be aided by the photographs of the target taken by reconnaissance aircraft after the mission. Assessment of the mission continued in the intelligence sections of high command for some days following the operation, by which time the combat groups had relegated it to recent history.

Left: Ground crews at Snetterton Heath get to work on an engine. Some of the men are wearing the Shearing type sheepskin jackets and trousers issued to mechanics. These were of lower quality to those worn by flight crews.

Below left: *Evelyn, the Duchess* requires an engine change. Cpl Boyd Cooper and Pfc Charles Striegel at work in a Hardwick hangar. Note twin .50s in nose of this B-24D.

Below: When the work was done there might be time to paint a nickname on a new bomber. J. Hoff uses the brush while Ray Bailey and George Hillard give support. B-17G 42-107078 N7:U of 398th BG.

Bottom: Armourers hard at work preparing .50 ammunition belts, passing them through an aligning machine.

Top: Relaxation and keeping up the tradition. At Thurleigh the 306th BG's major missions were recorded with candle smoke on the Officers' Club ceiling. Lt Col George Buckey and Major Richard Walck support Lt John Stolz.

Above: Capt Nicholas Rifkin, Intelligence Co-ordination Officer at 1st Division, appraising bomb damage from strike photos aided by WAC Pfc Virginia Scheuer. All Command and Divisional HQs had a WAC contingent.

1st DIVISION SQUADRON CALL-SIGNS: SPRING 1944 TO VE-DAY

322BS	Lingers	325BS	Sandpipe	358BS	Whipcream	364BS	Liftboy
323BS	Oboe	326BS	Goldfinch	359BS	Eavesdrop	365BS	Monsoon
324BS	Dimple	327BS	Davey	360BS	Toydoll	366BS	Grubby
401BS	Mutter	407BS	Quilpen	427BS	Newrow	422BS	Ancient
367BS	Morepork	508BS	Carlton	524BS	Nightjar	532BS	Afghan
368BS	Nular	509BS	Hotmint	525BS	Haircut	533BS	Tabby
369BS	Baema	510BS	Tipstaff	526BS	Mystic	534BS	Midget
423BS	Eating	511BS	Partnership	527BS	Heartstring	535BS	Colby
544BS	Clinker	600BS	Moorhen	612BS	Jabwock	748BS	Wedon
545BS	Splashboard	601BS	Newway	613BS	Marco	749BS	Eclipse
546BS	Luggage	602BS	Enclasp	614BS	Golfclub	750BS	Bluebell
547BS	Dragon	603BS	Adorn	615BS	Buzzard	751BS	Cutter

2nd DIVISION SQUADRON CALL-SIGNS: SPRING 1944 TO VE-DAY

66BS	Onward	328BS	Oxpug	564BS	Complex	576BS	Vitos
67BS	Backward	329BS	Furcoat	565BS	Protrap	577BS	Caldron
68BS	Smokeyblue	330BS	Maywind	566BS	Boorish	578BS	Hazard
506BS	Drivel	409BS	Thrufare	567BS	Lounger	579BS	Faceup
700BS	Displease	704BS	Headlock	712BS	Rocco	732BS	Lightman
701BS	Wallet	705BS	Accept	713BS	Egress	733BS	Tripup
702BS	Markum	706BS	Manage	714BS	Blitzer	734BS	Dizzy
703BS	Baffle	707BS	Loosend	715BS	Adal	735BS	Bowfinch
752BS	Hussar	784BS	Owlish	788BS	Shirtmaker	844BS	Steerage
753BS	Fiction	785BS	Eglan	789BS	Acford	845BS	Hourglass
754BS	Cotstring	786BS	Agram	790BS	Hamos	846BS	Ember
755BS	Affab	787BS	Behead	791BS	Baron	847BS	Gallop
852BS	Ballot						
853BS	Farkum						
854BS	Semen						
855BS	Quadrant						

3rd DIVISION SQUADRON CALL-SIGNS: SPRING 1944 TO VE-DAY

4BS	Daisy	331BS	Agmer	334BS	Neglect	337BS	Paintbrush
7BS	Extol	332BS	Rotate	335BS	Inland	338BS	Grating
18BS	Bawdry	333BS	Cedar	336BS	Landberg	339BS	Bookie
391BS	Laurel	410BS	Total	412BS	Abush	413BS	Cabbage
349BS	Kidmeat	548BS	Summer	560BS	Soapdish	568BS	Cavort
350BS	Poohbah	549BS	Fancyfrock	561BS	Caprice	569BS	Boaster
351BS	Mafking	550BS	Alfrek	562BS	Darklock	570BS	Anteat
418BS	Rubber	551BS	Boston	563BS	Fairman	571BS	Longshore
708BS	Munru	728BS	Pinetree	832BS	Trappist	836BS	Winner
709BS	Kirkland	729BS	Instinct	833BS	Pebbly	837BS	Rathmore
710BS	Inlay	730BS	Spencer	834BS	Deepseat	838BS	Entrap
711BS	Curlhair	731BS	Acquit	835BS	Nightdress	839BS	Bluntish
848BS	Ratchet	860BS	Shunter				
849BS	Abrade	861BS	Begman				
850BS	Baddog	862BS	Compar				
851BS	Gotam	863BS	Pilar				

COMBAT BOMB WING CALL-SIGNS

		15 Sep 43 – Mar 44	Apr 44 – VE-Day
1st Division	1CBW	Goonchild	Swordfish
	40CBW	Bullpen	Foxhole
	41CBW	Fatgal	Cowboy
	94CBW	Ragweed	Woodcraft
2nd Division	2CBW	Winston	Bourbon
	14CBW	Hambone	Hardtack
	20CBW	Pinestreet	Bigbear
	95CBW	Shamrock	Shamrock
	96CBW	Redstar	Lincoln
3rd Division	4CBW	Franklin	Hotshot
	13CBW	Zootsuit	Fireball
	45CBW	Wolfgang	Vampire
	92CBW		Gocart
	93CBW		Clambake

SPECIAL BOMB SQUADRONS

Spring 1944 to spring 1945

812BS	Lasthouse
813BS	Hermanson
814BS	Jetty
856BS	Reachfirth
857BS	Nextmorn
858BS	Garbage
859BS	Punchard
36BS	Picnic
406BS	Globy
652BS	Rator
653BS	Paintjar
654BS	Smalleck

Formation Assembly

Assembling its heavy bombers into battle formations was never an easy process for the 8th Air Force. Even with 'unlimited visibility' the task demanded precise control in order to form and place each bomber 'box' at the required position and altitude at a given time. Overcast was a more frequent morning condition in the area of bomber bases making assembly difficult and on occasions, with cloud too extensive, causing missions to be abandoned. Nevertheless, procedures were eventually developed whereby time and again a thousand bombers penetrated a heavy overcast to formate successfully above.

In the first missions of summer 1942 heavy bombers assembled into squadron and group formations while orbiting home base. After take-off the lead bomber climbed straight out for two minutes, or a similarly advised time, generally at 150 mph IAS and climbing at about 400 feet per minute. This placed the bomber five to six miles from base at some 800 feet when it began a gentle curve left. Other bombers of the first squadron followed at 30 second intervals turning progressively inside the leader's curve until all six aircraft were in the desired positions. The following squadron did likewise and positioned on the lead squadron, usually in an orbit and a half of the airfield, flying above a five mile radius. With a 12-plane group formation assembly could take as little as 18 minutes to effect; with a three-squadron 18-plane group, longer, 25 to 35 minutes. The orbits were always anti-clockwise. To aid turns in assembly the low squadron was kept a squadron's length behind the lead.

A heavy overcast, or more than 7/10th cloud extent, precluded operations in the early days and during the winter months of 1942–43 conditioned the slow pace of operations. Occasionally, when overcast was low and not too deep, individual bombers were briefed to climb through this cloud by flying a reciprocal course of, usually, five minute legs by Dead Reckoning (DR), repeating the manoeuvre until breaking out into the clear. Even if strict timing and climb rates were adhered to, attempts at assembly above an overcast in this way found aircraft emerging scattered over a wide area increasing assembly time. Some bombers, not locating their own group, often had to join a formation from another station. Moreover, even if group assembly was achieved the formation could be so far behind in the time schedule that correct rendezvous with the combat wing could not be made. Sometimes there were stacked layers of cloud through several thousand feet and a group might find it was assembling between layers. Assembly beneath an overcast was not tenable because of the danger of collisions in trying to take the formation up through the cloud.

To distinguish circling formations the firing of coloured flares from the lead aircraft was authorised during the autumn of 1942. Each group had a two-shot colour combination shell detailed for use in forming and these were fired as directed by a waist gunner of the lead bomber, using a flare pistol through the radio room hatch on B-17s and from the waist windows of B-24s. Colour range was red, yellow and green and combinations of these. Additionally an Aldis lamp was used to flash the group code letter from the leadplane's rear gunner compartment – which was usually manned by a displaced co-pilot.

Missions were generally restricted to days when weather conditions were suitable, both at the target and over home bases, during the first winter. Often suitable targets were in the clear but the bombers were held on the ground because of a 'solid overcast' above their bases. Also with new bomb groups arriving, adding to the congestion over East Anglia, chaos could result if weather deteriorated after take-off – as it frequently did. Planners at VIII BC recognised that the rate of operations could be improved if the problems of assembly could be solved. To achieve more precise control over the formating bombers the use of radio beacons was mooted where transmissions could be used as fixed points of reference by

individual aircraft. Through the rotating loop aerial on his bomber, a navigator or pilot could obtain a bearing on the beacon, indicated on the dial of the radio compass.

The British had developed a system of medium frequency radio beacons called Splashers. Each beacon site had three, later four, transmitters operating simultaneously at different frequencies but pulsing the same call-sign. The frequencies were interchanged between Splasher sites on a pre-arranged daily time schedule. The purpose was to confuse the enemy as to which MF beacons were in use and to ensure that the effect of his jamming (over-riding the signal with one of his own) or meaconing (keying a signal in step so an aircraft might be drawn towards the enemy source) was minimised. The radio operator of a bomber was provided with a schedule of times and frequencies, tuning the radio compass set accordingly.

In April 1943 the 8th AF made arrangements with the RAF for use of Splasher beacons during missions from take-off to return. These became available on 10 May and thereafter bomber crews were given a list of call-signs and frequencies for Splashers selected for the day's operation. At this date the RAF had 12 Splasher sites, increased to 15 during the summer of 1943 with a further site added in the following winter. Only eight or nine Splashers were in operation at any one time, although the 8th AF used only those situated within or near its general base area. These were Splashers No 4 Louth, No 5 Mundesley, No 6 Scole, No 7 Braintree, No 10 Windlesham and, when opened, No 16 Brampton Grange.

Initially Splashers were used as rendezvous points for groups of a combat wing, group formation leaders monitoring the signal so that they would be able to locate the other groups over the Splasher at the stated time. The value of Splashers as an aid to assembling combat wings was evident during June and July 1943. On 24 July a mission was despatched to targets in Norway where clear conditions were forecast even though extensive cloud covered England. In fact, an 8/10ths overcast shrouded East Anglia but its base was 1800 feet and it extended upward only a few thousand feet. On this occasion the participating bombers were briefed to climb through the cloud and make group assembly on a Splasher when in the clear. Positioning formations for the bomber column was then achieved by using a line of three Splashers for rendezvous points as combat wings flew north.

This experiment proved very successful and the procedure was repeated in following weeks. However, the use of a single Splasher beacon by several groups at the same occasion presented problems of spacing in time and altitude that were difficult to control, traffic congestion leading to some desperate manoeuvres to avoid collision. Since more beacons were desirable this led to conferences with the British to explore a proposal for a series of low-powered radio beacons specifically for assembling US heavy bombers. In October 1943 three such beacons were set up in each of the current combat wings. Known as Bunchers, the sites were adjacent to operational bomber airfields and operated by USAAF personnel. With an effective range around 25 miles, each Buncher in use transmitted once per minute using a morse call-sign followed by a long keying-in pulse. The original Bunchers in the autumn of 1943 were Nos 1 to 9 at Bassingbourn, Thurleigh, Molesworth, Shipdham, Hardwick, Hethel, Bury St Edmunds, Framlingham and Snetterton Heath respectively. During the winter of 1943–44 others were added to make the total 24 by March, and 33 by the end of hostilities.

Bunchers came to be used for all mission assemblies regardless of weather conditions. In good visibility or when only light cloud was present, group assembly took place using the assigned combat wing Buncher with all three groups flying the same orbit at different altitudes. The usual procedure following take-off was for individual aircraft to follow a briefed bearing for the required number of minutes, generally five, and then make a turn towards the Buncher. They then orbited the Buncher or flew a reciprocal pattern that took them to and from it as they climbed at the prescribed rate – 130 to 150 mph IAS and 300 to 350 feet per minute. Orbits took from six to ten minutes. Assembly into flights and squadrons was effected during this circling climb with a levelling out at a briefed altitude. Squadrons within a group assembled at different altitudes as did groups of a combat wing, relative to their briefed position – lead, high or low, the separation being 1000 feet between groups in the circuit. In cases where groups of a combat wing were using different Bunchers the same relative altitude separation was used, the coming together being timed over one or other of the Bunchers.

In May 1944 1st Division put more order into this technique by having the lead bombers of the three groups of a combat wing climb individually to a given altitude and take up their briefed positions relative to one another. With this change the whole combat wing formed together round the Buncher far quicker than previously.

When instrument procedures had to be used in association with Bunchers to penetrate an overcast or layered cloud, groups were allocated separate isolated assembly areas to minimise the risk of collisions. It was imperative that the approach course to these was accurately followed. Bombers took off at 45 second intervals and climbed ahead for two to four minutes before turning on to the prescribed course. For some groups this turn was to the right as an added safety measure. On reaching the group assembly area each bomber commenced a reciprocal course across it, using the Buncher signal to maintain position while climbing in the murk. After breaking out above the cloud group assembly took place over the same course, in most cases a 15 mile stretch aligned on the Buncher. The 'width' of the area was some five miles – the distance needed to turn the formation through 180 degrees.

A few groups were allocated a circular course around their home base for instrument procedure assembly, while it was necessary to place others some miles away out over the East Anglian coast to achieve safe separation. This applied to all 2nd Division groups, several of which used the same Buncher, taking a bearing on it as a timed run in their assembly pattern. There were also three groups that continued to make use of Splasher beacons for assembly purposes. For the most part however, the more powerful Splashers were used as rendezvous points for Division task forces and as such became Control Point 1 for a mission route. Splasher No 5 at Mundesley – often

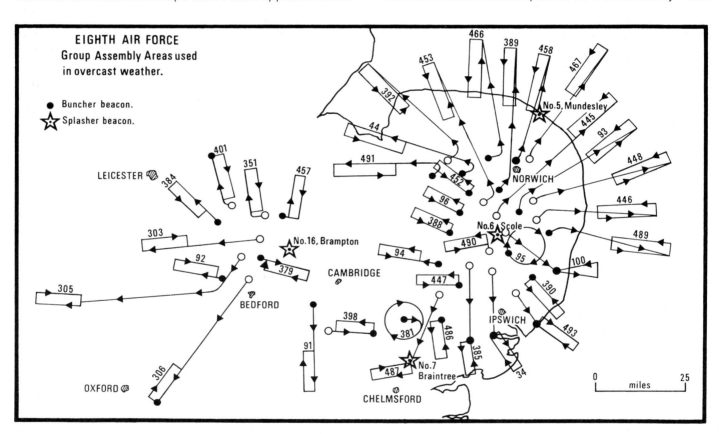

EIGHTH AIR FORCE
Group Assembly Areas used
in overcast weather.

● Buncher beacon.
☆ Splasher beacon.

1 Bassingbourn	12 Bury St Edmunds	23 Horham
2 Podington	13 Boxted	24 Hemsby
3 Kimbolton	14 Ridgewell	27 Bawdsey
4 Cottesmore	15 Horsham St Faith	28 Leiston
5 Shipdham	16 Rattlesden	29 Grafton Underwood
6 Hethel	17 Debden	30 Glatton
7 Hardwick	18 Mount Farm	31 Old Buckenham
8 Halesworth	19 Manningtree	32 Kings Cliffe
9 Snetterton Heath	20 Deopham Green	33 Harrington
10 Knettishall	21 North Pickenham	35 Attlebridge
11 Framlingham	22 Sudbury	

(No 8 moved to Bungay in winter 1944–45. No 31 was originally Toome.)

referred to as Cromer, the nearby seaside town located on the north Norfolk coast – became the most frequent departure point for missions to northern Germany.

Each Division developed its own approach to mission assembly and by the summer of 1944 every group in both 1st and 3rd Divisions had an individual Buncher or Splasher allocated for its use. The 2nd Air Division did not move towards such an arrangement until the last two months of hostilities.

Although Splasher and Buncher beacons allowed the 8th AF to assemble heavy bomber formations in conditions that would previously have seen missions abandoned, there still remained the problem of individual aircraft distinguishing their own group in the combat wing orbit, particularly if visibility was poor or the mission had been launched before dawn. Bombers did occasionally join with the wrong formation and squadrons with the wrong group. During the winter of 1943–44 a number of procedures were experimented with to try and lessen such occurrences. Colonel Castle, the 94th Bomb Group commander, was particularly interested in this matter. In December 1943 he experimented with smoke flares fixed outside the radio room hatch of the lead bomber, but it was found that the slip-stream dissipated the smoke trail. On 16 December, while his group flew a reciprocal course always passing over the Buncher, he had every bomber that had made formation fire flares every time the lead plane did. A later experiment involved a smoke flare in the tail, the white smoke trail being visible over a much greater distance than flares. A later experiment with an M-26 colour flare reeled out from the rear gun compartment was more successful and, together with the mass flare pistol discharge idea, was adopted for most 3rd Division assemblies. The towed flare was also used by 1st Division B-17 groups. However, the approach to assembly aids was very much one for individual groups and combat wings.

In November 1943 the 93rd Bomb Group at Hardwick decided to fit out a B-24 especially for assembling formations. A 'battle-weary' B-24D was stripped of most combat equipment and then painted overall in a bizarre fashion – initially with yellow and black stripes. A series of electric light ports were made in the fuselage sides and wired to give a flashing signal. The procedure was for this aircraft – variously known as an Assembly Ship, Forming Plane or Lead Ship – to take off first at a mission launch, proceed to the assembly area to orbit while following bombers formated behind. All the time while circling the fuselage lights flashed a signal and volleys of flares were discharged from the waist windows. The formation established, the Assembly Ship's job was completed and it returned to base. Proving extremely useful for the identification of a formation the idea was adopted for the whole 2nd Division and employed with varying enthusiasm and ingenuity by its groups during the remainder of operations.

During the last year of hostilities VHF radio became much more freely used for assembly. Except for emergencies, its use was restricted to formation leaders for giving directions and this only when the formation was high enough to be in view by enemy radar. Following the cross-Channel invasion and liberation of France, enemy interference with radio beacons was less severe leading the RAF to simplify MF beacons by discontinuing the Splasher system of four separate transmissions. The same sites were retained but from the late summer of 1944 only a single MF beacon operated. The term Splasher was still commonly used for these beacons by some 8th AF units.

Following the liberation of France and Belgium, radio beacons were established on the Continent and by the spring of 1945 were available for use in heavy bomber assembly if conditions over the UK were particularly poor.

Heavy Bomber Formations

More than any other feature, the large formations of heavy bombers typified USAAF bombing operations of the Second World War. To the uninformed observer there may have appeared little, if any, order in such formations, which were, in fact, both carefully planned and executed. Viewed either from the ground or in the air it was difficult to identify any set pattern. But not only were their arrangements complex, their positioning was difficult to maintain, principally because of the turbulence created by the leading aircraft which mitigated against perfect composition. The formation served two main purposes: defensive in that it massed the fire-power of the bombers' guns, and offensive in that it concentrated the mass release of bombs on a target.

Formating as a bomber tactic had originally been nurtured by the US Army Air Corps solely for defensive purposes, security of the force being seen as the dominant factor in conducting operations during daylight. With the development of the technique of high altitude daylight bombing, in which the 8th Air Force became the major exponent, other factors arose: bomb strike pattern, flexibility, visibility and control. The changing shape and composition of 8th Air Force formations reflects the quest to adequately meet all these requirements while defence remained the paramount consideration. With the advent of long-range fighter escort there was a need for formations that

could be more easily escorted. Still later when ground anti-aircraft fire became the major threat, formations had to be re-shaped and re-scheduled to minimise this danger. The progression in formations throughout the 8th's campaign was never uniform. Individual units had some latitude in this respect and with the three Bomb Divisions each tended to develop and pursue its own policy on formations. There were a dozen major formation patterns during the campaign and these are described and illustrated.

From the outset it was usual to talk of a unit formation as a 'box'. This arose from the practice in designing formations whereby each individual bomber was positioned within a box-shaped area which could be easily explained by plan, profile and front elevation drawings. In operational planning an ordered formation was projected as flying in an invisible box, the term 'box' coming to mean a concentrated formation.

On the first VIII BC mission, 17 August 1942, the 97th BG flew as two squadrons of six B-17s each. The squadrons, separated by approximately two miles, did not permit mutual fire support, although there was plenty of flexibility to manoeuvre. Each squadron formation was composed of a lead bomber with a second staggered off its right rear quarter at the same height. A third and fourth bomber flew above and on either side and slightly to the rear of the first two in a staggered formation. The fifth and sixth bombers flew below and directly behind but closer together than the third and fourth.

Top: **Basic 3-plane element of bomber formations displayed by shimmering 401st BG B-17s.** (V. Maslen)

Above: **Although the lower 9-plane squadron formation appears to have no order it is, in fact, composed of three 3-plane vee elements. In a perspective view formations always appeared confused due to the staggering of elements. The B-17F in the foreground, 42-3412, XK:M, is of significance in that it was one of only two 305th BG aircraft to survive the debacle at Schweinfurt, 14 October 1943.**

On its second mission, 19 August, the 97th BG flew four such squadron formations spaced in a diamond pattern. The distance between the squadrons was four miles for those on either side of the lead and three miles between the lead and the rear. The difference in elevation for each squadron was 1000 feet below and a mile and a half behind the lead for the left and right formations. The trailing squadron was 1000 feet above the lead's level. (1)

Missions during the remainder of August and early Sep-

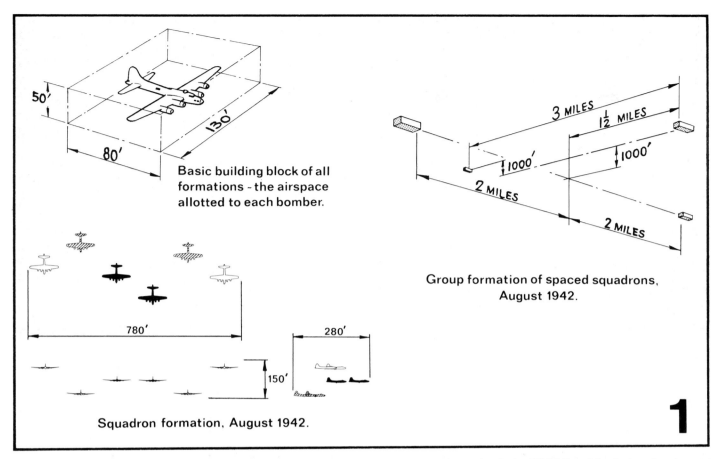

50'

130'

80'

Basic building block of all
formations - the airspace
allotted to each bomber.

3 MILES

1½ MILES

1000'

1000'

2 MILES

2 MILES

Group formation of spaced squadrons,
August 1942.

780'

280'

150'

Squadron formation, August 1942.

1

tember 1942 were based on six-plane squadron formations with additional aircraft or flights added when available. On all these shallow penetration missions RAF Spitfire escort and support deterred enemy interception, but it was evident that more compact and larger formations were necessary to mass defensive fire, particularly if the bombers were to range beyond available escorts. The basic element of three aircraft flying as a Vee – a leader with a trailing aircraft off its left and right wing – had long

been a basic formation in the USAAF and, for that matter, in most air forces.

Experiments were conducted during September 1942 to build squadron and group formations using the three-plane Vee element. (2) The squadron formation was increased to nine bombers in three elements, all flying at the same level. A second squadron, made up in the same way, flew 500 feet above the lead squadron to the right and trailing. While this was more

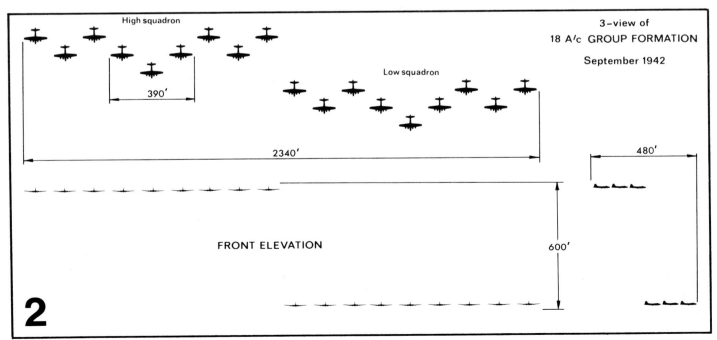

High squadron

390'

Low squadron

3-view of
18 A/c GROUP FORMATION

September 1942

2340'

480'

600'

FRONT ELEVATION

2

compact than previous formations it proved less flexible. During turns the pilots in the outside-flying aircraft lost sight of the bombers in the centre during completion of the manoeuvre. Outer elements tended to lose position to the extent that some blocked the fields of fire of other bombers. This formation was first given an operational trial on 26 September in an abortive bombing mission by 97th BG. An alternative formation developed during September 1942 provided for 36 bombers. (3) Although called a group formation it actually provided for the aircraft from two groups. Squadrons were made up of four three-plane Vees, two on one level and two trailing on a lower level and echeloned down towards the sun. The three squadrons were staggered in echelon and aircraft positioned so as to give gunners less restricted fields of fire and, as far as was possible, enhance mutual protection of the whole 36-plane group. The altitude separation was 500 feet between squadrons with the lead lowest. The second squadron was echeloned left and trailed the group leader by 160 feet; the third was echeloned right and trailed the leader by 320 feet. This 36-plane formation provided protection for its inner elements but did not actually improve on the 18-plane formation as far as fields of fire were concened. Like the 18-plane group it suffered from inflexibility. The greatest drawback however was that the group leader flew out of the line of vision of many elements and made the maintenance of a cohesive formation exceptionally difficult.

Both the 18- and 36-plane group formations and variations on these were used in October and November 1942 although often the high number of aborting bombers made a set keeping of formation impossible. Nevertheless, Luftwaffe fighters were finding such large assemblies of bombers difficult to deal with. The conventional fixed-gun fighter attack from the rear was largely thwarted by the massed firepower of the American bombers.

Each of the four B-17 groups experimented with formations, particularly the 305th, mainly to enhance mutual firepower. On

Below: **Two 18-plane group javelins of 91st and 351st BGs forming part of a combat wing, November 1943.**

Bottom: **The 448th BG assembling above an undercast in July 1944. Lead squadron has an extra B-24 filling in the 'diamond' of the last element. Wing men in several elements still have to close up. Separation between lead and high squadron is also too great.**

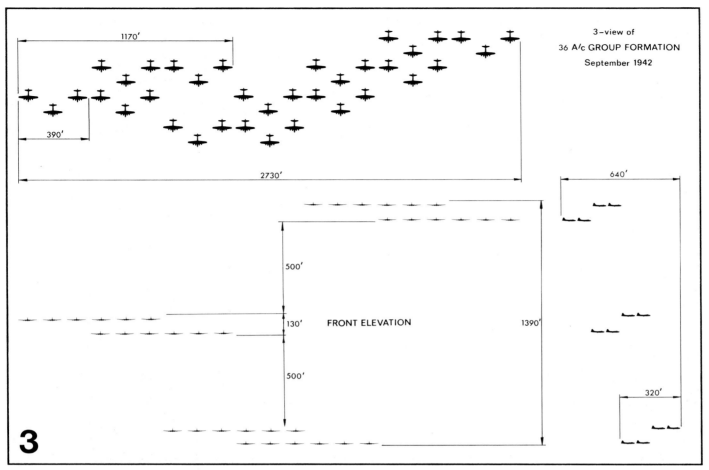

3-view of
36 A/c GROUP FORMATION
September 1942

1170'

390'

2730'

640'

500'

130'   FRONT ELEVATION   1390'

500'

320'

3

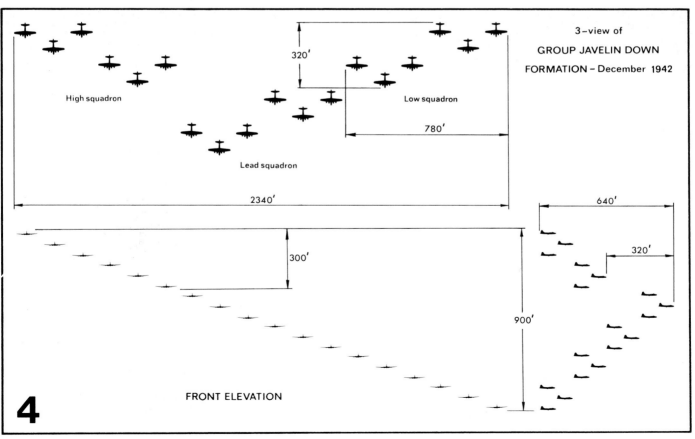

3-view of
GROUP JAVELIN DOWN
FORMATION – December 1942

320'

High squadron

780'

Low squadron

Lead squadron

2340'

640'

300'   320'

900'

4   FRONT ELEVATION

6 December 1942 the 305th BG introduced what became known as the Javelin Down formation, the basis of which influenced most formations for the rest of hostilities. (4) Perfected during subsequent operations that December, it was adopted by the other three B-17 groups of the Command. Based on an 18-plane group of three six-plane squadrons, the aircraft were all echloned down towards the direction of the sun, so that the highest aircraft could observe the lowest without the problem of glare. The lead squadron was in the centre position with the other two trailing it, one high and the other low, but both approximately 320 feet behind the group leader. The principal advantage of this arrangement was the greater firepower afforded each individual aircraft. In previous formations many gun positions had remained 'covered' in that the gunner's field of fire was severely restricted by other aircraft in the formation.

fethe Javelin Down placed each squadron in a better position to support the others, giving the whole group enhanced firepower. Positioning of the squadrons relative to one another also allowed much more flexibility and easier control than with previous formations. However, at this time the Luftwaffe was exploiting the vulnerability of the lightly defended nose area of the B-17s and B-24s with much success. On some missions losses rose to 10 per cent of sorties, allegedly due to frontal attacks by enemy fighters.

In a move to reduce losses due to frontal passes, groups were flown in trail, stacked behind and above the lead group and echeloned towards the sun. About a mile and a half separated each group box which was beyond the range of mutual fire support but the column tended to restrict head-on fighter attacks to the lead box. This arrangement of the four B-17 groups was used during January 1943 together with experimentation in dropping on the group leader's bomb release instead of by individual squadrons, thus allowing groups to maintain their defensive formations across the target. But it was found that stacking in trail at increasing altitudes caused varying speed differentials between the lead and the higher groups. This resulted in the column becoming strung out with elements or individual aircraft being unable to keep up, leading in turn to engine strain, stragglers and abortives.

In an attempt to prevent stringing-out by reducing the speed differential between boxes, the lead group was repositioned from the lowest level and placed mid-way between the highest and lowest levels. The other boxes were then echeloned back on opposite sides above and below the lead to form a wedge of groups. When this was practised on 16 February the Liberators flew as a fifth group in a low position, better suited to their altitude performance. This development shortened the column of groups, (5) but still did not entirely overcome the tendency of formations to string out caused by the difference in altitude between high and low boxes. In a further attempt to minimise stringing-out and at the same time build an even larger formation for defensive purposes, three 18-plane group boxes were brought into close proximity and staggered as squadrons within a group – lead, low left and high right. Known as a combat wing box this huge formation was composed, ideally, of 54 bombers but in practice ranged from 30 to 70. It was first tried with the three group boxes side by side at lead, high and low levels. This proved too unwieldy and an improvement was obtained by placing the high and low groups slightly in trail of the lead.

The chief advantage of this combat wing box was the increase in mutual firepower support to meet frontal attacks. Even so, it did not outweigh the difficulties of flying and maintaining such a vast formation which stretched vertically through 3000 feet and horizontally through an area roughly 2000 by 7000 feet. Moreover, the strength of VIII BC at this time – April 1943 – was still only four B-17 and two B-24 groups. Apart from being undesirable to fly the two types in adjacent formations because of the differing performance, there were frequently insufficient bombers to compose two full combat wing boxes and yet too many for one. When it was a situation of too many, a solution was to fly a fourth group box behind the combat wing in a high or low position. Alternatively group boxes could be increased to 21 bombers by either adding an extra element in the high squadron, or an extra bomber in the rear of each of the three squadron lead elements. This latter position was known as the diamond. Even so, the three-group combat box appeared to offer the best arrangement to combat the increasingly costly opposition from enemy fighters.

To further tighten up the group box the outer of the two elements forming a squadron was pulled in more behind the lead which had the effect of aircraft within each element being stacked in one direction while the elements and squadrons were stacked in the opposite direction. (6)

With the introduction of the combat wing box, Luftwaffe tactics changed to attacking the extremities – the high squadron of the high group or the low squadron of the low group – which received little firepower support from other parts of the box. Such was enemy concentration on the low squadron of the low group that this position became dubbed Purple Heart Corner in consideration of the chances of being killed or injured while flying there. In the summer of 1943 measures explored to lessen this vulnerability led to a modification of the formation flown by exposed squadrons; the echelon of their elements was reversed, having the effect of tucking in these bombers more behind the lead squadron. While also giving greater lateral compression of the formations this, and the previous measure, did little to improve the control of the combat wing box. The groups frequently became disarranged in turns where the high group often had difficulty in seeing the lead group.

The enemy was quick to take advantage of any disarray; a bomber with mechanical trouble or inexpert pilotage becoming a straggler had a high chance of being shot down. On some missions over 50 per cent of losses were straggling aircraft. Apart from emphasising formation discipline and fostering good maintenance there was little that could be done about stragglers. Without benefit of long-range fighter escort on deep penetrations the large combat wing box remained standing operational procedure until the winter of 1943 and thereafter as an optional formation until July 1944. Originally a one minute separation (3 miles) was planned between combat wings. From

DEVELOPMENTS in the DEPLOYMENT of GROUP FORMATIONS.

JAVELIN of Groups – December 1942

1 GROUP - 18 A/c

WEDGE of Groups – February 1943

1 GROUP - 18 A/c

5

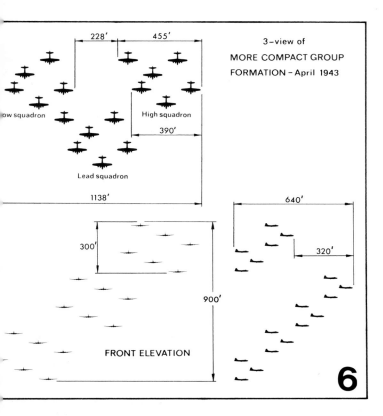

3-view of
MORE COMPACT GROUP
FORMATION – April 1943

228' 455'

ow squadron   High squadron

390'

Lead squadron

1138'

300'   640'

320'

900'

FRONT ELEVATION

6

Although by mid-January 1944 the 36-plane box had been accepted by most units, the 54-plane combat wing continued to be used when enemy fighters were expected. A doubling of unit establishment at 8th AF bomber bases beginning in October 1943 led to many groups flying two formations on a mission by January 1944. Composite groups, made up of squadrons from different groups in a combat wing, had been used for many months and this now became less common. Nevertheless, combat attrition, damage and repair often found groups unable to despatch high numbers during winter 1943–44 and spring 1944. For this reason many 18- and 21-plane group formations continued to be flown.

From the spring of 1944 ground anti-aircraft fire assumed the major threat to the 8th's bombers. This changed the requirements of a formation to one where mutual fire support could be relaxed and the emphasis placed on combining bombing efficiency with minimum exposure to flak.

In May 1944 the 1st Division experimented with a rearward spread of the elements in a 12-plane squadron, primarily to remove the danger of bombs falling on the lower aircraft. For the many tactical missions flown during 1944 against targets of small area at locations requiring only shallow penetration of hostile airspace, the 12-plane squadron box was the predominant formation, albeit that it was basically a section of the 36-plane group box. There were further trial formations but the 27- and 36-plane group boxes were still considered as standing operational procedure.

During the winter of 1944–45 further experiments were made with formations arrayed to minimise losses to flak, as concentrations of this formidable weapon grew. Using the basic 27-plane box, a slight lateral spread of elements within a squadron, and more space between squadrons, lessened the damage that any one shell burst could cause. At the same time the wing elements were brought further forward so that the whole group formation was both longitudinally and laterally more compact, offering a smaller plan target to flak gunners. When required a fourth 9-plane squadron could be added in a low-low position. This new 27- or 36-plane group formation proved easier to control and fly, the enhanced cohesion producing better bomb patterns. First introduced in February 1945, it remained the principal B-17 formation until the end of hostilities. (7)

B-24 groups of the 2nd Division used basically the same formation as the B-17s during 1945, but with modifications to

January 1944 this was extended to two minutes (6 miles) to allow for manoeuvring, particularly on IP approach when groups positioned in train for the bomb run. In practice the separation between combat wings was usually much greater.

Although VIII BC strength quadrupled during the spring and summer of 1943, Luftwaffe tactics and new weapons took an increasing toll of the bombers. Particularly threatening was the use of air-launched rockets fired from outside the effective range of the bombers' .50-calibre machine guns. By mid-October penetrations were restricted until more long-range fighter escort was available, although deterioration in the weather was the major obstacle to the pace of bomber operations for the rest of that year.

In mid-October 1943 experiments were again conducted with a 36-aircraft group formation, primarily to concentrate as many bombers as possible in a compact mass to take full advantage of the few radar Pathfinders then availalbe. The inclined group wedge was retained but the number of elements in a squadron was doubled. Aircraft within an element then flew on the same level while the elements were separated in altitude but had only a little stagger in what amounted to lead, high, low and low-low positions. With the new 36-plane group box a bomber column with groups in trail was also revised, each flying at the same altitude and separated by some four miles. Not only did it prove a much more satisfactory formation for 'blind' bombing, but was also easier for fighters to escort in that it was less given to disruption. Even so, as with all large formations, it was still difficult to fly. Where visual bombing was anticipated the low-low element of a squadron was often omitted making a 27-plane group which provided a greater safety margin when bombing – less risk of a bomber being struck by the release from a higher aircraft. These two formations, the 27- and 36-plane box, became standing operational procedure for most of 1944 with some variations introduced by individual combat wings. B-24 groups experimented with three distinct 12-plane squadron boxes with the introduction of the 36-plane group in an effort to reduce the straggling common to all large close-knit formations.

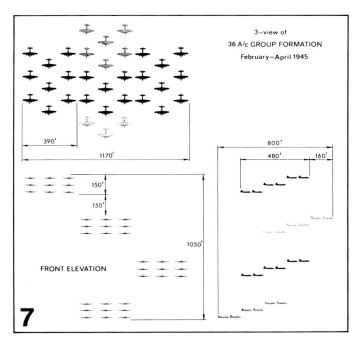

3-view of
36 A/c GROUP FORMATION
February–April 1945

390'

1170'

800'

480'   160'

150'

150'

1050'

FRONT ELEVATION

7

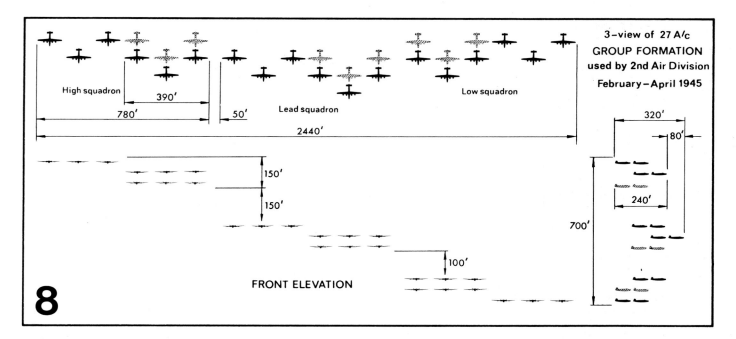

8

3-view of 27 A/c
GROUP FORMATION
used by 2nd Air Division
February–April 1945

High squadron
390'
780'
50'
Lead squadron
Low squadron
2440'

FRONT ELEVATION
150'
150'
100'

320'
80'
240'
700'

meet the peculiarities of their type. (8) B-24s were more difficult to fly in high altitude formation and pilots had more restricted visibility. Nevertheless, with the aim of obtaining a wider bomb pattern one element in each squadron – either in a high or low position – was flown to one side. A variation was for No 2 or No 3 aircraft of a squadron side element to cross over while the two other aircraft of the same element closed in. This put two aircraft on one side of the squadron's main flight of six and one on the other side, a manoeuvre conducted before the bomb run and designed to meet bomb pattern requirements.

arthe 96th Combat Wing groups of 2nd Division developed and used a variation of this formation. (9) Instead of flying the three squadrons as lead, high right and low left, they were stacked in trail as lead, low and low-low. While increasing the time individual squadrons took to pass over a defended target, their forward stagger enabled groups to fly at much closer intervals on the bomb run. This halved the time taken to get the whole combat wing across a target, lessening the time they were exposed to flak. Moreover, condensing the size of the group box longitudinally improved the bomb pattern, and the formation allowed each group to give one another good fire support. The use of this formation contributed in some measure to the superior bombing results of this wing during the final months of the war. On the route to the IP and after the target the 96th Combat Wing flew its groups as a low lead, a left high and a right high-high.

The terminology for describing the various formations – squadron, group and combat wing boxes – was derived from the size of unit that would be expected to fill a particular formation. In practice even a squadron formation could be composed of aircraft from two or more different squadrons. With the changes in formation strengths there arose some confusion in termin-

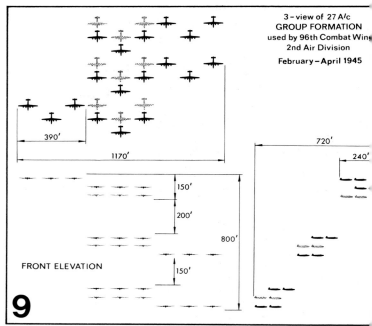

3-view of 27 A/c
GROUP FORMATION
used by 96th Combat Wing
2nd Air Division
February–April 1945

390'
1170'
150'
200'
800'
150'
FRONT ELEVATION

9

720'
240'

ology in that by 1944 the 36-plane group was also referred to as a combat wing while a 12-plane squadron passed as a group in some quarters, principally in 3rd Division. These anomalies seem to have disappeared by the end of that year. In the 2nd Division the squadron formation was commsily called a section and in some instances an element was referred to as a flight.

Visual Bombing

The visual bombing technique employed by the 8th Air Force heavy bombers was based on the use of the Model M sight, popularly known as the Norden. If correctly operated this instrument was capable of precise aim, but in practice the vicissitudes of combat and the very high altitudes at which it was employed mitigated against perfection. To reduce the danger of enemy anti-aircraft fire the bombers normally flew at around 25,000 feet when, for accuracy, much lower levels were desirable. Bombing accuracy decreased in direct proportion to increase in altitude. Where flak defences were considered meagre, attack altitudes were often reduced with a general improvement in the number of hits on target. Nevertheless, the correct adjustment of the bombsight remained paramount in the success of any visual attack.

Visual bombing equipment was basically the same in both the B-17 and B-24. Many modifications were made between 1942 and 1945 but the overall functioning of the equipment, and the technique for its employment, remained little changed. On the left of the bombardier's position in both aircraft was the bombing control panel. It incorporated an airspeed indicator and altimeter together with a number of switches and indicator lights, notably those for the predetermined selection of the order and interval of bomb releasethrough a system known as the intervalometer. Below the control panel was a quadrant with two or three levers. If there were two, the left-hand lever was pulled to engage the order of drop pre-set on the intervalometer or pushed fully forward for a salvo – instantaneous release of all bombs in the bay. The other quadrant lever opened the bomb-bay doors. On a three-lever quadrant the additional lever, located on the extreme left, controlled external bomb racks when fitted.

The bombsight was situated centrally and overhanging the flat glass nose panel which had anti-distortion properties. The sight instrument proper was mounted on a base box unit called the stabiliser, housing gyroscopic stabilising equipment and electrical components for the bombsight flight directional controls. Through these the bombardier's desired changes in course, made by manipulation of the bombsight, were conveyed to the Pilot's Directional Indicator (PDI) on the cockpit instrument panel for the pilot to follow, or to the automatic pilot (A-5 or C-1 models). The latter system was known as Automatic Flight Control Equipment (AFCE) but the term was later superseded.

The sight proper was the intricate instrument into which the bombardier fed figure data, mostly interrelated, affecting the fall of a bomb. These factors were: aircraft altitude, determining the time a bomb took to drop; forward speed affecting the distance the bomb would travel from its initial forward impetus on leaving the aircraft to its point of impact, trailing some distance behind the aircraov; atmospheric conditions, particularly wind strength and direction causing bomb deflection – in a cross-wind of the distance of drift from the aircraft's track towards the target; and bomb ballistics, the shape, size and weight of the bomb offering various degrees of air resistance, so affecting its dropping time and trajectory.

The bomb ballistic figures were obtaines by the bombardier from a table prior to the mission. While both attack altitude and airspeed were planned beforehand, precise data on these had to be observed from instruments at least five minutes before reaching the IP. Drift also had to be determined from instruments – the ABC computer – at this time. Whether PDI or AFCE was used on the bomb run it was absolutely essential that altitude and airspeed remained constant while the bombardier synchronised his sight. A barely perceptible increase in airspeed, a dip or skid at this time could unbalance the mechanism and affect the accuracy of the drop. In synchronising the sight the bombardier would first set in the figures for drift and drop-ping angle, taking into account bomb ballistics, trail, altitude and speed. As soon as the target was identified the bombardier asked the pilot for control on the C-1 auto-pilot – if AFCE was being used – and then proceeded to try and pick up the target aiming point through the optical part of the sight. This was a telescope with cross-hairs: the vertical cross-hair established course and the horizontal, the rate of closure – the range. By manipulating a control on the left of the sight the bombardier couh centre the vertical hair on the target; what he was in fact doing was altering the course of the aircraft through the automatic pilot (or directing the pilot to do so by PDI). Turning a control on the right of the instrument brought the horizontal hair across the target aiming point. The bombardier checked that the sight was stabilised by observing the bubble level of the gyros, and clutched in the electrical drive motor. The sight then automatically computed the time point for release. On the right of the sight were two indices, one indicating the bombing angle set-in by the bombardier, the other the 'rate' factor established by alignment of the horizontal cross-hair. The rate indicator, synchronised to the forward speed of the aircraft, gradually moved towards the other and when the two indices met the bombs released automatically.

A device known as extended vision allowed extra adjustment of the telescope angle to pick up the target at greater range. It was essential to return the telescope to normal position before making final adjustments to the sight or the bombs would drop short of the target, which happened on more than one occasion.

Even from 25,000 feet remarkable accuracy could be obtained if a Norden was correctly set and synchronised. There were, however, many factors that could contribute to poor bombing. The complex electrical system of sight or associated equipment might fail, although more trouble was experienced with the malfunctioning of the intervalometer and bomb release mechanisms than the actual sight apparatus. Freezing up of equipment and damage caused by enemy action were other reasons for failure. Human error, directly or indirectly, was the most frequent cause of inaccurate bombing, with inability to identify the target in time due to a wrong heading or poor visibility being high on the list.

The bombsight automatic system could be by-passed by the bombardier and bombs released by a toggle switch when he saw the indices meet. There was, however, no mechanical release for the bombs and they could only be liberated by physical force on the shackles. The 'in train' (dropping at intervals) and salvo electrical release systems were independent. There was also a salvo release switch in the cockpit for emergency use by the pilots.

When targets were partially obscured by smoke screens or small amounts of cloud, preventing the bombardier picking up his aiming point, it was possible to make a successful release by resorting to what was termed 'grid bombing'. This involved the use of a plexiglas overlay marked with vertical and horizontal lines to form a scaled grid, the preferred type being the RAF's Ground Speed – Second Delay Grid. The grid was placed over the target area map with its central vertical line aligned to the aircraft's track and a base horizontal line to an identified checkpoint ahead. Another horizontal line of the grid that intersected the target on the map provided the time in seconds that bomb release was to be delayed in relation to the speed and distance involved in the bomb run. The bombardier could then synchronise his sight on the identified checkpoint he could see, but delay the actual release for the specified number of seconds indicated on the grid. Successful use of this system usually required the navigator to assist with stop-watch and to operate the toggle switch, leaving the bombardier free to re-synchronise his sight should the cloud or smoke clear from the target. Grid bombing was occasionally employed with varying results at targets where radar aids would not be effective. Much depended on the skill of individual bombardiers, particularly in identifying checkpoints accurately and in sufficient time to make use of the grid.

Bombardier training in the United States had originally been based on the lead aircraft of each element or small section sighting for range and deflectioenwhile all others sighted for range only. This was quickly shown to be impracticable and dangerous in large formations where even slight bombardier-controlled manoeuvring on the bomb run might lead to collisions. In September 1942 it was accepted that bombing would have to be on the squadron formation leader's aim and that element leaders would set their sights for range only. This meant that from the IP squadrons manoeuvred to approach the target in train. By December that year the increase in enemy fighter opposition and the need to maintain large defensive formations influenced moves to drop on a group box leader's aim so that squadrons would not have to separate at the IP. With this change squadron formation leaders sighted for range only. Although the drop-on-group-leader held sway until the spring of 1944, against small targets or those where fighter opposition was not anticipated, bombing was still on a squadron formation basis. There was variation too in the positioning of deputy leaders depending on the size of formation. In group bombing the deputy was frequently the leader of the high squadron during 1943. Sometimes a wing aircraft in the lead element was so designated and with the introduction of Pathfinder leaders the deputy nearly always took this position.

While the drop-on-leader technique concentrated a pattern from a single formation, it had the disadvantage of a fractional time delay between the release of the lead plane's bombs and those of the rest of the formation. Much depended on fast human reaction as other bombardiers watched for the leader's bombs to fall away. To achieve a good pattern around the Mean Point of Impact, the planned centre of destruction, the Aiming Point for the leadplane was short of the MPI to allow for the delay in releases by the other aircraft.

In an effort to make the leadplane's drop more visible, in the early spring of 1943, 1st Bomb Wing groups began a practice of painting the bombs carried in bright colours – red, yellow or white and, more usually, striped in these colours. Later in 1943 coloured cloth streamers were fixed to the bomb fins and there was some experimentation with smoke flares strapped to bombs. The smoke plumes were found thin and were too quickly dissipated to be of benefit. The use of the powerful Skymarker smoke trail bomb for pathfinder work in the autumn of 1943 led to its general adoption for inclusion in all loads carried by lead bombers, whether the attack was visual or by radar means.

The desirability of having all aircraft in a formation release instantaneously with the leader led to the consideration of the use of radio triggering. As often happened, the genesis of such devices was in combat units.

During the 1943–44 winter Capt William M. Miller and T/Sgt Beljan of 413th Squadron, 96th Group successfully developed a system whereby the meeting of the indices on the Norden bombsight caused a radio signal to be transmitted to receivers in other aircraft close by, triggering release of their bomb loads. US heavy bombers were fitted with a radio marker beacon set intended for aiding location should an aircraft be forced down in a remote area. This equipment, not used in the ETO, was utilised as the transmitter for these experiments. During the initial trial of the Radio Bomb Release (RBR) a premature release was experienced suggesting interference by some other radio transmission on the same frequency. Nevertheless, high command was sufficiently impressed by the RBR to despatch Miller and Beljan to the US at the end of March 1944 to work on further development. As the original system was vulnerable to interference and jamming, interest centred on using the radio equipment for the *Azon* controllable bomb. By having three different frequencies transmitted simultaneously this radio was practically immune from jamming.

Meanwhile in the UK an improved RBR using the original aircraft marker beacon was made in two B-24s of 392nd Group by 3rd SAD at Neaton and successfully tested the following month. The equipping of 14th Combat Wing began and it was planned to make the RBR standard in all 2nd Division B-24s. However, concern over the possibility of the enemy jamming the system, shortage of items to effect modifications and the time involved in installation saw the plan abandoned in fdsour of the more promising *Azon* types.

After successful trials in the US, 12 B-17Gs with *Azon* RBR were sent to the UK in June 1944 and assigned to 96th Group. A further 14 96th aircraft were fitted with *Azon* receivers and after two highly successful trial bombing over UK ranges, the system was first used operationally on 11 August. Although bombs failed to release automatically from the signalling lead bomber because of a rack malfunction, all loads were triggered in the other 13 Fortresses. Resultant bomb pattern at the target, Mulhouse, was very concentrated and judged as no more than 600 feet long. Plans to equip the whole 3rd Division with *Azon* RBR – later given the cover name *Crawfish* – were frustrated by the need for further refinements and the low priority accorded to the delivery of transmitters and receivers from the USA. Not until the final month of the war was *Crawfish* generally available to all 3rd Division units and there was little opportunity for its use before hostilities ceased.

Overcast Bombing

The predominance of cloud in the north-western European sky was a major obstacle to visual bombing and the principal limiting factor in VIII BC operations, grounding bombers on an average four days out of five. During the winter fo 1942–43 it became obvious to even the most ardent promoter of visual attack that other means had to be sought to pursue the campaign during inclement weather. An inrbrest in the radars (high-powered radio pulses, reflected or regenerated, for locating objects or determining one's own position) developed by the British for night operations eventually led to an 8th Air Force Pathfinder Force and, subsequently, to a bombing-through-overcast capability. While radar techniques never achieved the accuracy of visual bombing, they greatly increased 8th Air Force operating capability. Radar-guided bombing received a number of descriptive terms in the 8th Air Force, namely Blind Bombing, Bombing Through Overcast (commonly just BTO), Overcast Bombing, but the most persistent term was PFF derived from Pathfinder Force.

MOLING

The first venture in overcast bombing was aimed more at interruption than destruction. Appreciating that winter weather would curtail normal bombing operations, VIII BC became interested in small-force harassing raids using British navigational radar to operate over enemy territory in thick cloud. The primary objective was to keep the enemy's air-raid and defensive measures alerted and thereby disrupt industrial production; bombs carried would be unlikely to have much direct effect. A plan to train and equip a single B-24 squadron for this task was approved by 8th Air Force on 24 October 1942. Originally the intention was to use a squadron of the recently arrived 44th Bomb Group, but as this organisation had only three squadrons instead of the normal four, it was decided not to further reduce the Group's strength and instead use a squadron of the operational 93rd Bomb Gr P. The 329th Bomb Squadron under Major George S. Brown (Head of the US Combined Chiefs of Staff in 1970s) was selected and moved to the satellite airfield at Bungay early in December and had its eight B-24Ds fitted with *Gee* sets.

Gee was the cover name for the secret equipment which allowed precise position fixing by an aircraft over some 350 miles through signals beamed from three beacons in England. The signals were displayed as pulses of light on the small screen of the '*Gee* box' receiver at the navigator's position which was moved from the nose to the flight deck behind the pilots. The fix was determined by measuring the relative time required for pulses of energy to travel from the ground stations to the aircraft. With *Gee* a trained crew could fly a completely 'blind' course in cloud and always know their exact location to within five to ten miles.

Under the code name *Moling*, operations were to involve single aircraft but with strictly observed limitations. A pilot had to abandon the mission if icing or other severe weather was encountered and if armament or radio failed. Over enemy territory the bomber had to fly within or near the top of cloud cover and continually engage in systematic evasive action in accordance with prescribed procedures. Ideal weather for *Moling* was defined as 10/10 cloud and if there was insufficient cloud then an operation had to be abandoned. Dead reckoning was to be the primary means of navigation with *Gee* as a check. The initial *Moling* operations were to be considered experimental with a view to developing technique and tactical doctrine which might be extended to include the use of specially equipped bombers as guides to lead formations over cloud cover to targets in the clear, or to engage in 'blind' bombing.

From 16 December 1942 the 329th Bomb Squadron prepared for *Moling*. The Ruhr was to be the prime target area, but suitable weather did not arrive until 2 January 1943. That day four B-24Ds left Bungay but over the sea the cloud thinned and all the bombers returned to base; further attempts on 11 and 13 January were also abandoned for the same reason, as were three in February. In March, the 329th Bomb Squadron rejoined its parent group and participated in normal daylight missions although a final *Moling* operation was attempted on 26 March, only to be thwarted again by thinning cloud. Thereafter this form of operation was abandoned. Ironically, when visual bombing had so frequently been adversely affected by cloud, there was never sufficient to allow a successful *Moling* operation. One outcome of this abortive experiment was the general appreciation of *Gee* as a navigational aid and plans were put in hand to install it in all VIII BC bombers.

Mentor to the 329th Bomb Squadron's endeavours was Major William S. Cowart, an VIII BC Hq officer who had been instructed by General Eaker to specialise in new radar developments. He had been one of the original six members of Eaker's staff who arrived in Britain in February 1942 – then as the General's personal aide. Cowart enthused about the potential of 'blind bombing' aids, and the benefits of establishing a Pathfinder

Force similar to that in RAF Bomber Command. With Eaker's approval, he went to Washington to obtain sanction to form a special organisation to experiment with and conduct such operations.

Meanwhile, discussions with the Air Ministry and RAF resulted in agreements that the British would supply two types of 'blind bombing' radar known as H2S and *Oboe*, assist with their installation in US bombers and train personnel in servicing and operating. Further, the RAF suggested that 8th Air Force establish a unit to specialise as a pathfinder force. As VIII BC would be predominantly a B-17 force during 1943, it was decided to concentrate initially on adapting Fortresses to radar uses.

THE PATHFINDER FORCE

The original plan for a pathfinder force called for a separate unit directly under VIII BC control. Alconbury was selected as force base in April 1943, mainly for its proximity to RAF pathfinder headquarters at Wyton. The 325th Bomb Squadron of 92nd Bomb Group was nominated the nucleus for operationally experienced crews, drawn from other units, to train to operate the new equipment. The force was required to be ready for operations by 1 September, when it was envisaged that its aircraft would be employed to lead combat wing formations. It was planned that two other squadrons would be added before that date, so with this in view in July it was decided to move the 92nd Bomb Group from Alconbury to Podington. Owing to improvements being made to the runways at Podington the move was postponed until mid-September.

In August 1943 Hq USAAF gave its approval for the formation of a new bomb group devoted to the development of bad-weather pathfinding. This was to consist of three squadrons, one operating the American version of H2S, one using British H2S and *Oboe* in B-17s and the third having the same equipment in B-24s. Official activation was at Alconbury on 20 August 1943 as the 482nd Bomb Group, with Col Baskin Lawrence, a former commander of 92nd Bomb Group, the CO, while Lt Col William Cowart, the pathfinder expert, was nominated Air Executive. Of its three squadrons, the 812th Bomb Squadron had Capt Fred Rabo, formerly of 305th Group, as commander who was despatched to the USA to bring back the first B-17s fitted with the American-built version of H2S. The 813th Bomb Squadron, under Capt William C. Anderson, was a redesignation of the 325th Bomb Squadron that had been conducting pathfinder training at Alconbury. The 814th Bomb Squadron (at first inadvertently advised as the 819th) under Capt Clement Bird, was to operate the B-24s, its personnel including men who had been connected with the abortive *Moling* enterprise. Apart from the 813th Bomb Squadron with four *Oboe* and two H2S-equipped B-17Fs, the 482nd Group had little substance on activation and continued to be in a formative state for several weeks.

A major set-back was the loss of the CO and most senior personnel of 813th Bomb Squadron flying in a B-17E which struck Skiddaw mountain in the Lake District on 14 September. Major Bird became the new 813th commander and his place in the 814th was taken by Major John Roche, a 29-mission veteran from the 93rd Bomb Group. The 814th was hampered by lack of personnel and equipment until the new year. In October 1943 the 479th Antisubmarine Group equipped with B-24s was disbanded in England and many of their personnel were used to enlarge the ground echelon of the 482nd. The aircraft of three of the 479th's squadrons were sent to Alconbury for possible use in pathfinder work. Each was already fitted with SCR-717 sea-search radar but following tests it was decided that this equipment, intended for locating vessels at sea, was quite unsuitable for adaption to VIII BC requirements. However, the radar mechanics of the 19th Antisubmarine Squadron were retained to become the nucleus of personnel to service 814th Bomb Squadron radars.

The 482nd Group participated in its first pathfinder operation on 27 September 1943 using H2S over Emden. Although it continued to provide pathfinder lead aircraft for 8th Air Force throughout the winter of 1943–44, a decision to eventually terminate its operational role was made soon after this debut. As more equipment and trained personnel became available it was planned to decentralise radar squadrons and to establish pathfinder capability in each conventional bomb group. The 482nd would then operate as the theatre radar school and conduct experiments with new equipment. The Group was taken off regular operational status on 26 March 1944.

H2S

The first pathfinder bombing aid used operationally by 482nd Bomb Group was the RAF's 10 centimetre frequency airborne terrain scanning radar, originally developed for use in night area bombing, which had that service's cover designation H2S. In the 8th Air Force it was popularly known as 'Stinkey'. Its potential for use in bombing through overcast led to USAAF interest and while arrangements were made for production and development in the USA, the British initially released eight sets for installation in US heavy bombers in the UK. The H2S set transmitted high frequency electrical impulses downward through a revolving antenna, these impulses being reflected back and converted into light images on a cathode ray tube. The reflections, varying in intensity depending on the nature of the terrain below, were discernible on a screen, popularly known as the 'scope'. The contrast between land and water was particularly clear; built up areas could also be discerned and, with skill, identified. At 25,000 feet the cover of H2S was a radius of about 50 miles.

In March 1943 four radio mechanics and two officers were sent to the Telecommunications Research Establishment (TRE) at Great Malvern to learn about H2S at this British establishment. That same month a 92nd Group B-17F, serial number 42-5793, was sent to RAF Defford for installation of H2S. Initial proposals were to site the scanner in the ball turret well but General Eaker did not wish to sacrifice armament. Instead, the scanner was placed below the B-17's nose where, shielded by a bathtub-shaped plastic cov b, it was well clear of the ground during take-offs and landings, and also gave anti-interference advantages. The radar scope and tuning set were situated on the left side of the navigator's position and necessitated the left-hand nose gun being repositioned further forward. Although the primary installation made at Burtonwood was completed in April, many difficulties arose in trials at Defford and were not satisfactorily overcome for several weeks. The aircraft was returned to Alconbury in August and later that month a second B-17F with H2S was received and put into the intense training programme. However, the radar sets were found somewhat temperamental, and polar diagram troubles were a recurring problem at this time. A further two H2S B-17s arrived in the first weeks of September and all four aircraft of 813th Bomb Squadron took part as combat wing leaders on the first combat mission, 27 September 1943. H2S pathfinders were used on several missions during the following winter but continuing difficulties with the equipment caused their relegation to deputy leads when the H2X B-17s began operations on 3 November.

H2X was an improved version of H2S built in the United States. Nevertheless, it was an H2S B-17F that led the first 8th Air Force bombing raids on Berlin, 4 March 1944, but 42-30731, piloted by 1/Lt William V. Owens, had its radar fail on the bomb run. Two days later the same aircraft was more successful, taking over the lead when an H2X aircraft aborted in the major attack on the German capital.

Much more difficulty was experienced wid installing H2S in a B-24 than in the B-17 and although the initial adaption had been started at Burtonwood in April 1943, the problems were still not fully resolved when the aircraft was delivered at Alconbury in October. The close proximity of the fuselage to the ground meant that the scanner had to be retractable and after some experiments it was placed in the rear fuselage. On following B-24 adaptations the ball turret was removed and a retractable scanner located in the well. The prototype B-24D H2S installation was the subject of constant modification and repair. The first operational H2S B-24H did not arrive until December and was first used on operation, 11 January 1944 when four led the combat wings of 2nd Division to the Brunswick area. H2S B-24s were retired as soon as sufficient H2X-equipped models were available. All told, the 482nd Group received eight B-17Fs, one B-24D and eight B-24Hs with H2S installations.

OBOE

The first 'blind bombing' radar taken up by 8th Air Force was Oboe, an extremely accurate technique for positioning an aircraft providing the range was within 250 miles. A beam system, two ground stations controlled each Oboe aircraft. One station sent 'cat' transmissions to the pilot to enable him to fly the arc of a circle that passed directory over the target. These signals were received aurally in the form of a steady note when the aircraft was on the correct course, as 'pips' when it was to the left, and as 'peeps' if it veered right. The other ground beacon was known as the 'mouse', its controller calculating the speed of the aircraft along its track and informing the navigator by aural signal when bombs should be released. It took approximately 10 minutes to control an Oboe bomber on a target run. The Oboe apparatus in the aircraft consisted of a receiver-transmitter automatically triggered by the pulses from the ground stations.

The RAF use of Oboe in the 1942–43 winter was confined to fast Mosquito aircraft operating at night. The British feared that the equipment might prematurely fall into enemy hands if fitted in slow bombers and cause the frequencies used to be compromised. Therefore, in March 1943, 8th Air Force agreed not to use Oboe in daylight until this equipment was available on a larger scale, and an advanced development, Oboe Mk II, was in production in case the enemy were able to neutralise the original type by jamming. Meanwhile Oboe Mk I installations would be made in US heavy bombers and personnel trained in its use.

In February 1943 six VIII BC men were sent to the TRE to learn about the Oboe technique. The following month two 305th BG B-17s (42-5745 and 41-24359) were sent to Wyton, the RAF pathfinder base near Huntingdon, for installations to be made. The mechanics who had trained at TRE helped with these installations and maintenance of the sets while trials were undertaken from Wyton. The Oboe B-17s on transfer to Alconbury were used to train more personnel. Two more B-17s with Oboe arrived during the summer and the total reached 12 by the late autumn. Six B-24s were also fitted with Oboe. There was experimentation with the equipment at Alconbury and an attempt was made to link Oboe signal with the B-17's AFCE system, a trial installation being made. Oboe was not released for operational use by 8th Air Force in daylight until 15 October 1943, the first mission led by Oboe B-17 pathfinders being to Düren five days later. Of the two aircraft involved, one aborted early and the other could not pick up signals in the target area.

Five more missions were led by Oboe B-17s during November but none of these was totally satisfactory. Following failure on the last, when deterioration of signal strength was apparently due to atmospheric conditions prevalent at the high altitude, Oboe-led operations were suspended. However, operational tests were conducted at night with B-17s equipped with Oboe II. Oboe Mk II used 9 cm wavelength compared to the 1½ metres of the Mk I but while the later model was practically free frogjamming it had slightly less range. By the end of January 1944 it was apparent that other radar bombing devices then in use would more satisfactorily meet 8th Air Force requirements and a decision was made to relinquish all *Oboe* equipment – which required rigid scheduling in operations and was not easily decentralised – to the 9th Air Force, other than sets used for operational experimentation. The range limitation and the fear that *Oboe* Mk I would be jammed were the major considerations leading to discontinuing its use in 8th Air Force heavy bombers. The B-26 Marauder mediums needed an overcast bombing aid and *Oboe* was ideally suited to their short range requirements and medium altitude attacks. Indeed, *Oboe*-guided bombing by the 9th Air Force became noted for remarkable accuracy. Most *Oboe* Mk II equipment and trained servicing personnel were transferred to the 9th Air Force as of 7 February 1944, together with five *Oboe* B-24s. These aircraft, in which *Oboe* Mk II sets had been installed, were later returned to 8th Air Force after the sets had been removed at Stansted.

H2X

The Massachusetts Institute of Technology at Boston was the principal agency involved in micro-wave research and radar development for the US Government in the early 1940s. Arrangements were made for construction of airborne radars similar to the British H2S but of 3 centimetre capability at the Institute's Radiation Laboratory, and for an initial 12 sets to be installed in B-17s and readied for delivery to the 8th Air Force by September 1943. All 12 sets were hand-built by 16 USAAF radar specialists under the supervision of two officers and several technicians from the Radiation Laboratory. The official designation for the set was AN/APS-15 although in the 8th Air Force it became known by the cover terms H2X and *Mickey*. While these sets were under construction the wiring, antennae and retraction gear (known as Group A parts) were being prepared and installed in Fortresses at Rome Air Depot, New York state. The first installation was in a B-17F, the following eleven on new B-17Gs. The scanner was positioned like that of H2S under the nose but in a cylindrical radome which was semi-retractable. With the radome extended these B-17Gs appeared to the uninitiated as having double chin turrets.

Major Rabo, who had been despatched from Alconbury in the summer to organise the collection of these H2X aircraft, arrived back with the first aircraft on 21 September. Others followed, and after hurried theatre modifications the aircraft were available for their first operational use on 3 November when they placed target markers for 2nd Division Liberators. The H2X sets were not without their problems, as was only to be expected in this comparatively new technology. Even so, they produced images with much greater definition than H2S, and from mid-January 1944 the policy was for an H2X B-17 to lead with an H2S as deputy. As with H2S, the bomb release was made on the radar operator's verbal signal to the bombardier to toggle the bombs when the aircraft's position was at the desired point on the scope relative to the target image.

Further H2X-equipped B-17s did not arrive until the end of January 1944, the first pre-production aircraft landing at Alconbury on the 30th. Thereafter there was a steady flow, and 26 B-17Gs and 14 B-24Hs equipped with H2X arrived in February. The most notable difference between the original 12 H2X B-17s and the newcomers was that the retractable radar scanner was positioned in the ball turret well, the turret having been removed. There were the usual delays for modifications before these aircraft could be hastened into service. With the influx of new H2X-equipped bombers the plan to decentralise the radar PFF squadrons was put into effect.

In January the first contingent of trainees arrived from the divisions for instruction as *Mickey* operators. The plan was to first form a PFF squadron in each division, later in each combat wing and eventually in each group. The initial units selected were the 422nd Bomb Squadron of 305th Group, the 564th Bomb Squadron of 389th Group and the 413th Bomb Squadron of 96th Group. However, there was some shifting of personnel to other squadrons of the parent groups as the PFF squadrons were to receive several crews drawn from other units. In February each group in each division sent two crews to Alconbury for training and assignment to the squadron supporting their division. On completion of the course in mid-March, the squadrons returned to their home bases with 12 new H2X aircraft each and from 22 March began providing PFF leads for their respective divisions. Whenever possible, the crews selected to lead specific groups were those who were on detachment to the PFF unit from that group.

A doubling-up of strength occurred on 1 May when the 324th Bomb Squadron at Bassingbourn, the 66th Bomb Squadron at Shipdham and the 333rd Bomb Squadron at Bury St Edmunds were established as H2X pathfinder units. These were to serve the 1st and 94th, 14th and 20th, and 4th Combat Wings respectively. The third stage was reached on 1 June when five B-17s went to 1st Division to form a new unit and ten B-24s to 2nd Division to expand existing PFF units. By August there were PFF squadrons in each combat wing and by December all groups had their own PFF aircraft. In some case PFFs were concentrated in one squadron while in others each squadron in a group had one or two PFF aircraft. By the end of hostilities there was an average 12 PFF bombers in each group.

STANDING OPERATIONAL PROCEDURE (SOP)

The SOP established during the early H2S, *Oboe* and H2X-led missions was applicable to all pathfinder techniques. The PFF bomber, loaded with two target smoke marker bombs, would proceed to the airfield of the group scheduled to lead the mission for the division, arriving before briefing. While the aircraft was refuelled and bombed up its crew participated in the host group briefing. The combat wing commander for the mission and the lead navigator flew in the lead PFF aircraft. A DR navigator furnished by the host group flew in the deputy PFF aircraft if one was assigned. All other personnel on the PFF bombers were furnished by the PFF squadron involved, although often the rear gunner of the lead aircraft was replaced by an officer of the host group to monitor the formation. If weather prevented the PFF bomber arriving at the host group airfield in time for briefing, this was conducted at the home base and the PFF bomber took off and joined the assigned group at its assembly area. Except in emergencies, all PFF aircraft returned directly to Alconbury when 482nd Group conducted this service and the host group had to collect their aircrew from there. After decentralisation they landed at the host group station for debriefing.

During the mission the lead PFF bomber was responsible for navigating the briefed course, signalling when to open bomb doors and the dropping of marker flares. The host group provided a deputy for visual bombing who flew the other wing position of the lead element. If bombing was to be by visual means the PFF lead signalled by Aldis lamp to the visual deputy to take the lead at or before the IP and this aircraft pulled forward slightly ahead of the PFF bombers. At the IP the PFF lead fired double yellow pyrotechnic flares and double red at 'Bombs Away' when the smoke markers were also released.

In the first PFF missions there were only sufficient aircraft to mark for the leading combat wings of a division, succeeding wings having to bomb on smoke trails left by the groups ahead, which were often dissipated by winds. More smoke bombs were dropped by succeeding group leaders as replenishment of the marked spot but this was far from accurate and led to bomb loads being widely scattered. As soon as more aircraft were available an H2X pathfinder was placed to lead each combat wing, but it was obvious that to achieve a more accurate concentration of bombs a PFF lead was desirable in each group.

Procedure for PFF attacks remained little changed once a pathfinder could be provided for each group box. The PFF lead also assumed responsibility for visual sighting and carried the group bombardier for the mission.

SYNCHRONOUS H2X BOMBING

With the arrival of production H2X there was a greater effort towards improving the concentration and accuracy of bombing by this technique. While in general H2X could not locate the average pin-point target, it could locate sufficient area targets through cloud to increase 8th Air Force's bombing capability to a marked degree. Additionally, it was found to be of great value in locating targets on visual days by aiding the finding of check points and correcting navigation over cloud on the way to the target. Photographs of the images on H2X scopes taken over enemy territory were used to train radar operators in identifying precise locations. From study of such photographs operational analysts concluded that there were industrial targets situated beside cities or shore lines that might be pin-pointed with some accuracy through reference to the irregular shape of the landmark image. These light images were known as 'blips' – a few very large targets produced a blip of their own discernible on the H2X scope. By approaching the identifiable landmark from the appropriate direction, a target could be bombed by the aid of its known distance and direction from the landmark. This led to intensive investigation and ultimately the institution of a technique using H2X in conjunction with the Norden bombsight and automatic pilot system.

Where a landmark could be positively identified from the radar scope blip, a calculation of altitude and distance from a nearby target gave a sighting angle, enabling a bombardier to incorporate this setting in the Norden to synchronise the instrument. As the bomber proceeded along the track towards the target the H2X operator provided additional sighting angles to the bombardier to allow him to recheck the synchronisation of the sight. The bombs released automatically at the point computed by the sight, as if it were a visual drop. A further benefit of this link between radar operator and bombardier was that in cloud breaks the bombardier could easily take over for visual sighting as only minor corrections would be necessary. To aid this development tables were prepared for use in converting distance and altitude into sighting angles for the bombsight. By adding sighting angle data to the H2X computer drum the radar operator had the means of furnishing the bombardier with data on ground speed, drift and distance for every mile until the aircraft was within four or five miles of the target.

This co-ordinated method of bombing was first tried in April 1944 and was soon shown to improve overcast bombing with H2X. Its most notable application, in the early period of development, was the bombing of coastal defences in Normandy on D-Day, 6 June. As a lateral bomb pattern was required, multiple elements of 18 to 36 bombers flew line abreast with an H2X pathfinder in the centre of the line. The radar operators had been intensively trained to recognise the coastline patterns on their scope and, despite a complete overcast, bombing was accomplished without any of the 1000-plus bombers dropping short of a line 300 yards beyond the beaches.

On 24 June the first major attempt to bomb an important strategic pin-point target by synchronous H2X was carried out against an oil refinery at Bremen where there were clear coast and river images on the radar scopes. The target survived but several bomb patterns were very close showing that this technique had great potential. Further study of synchronous bombing established that while a reasonable degree of success could be achieved against city areas or isolated industrial complexes, its use against small targets gave only a slight chance of bombs being placed on the desired MPI. Several other factors affected the accuracy of H2X attacks, most notably that one out of every four sightings proved ineffective because the H2X equipment failed, although this position improved during the final months of the war. It was also found that a much longer bomb run was required than for visual attacks, approximately 40 miles to give a higher chance of success. Moreover there was a striking correlation between the degree of cloud cover on the bomb run and bombing errors. Even a small break in the overcast enabled the bombardier to synchronise his bombsight and achieve considerable accuracy.

The 511th BS became the 351st BG's pathfinder squadron in October 1944, providing leads for all the Group's missions. *Partnership M for Mike* **is seen at 27,300 ft with H2X radome fully extended and bomb doors just beginning to open at the start of a PFF run on Kassel, March 1945.** (via K. Harbour)

GEE-H

Because H2X was completely self-contained and was not tied to ground station signals, it became the main PFF aid in the 8th Air Force. The beam-based radars however offered much greater accuracy, their primary drawback being range limitations. During the summer of 1943 there was interest in another British beam radar called Gee-H (or sometimes G-H) which incorporated the Gee box and was originally intended as a sophisticated navigation system. In September a B-17 (42-29994) and three mechanics were sent from Alconbury to RAF Newmarket for an initial installation. This aircraft was flown extensively after its return to Alconbury but as Oboe was at that time the chosen beam radar for B-17 pathfinders, Gee-H was eventually earmarked for B-24s. After eight test installations were made in early November it was decided that this device should be operationally employed by a 2nd Bomb Division unit leaving the 482nd Group to concentrate its efforts on perfecting Oboe, H2S and H2X.

The eight Gee-H B-24s were transferred with one officer and two mechanics to the 329th Bomb Squadron at Hardwick, the unit which had pioneered 8th Air Force Gee box bad weather operations a year earlier. The first operational use of Gee-H was on 28 January 1944 when four 329th Bomb Squadron pathfinders led the parent group, the 93rd, and the 446th Group to bomb a flying bomb site near Bonnières, France. V-weapon sites were almost the sole target type in the 31 Gee-H missions flown up to the time of the Allied cross-Channel invasion in June.

A basic difference between Gee-H and Oboe was that the interrogating transmitter was carried in the aircraft and not situated at the ground stations and has been described as 'Oboe in reverse'. Also its presentation was visual instead of aural. Effective range was 170 miles at 20,000 feet and 200 miles at 25,000 feet. The system was controlled by the navigator of the Gee-H bomber who turned on his equipment after leaving the English coast. The transmitter unit pulsed a signal which actuated the two Gee-H responder ground stations which pulsed answering signals on another frequency that were picked up by the receiver unit in the bomber and presented as two blips – one from each station – on the scope of the Gee box. One ground station pulsed a range or 'cat' signal, the other pulsed the releasing 'mouse' signal. The navigator watched the 'cat' blip to ensure the bomber was following the desired course which was an arc of a circle that cut through the target location. Any deviations from this course were immediately countered by corrections given to the pilot. When some 15 to 20 minutes off target the navigator operated another control which instantly gave calibration figures for the position of the 'mouse' blip. A chart beside the Gee scope listed a series of pre-determined figure/time check-points computed for each operation by Gee-H experts. The navigator compared the calibrations on his scope with this data which gave him his progress towards a final check-point known as the 'warning point'. The instant the 'mouse' blip reached the warning point he called 'Check' over the interphone to the bombardier. The bombardier carried a stop-watch set for a timed run on a figure previously supplied by the navigator and derived from the 'warning period' tables based on true altitude, ground speed and type of bomb. At the end of the timed run the bombardier used the toggle switch to release the bombs, other aircraft in the formation bombing on the leader's release of bombs and skymarkers.

While on average never as accurate as visual bombing, Gee-H was far superior to H2X against small targets as the point of attack could, theoretically, be pin-pointed by the ground station to within a few feet.

In May 1944 Gee-H equipment was fitted in selected B-17Gs of the 41st Combat Wing at Grafton Underwood, Kimbolton and Molesworth, and while these were used predominantly to lead their own group formations, they also provided leads for others in 1st Division. Gee-H was also allocated to 3rd Division's 486th BG and when this unit converted to B-17s in July 1944 the Gee-H B-24s were passed to 34th BG. After D-Day Gee-H attacks were expanded to many other types of targets, notably airfields, bridges, rail junctions and arms dumps. After June however there was a decline in this type of PFF bombing as Allied advances put most targets beyond the range of the ground stations in England, and by mid-August all were out of reach. Gee-H was not resumed until late September when the British, who operated the ground stations, established new sites on the Continent.

Meanwhile a programme of analysis and experimentation had resulted in a refined Gee-H method of operation. This was first put to use by 2nd Division when Gee-H operations recommenced in September 1944. As had been successfully done with H2X, a method of linking the Norden bombsight with the Gee-H technique was devised. Basically, it consisted of synchronising the bombsight at a number of Gee-H check-points. At briefing both navigator and bombardier received data for a series of check-points which had been computed to a high degree of precision by the Gee-H section at higher command. During the course of a mission the navigator advised and identified each check-point to the bombardier. At the first he called 'Check 1', the bombardier immediately adjusting his bombsight to the pre-determined sighting angle listed for that check-point in the Gee-H data sheet. This procedure was repeated as each check-point was reached and, if necessary, corrections made, until the bombsight automatically released the bomb load. This method was considered superior to the original in that it gave less margin for error at the critical point, that is the warning point. The 1st Division Gee-H units continued to use the original warning-point method of operation for some time but during October and November 1944 gradually went over to the new synchronous technique. From December 1944 all Gee-H operations were conducted in this way.

MICRO-H

Another type of radar for overcast bombing was under intensive development at Alconbury from the spring of 1944. Known originally as Microwave-H and later Micro-H, it went some way towards combining the advantages of beam radars with H2X. Introduced operationally by the 3rd Division on 1 December 1944, it was used exclusively by that Division's B-17s until the end of hostilities. However, both the 1st and 2nd Divisions trained to use Micro-H because of the risk of Gee-H being successfully jammed by the enemy. Micro-H could not be jammed. In the event, Gee-H, operating on the same frequency as Gee which had already been jammed successfully by the enemy, was never seriously interfered with.

Micro-H used two transmitting stations and these were set up near Namur, Belgium and Verdun, France. Like other beam radars, range was affected by the curvature of the earth and Micro-H could only be used reliably up to 180 miles range if the bomber was at 25,000 feet. Transmissions from these stations were received and presented to the radar navigator as two bright white dots on the H2S scope. The dots had to remain approximately equidistant from the centre of the scope for the bomber to be following the correct course – as with Gee-H, this was an arc running through the target. At the commencement of the bomb run the radar navigator set up his first check-point on the scope in the form of a range circle. As the aircraft moved towards the target the two white dots moved simultaneously towards the circumference of the range circle. When they touched it the navigator called the bombardier 'Check 1'. The bombardier immediately synchronised his sight to include the sighting angle from the pre-determined data in his brief. Likewise each check-point was synchronised into the bombsight until the aircraft reached the release point, a similar procedure to that of synchronous *Gee-H*.

Unlike *Gee-H* and *Oboe*, *Micro-H* was primarily an 8th Air Force service. The beacon personnel were on detachment from 482nd Group and all the computations were made by the *Micro-H* section at High Wycombe. While Micro-H was even more precise than *Gee-H*, in its original form it had three inherent restrictions – range, target handling capacity and course. Nothing could be done about range but means of reducing the other two restrictions were found. This was achieved by adapting the ground stations to pulse range and release signals as was done for *Gee-H*. The two white dots on the H2X scope thus represented 'cat' and 'mouse' and could be utilised in a similar way. Instead of the sole approach course and single target of the original *Micro-H* concept, four target approaches were possible and, by setting up the beacons to pulse several 'cat' ranges for tracking and 'mouse' signals to give different release points, four targets could be attacked. Cat and mouse *Micro-H* bombing began on 18 December 1944. Most of the 38 attacks made by 3rd Division employed this more flexible technique which was enhanced by the opening of another *Micro-H* beacon at Nijmegen, Holland, in January 1945.

Other types of radar bombing apparatus used by the 8th Air Force never passed the operational experimental stage, as mentioned under other headings.

Lead Crews

From the start of bombing operations it was policy to have the most experienced and practised crews fly the leading positions in group and squadron formations. It was soon evident that the success of a mission depended largely upon the abilities of the men in the lead bombers, and individual groups instigated their own programmes for fostering leadership skills. The first general acknowledgement in VIII BC of a lead crew policy was an announcement in July 1943 that each squadron would select four of its most experienced crews for leading. They then underwent additional training and always flew the lead position on combat missions. In order to conserve their experience, they only participated in every fourth mission by their unit. At the same time two aircraft in each squadron were fitted out with all the latest aids – notably *Gee* – and whenever possible were reserved solely for leading.

The key figures in a lead crew were pilot, navigator and bombardier who all underwent particularly intensive training when not engaged in operations. A supplement to a lead crew on many combat missions was a Command Pilot who usually flew in the co-pilot's seat of a group lead, acting as Combat Wing or Task Force commander as required. By 1944 the practice had changed and an air commander usually occupied a jump seat behind the pilots on the flight deck.

With the regularity of cloud over north-west Europe making navigation difficult, the task force lead crews during the summer of 1943 frequently had the services of an additional navigator who practised pilotage. The introduction of H2X radar during the following winter provided another navigational aid, for while this instrument was primarily intended for the direction of bombing through overcast, it could give a guide to the operating aircraft's position. When the 482nd Group furnished pathfinders that led divisions and combat wings, the host units supplied bombardiers, DR navigators and air commanders.

The early PFF missions were always accompanied by a deputy with a regular lead crew. When separate PFF units were formed in each division in March 1944, only an air commander was usually provided by the host group. Eventually H2X, *Gee-H* or *Micro-H*-equipped aircraft were available in every group for the use of lead crews. As soon as sufficient PFF aircraft were available in each group the deputy lead was also so equipped. In many groups, lead squadrons were formed; that is, all lead crews were concentrated in one existing squadron by shifting personnel among units in a group. When groups acquired their own PFF aircraft it became standard practice for group leads to carry three navigators: DR, pilotage and radar. Each squadron maintained four lead crews and always had two in training. If the policy was for all lead crews to be concentrated in one squadron, the total was 16 operational and eight in training. When training leads flew combat they headed elements or took a squadron deputy lead position. Lead crews were expected to fly 30 missions instead of the regular crews' 35 to complete a tour. They were also authorised to wear a special combat patch of blue and gold in their uniform.

A lead pilot was selected for his special abilities, as the compactness and smooth passage of a formation was largely dependent upon his skill and judgement. Changes in speed, altitude and course had to be made smoothly and gradually. If a leader flew erratically, it would be difficult for following aircraft to hold a compact formation. Pilots of squadron leads were trained not to keep their eyes fixed continually on the group lead, as this tended to make them fly erratically. The preferred way was to continually shift one's gaze from horizon to the group lead. Turns had to be made slowly for if too fast the formation would become scattered in trying to follow. Likewise abrupt increases in speed had similar effect; applications of power through a succession of small increments avoided this.

When flying S-turns, trying to lose time to make a control point, the indicated airspeed had to be reduced to 150 mph and the formation warned by radio. The turn at the IP had to be a definite bank of eight or ten degrees so that following units had no doubt that it was the IP turn. At all times the lead pilot had to fly a smooth, steady course with no abrupt changes of speed or altitude which could make difficulties for the rest of the formation.

The regular navigator of a lead crew practised DR (Dead Reckoning). He maintained a constant Air Plot which, apart from being the simplest and most accurate means of determining winds encountered, provided both pilotage and radar navigators with key information for commencing or recommencing their methods of navigation. While the DR navigator calculated the course by reference to time, ground-speed and drift, with confirmation from his *Gee* set while in range, the pilotage navigator of the combat wing or group leadplane pin-pointed landmarks he could visually identify. His work, of course, was made more difficult when there were only a few breaks in an undercast on which to make a contribution to confirming correct course.

A pilotage navigator was usually a senior group or squadron navigator who flew with a map in the nose turret of a B-24 or from a position behind the bombardier in a B-17. Sometimes pilotage was performed by the bombardier in lead B-17s. By using his H2X equipment to make regular fixes from radar scans the

Mickey operator (Radar Navigator) provided a third source of navigation. With dense undercast his work was particularly necessary. A regular dialogue was conducted by all three navigators to ensure confirmation of course and time at control points. If cloud was present on the bomb run from the IP the radar navigator worked in co-operation with the bombardier. Correct navigation of the planned route was the most critical factor in the execution of a bombing mission. Not only did it position the bombardier to perform his work at the target, but ensured that the formation would make correct rendezvous points with the escort and avoid the heavy concentratons of flak on route to and from the target.

All gunners on a lead crew were instructed to observe and report to the pilot on the position and behaviour of all other aircraft and constantly monitor the formation throughout a mission. Radio communications between other formation leaders, weather scouts, escort and command in the UK were all conducted by the combat wing lead.

Medium and Light Bomber Operations

As originally projected, 8th Air Force was to have both medium and light bomber units. Delays in establishing this force resulted in only four B-26 Marauder groups becoming operational before these medium bombers were transferred to a new tactical air force, the 9th. Nevertheless, there was a substantial operational period under 8th Air Force when the basic theatre procedures for medium bombers were developed. A-20 Havoc light bombers subsequently reaching the 9th Air Force in England employed similar procedures to the B-26s. Initially the sole light day bomber unit operational in 8th Air Force was the 15th Bomb Squadron which inaugurated all USAAF bombing from England on 4 July 1942. Its operational techniques were exclusively those practised by RAF light bomber squadrons at that time.

MEDIUM BOMBER PROCEDURES

In matters of servicing, briefing and other base procedures, the B-26 Marauder groups followed that of B-17 groups operating in 1943. Once airborne the requirements of low and medium altitude attack dictated other procedures. Initially the B-26 was to be used in low-level attack, a mode successful in the South-West Pacific Area. There was also some consideration of using the type for low-level shipping strikes and medium altitude bombing but the first concept held favour. In part this was determined by the fact that the Sperry D-8 bombsight fitted to the B-26B was inaccurate if used above 400 feet against small targets. Also, low-level operations would be less hindered by

Practising low-level attack *Mary V*, **41-17921 skims over the East Anglian countryside in March 1943. The right engine of this B-26 is not on fire – the smoke is coming from a locomotive hauling a coal train.**

weather than those at medium altitude. However, enemy light flak weapons were at their most effective against aircraft flying between 200 and 500 feet and even lower attack was highly desirable. It was decided to dispense with the nose-mounted D-8 bombsight and fit a modified N-6 or N-3A reflector gunsight in front of the co-pilot who would sight on the target and drop the bomb load via a special release rig. This allowed attack at 50 feet and also permitted the bombardier/navigator in the nose to apply himself to pin-pointing the course.

Only two low-level missions with B-26s were carried out using no more than a dozen aircraft from two squadrons on each occasion. Take-off was made at 30 second intervals with a climb to 250 feet to establish formation. The leadplane flew straight ahead after take-off for 2 minutes before commencing a gentle left-hand turn. Following aircraft of the first six-plane flight shortened the turn and gained their positions within an orbit of the airfield. The second flight followed immediately and took similar action in forming to position about a mile behind the lead flight. Each flight was composed of three two-plane elements. The Number 2 aircraft flew approximately a fuselage length behind the leader and a wingspan in separation to one side. Wing elements flew some 1000 feet from the lead, echeloned back so that the whole flight was of javelin form with all aircraft at the same elevation.

Having assembled, the formation passed over home base taking up a heading to the briefed coastal check point. On reaching this a turn was made and a heading taken for the briefed landfall on the enemy coast. Fifteen miles out from England the IFF set was switched off by pilot or navigator and height reduced to 50 feet to avoid radar detection. If enemy shipping or aircraft were encountered on route the mission had to be abandoned, the supposition being that enemy defences

would be alerted and the element of surprise – essential if losses were to be minimised – lost. Five minutes from the enemy coast engine power was advanced to increase speed from 200 to 240 mph. At landfall the forward-firing guns of the B-26 were used to suppress any ground fire that might be encountered. Navigation after crossing the coast was by DR and identification of landmarks highlighted at briefing.

Evasive action could be exercised at pilots' discretion although the very low altitude – tree top height – gave little room for safe manoeuvre. Bomb-bay doors were opened on identification of the IP – a prominent landmark – and bombing carried out by each individual aircraft as it crossed the target in formation, although wing elements might have to manoeuvre for position. Co-pilots, using the modified gunsights, aimed over the nose of their aircraft and released the bombs, which had 30 second delay fuses. Following the attack the formation withdrew

Left: **A trailer load of 500 lb M-43 bombs being delivered to 386th BG's *Hell's A Poppin'* 41-31614, at Boxted, August 1943. The Marauder could take the same bomb tonnage to short-range targets as the Fortress took to central Germany.**

Below left: **The undercarriage tucks away as 455th BS's *Sea Swoose* climbs away from Earls Colne, August 1943. The Marauder was one of the most heavily armed medium bombers of the war – ten of its 12 .50 guns show in this photograph.**

Below: **The 36-plan formation that became standard for VIII ASC B-26 groups in August 1943. Second 18 (shown in white) flew just below the level of the first, but between 2000 and 2500 feet to the rear.**

at low level and did not increase altitude to 1000 feet until nearing the English coast. At home base the landing pattern involved the separation of individual aircraft in sequence from the left during a wide orbit to line up for the runway.

The disastrous low-level B-26 mission of 17 May 1943, flown by 322nd Group, resulted in a review of tactics. It was deemed that the B-26, too slow and large for this mode of attack, was exceptionally vulnerable to light anti-aircraft fire. The use of the B-26 in low-level shipping strikes was revived and 322nd Group spent several weeks practising for such attacks. It soon became evident that the B-26 would be equally vulnerable to defensive fire in shipping strikes and the plan was abandoned. In June 1943, the second B-26 Group assigned to 8th Air Force, the 323rd, commenced training for medium altitude bombing, 10,000 to 14,000 feet and, after this proved successful during a series of combat missions flown in the second half of July, all B-26 units in England were so committed.

The change to medium altitude operations required the development of new formations, modification of aircraft and additional crew training. An initial obstacle was the acquisition of sufficient Norden M-7 bombsights; the first of these was not forthcoming until the last day of June. Bombardiers had to be trained or refreshed on the operation of this sight and pilots on the use of the Pilot's Directional Indicator, the cockpit instrument which displayed the flight movements required of the pilot when the bombardier manipulated his bombsight controls.

The operational plan for medium altitude bombing by B-26s underwent few changes during the type's service with 8th Air Force. Twenty-five minutes were allowed for briefing crews. A minimum 15 minutes for crews to arrive at aircraft before engines were started. Engines were started 15 minutes before take-off. Assembly of formation by 300 feet and climb to a 12,000 feet rendezvous with fighter escort at the English coast averaged one hour and five minutes, leaving an hour for penetration to maximum radius of action. Initially the area of suitable targets ranged from the Hook of Holland to Caen in France.

The formations used were influenced by B-17 heavy bomber operations. The basic element was a three-plane Vee with two elements comprising a flight, and three flights making the standard 18-plane group. In the leading element the wing aircraft flew to the rear and slightly above the leader. The second element was behind, below and to the right of the lead element and its wing aircraft behind and below its leader. The other flights were similarly composed, with the second behind and to the right and above the lead flight, and the third behind, below and to the left. As with the heavy bombers, the staggered nature of the formation was primarily to uncover as many defensive gun positions as possible.

The authorised strength of a B-26 group at summer 1943 was 64 aircraft, and an 18-plane strike force under-utilised the capability available. The limitation was dictated by the RAF's view that a four-to-one ratio of fighters to bombers was essential for escort. On some of the early missions the ratio was as much as six-to-one but when two or three B-26 groups were operating on the same day, RAF resources were strained. After encountering only limited enemy fighter opposition to early medium-level raids, 3rd Wing, the controlling organisation, were prepared to accept a two-to-one escort ratio and from early August two 18-plane formations per group were despatched on most occasions. Subsequently, 36 became the normal group force for operations. The second 18-plane box flew below the lead and about a half mile behind to either left or right.

Penetration of the enemy coast was, whenever possible, made at a point away from flak areas. Evasive action was flown from just before landfall to the Initial Point, a series of brief deviations from course in an effort to hamper the aim of anti-aircraft gunners. The bomb run from the IP was normally straight with a turn after bombing, usually to the right. If flak was encountered on the bomb run the lead bombardier directed his pilot on

Marauder squadron makes formation against a background of summer cloud, Boxted, August 1943.

any evasive action taken. Bombsights were carried by the lead and deputy lead aircraft of each flight but only the bombardier in the lead flight sighted for course and range, the other bombardiers sighting for range only. Experimentation with dropping-on-the-leader during August 1943 resulted in orders at the beginning of September for only the lead and deputy lead aircraft to an 18-plane group to carry bombsights and sight on target, although sights could be placed in other aircraft at the Group Commander's discretion. By October bombing was consistently on the leader of an 18-plane group.

The lead and deputy lead aircraft of each flight also began to carry an extra officer so that bombardier and navigator duties were handled by two men instead of one. The three gunners on a B-26 doubled as armourer, engineer and radio-operator, but on lead aircraft a full-time radio operator was carried and an additional gunner to take his place at the beam guns. Radio operators in box, group and deputy group lead aircraft maintained a constant listening watch on the wing operational frequency during the entire mission. All other radio operators went to their gun positions before the enemy coast, leaving their receivers set on the MF/DF section assigned.

As attack altitudes varied between 10,000 and 14,000 feet, B-26 crewmen did not need oxygen provision. Battle armour was provided for medium altitude operations, the flak suits and helmets being those already developed for heavy bomber crews.

LIGHT BOMBER PROCEDURE
The 15th Bomb Squadron's first operation on 4 July 1942 was performed with RAF Douglas Bostons as part of a combined RAF/USAAF formation. This attack on Dutch airfields was made at 'hedge-hopping' height, the aircraft flying in loose three-plane Vee formations. Later operations by 15th Bomb Squadron were at medium levels of 8000 to 12,000 feet. Formations were composed of loose Vees and bombing was by individual aircraft. These later operations were all escorted by substantial numbers of Spitfires with whom rendezvous was made at the English coast.

Fighters

Fighter Operations

Whereas the method of employment of 8th Air Force heavy bombers remained basically the same throughout hostilities, that of its fighters was subject to change in meeting new operational requirements. The original fighter contingent trained for support of a projected cross-Channel invasion in air defence and air superiority roles. RAF Fighter Command was its mentor and these early fighter units were not only trained in British procedures, but went into action under the Command's tactical operational control. When in the late summer of 1942 the cross-Channel venture was replaced by the plan to invade North Africa, the fighter units not taken to support that force were assigned to the defence of heavy bomber bases and escort duties.

Bomber support and escort became the primary role in the spring of 1943 and continued to be so to the end of hostilities. However, at the end of January 1944 8th Air Force fighters were additionally given an offensive role in seeking and destroying enemy aircraft away from the bomber column and on their airfields. Ground attack was soon expanded to include communications, notably railways. Use of the long-range fighter as an offensive weapon became more frequent and more important in the closing months of hostilities, the fighter force assuming an importance that had never been envisaged at the inception of offensive operations.

Because of the original tuition, operational procedures of VIII FC had much in common with that of the RAF. Inevitably, once the Command assumed combat control of its own units, 8th Air Force fighter procedures developed to meet special requirements, albeit that the basic procedures and control factors were always similar to those of the RAF. The description following of fighter mission procedure is typical of that from the spring of 1944 when VIII FC was nearing full strength and escort and support policy was, to a certain degree, stabilised. Aspects subject to considerable change or variation during the course of the war, together with specialised operations, are covered later.

MISSION PROCEDURE

The chain of command affecting orders for the fighter operations came from RAF Fighter Command while that organisation had tactical operational control, but in liaison with Headquarters of both 8th Air Force and VIII Fighter Command. When VIII FC assumed full operational as well as administrative control of its groups in the spring of 1943, the first priority was the escort and support requirements of VIII BC. Close liaison with the RAF continued as did combined support of VIII BC bomber missions throughout 1943, the degree of British contribution being reduced as VIII FC strength grew; there were only occasional requests for RAF fighter support after April 1944. VIII FC had authority to plan its own operations when the services of its units were not required by the bombers, and with the division of VIII FC units amongst three fighter wings in the summer of 1943, these headquarters could also plan and execute their own limited operations subject to VIII FC approval. When each of the three fighter wings were assigned directly to one of the three air divisions in October 1944, the chain of command was 8th Air Force Operations, Division, Fighter Wing and then Group. While after this date fighter groups were usually briefed to support the bombers of their parent division, this was not always the case, as often 8th Air Force required a heavier escort for support of one arm of its bomber operations than another.

COMMAND AND WING FUNCTIONS

A warning alert from 8th Air Force to VIII FC Hq or Division for a major escort operation was usually given in the late afternoon of the preceding day. This alert was immediately passed down the chain of command so that the various duty officers were prepared for the advance to a Field Order. The teletype advance usually came mid-evening and detailed the routes, check points, size of the task forces involved and the targets. Armed with this information, VIII FC Combat Operations staff consulted the wall Status Board recording current availability of aircraft and pilots to decide which groups were to be assigned to make the rendezvous check points. Two main factors influenced this selection and assignment along the route:

a The range of the types of fighter, estimated as 400 miles maximum for the P-47, 600 miles for the P-38 and 700 miles for

Country mansions served 8th Air Force as headquarters buildings. Bushey Hall near Watford housed VIII Fighter Command. (L. Chick)

the P-51. The capacity of drop tanks available at each fighter station was also a controlling factor.

b The ability of individual groups, placing the most experienced at expected points of contact with the enemy. Less experienced groups were mostly placed on withdrawal escort.

The selection data was telephoned to 8th Air Force and confirmed by teletype. A further advance from 8th Air Force by telephone gave the times bombers would be at each rendezvous point, their altitude, time of leaving the English coast, and time in at the enemy coast. With this information VIII FC had all that was required for framing a Field Order (FO) to which an operation conference was a regular prelude. This was usually attended by the Commanding General, his Chief of Staff, senior Combat Operations and Intelligence Officers, the duty Y-Service Officer and Weather Officer. The meeting in the Combat Operations Room reviewed possible German reaction with regard to the Luftwaffe's known strengths and dispositions. The command staff also considered other factors which might influence the operation and made points to be incorporated in the Field Order.

The Order was drafted by the Duty Operations Officer, a tour-expired operational combat squadron commander, typed, proof-read by him and an assistant, and when approved passed to the teleprinter office. From here the FO was simultaneously distributed to the three Fighter Wings and all fighter groups, all being on the same teleprinter circuit. Sometimes, with very complicated FOs, preparation was protracted and not completed until the small hours of the morning; in certain cases they were so delayed by 8th Air Force Hq revisions as to reach the

Groups only just in time for a hurried briefing of pilots before take-off. In one case a group received its FO just in time to give it to the Group CO already in his cockpit. In one very exceptional case a squadron left without knowing where it was bound until the rendezvous point was transmitted to the leader in the air by the chief controller of a fighter wing. The causes of such delays were many, most often, however, the very changeable weather.

When in the autumn of 1944 the fighter wings were assigned to the divisions, fighter requirements were assessed at that command level in a similar way and FOs issued to the wings at that source.

Although the mission Field Order went directly from VIII FC to the fighter groups it was the responsibility of each fighter wing to see that it was immediately acted upon. In some cases, when time did not permit transmission of a teletype Field Order, the details were passed to the fighter wing which telephoned them to its groups. Fighter Wings acted as consolidating agencies. On receipt of a teletyped Field Order the Operations Room staff at Fighter Wings laid out the entire mission on the operational map and studied it for any possible errors or ambiguities so as to anticipate any questions from the groups. Approximate take-off times were calculated and passed to the Control Center. Weather predictions for each base at take-off time were checked and, if doubtful conditions were anticipated, a local weather reconnaissance flight was ordered. Wing also arranged the required number of airborne relays – fighter aircraft despatched to high altitude near the enemy coast to relay VHF messages to and from US fighters on deep penetrations. All last minute telephone instructions from Command passed

Left: **Operations Room at VIII FC Hq was manned throughout a combat mission and received information on associated allied and enemy activities, passing relevant details to the fighter wing control rooms. Experienced fighter pilots, who had completed their combat tour, acted as control officers. Lt Col Roy Webb, formerly with 361st FG, sits in front of doorway. On his right is Major Robert Lamb and standing on his left Capt Russell Westfall. At extreme right of picture is Capt Jack Brown. These last three officers had all served with 56th FG (Lamb was an ace with seven victories). Other personnel are: upper dais (l. to r.): Pfc Milton Jacobs, Pfc Paula Gemmer, Major Theodore Wickwire, Sgt Dorothy Clark and on far side Cpl Hedwig Fritz and Cpl Jean Martin. On lower dais are: Pfc Thelma Frisch, 1/Lt Ruth Adams, Sgt Jack Dyer and Pfc Louise White. September 1944.**

Below: **Controller's level overlooked a plotting table on which mission progress was displayed with symbols. Information was relayed from fighter wing operations rooms and other centres. Plotting was done by WACs – in this instance pretty Pfc Thelma Frisch – each being connected to a fighter operations room or other source by telephone line.**

through Wing Combat Operations and were transmitted by telephone to the groups.

Each Fighter Wing had a Control Center manned by a Fighter Control Squadron. Modelled on similar RAF centres, each monitored its group's radio traffic and passed messages and information to group leaders during the course of a mission.

GROUP LEVEL

The alert to a fighter group came by telephone to the Operations Room message centre soon after a similar alert had been issued to bomber organisations. The controlling Fighter Wing telephoned or teletyped a warning message giving the approximate time of mission, number of aircraft to be prepared, fuel load and armament required, and type of operation to be conducted. With this information the Group Operations Duty Officer alerted the duty watch at squadrons and the various sections that would be involved in initial preparations – armament, engineering, weather, flying control and messes. The time of this warning order depended on the required duty for the fighter group, but was generally an hour or two after bomber bases had come to life.

On receipt of the Field Order that came from VIII FC or Division, the Group Intelligence and Operations sections were really able to get to work. The first section of the FO listed Air Task Forces and detailed bomber numbers and targets (by code numbers) together with route check points for course changes. The times at these check points, worked out from Zero Hour, the planned time of departure from the English coast were given as Zero Hour plus the calculated number of minutes. The

areas and times for other Allied air operations were also given. The second part of the FO listed air task forces the fighter groups were supporting and the time of Zero Hour. Under numbered air task force headings, the third part detailed fighter groups assigned to each and the point of planned escort. It also covered any strafing or fighter-bombing operations that might be planned in conjunction with the bomber mission, the requirement for drop tanks and a disengagement time. The last was mostly given as 'to the limit of endurance', meaning until such time as fuel had diminished to a point where it was necessary to return to base. The final section of the FO gave control data, call-signs for fighter-to-bomber intercommunication, geographical check points, emergency homing call signs and the recall code-word.

The FO arrived at the Group between four to six hours before the scheduled Zero Hour and it was not usual to wake the ground men until four hours before Zero Hour. Operations and Intelligence sections, however, began their work immediately. In Group Operations, the Duty Officer with an assistant, or the Duty Intelligence Officer, first plotted the flight course from their base to rendezvous with the bombers through the escort period and back to base. Working backwards from Zero Hour, take-off, start-engines, briefing and breakfast times were fixed. Fuel consumption figures were produced to ensure the planned mission was within range capability. To ensure their accuracy, the given rendezvous points were cross-checked with other data in the FO. The Intelligence Officer and staff consulted filed records for the latest details of flak and enemy fighter strengths that might be encountered on or near the planned course. Operations contacted the Weather Section requesting the latest weather information, while the Staff Weather Officer, or his stand-in, was woken to prepare for his part in briefing.

Operations also alerted Flying Control who worked out marshalling and take-off order. A member of the Intelligence staff went to the Briefing Room and marked up courses on the wall map above the podium with pertinent details that had been worked out by Operations. The course of the bombers was usually represented with blue ribbon, pinned at each check point, and that for the Group's fighters with red. Directional labels, sometimes in the form of fighter plane profiles, were pinned to the map to indicate the rendezvous points of other fighter groups. Bomber units to be escorted were displayed as symbols incorporating identifying tail markings. On an adjacent blackboard times for engine start, take-off and rendezvous were chalked, together with radio call-signs and other flight details.

In squadron operations buildings the duty staff listed pilots and aircraft for the mission, based on availability and rotas for the men and maintenance status of the fighters. While fighter squadrons had far clearer identities within a group's operations than bomber squadrons, combat missions were nearly always based on a three squadron participation. With the increase in some groups of squadron aircraft complements to 32 and pilots to 45 in the winter of 1943–44, many stations were able to despatch two separate group formations on an escort mission to rendezvous with the bombers at different times and locations. For single group formations it was usual to schedule three squadrons of 16 aircraft; for A and B groups, three squadrons of 12 aircraft each.

Later in 1944, when bomber formations were smaller, it was sometimes necessary to divide an individual group effort into three; A, B and C groups, where a mixture of eight or 12-plane squadrons were flown with one or two of these groups having only two-squadron formations. Pilots were usually listed with the position they would fly by reference to the flight colour and numbered position within that flight. These flights and colours were purely for flight direction and were unconnected with the division of a fighter squadron into A, B, C and D Flights for administrative purposes.

Meanwhile at the time worked out by Operations, squadron

Right: **S/Sgt Harvey Pepperman pulling through a P-47 engine to clear cylinders, Metfield, October 1943.**

Below right: **The 61st FS Engineering clerks schedule available P-47s for a mission in November 1944.** (AFM)

orderlies telephoned to the various Charge of Quarters (CQ) to awaken the ground men. Ground crews usually went straight to their aircraft, cycling from their billets to and round the perimeter track. Each fighter had a crew chief, an assistant crew chief (both mechanics) and an armourer, although in some cases the armourer served two or three aircraft. The mechanics first removed covers from cockpit plexiglas and engine air intakes, pulled through the propeller to remove any accumulated gasoline from the engine cylinders, while the armourer took off the gun barrel covers. The crew chief then climbed into the cockpit, primed and started the engine. Once it was running smoothly he carried out oil pressure, fuel and other instrument checks, then increased engine revolutions to see that the magnetoes were functioning correctly.

Once the crew chief had finished the engine pre-flight and shut it down, the armourer began his inspections, opening the gun bays, testing firing circuits and solenoids. If these were functioning correctly he then fed the traced ammunition to each gun breech. He also shook each gun to ensure it was tight on its mount and examined the ammunition and chutes to see there were no obstructions or snags before closing the bay and double-checking that it was secure. The armourer also cast an eye over the gunsight to see that it had not been damaged during servicing.

While the armourer did his work, the crew chief and his assistant checked flight control surfaces, undercarriage and tyres. The 'gas wagon' arrived to fill the externally slung drop tanks and top up the internal tanks once the engine pre-flight was completed, the ground crew watching for leaks on the drop tanks, particularly where the break-free glass tubes were fixed with securing clips to rubber hoses. Once the fuel tanker had moved on, the 'oxygen cart' arrived behind a jeep or small truck, the operator replenishing the oxygen bottles situated in the fuselage behind the pilot. A radio mechanic was on hand in the squadron area to be available if any last minute radio trouble was reported, but he had no regular duties at this time. The armament men too, once having checked over guns and charged them, remained on hand for last minute emergencies, usually relaxing in the ground crew hut or tent. If either crew chief or assistant had not breakfasted at this time one was able to cycle off or thumb a lift on a passing truck to the communal site mess. The other mechanic, usually the crew chief, remained to await the pilot. He spent his time fussing over the fighter, running a chamois over the plexiglas to ensure that the canopy was spotless or polishing the leading edge of the wing if the surface had been waxed to gain extra speed.

Mission leaders were awakened approximately an hour and a half before the general briefing was scheduled, giving them sufficient time to study mission data at Group Operations and plan tactics. An hour before briefing and two hours before take-off, all other pilots scheduled to fly were awakened, which allowed time to wash and shave – although many chose to shave the night before – and be taken to the officers' mess for a breakfast of powdered eggs, toast, fruit juice and coffee, and then on to the briefing room.

The sequence of briefing varied between stations but the first man to mount the podium was usually the Duty Intelligence Officer. He reviewed the entire mission, detailing times and rendezvous points, indicating on the wall map where flak was

Top: **Sgt Henry Meyers, 355th FG, fits a film magazine into the 16 mm gun camera installed in the leading edge of a P-47's wing. Camera operated automatically when guns were fired and provided for a set-over run.**

Above: **Topping up fuel tanks in a 4th FG P-51D, 44-73021, April 1945. AN/APS-13 tail warning radar antenna can be seen projecting both sides of the fin.** (M. Weddle)

likely to be encountered, known concentrations of enemy fighters and tactics they might employ. He also dealt with escape and evasion procedures. The Staff Weather Officer then took over and with the aid of weather maps told pilots of the latest expectations of clouds and winds on route, temperatures and the altitude at which condensation trials would form. In some groups the Weather Officer started the briefing proceedings. Then the group leader for the mission recapped on salient details pointed out by the main briefing officer, gave instructions as to the tactics the group would adopt for its particular assignment and any special measures that had to be taken. Finally he called for synchronisation of watches, all pilots adjusting wrist watches as he counted down to set the instant with the call 'Hack'.

The mission leader could be the Group CO, Air Executive, a squadron commander or a flight leader. Whoever was selected to lead knew that his word was law from the moment engines were started until they landed from the mission. His prime responsibility was to see that the requirements of the FO were met, although he was normally at liberty to select the course that would be flown from base to bomber rendezvous. Briefing took from 15 to 20 minutes depending on the complexity of the mission.

Following briefing, pilots walked or were transported to individual squadron ready-rooms in a nearby or adjoining building. Here they turned in personal possessions to the S-2 officer or sergeant in the crew equipment or locker room and put on flight clothes. Before dressing pockets were emptied of personal items. Orders were that letters, diaries or anything written could not be taken into the air lest it yield valuable intelligence should the pilot go down in enemy territory. From the locker room orderly each pilot received his helmet, oxygen mask, flight coveralls, Mae West inflatable life-jacket, gloves, GI shoes (lace-up boots) and parachute. Although most units forbade the carrying of personal weapons, some pilots chose to carry a knife and a '.45' handgun, as well as candy and cigarettes for the return trip.

In the ready-room the squadron S-2 and assistants handed out course check cards, maps and escape kits which were placed in coverall pockets. In some squadrons a card showing the call-signs and positions of other aircraft was provided and placed in the clear plastic pocket on the right coverall leg. The S-2 also checked that pilots were wearing their 'dog-tags' (identity discs worn on light chain around neck). In addition to the S-2 and other intelligence staff, the squadron medical officer was on hand to help with problems, but also to watch for any signs of combat fatigue which might show in some form of personal behaviour. Pilots tried to relax while waiting for the time that they should leave for the aircraft. Most studied the course cards and wrote the important times on the back of their left hand in pen as a convenient reference. At about 20 minutes before engine start the squadron leader called time to move and pilots carried their equipment to waiting vehicles, generally Personnel Carriers, Command Cars and Jeeps. The aim was to allow a pilot at least 15 minutes at the aircraft before engine starting.

After vehicles had delivered a pilot to his aircraft's dispersal point he first placed his parachute and helmet on the wing or tailplane; never on the ground – mice were known to have taken refuge in the parachute so placed! The pilot then carried out a visual check of the aircraft with the crew chief, mostly while engaging in light-hearted banter – no pilot wished his crew chief to feel he really doubted his ability to have the aircraft anything but in first-class condition. It was always practice for pilots to have an individual aircraft assigned to them once they became established members of a squadron. This encouraged pilot confidence as he flew *his* aircraft whenever it was serviceable and knew that no other pilot would be abusing it. It also allowed for 'personal feel', those slight differences in handling, real or imagined, that made a pilot more at home in the aircraft

Left: **The ground crew of Nancy V take a break from their labours to have a warming cup of coffee from a British Church Army mobile canteen that appeared out of the early morning fog. Bodney, December 1944.**

Below left: **The 353rd FG CO, Lt Col Loren McCollom, briefs 352nd FS pilots at Metfield, October 1943. The second and third men in the front row, Bill Odom and Dewey Newhart, were later MIA, as was McCollom.**

Right: **Capt Jesse Daves (left) and Lt Tom Shepard collect personal flying equipment – helmet, Mae West and oxygen mask. Duxford, October 1943.**

Below: **P-38 pilots of 55th FG dressing for an operational flight, Nuthampstead, November 1943.**

Below right: **Lt Col Francis Gabreski receiving Holy Communion before a mission from Capt John McGettigan, Catholic Chaplain at Boxted, July 1944.**

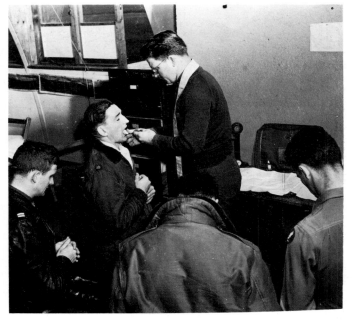

he was familiar with. The ground crews sometimes worked all night so that a pilot could fly his own aircraft on a mission. When pilot numbers per group increased later in the war, only senior pilots had personal aircraft, newcomers having to share. In practice, of course, senior pilots often flew other aircraft when their assigned aircraft were unserviceable and likewise junior pilots came to fly fighters assigned to old hands.

During his pre-take off inspection a wise pilot always noted the angle of the tail wheel to avoid an embarrassing swing when starting to taxi out. The pilot climbed up to the cockpit five minutes before the starting time, his last act on the ground probably being to urinate – use of relief tubes was awkward and something to be kept to a minimum. The crew chief handed up the seat pack parachute which the pilot then attached to the dinghy pack already placed in the well seat. Here again procedure varied depending on type of parachute and aircraft. Some pilots put on the parachute with dinghy attached before climbing into the cockpit, others preferred to place the parachute and dinghy in the seat and then fix the straps when in the cockpit. Before putting on his parachute a pilot always checked that the two retaining clip pins were not bent. Bent pins might bind and prevent parachute canopy release. Next, the quick-release safety straps were fastened, the helmet was donned, the radio cord from mask microphone and earphones plugged into the jackpoint and then the oxygen hose clipped to the harness and connected to the supply points and tested.

Above: **Pilots of 353rd FG leaving the crew equipment room for transportation to take them to their aircraft at Metfield, October 1943. Note parked bicycles issued for personal transportation around base.**

Left: **Lts Burton Wyman, Leighton Read and F/O Clemens Fiedler being transported in a light truck to their P-47s at Debden, October 1943. Wyman and Fiedler were both killed in action in 1944.**

Below: **P-38Hs of 55th FG taxiing to the runway head at Nuthampstead, November 1943. Lightnings were usually assigned target area support for the bombers at this date.**

Top: **With an audience of ground men, a 79th FS P-51D waits to taxi out onto the perimeter track to take up its correct position for take-off, King's Cliffe, August 1944. The aircraft has been partly sprayed with olive drab for camouflage. Drop tanks are 110 US gallon type.**

Above: **Ready to roll. P-47Ds of 350th FS gathered at the end of Raydon runway at the start of an escort mission in August 1944. All carry 150 gallon 'flat' belly tanks. Canopies will be closed before take-off.** (via K. Rust)

Left: **Heavily loaded and with throttle full open, P-51D 44-14827 of 435th FS becomes airborne from Wattisham. For the pilot the most anxious moment of a mission.** (V. Hooker)

Below: **With a full load of fuel, undercarriages were tucked away immediately after lift-off in order to build up speed. A 362nd FS element leaves Leiston main runway, February 1945.**

The radio was switched on, gun heaters turned on to prevent any moisture present freezing at altitude, gyro compass and altimeter set and the instrument panel clock checked against the pilot's wrist watch and adjusted as necessary. One of the mechanics removed wheel chocks, signalling this by a wave to the pilot. Checking that brakes were firmly on, the pilot shouted 'clear' – a warning repeated by the crew chief in acknowledgement. With main electrical switches on and engine primed, the pilot pressed the button for the inertia starter which whined as it built up speed and then turned the engine over. A second attempt was often needed before an engine fired and picked up revs. The crew chiefs on P-38s or P-51B/Cs closed hinged canopies which the pilots locked. Each pilot then watched for the aircraft that was to be ahead of his and taxied out after it onto the perimeter track. Because of the tail-down stance of P-47s and P-51s they had to be weaved from side to side for pilots to see ahead down the taxiway and care taken not to hit the tail of the aircraft in front.

On airfields with more than one runway, squadrons might be marshalled to use different runways to quicken take-off time and save fuel, provided crosswinds were not too strong. The first and third squadrons to take off would be marshalled for one runway, the second squadron at another and while this was taking off the third moved into position on the runway vacated by the first. Where standard 150-foot wide hard runways were in use, it was usual for a whole squadron formation to position at the head of the runway, staggered across it in the four-plane flight positions they would assume once airborne. At the marshalling area aircraft engines were run up as a final magneto check. Eight minutes were allowed from engine start for taxiing and marshalling before take-off commenced. Should there be a delay before take-off, engines might be shut down and restarted.

The occupant of the runway control van signalled take-off by flashing 'a green' with a shielded Aldis lamp. The group leader released brakes and began his run with his wingman following, each fighter keeping to its appropriate side of the runway. Every 30 seconds two more aircraft commenced their runs together as element leader and wingman. If a heavy load of drop tank fuel was being carried, the main wheels would be kept on the runway until near the end in order to build up as much speed as possible for lift-off. At grass fields, such as Duxford and Bodney, complete four-plane flights could take off together giving an even greater saving in time. Once airborne, the leader's element flew approximately two miles out from the airfield before beginning a gentle left turn. Following elements turned within the leader's curve so that all were in squadron formation position by the time 180 degrees had been made back over the

airfield. A squadron was airborne in four to five minutes and a whole 48-plane group in twelve to fifteen if all went smoothly. In practice, a group take-off would take anything from ten to twelve minutes, depending on numbers of aircraft involved, visibility and other factors. If there was very low and thick cloud, formations would be made above in the clear, fighters climbing through in elements.

Because of the need to extend escort time to the maximum the three squadron formations set course immediately after a single orbit of the base, each initially trailing the other but the second and third squadrons gradually taking up positions on either side of the lead a mile away. In the climb-out over the English coast and North Sea the fighters took a direct course to the bombers for their rendezvous, climbing to 20,000 to 25,000 feet to penetrate enemy air space. The three or four flights of a squadron were stepped down behind the leader's flight on this outward journey so that all pilots could easily keep it in view. Separation of flights was 100 to 150 feet and that of aircraft within each flight 25 to 50 feet. Once in formation, P-47s and P-38s were switched from main to drop tank fuel but for stability reasons the P-51 fuselage tanks were reduced to about 30 gallons or less before switching to wing drop tanks. To maintain balance, fuel was drawn alternately for 30 minutes for each wing drop tank.

Each squadron leader concentrated on the course which was by dead reckoning, perhaps with a few visual checks of landmarks if visibility was good. Other pilots watched the leader and their oil and coolant temperatures, engine revolutions and manifold pressure for any sign of engine trouble. Turnbacks for mechanical reasons were unpopular, but prudent in single-engine aircraft. Above 10,000 feet the oxygen began to be automatically supplied to the face mask, buttoned to the helmet before take-off; this also held the radio microphone. As far as possible radio silence was observed once airborne, although the home base directional finding station and Fighter Wing Control Center were listening on assigned frequencies. Group leaders were often required to indicate making landfalls and check points by coded radio calls. Every fighter had VHF radios equipped with four press-button-change channels allocated for specific communication purposes. Climb-out was made at 700 feet per minute in P-51s and the cruise speed varied between 240 and 270 mph IAS.

Tails lift as P-47Ds 42-25517, LM:X and 42-26636, LM:X accelerate past the half way mark on Boxted runway 42, July 1944.

Approaching the enemy coast each flight spread out until there was approximately 500 to 700 feet between each aircraft. Positioning of flights relative to one another within a squadron and squadron within a group varied with the favours of different groups and the type of operation. Individual groups were allowed to experiment with formations, but by the spring of 1944 the standard squadron battle formation positioned each flight with from 1000 to 3000 feet separation abreast, two leading and two covering them above and behind. If the whole group remained in close proximity during the penetration of enemy air space, the high flights flew nearer to the lead flights. Any attempts at interception by enemy fighters during this stage of the mission were met by the high squadron or a high flight. The paramount duty of the fighter force was to reach the bombers and provide escort. Engaging the enemy meant releasing external fuel tanks and thus reduced range, action that was to be avoided if at all possible during penetration. Also, prior to summer 1944, drop tanks were often in very short supply and were only to be jettisoned if absolutely necessary.

Rendezvous with the bombers was made on a time and location basis that had to be strictly adhered to. In practice navigational errors, weather, flight delays and many other factors not infrequently disrupted planned escort, but as the numbers of 8th Air Force fighters available for escort rose so did the reliability of the cover that could be provided. In good visibility a visual contact with the bombers could be made from 25 miles but radio could be used to locate if necessary. By the spring of 1944 one fighter group was usually assigned to cover each bomber combat wing box. On making contact the three squadrons of the fighter group took up positions as decided and advised by the leader at briefing. If changes were desirable to meet the tactical situation found at rendezvous, the leader gave directions over the radio. One squadron would overtake the bombers and position above, dividing into two sections, one some miles ahead of the other. A second squadron also divided into two sections and positioned above and about a mile out from the bombers on each side of their box. The third squadron acted as top cover some 4000 feet above the bombers, one section directly above and the other about ten miles ahead towards the sun where it would be ready to intercept any attacks from this 'blind spot'. This was the general escort layout but there were many variations and developments are covered later.

Above: **Squadron formation quickly established in a half circuit of the base, P-47Ms of 63rd FS turn south over Thorington Street, Suffolk to cross home base and set course for their rendezvous point.**

Below: **A squadron of P-47s weaving high above bomb formations is revealed by tell-tale contrails.**

Sections orbited or weaved as necessary to compensate for the speed differences between bombers and fighters. If enemy aircraft were not present once escort had been established, fuel was conserved by retarding throttle and mixture settings until the engine 'coughed' and then advancing them to smooth running. Pilots continually searched the sky for enemy aircraft. Mirrors on the windshield framing aided observations to the rear, but images were small and cover limited, so it was prudent to frequently look behind to gain a broader vision of any attack from this quarter. A pilot who survived in air combat was said to

be a good 'swivel-header'. Any attack or enemy aircraft sighting was called out by the observing pilot over the radio using the specified call-signs. A different word – generally two-syllable – identified each squadron and another the group which, in combat, meant the group leader. Flights were identified by a colour and the individual aircraft within each flight by numbers as leader and 2, 3 and 4. Any pilot knew instantly where the aircraft making the radio-call was situated as the location of colour flights within a squadron remained the same for each mission – most commonly white for lead, red for second, yellow for third and blue for fourth. The third flight usually covered the first and the fourth the second. However, while the same colours were used by all first 'A' group squadrons, the order varied from group to group. When a 'B' group formation was despatched its flights used additional colours to prevent confusion.

Bombers and fighters had joint radio communication over Channel C by which leaders of either could warn the other, and one pilot in each fighter squadron was briefed to monitor this channel. It was most used by bombers when under attack to call for fighter assistance. All air-to-air radio messages had to be kept to a minimum, to avoid blocking other urgent transmissions. The Fighter Wing Control Center could contact fighter leaders while in range with messages. Channel A was used for this purpose, each fighter group having its own frequency. Mission recalls or changes in the briefed plan came via this source. Occasionally information on enemy fighter movements derived from the RAF listening service (Y-Service) intercepts of radio traffic would be passed over Channel A. Other than the exception mentioned, all fighter pilots listened and communicated on Channel A.

Tactics employed against enemy fighters depended very much on the situation. If Luftwaffe aircraft were seen massing for an attack, a group leader could despatch one or two flights from a squadron to attack and break up the enemy concentration before it attacked the bombers. Prior to 1944 fighter escort was directed to remain with the bombers and interception of the enemy was largely confined to diving attacks on his aircraft as they approached the bomber boxes. With the change in policy in late January 1944, part of the fighter force was allowed to range away from the bombers and pursue enemy fighters. Groups were sent out with a ranging brief to locate and find enemy fighters that might be forming to attack the bombers.

The two-plane element, of which two made up the 'finger-four' flight, was the basic fighting element. The leader concentrated on attacking his quarry while his wingman, flying behind and to one side, kept a lookout for enemy interceptions and protected the leader's rear. For this reason wingmen were the most likely candidates for loss in an air battle, as well as having less opportunity to claim victories. As the principal enemy fighters, the Me 109 and FW 190, had advantages in acceleration in a climbing turning fight, US fighter tactics were usually to avoid this situation and after attacking to distance themselves from the enemy fighters before turning to make another firing pass.

When an attack developed it was prudent for the group leader to assign only sufficient fighters to effectively intercept, lest the enemy was trying to draw away fighters leaving the bombers open to attack from other quarters. After combat the group leader called over the R/T for his fighters to reform flights, if possible, and resume escort. He named an identifiable rendezvous point for this purpose – a town, column of smoke, etc. Only if fuel supplies were severely diminished, or for some other critical reason did individuals break away and turn for home. Escort was maintained until another fighter group arrived to take up its schedule, or to the 'limit of endurance' of the unit present. The relay system allowed each fighter group to escort a part of the bomber column for between 150 and 200 miles before being relieved. Sufficient overlap was always allowed in planning in case a group was late. Where continuous escort by relay was not possible because insufficient fighter units were

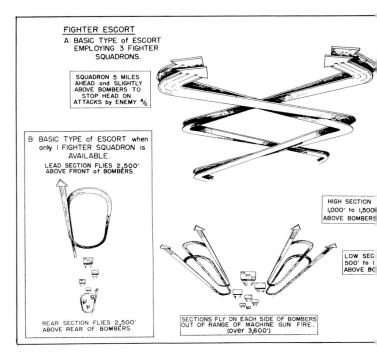

available, area support was used. This involved a fighter group flying to an assigned area on the bomber route and patrolling that area while the bomber column of boxes passed through. Sometimes continuous escort, giving close support, was combined with area support, tactics depending on the fighter forces available, the number and spread of targets attacked by the bombers, and depth of penetration into hostile airspace.

After January 1944, when a fighter group was relieved from escort and still had good fuel reserves, the leader was permitted to take his formations down to attack airfields in the vicinity, or enemy road and rail transportation. Strafing airfields, often heavily defended by light flak weapons, caused far heavier losses to fighters than those incurred on escort duties. To minimise enemy reaction it was important to obtain surprise and to limit the attack to a single pass as explained later.

After strafing or air fighting units were often widely scattered

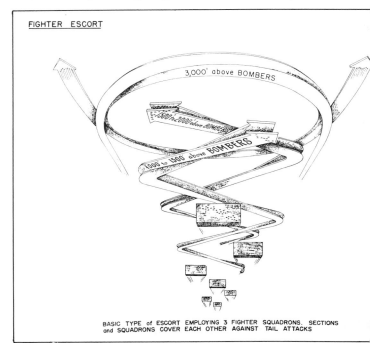

BASIC TYPE of ESCORT EMPLOYING 3 FIGHTER SQUADRONS. SECTIONS and SQUADRONS COVER EACH OTHER AGAINST TAIL ATTACKS

and frequently flights and sections returned 'home' on their own. In an air battle it was easy to become disorientated, so pilots would start for home on a compass bearing heading calling over the radio on D Channel for a 'fix' when in range. There were direction finder (D/F) stations at each fighter airfield to give homing bearings. Additional RAF D/F stations were situated along the coast of England. While over or near enemy territory it was necessary to remain 'swivel-headed', as small numbers of Luftwaffe fighters often operated to catch the unwary returning to England. Height was reduced over the North Sea or Channel and the oppressive oxygen mask removed when 'cigarette altitude' was reached (10,000 feet or less).

If the group was still together, flights flew a loose in-trail formation when there was a long journey through friendly airspace back to base. As a point of pride, formations were tightened on approach to the home airfield; a show formation was

Buzzing the field. A flight of returning 351st FS Thunderbolts sweep low across Metfield before peeling off to land. March 1944.

always appreciated by the ground men. Squadrons landed in order of trail and height, the highest squadron last. Each squadron flew across the airfield over the line of the runway in use for landing. Halfway along the lead flight 'peeled off', went into a climbing left hand turn and at the same time each aircraft separated from the others by slightly delaying this pull-up from the runway pass. Undercarriages were lowered and the aircraft of this flight curved round to the head of the runway in line for landing. There was about 15 seconds between each fighter's touch-down. The landing was normally made well down a runway as the full length was not usually required. Sometimes aircraft turned off at runway intersections to avoid taxiing long distances. During the first pass the second flight of the squadron also peeled off to make its landing when it reached the far end of the runway, while the remaining flights circled round again before making their break in a similar way. Other squadrons orbited the airfield further out to await their turn. At grass airfields such as Bodney, fighters often landed four at a time. After landing each fighter taxied back to its dispersal point where the crew chief was on hand to signal the aircraft into parking position and then chock the wheels.

The ground crew knew immediately if their fighter had seen action by broken tape seals on the gun muzzles. If victories were obtained a pilot signified these to the ground crew by holding up the appropriate number of fingers. As soon as the engine ceased the crew chief climbed up onto the wing to assist the pilot out of the cockpit – five or six hours' confinement made for stiff and sore anatomy. The crew chief's first enquiry inevitably concerned any successes in battle and how the aircraft had performed. A common ritual for the pilot after being helped out of the cockpit and down onto the ground was to relieve himself and light up a cigarette. Parachute and other personal equipment was placed on the wing or an off-the-ground object until a Jeep or personnel carrier came to collect the pilot. The crew chief produced Form 1 which had to be filled out by the pilot or on his direction with any mechanical or other problems that had been experienced during the flight. Mostly pilots completed the

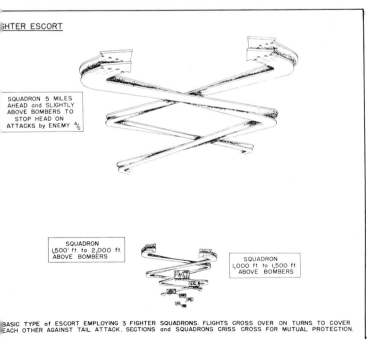

FIGHTER ESCORT

SQUADRON 5 MILES AHEAD and SLIGHTLY ABOVE BOMBERS TO STOP HEAD ON ATTACKS by ENEMY A/c

SQUADRON 1,500' ft. to 2,000 ft. ABOVE BOMBERS

SQUADRON 1,000 ft. to 1,500 ft. ABOVE BOMBERS

BASIC TYPE of ESCORT EMPLOYING 3 FIGHTER SQUADRONS. FLIGHTS CROSS OVER ON TURNS TO COVER EACH OTHER AGAINST TAIL ATTACK. SECTIONS and SQUADRONS CRISS CROSS FOR MUTUAL PROTECTION.

form while still sitting in the cockpit. If mechanical difficulties were entered on the form they had to be rectified before the aircraft would be released to fly again, a copy of the form going to the squadron engineering section.

Pilots were taken straight to their respective squadron ready-rooms where they first delivered any 'hot news' for 'flash reports' to the S-2 officer on hand, and then deposited personal flying equipment in the locker room. Refreshments in the form of coffee, hot chocolate, sandwiches and doughnuts, plus a two-ounce 'slug' of whisky, were available and consumed while the S-2 carried out interrogation. Fighter interrogations were far more informal than with bomber crews although similar questions were asked regarding enemy fighter opposition, tactics, markings, friendly aircraft in distress or shot down, enemy sea or ground movements, all with location and time. Those pilots claiming victories had to submit a written claim, and if there were witnesses to the action they were required to provide a written confirmation. These were usually dictated to a member of the Intelligence staff who typed out the report and returned it to the pilot for signature. Any claims were subsequently assessed against the gun camera film removed from the aircraft by the armourer and sent for processing (via Wing to Kodak at Harrow). Six copies were made and distributed to various headquarters,

with one earmarked for the pilot. After all pilots had been interrogated the squadron S-2 prepared a concise report and telephoned it to group Intelligence office where staff prepared a general group report for transmission to wing headquarters, initially by telephone and then a fuller version by teletype machine within two hours of the group landing. As soon as available processed combat film was despatched by courier to Fighter Wing headquarters.

Weary pilots went to the mess to eat and back to their quarters to shower and sleep. The more resilient were soon back in the officers' club 'hangar flying' the mission again.

Right: Pilots of the 61st FS at a relaxed interrogation in their ready room. Flight Surgeon 'Doc' Horning helps with refreshments and keeps an eye open for any signs of battle fatigue. At far right of front row is 'Gabby' Gabreski.

Left: **Over the threshhold. Flaps down, 356th FG P-51D** *Naughty Nordie*, **44-72377, flown by Lt Col James Wood, comes home to Martlesham. A five or six hour mission in a fighter was particularly demanding of a pilot.** (D. Morris)

Below left: **How did it go? Crew chief Sgt John Ferra, Form 1A in hand, greets Capt Don Gentile on return from a mission.** (G. Weckbacker)

Right: **New drop tanks are lifted into place on a 56th FG P-47 at Boxted, November 1944.**

Below: **A 4th FG armourer replenishes the gun bays of a P-51B with .50 calibre ammunition.**

For the base ground contingent there was at least two hours work after a mission returned and more for mechanics with a fighter requiring major repairs. The crew chief and his assistant carried out the required servicing of their charge and, if appropriate, performed a 50- or 100-hour inspection as detailed in the maintenance manual for the aircraft type. Spark plugs had to be changed every 16 to 20 hours and this was a laborious and difficult task. The interval depended on type of plug and condition of engine. New drop tanks were installed under each wing or under the belly of P-47s, the armourer assisting as three persons were required to do the job quickly. The armourer inspected the gun bays and if the guns had been fired he removed them for transport to the armoury, where each would be cleaned and carefully examined for distortion or damage. Rounds left in the bays were removed and returned to the tracing shed at the squadron armoury site for processing through a repositioning machine. The armourer's task was not complete until he had mounted the guns and filled the magazine bays with the authorised number of rounds – usually the maximum specified for the aircraft type. He also had to install a new gun camera magazine and tape the gun muzzles to keep out damp and dirt. One of the mechanics usually helped with the ammunition as the linked rounds had to be treated carefully to preserve alignment. The main fuel tanks were replenished by the gasoline crew who went from one dispersal to another with their tanker – there were generally two available to each squadron. Oxygen was also conveyed and pumped into the aircraft's system and the fighter brought to immediate availability.

The turn-round time depended on the mechanical condition of the aircraft and operational requirements. This could amount to as little as 15 minutes if the guns had not been fired or drop tanks released, to several hours if plugs or a tyre had to be changed. Generally a fighter's ground crew could complete their work within two hours. The last servicing task performed on the fighter was a radio test by the specialist team in each squadron. This was best performed after engines were shut down to avoid interference. When the radio men had departed in their Jeep, the crew chief could put the covers over the plexiglas and set off on his bike for the mess hall. Some ground crew men preferred to live in the dispersal tent or hut near aircraft to avoid long trips to their quarters, most likely a Nissen hut a mile and a half's ride away. Dispersal areas had a night guard from the station defence section but individual fighters were not guarded.

Fighter Ground Attack

The employment of the 8th Air Force fighters in attacks on ground targets evolved from a desire to make the maximum use of forces available when heavy bombers were not operating. Initially attention was chiefly focused on developing techniques of attack with bombs, termed fighter-bombing. With the order in January 1944 to take the offensive against the Luftwaffe, the predominant form of ground attack that developed was strafing – the destruction or damage of enemy personnel, installations and equipment by machine gun fire. Fighter-bombing, however, continued to feature in tactical operations in support of the cross-Channel invasion of June 1944 and the subsequent Allied advance until suitable targets were out of range. In the last year of hostilities strafing of enemy airfields, railways and other military targets was practised as a post-escort activity with some regularity. Ground attack presented far more danger to fighter pilots and the ratio of losses in these actions compared to those in aerial combat was in the region of five to one.

STRAFING

Strafing was a German term adopted by the Allies to describe aircraft shooting up the enemy on the ground. Spitfires of 4th Fighter Group had indulged in shooting at ground and sea targets on several occasions during the autumn and winter of 1942–43, chiefly during the execution of *Rhubarb* sorties. With the arrival of the P-47 and concentration on escort duties, VIII FC fighters kept to high altitudes. The first known instance of P-47 strafing occurred on 28 July 1943 when Lt Quince Brown of 78th Group decided to make profitable use of remaining ammunition when having to return from an escort mission at 'hedge-hopping' height across north-west Germany. Other incidents occurred in following months although the first planned strafing mission was not flown until 11 March 1944 when 352nd Group made a low-level sweep over airfields behind the Pas de Calais area, resulting in the loss of two P-47s and the crash landing of another on return, all due to small arms fire. Following this, planned strafing operations involved high altitude penetration of hostile territory, the fighters descending to strafe when in the area of their objective.

Individual groups were left to develop their own tactics for ground attack but a fuller appreciation of the dangers involved led Major General William E. Kepner to institute formation of a special detachment to explore the best methods of conducting strafing. Dubbed *Bill's Buzz Boys* as a gesture to its sponsor, this detachment at Metfield was officially known as the 353rd 'C' Fighter Group under the Group CO, Colonel Glenn Duncan, who had originally suggested the idea to Kepner. Composed of 16 pilots and P-47s drawn from four different groups, *Bill's Buzz Boys* flew six missions between 26 March and 10 April, whereafter the detachment was dissolved and the surviving pilots – two were lost – returned to their regular units. From their experience general rules for strafing airfields were formulated and circulated to all VIII FC groups. The salient points were: approach the target at medium altitude; let down when far enough away so as to be unobserved and, to avoid alerting the defences, fly at tree top height for a few miles before reaching the target so as to achieve surprise; make only one line abreast pass to keep losses to a minimum. It was further emphasised that pilots should make a thorough study of the target and its locality at briefing so as to be familiar with landmarks and the layout of the enemy airfield.

Planned mass strafing operations by VIII FC fighters, such as the *Jackpot* series against airfields in Germany and the *Chattanooga* attacks on rail and other transportation in the spring of 1944, generally made use of these tactics. Freelance strafing of German airfields was permitted after groups had completed their escort duties, and in these instances an impromptu method of attack had to be practised.

By the summer of 1944 the technique of impromptu strafing had been considerably developed through experience. After escort, squadrons of a group would separate by several miles and fly at between 12,000 and 15,000 feet, an altitude from which it was able to spot enemy aircraft on airfields and moving trains. When a suitable target was seen the squadron leader separated his force into two sections, one to provide top cover. The attack section continued on past the target for some 10 to 20 miles before coming down in a curving dive to approach it.

Wind direction and strength was a major factor influencing the target approach route, down-wind being preferred so that smoke from targets fired by the first wave of fighters did not obscure targets for the second. Flying across a strong wind was avoided as drift could affect accuracy of fire. If the sun was low in a clear sky an approach from that direction was often used. Flights attacked line abreast or staggered astern of one another at about 3000 feet intervals. This allowed enough distance to prevent damage to aircraft in preceding flights from ricochets of

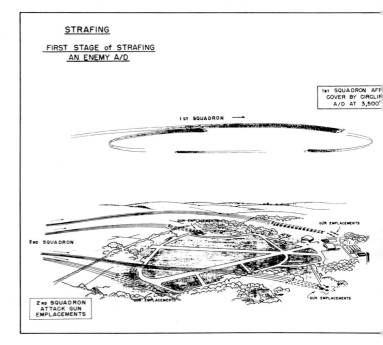

Right: **The lower the safer. This gun camera frame gives an indication of just how low the 355th FG P-51 was when opening fire on parked Me 110s.**

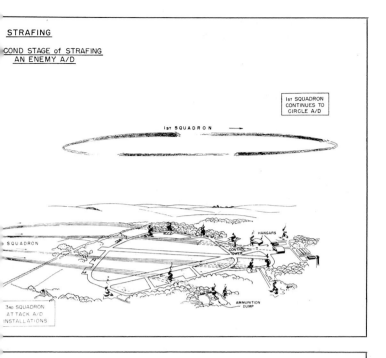

STRAFING

COND STAGE of STRAFING
AN ENEMY A/D

1st SQUADRON

1st SQUADRON
CONTINUES TO
CIRCLE A/D

SQUADRON

HANGARS

CONTROL
TOWER

3rd SQUADRON
ATTACK A/D
INSTALLATIONS

AMMUNITION
DUMP

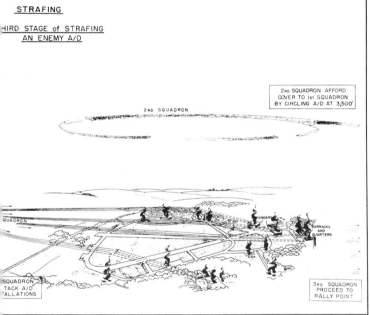

STRAFING

HIRD STAGE of STRAFING
AN ENEMY A/D

2nd SQUADRON

2nd SQUADRON AFFORD
COVER TO 1st SQUADRON
BY CIRCLING A/D AT 3,500'

QUADRON

HANGARS

BARRACKS
AND
QUARTERS

SQUADRON
TACK A/D
TALLATIONS

3rd SQUADRON
PROCEED TO
RALLY POINT

fire from those following. The staggered flights astern arrangement also allowed those trailing to identify ground defence points firing at those ahead and so attack those gun positions.

Lead flight or flights generally made the initial pass at 300–350 mph, and if intense ground fire was encountered their leader radioed for following flights to break off their runs and climb away. If negligible opposition was encountered, following passes would be made at a reduced speed to obtain greater accuracy. Long bursts – two to three seconds – commencing as much as a half mile from the selected target, were practised to ensure hits. Slight back pressure was applied to the control column when firing to correct for bullet drop. After attacking, aircraft continued to fly low, under 50 feet if possible, for some distance, avoiding any area that might be defended when climbing back to high altitude. Mostly squadrons worked independently when strafing, although similar tactics were used when two or three squadrons were involved. Despite these

precautions losses to ground strafers rose steadily during the final nine months of the war and opportunity strafing was banned by the beginning of 1945.

The P-51, eventually equipping all but one of the 15 fighter groups, was particularly vulnerable to small arms fire because of the engine's easily punctured liquid-cooling system. General strafing techniques for a group attack on an airfield had by 1945 evolved to an even more cautious pattern. The three squadrons of a group would drop down from high altitude to make low-level approach with all flights in a squadron line abreast. About one mile from the airfield the lead squadron would commence a climb which would put it at sufficient height over the target to be out of range of small arms fire, but hopefully distracting enemy gunners. This squadron would orbit, providing top cover against enemy fighter interceptions or engage in simulated dive-bombing to draw fire while at the same time its pilots could observe enemy defence reaction to the attack of the second squadron. This unit concentrated on gun emplacements and anti-aircraft batteries as it swept across the airfield and continued flying low until out of range. The third squadron followed immediately and shot up parked aircraft and airfield installations before making its getaway. By this time the second squadron had climbed to give top cover and replace the first which descended to shoot at installations or aircraft missed by the initial waves of strafers.

If the defences were too fierce the assault was often abandoned after the first pass; if they proved negligible each squadron would make further passes until ammunition or worthy targets were exhausted. To confuse the defences, squadrons of a group were sometimes briefed to make approaches to the enemy airfield from different directions, requiring precise co-ordination lest collisions or the shooting down of friendly fighters occurred – as it occasionally did.

It was accepted that the lower and faster an aircraft flew, the less the chance of it being hit by enemy gunfire. But in speeding low over the ground it was difficult to sight accurately and the risk of flying into obstructions was increased. Airfields sheltering fighter aircraft were usually heavily defended and more so during the closing stages of the war, as the enemy's shrinking front line allowed some measure of concentration.

Since guns in fighter aircraft were aligned to fire directly forward for air fighting, strafing ground targets involved diving, unless a pilot risked truly skimming the ground to be on a level with parked aircraft and installations. Pilots found the most assured way of hitting a selected target was to open fire short and trace the bullets into the target. While wasteful in ammunition, the swath of bullet strikes on the ground ahead gave a definite indication of aim.

Attacks on trains were usually carried out at right angles to the target with first efforts aimed at puncturing the locomotive's boiler to bring the train to a standstill. Approach along the length of the train was potentially less wasteful of ammunition, but far more dangerous if there were wagons with flak or machine gun installations. Attacks on most forms of transportation were carried out by elements in line astern.

FIGHTER-BOMBING
The adaption of fighter aircraft for use in ground attack by fitting external bomb racks was well practised by all protagonists during the Second World War. Such employment for USAAF fighters in the UK was first proposed in 1942 and then neglected while escort activities were promoted. It was logical that the shackles (racks) installed on 8th Air Force fighters for holding external fuel tanks should eventually also be utilised for ordnance.

In the autumn of 1943 VIII FC instructed 353rd Group to investigate the use of the P-47 in dive bombing. Three pilots with experience of bomb-carrying P-40s were despatched on 22 October to Llanbedr in Wales to carry out experiments using

100 lb practice bombs on a small target island nearby. Conclusions drawn from these and later trials on The Wash ranges advocated a 60 degree dive from 10,000 feet, with bomb release and pull-out at 4000 feet. While greater accuracy could obviously be obtained by closer target approaches, the P-47's build up of speed in a long dive precluded a lower altitude pull-out. Dives from over 20,000 feet with release and recovery at 16,000 feet could give a fair amount of accuracy if the dive angle was increased to 70 degrees. The only sight used in these experiments was the normal 100 mil reflector gunsight.

These findings were used as the basis for tactics on the first dive bombing operation on 25 November 1943 conducted by 353rd Group, the object being to arouse enemy fighters to intercept through an attack on their base, St Omer/Ft Rouge. Carrying a 500 lb GP bomb each, the P-47s dived individually from about 14,000 feet, releasing at 8000 feet; the results were assessed as poor, with bombs widely scattered. Nevertheless, high command was impressed with the possibilities of the technique if not the results. The Group made further dive bombing attacks on enemy airfields during the following weeks, when released from escort duties and if the weather was favourable. Tactics remained broadly the same: a fast approach by flights in battle formation, individual aircraft rolling into a 50–75 degree dive commenced between 15,000 and 18,000 feet, with pull-out and release of bombs at 6000 to 10,000 feet. Other fighter groups subsequently took up the practice and various angles of attack were used including a vertical plunge from about 10,000 to 6000 feet which was considered to produce more accuracy in aim, but the length of dive had to be restricted lest there was difficulty in recovery. As a guide to obtaining the desired dive angle coloured lines were painted on either canopy panels or wing leading edges. By aligning the appropriate line with the horizon when commencing an attack a pilot knew he had the desired dive angle. P-47s were also used for dive bombing with two 500 lb bombs on wing pylon shackles. Two 1000 pounders were also used but this had to be stopped as there were several cases of wings becoming over-stressed and developing a considerable increase in dihedral.

Dive bombing using P-47s and P-51s was often described as 'by guess and by God' since the nose obscured the target before release. Pilots developed their own 'counting system' after the target disappeared before releasing, depending on dive angles.

Two other forms of delivery were also developed: glide bombing entailing a gentle angle approach to low altitude – 100 to 500 feet – before release, and skip bombing, fast, very low-level approach and level release of bombs so that they would skim rather than drop into the target. During the two months following the cross-Channel invasion, VIII FC groups regularly engaged in fighter-bombing in support of the ground forces. Dive bombing was chiefly undertaken by the four remaining P-47 groups in the Command. While P-51s were used in this role, there was a degree of risk of structural failure in sharp pull-outs, so P-51s mostly used shallow angles of attack or glide bombing.

On the same occasion that the 353rd Group had initiated dive bombing in the ETO, the 56th Group, under its innovative leader Hubert Zemke, had carried out a high level formation bombing attack on St Omer/Longuenesse airfield. Each P-47 carried a 500 lb bomb and dropped on the signal of a B-24 which led and sighted for the fighter formation at 24,000 feet. Results were poor as most bombs overshot the target. This form of high altitude formation bombing was not repeated primarily because the B-24 lead aircraft, being too slow, made the formation vulnerable to anti-aircraft fire. Nevertheless, the idea of a tight formation of fighters dropping bombs from high or medium altitudes retained an appeal for some 8th Air Force tacticians.

A concentrated pattern of drop might be obtained by such a force with less vulnerability to flak if a fast aircraft could be used to sight on target. To this end a P-38 at Langford Lodge had its armament removed and the nose modified to take a bombar-

The 353rd FG pioneered dive-bombing with the P-47. Here M/Sgt Clarence Piffer, Sgt Tom Zetterval and Cpl Dave Winner adjust braces to prevent oscillation of a 500 lb bomb attached to the belly shackles of P-47D 42-8602:YJ:E, nicknamed *Sis*. Metfield, November 1943.

dier, Norden sight and associated equipment. Proving successful, it was planned to provide four similarly modified P-38s, termed 'Droop Snoots', for each fighter group.

First operational employment was on 10 April 1944 when 20th and 55th Groups bombed enemy airfields from 18,000 feet with variable results. Subsequent Droop Snoot bombing operations were carried out at between 15,000 and 18,000 feet, depending on the strength of anti-aircraft defences to be faced.

Experiments continued with various types of close formation to concentrate the bomb pattern. Two squadrons totalling 36 aircraft flying a diamond pattern was the preferred maximum, but group formations were also tried with the two squadrons on either side of the Droop Snoot and the third directly aft. In the first Droop Snoot operations the force tightened formation on approach to the target and made a long level run. However, the intensity of anti-aircraft fire encountered at targets demanded a change of tactics to an approach in very loose formation, tightened for only 30 seconds and an immediate scatter of flights and squadrons after bombs were released on visual and radioed signal. Maximum bomb load per aircraft was two 1000 lb bombs but more usually two 500 lb. When range was a factor one 1000 lb bomb was carried on one rack and a 150 US gallon drop tank on the other.

Overall, the results of Droop Snoot bombing were variable, mainly because these operations were somewhat intermittent due to the priority of escort and support missions and insufficient practice in this technique. In particular, the bombardiers, recruited from bomber units, had great difficulty in setting up their sights, especially in poor weather, for runs at almost twice the speed that they were accustomed to in heavy bombers.

Some experimentation occurred with the use of individual Droop Snoots for precision attacks on special targets. On 14 July 1944 the 55th Group conducted a dive attack on an ammunition dump in France, dropping a 200 lb incendiary with two 150 gallon fuel tanks fitted with the tails from 2000 pound bombs. The release was made from 5000 feet at a speed of 200 mph indicated. Similar use of full fuel tanks as fire bombs was made by P-51s in low-level attacks on suitable ground targets, the gasoline then being ignited by firing tracer. This method, requiring a high degree of skill, was often unsuccessful.

Taken as a whole, VIII FC fighter-bomber operations were marked with very variable success. Even the four P-47 groups that had undertaken most of this work were never able to achieve a consistent standard of accuracy, and the dive bombing attacks against airfields and bridges were eventually viewed as unsatisfactory. With the conversion of all but one group to the more vulnerable P-51, fighter-bombing operations ceased in the autumn of 1944 and thereafter were only very occasionally revived.

AIR TO GROUND ROCKET PROJECTILES
In August 1944 the four VIII FC P-47 groups were each issued with four sets of equipment for air launching 4.5-inch rockets of the type developed from the infantry tube launcher. These weapons were used operationally but only for a limited experimental period and no firm tactical doctrine for their use was established. The rockets were launched in shallow dives of not more than 30 degrees at a range of 1200 feet. The peculiar trajectory of these projectiles made them very difficult to aim and they were not viewed with favour by pilots using them. During the autumn of 1944 the 434th Fighter Squadron of 479th Group received British short-rail rockets for trials. However, this weapon was never employed operationally by this unit.

Fighter Formations
The purpose of fighter formations was basically one of control. There were other influencing factors but control was always paramount. In the United States the traditional fighter formation was composed of elements of three aircraft in a V-arrangement similar to that used by bombers. When the United States entered hostilities this was soon abandoned in favour of the British system, this having in turn been influenced by Luftwaffe fighter formations employed during the battles of France and Britain in 1940.

The basic fighting unit was two aircraft, a leader and wingman – in RAF terminology the latter was often referred to as the 'No 2'. The leader attacked the enemy while his wingman guarded him from interception from the rear. Known as an element, all larger combat formations were composed of these two-plane units. The Flight consisting of two elements was considered the most efficient combat formation for attack and defence, being highly flexible with each element readily supportive of the other. The flight leader was also the leader of one element. Two flights formed a Section which became the usual self-sustaining unit for bomber escort and support. Two sections made up the standard Squadron of 16 aircraft, although initially squadron formations were composed of three 4-plane flights.

The first four fighter groups to arrive in the UK – the 1st, 14th, 31st and 52nd FGs – were all tutored in RAF fighter tactics and formations. The 31st and 52nd, equipped with Spitfires, generally employed flights of in-trail aircraft, each stepped down behind the leader with about 150 feet separation. This was easy

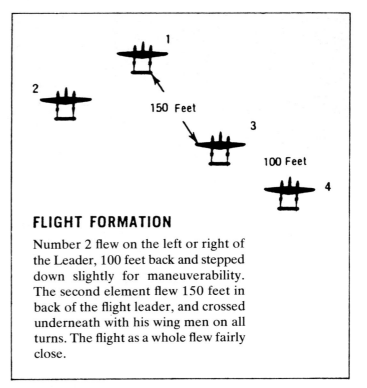

FLIGHT FORMATION
Number 2 flew on the left or right of the Leader, 100 feet back and stepped down slightly for maneuverability. The second element flew 150 feet in back of the flight leader, and crossed underneath with his wing men on all turns. The flight as a whole flew fairly close.

to fly and the movements of the leader could be easily observed by those following. Squadron formations were normally of 12 aircraft, made up of three flights flying side-by-side with some 1200 feet separation. The flight nearest the sun flew 200 feet higher than the leading, central flight, with its leader about 100 feet back from the lead flight leader. The other flight, furthest from the sun, flew 500 feet above the lead flight and with its leader some 200 feet ahead. On 90 degree turns the flanking flights crossed over, the flight turned into by the lead flight crossed under, and the flight turned away from crossed over. The distance between each flight was sufficient for each to make a 180-degree break turn without overrunning adjoining flights. This formation was one developed and employed by the RAF for patrol.

The P-38 pilots were schooled in a flight formation known as the 'Vickers Vee' which consisted of two elements positioned like the fingers of a hand; in fact, this formation later became generally known as the Finger Four. The flight leader's wingman flew about 100 feet back on either right or left. The second

Top: **Finger-Four squadron formation flown by 84th FS P-47s. Flying slightly below and back from the leader allowed wing pilots to follow with ease and safety.**

Above: **Squadron sweep formation used by 4th FG in early operations with P-47s. Wingman of second element in each flight flew to the right of his leader and lower than the other three aircraft. Flights flew line abreast, slightly echeloned back of the lead flight.**

element leader – No 3 – was on the opposite side and about 150 feet back with his wingman – No 4 – 100 feet further out. The second element crossed underneath on all sharp turns. The usual squadron formation consisted of three such flights abreast with about 450 feet between flight leaders. On the few sweeps or bomber support missions undertaken by 1st and 14th FG squadrons the formation flew in conjunction with other US and RAF squadrons at various flight levels.

With the departure of the original four fighter groups to North Africa late in 1942 only the 4th FG remained operational and continued to fly under RAF control using RAF Fighter Command formations. With conversion to P-47s and the operational debut of 56th and 78th FGs in April 1943, the emphasis was on bomber support and escort. The 'Finger Four' flight formation was employed and missions conducted with individual aircraft separated by some 50 to 75 feet. Umbrella support of B-17 boxes consisted of placing squadron formations at varying altitudes above the bombers, varying from 2000 to 5000 feet. An RAF tactic, it proved rather ineffective in affording protection as enemy fighters, attacking at the level of the bombers from front and sides, were gone before they could be attacked by the escort. In June 1943 it became policy for squadrons, flights and elements to open out on reaching the enemy coast to cover more air space and more easily detect the enemy. At first about 300 feet between aircraft but by the late summer this spacing had increased to around 750 feet.

Group commanders were encouraged to develop new formations to better their tactics and while the four-plane flight remained sacrosanct there was considerable variation between groups in the form of squadron and section deployment. Nevertheless, by mid-summer of 1943 the P-47 groups were using fairly uniform formations for the climb-out to enemy territory and penetration of hostile airspace. On leaving home base close 'Finger Four' flights would be separated by no more than 150 feet stacked down one behind the other in squadron formation. This eliminated stragglers and allowed penetration of light cloud without disruption and spreading. The three squadrons of a group flew about a mile to a half mile apart, the two flanking squadrons slightly above the lead squadron. About three minutes before crossing the enemy coast the group leader signalled battle formations by waggling his wings, whereupon a general spreading of all squadrons began. Aircraft within each flight positioned about 750 feet apart, a distance judged by the ability to read squadron letters on fuselages. A wingman flew with the nose of his aircraft level with the canopy of the element leader, and the second element leader, No 3, with his nose in line with the canopy of the flight leader. This contrasted with keeping the nose in line with the leading aircraft's tailplane in the close, climb-out 'Finger Four'. All aircraft in a flight flew at the same altitude. At the same time the trailing flights of a squadron pulled out, usually to the left of the lead, to form two sections.

The lead section, formed with the first and second flights, flew 50 feet below and 50 feet forward of the second or high section composed of the third and fourth flights. The aircraft of each section were at the same altitude. Squadrons within a group remained about a mile apart while making Battle Formation but one flanking squadron kept about a thousand feet higher than the lead and the other about a thousand feet below. Thus widely spaced, a single group was spread across nine miles enhancing its opportunities of seeing any enemy air activity. This string battle formation also allowed maximum manoeuvrability to each aircraft and good control to flight and section leaders. The relative positions of the two flanking squadrons to the lead varied with individual group preference, although the squadron furthese from the sun was always positioned highest where it could see any attacks out of the sun on the other squadrons. To keep a flight together and abreast when a 90-degree turn was made in battle formation, the second element passed under the lead and the aircraft of the flight repositioned in the converse of their original formation.

The wide front battle formation was maintained until rendezvous with bombers when it was necessary to position squadrons above and around the bomber boxes. It became general practice to divide the squadrons into sections with one of the two flights covering the other. The covering flight was normally from 500 to 1000 feet behind and above the leading flight and slightly to the sun side. This arrangement allowed the leading flight to concentrate on searching the sky for enemy attacks on the bombers while the cover flight watched for enemy attacks from

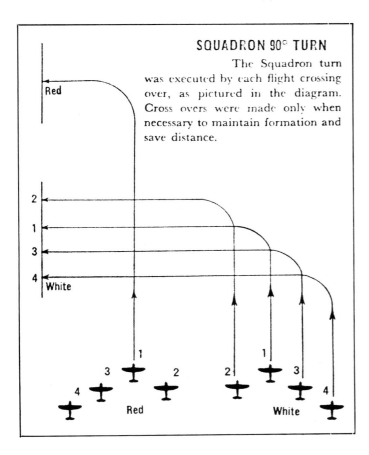

SQUADRON 90° TURN

The Squadron turn was executed by each flight crossing over, as pictured in the diagram. Cross overs were made only when necessary to maintain formation and save distance.

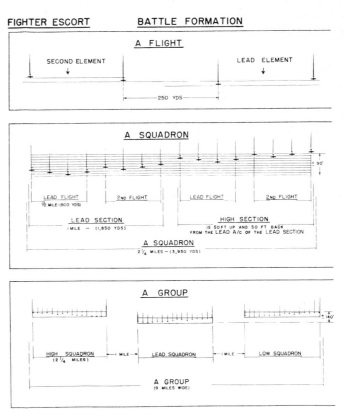

above. Thus stacked, flights orbited over the bombers in trail, extending separation to 1500 to 2400 feet. Eventually the section escort formation was adapted to provide a new squadron battle formation whereby two sections with stepped-up flights flew parallel as soon as the enemy coast was reached, having between 1000 and 2000 feet separation. Squadrons still flew line abreast but were now two to three miles apart. By the spring of 1944 this had generally superseded the wide front battle formation formerly used on penetration.

Unless separated by action, the stepped two-flight formation was used continually while in hostile airspace. If a squadron had not seen action and was still together, on leaving the enemy coast flights closed up and went into trail.

From D-Day to the end of hostilities there were no important changes in fighter formations. Experimentation that occurred with individual groups involved the positioning and spacing within the accepted formations. The Finger Four flight formation remained the basis of all larger formations.

While the positioning of the flight leader's wingman was originally optional, in most groups the position occupied by No 2 was on the left. The 353rd FG, however, was one group where the No 2 was mostly on the right.

Fighter Air Combat Tactics

The basic tactics of air fighting were common to both sides, the most notable being: use of the sun glare for surprise in diving attacks, turning into the attacker if he was apprehended in time, tightening a turn to gain the advantage and position behind an adversary, rolling out and diving to escape from a position of disadvantage. However, the performance and handling characteristics of the fighter types involved had a distinct bearing on the tactics employed.

The P-47 Thunderbolt was large and heavy in comparison with its main adversaries, the Me 109 and FW 190. At low altitude it exhibited poor acceleration and rate of climb and could be out-turned by both German types unless a high speed was maintained. With increases in altitude above 15,000 feet performance gradually improved and at the heights at which the US bombers operated the P-47 was faster than its adversaries in level flight and far superior in dives. Its acceleration and rate of climb remained poor by comparison. To fight effectively in a P-47 it was essential not to let the indicated airspeed fall below 200 mph, preferably launching an attack in a dive so that after opening fire the momentum of the dive was sufficient to aid the break-off climb – prudently towards the sun. Because of the P-47's poor climb performance it was advisable to gain height in gentle turns once the initial momentum obtained from a dive was gone. At high altitude the turning circle of a P-47 was equal to that of the Me 109 and FW 190 if the speed was kept to a minimum of 200 mph.

A well aimed, short burst of fire at the right range from the Thunderbolt's eight .50-calibre guns had a crippling destructive effect on an enemy aircraft. However, the converging harmonisation of the guns necessitated a maximum range of 900 feet and preferably much less. Although a large machine, the P-47's rate of roll was surprisingly good and served well in evasive manoeuvres. If an attack by enemy fighters was anticipated, the standard action was to turn sharply to meet the attacker head-on. While turning fights were inadvisable with a P-47, a manoeuvre to gain position on the enemy, when being out-turned, was to pull the nose up and with violent use of rudder, skid the aircraft down and round to shorten the turn. Another method of tightening a turn was to put the propeller into fine pitch and lower 10 degrees of flap. If caught in an extremely disadvantageous position, the standard evasive manoeuvre was to turn into a 50-degree dive, immediately executing 'sloppy' aileron rolls until sufficient speed was built up to out-run any pursuer. Evasive action was necessary as although the P-47 could out-dive both Me 109 and FW 190, in the initial stages of the dive its acceleration was much slower than that of the German fighters.

Once the pursuer had been out-distanced or lost in the dive, the P-47 continued at high speed away from the general battle area before commencing a climbing curve and rejoining its unit. If the enemy was not shaken off in the dive the P-47 sought cloud cover to evade or continued to 'the deck' where high speed was maintained and combined with jinking and skidding evasive action. Below 15,000 feet the P-47 had distinct performance disadvantages to both Me 109 and FW 190 and a prudent pilot did not attempt to engage in a turning fight. At the end of 1943 P-47s were modified to receive water injection equipment and wide-blade propellers. These greatly benefited sprint performance and it was then possible for the Thunderbolt to out-turn enemy fighters at low altitude if high speed was involved. Many turning combats took place between P-47s and FW 190s at very low altitude where the former was successful, but the German pilot's awareness of the violent steep turn stall characteristics of his aircraft was probably a cautioning factor in such circumstances.

Much of the original combat successes with P-47s was due to the use of the wrong evasive tactics by many Luftwaffe fighters. During the early war years the Luftwaffe had developed a standard evasive measure which had proved reliable when fighting Spitfires. If 'bounced', the German pilot immediately rolled his aircraft into a steep dive, reversing his direction of travel. Turning to meet a Spitfire and engaging in a turning fight was unwise because of the British fighter's superior manoeuvrability, but in a dive both Me 109 and FW 190 could quickly and easily out-run

'Get in close, then you can't miss' was a dictum in VIII FC followed with much success. The detail in this gun camera still shows how closely a 355th FG P-51 pilot pressed his attack on an FW 190.

a Spitfire. As RAF procedure favoured breaking off the attack in such circumstances, the German fighters simply recovered safely at lower altitude. Many Luftwaffe pilots continued to use this tactic when 'bounced' by P-47s and found to their cost that the Thunderbolt eventually overhauled them in a dive. Although P-47 performance remained inferior in some respects to that of its opponents, by prudent exploration of its superior qualities with suitable tactics the type proved a formidable and successful fighter.

The early 8th Air Force Lightning units with P-38F models did not see combat while based in England. A year passed before other P-38 groups commenced operations, with their long range allowing the much needed support to heavy bombers at distant targets. However, the P-38 was beset with technical problems, notably with the limitations of their Allison engines at high altitudes in the extreme cold and high humidity atmosphere of north-west Europe. Frequent cases of complete engine failure in high altitude combat eventually led to P-38 units being restricted to a maximum 20,000 feet whenever possible. Modifications improved high altitude operating ability during the summer of 1944, but by that time VIII FC was converting all P-38 groups to the P-51.

The P-38J, the standard model used by the 8th Air Force's four Lightning groups, was equal in level flight speed to most, and better than some, Luftwaffe single-seat fighters at medium altitudes, as also was its rate of climb. But the risk of engine failure cautioned pilots on power settings and inhibited combat tactics. Although a large twin-engine aircraft, the P-38 was exceptionally manoeuvrable even with drop tanks. Without them it could turn with, and often out-turn, both Me 109 and FW 190. Its particularly good stall characteristics allowed very tight turns without danger of spinning, whereas the FW 190 in particular could not follow without falling out. Very fast turns could be made by varying the speed of each engine. In consequence P-38 pilots exploited the turning combat unless outnumbered. Even than a flight of P-38s formed a tight follow-my-leader turning circle (a Lufbery) and another flight a similar circle about 500 to 800 feet above, going in the opposite direction, as one of the best ways of resolving the situation.

The Lightning was an excellent gun platform with heavy nose-mounted armament including cannon. Unlike the P-47 and P-51 with their wing guns, fire did not converge thus allowing more flexibility in range. Although the P-38 was faster on entering a dive than the Me 109 and FW 190, it had an inherent tail buffeting problem at very high speed which could endanger the aircraft and cause loss of control. Therefore, pilots had to restrict diving speeds to 325 mph indicated which mitigated against both catching up and escaping from the enemy. A good P-38 pilot survived in an unfavourable situation by sharp turns and evasive action until he could reach the safety of cloud. With one engine failed the aircraft became particularly vulnerable to attack. Another disadvantage was the distinctive twin-boom configuration which made the P-38 readily identifiable to enemy interceptors. General P-38 escort tactics involved gaining altitude above the bombers and intercepting enemy attacks on them with shallow dives, attempting to engage individual enemy fighters in turning fights.

P-51 Mustang units initially used similar tactics to those practised with P-47s. The Merlin-powered Mustang was aptly named, being of wild temperament; the torque of its powerful engine, and the low-speed stall characteristics of the laminar-flow wing, demanded prudent handling. Nevertheless, these allowed the P-51 to be manoeuvred in a very erratic fashion and save many a pilot's life when 'bounced'. In all-round performance the P-51 was superior to most models of the Me 109 and FW 190. Being a little heavier and larger, its rate of climb from level flight was, at all but very high altitudes, slightly inferior to that of the enemy. In level flight the P-51 could overhaul both FW 190 and Me 109 at all heights. In high speed dives it could catch both enemy types, although there was more difficulty with the Me 109 if it had a good lead. In turning fights the Me 109 could usually be easily out-turned; the FW 190 proved more difficult but often spun out if tightening too much. P-51B armament was light by comparison with the other US fighters, so close range was recommended to destroy an enemy, but there was also a problem of guns jamming. The later P-51D overcame these problems with armament increased to six .50 weapons. Directional stability was not considered as good with this model and accurate shooting more difficult to master. The P-51 did not have the inhibiting performance and handling characteristics of the other two American fighters, thus allowing pilots greater flexibility in combat and more confidence to engage the enemy.

For high altitude actions both the P-47 and P-51 possessed the two most important performance characteristics evidenced by air fighting during the Second World War – high top speed and superior diving speed. These allowed swift attack and pursuit plus the means of escape. All the successful fighter pilots who survived practised hit and run, endeavouring to avoid dog-fighting. In fighter/fighter interceptions the element of surprise was often decisive. It has been estimated that 75 per cent of victories were obtained in this way – equally, this probably applied to Luftwaffe successes against US fighters. Once alerted to being attacked, a fighter pilot engaging in evasive action could outwit his adversary.

The most promising form of surprise approach was to dive to a point slightly beneath the enemy aircraft and then climb up astern sighting on the underside of the victim. When an element commenced an attack the wingman dropped back to follow his leader by about 500 to 1000 feet and out to one side by 500 to 700 feet. He was then in a position to fire on the enemy if the leader overshot. But in all circumstances the wingman had to remain covering his leader. When the wingman was in a more advantageous position, the element leader would call on him to attack. While policy varied between groups and even squadrons within a group, generally flight or element leaders would automatically initiate attacks on the enemy, calling 'the bounce' over the radio as they went down. If the enemy was first spotted and reported by a wingman he would be directed to lead the attack if element or flight leaders could not see the objective.

Group leaders often positioned themselves relative to their squadrons so that they commanded an overall view of an air battle which allowed them to give directions over the radio. However, a major factor in all air fighting was seeing your enemy first. In both attack and defence situations spotting your adversary could be the crucial factor. Sharp eyesight was the fighter pilot's most important asset, but continued observation under sun glare through a canopy and goggles was both difficult and tiring.

Ground Control of Airborne Fighters

RAF Fighter Command had developed an extensive system of directing its fighter units when airborne from establishments known as Sector Control Centres. Via VHF radio, ground controllers vectored fighter leaders towards enemy formations identified by radar, ground spotters or other sources of intelligence. Early VIII FC operations were conducted under this RAF control system and plans were made to provide a similar system when the Command had operational control of its own units. To this end three Fighter Control Squadrons were formed in the USA and despatched to the UK in 1943 to man centres at each of the fighter wing headquarters.

The first operational fighter wing was the 65th which took over the RAF Sector Control Centre at Debden, actually located in a disused school building near Saffron Walden. It commenced radio control of all VIII FC fighter groups on 1 July 1943 using the call-sign *Morelight*. The call-sign was changed to *Warmsun*, then *Tackline* and finally, early in 1944, to *Colgate*. Hub of a fighter control centre was the Plotting Room. A large table-top map of south-east England and the adjacent continental area covered by VIII FC operations was the central feature. A plotting crew of enlisted men moved numbered counters to display salient data concerning fighter units involved in a mission, the

information coming chiefly from radio communication with the force and from coastal radar stations. The duty controller and his assistants sat on a raised dais around the sides of the room where they could overlook the visual display and receive telephoned or radioed information. Land-line input came chiefly from VIII FC (*Ajax*) and VIII BC 8 AF Hq (*Pinetree*).

The duty controller had the means of direct aural contact with fighter leaders on a mission through 'A' Channel, one of the four press-button radio channels available to fighter pilots on their VHF set. 'A' Channel was utilised for direct contact with group leaders and used to pass on pertinent information as well as to receive messages. These usually concerned time changes because other fighter or bomber formations were going to be late or early at check points, mission recalls, and similar matters. These radio exchanges were all logged by the control centre as were those monitored on 'C' Channel, the common fighter-to-bomber frequency. A different frequency was used for each participating group in 'A' Channel radio control so that there would be no confusion as to source. In emergencies when a warning was sent to all groups, 'D' Channel was sometimes used as the frequency was common to all groups. 'D' Channel, however, was that on which pilots normally called for a navigational 'homing' or 'fix'. A number of D/F (Direction Finding) stations, eventually 12, were set up for this purpose, mostly near

the English coast. These were initially manned by the 52nd Fighter Control Squadron, also staffing the *Colgate* control centre.

From July 1943 the 65th Fighter Wing operated the Air/Sea Rescue (ASR) radio fixer service, initially for fighters but from January 1944 for all 8th Air Force aircraft. 'B' Channel was utilised exclusively for ASR emergency calls by pilots and received by coastal ASR fixer stations. These reported to the ASR plotting and control room in a separate building at 65th Wing where the required fixes were established by triangulation methods. 'D' Channel was often used as an auxiliary ASR channel if 'B' was busy. The range of 65th Fighter Wing radio contact was extended by employing forward relay stations along the east and south coasts of England. Two of these were manned by 52nd Fighter Control Squadron personnel. VHF radio receivers were also installed in VIII FC's Operations Room and through relay staff could listen to fighter radio traffic.

'Y Service' was the cover name given to the RAF organisation that constantly monitored enemy radio communications to gather intelligence. Their centre at Kingsdown processed this data and was often able to advise on enemy air activity while an Allied raid was in progress. In September 1943 the Y Service was made directly available to VIII FC, where information on the reaction and movement of enemy fighters during 8th Air Force operations was passed through its plotting room to *Colgate* and used to warn or vector fighters over enemy territory. Y Service radio intercepts were limited by range factors and most information deduced was on Luftwaffe air movements within 200 miles from the English coast. By using Y Service reports the fighter controllers were occasionally able to warn their charges of the presence of enemy formations. It also provided useful intelligence on where the Luftwaffe assembled its fighters to meet US bomber raids.

A more extensive control of fighter units and better vectoring to meet enemy aircraft was available with the RAF-manned Type 16 system. These were high-definition radars located on the coast; one at Beachy Head (original call-sign *Jensen*) used by the USAAF had an operational range of 120 miles. It could present on its screen all air activity within range and its operators were, through direct radio communication, able to advise Allied fighter leaders of the direction and altitude of enemy fighter aircraft. Type 16 was limited to short-range missions and only two fighter units in one area could be handled at one time. When it was desired to use this system, control of the fighters involved passed from the fighter wing centre to the Type 16 operators; the hand-over normally taking place mid-Channel. Type 16 was first utilised by VIII FC fighters in December 1943 and thereafter periodically until October 1944

Left: **Plotting table and mission display board in the Operations Room at Saffron Walden from where all fighter missions were controlled from the end of December 1944. Mission details are fictitious but show the information displayed based on operations as planned. Plotting table carried operations as they were actually being flown. The photograph was taken from the dais position of the controllers who were in radio contact with airborne fighters.**

Above: **Radio reliability was of great importance in fighter control. Cpl Mickey Balsam, 50th Fighter Control Squadron, was one of several radio repairmen who regularly checked equipment. He also had the distinction of being the composer of the well known ditty, 'Lily from Piccadilly'.**

On 18 November 1943 the 66th Fighter Wing at Sawston Hall (now the Cambridge Language Centre) took operational airborne control of its assigned fighter units, and on 4 December the 67th Fighter Wing did likewise from Walcot Hall, just south of Stamford. These centres, known by the call signs *Oilskin* and *Mohair*, were manned respectively by the 50th and 57th Fighter Control Squadrons. They also took over some of the D/F stations which had previously been serving 65th Fighter Wing control centre. However, the 65th Wing continued to control all ASR calls.

To extend the VHF radio link with fighters the control centres employed radio relay aircraft. These were usually fighter aircraft drawn from different groups and assigned to fly at specified altitudes and time periods, orbiting over the North Sea or other designated area, picking up messages on 'A' Channel and retransmitting them so that they could be received by the fighter control centres. From the spring of 1944 each fighter wing was assigned a heavy bomber which was maintained on a bomber base but operated for the fighter wing as an airborne radio relay station.

A further advance in offensive control was the introduction of the AN/CPS-1 Micro-Wave Early Warning (MEW), a radar technique similar to Type 16 but with better definition and longer range. The maximum was 200 miles with operational control range for vectoring of two or three fighter groups being 165 miles. The first installation at Grey Friars began operations in July 1944 using the call-sign *Dwarfbean*. On several occasions its operators, 401st Signal Co, were able to successfully vector fighters towards enemy aircraft.

In November 1944 MEW was established at Gulpen, just west of Aachen and provided detection over a large part of northwest Germany. Two other MEW installations were placed on the Continent before the end of the war. One of the most successful uses of MEW occurred on 27 November 1944 in a unique operation when the 8th Air Force bomber effort was subordinate to that of the fighters. A cleverly managed despatch of fighters, coupled with radio countermeasures, led German radar monitors into mistaking the large force of fighters despatched to strafe targets in north-west Germany for bombers. Y Service was able to deduce this error from radio intercepts and MEW was able to observe Luftwaffe reaction and vector US forces to where large numbers of enemy fighters were assembling to meet the expected bomber threat. As a result 8th fighters were able to claim many victories, 98 being credited.

Operational radio control of airborne fighter units was returned to 65th Fighter Wing at Saffron Walden when 8th Air Force decided it more efficient and effective to have all monitoring at a central point. The 66th Fighter Wing operational control centre ceased operations on 1 January 1945 and that of 67th Fighter Wing a month later. All the D/F stations operated by these two wings were passed to 65th Wing control. As there were now too many aircraft operating on D Channel it was divided into two different networks termed Red and Blue, using two different frequencies, seven groups assigned to use one and eight the other. It was planned that the 50th and 57th Fighter Control Squadron would move to the Continent and operate MEW facilities.

In February 1945 the 65th Fighter Wing's 52nd Fighter Control Squadron was manning 12 D/F fixer, eight ASR fixer and two Forward Relay stations with three officers and 239 enlisted men. At *Colgate* control room it had two officers and 27 enlisted men. Following the end of hostilities the remaining six ASR fixer and the two relay stations were closed down in mid-July and the remaining fixer stations a month later.

FIGHTER CALL-SIGNS: MAY 1943 – 22 APRIL 1944

Debden — Carman		Duxford — Rutley	
4FG	Upper	78FG	Greywall
334FS	Pectin	82FS	Stedman
335FS	Greenbelt	83FS	Lockyear
336FS	Shirtblue	84FS	Bayland
Halesworth — Sturdy		78'B'FG	Bakehouse
56FG	Yardstick	82'B'FS	Churchtime
61FS	Keyworth	83'B'FS	Cleveland
62FS	Woodfire	84'B'FS	Clinton
63FS	Postgate		
		Nuthamstead — Rockcreak	
56'B'FG	Ashland	55FG	Smallboy
61'B'FS	Halsted	38FG	Swindle
62'B'FS	Groundhog	338FS	Warcraft
63'B'FS	Northgrove	343FS	Careful
Steeple Morden — Towrope		Metfield — Boyhood	
355FG	Sunshade	353FG	Slybird
354FS	Haywood	350FS	Pipeful
357FS	Blowball	351FS	Roughman
358FS	Trooptrain	352FS	Wakeford
Martlesham — Recount		Leiston — Earlduke	
356FG	Soundwave	357FG	Rightfield
359FS	Beachhouse	362FS	Judson
360FS	Plaster	363FS	Chamber
361FS	Molecat	364FS	Cowdy
Bottisham — Lakepress		Bodney — Speedboat	
361FG	Wildcat	352FG	Hatfield
374FS	Hubbard	328FS	Turndown
375FS	Wabash	486FS	Handspun
376FS	Gaylord	487FS	Crownprince
Kings Cliffe — Churchpath		East Wretham — Woodbrook	
20FG	Denton	359FG	Wallpaint
55FS	Towntalk	368FS	Jackson
77FS	Rebuke	369FS	Tiretread
79FS	Crownright	370FS	Wheeler
Raydon — Westland		Boxted — Goodhall (9AF)	
358FG	Tapdance	354FG	Flosmoor
365FS	Barnshoe	353FS	Jacknife
366FS	Snowpass	355FS	Vinepress
367FS	Outdress	356FS	Starstud

The 62'B'FS was originally Keeler but changed as could be confused with 61FS Keyworth. 343FS was originally Whiteman.

FIGHTER CALL-SIGNS: 23 APRIL 1944 TO MAY 1945

65 Fighter Wing — Colgate

Debden — Diction

	'A'	'B'	'C'
4FG	Horseback	Amber	Mascot
334FS	Cobweb	Tiffin	
335FS	Caboose	Supreme	
336FS	Becky	Ronnie	

Steeple Morden — Tworoom

	'A'	'B'	'C'
355FG	Uncle	Hornpipe	Borax
354FS	Falcon	Chieftain	
357FS	Custard	Moses	
358FS	Bentley	Beehive	

Little Walden — Darkfold

	'A'	'B'	'C'
361FG	Glowbright	Filly	Magpie
374FS	Ambrose	Ripper	
375FS	Decoy	Dishcloth	
376FS	Yorkshire	Skyblue	

Boxted — Dogday

	'A'	'B'	'C'
56FG	Fairbank	Subway	Pantile
61FS	Whippet	Household	
62FS	Platform	Icejug	
63FS	Daily	Yorker	

Bottisham — Lakepress

	'A'	'B'	'C'
361FG	Cheerful	Marble	Maltese
374FS	Noggin	Kingdom	
375FS	Cadet	Daydream	
376FS	Titus	Style	

Wattisham — Heater

	'A'	'B'	'C'
479FG	Highway	Snowhite	Flareup
434FS	Newcross	Reflex	
435FS	Lakeside	Haddock	
436FS	Bison	Springbox	

66 Fighter Wing — Oilskin

Duxford — Rutley

	'A'	'B'	'C'
78FG	Phoenix	Slapstick	Boycott
82FS	Surtax	Rainbox	
83FS	Cargo	Turquoise	
84FS	Shampoo	Spotlignt	

Raydon — Cockle

	'A'	'B'	'C'
353FG	Jonah	Keylock	Muffin
350FS	Seldom	Persian	
351FS	Lawyer	Squirrel	
352FS	Jockey	Bullring	

Fowlmere — Gaspump

	'A'	'B'	'C'
339FG	Armstrong	Student	Pretend
503FS	Beefsteak	Unique	
504FS	Cockshy	Gluepot	
505FS	Upper	Slapjack	

Wormingford — Fusspot

	'A'	'B'	'C'
55FG	Windsor	Graphic	Kodak
38FS	Hellcat	Program	
338FS	Accra	Richard	
343FS	Tudor	Saucy	

Leiston — Earlduke

	'A'	'B'	'C'
357FG	Dryden	Silas	Eyesight
362FS	Dollar	Rowntree	
363FS	Cement	Diver	
364FS	Greenhouse	Hawkeye	

67 Fighter Wing — Mohair

Kings Cliffe — Churchpath

	'A'	'B'	'C'
20FG	Walnut	Oatmeal	Katie
55FS	Sailor	Pator	
77FS	Outcry	Glory	
79FS	Primrose	Screwgun	

Martlesham — Recount

	'A'	'B'	'C'
356FG	Lampshade	Notebook	Seaweed
359FS	Farmhouse	Bucket	
360FS	Vortex	Deansgate	
361FS	Chinwag	Webber	

Honington — Outside

	'A'	'B'	'C'
364FG	Sunhat	Weekday	Harlop
383FS	Escort	Tantrum	
384FS	Goldfish	Zeeta	
385FS	Eggflip	Pillow	

Bodney — Speedboat

	'A'	'B'	'C'
352FG	Topsy	Bearskin	Cloister
328FS	Ditto	Tarmac	
486FS	Angus	Rocket	
487FS	Transport	Vicar	

East Wrethem — Woodbrook

	'A'	'B'	'C'
359FG	Chairman	Cavetop	Ragtime
368FS	Jigger	Handy	
369FS	Tinplate	Earnest	
370FS	Redcross	Rollo	

In April 1945 Bodney became Beachhouse, 352FG — Packload, and 328FS — Screwcap.

Air/Sea Rescue

5ERS	Teamwork

Scouting Force

1SF	Borax (to Sep 44)
1SF	Buckeye (Oct 44 – Apr 45)
1SF	Cavalry (Apr 45 –)
2SF	Bootleg
3SF	Kodak

Reconnaissance

Photographic Reconnaissance

Prewar aerial photography conducted by the US Army Air Corps was mostly in connection with the preparation of maps of the remoter areas of continental United States. Hitherto without any such requirement, the USAAF was quick to appreciate the necessity of photographic reconnaissance in support of strategic air operations as highlighted during the first two years of the war in Europe. While long-range bombers were fitted out for this role it became evident that there was a need to develop a fast photographic aircraft to operate with a degree of immunity in hostile airspace along the lines of the successful British innovations. The Lockheed P-38 Lightning twin-engine fighter lent itself well to this task, being extremely fast, very stable in level flight, and having a weapon bay in its nose that could be converted to hold various camera arrangements. When the US entered hostilities this aircraft was only in limited production and much in demand for fighter units. Nevertheless, it was on the use of the Lightning that USAAF photographic reconnaissance was to be largely based.

OPERATIONS

The first unit with a photographic mission to arrive in the UK was the 5th Photo Reconnaissance Squadron with five officers and 158 other ranks who disembarked on 14 August 1942, its F-4 aircraft (the designation for the photographic version of the P-38F) to follow at a later date. Another four F-4 squadrons and one with F-9s (photographic version of the B-17), to be part of the 3rd Photographic Group, were scheduled to arrive in following weeks and General Eaker was anxious that immediate attention be given to a plan for their employment. Aware of the almost total lack of expertise in the art of modern photographic reconnaissance, Eaker wanted these units to have the RAF as their mentor, further suggesting that initially they be stationed at the British photo reconnaissance base at Benson, near Oxford. In discussions with the appropriate RAF authorities agreement was reached that units of 3rd Photographic Group would be based at the Benson satellite, Mount Farm, but as this airfield was not readily available the Group would temporarily use Steeple Morden. However, operation *Torch*, the Allied invasion of North Africa, claimed the 3rd Photographic Group and on 16 October 1942 it was transferred to the 12th Air Force before ever becoming operational. The Group departed for North Africa minus three of its assigned squadrons which were still in the US or on route to the UK – one, in fact, was eventually diverted to India. Another one of the delayed squadrons, the 13th, finally arrived in England on 1 December 1942 and was retained to become the 8th Air Force's first operational photographic reconnaissance unit. Initially established at Podington, where F-5As (photographic designation for P-38G) started arriving on 9 January 1943, the squadron was moved to Mount Farm with its complement of 13 aircraft in mid-February.

Intensive training under RAF guidance resulted in the first combat sortie being flown on 28 March by the unit CO. This, as with most other early sorties, was to coastal regions of occupied France to engage in area strip photography, the resulting prints providing intelligence on enemy activities within these locations. Bomb Damage Assessment sorties to photograph targets attacked by 8th Air Force bombers began on 16 April 1943 and became an increasing part of the squadron's operations. Two other photographic squadrons arrived at Mount Farm in May 1943 and in early July all were established under the 7th Photographic Group. In the following December a fourth squadron was assigned.

Prior to the debut of the 13th Photo Squadron, 8th Air Force relied entirely upon RAF sources for all photographic requirements. An 8th Air Force officer was placed in the office of the RAF's Assistant Director of Intelligence, Photography, to process requests, most commonly that for damage assessment cover of targets attacked by VIII BC. The RAF continued to provide such cover until early 1944 when US units were sufficiently numerous to handle all 8th Air Force requirements, although an exchange of photographic intelligence continued until the end of hostilities.

Initially the RAF's Central Interpretation Unit at Medmenham scrutinised and processed all photographs taken by Mount Farm aircraft. A provisional 8th Air Force photographic interpretation unit, established at Medmenham in August 1942 to train US personnel in RAF techniques, was eventually absorbed (in February 1943) by the 1st Photo Intelligence Detachment at 8th Air Force Headquarters. Ultimately 8th Air Force established an extensive photo interpretation organisation at High Wycombe but Medmenham continued to shoulder the major proportion of this task throughout the war.

The major assignment of 7th Photo Group throughout its operations was obtaining photographs for damage assessment of targets attacked by the Eighth's bombers or fighters. Next to this, frequent photographic cover of installations of target interest was maintained to supply intelligence for planning strikes. Area cover was flown in an endeavour to record enemy activity that might establish new targets for attack or provide other important intelligence. Another requirement was photography for the preparation of maps and a third of the Group's total sorties were for this purpose.

Even before the first 8th Air Force F-5As became operational, some disquiet was expressed in USAAF circles as to their suitability for the task. This was chiefly based on experience in North Africa where the President's son, Colonel Elliot Roosevelt commanding a photographic unit, had expressed preference for the RAF's Mosquito in high-altitude long-range photographic work. US efforts to procure Mosquitoes from the British were eventually successful although delivery was protracted due to demands for this aircraft in other roles and they were rarely used for daylight damage assessment sorties.

Dissatisfaction with the current F-5 Lightning continued to be aired by 8th Air Force Headquarters and in October 1943 General Eaker requested the loan of 12 photographic Spitfires until improved models of the F-5 became available early in 1944. Shortcomings of the F-5A and F-5B were principally insufficient ceiling and range for the type of operations conducted. Further, it could not accommodate cameras of 36-inch (914 mm) focal length which were desirable to obtain more detailed images. Despite the limited production of the photographic Spitfire XI, the RAF responded favourably and 12 were supplied to Mount Farm in October/November 1943. Initially distributed among all squadrons of the 7th Group, they were later concentrated in the 14th Photo Squadron. The Spitfires were used almost exclusively on the very long range damage assessment sorties. In March 1945 all Spitfires were ordered to be returned to the RAF in line with a USAAF high command policy that the 7th Photo Group should operate only US-built aircraft. By this time most of the deficiencies of early F-5s had been eliminated in newer models although the type still required much more maintenance than the Spitfire. The F-5 was, however, the preferred camera platform by many pilots. Additionally a P-51D, specially modified to take a 24-inch K-22 camera in each wing, was brought into service for high altitude photography in the final weeks of the war.

The second 8th Air Force reconnaissance group, initially the 802nd Provisional, later the 25th Bombardment (Reconnaissance), did not normally engage in daylight photographic sorties. They operated one B-17/B-24 and two Mosquito squadrons, one of the latter engaging in night photography and the other, with the heavy bombers, was used primarily for weather reconnaissance.

OPERATIONAL PROCEDURE: DAY

All requests for photographic coverage of enemy territory were originally channelled through 8th Air Force Headquarters. From early 1944 requests were made directly to the 8th Reconnaissance Wing (P) – and later its formal successor 325th Reconnaissance Wing – located at High Wycombe adjacent to 8th Air Force Headquarters.

Orders for specific missions were received at Group Operations at Mount Farm through the teleprinter network, usually in the early morning if they involved damage assessment. Each squadron had a rotation list of pilots and a specified number were alerted to be at readiness. Duty pilots usually went to their respective squadron Ready-Rooms to await a telephone call from Operations. As it was mostly desirable to obtain photographs without long shadows the preferred time over target was mid-morning or mid-afternoon. However, weather was the dominating factor in all photographic sorties as the target had to be clear of cloud for a successful run. When a damage assessment sortie had to be flown following an attack by bombers, it was desirable to leave a few hours between the bombing and photography to ensure smoke and dust were not obscuring the target.

Pilots, usually individually, were called to Squadron Operations adjoining the Squadron Ready Room, for briefing conducted by the Squadron Intelligence, or Operations Officer, together with the Squadron Weather Officer. This consisted of giving the pilot his target cover required and scale of photographs, the latter dictating the altitude for the camera run. Detailed weather forecast for the route was also discussed. The pilot then planned his own route unless for special reasons, such as other Allied air operations, this was given in instructions from higher command. Prominent landmarks visible from high altitude were selected as check points along his planned route. When satisfied with his briefing the pilot collected his personal flying equipment, helmet, gloves, parachute, Mae West, escape kit, etc. The inefficient cockpit heating in the F-5 made it necessary to wear a heavy sheepskin flying suit, RAF type fleece-lined boots and silk gloves under the standard deerskin pair. Because of the risk of heating failure, F-5 and Spitfire pilots always wore heavy clothing on long high-altitude missions.

When ready the pilot was transported to his aircraft, usually by Jeep. As with fighters, individual pilots preferred always to fly the same aircraft, but due to maintenance and camera installation requirements this was not always practicable. Several configurations of K-17 and K-18 cameras were set up in the F-5s to suit particular missions and although these could be and were changed, it was practice to maintain available aircraft with different combinations to save time in despatching a mission. On all but shallow penetrations of enemy territory, two 150 US gallon drop tanks were carried plus a full internal fuel load.

After checking the maintenance Form 1 and discussing the serviceability of the aircraft with the crew chief the pilot donned his parachute and climbed into the cockpit. One of the pilot's first actions, after securing his safety harness, was to test camera mechanisms by taking a few 'clearing shots' – place the intervalometer switches 'on' and expose a few frames of film. Starting and taxiing procedure was similar to that followed in fighter units. However, reconnaissance pilots at Mount Farm made contact with the control tower via the operational channel of their radios. This was permissible as the airfield's location far inland gave no risk of radio conversations at ground level being monitored by the enemy. The pilot informed the tower when he started taxiing and was directed by them when clear to take off. Once airborne, radio silence was maintained.

After a left-hand turn, the pilot immediately took up the precise bearing for his coastal cross-out point and began his climb. Normally the target bearing was taken over briefed coastal landmarks but some long range sorties were made by a direct line from base to objective. On extreme range missions the PR aircraft landed at an RAF coastal airfield to top up tanks. Rate of climb-out from base depended on the distance to land-

Left: 'Split-verticals', twin K-17 cameras of 24-inch focal length being removed from F-5A 42-12778 at Mount Farm, July 1943.

Below: **Manhandling an F-5A into a Mount Farm blister hangar, July 1943.**

fall over the enemy coast where it was desirable to be at operational altitude. As a rule the enemy coast was crossed at not less than 20,000 feet and usually between 25,000 and 28,000 feet, the climb being terminated as soon as contrails started to form behind the aircraft. The pilot then reduced altitude by 500 feet to ensure no further contrails were made to advertise his presence to the enemy. The contrail-producing altitude band varied due to atmospheric conditions, but was usually two miles deep. If contrails already existed PR aircraft often flew along them. With overcasts they flew just below, going in and out of cloud.

While there was normally no time schedule to follow for a mission it was flown at maximum cruise speed in order to minimise the likelihood of interception. In the Lightning this was 240 mph IAS at 28,000 feet giving a true airspeed of 360–380 mph using 35 inches manifold pressure and 2600 rpm. On long missions where fuel had to be conserved, power settings were reduced to 160 mph IAS with 31 inches and 2200 rpm. While continuous high speed operation gave higher engine oil temperatures than with the fighter Lightnings, it was still necessary to periodically run up the rpm and bring down manifold pressure to keep crankcase oil sufficiently warm. Spitfire XIs were frequently climbed to over 30,000 feet and flown at a true airspeed of 400 mph. While there were no heating problems for pilot, engine or cameras, the cockpit was extremely cramped for flights of over four hours' endurance.

Although a straight course was flown it was sometimes necessary to detour round flak areas when flying at reduced altitude below contrail level; at over 30,000 feet there was little danger from flak. In the F-5 a distinctive buzz from the radio receiver was an indication that the aircraft was being tracked by *Würzburg* ground radar. Interception by enemy fighters could usually only come from those above or ahead (until jets appeared on the scene). If intercepted the reconnaissance aircraft, being unarmed, could only hope to evade by high speed and sharp manoeuvres. Standard Luftwaffe day fighters were rarely a threat but those with improved high altitude performance, particularly jets, began to take such a heavy toll of 7th Photo Group aircraft during the summer of 1944 that as often as

possible fighter escort was provided in likely danger areas. This consisted of a flight of P-51s, the F-5 flying to their base and while it was refuelled the pilot briefed the escort. The fighters provided close escort to mid-Channel, then took up battle formation, positioning behind and above their charge. From January 1945 the 7th Group was assigned its own P-51Ds for escort purposes and thereafter used them to accompany most reconnaissance missions. The Group had to train its own pilots for this purpose. Previous to the provision of escorts, F-5s and Spitfires were often warned of the presence of enemy aircraft by radio messages from an RAF control centre. Usually this would be a recall. The warning was derived from knowledge of Luftwaffe fighter movements through Y-Service intercepts.

In aligning his target a pilot would occasionally roll his aircraft up on a wing to obtain a better view of the ground. Once identified, an approach was made at 30 to 45 degrees to the desired photographic run. At the appropriate point the pilot banked the aircraft round towards the target, this procedure allowing him to line up accurately as once the run began the aircraft nose would obscure the target from view. It was now essential to fly level at a constant height and airspeed to achieve the correct overlap in exposure and maintain the scale. To start the cameras the switches of the pre-set intervalometer were 'flipped'. The scale of the resultant photographs depended on altitude and camera focal length. A 6-inch (152 mm) focal length camera provided a scale that was twice the altitude of the aircraft, a 12-inch (305 mm) a scale equivalent to the altitude figure and a 24-inch (610 mm) a scale half times the altitude. A 60 per cent overlap of frames was desirable and set into the intervalometer. It was usual to make two runs

Above left: Special cases were provided for handling exposed film magazines to prevent the risk of light damage while in transit.

Left: Intelligence officers at Mount Farm examining a developed film in order to select frames for 'rush prints' for target damage assessment.

Above: The automatic Wilkinson Multiprinter could produce 900 nine-inch square contact prints an hour if necessary. The number required from each negative could be set in.

Right: Although photo-interpretation was carried out at Mendmenham, preliminary print examination was often performed at Mount Farm. The magnification instrument in use is a stereoscope which combined the images of two photographs taken with a brief time lapse to give a three dimensional effect.

across the target, the second usually at between 35 to 50 degrees to the first. If cloud partly obscured the target further runs might be made, but the longer the reconnaissance aircraft remained in the target area the greater the danger of interception.

Area cover sorties for intelligence search or mapping purposes were flown by up to nine but more usually four or five F-5s in spaced formation. Camera equipment and altitude dictated the spacing, aircraft being echeloned back from the leader. Measured parallel runs were made, and sometimes the same area was covered by second runs at 90 degrees to the first.

The return journey was flown at the same high altitude and also at maximum cruising speed until out of hostile airspace. Any interesting targets of opportunity were photographed to use up film. Thereafter a rapid descent would be made to clear oxygen level. On reaching Mount Farm pilots were permitted to 'buzz' its airfield to alert the intelligence and camera personnel to be on hand to remove the film as soon as the aircraft landed and arrived at its dispersal point. The pilot went immediately to a debriefing session in the group operations room, usually with the two officers who briefed him. Opinions on his visual impression of target damage were elicited plus precise details of weather encountered. Coffee and 'two slugs' of rye whisky were available during his debriefing, which might take from ten to 15 minutes. Following this a pilot was released to eat or sleep as desired.

Processing of film was performed at Mount Farm. Each film magazine held approximately 200 to 500 feet and the wet negatives were fixed within 30 minutes of the aircraft's return. Prints were available within the hour. The work was highly mechanised, a Williamson Multiprinter performing processing, drying and printing in one operation. A first interpretation was generally carried out by 7th Photo Group intelligence staff before prints were forwarded to higher headquarters and Medmenham for more detailed analysis.

LOW-LEVEL OPERATIONS
Prior to the Allied cross-Channel invasion of June 1944 there was a demand for photographic cover of German defence installations along the French and Belgian coasts. Although this was primarily undertaken by the British and American tactical air force units, the 7th Photo Group was called on to contribute to this extensive task. The Group employed F-5s exclusively for this work, with arrangements of one or two side cameras for left and right obliques and a forward and down-looking camera fixed behind a special aperture in the nose.

The mission requirements for this low-level work did not usually involve deep penetration of hostile territory but it was nevertheless fraught with great danger for unarmed reconnaissance aircraft as a constant height and speed had to be maintained when photographing. Known as *Dicing*, a term derived from the RAF slang 'a dicey situation', these missions were generally undertaken by a pair of aircraft flying in close proximity to make the most of the element of surprise. After take-off an altitude of between 10,000 and 15,000 feet would be reached and held until mid-Channel when a descent to 50 feet was made to conduct the camera run. Following this the F-5 climbed back to medium altitude for the return to base.

Medium-level photography missions at 10,000 to 12,000 feet were conducted on a very limited scale by 153rd Reconnaissance Squadron of 67th Reconnaissance Group during the high summer of 1943. This unit, based at Keevil, was equipped with Douglas A-20Bs for use in a tactical role, originally ground

attack. Later some of these Havocs were modified to take camera installations in the nose and rear fuselage. Operations were mostly over the Brest Peninsula and no more than two A-20s were involved at one time. Escorted by RAF Spitfires, these missions were in part diversions for B-26s bombing targets in north-west France.

OPERATIONS: NIGHT
To supplement its daylight photographic effort, in the spring of 1944 8th Air Force used one of its newly formed Mosquito squadrons to engage in night photography. Cloud was a frequent foil to daylight operations in north-west Europe whereas the sky often cleared during darkness. Mosquito XVIs flying from Watton were used for a variety of night photographic missions, known as *Joker*, usually where long range was required. Flight altitudes were normally in excess of 20,000 feet to the target area where a descent to under 15,000 feet was made. On the target run a flash bomb was released to ignite at a predetermined height, the camera shutter having been opened and kept open until this occurred.

In the summer of 1944 the Watton unit, 654th Bpmb Squadron (R), received three B-26G Marauders which were used in the *Dilly* project for photo-flash cover of V-weapon sites during darkness. The ageing Mount Farm B-25 Mitchell was also employed on this task until sufficient B-26s were available. Following the capture of French V-sites by Allied forces in August these B-26s remained with the 25th Group at Watton but were thereafter used for operational training.

USE OF HEAVY BOMBERS
While no true photographic models of the B-17 or B-24 were used operationally by 8th Air Force from England, both types were occasionally fitted out with K-17 or other cameras on a hand-held rig at open waist windows for use in specific non-combat operations. These included the required aerial photography of US military installations in Europe, and those

Right: **Oblique-facing camera in low-flying 7th PG F-5 photographs aircraft's shadow as well as defences on French beach, May 1944.**

captured from the enemy. The camera crew was usually provided by the 1st Combat Camera Unit which was attached to 8th Air Force Hq.

The 1st Combat Camera Unit also manned cameras in heavy bombers on combat missions to obtain action pictures, both still and ciné. Additionally, a photographer acting as a waist gunner was present in bomb group formations on most combat missions to obtain obliques of the attack on the target. Photographs so obtained, together with the strike photos from the fixed K-21 strike cameras, which the radio operator of a B-17 and waist gunner on a B-24 put in motion at bombs away, provided other valuable intelligence imagery.

Assigned to USAAF Hq but attached to the 8th and 9th Air Force for support, the 19th Reconnaissance Squadron was engaged in high-altitude photography of western Europe for mapping purposes at the end of hostilities. Based at Watton and Thurleigh between April and August 1945, the unit was equipped with F-9Cs, the camera-equipped version of the B-17G.

Weather Reconnaissance

Initially 8th Air Force saw no requirement to supplement the RAF meteorological flight programme over and around the British Isles, but it soon developed that in VIII BC operations there was often need for up-to-date local weather information during the launch of a mission. The state of the elements could change so rapidly that exploration of conditions prevailing at high altitude in the area of bomber bases became a prudent policy. Thus, from the summer of 1943, whenever there was doubt about atmospheric conditions that would be encountered in a bomber assembly area, a B-17 was despatched to reconnoitre about an hour to a half hour before scheduled mission take-off. A volunteer member of the base weather detachment often joined the crew in this flight, which generally took an orbiting climb up to the optimum operational altitude – 25,000 feet. Information gathered concerned cloud extent and height, ice formation levels, the intensity, persistence and height of contrail formations, and visibility. The 'weather ship' landed back at base to report prior to mission take-off but, if unexpected adverse conditions were encountered, the details might be radioed back in code to base Flying Control. Pre-mission local weather flights proved so valuable that it became regular practice for the three groups of a designated combat wing to take turns in providing an aircraft and crew for this flight. Subsequently all three Divisions authorised local weather flights and detailed units to perform them as required.

HEAVY WEATHER SQUADRON
Weather proving a major limiting factor to 8th Air Force bombing missions during the first year of operations, there was need to improve meteorological information available for mission planning. In early August 1943, General Eaker expressed to the RAF a wish to extend the weather service as VIII BC daylight bombing operations required weather data 12 to 18 hours in advance of a projected mission. Inadequate information was available covering the Atlantic approaches, from whence most weather fronts arrived. While aware the RAF intended to re-equip some meteorological units with Halifaxes for long-range weather duties, Eaker suggested temporary help from American aircraft and crews. The offer was accepted and an agreement was reached that a small number of Fortresses and their crews would conduct weather flights over the eastern Atlantic under RAF guidance.

On 8 September 1943 four B-17Fs and crews were sent to St Eval. There they were attached to No 517 Squadron RAF who initially provided ancillary equipment and weather personnel. On 27 October the US flight moved to St Mawgan where another four B-17s arrived on 5 November to swell the long-range meteorological capability. However, as it was desirable to have the B-17s on a USAAF base for maintenance and supply, on 23 November the flight, under Capt Alvin Podjowski, was moved to Bovingdon. From here the flight flew regular Atlantic sorties staging through RAF St Eval. Although it was planned that B-17s and crews would return to their units when the RAF Halifaxes were ready, the British said this would not be before the spring of 1944 and wished 8th AF Atlantic meteorological flights to continue. On 21 April 1944 the unit was designated the 8th Reconnaissance Weather Squadron (Heavy) and moved to Wat-

Right: **Until sufficient USAAF-trained weather observers were available, some RAF personnel flew with the provisional Heavy Weather Squadron. In this photograph Capt A. E. Podjowski, the unit's commander, holds a psycrometer in place while Sgt W. H. Timms, RAF, secures it to the supports on a B-17F's nose. The instrument displayed data which allowed an observer inside the aircraft to record outside temperatures and humidity. Bovingdon, February 1944.**

ton where all weather reconnaissance units were being concentrated under a single headquarters, the 802nd Reconnaissance Group (P).

At Watton the Squadron absorbed a few B-17Fs of the 8th Reconnaissance Courier Squadron (P), a unit originally formed at Cheddington on 4 March for local weather flights. The unit also had three L-5B Sentinel light and six UC-64 Norseman utility aircraft which ran a daily courier service from reconnaissance bases carrying photographs and documents to Booker, a small grass airstrip near 8th Air Force Hq. This element was disbanded by 31 May and the Squadron was then solely concerned with long-range weather flights.

There were two regular kinds of sortie, those to land in the Azores, code named *Sharon*, and those over an 800-mile triangular course south-west of Ireland, code named *Allah*. Point of departure from England for both kinds was over Lands End. In June the complement of B-17F/Gs was scheduled for replacement with B-24Js, in line with a policy of conserving the supply of Fortresses received in the UK for bomber units, there being a forecast shortage of the type, whereas Liberators were already exceeding production estimates. The Squadron, loath to part with its B-17s, managed to avoid conversion until August, the same month that it finally received an authorised designation and Table of Organisation as the 652nd Bomb Squadron (Recon). It was quickly discovered that the B-24s did not behave as well as the Fortress at the high altitudes necessary for some meteorological observations. In particular the heated wing arrangement for de-icing proved unsatisfactory. After a few dangerous spin-outs due to wing icing, a convincing case was made for a return to B-17s. At this time, late September, the 652nd had 11 B-24Js on strength. By the end of the year it was completely re-equipped with B-17Gs.

On 1 August 1944, the 652nd made its first round-trip flight to the Azores. Known as *Epicure*, such sorties were often over 14 hours' duration, made possible through the use of two 410-gallon bomb-bay tanks to boost total fuel in the B-17 to 3,630 US gallons. Eventually the Squadron was flying sorties to eight different areas around the British Isles although the regular hauls remained *Sharons* and *Allahs*.

As flights were over areas where contact with the enemy was considered highly unlikely, most armour and armament was removed to improve performance and the crew reduced to seven: pilot, co-pilot, navigator, weather observer, flight engineer, radio operator and tail gunner. During these over-water flights meteorological information would be gathered every 50 miles from altitudes extending from a few hundred feet to 30,000 feet, with coded data being encoded and radioed back to a RAF collating station. The course was flown in a series of long climbs and descents. Between two and four heavy weather sorties were flown in each 24-hour period.

LIGHT WEATHER SQUADRON

On several occasions during the spring and summer of 1943, 8th Air Force bombers reached a target area only to discover that the forecast for clear conditions was incorrect. From the frustration of group leaders on such occasions was born the idea of fast weather scouting aircraft preceding the bombers to a target area to report prevailing conditions. The foremost enthusiast for such assistance was Col Bud Peaslee of 384th Group who took his ideas to General Eaker. Unfortunately at that time, August 1943, there were no aircraft 8th Air Force could utilise for such a purpose. Eaker did consider using F-5 Lightnings, but this did not ensue, chiefly for technical reasons. Aware that the USAAF had negotiated a supply of de Havilland Mosquito aircraft, a type possessing the necessary range, speed and altitude requirements for the job, Eaker approached the British in September 1943 with a request for 30 Mosquito VIs to establish a target weather reconnaissance unit at Mount Farm in the 7th Photo Recon Group. Although the RAF agreed to make the required Mosquito VIs available, USAAF investigation of this fighter model found it unsuitable for the proposed mission, particularly as extensive modifications would be required. Instead USAAF preferred to wait for the Mk XVI photographic reconnaissance model of which first deliveries were promised in February 1944.

With the availability of the first Mosquito PR XVIs, a decision was taken in late February to use the aircraft not only for target weather scouting, but radar and night photography. The weather reconnaissance element was to utilise the personnel of 50th Fighter Squadron at Nuthampstead, this unit having recently been brought in from Iceland. Mosquito XVI MM338, the prototype for the weather reconnaissance requirements, was duly fitted with special radio and other instrumentation at Burtonwood depot. The 8th Reconnaissance Weather Squadron (Light) (P) was activated on 4 March to operate the aircraft from

Light Weather Squadron Mosquito (NS569) and Heavy Weather Squadron B-17G (43-38867) at Watton. Turrets have been removed from Fortress. (Flight)

Cheddington where training commenced. Because of the required modifications and pilot training several weeks were to pass before the first operational sortie. This was flown by NS510 on 23 May – a week later than the planned debut – from Watton, where the unit had moved on 22 April as part of 802nd Group. The squadron did not receive its full complement of aircraft until early June, but thereafter the pace of operations increased dramatically.

Target weather scouting was run under the code name *Scout*. Mosquitoes were despatched singly on scouting operations to arrive in the bomber target area 10 to 15 minutes before the first bombers. On the route out the scouts would climb to an optimum 30,000 feet and radio code weather observations as soon as they were ahead of the bomber stream. The scout aircraft could not arrive in the target area too early as the enemy, aware of their purpose, would be alerted as to the target about to be attacked. A further measure to secure the bombers' destination was for the Mosquito scout to extend its search over a wide area. As the bombers approached the Mosquito circled the target and continued to radio weather and general reports on smoke at the target and other enemy activity. Observations were made and broadcast by the navigator in the nose of the aircraft. If weather deteriorated on the return flight this information was radioed to following bombers. During some operations, notably the *Frantic* shuttle missions, scout Mosquitoes landed in the Soviet Union and Italy.

The Mosquito was sufficiently speedy to encounter little trouble from enemy fighters. Indeed, judging by the number of interceptions by bomber escort Mustangs it was more in danger from friends than enemies. Following the shooting down of a Mosquito on 12 August by a P-51 pilot who identified it as a Ju 188, the tails of the Light Weather Mosquitoes were painted bright red as an identification feature. Encounters with enemy jet aircraft were a matter of concern and led to P-51 escorts being provided for many Mosquito reconnaissance flights during the last six months of the war.

In July and August 1944 regular target scouting by unarmed Mosquitoes was superseded by Mustangs operating at flight strength. The fighter weather scouts had the advantage of being armed if intercepted and were also less likely to reveal target intentions to the enemy, who had difficulty in distinguishing their activity from that of the van of the bomber escort. Although Mosquito target weather scouting missions were occasionally flown to the end of hostilities, after September 1944 they were of a more specialised nature or as a supplement to the P-51 scouts.

From the summer of 1944 the 653rd Bomb Squadron (R) (L), as the unit had been formally designated in August, concentrated on strategic weather reconnaissance sorties code-named *Blue Stocking*. Flown in daylight and darkness these were carried out principally to provide the weather forecasting service with detailed knowledge of conditions over or near enemy held territory. Occasionally *Blue Stockings* were flown over the Atlantic approaches to supplement the work of the Heavy Weather Squadron. Planned cover of the continent involved four sorties each 24 hours although timing and routes were varied constantly to minimise the chance of interceptions.

In addition to its *Blue Stocking* duties, 653rd Bomb Squadron also took on the anti-radar *Chaff* dispensing role (code-named *Graypea*) at the end of 1944, and from February 1945 made available one Mosquito to each Division for command purposes on bomber missions. This involved a 653rd crew flying their aircraft to a designated bomber base to pick up the mission task force air commander for the day. The Mosquito would then accompany the division formation to the target while the air commander monitored formations and gave any necessary directions or advice to bomber leaders by radio.

On 13 February 1945 the 653rd Bomb Squadron flew its first *Skywave* sortie. This was the cover name for *Loran* navigational

calibration flights. *Loran*, a US-improved and longer-ranged version of *Gee*, was being introduced as a replacement and required the preparation of navigational grid maps. These flights were also utilised for weather reporting.

By VE-Day 653rd Bomb Squadron, with 40 Mosquitoes on strength, had the largest complement of any 8th Air Force squadron.

WEATHER SCOUTING FORCE

From pioneering target weather scouting with Mosquitoes, Colonel Peaslee turned to the P-51 as better suited to his venture. He obtained permission from General Doolittle to form a special flight at Steeple Morden to try out his ideas. Using P-51Ds borrowed from the resident 355th Group and a few former bomber pilots, Peaslee despatched his first scouting force mission on 16 July 1944. Although in early experimental sorties it proved more difficult to locate targets than with the Mosquitoes – which had navigators – the service was quickly acknowledged as most valuable by bomber leaders. Most of Peaslee's pilots formerly held a command pilot or lead crew position in a bomb group prior to finishing a combat tour. Peaslee's logic was that these men, versed in the problems of bomber operations, would be better suited to the task in hand than fighter pilots.

In August General Doolittle authorised the formation of a scouting force in each division. Peaslee's unit became the 1st Scouting Force and moved to Honington, a 1st Division base, to use aircraft of the resident 364th Fighter Group. At this time command of the unit was taken by Lt Col Allison Brooks, former B-17 pilot and executive officer of 401st Bomb Group. A new scouting force was formed at Steeple Morden, a 2nd Division base, designated 2nd Scouting Force. Lt Col John R. Brooks, previously with 389th Bomb Group B-24s, was given command and selected other former Liberator pilots for his scouts. In the 3rd Division the job of organising and commanding its new scouting force went to Major Vincent W. Masters, a former lead pilot of 385th Bomb Group with 28 missions to his credit.

Initially the total pilot strength of each unit was eight. They received instruction on weather observation and then took a conversion course on P-51s at Goxhill where each received an average of about 20 hours on the type. Lacking a Table of Organisation, the formal authorisation for a unit, equipment and personnel for the scouting forces had to be 'borrowed' from existing organisations. P-51 aircraft, ground crews and complete operational back-up was obtained from an existing fighter group's facilities. The 364th Fighter Group was host to the 1st Scouting Force, the 355th to the 2nd and the 55th to the 3rd. Additional aircraft were assigned to these groups who were also called upon to provide pilots and aircraft to fly as wingmen on most scout missions. This meant additional work and strain on the resources of already busy fighter bases, and while the newcomers were hospitably received, they were not particularly welcome. First missions of the 2nd and 3rd Scouting Forces were on 26 and 15 September. Thereafter P-51 scouts were active on all bomber missions for their respective divisions.

Scouting force pilots were billeted separately to other fighter pilots but used all base facilities in common with fighter pilots of the host group. Their alert came from the group field order, but briefing was separate and usually about a half hour before that for fighter pilots. Briefing normally involved two or four scout pilots plus their wingmen and was conducted at Group Operations by the Intelligence Officer, Weather Officer and the Scouting Force commander or his deputy. The briefing concentrated on target identification, order and position of bomber forces and weather forecasts. One or two flights of four P-51s were despatched, depending on the scale of the operation. Take-off was timed so that in a direct flight to the target area the scout Mustangs would overtake the bombers on route and arrive in the general area about ten minutes ahead of the bombers. On route scout leaders used radio to advise bomber combat wing leaders of any changes to the forecast weather. Particular notice was taken of visibility, smoke screens, cloud extent and changes in wind direction and velocity. A four-plane flight was the usual maximum strength for the scouts in one target area where their leader would frequently advise bomber leaders on bombing results, errant formations or action to be taken if weather deteriorated. Weather reports were also given to the bombers on the return journey.

P-51Ds used by scouts were normally fighter aircraft without any special equipment. Pilots were under strict instructions only to engage in combat if attacked and when possible avoid interception. Nevertheless, actions did occasionally take place and by the end of hostilities the 1st Scouting Force had one confirmed victory, the 2nd 12 and the 3rd four.

In January 1945 the 3rd Air Division decided to expand its weather scouting units' duties to bomber assembly areas and the North Sea, replacing the pre-mission local weather flights performed by designated bomber units. Using eight stripped-down B-17Gs this extension of operations began at the end of the month. The host 55th Group at Wormingford, becoming

Above: **Pilots of the 2nd Scouting Force making notes on special tabulated forms during a briefing at Steeple Morden. They are (l. to r.): Capt Henry Hays, 1/Lt Charles Rodesbaugh, 1/Lt John Gerber, 2/Lt George Rossman, 2/Lt David Allen and 1/Lt John Wilkins, April, 1945.**

Left: **Col 'Bud' Peaslee and Major Allison Brooks, pioneers in the use of fighters for weather scouting. Brooks commanded the 1st Scouting Force.** (Q. Bland)

somewhat overcrowded, saw no merit in the distinction that it was the only combat base in 8th Air Force operating both bombers and fighters. This growth of a provisional unit was felt to need the formal accolade to placate USAAF Hq bureaucracy, and so on 17 February 1945 it became the 862nd Bomb Squadron, a unit of the 493rd Bomb Group. Most personnel and bombers of the 862nd remained at Debach attached to other squadrons of the 493rd. Some ground personnel did move to Wormingford to fill out the B-17 maintenance section. The 862nd Bomb Squadron was re-established in the 493rd Group on 18 May 1945 when both the 2nd and 3rd Scout Forces were dissolved and personnel returned to their original units.

The 1st Scout Force survived in the immediate postwar period as the 857th Bomb Squadron, having been assigned this designation on 10 March 1945. This 'regularising' of the unit coincided with a move from Honington to Bassingbourn, near to 1st Division Hq. Following VE-Day the squadron was moved to Alconbury where in addition to its P-51s it received a dozen war-weary B-17F/Gs which were used for weather reconnaissance during the following summer months. The 2nd Scouting Force was planned to move to Halesworth had hostilities continued but never achieved squadron status.

Special Operations

Night Bombing

From the outset of USAAF moves to establish a heavy bomber force in the United Kingdom there was pressure from some quarters, mostly British, for the force to engage in night bombing. This was based principally on the belief that B-17s and B-24s would be unable to conduct operations beyond the range of fighter escort without incurring prohibitive losses. The USAAF successfully resisted this pressure through initial successes with their system of conducting daylight bombing and also by poining out that their two bomber types had been specifically developed for daylight operations and could not economically be converted to night attack. Nevertheless, the stiffening resistance met and increasing losses suffered by VIII BC during the summer of 1943 caused General Eaker to order the necessary preparations in case his bombers were forced to seek the cover of darkness.

In July it was planned to equip and train six B-17 groups, three in each Division initially, the 92nd, 94th, 96th, 305th, 306th and 385th, to join in raids by RAF Bomber Command. Thirty aircraft in each were to be modified for the task, receiving resin lights, engine exhaust flame dampers and blackout curtains for the navigator's compartment. Gun barrels would need flash eliminators to prevent gunners being temporarily blinded when firing. Additionally, night adaption goggles had to be supplied for the crews. It was also desirable that the B-17s involved had

Gee and Standard Beam Approach equipment, while it was essential that only those with long-range wing tanks were selected.

On 20 July the 422nd Bomb Squadron of 305th Group was selected to act as a trials squadron to co-operate in RAF night bombing attacks. An RAF Bomber Command liaison officer was later attached to the unit at Chelveston where night flying training began on 2 August 1943.

Modification of the B-17s proceeded as far as normal missions would allow, but several aircraft partially modified were lost on daylight raids. It was further discovered that illuminated reflector sights would be necessary for the guns, which the 422nd Bomb Squadron had made temporarily out of plexiglas claiming that they could be used successfully in the dark. This squadron attacked coastal defences near Boulogne on 8 September for its first night bombing mission and during the following four weeks flew seven more to targets with RAF Bomber Command. The B-17s took off from Chelveston and individually flew the briefed course and time schedule to the target where

Below left: **The crew of the 385th BG's *Fighting Cock* boarding a truck to be taken to their aircraft for a practice night mission. September 1943.**

Below: **Flame damper on turbo exhaust of 385th BG's *Shack Bunny.***

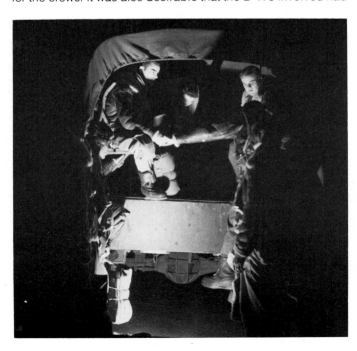

bombing was on target indicator flares previously dropped by the British force. The crews found difficulty in distinguishing these flares and there was some confusion over radio signals. Bombsights were also found unsuitable. No more than five aircraft were despatched on any one night and the total of effective sorties for the eight raids was 32. Two of the B-17s were shot down by night fighters, one on the night of 4/5 October when only three B-17Fs had been despatched. Following this 422nd Bomb Squadron night bombing operations were terminated, but crew training was not wasted for this unit then commenced operations dropping leaflets over enemy controlled territory during darkness.

Throughout September the six groups assigned to night bombing preparations had been carrying out modifications and training and by October several crews were considered ready to participate in operations. However, all night training was stopped when, following a conference at VIII BC, the decision was made not to proceed with the plans for night bombing. Factors influencing this move were: despite heavy losses the day bombing brought positive destruction of industrial targets while there was no immediate hope of any such accuracy in the night attacks; 422nd's performance had shown that losses would not be substantially reduced by operating in darkness; if night bombing was continued the assigned groups would have to practise this exclusively thus weakening the daylight effort; the anticipated availability of long-range fighters for escort should reduce day bomber losses.

For the next year the only night bombing operations carried out by 8th Air Force units were the experimental sorties conducted by 482nd Group to test new radar equipment and techniques. Nevertheless, 8th Air Force had not completely lost interest in bombing during darkness for in October 1944 it again set about organising such a force, albeit small. The 492nd Bomb Group at Harrington had a reduced work load when its primary task of clandestine supply to the resistance movements on the continent during darkness, known as *Carpetbagging*, had been concluded due to the advances of the Allied armies. On 20 October 1944 three of the four squadrons of the 492nd were instructed to prepare for night bombing operations. Bombing equipment that had been removed for *Carpetbagger* work had to be reinstalled and training was protracted due to technical and personnel problems, together with the apparent uncertainty about the project at higher command. Sperry S-1 bombsights were installed as the Norden was not suitable for the operations planned.

In November six B-24s with H2X were assigned and the Group prepared to use these as its pathfinders to drop target markers on which following Liberators could aim. Before the Group could become operational in its new role, one squadron was despatched to Italy in mid-December to conduct *Carpetbagger* sorties over the Balkans, its already modified B-24s being concentrated in the remaining two squadrons scheduled for bombing. A trial mission was carried out in daylight on 24 December when 12 B-24s set off to attack coastal batteries at La Pallice, an isolated German pocket holding out on the French Atlantic coast, where enemy fighter interception would not occur. The same target was attacked in darkness a few days later.

The technique for attack was basically as used by the RAF with the PFF aircraft dropping marker flares, and those following at approximately 45 second intervals dropping individually on these. The results of three operations were not considered all that creditable and 857th and 858th Bomb Squadron were put to further training while there was some discussion with the RAF as to potential targets. This subsequently led to the 492nd Group acting as a diversion force in conjunction with RAF No 100 Group, the organisation based in Norfolk supporting RAF Bomber Command operations through deception and destruction of enemy air defences,. The targets and all orders for procedure for the small 492nd Group force came from No 100 Group, the object being to use the American Liberators in conjunction with the Group's own screening and 'spoof' activities to try and mislead the enemy defences as to the main thrust by RAF Bomber Command.

The first of these co-ordinated missions was conducted by 30 B-24s in the evening of 20 February 1945 and during the next four weeks 11 more were undertaken. Some opposition was encountered on two occasions with two B-24s being shot down and two others severely battle damaged. The force strength declined in early March when the 857th Bomb Squadron was disbanded and reformed elsewhere with a different task. The B-24s and crews, however, remained and were distributed among the remaining two squadrons. There was a lull in night bombing after the night of 13/14 March due to renewed *Carpetbagger* activity with 858th Bomb Squadron joining the 856th in operations over Norway and Denmark. Night bombing by 858th Bomb Squadron was resumed in April when four more missions were carried out in co-ordination with RAF No 100 Group. The last of these took place on 13/14 April when 12 B-24s attacked a rail junction at Beizenburg.

The total 8th Air Force night bombing sorties, excluding special radar tests, was 343 despatched and 307 effective, dropping 745 tons of bombs for the loss of two B-24s plus two B-17s missing and two B-24s written off as Category E.

Leaflet Dropping

An important element of the psychological warfare programme developed by the British in the early war years was the dropping of propaganda leaflets over enemy held territory. The cynicism of RAF Bomber Command crews that they were 'simply providing toilet paper' was not misplaced during the period when Germany's fortunes were in the ascendancy. However, once defeat seemed inevitable these leaflets did help to further undermine enemy morale. Just how effective this psychological weapon proved against the Germans is difficult to assess, whereas leaflets directed at populations in occupied lands were, without doubt, extremely advantageous in boosting morale. In this latter case news or general messages were sent which could only otherwise be conveyed over the radio, a medium to which few people had access.

US interest in psychological warfare resulted in a joint agency to direct a whole range of activities from the UK. USAAF participation in leaflet dropping was a natural development resulting from this combined venture and in the summer of 1943 the 8th Air Force was given the task of delivering 45,000 lb of leaflets per week during the course of regular bombing missions. Further delegated to 1st Wing and its five oldest groups, the leaflets, code named *Nickels*, were to be dropped on every mission over Germany after 14 July. Within a week of this date a bundle consisting of 6500 leaflets, weighing 23 lb in 8½ ×

10½ × 7¼ inch packages, had been adopted as standard. Hand-dispensing through flare shutes and windows was not satisfactory and special containers were devised to be carried in bomb bays. These were adapted wood packing cases with hinged lids. Filled with bundles, the case was then inverted between the outboard and inboard bomb racks in a B-17 with a releasable shackle attached to the lid. Release of the shackle through the normal bomb control system let the lid swing free and the leaflet bundles tumble out. The leaflets were released after a formation's bombs had been dropped.

Leaflets arrived in bulk from the British printer and were packed into bundles by the S-2 staff on the combat base. Each bundle had a card wrap and was secured by a cord with a barometric release, a canister of approximately 4 inches diameter containing a bellows which compressed when reaching heavier atmosphere, eventually pulling a pin to release the cord. The device was generally wanting in that to function correctly the securing cord had to be neither too tight nor too loose, a desirable state apparently rarely achieved. Most bundles came apart in the slipstream immediately after release while any secured too tightly fell brick-like to the ground. It was rumoured that people had been killed by leaflet bundles and a wooden barge holed and sunk by these paper missiles. Loose leaflets also posed a threat to bombers following a *Nickel* dispensing aircraft as this paper could easily clog the engine air intakes. Moreover, as the B-17s were operating at a mean 25,000 feet it was apparent that most of the leaflets were ending up as much as fifty miles from the release point if there were strong winds at altitude. In fact, it was later estimated that an average of only four per cent of total leaflets discharged in this fashion on a mission were ever picked up by the people for whom they were intended.

The general disenchantment with leaflets in VIII BC was resolved by handing the task to one unit. In the late summer of 1943 the 422nd Bomb Squadron of 305th Bomb Group at Chelveston was used to explore the viability of using B-17s in night bombing operations. A few sorties were sufficient to convince VIII BC leaders that what they had suspected, the Fortress could not economically be employed in the type of night attacks performed by the RAF. The training and modification of the Squadron's aircraft for night flight was not wasted, for it was seen that the leaflet dropping task was well suited to individual aircraft flying under the cover of darkness. Thus, commencing with a visit to Paris on the night of 7/8 October 1943, the 422nd Bomb Squadron undertook regular leaflet delivery, principally over occupied territory. Selected aircraft in regular bomb groups were still required to carry and dispense leaflets on occasions, normally when visiting German targets.

The Special Leaflet Squadron, or later the Night Leaflet Squadron, as the 422nd became known, normally despatched between two and eight aircraft on a night's operations during the first six months of activity. Aircraft operated individually, each often visiting four to seven locations to drop leaflets. Most sorties were at very high altitude to enable release to be made on a *Gee* fix when possible. Flying at over 30,000 feet also helped minimise the chance of interception by night fighters, and as a further safety measure the course was planned to include frequent changes of direction. A normal B-17 crew was carried, the bombardier releasing the leaflets from the bay.

Dissatisfaction with the methods of carrying and dispensing leaflets led Squadron personnel to explore ways of making improvements. Foremost in this was Capt James L. Monroe, the Armament Officer, who concluded that what was required was some form of leaflet 'bomb' which would function like the new M-17 Aimable Incendiary Cluster, breaking apart to release its contents at lower altitude. He then hit upon the idea of using the stout laminated card containers in which the M-17s arrived on the base. These containers were cylindrical, 48 inches long with a diameter of 16½ inches, and had two cardboard end caps. They were considered as scrap once the incendiary had been removed in the chemical bomb store. With light steel bands and U-brackets a container could be easily adapted to hang from a standard bomb shackle and be carried and released like a conventional bomb.

Leaflets to a weight of 300 lb could be packed into the container but its fall characteristics would only be known by tests. Monroe's next problem was to get the leaflets out of the container at the desired height. His ingenious solution was to drill a series of ½ inch holes along the tube container, across one end cap, and then back on the opposite side of the tube. He then passed double strands of standard explosive primer cord through the holes, securing both ends to a T-39 time fuse, which was fitted into a wooden block on the other end cap. A static test of the explosive charge resulted in the container being split neatly in two. Known in the Squadron as the Monroe Bomb, more were constructed for testing, but air tests were delayed due to the inventor being sent on detached service to London.

The first trial drop eventually took place over The Wash on 21 January 1944 when a B-17 dropped the leaflet bomb from 30,000 feet while Monroe and Major Earle Aber, the 422nd CO, flew in a Boston at 5000 feet to observe the planned burst. Disappointingly nothing was seen of bomb or leaflets following the drop. The next test over The Wash did not take place until 4 February but proved very successful. This time a 'bomb' with a five-second fuse was dropped from 10,000 feet and was seen to have opened as planned by an observing crew in another B-17 at 6000 feet. Using this type of container it was at last possible to drop from high altitude and with the correct time fuse cause the

T-2 Leaflet Bomb fitted with 860 Mk II fuse photographed at Lavenham, February 1945.

The aneroid used to set a pre-determined altitude for discharge of leaflets in the Monroe leaflet bomb.

'bomb' to blow at 2000 or 2500 feet to concentrate 80,000 leaflets over a square mile, or to cover larger areas as desired by fusing for higher release Following further trial drops, four Norwegian towns were the targets for the first operational use which took place on the night of 18/19 April 1944. Subsequent intelligence revealed that the fuses had been set for too low release and distribution had been poor. Technique improved rapidly and Monroe Bombs proved most effective.

The next problem was one of supply for the limited facilities of the Leaflet Squadron could in no way meet the construction of the number of 'bombs' required. Monroe and Aber persuaded higher command to instruct a chemical company in charge of the nearby Sharnbrook incendiary bomb dump to undertake manufacture of the leaflet bombs, a temporary measure until a large organisation for ordnance maintenance at Melchbourne Park was ready to undertake the work. Melchbourne Park commanced production in mid-May and quickly incorporated improvements. Specially made laminated card cases were obtained from a British contractor in place of the M-17 incendiary cases originally utilised. The primer cord was now fixed under a paper strip with adhesive and a more suitable 860 type fuse was then used. Fins could also be attached to give the 'bomb' better stability when dropped. The revised leaflet bomb, designated the T-2, was usually fused to burst at 2000 to 2500 feet and cover an area 200 by 50 yards with leaflets. It was first employed operationally on 20 June 1944 and thereafter became the standard leaflet container used by 8th Air Force heavy

bombers. All told Melchbourne produced 75,277 T-2s of which approximately 55,000 were used operationally, conveying about 90 per cent of the USAAF leaflet total during the rest of hostilities. A T-3 leaflet bomb was also produced by US ordnance facilities in the UK. This container, developed by an RAF officer, was derived from a converted M-26 parachute flare case and was mostly used for low altitude drops.

During the spring of 1944 the 422nd Bomb Squadron also functioned as the Pathfinder unit for 1st Bomb Division. With different aircraft and crews for both the PFF and leaflet mission it became two squadrons in one, a situation finally resolved in June when the leaflet element moved to Cheddington and assumed the designation 858th Bomb Squadron. In August it had a further change of number, becoming 406th Bomb Squadron. Fourteen B-17s and 16 crews moved to form the new unit at Cheddington. Another change was conversion from B-17s to B-24s, in common with all other special units due to an anticipated shortage of Fortresses. Although the B-24 bay could hold 12 leaflet bombs compared with nine in the B-17, the move was far from popular as a loaded B-24 was more difficult to fly at the high altitudes used by the Leaflet Squadron. Further, the majority of the Fortresses assigned were the older models and would not be wanted in regular bombing units. A compromise was reached whereby new aircraft received would be B-24s replacing the B-17s by natural wastage. In the event the B-24s – the first two being received in July – were used to expand the Squadron to meet an increasing workload and by October, when double the tonnage of paper was dispensed compared with the previous May, it had 12 B-17s and eight B-24s on strength.

A continuing expansion of operations could not be met by the assigned personnel and in November 1944 seven crews and aircraft from 492nd Group were detached to Cheddington for a month to aid the Night Leaflet Squadron.

While the number of B-17s gradually declined a few remained at the end of the year, and two were retained until the end of hostilities for use in very high altitude releases over dangerous areas. By April 1945 a peak of 22 B-24s and six B-17s was reached. It was in one of the remaining B-17s that the unit CO, Lt Col Earle J. Aber, was killed when returning from his 51st mission. His aircraft was shot down by anti-aircraft fire near

In all-black dress Night Leaflet Squadron's veteran, _Miss Mickey Finn_ sits on hardstone 22 at Harrington, May 1945. The B-17F, which started missions with 305th BG in the summer of 1943, displays symbols for completion of 151, a total greater than achieved by any other 8AF B-17F. Note flash eliminators on ball and rear tail guns. (P. Carty)

Harwich during one of the last Luftwaffe air raids on England. Aber had been given command of the Squadron in November 1943 and was personally responsible for developing much of its expertise.

In July 1944 six regular heavy bomb groups, two in each division, were designated to carry leaflets when required. Commencing 5 July an average eight aircraft in every mission carried only leaflets to discharge over the target area. The six groups involved in regular leaflet carrying were the 91st, 306th, 445th, 447th, 487th and 491st. These groups continued to provide one or two bombers per mission for the rest of hostilities to carry only leaflet bombs. In fact, the last 8th Air Force heavy bomber operation during the war, flown on 8 May 1945, was carried out by 12 B-17s of 306th Bomb Group dropping leaflet 'bombs' over German cities.

In March 1945 the Night Leaflet Squadron moved from Cheddington to Harrington from where operations continued until the night of 6/7 May. Post-war distribution of leaflets over Germany was carried out in daylight. Some 3734 tons of leaflets were dropped by the Squadron during hostilities, which compares with 2086 tons delivered by regular heavy bomb groups on bombing missions.

Radio Countermeasures

The war of radio waves became extraordinarily sophisticated as hostilities progressed, as each side attempted to counter advantages gained by the other in detection and direction. Another facet was deception which the British had advanced to a high degree, particularly to protect their vulnerable night bombers from interception. Radio countermeasures became a special art in the RAF with, eventually, a whole Bomber Group engaged in the practice.

USAAF interest in the various techniques and devices was enthusiastic although initially these appeared to have little application to their day bomber operations. Nevertheless, co-operation between British and American agencies engaged in the development of electronic aids resulted in some significant developments. The extensive technological and production facilities available in the US provided much of the best equipment towards the end of the war.

During the first eighteen months of the day bomber campaign, 8th Air Force was primarily concerned with protecting its B-17s and B-24s from fighter attack. However, as early as the winter of 1942–43 interest was shown in British devices designed to jam or smother enemy gun-laying radar transmissions. Arrangements were made for development to be undertaken in the US, and manufacture of a jamming radio set known as *Carpet I*. This was specifically designed to disrupt *Würzburg* radars feeding most of the enemy's major flak batteries with location, height and speed data for directing their fire.

Carpet I was a barrage jammer, transmitting a continuous signal on a pre-set frequency range when in operation. Its compact transmitter could easily be installed in the radio compartment of a B-17 or B-24. To be effective with the large B-17 and B-24 formations it was necessary for at least half the bombers in a group to be equipped with *Carpet* so that a more powerful jamming effect could be brought to bear against the frequency range the enemy might be using.

Initial arrangements were the installation of 40 *Carpet I* sets in the B-17s of 96th and 388th Groups, which first used them 8 October 1943 when attacking Bremen. On this and subsequent missions formations with *Carpet* protection were usually found to have suffered far less relative flak damage, the accuracy of fire against these formations being considerably reduced. Plans were made to equip more B-17 groups but the hard-pressed US electronics industry could not meet orders quickly due to other priorities.

An installation policy was implemented whereby two groups in each combat wing received *Carpet*.

During the second half of 1944 *Carpet III* for selective spot jamming became available. It consisted of a transmitter, receiver set and indicator unit. The receiver, via a short aerial, 'swept' automatically for *Würzburg* transmissions. On receipt of a signal the automatic sweep stopped and a noise modulated transmission was made to jam it. The new device was introduced into the programme, which was revised so that 12 aircraft in each group had *Carpet III* spot jammers and the rest, except those with PFF radars, two sets of *Carpet I* each. Installations were made a group at a time, the whole programme being completed by the late autumn.

To meet German countermeasures of using a wider band of frequencies to overcome the jamming problem, a further installation programme was planned during the 1944–45 winter to increase the number of *Carpet I* sets in all bombers from two to three, but never completed due to supply difficulties from the US. The effectiveness of *Carpet* jamming varied from mission to mission, but remained a constant problem throughout for *Würzburg* radars.

Another form of radar countermeasure that came into regular use on heavy bomber missions was a simple yet effective technique known by the general code word *Window*. It consisted of dispensing large quantities of metallised paper strips for which the US code name was *Chaff*. As the cloud of *Chaff* descended it reflected radar beams, simulating aircraft on radar receivers, obscuring the true size and position of a bomber formation and frequently reducing the accuracy of radar data used for gun-laying. First used by the 8th Air Force on 22 December 1943, the cylindrical bundles containing 2200 strips of *Chaff* were thrown out of waist gun windows to disperse in the slipstream. This was not satisfactory and special dispensing chutes were manufactured and installed in the radio operator's room on B-17s and near a waist window in the B-24. One bundle of *Chaff* produced a response on enemy radar equivalent to a single heavy bomber. Each bomber delegated to dispense *Chaff* normally carried two to four cartons, each containing 72 bundles known as units of *Chaff*. When released *Chaff* did not offer protection to the discharging formation, but those following. For this reason it was usually carried only by the leading combat wings or groups of a formation.

The technique varied to suit prevailing weather conditions, attack altitudes and the type of radars it was aimed to smother – for which different types and lengths of *Chaff* were available. In general, a formation approaching a gun defended target area commenced discharging *Chaff* two or three minutes before the target, continuing to do so until clear of the flak area. The rate of discharge for each aircraft was detailed in briefing; in early operations this was usually 15 units per minute from each aircraft. *Chaff* fell at a rate of around 300–400 feet a minute. With improvements in enemy flak technique *Chaff* dispensing increased in range and intensity. By the spring of 1944 some target requirements called for release to commence 35 miles from the target and to continue for 13 miles past. First groups to receive *Chaff* dispensers were those of the 14th, 40th and 45th Combat Wings. The original chute was developed in the theatre, a US production model being received at a later date. By the winter of 1944/45 all operational 8th Air Force B-17s and B-24s had *Chaff* dispenser chutes. From October 1944 special *Chaff* dispensing formations of six to twelve B-17s or B-24s were sent ahead of the main force to screen the leading formations. Subsequently, the speedier and less vulnerable Mosquito was also employed on these duties.

In addition to the measures against enemy radar warning systems the 8th Air Force also practised radio deception. Initially this was limited to the broadcast of false VHF radio messages during the assembly and the early stages of a mission. A practice introduced and used selectively during the winter of 1943–44, it was aimed at the German listening service in the hope that spurious information might confuse the enemy as to the scope and route of an operation. During the spring of 1944 special German-speaking radio operators were trained and flown as additional crew members on selected B-17s to monitor the Luftwaffe radio control network as an extension of the Y-Service. A selected few were instructed in broadcasting bogus messages when opportune. The aircraft used carried additional radio equipment for use by the Y operator.

In November 1943 RAF Bomber Command formed a special organisation, No 100 (Special Duties) Group, to confuse enemy opposition to its night bombers. A major element of this force was a half dozen squadrons specialising in radio countermeasures (RCM) and employing an array of electronic devices. One was a powerful new jammer for use against enemy radio communication transmissions known as *Jostle*. The transmitter was contained in a pressurised cylindrical casing which was required to be mounted vertically and would not fit in the low-profile bomb-bays of any of the current British four-motor bombers. However, the deep bomb-bays of the B-17 and B-24 were well suited to encompass the *Jostle* transmitter which led RAF Bomber Command to request 14 B-17s from the 8th Air Force to be off-set against Fortresses due for delivery to the British through Lend-Lease. Additionally, the high altitude capability of the B-17 would also be a useful attribute in some of the operations envisaged by the RAF.

The request was met by well-worn B-17F/Gs being sent to 214 Squadron at Sculthorpe during January 1944, while in return the RAF agreed to supply a dozen Mosquitoes for special purposes. While 8th Air Force had no current requirement for RCM support in night operations, in furtherance of the policy of participation in all new technology it was proposed that a US-manned unit be set up in 100 Group to specialise in RCM operations. This proposal being accepted, a small detachment under Capt G. E. Paris went to Sculthorpe on 17 January to assist the RAF Fortress squadron in conversion and to be made privy to the mysteries of RCM.

In March the 8th Air Force RCM Detachment, as it was known, received six B-17s from the 96th Group equipped with *Mandrel*, a jammer designed for work against the German long-range early warning ground radars. On arrival at Sculthorpe these aircraft were fitted with flame-damping exhaust manifolds and other modifications deemed necessary for night operations. Sets of *Carpet* were also installed, the mix of *Mandrel* and *Carpet* varying between individual aircraft. By the end of March a provisional number designation had been conferred on the American unit, 803rd Bombardment Squadron (P). A command decision was made around this time that the unit would initially operate with 100 Group in support of RAF Bomber Command night attacks.

Training was intensified and 8th Air Force assigned further

Chaff dispenser installation in a B-17, May 1945. Key: 1/ Stripper unit; 2/ Chute; 3/ tape collection bag; and 4/ shelf for chaff cartons.

personnel and equipment. On 14 May the squadron's aircraft complement was raised to nine when three ageing *Carpet*-equipped B-17Fs from 95th Group were added and was increased again in June to 12. One aircraft was a new Fortress recently arrived from Wright Field, carrying the new *Jackal* and *Rug* devices. *Jackal*, designed to jam enemy ground VHF radio communications, was restricted to 20 miles beyond Allied ground forces, as it could otherwise equally interfere with friendly R/T. *Rug* was a development of *Carpet*. This B-17G, serial number 42-97691, was sent to 803rd Squadron to have *Mandrel* additionally installed. However, the days of these Fortresses were numbered. In June 1944, due to a shortage of Fortresses by the impending conversion of five 3rd Division bomb groups from B-24s to B-17s, 8th Air Force decided to convert all special units using B-17s to B-24s.

The squadron, having moved to Oulton, flew its first sortie over enemy territory in darkness on 3 June, when B-17 42-3518 equipped with electronic search devices monitored two British ground radar stations on the Suffolk coast from Belgian airspace. Their first jamming operation was on the night of 5/6 June when they joined RAF RCM aircraft in putting up a *Mandrel* screen to smother enemy radars that might otherwise detect the Allied invasion fleet. The four B-17s participating operated their sets for 6¼ hours at 15,000 feet.

Thereafter the 803rd regularly participated as part of the *Mandrel* screening force, in conjunction with 100 Group, for the rest of 1944. The general procedure was for crews to be briefed with an RAF squadron and be given positions in the *Mandrel* chain set up to screen an RAF Bomber Command operation. Aircraft were despatched to work in pairs in designated areas at a given distance from the enemy coast; in early operations 40–50 miles. The line of the *Mandrel* chain was usually based on *Gee* navigational co-ordinates. On reaching the specified area a pair of B-17s would fly a 10 mile anti-clockwise racecourse pattern circuit, each commencing jamming transmissions at opposite ends to average the intensity of jamming. Each circuit took exactly ten minutes and adjustments were continually made to allow for wind strengths so as to maintain a precise schedule. Separation of the two B-17s on passing in the circuit was about two miles and the usual height for transmission

RCM B-24 *Beast of Bourbon* with monster nose decor, taxies past the technical site at Cheddington. Early 1945.

19,000–20,000 feet, although some early operations were at lower altitudes.

A B-24 conversion programme began in mid-June. Scheduled to receive nine first-line and two second-line aircraft, the last was not received until 1 August. The first-line B-24s had *Mandrel III* (AN/APT-3) equipment installed in the rear bomb-bay together with facilities for an operator. Four aircraft had one set each, two three sets each and three six sets each.

Additionally, *Carpet* sets were fitted in several aircraft while four were fitted with *Jackal* for jamming enemy battlefield VHF communications. At the end of August a twelfth B-24 was received for fitting out as an ELINT aircraft. The term derived from *el*ectronic *int*elligence, which was gathered with the equipment carried – S27 and SCR-587 search receivers. A B-17 had previously been maintained for these duties, primarily the monitoring of enemy radar transmissions to determine frequencies, power, etc for use in developing countermeasures.

The first B-24 *Mandrel* sortie was flown on the night of 12/13 July, the last B-17 operating in that role participating 25/26 July. Only the ELINT Fortress remained by the end of August, the rest of these well-worn aircraft having been flown to Honington where most eventually ended their days as radio-controlled *Castor* 'flying bombs'.

During early August 8th Air Force was instructed to dispense with the several provisional organisations it had created by regularising the units involved with formal designations. In the number shuffling that occurred the 803rd BS (P) became the 36th BS (H). At the same time it was placed on an 8th Air Force station by moving the unit to Cheddington. Although separated from its British associates, the American RCM squadron continued to operate in support of RAF Bomber Command. However, in the autumn, 8th Air Force became interested in using the unit to support their own forces. On 10 October, when there was no daylight heavy bomber mission, six RCM B-24s attempted to simulate an assembling bomber force by 'spoof' electronics and VHF radio traffic, a task they had previously practised for the RAF. The success of this operation and an increase in the RAF's own RCM capability were influential in an arrangement, concluded that November, whereby 36th Bomb Squadron would be used to screen for 8th Air Force operations but still support RAF Bomber Command on request.

From 25 November the Squadron regularly sent out aircraft over the North Sea to make continuous *Mandrel* transmissions to screen the VHF radio messages of assembling 8th Air Force bombers. This duty, plus jamming of enemy early warning radar during the preliminary stages of a mission, became their primary role until the end of hostilities. Other activities included occasional spoof jamming of enemy VHF or electronic intelligence sorties.

VHF screening was usually conducted by four to eight aircraft taking off about 30 minutes before the bombers to position singly, about ten miles apart, in an arc 50 miles east of the bombers' assembly area. Each RCM B-24 flew a race-track circuit and began jamming transmissions as altitude was increased for two to three hours, until the bomber formations were about to penetrate enemy airspace. During this period the jamming screen would gradually be advanced towards enemy territory. These tactics were frequently modifed to ring the changes and so prevent enemy monitoring services detecting a particular pattern. Spoof operations were conducted along the same lines but included the broadcast of pre-recorded VHF radio exchanges to simulate the usual R/T transmissions associated with bomber assembly.

Jackal operations involved orbits over the front lines at reduced altitude with jamming transmissions directed at enemy armour VHF radio communications. The two B-24s fitted out as ELINT aircraft operated individually with escort, normally off the enemy coast or front line, to detect and monitor his defence radars. Faster, less vulnerable aircraft were required for penetration of enemy territory. In the summer of 1944 three P-38Js with special electronic detection equipment were prepared. Assigned to the 7th Photo Group at Mount Farm, these aircraft were operated as a special detachment from the RAF 100 Group base at Foulsham from August 1944 until March 1945 when they joined the RCM squadron which had recently moved to Alconbury. The P-38Js used were *Droop Snoots*, modified to carry a crewman in the nose, in this case a radar operator who used the equipment carried to monitor enemy radar transmissions. ELINT P-38s were used for lone high-altitude penetrations of airspace to areas where new radar developments were known to be tested. One of these aircraft with its crew was lost to unknown causes in the North Sea during October 1944.

The increase in German radars made it necessary to boost the strength of the RCM Squadron in January 1945 to 18 aircraft and 24 crews. Many equipment changes were also made. *Mandrel III* spot jammers were replaced by *Dina*, a US development of

Mandrel, possessing a much wider band range to meet the German attempts to avoid jamming by use of more varied frequencies. *Carpet* sets were carried for spot and barrage jamming and more *Jackal* transmitters for interfering with enemy ground VHF communications. RCM operations by 36th Bomb Squadron continued until 25 April 1945.

Although its aircraft complement was reduced to six B-24s shortly after VE-Day, the unit conducted experimental work with RCM techniques and equipment for several weeks. In fact, it was one of the last 8th Air Force flying units to leave the UK. During the course of operations the RCM Squadron flew a total 1159 sorties in which 1110 were considered effective. Two aircraft and 18 men were missing in action and nine men killed in crashes involving three B-24s.

Azon

One of the weapons developed under the auspices of the National Defense Research Committee for the USAAF was a radio controlled tail unit to fit a standard bomb, enabling the missile to be steered laterally as it fell. Known as the *Azon* bomb, a name derived from the fact that it could be controlled in *az*imuth *on*ly, it appeared to have considerable potential for use against small pin-point targets. The enthusiasm for the *Azon* bomb shown by agencies in the United States led General Spaatz on 8 May 1944 to urgently request General Arnold that a B-24 unit, specially trained in *Azon* delivery and on route to another war zone, be immediately diverted to the 8th Air Force, where it could be used to attack vital targets such as bridges and coastal batteries during the pre-*Overlord* period. His request was favourably received.

The unit, under Capt Maurice E. Speer, had no formal designation, being simply ten B-24 crews with key men specially trained in the *Azon* technique. Their new B-24Js, fitted with the special control apparatus at Orlando, Florida, reached England via the south Atlantic route, arriving on 14 May. Before leaving the US each aircraft was loaded with as many *Azon* tails as could be safely carried. While the B-24s went to Warton to receive theatre modifications, the crews were sent to Northern Ireland for an indoctrination course. The 2nd Division planned to assign the *Azon* unit to 467th Bomb Group, which the crews joined on 21 May. However, prior to this the mentors for the *Azon* project, Majors Henry J. Rand and Robert K. Holbrook, had arrived at Rackheath where a decision had been made to distribute the *Azon* crews and aircraft among all four squadrons of the 467th.

Rand insisted *Azon* should be concentrated in one unit and as no agreement could be reached with 467th HQ on this matter, the *Azon* project was transferred to 458th Group at Horsham St Faith two days later. Here the unit became part of the 753rd Bomb Squadron which had been operational in a conventional day bombing role since the previous February. It was planned that other aircraft of the Squadron would be fitted with *Azon* transmitters and antenna when this equipment became available. Meanwhile all haste was made to get the present *Azon* crews and aircraft operational – they were labelled 'the Buck Rogers Boys' by the other 458th squadrons.

Clear weather conditions, essential to the control of the *Azon* weapon, delayed the first opportunity until 31 May. Five *Azon*-armed B-24s were despatched and shepherded by 48 P-51s to bridges in the Paris area. Each bomber carried five M-44 1000 lb bombs, one of which was fitted for *Azon* control. By mixing the load for release, it was hoped that the enemy would not detect the use of the new weapon. One Liberator aborted, and while bombing was hindered by a fair amount of cloud in the area of the targets, the attacking aircraft were apparently without success.

Operational procedure at this time called for the bombers to break formation and take up in-trail position at the IP. Flying between 10,000 and 20,000 feet they then attacked individually. Higher altitudes could not be used as the bombs were uncontrollable at terminal velocity. A bombardier in the nose of the B-24 operated the standard Norden sight and used normal procedures to sight for range and release of bombs. At 'bombs away' the bombardier transferred his attention to a special window in the floor behind the bombsight. This enabled him to watch the bombs fall and see the flare ignite in the *Azon* tail. By use of a simple left-right toggle switch he altered the direction of the bomb as it descended towards the target. Signals transmitted from the directing aircraft adjusted the two movable tail rudders on the bomb, which was prevented from rolling by the automatic action of two gyro-stabilisers. The azimuth control allowed approximately 2000 feet deflection on either side of what would have been the normal impact point. The forward trajectory of the bomb could not be altered. After all aircraft had made their runs, formation was resumed for the home journey.

The chief advantage of the *Azon* bomb lay in attacks on 'long targets' which could be approached along their length so that some over or under sighting for range was not critical. Thus all

Shack Time displays three masts under the rear fuselage, identifying it as an Azon delivery bomber. (J. Archer)

targets selected in the first operational phase were suitable bridges or embankments. One of the targets for the opening missions was the 5300-feet long Melun bridge embankment and this was also selected for the second operation, flown on 4 June. Heavy haze made it difficult for the *Azon* directors and results were inconclusive. Twice on 8 June a maximum effort mission was despatched to the same target but cloud frustrated both attempts. During the morning the objective was circled three times in an attempt to get a sighting. The 8 June missions saw a change of tactics forced by the vulnerability to flak of individual aircraft lingering too long in the target area. These tactics were also used on 14 June when part of the 15 plane strong force bombed in flights of five, the lead aircraft performing normal sighting while the four wing aircraft sighted for range only. In all subsequent missions flights of five or six B-24s all dropped on the lead plane which performed normal sighting while all aircraft controlled their *Azon* bombs individually.

Following another unsuccessful mission, on 19 June General Doolittle stated he was not impressed with *Azon* and felt that with the current strain on 8th Air Force facilities it would be better to leave further tests until more forces were available and there was less chance of the weapon falling into enemy hands at an early date. Postponement of the project followed but not before nine *Azon* bombers achieved a direct hit on the Tours Le Riche rail bridge, one of two targets visited on 22 June. Thereafter the 753rd returned to regular operations although its *Azon*

aircraft with their secret equipment could not be used and B-24s had to be borrowed from other squadrons. Three of the *Azon* B-24s and crews were detached to work with Project *Aphrodite*, the crews never to return to the 753rd.

In August 1944 a further phase of experimentation with the *Azon* bomb was ordered. The 753rd BS then had 18 aircraft on hand with transmitting equipment. In the six missions run between 17 August and 3 September aircraft attacked in flights of five or six, releasing on a leader's sighting. With little success a decision was made to terminate *Azon* operations completely and again return the 753rd BS to regular missions.

An analysis of the project found that the equipment was satisfactory but unsuited for the ETO where the enemy's anti-aircraft defences made the necessary medium altitude approach and long target loiter untenable. Weather conditions were another critical factor as more than 4/10ths stratus or strato-cumulus precluded use of the weapon. In order to take advantage of favourable weather a constant state of alert had to be maintained among crews and, as so few missions resulted, morale suffered. Further, it was proved that regular precision pattern bombing could do any task that had been assigned to the *Azon* squadron.

After the removal of the B-24s the *Azon* transmitters were sent to other groups for use in the Radio Bomb Release programme, for which they could be easily adapted.

Aphrodite

On 13 June 1944 the Germans opened their 'flying bomb' offensive against London from launching sites in the Pas de Calais. The V-1 was in reality a purpose-built, pulsejet-powered expendable pilotless aircraft for conveying a warhead. While this was not the first 'guided weapon' to see operational use, its mass employment intensified interest in the Allied camp in expendable delivery systems. The use of pilotless conventional warplanes loaded with high explosive and equipped for radio-control had been mooted in several quarters but now incorporated in a positive proposal with USSTAF and taken up by General Spaatz in view of the V-weapon menace. Obsolete or long-serving heavy bombers that had been retired from first line service were to be stripped of war equipment, fitted with radio receiving sets linked to the auto-pilot and filled with some ten tons of explosives. The aircraft would be flown off the airfield manually and taken to altitude, the two-man crew – pilot and his radio engineer – parachuting once flight control had been established by the transmissions from a 'mother' aircraft which would then guide the robot aircraft to and into a suitable target.

On 20 June 1944 Spaatz notified General Arnold that the project had started, requesting that related experimentation be conducted in the US. As a result a programme was instituted at the Air Force Proving Grounds in Florida under the cover name *Weary Willie*, although it appears to have been of a protracted nature and had little bearing on the work in England.

Project *Aphrodite* was ordered by USSTAF Hq on 23 June 1944 with the requirement that 8th Air Force conduct development and operational trials. The Operational Engineering Section being immediately involved indicated that the most suitable radio control unit at hand would be that currently used in the *Azon* bomb experiments. This was essentially a makeshift system pending the arrival of special equipment from the USA.

Major Henry Rand, the *Azon* technical expert, was directed to leave the *Azon* bomb unit at Horsham St Faith and go to Burtonwood while three *Azon*-trained crews went to Bovingdon, where the first radio-controlled robot would be tested.

Meanwhile, 8th Air Force had given 3rd Division the task of forming the *Aphrodite* unit. Pilot and auto-pilot engineer volunteers, recruited for a 'secret and dangerous' mission from among the Division's bomb groups, assembled at Honington air depot where the 1st SAD was busy stripping down ten war-weary B-17F/G models with, ultimately, 65 planned. All armour, turrets, bombing and oxygen equipment, the co-pilot's seat and anything else superfluous to requirements of the one-way flight were removed. The Fortresses were lightened to some 32,000 pounds. This 5000 lb weight reduction affected flight characteristics and data had to be obtained on how such aircraft would perform in dives. Much of this information was obtained by using General Partridge's transport B-17F which was of similar overall weight.

Each B-17 after stripping at Honington was flown to Burtonwood where two *Azon* receivers were installed and linked to the auto-pilot, together with antenna, wiring and an automatic radio altimeter. The bomb-bay was also strengthened by cross beams to support seven tons of the total ten tons of explosive planned. Three *Azon* B-24s of 458th Group were initially used as director aircraft although a B-17G was also fitted out with *Azon* transmitters at Burtonwood. After conversion the aircraft were flown to Bovingdon where training commenced under great secrecy on 1 July. Crews were given 25 hours' flight training plus intensive target and route navigation study. The *Azon* control appeared to function reasonably well, stability of the robot being the only major problem. In all trials of this robot bomber, termed the 'baby', a pilot was in the cockpit even when under radio-control. No robots were actually expended in trials.

The construction of the large V-weapon structures being pre-

echelon moved from Knettishall to Fersfield in August to act as a manning unit and the Squadron CO, Lt Col Roy Forrest, was placed in command at the base. Meanwhile, the 560th BS B-17s and crews at Knettishall continued to participate in regular combat missions, with support from the other three squadrons of the 388th.

Among interested parties moving into Fersfield was the US Navy's Special Air Unit No 1, intent on participation, having recruited volunteers from the anti-submarine patrol wing at Dunkeswell in south-west England. The US Navy had already considered a similar project for use in the Pacific war, flying radio-controlled drones from carriers on one-way missions, and wished to share in this first US venture into robot warfare. Their operation at Fersfield functioned under the code name *Anvil*. To complicate matters still further, the special Wright Field detachment that had recently arrived in the UK to run operational experiments with television-guided bombs was also assigned to Fersfield with the cover name *Batty*.

Although alerted several times in previous weeks, the first *Aphrodite* mission was finally launched in the early afternoon of 4 August when two 'babies', grossing 64,000 lb each, were flown off from Fersfield at five minutes apart to be directed to large concrete V-site structures near the French Channel coast. The two *Azon* controlling 'mother' aircraft had taken off 45 minutes previously to climb to 20,000 feet over a designated control point. The 'babies' were led to the control points by a navigational B-17, where the 'mothers' established radio-control. The robots at 2,000 feet were then guided around a 50 mile rectangular course while control apparatus was tested. Each 'baby' had a B-24 'mother' and B-17 back-up 'mother' in case of transmission failure on route to target. The upper surfaces of the 'babies' were painted white to make them more visible. A weather scouting Mosquito flew ahead and another B-17 acted as a relay for weather information. The first 'baby' crew successfully vacated the aircraft between Woodbridge and the coastal departure point at Orfordness but catastrophe overtook the second 'baby'. When radio control was established prior to the crew parachuting the aircraft went into a shallow climb, the pilot re-established level flight but the aircraft still climbed when radio-control was switched in. On a third attempt the climb resulted in a stall and the Fortress went into a spin. The radio man baled out safely but the pilot, Lt John Fisher, was killed only just clearing the aircraft before it impacted and exploded in a wood at Sudbourne.

The first 'baby' was successfully guided across the Channel only to suffer a failure of the down control and in subsequent manoeuvring crashed north-west of Gravelines, some distance from the target at Watten. Flak damage was suspected of causing the failure. The explosion reduced the B-17 to tiny fragments scattered over an area of 3½ miles. When the 'mother' aircraft returned over home base two more 'babies' were flown off, this time with V-sites at Wizernes and Mimoyecques as the targets. A similar course was followed over Suffolk with the same point of departure. Both 'baby' crews parachuted clear but two men were slightly injured on landing. The Wizernes drone was unfortunately lost from view in low cloud on approach to the target and crashed beyond it. There was no success at Mimoyecques either – the 'baby' impacted short due to error in the controller's

pared in France was viewed with increasing alarm. There were pressures to run the first missions at the earliest opportunity and agreement was reached with the RAF for use of the extra long runway at Woodbridge as a launch point. On 7 July, Lt Col James Turner, commanding the *Aphrodite* unit, moved to Woodbridge with ten B-17 'babies', one B-17 and three B-24 'mothers' for direction and observation, and eight P-47s on detachment from a fighter group to fly escort. Nine of the robots were loaded with 20,000 lb TNT, the tenth with the same weight of jellied petroleum, then dispersed among the pine trees. This caused station staff some apprehension, as the airfield continued to function as a 'crash' site for damaged aircraft returning from operations. Many of the 'lame ducks' went out of control on touching down and the prospect of one careering into a loaded *Aphrodite* was daunting.

Because of radio frequency restrictions only two robots could be launched at one time. The plan called for two task forces, each consisting of two 'mothers' and one 'baby'. These would take off, fly a prescribed route during which control would be checked and the robot crews would bale out. After guiding the first two 'babies' to their targets the 'mother' aircraft were to return to base areas and take over two more robots, flown off to meet them, to be directed in the same way. The jellied petroleum robot was to be kept on alert to be aimed at one of the targets successfully struck by a blast load.

Clear weather was essential for launching an operation, but in the days following the arrival of the *Aphrodite* unit conditions were never favourable in target areas. Meanwhile, a decision was made to establish *Aphrodite* on an isolated base, Fersfield, a standard bomber airfield built for the 8th Air Force but not hitherto occupied by a combat organisation. This was allocated on 12 July and three days later *Aphrodite* started moving in from Woodbridge.

At Fersfield the establishment was run as a detachment of the nearby 388th Bomb Group. Its 560th Bomb Squadron's ground

judgement of application of the down control. The Germans apparently did not recognise these two incidents as being a special weapon. They did, however, investigate the Watten explosion where observations by the flak crews on the behaviour of the B-17 they claimed to have shot down had aroused suspicions. The absence of human remains, defensive guns and the extent of the explosive force did not go unnoticed.

The next *Aphrodite* operation was on the morning of 6 August when two 'babies' were launched. Similar procedures were carried out to the first mission with a primary and secondary 'mother' flying 15,000 feet above each 'baby' in a test course over Suffolk before landfall out at Orfordness. The crew baled from the first 'baby' successfully, but nearing the enemy coast the radio-controller in the 'mother' B-24 lost control and the explosive-filled Fortress dived into the sea. Control difficulties were also experienced with the second 'baby' following ten minutes behind, for after the crew had jumped and the English coast crossed it went into uncontrollable left turns, also crashing into the sea.

Dissatisfaction with the limitations of the *Double-Azon* receiver control, essentially a temporary experiment, led to its abandonment in favour of more sophisticated equipment that had arrived from the US and promised more precise and responsive control. While installations and tests were made further *Aphrodite* launches were delayed for a month. In fact, the new cover name *Castor* was given to robots with the new equipment, although the name *Aphrodite* remained in use as an overall term for the USSTAF guided missile programme at Fersfield.

The US Navy despatched its first robot under the *Anvil* banner on the afternoon of 12 August, the objective being the destruction of the V-site at Mimoyecques. True to pursuing its separate identity, the US Navy had brought in and prepared its own 'mother' aircraft, two PV-1 Venturas. The 'baby' was a Navy PB4Y-1 Liberator piloted by Lt J. P. Kennedy, son of the US Ambassador to Britain, accompanied by radio-control engineer Lt W. J. Willy.

With an escort of P-51s, plus navigational and other support aircraft from Fersfield, the Navy strike was assembled and headed towards the coastal point at Southwold, when the 'baby' suddenly exploded at 2000 feet. Nothing was found among wreckage scattered widely in the neighbourhood of Blythburgh that could suggest a cause; detonation of 24,240 lb of high explosive had fragmented almost everything but the engine blocks. Subsequent investigations concluded that the most likely cause was a fault in the electrical system, switched in before the crew was due to parachute.

During August 1944 three *Batty* operations using the GB-4 television guided bomb were conducted. These missions were not characterised by any outstanding success, chiefly due to poor resolution from interference by water reflections and radio equipment. Built around a standard 2000 lb bomb, the GB-4 had small glider wings, moveable tail surfaces, a radio-control unit and a television camera mounted in a nose piece. Two of these weapons were carried on underwing racks fitted to a B-17 'mother' aircraft. The same B-17G, 42-40043, and a 388th Group crew were used on all operations.

Following three trial releases of GB-4s over English ranges the first combat delivery took place on 13 August. The target was the port of Le Havre. An observation B-17 accompanied the *Batty* aircraft; included in each crew were two and five Wright Field experts respectively who had been involved in the development of the weapon. Colonel Forrest accompanied the mission in a *Droop Snoot* P-38 to observe proceedings. A Mosquito, assigned to take photographs, venturing too close to one of the weapons after release, was struck by fragments when it detonated causing its loss. The television receiver in the 'mother' aircraft, not functioning properly, gave pictures too faint to be of practical use in directing the weapons. One bomb fell a mile short and the other about a mile to the right of the port.

Above: **B-17G 42-400043 carrying two GB-4s on the first *Batty* mission, 12 August 1944. The accompanying Mosquito, MM370, was lost when it flew too close to one of the weapons as it detonated.**

Right: **The two GB-4s can just be discerned under B-17G 42-400043 flying in the sun's glare.**

The second *Batty* mission, run a week later against La Pallice U-boat pens, was particularly unsuccessful. On the first weapons released the camera shutter closed, preventing transmission of pictures. For some reason the second GB-4 went into an uncontrollable spin. The third and final attempt with the GB-4 took place on 26 August when enemy installations at Ijmuiden were to be attacked. Eight-tenths cloud obscured the target area and the mission was abandoned. Following this abortive sortie, Command decided to refer this project for further development. In retrospect the technology of the time was not sufficiently advanced to afford the required control and reliability.

The US Navy ran its second and final *Anvil* operation on 3 September. Allied land advances had overrun the large V-site structures so the island U-boat base of Heligoland was the target. This time the mission suffered no mishap but the controller mistook nearby Düne Island for Heligoland and impacted the Liberator there. The explosion destroyed several houses over a half mile from the impact. The FM system used by the Navy employed a television camera mounted in the nose of the robot, transmitting pictures to the 'mother' ship.

Castor missions commenced in September, with control equipment similar to that of the Navy FM employing a television camera in the nose of the robot. Heligoland and Heide/Hemmingstedt were chosen as targets because they involved only a short penetration of enemy territory, reducing the chances of the robot being shot down by flak. In place of *Double-Azon* a standard radio-control receiver apparatus AN/ARW-1 was fitted in the robot and the complementary transmitter AN/ARW-18 in the 'mother'. Although a two-man crew was still used to fly the robot off, the AFCE specialist was replaced by a co-pilot. *Eureka/Rebecca* sets were used to aid location of

the robot in poor visibility should it become lost to the controller's sight. Aids to maintaining visual contact were a smoke dispensing tank on the robot that could be operated by radio signals and the painting of the upper surfaces in bright yellow.

First *Castor* launch was made on 11 September when a single 'baby' loaded with 21,855 lb of Torpex was aimed at Heligoland. Mission procedure was similar to that employed with the *Double-Azon Aphrodite* except that the 'mother' aircraft flew at the same altitude as the 'baby', 2000 to 2500 feet on route but some one to two miles behind, lengthening the gap to six to eight miles nearing the target. Control was described as 'perfect' during the 355 mile flight, but when only ten seconds from the target the 'baby' was hit by flak and deflected into the sea, exploding about 200 yards from the shore. While *Castor* showed a great improvement over previous equipment, the mission was marred by a fatality. When the pilot, 1/Lt Richard Lindahl, baled out of the robot his static line was apparently incorrectly attached and he broke his neck. Three days later two *Castor* drones were sent against an oil refinery complex at Hemmingstedt, only to miss the target primarily due to poor weather conditions.

Heligoland was once again the objective for two double launches on both 15 and 30 October, all of which failed to hit the mark. One struck near the town of Heligoland and two went into the sea, while there was a complete loss of the radio link with the fourth which flew off on a north-easterly course and finally exploded 325 miles away on a farm near Trollhättan in Sweden. Apparently the patient Swedes took this to be yet another incident of a crippled Allied bomber attempting to seek sanctuary in their country, particularly as they reported the crew as having baled out over Denmark!

On 27 October instructions were received from USSTAF to use the remaining *Castor* robots in attacks on industrial objectives in large German cities as far inland as possible. To accomplish this it was necessary to add throttle controls to the system in order that penetration of enemy territory could be made at 10,000 feet followed by a let down to 250 feet in the target area. A higher penetration altitude was desirable but prohibited by the robot's oil-regulated supercharger controls which had a tendency to freeze and become inoperative.

By November, with the *Batty* and *Anvil* projects departed, 3rd Division decided to transfer *Aphrodite* to the parent base of the manning unit, Knettishall, the move being accomplished at the end of the month. The first pair of launches from Knettishall took place on 5 December when the marshalling yard at Herford was the target. The weather deteriorated on route and extensive cloud was encountered making it impossible to locate Herford. Breaks in the cloud near Dummer Lake allowed descent to find targets of opportunity. The first 'baby' was directed at Haldorf and exploded south of the town. The second robot began to lose power and sink, most probably due to carburettor icing, and finally mushed into a field without exploding. To the crew of a Mosquito flying as mission observer, the robot appeared intact! Escorting fighters were ordered to strafe the robot; these failed. While Command believed that an intact robot had fallen into enemy hands, it appears that this was not the case. One report suggests that the *Castor* bomber exploded shortly after crash-landing, killing some German troops who had started to inspect it. German records on *Aphrodite* operations indicate that they did not identify any such attack on that date, leading to the assumption that if the robot exploded after crash-landing, it was taken to be a normal B-17 with bomb load.

Ironically, the *Aphrodite* that did fall into enemy hands, albeit broken, was unknown to the USAAF at the time. On New Year's Day the last two *Castor* B-17s on hand were directed to a power-station at Oldenburg. The first 'baby' to approach the target was damaged by flak and crashed into a field just outside the town, breaking up but not exploding, a situation not appreciated by the supporting force. Luftwaffe investigators were able to fairly accurately assess the *Castor* bomber, retrieving much of the radio equipment and control system. The second 'baby', also apparently hit by flak, crashed and exploded some miles to the south-west of Oldenburg. As it happened this was to be the last operational use of *Castor* robots, primarily because it suddenly became a political issue.

In November USSTAF had proposed moving the launch base for *Aphrodite* to the Continent where the robots could be used against the industrial area. When put to the British Joint Chiefs of Staff, they expressed some concern that as the weapon was to be used against highly populated areas it might invite similar retaliation against London, currently suffering V-2 bombardment. It was pointed out that the Luftwaffe had already used pilotless explosive-laden aircraft against Britain, three crashing in rural locations during the late summer. Reluctantly, final British approval was given to the plan on 15 January, despite disquiet in some quarters which continued and resulted in approval being withdrawn 11 days later. British misgivings were, in part, due to an about-turn on the value of the bombing of areas of high population to break morale.

USSTAF, still anxious to proceed with the experimental attacks, by representations via Washington persuaded President Roosevelt, in a telegram sent on 29 March 1945, to repeat the request for British approval to the plan to use *Castor* against the Ruhr. British procrastination won the day, for Churchill felt strongly that 'no unnecessary damage should be done to German habitation'. Nevertheless, the Prime Minister's cable to the President of 14 April gave full approval, but was framed with typical Churchillian skill to convey such obvious concern that Roosevelt would have probably been reluctant to proceed. As it was, events took a hand for the untimely death of the President and the final collapse of Nazi Germany terminated furtherance of the plan. No more *Castor* robots were made available for despatch from Knettishall and cancellation of the project was anticipated by those involved; *Aphrodite* 'mother' crews and aircraft meanwhile remained in limbo for several weeks. Not until 27 April was the operation, constituting the largest single mass of conventional explosives launched against an enemy target during the Second World War, finally terminated.

Aphrodite Operations: Aircraft and Launch Crews

Date	Target	Baby	Crew
4 Aug 44	Watten	B-17F 42–30342 (ex-95BG *Taint A Bird*)	1/Lt F. H. Pool, S/Sgt P. Enterline
4 Aug 44	Siracourt	B-17G 42–39835 (ex-351BG *Wantta Spa*)	1/Lt J. W. Fisher (KAS), T/Sgt E. Most
4 Aug 44	Wizernes	B-17F 42–3461 (ex-92BG)	1/Lt F. L. Houston, T/Sgt W. D. Smith
4 Aug 44	Mimoyecques	B-17F 41–24639 (ex-91BG *The Careful Virgin*)	1/Lt C. A. Engel, T/Sgt C. A. Parsons
6 Aug 44	Watten	B-17F 42–30212 (ex-388BG *Quarterback*)	1/Lt J. P. Andrecheck, T/Sgt R. Healy
6 Aug 44	Watten	B-17G 42–31394 (ex-379BG)	1/Lt J. Sollars, T/Sgt H. Graves
12 Aug 44	Mimoyecques	PBY-1 32271	Lt J. Kennedy (USN) (KAS), Lt W. J. Willy (USN) (KAS)
3 Sept 44	Heligoland	B-24D 42–63954	Lt R. Spalding (USN)
11 Sept 44	Heligoland	B-17F 42–30180 (ex-96BG *Guzzlers*)	1/Lt R. W. Lindahl (KAS), 1/LT D. E. Salles
14 Sep 44	Hemmingstedt	B-17F 42–30363 (ex-96BG *Ruth L III*)	1/Lt M. P. Hardy, 1/Lt E. Hadley
14 Sep 44	Hemmingstedt	B-17G 42–39827 (ex-306BG)	1/Lt W. G. Haller, 2/Lt C. L. Shinault
15 Oct 44	Heligoland	B-17F 42–30039 (ex-384BG *Liberty Belle*)	1/Lt R. Betts, 2/Lt M. Garvin
15 Oct 44	Heligoland	B-17G 42–37743 (ex-94BG)	1/Lt W. Patton, 1/Lt J. W. Hinner
30 Oct 44	Heligoland	B-17F 42–30066 (ex-100BG *Mugwump*)	1/Lt G. A. Barnes, 1/Lt R. McCauley
30 Oct 44	Heligoland	B-17F 42–3438 (ex-96BG)	1/Lt W. C. Gaither, 1/Lt W. M. Dunnuck
5 Dec 44	Herford	B-17F 42–39824	1/Lt T. H. Barton, 1/Lt F. E. Bruno
5 Dec 44	Herford	B-17F 42–30353 (ex-95BG *Ten Knights In The Bar Room*)	1/Lt R. F. Butler, 1/Lt K. T. Waters
1 Jan 45	Oldenburg	B-17F 42–30178 (ex-95BG *Darlin' Dolly*)	2/Lt J. Stein, 1/Lt E. Morris
1 Jan 45	Oldenburg	B-17F 42–30237 (ex-397BG *Stump Jumper*)	Cpt J. Hodson, 1/Lt L. Lawing

Resistance Forces Support and General Supply Dropping

By their encouragement of resistance movements in occupied countries the British had built up an extensive support network by the time the United Stated entered hostilities. One venture was the forming of special RAF squadrons to fly agents and supplies into France, Belgium and Holland as required by the Special Operations Executive (SOE), which conducted or organised most of the clandestine activities in those countries. With preparations for *Overlord*, the cross-Channel invasion, set for the spring of 1944, it was desirable that French partisans should be further encouraged and supplied. To this end the Combined Chiefs of Staff recommended USAAF participation in expanding activities of the Office of Strategic Services (OSS), the American counterpart of SOE.

At this time, September 1943, 8th Air Force was to acquire most of the personnel and aircraft of the 479th Antisubmarine Group based at Dunkeswell, Devon. The 479th was to be disbanded following an agreement whereby US Navy units would assume responsibility for all anti-submarine activities. Part of the group was to be used to equip and man the new pathfinder organisation at Alconbury, while its 22nd Antisubmarine Squadron, under command of Lt Col Clifford Heflin, would form the nucleus for a special operations unit for resistance movement support. On 26 and 27 October the aircraft of this unit arrived at Alconbury and were later surveyed by RAF officers from Tempsford, home of that service's special duties squadrons, who advised on modifications and suitability.

The B-24Ds were to be fitted with four main aids for the task. An absolute radio altimeter for accurate height information was essential. *Gee* was required for precise navigation although it was eventually planned that *Loran*, a US development of *Gee*, would be fitted. To locate dropping points *Rebecca* sets were to be used, initially obtained from the British but those from US production were to be supplied when available. *Rebecca* worked in conjunction with *Eureka*, a ground beacon set supplied to the partisans. With *Eureka* switched on, radar impulses sent from *Rebecca* were returned as a directional blip on the navigator's grid screen and provided accurate location. A further fitment was the 'S-phone', a two-way radio which allowed vocal communication with persons on the ground at short range. Sent for modification to Burtonwood, the B-24Ds had waist guns and ball turret removed. The circular opening in the underfuselage left by the ball turret was used as a hatch through which parachuting agents could drop. Other modifications included the removal of oxygen equipment, the fitting of plywood flooring to facilitate movement within the rear fuselage, blackout curtains for the waist windows and navigator's compartment, and blister side windows at the cockpit.

On 11 November 1943 the 22nd Antisubmarine Squadron became the 406th Bombardment, and on the same date the 36th Bombardment Squadron was established at Alconbury as a second special operations unit, its ground personnel coming chiefly from the 4th Antisubmarine Squadron. These new formal designations were re-allotted from units recently disbanded in Alaska. By early December the 36th and 406th had complements of 16 B-24Ds each although many still required modifications or lacked special navigational aids. Night flying and training for special duties was pursued during November and December under the guidance of RAF Tempsford, and it was from this base that the first sorties were undertaken on the night of 4/5 January 1944.

CARPETBAGGER OPERATIONS

Patriot support operations were code named *Carpetbagger* (an opportunist visiting salesman) and this also became the popular name for the organisation conducting them. The Liberators, having long range, were mostly given supply missions to south and central France where there were flourishing resistance groups. Operations were co-ordinated with the British and the early sorties were flown under the watchful eye of Tempsford personnel, who also arranged for much of the loads carried. As Alconbury was becoming overcrowded, in February a move was made to Watton where the 328th Service Group provided an administrative headquarters. This, however, was a temporary arrangement pending the acquisition of a separate airfield for *Carpetbagger* units. In March a move was made to Harrington, west of the general 8th Air Force area and 35 miles from the packing and storage facilities at Holme and other US and British installations concerned with resistance support. Just prior to the move to Harrington the *Carpetbaggers* were established under a revised headquarters as the 801st Bomb Group (Provisional), with Lt Col Heflin in command.

In May 1944 with D-Day imminent, the requirements of OSS and other agencies were far more than 801st Group could meet. To overcome this, 8th Air Force removed a B-24 squadron from each of the 2nd and 3rd Divisions and sent them to Cheddington for training and then to Harrington; these, the 788th and 850th Bomb Squadrons, left their B-24H/Js with their parent groups. 801st Group immediately suffered an acute shortage of suitable aircraft although as many B-24Ds as were available were readily sent to Harrington. This model was desirable for *Carpetbagger* work because of the better outlook from the nose and its superior handling qualities. Nevertheless the Group was forced to use some H models, Burtonwood removing the nose turret and replacing it with a special faired section. By the end of June the Group had 69 aircraft assigned, of which nine were counted as reserves. During this month the Liberators received an overall gloss black finish whose reflective qualities had been found to aid in escaping searchlight illumination.

July 1944 was the peak month of operations with 592 sorties despatched, 437 being effective. One hundred agents, 5103 weapon containers and 3122 other packages were parachuted during the month. Thereafter activity declined as more and more of France was liberated by the ground forces. During July the Group acquired four C-47s which it used on 35 occasions to land at 12 specially prepared airstrips. The first of these was flown by Col Heflin to a secret strip in the Ain department on the night of 6/7 July. The last *Carpetbagger* operation to France was flown on the night of 16/17 September.

In August the 801st Group and its squadrons became the 492nd Group and 856th, 857th, 858th and 859th Bomb Squadrons in an extensive shifting of unit designations to conform with USAAF Hq's requirements for dispensing with provisional units. Following the completion of *Carpetbagger* operations over France the Group engaged in hauling fuel using liberated airfields in Belgium, and later prepared for night bombing. The 859th Squadron was sent to Italy from December for *Carpetbagger* operations over the Balkans.

In the UK only the 856th was retained for *Carpetbagger* work, taking part in occasional sorties to the Netherlands, Denmark and Norway. Sorties over the two Scandinavian countries increased in the early spring of 1945 when 858th BS contributed to the effort using H2X-equipped B-24Hs and Ls for dropping zone approach at 300 to 500 feet. In March, a few Mosquitoes and A-26s were used by a detachment from 856th BS for dropping agents in Germany and monitoring their radio signals, using Dijon, France, as a forward base. A-26 flights were made during bright moon periods at low level, with two navigators in the nose 'pin-pointing'. The last *Carpetbagger* operation by B-24s was flown over Norway in the night of 26/27 April 1945.

In the course of its wartime operations the *Carpetbagger* organisation despatched a grand total of 2857 sorties of which 1860 were deemed effective. Its deliveries included 1043 persons, 20,295 weapon and equipment containers, 11,174 other packages, 21 pigeon hampers and 7956 leaflet bundles. During the course of these operations 25 B-24s were missing in action with 197 men, and another 8 Liberators were written off in mission accidents killing 11 men.

OPERATIONAL PROCEDURE

Requests for an agent or supply dropping operation originated through activities associated with OSS and SOE. The Special Force Headquarters in London had sections with responsibility for such deliveries to resistance organisations in several occupied countries. Priority requirements were agreed by the air operations section of OSS and these with the delivery points passed to Hq 8th Air Force for approval. After receiving this endorsement OSS dealt directly with *Carpetbagger* Hq via telephone, detailing the coded target list to the duty Intelligence Officer. Usually 24 hours' notice was given to allow a thorough preparation by all involved. Dropping points were determined from the coded information by reference to cypher documents and a folders cabinet kept under lock and key. The next task for Intelligence staff was to pin-point the targets on their large wall map, using coloured tabs to indicate the priority standing of each required drop. S-2 also extracted all pertinent details on the drop zone (DZ) and these were discussed with the Group commander or his deputy. If there was some practical reason why certain of the DZs should not be visited, Intelligence would discuss this with the appropriate OSS section over the scrambler telephone. Once the drop point list had been agreed, OSS notified its agents in occupied territory of impending operations. Signals for despatch of reception parties to dropping points were generally given through coded references in BBC radio programmes.

An OSS officer attached to the *Carpetbagger* base was responsible for organising delivery of the required loads. Most of this arrived by road from the special packaging station at Holme and was stored in Nissen huts adjacent to the perimeter track until required. Certain categories of loaded container – those with munitions and arms – were usually on hand in the bomb dump area. The more frangible items – such as radios – went into containers which had shock-absorbing ends.

Col Heflin studying drop zones on map of France. (via M. Gibson)

Around mid-morning, the squadron commanders or their deputies were normally called to the Group Intelligence office to be shown the 'targets' for the forthcoming night. They were usually allowed to allot targets to crews of their own choosing if the night's operation involved several aircraft and objectives. The more difficult locations were given to the more experienced crews, but an attempt was always made to share the workload fairly. Group operations would then allocate crews and aircraft and inform the various service organisations. B-24s scheduled would often be given a short test flight before loading.

Group ordnance collected, delivered and loaded the containers, first attaching parachutes. The C-3 containers were hung from shackles in the bay and were discharged by the bomb release apparatus. A full load was 15, each weighing about 300 pounds. Packages with parachutes attached were hauled and loaded by the armament section. These were normally lifted through the waist windows and stacked and secured ready to be pushed out of the 'Joe Hole' – the popular name for the ball turret well through which 'Joes' (agents) departed. During the course of operations some 450 different items were conveyed in containers or packages and, apart from weapons and munitions, included radio equipment, specialised tools, money, forged documents, medical supplies, foodstuffs and clothing. A regular extra on the majority of *Carpetbagger* sorties was six to ten leaflet bundles containing some 4000 sheets each, from the same warehouse supplying the Night Leaflet Squadron. The reason for carrying and releasing propaganda leaflets was the hope that the enemy would identify these sorties as being made solely to dispense leaflets – bona fide leaflet dropping aircraft frequently operated over occupied territories on the same nights as *Carpetbagger* activities. After each aircraft had been loaded the OSS liaison officer checked to see that all load items were as required.

As soon as the necessary maps and data sheets on each drop point were available, all scheduled navigators were called to Operations and allowed two to three hours' study, each to draw up individual flight plans. Drop zone maps were scaled five miles to an inch to enhance accuracy. Flight plans were given to the Squadron Navigator and checked at Group Operations, for while each navigator was allowed to plan his own route it was necessary to see there was no timing which might present a collision hazard or confusion at a dropping point. When all flight plans were approved the Group Navigator fixed scheduled take-off times.

Pilots and bombardiers then arrived for pre-briefing to study the flight plan and dropping zone information for an hour or so, following which they were joined for the full briefing by the rest of their crews in the main briefing room. Much along the lines of a normal bomber crew briefing, this involved addresses from the staff weather officer who dealt in detail with known and forecast conditions; the intelligence officer on dropping zone identification and related matters; a senior Group Hq officer covering required flight and dropping procedures, and finally, the group navigator on route details. Any special briefings for package despatchers and gunners were given after the main briefing. The normal crew consisted of pilot, co-pilot, bombardier (who released the bomb-bay load), navigator, radio operator, top-turret gunner, despatcher and tail gunner.

Crews then put on flying clothes and collected escape packages. Radio operators were given their signal code flimsies. Crews were driven out to the aircraft to arrive at least a half hour before take-off. Any 'Joe' scheduled to be on the flight was driven directly to the aircraft on which he or she would fly. They were under constant OSS supervision while on the airfield and conversation with the aircrew with whom they would fly was not encouraged. The crew were instructed not to ask questions of their passengers for if shot down and interrogated they would then not be able to give information that might endanger the agent.

Carpetbagger B-24s were despatched individually in accordance with the timed schedule. If several aircraft were to be despatched during a night's operations take-offs might be spread over several hours. Selected routes out over England had previously been notified to the British air defence organisation. Altitudes flown varied but were usually between 5000 and 10,000 feet with descent to 500 to 700 feet in the dropping zone area. Some landfalls of occupied territory in particularly well defended areas were made at low level but, whenever possible, penetration was made away from known flak areas.

In the area of the DZ a B-24 crew looked for signal fires while pilots tried to make contact with the reception committee via the S-phone radio. Various symbols formed with red and white lamps were another form of ground identification. Because of the danger that a reception committee might really be the enemy, recognition signals were constantly revised. If no pre-arranged signal fires or lights were observed and satisfactory contact by the S-phone was not possible, the B-24 would orbit while a member of the crew flashed the night's code letter with an Aldis lamp. An answering signal by flashlight with the correct code would establish contact. Alternatively, where a reception party had a *Eureka* set, the *Carpetbagger* pilot requested the code signal identification which was transmitted by the beacon and, if correct, verified by the *Rebecca* unit in the aircraft. In case of the presence of enemy forces in the vicinity, or other obstacles for the reception party so that contact was not possible or positive, the B-24 would return to base with its load. If satisfactory identification was made the pilot reduced altitude to about 600 feet, lowering flaps to bring the indicated airspeed down to 130 mph for a dropping run over the ground markers. This altitude gave sufficient height for static line controlled parachutes to open. Several runs were usually necessary to despatch a full load. The bombardier, who had previously opened bomb-bay doors, released the containers while, on his signal, packages were pushed out of the rear hatch and 'Joe Hole' by despatchers. If an agent was on board he or she would depart via the 'Joe Hole'. The red and green signal lights at this station were operated by the bombardier.

After leaving the DZ the despatchers prepared to dispense the leaflet bundles. These were normally pushed out of the 'Joe Hole' between 35 and 50 miles from the target area to disguise the purpose of the flight. However, the nature of most of these sorties was recognised by the Germans, although tracking and interception by night fighters were difficult to achieve at the low altitudes used.

Above left: **Loading free-drop supplies – including a new vehicle tyre.** (via M. Gibson)

Above: **Preparing C3 parachute containers for loading in a B-24's bomb-bay.** (via M. Gibson)

Below: **A 'Joe' about to release his grip on the sides of the 'Joe Hole' and fall clear of the aircraft. In foreground another agent sits awaiting his turn to jump.** (via M. Gibson)

The return flight to England was made at an optimum 5000 feet using recognised air corridors over England. After landing, each crew was carefully interrogated at Group Operations where OSS liaison officers were at hand. Much useful intelligence could be obtained, particularly as to how the reception committee performed. A reward for each crew member after a *Carpetbagger* combat sortie – which could last between four and eight hours – was a 2-ounce 'slug' of whisky and real eggs for breakfast.

MASS SUPPLY DROPS BY DAY BOMBERS

Following the break-out of the Allied forces from their Normandy beachhead and the subsequent drive across France, much reliance was put on the activities of the French Forces of the Interior and the Maquis – in hindering the movement of German reinforcements by direct attack and sabotage. The scale of French guerrilla intervention was dependent upon the availability of arms and munitions. To supplement the work of the *Carpetbaggers* 8th Air Force was requested by SHAEF to carry out a number of supply drops using day bombers over remote areas of south central France. The task was given to 3rd Division B-17 groups which undertook four major missions for this purpose. These involved 180 B-17s on 25 June, 324 on 14 July, 194 on 1 August and 70 on 9 September, and were planned so that 8th Air Force bombing elsewhere acted as a diversion. Heavily escorted, the B-17s flew in formation at medium altitudes, reducing to 500 to 900 feet in the vicinity of the DZ on the first of these missions and slightly higher altitudes on the last. Formations were loosened and undercarriages lowered to reduce speeds to 130 mph indicated for the dropping run. Each B-17 carried 12 C-3 parachute canisters of 300 lb each in its bay which were released over the dropping point by bombardiers. The B-17s climbed to medium altitude for the return journey.

In support of the beleaguered Polish resistance fighters in Warsaw 3rd Division B-17s dropped 1284 C-type containers during a shuttle to the Soviet Union on 18 September 1944. Release altitude had to be at the much higher at between 13,000

Above: **Final 8th Air Force supply drops were food deliveries to starving Dutch population during the first days of May 1945. As packages were free-fall from 500 ft, to lessen spread undercarriage and flaps were lowered to reduce speed to 130 mph. Here 96th BG's B-17G 44-8877 unloads over Schipol airfield. Formations flew in waves of six widely spaced aircraft.**

and 18,000 feet due to enemy defences. The high altitude was in some measure responsible for most of the containers landing in enemy held areas.

Supplies were also dropped to Allied ground forces during both the Allied airborne landings in the Low Countries on 18 September 1944 and at the crossing of the Rhine on 24 March 1945. B-24s of the 2nd Division carried out both these operations. For the September drop 252 B-24s were involved. After flying in loose formation at 1500 feet to the IP, height was reduced to 300 feet to cross the DZ, thereafter making a climbing turn to 1500 feet to withdraw. The formation consisted of 9-plane vees spaced in trail 30 seconds apart. A speed of 165 mph IAS on route was reduced to 150 mph IAS for the dropping run. Each aircraft had a trained dropmaster to direct two men in pushing packages through the open rear hatch and ball turret well. Every B-24 had about 2 tons of supplies in 20 containers. Some formations crossed the DZ at between 500 and 1500 feet and suffered heavy damage and losses to enemy ground fire.

For the Rhine crossing drop mission, 240 B-24s were scheduled. Each carried 2½ tons in 20–21 bundles of which a dozen were placed in the bomb-bay, five or six around the ball turret well and three near the rear under hatch. 'Indestructible' items were free-fall, the rest parachute assisted. Similar formations and tactics were used as in the previous September. The dropping altitude was again set at 300 feet. Despite efforts to minimise time over hostile territory, the force was exposed to concentrated small arms and light flak fire, sustaining heavy damage and loss.

Air/Sea Rescue

The pre-war USAAC, largely based in the land mass of the continental United States, had little need to give much attention to the safety of airmen who might be forced to abandon their aircraft over or in water. With the establishment of the 8th Air Force for operations from the United Kingdom, lack of training and equipment for such emergencies proved a serious deficiency when all combat operations involved crossing either the English Channel or the North Sea. Inevitably, some aircraft damaged by enemy action would not regain the English coast and would have to come down in the sea. As with other specialised services, 8th Air Force initially depended on the RAF which in this respect had developed an efficient organisation, known as Air/Sea Rescue (ASR), for plucking airmen out of 'the drink'. A system of pin-pointing distress signals through a network of coastal listening posts was used to alert or despatch search and rescue aircraft and vessels.

ORGANISING ASR

General Eaker and his staff had recognised the need to enlist the services of the RAF's ASR as early as March 1942 and to train American aircrew in its techniques. Arrangements were made in the following October for RAF personnel to give instruction in crash and rescue drill, the use of dinghies, markers, visual aids and emergency signals, as little action had been taken to improve sea rescue training in the US.

American equipment left much to be desired. While the B-17Es reaching the UK in 1942 had A-3 type liferafts (inflatable dinghies), rations, first aid kits, canned water and flares, most of this equipment was either of a makeshift nature or unsuitable. The K-rations provided were not only thirst-inducing, but had no waterproof packing. First aid kits and flares were also without waterproof protection. There was no automatic ejection of dinghies (immersion switch) and many were found to be improperly packed in the aircraft, having not been fully deflated after factory tests. In such cases the air in the dinghy expanded at high altitude and sometimes blew out of its stowage, endangering the aircraft. Furthermore, the B-17 and B-24 were not designed to withstand the strain of forced sea landings or to permit the speedy exit of their crews. Bomb-bay doors were weak and the bays deep, allowing the fuselage to be quickly flooded.

In the early months of 8th Air Force operations several successful sea rescues were made by the British organisation, but many American airmen perished due to poor survival equipment or lack of training in its proper use. Where possible these deficiencies were rectified locally and as a stopgap much British equipment was used. The RAF K-type one-man dinghy was used by all 8th Air Force fighter pilots and also, later, it was supplied for many bomber crews. Bomber dinghy survival kits were improved and British items were utilised for many months, but the British bomber J-type dinghy could not be stowed in American bombers.

The problem with the B-17 dinghy stowage persisted; the release mechanism was rather complicated and maintenance personnel had difficulty in adjusting it correctly. In December 1942 one bomb group discontinued using the stowage provided and carried the dinghies inside the aircraft, following five cases of inadvertent release in the air. The designed stowage being in the upper deck of the fuselage, just aft of the top-turret, meant that when a dinghy was released in flight it might foul the tailplane. There were at least three instances when this caused fatal crashes. Although modifications to the B-17 dinghy release mechanism were advised in February 1943 as a measure to prevent accidental discharge in flight, this problem was not satisfactorily overcome until much later in the year.

Despite undesirable features for ditching, such as the weak plexiglas nosepiece and open waist windows, some Fortresses put down on the sea stayed afloat long enough for the crews to evacuate safely, particularly if the landing was made parallel to the swell to minimise the force of the impact. The Liberator, however, with its shoulder-wing configuration and weak bomb-bay doors, invariably broke aft of the wing or nosed under and sank rapidly. In January 1943 the advised ditching drill in B-24s was for six men to gather on the flight deck to escape through the top hatch and the remaining four to stay in the rear of the aircraft against a wide ditching belt strung between the waist gun posts. The ditching belts were manufactured by VIII AFSC in accordance with an experimental model fabricated at Burtonwood in December 1942. This was looked upon as a stopgap until a more satisfactory solution could be found. Eventually, the establishment of a ditching deck above the bomb-bay was advised. This involved relocating the oxygen bottles and constructing a small escape hatch above this deck. A B-24 incorporating this modification was sent back to the US; although scheduled for embodying on production it was never introduced. In the second half of 1944 a simplified modification kit became available for providing this deck, but due to the man hours involved the programme was very limited.

Another means of improving the chances of successfully ditching a B-24 was by strengthening the bomb-bay doors. To avoid the necessary major redesign and disruption of production, a compromise solution was the provision of strengthening formers, carried in the aircraft, that could be placed in position above the doors prior to a ditching. Available for late production aircraft they were fabricated in the UK. Nevertheless, the poor record of successful ditchings with B-24s was an undesirable morale factor for their crews and remained so throughout hostilities.

Ditching fighter aircraft was extremely hazardous and not advised. Few who attempted it survived. Instead, pilots were told to parachute into the sea. The number of 8th Air Force fighter pilots who survived putting their disabled aircraft down on water was probably only in single figures. Most of these lucky few were in the large twin-engined P-38, there was only one known instance of a P-51 having been ditched successfully. The records, did not, however, cover POWs, a few of whom had survived water crash landings.

Through arrangements with the British all US fighter pilots were issued with the K-type dinghy which was attached under the parachute harness and was readily available for inflation once the harness was discarded. Eventually all fighter pilots were given instruction in a pool or lake on freeing parachute harness in water and the correct method of climbing into a dinghy. Intensive courses for making USAAF officers thoroughly conversant with ASR equipment and procedures were set up at Toome and other officers attended the RAF School of Air/Sea Rescue at Blackpool. Training in correct procedures was a major factor in the improving survival rate of all 8th Air Force men down in the sea, the percentage of those rescued to those known down in the sea rising from 23.5 in 1943 to 45.4 for 1944. A higher proportion of fighter pilots than bomber crewmen were always rescued and the rate for all was nearly doubled for summer months when sea temperatures were higher.

The formation of the 8th Air Force's own Air/Sea Rescue organisation took place in stages over several months. On 7 July 1942 Headquarters recommended to Washington that four Lockheed Hudsons with crews, and one Hudson and crew each month thereafter, might be furnished to augment the RAF ASR service and to support American operations. This was turned down as the aircraft and crews could not be spared. Instead, a counter recommendation was that for the time being 8th Air Force rely entirely on the British services. On 8 September the 8th Air Force were notified by the RAF that all their ASR resources and facilities were at American disposal, provided that they became familiar with their procedures. Nevertheless, 8th Air Force was to become involved in ASR through VIII Fighter

Command's adoption of the RAF fighter control system. With the allocation of specific RAF Fighter Command sector areas in the eastern counties to VIII FC early in 1943, it was planned that the sector control centres would eventually be taken over and operated by US personnel. Linked to the main function of airborne operational control by radio was the direction finding services of which one branch dealt with aircraft in distress and alerted rescue services. As the first American fighter wing headquarters was committed to take over the Debden sector with its control centre at Saffron Walden, this organisation was also to shoulder the D/F responsibility.

The 52nd Fighter Control Squadron, which arrived to man the control room, was initially given the task of operating part of the ASR direction finding network. With three reporting D/F 'fixer' stations at Palling, Leiston and Tolleshunt D'Arcy, and a triangulation room at Hornchurch, the unit became operational on 14 June 1943. Each fixer station had a radio receiver with directional antenna which could be turned to pick up a distress signal and obtain a compass bearing. The bearing was then telephoned to an operator at the Hornchurch triangulation table, displaying a grid map of the coastal area of the southern North Sea. The operator placed a string from the position of the reporting fixer station on the map along the line of the bearing given. Reports from the other fixer stations were similarly handled and where the strings crossed a location point was established. This map reference was then passed to the control room at Saffron Walden for action. The only distress calls which 52nd Fighter Control Squadron received were those of the three P-47 groups which made use of the 66.50 mcs frequency on VHF radio sets. Each P-47 VHF radio had four channels selected by pushbuttons. That reserved for ASR distress calls was Channel B. Such calls were prefaced with the international distress call *Mayday*, repeated three times. Next the aircraft call-sign was given and a count of 1 to 5 and back to 1 to give time for a bearing to be taken.

The Hornchurch organisation was short-lived for the 65th Fighter Wing, and its 52nd Fighter Control Squadron, took over the Debden sector control at the beginning of July 1943. The triangulation team was moved into an attic at Saffron Walden Grammar School where two triangulation tables were set up covering north and south approaches to the sector area. Additional ASR fixer stations were established and two were moved. By the end of the month seven were in operation, at Hemsby, Leiston, Wix, Monkton, Beachy Head, Halnaker Hill and Wittersham. Additionally the triangulation room then served Channel D fixer stations used to home non-distressed aircraft of the Wing.

The actual rescues of US airmen were still made by the British: RAF ASR squadrons using Walrus amphibians to make pick-ups, or Hudson and Warwick aircraft to drop airborne lifeboats, but chiefly by the RAF-manned High Speed Launches (HSL) or Royal Navy Rescue Motor Launches (RML). RAF ASR aircraft mainly concerned with 8th Air Force rescues were those based at Martlesham, Bradwell Bay and Bircham Newton in conjunction with the marine craft unit bases at Harwich and Gt Yarmouth. The 65th Fighter Wing ASR controller had direct communications with the appropriate headquarters for requests to despatch rescue craft. For spotting and search he was also able to obtain the occasional use of aircraft and crews from both VIII FC and VIII BC to cover the area where an aircraft was believed, or known, to have gone into the sea. Later it was occasionally possible to arrange for a small number of fighter aircraft which could be spared from operations to patrol specific sea areas when a major combat mission was in progress.

In January 1944 8th Air Force bombers were equipped with new VHF crystals permitting distress calls on Channel B. Previously their distress calls were by wireless transmissions in morse code fed into the ASR network by both US and RAF receiving agencies. Inevitably, there was some delay in the transmission and handling of such messages whereas a vocal call via VHF could take as little as 13 seconds to alert rescue services. With the addition of all bombers to Channel B on 14 January 1944 and the growing scope of combat operations a vast increase in D/F bearing calls occurred; for December 1943 this was 185, but for June 1944 the figure had risen to 243, placing considerable strain on the ASR reporting network.

A special spotter aircraft squadron was to be set up by 8th Air Force whose trained pilots would be better able to conduct searches than those occasionally employed from combat units. To speed rescues it was agreed with the British that there should be VHF communication direct with rescue launches on standing patrol to avoid the inevitable delays, be they short, of telephoning through authorised channels. To further speed communication and action, the Saffron Walden ASR centre would use its spotter aircraft to relay messages to rescue vessels when these were beyond normal VHF range. Two RAF Warwick squadrons with airborne lifeboats also had their aircraft fitted with Channel B crystals, to effect direct communication with 65th FW ASR control. To reduce the traffic load on Channel B, all ASR communication between control, rescue aircraft and vessels would be carried out on a separate frequency. Final agreement on these changes was reached at a meeting between the three interested parties, RAF, Royal Navy and USAAF, on 8 May 1944, following successful experimental trials made during the previous month, RAF augmentation including six Warwicks with airborne lifeboats and two Walrus at Martlesham available for each 8th Air Force operation.

ASR fixer stations were increased to nine in February 1944 when Cockthorpe and Skidbrooke were opened and extended cover northwards to cater for heavy bomber missions routed far out over the North Sea. During June 1944 when there was intensive air activity around the Normandy bridgehead, mobile ASR fixer stations were set up temporarily at Warmwell and

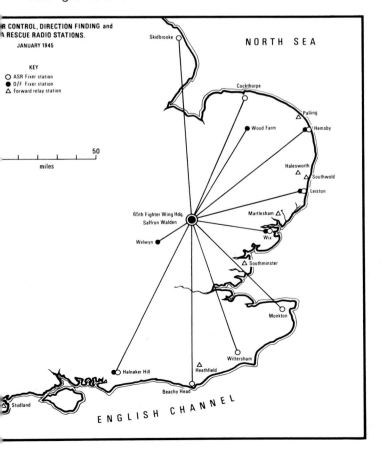

R CONTROL, DIRECTION FINDING and
RESCUE RADIO STATIONS.

JANUARY 1945

KEY

○ ASR Fixer station
● D/F Fixer station
△ Forward relay station

NORTH SEA

Exeter in south-west England in anticipation of increased ASR calls in that area. These stations were removed in August.

Following the liberation of France the south coast fixer at Halnaker Hill was closed in December 1944.

CONTROL PROCEDURE

Although two other fighter wing control centres were opened by VIII FC, the ASR commitment remained solely with the 65th FW at Saffron Walden. Procedure remained broadly little changed throughout the full operational period. The following outline is typical of procedures for the last year of the war.

A team of a dozen men, two commissioned and the rest non-commissioned officers, was assigned to operate the ASR Control under 1/Lt, later Captain, Fred W. Graf. ASR Control was housed in a glass panelled booth overlooking the large table display in the 65th FW operations control room. The ASR duty crew consisted of the Duty Controller, his Liaison Sergeant, a plotter and a message recorder. The Duty Controller had his Channel B microphone and telephone communications 'hot lines' in front of him. On his immediate right was a plotting table map to which was attached an adjustable computing device used for quick establishment of a course. A plotter worked at this table map. On the Duty Controller's left sat a clerk who recorded all messages in a log. To his left was the Liaison Sergeant with radio and telephone communications. All men wore headphones.

When a mission was laid on the Duty Controller received a copy of the field order and extracted over-water routes and timings. He or his Liaison Sergeant first notified the RN and RAF rescue launch bases, as they required at least three hours' notice to have boats in position under the route out from England. The American spotter squadron and RAF ASR units that would be involved were alerted and all scheduled flights by the US spotters notified to higher headquarters and to British defence organisations. ASR fixer, radio relay and other communications stations were also alerted. Any airborne radio relay aircraft that were required were arranged through 65th FW and other headquarters.

The Duty Controller received all Channel B radio traffic in his headphones via the coastal relay stations. If a *Mayday* was faint or insufficiently long for the direction finding stations to make a fix, he would call the distressed pilot to transmit for a long count. As soon as the triangulation room plotters received sufficient bearings to make a fix on their grid map the position was passed through the internal telephone system to ASR control. The plotter marked the fix with grease pencil on the table map while all details were recorded by the clerk. The Duty Controller called this course to the pilot and on another frequency vectored spotter aircraft towards the distressed aircraft. The Duty Controller continued to talk to the *Mayday* pilot both to enable a check to be kept on his position and to raise his morale. As soon as a spotter pilot found the troubled aircraft or its crew in the sea he informed the Duty Controller who would then instruct him as required, usually to call the nearest rescue vessel. Meanwhile the Liaison Sergeant informed the rescue vessel base of proceedings using Royal Navy W/T channels. If the rescue could be better effected by an amphibian aircraft the Duty Controller radioed for these. Once a rescue was made information on the names and condition of the men saved was radioed to the Liaison Sergeant who informed their home base and made arrangements for their reception once ashore.

THE 5th EMERGENCY RESCUE SQUADRON

Like so many specialised units established in the 8th Air Force, the decision to form a flying unit for ASR search and support faced the formal obstacle of obtaining a Table of Organisation (T/O). Without this authorisation personnel or equipment would not be forthcoming from the United States and the delay in

obtaining an authorised T/O 'through the proper channels' was notorious – and some thought outrageous when the saving of life was often ultimately involved. It was therefore necessary to form a provisional unit, staffing and equipping it by drawing on other units in the Command. In the case of the spotter squadron, instead of producing a provisional number, its creators simply chose to identify it as 'Detachment B, Flight Section, Hq, 65th Fighter Wing'. While it would be accounted in the records as Detachment B, it became generally known as the Air/Sea Rescue Squadron. Command and formation of the unit was vested in a former ASR controller, Captain Robert Gerhart.

The aircraft type selected was the P-47 Thunderbolt. RAF experience had shown that fighter aircraft were well suited to the spotting role and could operate closer to the enemy coast, being better able to meet any interceptions that might occur. While not the most desirable type because of its limited endurance, the P-47 was the only fighter that could be spared in the spring of 1944. In fact, on long range searches P-51 Mustangs and their pilots from combat groups were occasionally requested and employed. To equip the ASR squadron each of the remaining P-47 groups in VIII FC supplied aircraft with high operational hours. These were 'war-wearies' – aircraft that were due for retirement. The base selected for the new squadron was the P-47 airfield at Boxted and from its resident unit, 56th Fighter Group, Gerhart received much help and equipment, chiefly through the good offices of its commander, Col Hubert Zemke. In addition to 25 ageing P-47Ds, an equal number of pilots and 90 or so mechanics, plus a support team were obtained, all on detached service. All other equipment had to be begged or borrowed. Gerhart was given a group of dispersal points at the northern end of Boxted and set up his headquarters in a deserted farmhouse. For maintenance, a blister hangar was later erected by the Squadron.

Rescue equipment was obtained from the British Air Ministry and the initial load for a P-47 was a double M-type dinghy pack under the fuselage, two 108 gallon drop tanks on the wing racks and a British four-unit smoke marker rack under each wing.

The first attempted test flight proved that this arrangement produced too much drag, the smoke flare racks acting like dive brakes. A successful rearrangement placed a single M-type 4-man dinghy pack on each wing rack, a single 150 gallon drop tank on the fuselage shackles and a smoke flare rack immediately aft of the tank under the fuselage. Armament was reduced to two .50 calibre guns in each wing to lessen weight. With low power settings a five hour endurance could be obtained from a P-47 so modified.

Operations by the ASR Squadron from 9 May 1944 were based on regular patrols during the whole period of a combat mission. A minimum one hour's notice was given on the alert from ASR Control at Saffron Walden. Spotters were despatched in pairs, the first being in position over the sea patrol area by the time bombers started to leave the coast. Depending on the spread of mission task forces, two or more pairs might be despatched to patrol different areas. When a pair had reached the time point for return to base, usually after a two hour patrol, it would be relieved by another two P-47s. Patrol altitude was determined by the prevailing weather and the distance from the radio relay stations. At 100 miles 8000 feet was needed to receive VHF signals and for 150 miles it was necessary to fly at 15,000 feet. On receipt of a distress call, control advised the P-47s of position and all other useful information. Normally the No 2 aircraft would retain VHF altitude while searching at the detailed spot while No 1 went to low level. This enabled No 1 to be informed of any further fixes or information on the distressed aircraft. If the distressed aircraft was located still in flight, efforts were made to establish plane-to-plane radio communication using Channel C and then to try leading it to the nearest friendly airfield or to the location of a patrolling HSL or RML. If the disabled aircraft had already crashed or ditched, the spotters

P-47D 42-8410 rises past Boxted hangar No 2 as it sets out on an ASR patrol

tried to locate the crew and if successful radioed to the nearest rescue vessel or amphibian aircraft while orbiting the spot. Wing pack dinghies were released if it appeared the downed crew were in need, and smoke markers when a rescue boat or aircraft approached. Where a search had to be carried out a definite technique was employed, first defining the limits of the search area by dropping smoke markers or getting repeated fixes from the controller. The search patterns were ribbon, circular or square, depending on weather conditions and value of fixes obtained. Once a dinghy was seen the No 1 spotter orbited at low altitude so as not to lose sight of it. If a rescue vessel was some hours away this aircraft would ge relieved by another spotter.

Although 8th Air Force had requested amphibian flying boats for use in ASR during the winter of 1943–44, more than a year elapsed before they were available. Originally plans were made to lay additional hardstandings at Boxted to receive these aircraft, but in January 1945 the ASR squadron moved to the vacant bomber airfield at Halesworth with ample parking space and where the first OA-10 Catalinas were received. Shortly after arrival the unit received formal T/O authorisation with the designation 5th Emergency Rescue Squadron. With the amphibians the Squadron had the facility to conduct rescue, the first taking place on 3 February 1945 when an OA-10 on a local indoctrination flight was diverted to pluck a bomber crew from near the Dutch coast. Eventually nine OA-10s were assigned although the spotter strength of P-47Ds was maintained at 25. Additionally the unit received the US-designed airborne lifeboat in March 1945 with six 'war weary' B-17Gs to carry them. One of these boats, the Higgins type A-1, was successfully dropped to a bomber crew off Denmark on 31 March.

The only ASR Squadron aircraft known lost to enemy action was an OA-10, shot up on the sea by an Me 262 jet on 31 March 1945. Only one P-47 was listed MIA, believed due to having been flown into the sea on 1 August 1944. This, incidentally, was the only 'silver' finish aircraft received by the unit prior to 1945. Most of the original war-wearies soldiered on until May 1945. Two, together with their pilots, were lost in a collision over Fritton Broad in April 1944.

Experimentation and Training

Pathfinder School

The main purpose of the 482nd Bomb Group, formed at Alconbury in the high summer of 1943, was to provide radar leads for bombing missions in inclement weather – pathfinders. Alconbury became the 8th Air Force radar establishment and in addition to participating in regular daylight bombing missions the 482nd was also heavily involved in the development and trials of new radar devices together with the training of both radar operatives and servicing personnel. On 4 November plans were drawn up to eventually remove the 482nd from regular combat operations to concentrate on training and experimentation. As a training establishment it became known as the Pathfinder School and became the major American centre for radar, and associated electronic arts, in the theatres of war with Germany.

TRAINING

Tuition for the first 8th Air Force radar operators and mechanics was given at RAF establishments, the equipment they would use being predominantly of British origin. An RAF contingent was also present at Alconbury during the formative months, mainly involved in instruction on technical matters. The first trainees coming from outside the 482nd Bomb Group were a detachment arriving from the 15th Air Force in Italy during December 1943.

With, as related, H2X adopted as the principal blind bombing device to be employed by USSTAF forces, a training programme on this aid started in February 1944. The eight original RAF instructors assigned as British H2S experts quickly made themselves familiar with American H2X. The first class of 42 officers from the three bomb divisions began the course on 21 February and graduated on 18 March. The next 'Mickey School' class completed its course on 27 April, and others thereafter at monthly intervals. An expert H2X navigator was assigned to each bomb division to further the training of the initial graduates when they returned to their units to engage in combat operations.

Training courses for other types of radar bombing and navigation aids were also established, together with those for mechanics. During the final months of the war classes in *Micro-H*, G-H, RCM and *Loran* were included. The revised complement of aircraft in the 482nd Group was engaged principally in training activities. To ease the maintenance requirements of the 814th Bomb Squadron, originally a B-24 unit, it converted to B-17s for its training role. However, it continued to operate the Group's B-24s involved in experimental work. Training flights were usu-

ally carried out in daylight, with pupils operating H2X equipment in high altitude runs on selected British towns and cities.

OPERATIONAL EXPERIMENTS

Although the 482nd Group was removed from regular combat operations on 26 March 1944, it continued to fly combat missions for experimental purposes until the end of hostilities. With few exceptions these missions were conducted at night to reduce the chances of enemy interception and rarely involved more than two to four sorties. Although bombing was not the object of these flights, bombs were often carried and unloaded over suitable targets in order that their activities appeared to the enemy as planned nuisance raids.

In June 1943 three scientists from the Radiation Laboratory arrived in England to work on an Anglo-American project to develop *Oboe II*. The result was a system using part British, part American components. A prototype installation was made in B-17F 42-3525 and the first experimental sortie flown on the night of 11/12 November 1943. This form of *Oboe II* was code named *Albumleaf*, and a further ten night missions were flown by the same Fortress until 24 January when, landing at Alconbury in the early hours, it struck an obstruction damaging a wing and propeller. The first aircraft received from the USA with production installations for *Albumleaf*, B-17G 42-31106, flew its first test sortie over enemy territory on 14 January. The components of *Albumleaf* were an *Oboe* Mk II receiver used in conjunction with a transmitter and modulators of the US Navy sea-search ASG-3 radar which, it was hoped, would enhance signal strength. After four more night missions that month by this aircraft, *Oboe* and *Albumleaf* were made a 9th Air Force responsibility, the equipment being removed from the 482nd's aircraft at the Stansted depot early in February.

Following the transfer of *Oboe* there was a lull in combat sorties by the 482nd until April when a regular programme of night operations was commenced to obtain H2X scope photographs of selected targets in enemy territory. To aid radar navigation, photographs of the images produced by specific targets on the scope of an H2X set were rephotographed. This provided a visual record which could be used to compare with images received on H2X scopes during an actual attack. Provision of photographs, superimposed on grid maps, was an obvious aid to ensuring a higher degree of accurate target identification.

A programme to obtain scope photographs was instituted at Alconbury late in 1943. A K-24 camera, mounted above the scope in a B-17, was first used during the mission to Bremen on 16 December. This arrangement, however, was cumbersome and not practical for the required photographs to be obtained by pathfinders engaged in leading daylight missions. With the arrival of more H2X-equipped B-17Gs in February 1944, it became possible to assign two aircraft specially for modification as 'camera scope ships'. To cover distant and heavily defended targets, faster aircraft were desirable, leading to 8th Air Force asking the British that two Mosquito XVIs, scheduled for delivery for photographic reconnaissance, be modified to carry H2X sets. This being agreed, the first of these aircraft with the scanner mounted in a bulbous nosepiece, was delivered to Alconbury on 28 April 1944; eventually 12 were so modified.

The first night 'scope photo' sorties with B-17 Fortresses, confined to a dark moon period, were carried out over Holland on 20 April. This type of operation continued periodically to the end of hostilities to build up a print library of H2X target images. Initially two B-17Gs, 42-97623 and 42-97692, were used to prove the technique and overcome the technical problems. They were used with particular success in making scope pictures of the D-Day landing areas. In July and August 1944 an expansion of the task was effected by increasing the number of B-17s modified to carry K-24 cameras over the radar scopes to eight. This allowed sorties flown per night to be doubled when required.

The operational procedure adopted called for an aircraft to take off and climb to high altitude on route to enemy territory, avoiding RAF bomber stream areas. Climb would be continued until the briefed height was reached, this corresponding to daylight attack altitudes on enemy targets at 18,000 to 27,000 feet. A number of locations would often be visited by each participating aircraft with approaches made from different directions, lest the enemy became aware of the true nature of these activities and deduced the desired route day bombers would take in their approach. When bombs were to be dropped at a target being photographed, more than one run across was made before release for the same reasons. Leaflets were often dropped alternative to bombs. The 482nd's B-17s carried a full crew and often an extra radar navigator. During the course of over 200 H2X scope photo sorties no losses were sustained due to enemy action, due chiefly to the high altitude for these missions, although a few aircraft were slightly damaged by flak.

Operations by the H2X-equipped Mosquitoes commenced on the night of 1 May 1944 with Mk XVI, serial MM311 successfully completing a mission over the Continent. These were flown by trained crews of the 802nd Reconnaissance Group (P), which was then equipping with Mosquitoes at Watton. The H2X Mosquitoes were transferred from the 482nd to the 802nd in May, but they continued to be operated from Alconbury as the surface of their home airfield, being grass, was too rough for the delicate H2X instrumentation. Unhappily, the career of one Mosquito (MM308) was short for, attempting to land after a sortie on the night of 12 May, it overshot the runway and crashed, injuring the crew. The Mosquito detachment received two more aircraft in June, only to lose one and its crew to a balloon cable during a training flight near Gravesend. Mosquito night flights over German locations continued until 24/25 July, when the 802nd Group detachment moved to its home base where a new concrete runway was then available.

On occasions the 482nd Group was used as a reserve to bolster normal daylight operations. For the pre-landing bombing of enemy coastal positions in Normandy on 6 June 1944, eighteen 482nd Group pathfinder crews and aircraft were employed as additional pathfinder leads, flying 24 sorties. On Christmas Eve that year 12 B-17s, four from each squadron, flew in formation out over the North Sea to 50.00E – 54.00N as a diversion for the largest 8th Air Force mission of the war. Conditions deteriorated and on return all 12 Fortresses had to land at RAF Wratting Common.

The 482nd Group was involved in developing techniques for the *Micro-H* radar bombing system and started a programme of operational tests on 4 August 1944 when B-17Gs 42-97623, 42-97689, 42-97690 and 42-97717 were despatched to bomb a fuel dump at Bois-de-la-Houssire in France. A further 25 *Micro-H* combat tests, carried out during the following four weeks, established the accuracy of this device and developed a technique. Beacons for these *Micro-H* tests were set up at Beachy Head and Halesworth. In September the first aircraft equipped with the so-called *Eagle* radar, AN/APQ-7, arrived at Alconbury for trials. The B-17G concerned, 44-6252, was distinguished by a stub airfoil under the nose containing the radar scanner. Considerable trouble was experienced with the *Eagle* equipment although local flights were carried out almost daily. Other bombers equipped with this device were slow to arrive and a programme of operational flights to obtain *Eagle* scope photographs was not commenced until the night of 27 March 1945. At this time the 482nd had 11 B-17Gs and six B-24s with *Eagle* radar on hand. A total of 21 such sorties were despatched to locations in the crumbling Third Reich during April. Thereafter the *Eagle* B-17s were transferred to the 96th Group and the *Eagle* B-24s to the 44th.

Other radars tested by the 482nd were APS-15A, an improved H2X received in November 1944, and *Micro-H* Mk II. The first combat trial of the latter was on the afternoon of 20 March 1945 when B-17 42-97702 bombed a target at Oberursel. Further combat tests followed. *Micro-H* Mk III was under local test in the last month of hostilities, as was an experimental project code-named *Buzzard* which combined *Eagle* with H2X for better target location. Other devices for development and test installed in 482nd aircraft early in 1945 were: *Nosmo* (Norden Optical Synchronised with Mickey Operation), a device developed at Alconbury giving direct electronic coupling of Norden sight and 'Mickey' set; Radar-H, a system using radar echoes from cities and installations other than beacons using a special adaption of *Micro-H*; *Loran*, a radar navigational system similar to *Gee*; AN/APS-13 tail warning radar and *Shoran*, a US development for radar grid bombing similar to *Oboe*. All these did not pass out of 8th Air Force testing stage before the cessation of hostilities.

ENGINEERING AND GROUND FACILITIES

The Pathfinder School housed a number of radar specialist teams concerned with developing new equipment and solving technical difficulties for all USSTAF organisations. The expertise at Alconbury was such that in the summer of 1944 Washington mooted the transfer of the 482nd Group to the USA, but this was successfully resisted by General Spaatz. However, in October the 8th Air Force did agree to supply 61 radar navigators and some ground personnel to expand training in the US.

While the *Oboe* and G-H ground facilities used by 8th Air Force were manned by RAF personnel, 482nd also developed ground beacon installations and trained men to operate them. In connection with testing airborne sets of H2S and H2X, 'S' and 'X' band beacons were set up at Alconbury. In March 1944 another 'X' beacon was set up at Halesworth which could be received over the Frisian Isles at 193 miles range at 13,000 feet. Radar test beacons were then set up at Beachy Head, Tillingham and Winterton for the new Micro-H system. These were manned by 482nd Group teams each consisting of one radar officer, six beacon mechanics and three communications men. A reserve beacon was kept on each site. Three Micro-H beacons were established on the Continent during the final months of the year with the UK sites reduced to two and utilised for training.

Technical Operations

Technical advancement was a vital factor to the outcome of the Second World War and nowhere more so than in air operations. The USAAF was backed by the largest aviation industry and development organisations of any of the belligerents. Even so, considerable technical advance originated overseas within combat air forces, particularly in the United Kingdom. Indeed, of the operational engineering organisation supporting 8th Air Force, it can be said that it was responsible for developing equipment which made possible the Force's major contribution to victory in Europe – the gaining of air superiority over enemy-held territory.

The location of the 8th Air Force in the high technology environment of the UK was an important factor in the technical engineering support it received. In 1941 the US and British governments came to an agreement on the exchange of aviation technology which, on the US side, was the responsibility of a special observer group attached to the air attaché's office in the US Embassy. Some months after the Axis powers declared war on the United States the functions and duties of the special observer group were absorbed by a special staff section of Hq, European Theatre of Operations, US Army, known as the Air Technical Service (ATS). This organisation facilitated the interchange of technical information between Britain and America in the military aviation field, in particular by liaison between the USAAF's Materiel Command (which handled all experimental and development projects) and the British Ministry of Aircraft Production. Later, a scheme was set up whereby engineers and test pilots of Materiel Command came to the UK on temporary duty with ATS.

In February 1944 ATS was transferred to Air Service Command, USSTAF and redesignated Directorate of Technical Services, but retaining its experienced head, Col Howard G. Bunker. While ATS was independent of 8th Air Force it became heavily involved with it on technical matters, particularly during the first year of operations when much assistance was sought from Britain. It proved a useful key in affording other 8th Air Force agencies access to local aeronautical and industrial facilities. Nevertheless, ATS was primarily a clearing house for information on research and development.

The major technical engineering establishment within VIII Air Force Service Command was the Technical Services Branch of Maintenance and Repair Division. It included a factory service representatives section, composed of civilian technicians of the various US factories having their products in use by both USAAF and the RAF in the UK. This organisation rendered engineering advice, solved maintenance difficulties, instructed maintenance and operational personnel and located spares. An Engineering Section, at Langford Lodge, Northern Ireland, monitored engineering projects, prepared data and made trial installations as well as dealing with the technical aspects of modifications. Administered by three VIII AFSC engineering officers, other personnel were largely civilian engineers of the Lockheed Overseas Corporation. A Technical Data Section processed unsatisfactory reports received from flying and service units, and prepared technical circulars and instructions.

Both VIII BC and VIII FC developed technical sections which made modifications and investigated problems, although the Service Command considered that this was properly in their domain. There was also some friction with ATS and pleas to higher authority from VIII AFSC that it be allowed to absorb all technical engineering organisations in a single division under its control. These protestations were for the most part successfully resisted by VIII Fighter and Bomber Commands, although there was eventually some resolution.

The bomber technical investigation was centred on Bovingdon when this base became the first combat Crew Replacement Centre. As its B-17s were assigned to training duties they were more readily available for the Engineering Office to perform experimental modifications which could not be carried out on combat stations. During the winter of 1942–43 Major Robert J. Reed oversaw the extensive reworking of B-17s and B-24s at this base to improve defensive armament. But for the most part modification and experimentation on bombers was carried out in conjunction with VIII AFSC at its Honington, Little Staughton, Burtonwood and Warton depots during 1943.

From its inception, VIII FC had a more positive awareness of the need for on-the-spot technical expertise. Shortly after arriving in England a special section was set up which was so successful in solving operational engineering and tactical problems that it was later developed into a major unit charged with providing this type of service for all USAAF combat organisations in the ETO.

In the summer of 1942 VIII FC received the first two Lockheed P-38 fighter groups to be moved overseas. As this was a new and advanced type of aircraft Brig General 'Monk' Hunter took the precaution of seeing that specialists accompanied the movement to sort out any technical problems that arose. The task was assigned to Lt Col Ben Kelsey, the test pilot who had flown the prototype Lightning, and Major Cass Hough, another experienced pilot with a flair for innovative engineering. Both men flew P-38s of the 1st Group across the North Atlantic in July but Kelsey was soon to return to the USA and subsequently went to North Africa where the P-38 units moved in November. This left Major Hough to head VIII FC's Office of Flight Research and Engineering at Bushey Hall, Watford, using flight facilities at nearby Bovingdon. Hough recruited T/Sgt Robert H. Shafer, a talented crew chief he had met before the war, for promotion as his senior ground engineering officer. Hough, Shafer, plus a few mechanics and clerks, constituted what General Hunter decided, late in 1942, to call the Air Technical Section of VIII Fighter Command, although the abbreviation, ATS, caused some confusion with that of the Air Technical Service.

Hough's main occupation was trouble-shooting and as the only pilot he conducted all test flying. One of the first tasks involved investigation of high speed dives with P-38s, in order to advise on recovery techniques. He also conducted trials with the P-38F against Spitfires of the AFDU at Duxford and, together with Shafer, gave dive recovery lectures to P-38 pilots. Following the departure of all P-38 units, Hough and Shafer were confronted with the P-47 Thunderbolt and its teething troubles. The VHF radio installations suffered from excessive noise, diagnosed as interference from the engine ignition. Cracked leads and poor bonding were sealed with a special compound to cure this problem. A further P-47 difficulty was a lack of power at high altitude, traced to atmospheric conditions over the UK being sufficiently different from those in the north-east USA to require reworking the boost controls. Non-uniform cooling of engine cylinders was yet another problem for Air Technical Section and solved with baffles in the nose cowling.

The extension of P-47 range was of vital concern at this time and an obvious means to this end was the use of expendable, external fuel tanks. A 200 gallon ferry tank was available in the US and a consignment arrived in late February 1943. VIII AFSC immediately acquired two for tests at Langford Lodge but it was two weeks before Bovingdon could wrest one from the Service Command. It was quickly apparent to Cass Hough that these 'bath tub' tanks, aerodynamically imperfect and inclined to leak, were far from satisfactory. Moreover, some form of pressurisation was necessary as atmospheric pressure would prevent fuel being drawn from the tank at altitudes beyond 20,000 feet. Paper/plastic composition tanks of 108 US gallon capacity were procured from British sources, while Hough devised a means of pressure control by taking the bleed air from the instrument stability vacuum pump and using it to gradually pressurise the tank as altitude increased. These developments proved highly successful and allowed the P-47's radius of action to be doubled.

Air Technical Section's development of pressurised drop tank installations on the P-47, and later the P-51, proved to be one of the most notable technical advances of the 8th's campaign, providing the extra radius of action that allowed the US fighters to eventually range over almost all of the European enemy's territory and achieve air superiority.

The activities of VIII FC's Air Technical Section generated much bureaucratic disapproval in some offices of VIII Air Service Command and Materiel Command. Examples of the paper composition tank were required to be sent to Materiel Command at Wright Field for approval. Almost one year later to the day, when some 14,700 'paper' tanks had been used operationally, VIII FC received a report from Wright Field stating that the 'paper' tanks had been tested and found unfit for combat use! There can be little wonder that 8th Air Force high command wittingly protected units such as Air Technical Section from the clutches of Air Service and Materiel Commands.

By the end of 1943 Air Technical Section was recognised as having some of the most innovative aeronautical engineers in the UK. One recruit who particularly distinguished himself in several difficult projects was M/Sgt Walter Toczylowski, who had been crew chief on General Hunter's personal aircraft until August. A great many of the projects undertaken at Bovingdon came directly from the fighter pilots, the trouble-shooting prowess of Hough's unit being well respected by VIII FC fighter pilots. Indeed, it was David Schilling, 56th Group ace and leader, who bestowed its unofficial motto: 'Nil Excretum Taurus', which Cass Hough considered their greatest accolade – if somewhat unscholarly Latin.

When Lt General Doolittle took over 8th Air Force in January 1944 he was so impressed with the ATS of VIII FC that he decided to expand it into a single organisation to deal with bomber and all types of operational problems. Activated on 21 February as Operational Engineering Section (OES), two Bovingdon hangars were made available to house its projects and personnel increased to nearly 200. Col Ben Kelsey was transferred from the 9th Air Force to command and Lt Col Cass Hough became his deputy, although Kelsey considered it a joint command. Lt Col Algene E. Key was made head of bomber projects. There was, however, no separation of purpose as all members of the team worked on both bomber and fighter projects. Further, OES served both 8th and 9th Air Force with a brief as stated by General Doolittle: 'Combat evaluation of existing tactics, techniques and material. Development of new tactics, techniques and material to adjust to the tide of battle. Listen to field problems in all areas of the above and try to find fixes where indicated. And in these processes, be available to counsel operational units by flying missions with them.' The unit's relationship with VIII AFSC was also defined with a view to alleviating friction.

During the winter of 1943–44 Cass Hough, in co-operation with Lt Col Don Ostrander, the senior OES Ordnance Officer, adapted the P-38 for high-level bombing by removing all armament and modifying the compartment to take a bombardier and his bombsight apparatus. This was the *Droop Snoot*, its purpose to lead a formation of bomb-carrying Lightnings. The venture proved successful, although operational employment was somewhat negated by the conversion of all 8th Air Force P-38 fighter groups to the P-51 after D-Day. Reintroduced in 8th Air Force in September 1943, the P-38 had been dogged with high altitude engine troubles which, despite numerous modifications, were never really satisfactorily solved. In the spring of 1944 OES proposed that a P-38 be experimentally fitted with Rolls-Royce Merlin engines to enhance performance. While approved locally, with a P-38J despatched to the Rolls-Royce plant in May, there were immediate repercussions from Washington with orders that this project was not to proceed; a decision viewed as political by some of the senior combat officers in England.

For both Kelsey and Hough the P-38, despite its high altitude problems, was still a favourite and often used for operational excursions in connection with some specific problem. On 1 September 1944 they flew to observe the island of Cezembre, in the gulf of St Malo. A German garrison still held out in this rocky fortress which had batteries of heavy guns in protected and deeply recessed positions, thus denying the use of nearby harbours to Allied shipping. Repeated bombing had failed to resolve the situation and 8th Air Force asked OES to investigate and suggest suitable ordnance and techniques for removing the obstacle. On reaching Cezembre both pilots flew several orbits while making observations. Before departing Hough and Kelsey decided to fire some .50-calibre rounds into one of the casements, more as a gesture of frustration than anything else. Somewhat to their astonishment this assault produced an explosion, immediate fire and German troops on the top of the island waving white flags. While Hough continued to circle the island, Kelsey climbed to higher altitude and reported the surrender by radio to home base. The P-38s continued to circle for about an hour and a half until assault craft appeared and landed Allied troops on the island. This was the only occasion that enemy ground forces surrendered to 8th Air Force aircraft.

On 14 August 1944 OES became the Maintenance and Technical Services (MTS), apparently to placate the Materiel Command. This change was not popular with the unit who, as special staff section of 8th AF Hq, had no part in maintenance. On 17 March 1945 a more suitable designation was approved when MTS became the Technical Operations Section of 8th AF Hq, usually shortened to 8th Technical Operations. The mission remained unchanged, the organisation continuing to function as before, and by VE-Day having been involved in more than 350 projects since its inception. Among the most notable achievements were: front line marking devices to prevent bombing of friendly troops in tactical attacks; the development and testing of an integrating sight for dive bombing; a device on P-51s which provided constant automatic trim as engine torque increased (not beyond prototype stage before war ended); the counselling of B-17 pilots on engine cowl flap settings to prevent over-heating; the counselling of P-47 fighter pilots to conserve fuel by using high manifold pressure and low engine revolutions as against the tendency to use high rpm because the engine ran more smoothly; operational testing of the British 'Disney' rocket bomb for penetrating the thick concrete of U-boat pens; overcoming gun failures in P-51Bs; testing and programming installations of the K-14 gyro reflector gunsights; preventing top turret fires in B-17s by sealing electric cables against fraying with cement; designing a device to produce coloured smoke from engine exhaust to aid bomber formation assembly and a foolproof method of preventing loss of hydraulic brake pressure during the landing of heavy bombers.

Two dozen projects were often in hand at one time, ranging from simple investigations of component failures to major engineering such as the conversion of a B-24 to transport configuration. Most of the investigations or projects came from combat units, being passed to 8th TO for detailed study and advancement; others originated at Bovingdon. 8th TO possessed a variety of aircraft types for trials and experimentation. Technical details of many Bovingdon projects involving aircraft and equipment are given under appropriate headings elsewhere in this book.

Despite signified approval in high command, there were elements within both VIII Air Service Command and Materiel Command who viewed OES/8th TO as an illegal, buccaneering outfit. Indeed, OES/8th TO made no secret of its tendency to ignore 'the proper channels' in the cause of expediency to solve an operational problem it had been given. Much use was made of British facilities and agencies in meeting urgent requirements by direct approach. Nevertheless, there were occasions when the activities of the Bovingdon unit were subject to censure. Cass Hough was twice threatened with Court Martial, once for succumbing to a US congressman's demand to be flown over the enemy lines in the special two-seat P-38 conversion kept at Bovingdon, and on another occasion for recommending instructions for fuel usage contrary to those stated by the Service Command. Nevertheless, the endeavours and enterprise of Technical Operations were much admired and supported by the majority of 8th Air Force combat commanders and enthusiastically by Generals Doolittle and Spaatz.

Operational Training

In planning extensive USAAF operations from the United Kingdom there was early acceptance of the need to adopt many British services and procedures to ensure smooth functioning. Training establishments were to be set up to provide instruction in these theatre subjects and those which might arise from operational experience. Not only would new units require a period of indoctrination but provision had to be made for training replacement personnel to make good losses which, based on British experience, were expected to be 5 per cent per month for bomber crewmen and 3 per cent for fighter pilots.

Creation of a training organisation primarily concerned with the provision of fully trained replacement aircrew was an early task for General Eaker's staff at VIII BC. In March 1942 requests were made to Washington for the approval of Tables of Organisation for Combat Crew Replacement Centers (CCRC) and the necessary personnel to man them. Official sanction was to be long in coming. In the meantime the British were approached for an initial airfield allocation where such establishments could be formed much along the lines of the RAF Operational Training Units (OTU). Bovingdon in Hertfordshire and Oakley in Oxfordshire were originally proposed but as Oakley would not be available for some time Cheddington was substituted.

At first it was intended to use Bovingdon for bomber training and Cheddington for fighters, a short-lived plan as a US-British conference in May 1942 found this quite inadequate to sustain the combat forces proposed and agreed an eventual 16 airfields be allocated for 8th Air Force training purposes. These were to be concentrated in Northern Ireland to conserve airfields in England for operational units. Further, it was evident that training on such a large scale warranted a special headquarters to oversee this activity and on Independence Day 1942 the USAAF activated VIII Air Force Composite Command to fulfil this function. At the time 8th Air Force planned that Composite Command would eventually be responsible for the reception of new units and personnel, establishing replacement centres, and training all bomber and fighter units. An additional responsibility would be the defence of Northern Ireland. In the event, Composite Command was to have a very chequered career and only came to perform the training functions. The Headquarters, not arriving in Ulster from the United States until 12 September 1942, was temporarily accommodated at RAF Long Kesh until Kirkassock House, Lurgan, its planned location, became available the following November. Due to lack of resources to expand theatre training, VIII AFCC was unable to engage in its assigned task until the spring of 1943 and then only on a limited scale.

BOMBER TRAINING ESTABLISHMENTS

Initially all operational training was condicted by the two combat commands, primarily due to the urgent need to train the personnel of units newly arrived from the United States.

Although the allocation of Bovingdon and Cheddington for this purpose had been confirmed in May 1943, they did not come into operation until late in August that year when, failing provision of authorised units, two provisional units were activateddd at these bases. These were designated Nos 11 and 12 CCRC respectively. Hitherto theatre indoctrination had been conducted at appropriate RAF establishments while small numbers of RAF specialists had been loaned for instructing in the British system of flying control and communications at each combat base when a unit arrived from America. RAF personnel were also made available for Bovingdon where bomber crew training was to be concentrated.

In lieu of a Table of Organisation from Washington, Generals Eaker and Spaatz had no option but to use personnel and aircraft from a combat unit to man the CCRC establishments. In consequence it was decided to use the third Fortress-equipped group to arrive in the UK, the 92nd Group, transferring its B-17Fs to the operational 97th Group and using that unit's B-17Es, which lacked many combat refinements, for training. By early September No 11 CCRC – as the 92nd Group was then known – had acquired 28 B-17Es, generally considered in poor condition. Some 92nd Group men were used to form the nucleus of 12 CCRC at Cheddington. This was to be the B-24 training station and the intention was to use the 44th Group, then on route to the UK, as the flying element in a similar way to which the 92nd was being employed. General Eaker changed this plan on 9th September when it became known that there was no likelihood of further Liberator groups reaching the 8th Air Force for some months. As 1st Wing had no airfield ready for occupation by the 44th it was temporarily stationed at Cheddington until transferred to the 2nd Wing area in October. In fact, Cheddington did not function as a CCRC until June 1943 and had what amounted to no more than a holding unit for many months.

Ground schools were set up at Bovingdon and key men from the five new heavy bomb groups arriving during the autumn of 1942 were sent for a period ranging from a few days to two weeks to receive instruction. While the syllabus was frequently amended, the broad function of all bomber CCRCs remained the same, firstly assessing the state of training of an individual for his assigned duties and then to give him instruction in equipment and procedures pertinent to operating from the UK. Ground schools instructed pilots in the RAF flying control system, Standard Beam Approach (for bad weather landings) and various radio and visual aids. Additionally, the flight assembly and formation procedures, peculiar to 8th Air Force, were taught. Navigators were schooled in the use of British maps and radio and visual aids to navigation. Radio operators were given a thorough grounding in radio aids and cyphers. All gunners received an intensive course in aircraft recognition and practice in the use of their weapons.

The Fortresses at Bovingdon were utilised for navigational, formation and flying control procedure flights. A few were also used to test modifications and other trials work for VIII BC and

A general weakness in the training of most pilots received from the US was instrument flying. The Link Trainer, available at many 8AF combat bases, crudely simulated blind flying conditions and was used in the effort to improve pilot capability. Here Bovingdon instructor passes directions to a student in the Link by interphone while monitoring his performance by desk instruments. August 1943.

VIII AFSC. The 92nd Group crews became a reserve, some being transferred to operational groups as combat replacements. Additionally, on three occasions 11 CCRC was called upon to provide both aircraft and crews to participate in combat missions to boost the VIII BC strike force. It was planned that eventually 92nd Group would be rebuilt and become a combat organisation again, a move given impetus by the discovery that the actual flying requirement of a CCRC could be handled by a single squadron. Indeed, it was not until January 1943 that the first batch of 21 replacement bomber crews arrived at Bovingdon from the United States, prior to which the facilities were somewhat underused.

On 7 January the 92nd Group with three squadrons was moved to Alconbury, leaving the 326th Bomb Squadron on detached service at Bovingdon to act as the school flying unit. With arrival of several new bomb groups during the spring of 1943 facilities at Bovingdon were temporarily overwhelmed and Cheddington functioned as an overflow station. However, both bases were able to handle VIII BC heavy bomber training requirements satisfactorily until the autumn of that year.

During the winter of 1942–43 bomber crew training was predominantly for B-17 crewmen. There were only two B-24 groups with the 8th Air Force and for most of that period one was detached to North Africa. Nevertheless, there was need to improve the state of training of Liberator aircrews in matters which could not be satisfactorily achieved by the general course at Bovingdon. In March 1943 the 2nd Bomb Wing set up a Provisional Training Center at Hethel. Initially only ground

schooling was available and the first two classes totalling 83 men completed an aerial gunner course in April. These were men who previously performed ground duties in 2nd Wing and who had volunteered to fly because of the acute shortage of replacement aircrews. During May and June replacement crews from the United States were received at Hethel and given six days' ground training – the theatre indoctrination course. Additionally pilots from the two combat groups in the Wing received instruction in Standard Beam Approach and both pilots and navigators took refresher courses in British visual and radio aids.

Hethel had become the unofficial CCRC for B-24 crews but it was still VIII BC's intention that Cheddington should eventually handle this task and steps were finally taken in June to effect this. However, 2nd Wing's Provisional Training Center endured. A few crews and aircraft of the 44th and 93rd Groups were left behind when these groups moved to North Africa for the Ploesti raid. To keep these remaining crews in training the Center moved to Hardwick where all crews and B-24s were concentrated. Despite most of the instructors being transferred to Cheddington early in July, the organisation functioned in its new role until the combat groups returned from North Africa in late August. Although most B-24 replacement crews were passing through Cheddington by this time, it was felt that additional training, particularly in flight procedures, would benefit them and on 23 October 2nd Wing's Provisional Training Center was brought to life again, this time at Attlebridge. Using a dozen B-24Ds and some personnel of the about-to-be-disbanded 19th Antisubmarine Squadron, extra training for replacement crews was conducted from this airfield until Christmas. The organisation was finally disbanded on 26 December 1943 when facilities at Cheddington and a new CCRC in Ireland were providing an expanded programme of pre-combat training.

The arrival of B-26 Marauder units in March 1943 brought a requirement for a medium bomber CCRC. The 3rd Wing wanted to set up such an organisation at Rattlesden but VIII BC insisted that for the time being B-26 crews should use existing facilities

Above: **Veteran B-17F *Annie Freeze* was the first B-17 received by No 12 CCRC at Cheddington, still displaying the marking of its former operators, 381st BG, when it arrived in late June 1943. It was used for high-altitude oxygen training flights.** (via P. Carty)

Below: **Individual combat groups devised their own training equipment. This rig was constructed in a blister hangar at Kimbolton utilising chin, ball and top turrets, and nose side positions, from wrecked B-17s. Projected film provided target images and aim was checked with a recorder. April 1944.**

Right: **Lt Stirling May, 379th BG Gunnery Officer, also had a B-17 top turret fitted to the floor of a truck. While the vehicle was in motion, gunners practised their aim against aircraft flying over the airfield. Aircraft in background are from 1st Division Hq Flight, resident at Kimbolton in April 1944.**

at Bovingdon. With the presence of three more B-26 groups and the commencement of full scale combat operations with this type, a special training centre to handle replacement crews became a priority, and in July it was proposed to use the recently opened Toome airfield in Northern Ireland for this purpose.

On 23 August 1943 the 2902nd CCRC Group (Bombardment) (Provisional) was activated there together with the 2905th Replacement and Training Squadron, although it was not until 20 September that the school opened and the first men arrived for training. For flying purposes the station initially received the short-wing B-26Bs that had equipped the 322nd Group when it first arrived in England. By November there was a total of 32 B-26s and four Havocs on strength and more than 50 crews in training. Even though B-26 combat groups had been transferred to the 9th Air Force in the previous month, the 8th Air Force continued to handle all operational training for replacement crews.

The designation of the Toome CCRC was in line with the reorganisation of establishments and the use of four-digit numbers for provisional units that occurred in August 1943. Bovingdon became the 2900th CCRC Group and Cheddington the 2901st CCRC Group although more commonly they continued to be referred to by the original designations. However, early in November the long awaited Tables of Organisation were approved and the provisional designations discontinued. On 12 November 1943 the Bovingdon and Cheddington organisa-

tion became Nos 1 and 2 CCRCs respectively, and shortly thereafter Toome became No 3 CCRC.

Toome was the first CCRC station of Composite Command to come into full scale operation and at long last this Command assumed the primary function for which it was activated 14 months previously. CCRCs were set up at four other airfields in Northern Ireland: Cluntoe, which was acquired at the end of August, Greencastle, Maghaberry and Mullaghmore. In November No 4 CCRC was activated at Cluntoe to provide an additional source for training B-17 replacement crews. No 5 CCRC was established at Greencastle in December for B-24 fliers and in the same month No 6 CCRC was activated at Mullaghmore for bomber training activities. Maghaberry was originally to have been the seventh CCRC but as there was currently no requirement for this additional centre the airfield became the base for ferrying squadrons of VIII Air Service Command engaged in ferrying new aircraft from storage parks in Northern Ireland to England. Extra hardstandings for use as aircraft storage parks were planned for most VIII AFCC bases in Ulster, eventually only being constructed at Langford Lodge, Greencastle, Toome and Mullaghmore.

Although there was an influx of new heavy bomber groups for 8th Air Force during the winter of 1943–44, crew training was of a very much higher standard than with those received in the previous winter. In consequence, this, together with the smaller ultimate size of 8th Air Force due to the diversion of 15 of its new groups to Italy, rendered Composite Command's facilities in excess of requirements. It followed that when 8th Air Force sought to form a new provisional reconnaissance organisation and was again confronted with the requirement of obtaining an authorised Table of Organisation, use was made of the under-employed CCRCs in Northern Ireland.

In a reorganisation of VIII AFCC on 20 February 1944, Nos 5 and 6 CCRCs were transferred – on paper – to Cheddington while their personnel joined other units at Greencastle and Mullaghmore. No 4 CCRC at Cluntoe, having by this date processed 57 B-17 crews, was also transferred – on paper – to Cheddington while its 4th Replacement and Training Squadron was re-established at Greencastle to operate for the B-24 Gunnery School there. No 2 CCRC at Cheddington was moved to Cluntoe which then became a predominantly B-24 CCRC. Mullaghmore and Maghaberry were gradually run down and remaining units transferred elsewhere. Greencastle continued to function as the B-24 gunnery school from whence B-17s towed triple sleeve targets over the Derryogue coastal range where turrets mounting .50 weapons were situated. While the reorganisation reduced VIII AFCC operations in Northern Ireland, at the same date it finally acquired control of the bomber and fighter training airfields in England, together with the B-17 gunnery school at Snettisham. With the larger proportion of its training administration now in England, Hq Composite Command moved from Lurgan to Cheddington.

By the spring of 1944 the flying requirement of bomber CCRCs had been reduced and the four stations were operating with the following strengths in June 1944: 1 CCRC – 13 B-17; 2 CCRC – 7 B-17, 11 B-24 and 7 A-35; 3 CCRC – 27 B-26 and 12 AT-23; 4 R&T Sqdn – 2 B-17.

FIGHTER TRAINING ESTABLISHMENTS

Because the first USAAF fighter groups to arrive in Britain were required to operate within the RAF fighter control system, the three fighter stations and their satellite airfields occupied by the first arrivals became in effect training bases. In the original allocation of fighter airfields to VIII FC, Atcham, Goxhill and Eglinton plus their satellites were the intended operational stations, but their location, far from the cross-Channel area of offensive fighter action, ruled out use for operations. Thus VIII FC quickly came to use these stations for preparing new groups for operations prior to movement to bases in the south or south-east. In the first allocation of fighter training bases in August 1942, Atcham and Goxhill, plus satellites, were listed as staging posts while two airfields in Northern Ireland were also to be made available as fighter CCRC.

After the first flush of new fighter groups had departed for North Africa with the 12th Air Force, VIII Fighter Command found that Atcham and Goxhill were all that were necessary for its operational training requirements and the two satellites, High Ercall and Kirton, were returned to the RAF. The policy was to use Goxhill as a reception base for processing new units and in the year from December 1942 four such fighter groups received combat preparation at this station. Atcham was to be developed as an operational training unit, principally to process replacement pilots – although the term 'combat crew replacement center' was not used by VIII FC. The 6th Fighter Wing, originally sent to England to act as a headquarters for fighter groups, had been placed at Atcham in late August 1942 and became the controlling unit at this airfield. In November, the 109th Observation Squadron of the 67th Observation Group moved into Atcham to serve as the flying unit operating the OTU, with four experienced Spitfire pilots the original instructors. During that month a few Spitfire Vs were received and the training organisation was built up. Initially their activity concerned converting US pilots to Spitfires. By February Atcham had 40 Spitfire V, 5 Miles Master, 5 P-39M, 3 L-4B and a Lysander on strength. A tow-target flight was formed that month using Lysander tugs obtained from the British, operating from Llanbedr on the Welsh coast towing sleeves for Atcham fighters.

With Spitfire units converting to P-47 Thunderbolts and the knowledge that this type would henceforth predominate in VIII FC, Atcham prepared for change. As P-47s could be spared by the operational units, numbers at Atcham were built up and two provisional squadrons formed, enabling the Spitfire equipped 109th Obs Sqdn to return to its parent group at Membury in May. With the revised designation system for 8th Air Force provisional units introduced in August 1943, the controlling organisation at Atcham became the 2906th Observation Training Group (Fighter) (Provisional) replacing the 6th Fighter Wing, which was later disbanded. The two flying units were designated 2908th and 2909th Single Engine Flying Training Squadron (F) (P). These cumbersome provisional designations were in short use as authorised Tables of Organisation and approved designations came from Washington after seven weeks. The Group became the 495th Fighter Training Group and the squadrons 551st and 552nd Fighter Training Squadrons. It was planned that the 495th would handle all P-47 replacement training for both 8th and 9th Air Forces and that the 496th Fighter Training Group would be formed at Goxhill to provide a similar syllabus for P-38 and P-51 pilots.

The 496th Group was actually activated at Greencastle, but this was purely an administrative move with a minimum staff. On 27 December 1943 the Group was transferred to Goxhill, less all personnel, where its physical formation took place over the next few weeks. The two flying squadrons activated at the same time were the 554th FTS to handle P-38s and the 555th FTS to fly the P-51. Training classes commenced on 3 January 1944. At first there was an acute shortage of P-51Bs with which to conduct training and the position did not improve until the spring. In February 1944 VIII Composite Command was given control of both Atcham and Goxhill, promptly identifying these stations as Nos 7 and 8 CCRC, although the existing unit designations remained unchanged. At both fighter establishments courses lasted two to four weeks with frequently nearly double the number of trainee pilots on hand above the 250 planned.

The total of aircraft operated by 495th Group rose to nearly 70 by June 1944. For flying training purposes the aircraft were divided into four 'squadrons' identified as A and B (aircraft assigned to 551st FTS) and C and D (aircraft assigned to 552nd FTS) which were further identified by the P-47 cowlings and rudders being painted a different colour: A – blue, B – white, C – red and D – yellow. At this time the 496th Group had a strength of 24 P-38H/J and 30 P-51B fighters. With the conversion of several 8th Air Force groups from P-47s and P-38s to P-51s, there was an increased demand for P-51 replacement pilot training and in August 1944 P-38 training was transferred from the 496th to the 495th where Squadron A received 18 Lightnings. However, the P-47 total was not diminished, those displaced in Squadron A being transferred to the other units. Goxhill increased its P-51 complement to 65 in the same month.

Below: **The accident rate in the fighter training groups was high. One reason was the well-worn aircraft inherited from combat groups, usually after they had been reduced to 'war-weary' status. The pilot of 551st FS P-47D, 42-22543 had a lucky escape when after engine failure he was forced to belly-in through a hedge into a field of hay grass, June 1944.**

Above right: **The 496th FTG provide conversion training for pilots destined to fly PR Spitfires with 7th PG at Mount Farm. Clipped-wing Spitfire VC, W3815 was one of the aircraft used for this purpose at Goxhill.** (via P. Green)

Below right: **Night Leaflet Squadron mechanics at Cheddington receive instruction on revised oxygen systems from a Mobile Training Unit team. B-17F 42-3181, *Flak Alley Lil'* exhibits night camouflage.**

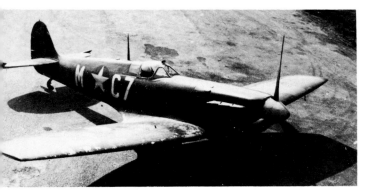

The accident rate at both Goxhill and Atcham was high, at the latter particularly so, as between 1 January and 31 October 1944 157 aircraft were involved in 137 accidents, resulting in 37 fatalities. Staff at Atcham considered that much was due to the generally poor standard of training pilots had received in the States prior to reaching Atcham. Another factor was the extremely hilly terrain around the airfield and the frequent low cloud which demanded constant caution.

DISSOLUTION OF COMPOSITE COMMAND

Following the cross-Channel invasion and deployment of many 9th Air Force units on the Continent, 8th Air Force planned to move CCRCs closer to its combat bases in south-east England. No 3 was to move to Welford, No 2 to Aldermaston, No 7 to Chalgrove and No 8 to Membury. That this was never realised was due to a major change in operational training policy. The 8th Air Force, no stranger to providing units to build other organisations, was in September 1944 once more subject to such depletion. USSTAF wished to form an Air Disarmament Command with a brief to disarm captured enemy air units, handle captured equipment and its disposal, and obtain technical intelligence from the Luftwaffe and the German aviation industry. Personnel and units having to be found to man this new Command led to the disbandment of Composite Command to use its remaining authorised units for this purpose. Thereafter theatre indoctrination and specialised training became the responsibility of combat groups and before participating in

operations replacement crews underwent a period of instruction at the combat group to which they were assigned.

During September training activities ceased at Cheddington, Toome, Cluntoe and Greencastle and their aircraft were flown to base Air Depots for disposal. No 1 CCRC was closed in October and under the new Air Disarmament Command Nos 1 and 2 CCRCs eventually moved to Boreham and Chipping Ongar prior to going to the Continent. The fighter training groups were re-assigned to the 1st and 2nd Bomb Divisions and moved to Cheddington and Halesworth. The 495th Group was, in fact, merely a headquarters staff in this move, P-47 training terminating by the end of 1944 and the aircraft being placed in storage. The 496th Group's 555th FTS did survive as an active flying unit until the early spring of 1945 before being disbanded.

To overcome the loss of Atcham and Goxhill, each 8th Air Force fighter group formed an OTU flight which adhered to a proper training syllabus and had use of a number of 'war-weary' P-47s and P-51s. Although not a general requirement until October 1944, there were such training flights in some groups as early as the previous May. While the OTU placed an additional work load on operational fighter bases, the system was soon preferred as a fighter pilot fresh from United States training grounds could be moulded to the particular operational procedures of the group with which he was eventually destined for combat.

MOBILE TRAINING UNITS

The frequent production changes to aircraft and equipment often caused difficulties in the combat theatres in that personnel were not trained to deal with these new developments. To overcome the problem, 8th Air Force requested teams of specially trained personnel who could be sent from base to base giving instruction. Known as Mobile Training Units, the first of these proved so useful during the spring of 1944 that in June 8th Air Force planned for 16 specialising in specific aircraft types or equipment. The personnel for each were trained in the US on the latest technical developments and then spent 60–90 days in the UK with an MTU. At the end of that period they were replaced by another team from the US, so that the instruction provided continually kept abreast of new technology. In August 1944 the Divisions were given control of the MTUs, each being lodged at a combat base as required.

COMBAT CREW REPLACEMENT CENTRES

No 1 CCRC
Activated under VIII BC as No 11 CCRC on 27 Aug 1942 at Bovingdon.
Reorganised 16 Aug 1943 with activation of 2900th CCRC Group (B) (P) and 2903rd Replacement & Training Squadron.
Regularised 12 Nov 1943 as No 1 CCRC with 1st R & T Sqdn (B). No 11 CCRC discontinued.
Assigned VIII AFCC 14 Feb 1944.
Assigned Air Disarmament Command, USSTAF 16 Sep 1944 and re-established Chipping Ongar with new personnel and no aircraft.
Principal aircraft: B-17E Aug 42 – summer 43; B-17F summer 43 – summer 44; B-17G winter 43 – Sep 44.

No 2 CCRC
Activated under VIII BC as No 12 CCRC on 27 Aug 1942 at Cheddington.
Opened for training 8 June 1943.
Reorganised 16 Aug 1943 as 2901st CCRC Group (B) (P) with 2904th R & T Sqdn.
Regularised 15 Nov 1943 as No 2 CCRC with 2nd R & T Sqdn (B). No 11 CCRC discontinued.
Assigned VII AFCC 14 Feb 1944.
Transferred Cluntoe 28 Feb 1944 less personnel and equipment. (Redesignation of No 4 CCRC.)
Assigned ADC, USSTAF 16 Sep 1944 and re-established at Boreham with new personnel.
Principal aircraft: B-17E & F June 43 – Sep 43; B-24D, H & J Sep 43 – Sep 44.

No 3 CCRC
Activated under VIII AFCC as 2902nd CCRC Group with 2905th R & T Sqdn (B) (P) on 23 Aug 1943 at Toome.
Regularised 21 Nov 1943 as No 3 CCRC and 3rd R & T Sqdn (B).
Assigned Air Disarmament Command 16 Sept 1943.
Principal aircraft: B-26B & C Aug 43 – Sep 44. Also AT-23 & A-20.

No 4 CCRC
Activated under VIII AFCC as 2915th CCRC Group on 1 Oct 1943 at Cluntoe.
Regularised as No 4 CCRC with 4th R & T Sqdn (B) on 23 Nov 1943.
Transferred Cheddington less personnel and equipment 28 Feb 1944. (Redesignation of No 2 CCRC.) 4th R & T Sqdn transferred to Greencastle.
At Cheddington No 2 CCRC functioned as a TO for radar and personal equipment schools.
Disbanded 5 Oct 1944.
Principal aircraft: B-17 Nov 43 – Feb 44.

No 5 CCRC
Activated under VIII AFCC in Dec 1943 as No 5 CCRC with 5th R & T Sqdn (B) at Greencastle.
Transferred Cheddington less personnel and equipment 20 Feb 1944.
Transferred Watton 12 Apr 1944 to provide a TO for 8th RW and 8th RG (P).
Inactivated 9 Aug 1944.

No 6 CCRC
Activated under VIII AFCC as No 6 CCRC with 6th R & T Sqdn on 16 December at Mullaghmore.
Transferred Cheddington less personnel and equipment 20 Feb 1944.
Transferred Watton 12 Apr 1944 to provide a TO for 8th RW and 8th RG (P).
Inactivated 9 Aug 1944.

No 7 CCRC
Organised as undesignated OTU under VIII FC at Atcham in Dec 1942. Used 6th Fighter Wing as an Hq and 109th Obs Sqdn as the flying unit.
Reorganised in May 1943 when 109th Obs Sqdn returned to parent group.
Reorganised 16 Aug 1943 as 2906th Observation Training Group (F) (P) with 2908th and 2909th Single Engine Fighter Training Sqdn (F) (P). The 6th FW disbanded Atcham 13 Sep 1943.
Regularised as 495th Fighter Training Group with 551st and 552nd FT Sqdns on 26 Oct 1943. (Redesignation of units.)
Assigned VIII AFCC 14 Feb 1944 when overall training establishment at Atcham designated No 7 CCRC without changes to existing unit designations.
Reassigned VIII FC 29 Sep 1944 with discontinuation of No 7 CCRC designation.
Assigned 1st Bomb Division 28 Nov 1944.
Moved Cheddington 15 Jan 1945 and reduced to an Hq.
Disbanded 21 Mar 1945.

No 8 CCRC
Activated by VIII AFCC on 11 Dec 1943 as 496th FTG with 554th and 555th FT Sqdns at Greencastle.
Assigned VIII FC and transferred less personnel to Goxhill 27 Dec 1943.
Assigned VIII AFCC on 14 Feb 1944 when overall training establishment at Goxhill designated No 8 CCRC without changes to existing unit designations.
Reassigned VIII FC 29 Sep 1944 with discontinuation of No 8 CCRC designation.
Assigned 2nd Bomb Division 28 Nov 1944 and reduced to an Hq with 555th FTS.
Moved Halesworth 15 Feb 1945, and later used as TO for 2nd Scouting Force.
Disbanded May 1945.

1st Combat Crew Gunnery School
Established under VIII BC at Snettisham in summer 1943 as a detachment of 2901st CCRC.
Activated as the Air Division Gunnery School on 12 Nov 1943 serving 1st Division.
Assigned VIII AFCC and redesignated 1st CCGS 14 Feb 1944.
Assigned VIII FC 29 Sep 1944.
Assigned 3rd Bomb Division 28 Nov 1944.
Disbanded Mar 1945.

Bombing and Gunnery Ranges

As the standard of training of bombardiers and air gunners left much to be desired, practice ranges were an early requirement of VIII BC. The RAF had a large number of ranges, predominantly in the western and northern areas of the UK, and several of these were offered for American use. An immediate problem was safety. The high altitude at which bombing and gunnery would be carried out increased the possibility of error and danger to civilians and property in the vicinity of ranges. Then the need for ranges within economical flying distance of airfields and avoiding interference with coastal defences restricted the number of available sites. As 8th Air Force grew in strength so did the problem of acquiring suitable ranges.

BOMBING RANGES

Bombing ranges originally provided by the Air Ministry were found to be too small in area both for safety and location from altitudes in excess of 20,000 feet. Only Breast Sands, in the south-east corner of The Wash, was acceptable to become the first range used by B-17s. Early missions by the Force revealed poor bombing results and intensified practice was undertaken whenever weather permitted during the winter of 1942–43. At least two additional ranges were required, but to reach those of suitable size round flights of 200–300 miles from bases were entailed. In conjunction with the frequently unfavourable weather, this resulted in aircraft being scattered at airfields throughout the west and north. As a result of further approaches, the Air Ministry offered Ot Moor in Oxfordshire which became available in April 1943. Additionally, Grassholm and Ynys-Gwylanfach islets, off the Pembrokeshire and Caernarvon coasts respectively, were allocated for use in the previous month. In the spring of 1943 13 ranges were scheduled for 8th Air Force use. Of these East Hatley, west of Cambridge, Redgrave Fen, near Diss, and Duck's Hall, six miles north-west of Sudbury, Suffolk, were used for low-level practice by B-26s of 3rd Wing. The radius of the danger areas at ranges used by the B-26s was from 500 to 650 yards, whereas the high level ranges were all in excess of 1000 yards.

In a rationalisation of range usage later in 1943, Breast Sands was allotted to 1st Division, Stockyard Green, between Milden and Lindsey, and Sutton Walks, near Woodbridge, both in Suffolk, to 2nd Division, and Tollesbury, near Maldon, Essex, to 3rd Division. Non-explosive M38 practice bombs were normally used on these ranges.

GUNNERY RANGES

The first air-to-air gunnery range used by VIII BG was 68A on the eastern side of The Wash near Snettisham. A second, shared with RAF Bomber Command, was made available at Jurby, Isle of Man, but it was considered too far from B-17 and B-24 bases for regular use. As the Wash range was inadequate for the growing force it was proposed to the Air Ministry in September 1942 that an over-water strip from Happisburgh to Southwold on the East Anglian coast could be utilised. Although RAF Fighter Command was concerned such an arrangement might complicate coastal defence against enemy air raids, in October the use of this stretch was approved, providing target sleeves were not towed closer to the shore line than a half mile and at altitudes of not more than 2000 feet. Thus restricted, VIII BC considered the range of limited value although later it was used extensively by 2nd Division B-24s and VIII FC aircraft. Early in 1943 another air-to-air gunnery range was made available on the west side of The Wash plus two more for use in cross-country exercises, one of Criccieth, North Wales, and the other over North Channel, between Scotland and Ireland.

Air gunners obtained ground-to-air practice first at Cornish coastal ranges and from autumn 1943 at Snettisham, near The Wash. On 12 November 1943 an Air Division Gunnery School was established there, providing such facilities at local ranges. This establishment catered for B-17 gunners, while those of B-24s received similar training at the Derryogue range in Northern Ireland.

The first air-to-air gunnery ranges for VIII FC, allotted in September 1942, were numbers 64A, located east of Holmpton, just north of the Humber estuary, and 23A to the west of Llanbedr in Tremadoc Bay. These served the fighter training stations at Goxhill and Atcham respectively.

The 68th Observation Group was initially the only unit requiring air-to-ground firing facilities and the RAF's Hilmarton site on the edge of the Marlborough Downs was assigned for this purpose on 5 January 1943. On 14 April 1943 the RAF air-to-ground range at Pepper Box Hill was also available for use by the Group's Spitfires and Havocs. Other ranges made available to VIII ASC in the spring of 1943 were Poole Bay for air-to-air, and Lambourn Downs for air-to-ground.

Until the late summer of 1943, the 8th Air Force Gunnery School used facilities at Mousehole, Cornwall where air gunners were sent for ground-to-air firing at towed targets. Water-cooled .50 guns were sited on the shore line, this one manned by Pfc Ken Chojnische.

Target Towing

When the first 8th Air Force flying units arrived in the United Kingdom they had no facilities for towing target sleeves for gunnery practice. As it was quickly evident that the standard of gunnery was poor in both bomber and fighter units, requests for assistance were made to the British. In response, during 1942 and 1943 the RAF made available a total of some 50 aircraft fitted out for target towing, mostly Westland Lysanders and older versions of the Douglas Havoc/Boston. One such aircraft was eventually assigned to each bomber group to fly for air-to-air firing over designated ranges off the English and Welsh coasts.

In the summer of 1943 the four B-26 groups that arrived in England received at least two, and in some cases three, ex-RAF Havocs or Lysanders to enable gunner performance to be improved. In addition to sleeves, British target gliders were also used during 1943. By the end of that year the volume of air traffic in the UK had increased to a point where air-to-air gunnery training for bomber crews had to be curtailed in operational units due to the congestion around ranges. Thereafter gunnery practice was confined chiefly to CCRC units until these ceased to function, by which time it was considered that new gunners were generally proficient from the training they received before coming overseas.

In VIII Fighter Command target towing for air-to-air gunnery was initially provided by special units flying from Llanbedr and Goxhill airfields close to the assigned ranges. Fighter groups sent detachments of pilots and aircraft to these airfields for short periods to engage in air-to-air firing against towed sleeves. The special units set up were originally known as the 1st and 2nd Provisional Gunnery Flights and assigned to the fighter training establishments at Atcham and Goxhill. The Atcham unit operated from Llanbedr as a lodger with the RAF. Both flights were initially equipped with four Lysanders and had complements of five officers and 30 enlisted men. In line with 8th Air Force's system of provisional designations, later in the month of their formation the units were redesignated as 2025th and 2031st Gunnery Flights. Formally authorised designations, the 1st and 2nd Gunnery and Tow Target Flights (Special) were bestowed in late August that year. The Atcham controlled flight moved to Warton in July 1943 and Templeton in December, continuing to use the Welsh coastal ranges. Lysanders and a Miles Master each were used by both flights until the Goxhill unit acquired six A-20B Havocs previously operated by the 67th Observation Group.

The 3rd Gunnery & Tow Target Flight (SP), activated at Goxhill on the last day of October 1943, acquired two Lysanders late in November and four more plus a Master after transferring to East Wretham in January 1944. Here it operated for VIII FC groups in air-to-air firing over The Wash ranges nearby. When the Lysanders were withdrawn in March, 'war-weary' P-47s were employed but the towing arrangement was not satisfactory. On 18 April the Flight received the first of six Vultee A-35B Vengeances that it was to be assigned. These two-seat aircraft, supplied to the RAF as dive bombers, were surplus to their requirements and converted into target tugs by the installation of light cable winches. Thirty were made available to 8th Air Force, those supplied to 3rd G&TT Flight still bearing their RAF roundels, which remained unchanged. This Flight retained their P-47s as gunnery aircraft raising their complement to 14 in June 1944, although their pilot strength was only six.

Whereas the first three tow target units served VIII FC, the 4th G&TT Flight was formed in December 1943 at Greencastle, Northern Ireland, to provide sleeve towing for the local CCRC units of Composite Command. Initially with a few Lysanders and ex-RAF Havocs, its complement grew to 14 in June 1944 – two Lysanders, five Havocs and seven A-35Bs – although the Lysanders and Havocs were soon withdrawn. Like the other flights only four or five pilots were on strength. Duties for the 4th G&TT Flight were chiefly towing for ground-to-air firing over the Derryogue coastal range used to train B-24 gunners. In February 1944 the 1st and 2nd G&TT Flights came under Composite Command control although their duties remained unchanged.

The A-35B Vengeance became the standard target tug for the gunnery flights in the spring of 1944, the 1st G&TT Flight receiving them and relinquishing its six Lysanders and single Master in July. The 2nd G&TT Flight, however, continued to keep its A-20Bs for some months.

Following a change of policy at the Atcham training establishment, the 1st G&TT Flight was moved from Wales to Sutton Bridge near The Wash. Here the unit commenced towing for ground-to-air firing under the Air Division Gunnery School at Snettisham, which had previously relied upon three Lysanders operating from RAF Docking. In the autumn of 1944, Composite Command was disbanded, and thereafter operational training was performed by the combat groups themselves. As a result, 4th G&TT Flight ceased to tow in September, its aircraft being disposed of at the end of that month when the unit moved to Chipping Ongar as a manning unit for Air Defence Command. The 1st and 2nd G&TT Flights were maintained and transferred to the 2nd and 3rd Bomb Divisions, respectively, in November. This brought moves into bases of these divisions, the 1st going to Little Walden, then to Halesworth, and the 2nd to Leiston.

During the final months of hostilities all three gunnery flights towed for air-to-air firing for the fighter groups of their respective divisions. However, the 1st also flew on the Kessingland range for B-24 gunners of 20th Combat Wing. Basically, the same procedure for air-to-air firing with fighters was followed during the whole period of operation. A small number of fighters would come to the tow target flight base and operate from there for a week's practice. Pilots would be briefed together and take off to follow the tug to ensure continuous visual contact and maintain safety. Ammunition loaded had different coloured bullets for each participating fighter, with the paint used marking the target sleeve. Firing passes were always pointed away from land, with attack instructions given by the pilot of the tow target aircraft, conducted in good visibility and never above 2000 feet. The standard sleeve was 20 ft long, but with the introduction of gyro-computing gunsights the length was increased to 30 ft for use with deflection shots. During the final period of towing activities each of the three flights had similar equipment – six A-35s, three P-47s and one A-20, while personnel averaged seven officers and 33 enlisted men per Flight.

The 1st and 2nd G&TT Flights were quickly disbanded in the final weeks of the war, their demise chiefly due to most individual fighter groups performing their own tow target activities. Following the break-up of the CCRC training units in Ireland, a number of AT-23B Marauder tugs became available in England and were distributed to fighter groups. Additionally, P-47s were used to tow sleeves using an extended cable to fly the sleeve straight off the runway, cable and sleeve being jettisoned before landing.

Top right: **The 2nd G & TT Flt's A-20B, 41-3983 over an east coast town. The tow cable attachment point can be seen under the rear fuselage.** (P. Green)

Centre right: **The 3rd G & TT Flt was given a few P-47s for target-towing as replacements for its ageing Lysanders. They were not satisfactory due to difficulty with sleeve cable attachment and damage to rudder. This example formerly served with 78th FG.** (P. Green)

Right: **A-35A FD217 taking off from Leiston. The type became 8th Air Force's principal tow-target aircraft from the spring of 1944.** (J. Gasser)

GUNNERY AND TOW TARGET FLIGHTS

1st G & TT Flt

Activated 1 Feb 1943 as 1st Provisional Gunnery Flight to serve the Atcham fighter training establishment of VIII FC. Redesignated 2025th Gunnery Flight (P) with an establishment of 5 officers and 34 enlisted men on 24 Feb 1943. Redesignated as 1st G & TT Flt (SP) on 26 Aug 1943. Assigned 14 Feb 1944 to VIII AFCC; 29 Sep 1944 to VIII FC; and 19 Nov 1944 to 65th FW, 2nd Bomb Division. Disbanded May 1945.

Bases		Aircraft	
Atcham	1 Feb 43 – 3 Mar 43	Lysander	Feb 43 – Jul 44
Llanbedr	3 Mar 43 – 6 Jul 43	Master	Mar 43 – Jul 44
Warton	6 Jul 43 – 14 Dec 43	A-35B	May 44 – Apr 45
Templeton	14 Dec 43 – 8 May 44	P-47D	Nov 44 – Apr 45
Atcham	8 May 44 – 10 May 44	A-20B	Nov 44 – Apr 45
Sutton Bridge	10 May 44 – 21 Nov 44	AT-23B	Jan 45 – Apr 45
Little Walden	21 Nov 44 – 10 Jan 45		
Halesworth	10 Jan 45 – May 45		

At Llanbedr, Templeton and Sutton Bridge the unit was a lodger with the RAF.

Commanding Officers	
Cpt Woodrow Hopkins	Jan 43 – Dec 43
Cpt Norman V. Crabtree	Dec 43 – 7 Aug 44
Cpt Roger L. Swain Jr	7 Aug 44 – 6 Nov 44
Cpt William F. Genheimer	9 Nov 44 – Apr 45

While Cpt Crabtree was on DS with RAF Typhoon sqdn in France 24 Jun to 7 Aug, 1/Lt Glenn F. Windell was acting CO.

2nd G & TT Flt

Activated 1 Feb 1943 as 2nd Provisional Gunnery Flight to serve the Goxhill fighter training establishment of VIII FC. Redesignated 2031st Gunnery Flight (P) on 24 Feb 1943 and as 2nd G & TT Flt (SP) on 26 Aug 1943. Assigned to VIII AFCC on 14 Feb 1944; to VIII FC on 29 Sep 1944; and to 66th FW, 3rd Bomb Division on 18 Nov 1944. Disbanded Apr 1945.

Bases		Aircraft	
Goxhill	1 Feb 43 – 18 Nov 44	Lysander	Feb 43 – May 44
Leiston	18 Nov 44 – Apr 45	Master	Apr 43 – Jul 44
		A-20B	Oct 43 – Apr 45
Commanding Officers		A-35B	Nov 44 – Apr 45
Cpt Dorsey L. Martin	Feb 43 – Nov 44	P-47D	Nov 44 – Mar 45
1/Lt Augusto M. Govoni	Nov 44 – 8 Apr 45	AT-23B	Oct 44 – Nov 44
1/Lt Alvin Levine	8 Apr 45 – Late Apr 45		

3rd G & TT Flt

Activated 31 Oct 1943 at Goxhill to serve VIII FC. Assigned 1st Bomb Division 15 Sep 1944. Disbanded Oct 1945.

Bases		Aircraft	
Goxhill	31 Oct 43 – 20 Jan 44	Lysander	Nov 43 – Mar 44
East Wretham	20 Jan 44 – Oct 45	Master	Feb 44 – Dec 44
		P-47D	Mar 44 – Sep 45
Commanding Officer		A-35B	Apr 44 – Sep 45
Cpt William R. Wallace	31 Oct 43 – Sep 45	A-20B	Nov 44 – Sep 45
		AT-23B	Summer 44

4th G & TT Flt

Activated 3 Dec 1943 at Greencastle to serve VIII AFCC B-24 gunnery school. Assigned Air Disarmament Command, USSTAF Sep 1944 as a manning unit. Transferred Chipping Ongar and later to the Continent.

Bases		Aircraft	
Greencastle	3 Dec 43 – 30 Sep 44	Havoc I & II	Dec 43 – Sep 44
		Lysander	Dec 43 – Jul 44
Commanding Officers		A-35B	May 44 – Sep 44
1/Lt John Teling	3 Dec 43 – 20 Dec 43		
1/Lt William C. Slade	20 Dec 43 – 7 Jan 44		
2/Lt Edward J. Krause	7 Jan 44 – 12 Jan 44		
2/Lt Harold A. Sabin	12 Jan 44 – 2 Mar 44		
1/Lt Edwin D. Woeliner	2 Mar 44 – 6 Aug 44		
1/Lt George W. Cowgill	6 Aug 44 – Sep 44		

Logistics and Other Support Services

Maintenance and Supply

For every combatant in 8th Air Force there were 20 personnel in a supporting ground role. The scale of the 8th Air Force's combat operations required an enormous logistical back-up and while the original strength planned was never realised, the service and supply organisation built up in the United Kingdom was unsurpassed in any other theatre of war. VIII Air Force Service Command (VIII AFSC) was the agency directly responsible to 8th Air Force for service and supply but it also served two other masters: Air Service Command in the United States and Services of Supply, European Theatre of Operations. Air Service Command in the United States scheduled equipment and supplies plus providing guidance on technical matters and to some extent dictated policy. Services of Supply, ETO, had

overall control of logistics for both land and air forces in the UK, but as it was concerned largely with shipping, port, and storage matters at a higher level, VIII AFSC had a high degree of autonomy. Nevertheless, during the 8th Air Force's campaign supply and maintenance organisation was subject to many changes, most units suffering more than one redesignation and reassignment.

Mechanics of 332nd Service Squadron put a new R-2800 on Capt James Cooper's *Hellza Poppin*, P-47C 41-6361, Duxford, September 1943. Engine changes were a frequent task for some service squadrons. On a P-47 it was usually a 12-hour job, depending on the help available.

SERVICE AT COMBAT AIRFIELDS

The early arrangements for the procurement of depots and other facilities from the British were conducted by the Services of Supply, VIII AFSC Headquarters being allocated some of these when established alongside that of 8th Air Force at Bushy Park in July 1942. While arrangements were made to place the substantial number of service units expected to arrive during the summer of 1942, a system of organisation was arranged varying from that prescribed by USAAF Hq. Aircraft maintenance had been classified as four distinct functional levels. That known as first echelon was the servicing that could be performed by the air crew, second echelon maintenance was that provided by the ground crew of the combat unit to which an aircraft was assigned, third echelon was more or less a mobile organisation with specialist teams and heavier equipment to handle such things as engine changes and component replacement, while fourth echelon was major overhaul and substantial specialist engineering carried out at the rear depot. In the cause of efficiency, 8th Air Force Hq decided that third echelon maintenance units would be assigned to the combat commands – bomber, fighter and air support. Instead of following normal procedure for third echelon maintenance where service group units operated from a service centre to serve three or four airfields, the group was divided between and stationed at two airfields on a more or less permanent basis. Further, the service element and all other support units would come under the station commander – who was normally the flying group commander. Only fourth echelon maintenance remained VIII AFSC's responsibility and was met with two types of depot: an advanced depot serving a number of operational airfields, and rear base depots which could carry out major modification and other engineering work with near factory type facilities. While decisions on this organisation were taken in June 1942, nearly a year passed before a general conformity of service and supply organisation in 8th Air Force was achieved. By this date a bomber, troop carrier, fighter or reconnaissance base had, in addition to the combat group and its three or four squadrons, a headquarters and headquarters' squadron of a service group or a detachment from it, one service squadron, a quartermaster company and chemical, signal and military police detachments.

At some stations the headquarters of a detachment would also be present and there might be detachments from other types of unit, such as finance or infantry. The total personnel of

---

SERVICE GROUPS AND SERVICE SQUADRONS SERVING FIGHTER GROUPS

Fighter Group	Service Group	Service Squadron
4	33A	45
20	97	384
55	97A	315
56	33	41
78	79	84
339	314A	464
352	1A	17
353	79A	378
355	1	5
356	85A	394
357	50	469
359	85	395
361	50A	468
364	314	467
479	331	364
495	333	356
496	333A	332

The 78FG was originally served by 333ASG and 332SS while 496FTG was served by 79SG and 84SS. When 496FTG was transferred from VIII FC to VIII AFCC in February 1944 the designations of service units at Duxford and Goxhill were exchanged to avoid splitting a service group between two commands.

SUB-DEPOTS SERVING 8AF BOMB GROUPS

The original 26 were:

440SD – 482BG		
441SD – 91BG	450SD – 401BG	459SD –448BG
442SD – 305BG	451SD – 96BG	460SD – 446BG
443SD – 384BG	452SD – 388BG	461SD – 93BG
444SD – 303BG	453SD – 94BG	462SD – 445BG
445SD – 379BG	454SD – 447BG	463SD – 389BG
446SD – 92BG	455SD – 385BG	464SD – 44BG
447SD – 351BG	456SD – 100BG	465SD – 392BG
448SD – 381BG	457SD – 95BG	
449SD – 306BG	458SD – 390BG	

Remainder formed during first half of 1944:

466SD – 452BG	471SD – 487BG	476SD – 491BG
467SD – 453BG	472SD – 466BG	477SD – 490BG
468SD – 457BG	473SD – 486BG	478SD – 398BG
469SD – 458BG	474SD – 489BG	479SD – 492BG
470SD – 467BG	475SD – 34BG	480SD – 493BG

service and support units on a combat base varied between 500 and 550 in the spring of 1943. The increase of combat strength in aircraft and crews during the winter of 1943–44 required increases in ground personnel, and by the summer of 1944 these averaged 700 men. This meant that the total personnel, combat and support, on a fighter station rose from 1400 in spring 1943 to 1600 by spring 1945, while for bombers the average figures increased from 2000 to 2600. With each combat base having service units assigned on a permanent basis and under the commander of the combat group CO, there was a general merging of personnel from various units, both service and combat, in performing specific duties. A man assigned to a service squadron might find himself regularly working with a ground team from a combat squadron on some specialised item of aircraft maintenance. The reverse was also true. There was also considerable flexibility as to who carried out third echelon maintenance and often this would be done by a mobile team from the local air depot. Within reason, in aircraft maintenance, bomb and ammunition handling, supply, transportation and many other ground duties there was no enforced demarcation for base component units, any more than there was in the actual tasks undertaken by individuals. Much depended on the pressure of work and the skills involved.

In the autumn of 1943 a reorganisation of VIII AFSC took place, primarily to improve work throughput. Among the changes was the Command's re-establishment of control of service units on bomber bases. The service group headquarters detachment, its service squadron and other elements were absorbed by newly activated sub-depots. The sub-depots were assigned to VIII AFSC which could exercise technical control of maintanance done by personnel through instructions and supervision. Although not assigned to the bomber group a sub-depot was under command of the combat commander. The situation on fighter bases remained unchanged, primarily because it was expected that fighter groups would eventually move to the Continent and each needed a more cohesive arrangement for its service elements. While the creation of sub-depots undoubtedly made a clear division between service and combat group ground crew responsibilities, in practice there was still a good deal of co-operation. The guideline for

combat squadron ground men was not to undertake any engineering task that required more than 36 hours. Eventually, on 8 December 1944, all sub-depots were assigned to the three Divisions, VIII AFSC retaining only technical supervision.

A further change in the structure of combat base service organisation occurred near the end of the war. As of 16 April 1945 an Air Service Group headquarters was activated at each 8th Air Force station to control all service, supply and support activities. Assigned to it were all units on the station other than the combat units. In some instances new service squadrons were activated. There was, however, no change of personnel or duties, the new system of designations being aimed at bringing some overall conformity to Air Service Command units.

A typical 8th Air Force heavy bomber group complement is shown for Chelveston, 10 May 1943:

Unit	Officers	Enlisted Men
Hq 305th Bomb Group	18	36
364th Bomb Squadron	59	316
365th Bomb Squadron	55	317
366th Bomb Squadron	60	310
422nd Bomb Squadron	57	313
Hq & Hq Sqdn 325th Service Gp (less detachment)	17	85
343rd Service Sqdn	6	205
1121st Quartermaster Company Service Group (less detachment)	1	35
876th Chemical Company (less detachment)	1	40
1632nd Ordnance Maintenance Company (Aviation)	2	38
Detachment A, 983rd MP Company Aviation	3	49
Detachment 105, 18th Weather Sqdn	2	7
8th Station Gas Defense Detachment (P)	0	4
Detachment B, Hq & Hq Sqdn 304th Service Group (Finance)	1	7
	282	1762

At this date the plan was to eventually build up bomber stations to have 2742 personnel when additional aircraft and air crews were assigned. In May 1943 the 305th Group's aircraft complement was 12 plus three reserves per squadron. On this base personnel from the various units were pooled for mess, transport, intelligence, operations, flying control and armament specialist duties.

Sub-depots had the responsibility for removing aircraft wrecks obstructing the airfield. When the left main undercarriage leg failed on landing, 486th BG's *Monty* ended up just off the main runway. Damaged beyond economical repair, the B-24H was quickly dismantled by 473rd Sub-depot using a heavy mobile crane.

Typical 8th Air Force fighter group complement is shown for Debden, 30 April 1943:

Unit	Officers	Enlisted Men
Hq 4th Fighter Group	22	51
334th Fighter Squadron	36	245
335th Fighter Squadron	38	242
336th Fighter Squadron	39	245
Detachment A, Hq & Hq Sqdn 33rd Service Group	20	60
45th Service Sqdn	2 (WO)	209
Detachment B, 1148th Quartermaster Company Aviation	0	19
102nd Station Gas Defense Detachment (P)	0	4
Detachment A, 1085th Ordnance Company Aviation (AB)	0	16
Detachment A, 1631st Ordnance (Motor Maintenance) Company Aviation	1	18
Detachment A, 1030th Signal Company Service Group	1	30
	159	1139

As with the bomber stations there was a pooling of personnel for many ground services.

ADVANCED AND STRATEGIC AIR DEPOTS

The first major service unit to arrive in England was the 2nd Air Depot Group, placed at Molesworth airfield in May 1942 to establish the short-lived 1st Mobile Air Depot, for after only a few weeks' residence 2 ADG moved to the Warrington area.

Prior to the decision to place field service units under the command of combat groups, a plan had been drawn up whereby service groups responsible for third echelon maintenance were to be based at ten bomber and three fighter airfields with extra accommodation and workshops, termed as Advanced Supply and Repair Depots. This plan, extended in July 1942 to 25 bomber, seven fighter and four air support command airfields, was discarded when the construction effort required was reviewed and found wasteful of resources. It was then decided to set up third echelon maintenance on each combat station.

With a definitive plan for 8th Air Force installations, accepted in August 1942, came the proposal to establish a single advanced air depot in each of the five bomb wing division areas to be known as Air Replacement and Supply Depots. Locations were Little Staughton for 1st Wing, Watton for 2nd, Honington for 3rd, Wattisham for 4th and Boreham or Ridgewell for 5th, but later settled at Stansted. Of these, only Honington, a few miles north of Bury St Edmunds in Suffolk, was ready for use and in September 1942 started to serve all bomber stations then operational. In April 1943 Honington depot was renamed the 1st Advanced Air Depot. Although handling all US bomber types in

Above left: **The men of 453rd Sub-depot boxing a worn Wright R-1820 engine with the aid of a 'home-made' hoist fitted to the front of a Cletrac. Personnel are (l. to r.): Sgt Wesley Narem, Pfc Bill Moran, Sgt Jack Turner (who designed the hoist), M/Sgt Alen Ries, T/Sgt Edward Lynch, and S/Sgt Abraham Myers. Outside Bury St Edmunds hangar No 1 on a long road trailer with other boxed engines ready to be transported to a Base Air Depot for reconditioning.**

Above: **Every combat station accumulated a 'graveyard' of wrecked aircraft. These become the source of many spare parts and components. The carcasses of five B-17s reposed near the Kimbolton technical site when this photograph was taken in January 1944.**

the early days, most work was on B-17s, in particular their armament modifications. Honington, however, was 50 miles from the general area of the 1st Wing's original B-17 airfields and a closer store of spares was desirable. Until Little Staughton depot was complete, stores at Thurleigh were used for B-17 parts.

VIII AFSC established a new headquarters, the Advanced Air Service at Milton Ernest, Bedfordshire in February 1943 to oversee and co-ordinate activities at the advanced air depots. The second to come into operation was Little Staughton in late April

serving 1st Wing area as the 2nd Advanced Air Depot. Stores were moved from Thurleigh and some work previously handled by Honington was taken over. Honington then prepared to serve 3rd Wing and its B-26s while Wattisham in the same county was taken over from the RAF to become the depot for the new 4th Wing and its B-17s arriving in May. However, before Wattisham could be brought into full use the 3rd and 4th Wing units exchanged base areas and Honington once again found itself serving B-17s. At this time, June 1943, Greenham Common and Stansted were being developed for air depot use but were far from complete. Aldermaston was therefore used as a temporary depot for B-26s of Air Support Command until Stansted was available. Wattisham then became the advanced fighter depot primarily concerned with P-47s. The Watton depot for 2nd Wing began its function as the 5th AAD in August and received its first B-24s to repair early in September.

In line with changes in VIII AFSC structure and terminology proposed earlier in the year, on 1 August 1943 the Advanced Air Service Headquarters at Milton Ernest became the Strategic Air Depot Area, retaining jurisdiction over the advanced depots which at the same time were redesignated as Strategic Air Depots. Function was unaffected. Honington became the 1st SAD, Little Staughton the 2nd, Watton the 3rd. Wattisham, originally the 3rd AAD, became a tactical air depot, but on 14 December 1943 was established as the 4th Strategic Air Depot. In early planning it was the intention that each advanced air depot airfield would also sustain an operational combat group.

While the advanced air depot would initially use existing airfield technical site buildings, a depot site complete with its own loop aircraft taxi track, hardstandings, hangars, workshops and living sites would be constructed at a point outside the perimeter track. Both depot and combat group aircraft would use the same flying field. Construction of air depot sites got under way in the spring of 1943, but work at Little Staughton was halted when it was decided to develop Alconbury instead because of better road and rail access. Movement to Alconbury took place in March 1944.

To distinguish the strategic air depot sites and avoid confusion with combat group facilities, they were given separate names in February 1944. Honington depot became Troston, Alconbury became Abbots Ripton, Watton, Neaton and Wattisham, Hitcham; names relating to parishes or places in the locality.

The principal manning units of the Strategic Air Depots were Air Depot Groups, two being assigned to each. The 9th and 40th ADGs served at Honington/Troston, the 5th and 35th at Alconbury/Abbots Ripton, the 31st and 46th at Watton/Neaton and the 21st and 44th at Wattisham/Hitcham. The 10th ADG was the original unit at Wattisham, specialising in medium bombers, but had been transferred to IX AFSC late in 1943.

Above: **Although a special air depot site was built at Honington, the 1st SAD continued to use all but one of the hangars on the airfield's main technical site as these were not required by the fighter group which shared the airfield. B-17s in various states of repair can be seen beside the C-type hangars. H-shaped buildings are permanent barracks (brick with flat roofs). Control tower and flying control ground symbols can also be seen.** (R. Zorn)

Above right: **The Instrument Shop at 3rd SAD, Neaton. Various rigs can be seen for testing aircraft instruments. Note particular cleanliness of room which was essential for this delicate work.** (via W. Noble)

Below right: **Veteran of 100 missions with 467th BG, *Prowler*, B-24J 42-110171: Q2:X, has guns and salvagable equipment removed by 3rd SAD personnel at Neaton before being broken up as salvage. This aircraft was considered too worn to be returned to the USA.** (T. Land)

With the proposal to place five groups of B-24s in the 3rd Division in the spring of 1944, there was need for an auxiliary depot to serve this element. Construction of a site adjacent to Snetterton Heath airfield and named after nearby Eccles was undertaken in March. The first unit to operate from here was the

15th Mobile Reclamation and Repair Squadron transferred from Neaton. However, work on Eccles ceased soon after conversion of the B-24 groups to B-17s was approved and it was used for storage until turned over to IX Troop Carrier Command in December 1944.

The liberation of large areas of France in the summer of 1944 enabled many 8th Air Force aircraft in distress to land there when returning from operations. Soon after D-Day VIII AFSC began sending mobile repair units to the bridgehead to deal with forced down aircraft. Although some assistance was obtained from RAF and IX AFSC establishments, the increasing number of 8th Air Force bombers and fighters coming down in France and the Low Countries demanded a repair depot on the Continent. Eventually Merville airfield in France was acquired and in December 1944 put into operation as the 5th SAD. Personnel to staff the new organisation were drawn chiefly from the four English SADs.

The basic function of the AAD/SAD was repair of aircraft. During 1942–43 modification of aircraft was undertaken but only when this could not be performed by the rear depots at Burton-wood, Warton and Langford Lodge. Nevertheless, AAD/SADs performed modification work when for some reason it was more convenient to have the work done by them. Major overhauls formed a large part of the work performed, aircraft that had reached the required number of hours flying being to the depots from their home bases. During early 1943 when there was an acute shortage of heavy bombers, many B-17s that had been overhauled or repaired tended to be used as replacements and sent to a group in need, rather than the group from which they had come. Later it was policy to return an aircraft to the group from which it had been received.

Aircraft returning from a mission with heavy battle damage were sometimes directed to land at the appropriate depot air-field rather than home base. If a wheels-up landing had to be made B-17s and B-24 were frequently directed to carry this out at the depot airfield where repair or salvage could be more easily facilitated. Crashed aircraft were also the responsibility of the SADs, although the actual retrieval operations were con-

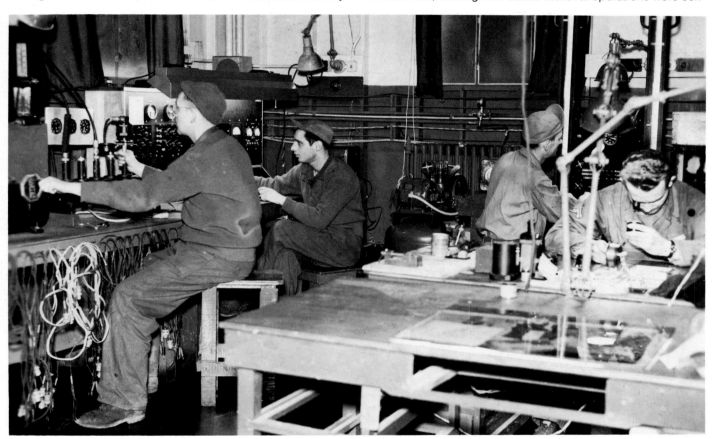

Top: **Pneumatic jacks (air cushions inflated by compressor) were by far the easiest method of raising a bomber with a collapsed undercarriage. B-17G 44-8306, CC:H of 390th BG sank into a filled-in bomb crater while taxiing at Merville, March 1945.**

Above: **A mobile repair unit replacing engines on** Stella, **B-17F 42-29651, which made an emergency landing at Lychet Minster in April 1943 after straying over France and sustaining flak damage during a transit flight to the UK. The bomber later served with 384th BG.**

ducted by No 43 Group RAF. Wrecked aircraft that could not economically be repaired were classified Category E. This was divided into E1 and E2, the former being wrecks rendering repairable or serviceable items for spares and the latter wrecks only suitable as scrap metal. E1 wrecks were usually returned to 8th Air Force strategic air depots whereas E2 wrecks were transported to RAF salvage dumps. While 8th AFSC did occasionally collect some American crash wrecks, the major proportion continued to be retrieved by the RAF throughout the war.

To expedite repair of aircraft that had landed away from home bases trials were made from September 1942 in taking the repair capability to the aircraft. There was a need for mobile repair crews to repair crash-landed or battle-damaged aircraft sufficiently to enable them to be flown to an air depot. The Lockheed Overseas Corporation at Langford Lodge, charged with designing and prefabricating such mobile repair units, completed the first early in December 1942. It consisted of two tractor units with semi-trailers, one 1½-ton truck and a Jeep. One semi-trailer contained the workshop and repair equipment and the other the living and sleeping quarters for the repair crew. The truck and Jeep were used for transportation, principally securing supplies. Early experience showed the trailer used as a billet was uneconomical and in January 1943 this was converted into a second trailer workshop. The men were then billeted local to their working. A second Jeep, truck and water tank were available when the situation demanded. From 16 to 19 specialists and drivers crewed the unit. The earliest completion of a mobile repair was 13 February 1943 when a 303rd Group B-17 that had forced-landed in a field at Dawlish, Devon, was flown out. During the first year of operations more than 500 bombers were repaired by mobile units. By November 1943 28 such units operated out of the four depots and were at that time organised into seven Mobile Repair and Reclamation Squadrons. These squadrons were later also used to carry personnel at the SADs. More were activated until eventually each SAD had five assigned.

Each Air Depot Group had one Maintenance and one Supply squadron. However, for practical reasons the organisation within an AAD/SAD was based on function and there was some intermingling of personnel from different units. To achieve more cohesion Strategic Air Depots were reorganised into Administrative, Supply, Maintenance and Transportation Divisions. This consolidated the assignment of personnel to function, although it meant that some units had men serving all four divisions. Nevertheless, this system proved successful and was retained until the SADs were disbanded.

The total personnel of a strategic air depot fluctuated between 4000 and 5000 as assignment and removal of component units occurred. Five of the Mobile R & R Squadrons were sent to France to become the backbone of 5th SAD. VIII AFSC activities in liberated territory were responsible for the return of 1221 repaired aircraft to the UK while another 67 repairable aircraft were transferred to other air forces. Additionally, useable parts were salvaged from 422 8th Air Force aircraft.

There was always a high degree of flexibility in the commitment of Strategic Air Depots and work was handled that, by the rules, should have been carried out by combat bases or base air depots. Manufacture and overhaul of components was often undertaken and although each depot supposedly served only one particular Bomb/Air Division, some work was done for the benefit of others. For example, 1st SAD fabricated components to allow *Carpet I* RCM sets to be installed in both B-17s and B-24s during autumn 1944. The 3rd SAD designed and produced a special gauge for all depots to measure the oil buffers in .50 guns, following the discovery that a manufacturing fault caused some guns to stop firing when elevated.

Another important aspect of AAD/SAD work was stores holding, particularly parts for the aircraft type operated by the division each supported. The truck companies at each AAD/SAD ran regular supplies to combat bases in their division and at times collected supplies from base air depots or other stores.

BASE AIR DEPOTS

One of the first tasks of those USAAF officers preparing for the establishment of 8th Air Force in the United Kingdom was securing suitable sites for the primary air force depots. These were to be in areas away from combat stations to give a degree of security from enemy air attack and to be reasonably close to

ports through which supplies would arrive from the United States. Under initial plans to establish an American military presence in Northern Ireland, arrangements had been made with the British to construct an air depot at Langford Lodge, a large estate west of Crumlin on the banks of Lough Neagh. Work began in February 1942 while arrangements were made with Lockheed of America to operate the base with civilian technicians from the USA supported by labour recruited locally. A second site for a major depot was acquired at Warton where construction started in the spring of 1942. While both establishments had a priority in the construction programme, it was apparent that the Force would need major depot services before completion. US observers in March 1942 inspecting facilities operated by the British requested the following month that Burtonwood be used on a joint basis.

Close to the port of Liverpool, Burtonwood had been developed during the early war years as a store and modification centre, specialising in the assembly and preparation of American aircraft arriving for the RAF. The first US units arrived on 11 June, followed next day by the 5th Air Depot Group which, initially, became the principal manning unit of the American section. The first aircraft were received for modifications in July and from September US civilian technicians arrived when aircraft engine overhaul was also concentrated at Burtonwood. As the American presence increased, arrangements were made for them to take over the whole base.

Langford Lodge began to operate in August 1942 and eventually Lockheed had some 2600 US civilian engineers on the base. Much of their work concerned special modifications for aircraft and this depot came to specialise in experimental engineering whereas Burtonwood, and later Warton, concentrated on proven modifications. Warton was able to receive aircraft for repair from April 1943. Until the end of 1943 the three base air depots, as they became known, dealt with all types of aircraft as required. While stores were concentrated in England the same specialised items were often held by both depots.

In the autumn of 1943 a number of organisational changes were made in VIII AFSC. The three base air depots, together with associated storage and transport facilities, were grouped under an administrative headquarters labelled Base Air Depot Area (BADA). Burtonwood, Warton and Langford Lodge then became Base Air Depots Nos 1, 2 and 3 respectively. The numerous units at each establishment were organised under four divisions or sections: maintenance, to perform engineering on aircraft and equipment; supply, to handle stores received and despatched to advanced depots; internal supply, to provide items necessary for the work performed at base air depots and administration. As had been proposed earlier, the services of the majority of civilians employed were dispensed with as quickly as possible. The majority of US civilians were returned to the US from Burtonwood and Langford Lodge between January and June 1944. There were plans for base air depots to specialise, with Burtonwood repairing and modifying B-17s, P-47s and P-38s, while Warton handled B-24s and P-51s; in the event this was not rigidly adhered to. All radial engines were overhauled at Burtonwood and all inlines at Warton, while Langford Lodge specialised in propeller overhaul and manufacturing modification kits. These arrangements facilitated production line methods for repair and overhaul bringing increased productivity during the winter of 1943–44. At this time BAD 1 and 2 had some 25,000 military personnel while facilities at both were still expanding. Burtonwood, the major depot, eventually had 44 hangar workshops and stores of various sizes adjacent to the airfield, to Warton's 16. Activities at Langford Lodge were gradually run down as Force activities in Northern Ireland were reduced and Burtonwood and Warton were, together, able to meet the requirements of combat units in England. By August 1944 regular maintenance activities had ceased at Langford Lodge, the 3000 men remaining being involved chiefly in research and development during the rest of hostilities.

Early in 1944 when the 8th Air Force Hq at Bushy Park was taken to become the headquarters of the theatre air force, United States Air Forces in Europe (USSTAF), the VIII AFSC Hq at the same location was also taken to become the theatre Air Service Command Headquarters (ASC, USSTAF). As BADA served both 8th and 9th Air Force this organisation was also transferred from 8th Air Force, although not officially until March. A new VIII AFSC Hq was created by redesignating the SADA Hq at Milton Ernest – officially as of 23 February 1944. This had little practical effect on the work of this establishment as from then on VIII AFSC's jurisdiction went no higher than Strategic Air Depot level.

In October 1943 the VIII Air Support Command became the nucleus of the US tactical air arm for support of ground forces in the forthcoming cross-Channel invasion of the Continent. Designated as the 9th Air Force its requirements were also met by BADA, the depot at Baverstock/Greenham Common, later becoming Base Air Depot 4.

One of the major functions of the base air depots was preparing new aircraft for combat units. Bomber aircraft flown across the north or south Atlantic ferry routes normally arrived in the UK at Prestwick or St Mawgan, St Eval and Valley. They were then ferried to a base air depot for inspection and modification or, if

Left: **Line-up of assembled Lightnings at Langford Lodge, February 1944. Originally operated by the Lockheed Aircraft Corporation for the US Government, it was often referred to as 'Lockheed City'. Aircraft in centre of picture is an F-5C (42-68196) with oblique camera windows in nose.**

Below left: **BAD 2 at Warton specialised in preparing new P-51s and B-24s. In the foreground new Mustangs, painted in type recognition markings, await delivery, August 1944. Behind the hangars B-24s are under repair, while other types to be seen are the P-47, UC-61, A-26 and P-38. August 1944.** (via H. Holmes)

Below: **When Stanstead was vacated by the 9th Air Force, BADA used it as a forward storage park for B-17s and P-47s. More than 200 aircraft were on hand when this photograph was taken in the spring of 1945.**

of repair or maintenance. While base air depots had the responsibility for 4th echelon maintenance, in practice they received those flyable aircraft that the strategic air depots could not deal with, the line between 3rd and 4th echelons being arbitrary.

Fighter aircraft, apart from a few early trans-Atlantic ferry flights, were shipped in deck-loaded on cargo vessels, mainly tankers. Their reception port was chiefly Liverpool, but some P-47s and P-38s arrived at Belfast and P-47s and P-51s via the Clyde. These aircraft were taken by road to the nearest suitable RAF airfield, from Liverpool to Speke which from mid-1944 became the main fighter assembly point; from Belfast to Sydenham and from the Clyde to Renfrew. After assembly at these stations they were flown to a base depot for inspection and modification.

Apart from the aviation supplies stored at the base air depots, VIII AFSC originally controlled several other supply depots in

facilities were overburdened, to a storage airfield. Greencastle, Mullaghmore, Toome and Langford Lodge were used for storage during the early part of 1944 but reduced to Greencastle and Langford Lodge later in the year. Both Burtonwood and Warton had extensive parking areas for aircraft storage. Aircraft were ferried by 27th Air Transport Group pilots from storage in Northern Ireland to Burtonwood or Warton as required. After modification and pre-delivery maintenance the aircraft were test flown and then ferry pilots delivered them direct to combat bases or, if the aircraft had radar, to Alconbury first. When the 9th Air Force moved to France, IX AFSC vacated Stansted air depot which was then taken over by BADA and used until the end of hostilities as an aircraft park for both bombers and fighters that had passed through the base air depots. Every new aircraft received at base air depots went through the current type-modification programme. This averaged 15 heavy bombers a day by summer 1944. In addition to work on new aircraft, there was a constant flow of aircraft from combat bases in need

the UK. These were either new utility buildings – generally erected in estate parks – or commandeered civilian factories and other suitable installations already used by British forces. Poynton was the first to be transferred to the USAAF and handled general stores. Initially such depots were controlled by Services of Supply but then transferred to VIII AFSC. By December 1942 general supply depots serving 8th Air Force were in being at Aintree (motor vehicles and parts), Ashchurch (motor vehicles and parts and chemical supplies), Melchbourne Park (vehicle storage), Rushden (motor transport maintenance and medical equipment maintenance), Thrapston (medical supplies), Wellingborough, Stowmarket, Thatcham, Kettering and London (quartermaster stores of all kinds) and Huntingdon (general engineering). There were also three ordnance and ammunition stores at this date.

During 1943 many more general depots were opened, for the most part administered by Services of Supply but often manned by units assigned to VIII AFSC. With the creation of ASC, USS-

TAF early in 1944, the only VIII AFSC stations other than the Strategic Air Depots were the truck depots at Stowmarket and Thrapston.

27th AIR TRANSPORT GROUP

From the earliest days of VIII AFSC operations in the UK there was a requirement for speedy delivery of urgently required materials and parts which could best be expedited by air transport. As the Command had no commitment to conduct its own air freight deliveries it had no assigned transport aircraft. When possible, use was made of the C-47s and C-53s of troop carrier groups during the summer of 1942, supplemented by Oxfords, an Anson and a Dominie borrowed from the RAF and flown by liaison pilots attached to the Command. During the winter of 1942–43 aircraft of the 315th Troop Carrier Group carried a large amount of freight between depots and combat airfields but VIII AFSC was endeavouring to establish its own flying organisation to meet these requirements.

In October 1942 the few pilots and British communications aircraft on hand were acknowledged as the Ferry and Transport Services. On 26 February 1943 this provisional unit became the 2008th Transport Group (P) until 15 April when Command received full authorisation to bestow the official designation 27th Air Transport Group. The two flying units in the Group were distinguished as the 86th and 87th Air Transport Squadrons. The 27th ATG Hq was based at Heston near VIII AFSC Hq; the 86th ATS at Hendon and 87th ATS at Warton. Both squadrons had detachments at other VIII AFSC airfields, the 86th being represented at Honington and Little Staughton, the 87th at Burtonwood and Langford Lodge. Suitable aircraft continued to be a major problem and it was several months before the 27th ATG acquired sufficient C-47s for its purpose.

In addition to flying supplies the Group was given the task of ferrying aircraft between depots and deliveries to combat bases. This became an increasinlgy important part of the Group's work and in the autumn of 1943 four ferrying squadrons were formed specifically for this purpose, while at the same time a further two transport squadrons were added to the Group. The 310th Ferrying Squadron was established at Warton and the 320th ATS at Honington. The other four units were formed in Northern Ireland: the 311th and 312th Ferrying Squadrons and 321st Air Transport Squadron at Maghaberry on 1 November, and the 325th Ferry Squadron at the same location on 9 December. Maghaberry, then a storage depot for new aircraft, became the main base in Northern Ireland for the ferrying units.

However, activities under VIII AFSC were short-lived, as in January 1944 the 27th ATG began working for ASC, USSTAF, although not formally until the following March. Also in January the 86th ATS moved into Cranford/Heston to join the Group Hq, and, with the general reduction of USAAF activities in Northern Ireland, during May 1944 the 311th, 312th and 321st Squadrons transferred to Langford Lodge and the 325th to Heston.

While with VIII AFSC, 27th ATG and its progenitors delivered 42,964 US tons of cargo, carried 20,000 passengers and ferried 10,500 aircraft.*

MUNITIONS STORES

The US Army Services of Supply made the initial arrangements with the British for munitions stores in 1942. The first VIII AFSC site was at Barnham in Suffolk, which was made available in

Above: **The RAF handled transport of USAAF aircraft arriving in the Clyde. These P-47D-2s were a shipment brought to Renfrew in August 1943, towed from the docks by modified lorries.**

Right: **Personnel of the Earsham ordnance depot unloading bombs from waggons at the railhead adjacent to the bomb storage area. Local English contractors regularly hauled these bombs in their lorries for the USAAF.**

Below right: **Many of the truck companies in VIII AFSC were manned by Negro personnel. This Dodge, belonging to the 2016 Quartermaster Truck Company, then based at Tostock, Suffolk, gets refuelled with 'pool petrol' in Surrey.** (V. Doone)

June 1942, and the following month Sharnbrook in Bedfordshire was acquired. These two ordnance stores provided VIII BC requirements during the early months of its operations. In July 1943 Braybrooke, Melton Mowbray and Wortley were assigned to VIII AFSC as munitions stores although the latter two eventually became truck depots. Earsham was brought into service in the autumn of 1943. In general 1st Division received bombs and ammunition from Sharnbrook, 2nd Division from Earsham and 3rd Division from the Warren Wood site at Barnham. During 1943 another site was prepared at Bures on the Essex–Suffolk border which eventually served 9th Air Force bomb groups. However, after the departure of the A-20 and B-26 units to France the remaining bombs in this store were used by local B-17 groups.

Other munitions parks were those established in the summer of 1942 at Melchbourne and Lords Bridge holding stocks of poison gas bombs and other special chemical weapons in case the enemy resorted to chemical warfare and reprisals became necessary. As it was, the knowledge of the ability to retaliate in this way proved an effective deterrent. When USSTAF took over the original VIII AFSC Hq and BADA early in 1944 it also assumed control of all the munitions stores outside those on combat bases. As a result, while 8th Air Force continued to draw bombs and ammunition from the same dumps and stores the manning units were no longer under its jurisdiction.

Bombs and ammunition arriving at a west coast port were carried by train to the railway station nearest the store to which they were assigned. Bomb store operatives unloaded the wagons and hauled the bombs into the store by 2½-ton trucks. Bombs and ammunitions would then be dispensed as required to combat airfields, again by truck. To prevent unnecessary

---

* Although constantly referred to as 27th Air Transport Group in official orders, it was actually constituted as the 27th Transport Group, an anomaly not corrected until late in 1944. As non-combat units, transport group and squadron designations were in a separate numbering system.

handling it became policy to send bombs by train directly to a rail station near a combat base where they could be hauled by military truck or contracted civilian lorry directly to airfield bomb dumps, thus leaving the area depot bomb store as a reserve. At depot stores the bombs were placed in rows on concrete standings, usually stacked as high as they could be rolled by hand from a 2½-ton truck. The concrete standings were spaced along hard surface roads, sufficiently apart so that an accidental detonation of bombs on one standing would not affect others. Existing civilian roads were embodied in the lay-out of some dumps, with bomb standings at intervals along them. Machine gun ammunition, supplied in wood boxes, was stored under cover, usually in widely spaced Nissen-type huts. Incendiary material was also normally stored under cover.

Incendiary and poison gas dumps were set up separately from other ordnance. Known as Advanced Chemical Parks, Melchbourne Park and Barnham were the first set up, with a third site to be selected later. Each site was to be provided with a storage yard for filled and empty chemical munitions, bulk storage installations for mustard gas and a filling plant for chemical munitions, smoke tanks and bombs. Six underground storage tanks, three at Melchbourne and three at Barnham, were to be provided. The British supplied a large proportion of the gas weapons.

FUEL SUPPLIES

One-thousand bomber raids on Berlin required 2,500,000 gallons of gasoline. Almost all petroleum fuels used in the ETO came from American sources, its distribution in the UK being, by agreement, the responsibility of the British. As a single heavy bomber raid could consume the whole supply for the minimum bomber airfield tankage of 72,000 gallons, the grey British 'Pool' tankers kept up an almost non-stop delivery service from rail terminals to base storage tanks. During 1943 the storage capacity on VIII BC bases was doubled to ensure a reserve. While there was never a prolonged delay in fuel replenishment, the strain on British rail transport was such that from October 1943 some fuel was shipped via the Thames and nearer the general area of major use. In addition a pipe line was laid from the Thames to the 1st Division area and by April 1944 Bassingbourn was reported to have become the first station to receive fuel direct from the shipping terminal. US military tankers were used on occasion to supplement the British effort, particularly when consumption threatened to deplete base supplies. Motor vehicle fuel was also supplied by British transport to combat bases.

REPLACEMENT CONTROL DEPOTS

To handle all personnel not assigned to a unit who arrived in the UK for duty, the 12th Replacement and Control Depot was established at Stone, but located two miles away at Yarnfield, Staffordshire, in September 1942, with detachments at Chorley and Bamber Bridge in Lanchashire. Its function was to receive, process and assign airmen. A second handling unit, the 14th Replacement and Control Depot, arrived in April 1943 and a third, the 16th, arrived in August, the 12th at Stone acting as the senior establishment. In March 1943 these depots were given the responsibility for reception of replacement combat crews, of which there were few until the summer. Less than 4000 persons passed through the centres before June 1943 when a sudden influx occurred. Efforts were made to increase both accommodation and staff to deal with increasing traffic, but the arrival of some 20,000 non-assigned personnel in October 1943 completely swamped facilities and substantial numbers of men had to be temporarily placed at other stations where accommodation was available. By December 1943 handling capacity had been increased to 32,000, and together with a more practised system of processing the two centres were able to meet demands on them for the rest of hostilities. The Stone, Chorley and Bamber Bridge units were transferred to ASC, USSTAF early in 1944 and all establishments came under a headquarters, the 70th Replacement Depot. This organisation also processed personnel being returned to the USA.

REST HOMES

Administered by the same section of VIII AFSC were the so-called rest homes. These were hostels to which combat men who showed signs of battle fatigue or had undertaken a great many combat missions could be sent on leave to relax. Large country mansions were mostly selected and what amounted to hotel service provided. Extensive sport and amusement facilities were available, although a visitor was at liberty to spend his time in any way he chose to relax. The period of stay was usually a week, depending on the recommendation of a combatant's medical officer. The first rest home acquired and opened, on 3 January 1943, was Stanbridge Earls at Romsey, Hampshire. The capacity was 30 officer guests. Moulsford Manor, opened in May 1943, was the first for enlisted men but later changed to officers. Other homes were added during 1944 but by then they were no longer under VIII AFSC jurisdiction.

REST HOMES USED BY 8th AF COMBAT PERSONNEL

	Opening Date	Developed Capacity
Stanbridge Earls (Romsey, Hants)	3/1/43	30 officers
Palace Hotel, Southport (Lancs)	19/2/43	50 officers & 100 enlisted men
Moulsford Manor & Bucklands (Berks)	13/5/43	25 officers
Combe House (Shaftesbury, Dorset)	20/9/43	50 officers
Walhampton House (Hants)	17/2/44	50 enlisted men
Aylesfield House (Alton, Hants)	15/3/44	25 officers
Roke Manor (Romsey, Hants)	10/4/44	25 officers
Pangbourne House (Berks)	1/5/44	30 officers
Spetchley Park (Worcs)	1/6/44	45 enlisted men
Furz Down House (Kings Somborne, Hants)	26/6/44	25 officers
Eynsham Hall (Whitney, Oxon)	22/7/44	65 officers
Keythorpe Hall (Tugby, Leics)	26/7/44	30 enlisted men
Ebrington Manor (Gloucestershire)	5/8/44	20 enlisted men
Knighthayes Court (Tiverton, Devon)	6/10/44	40 officers

Below left: Stanbridge Earls, the first 8th Air Force rest home to open, photographed in March 1943 from the rear garden side.

Below: Croquet on the lawn at 'Gremlin Gables', a popular name for the 400-year-old Moulsford Manor, first rest home for enlisted men. Standard of food was high – two real eggs for breakfast – and men could do as they wished with their time provided they were in by midnight.

Weather Service

Many American servicemen returned home after service in England with the conviction that the island was set in an intermittent downpour. While seasonal fluctuations may bring unusually wet periods, the fact is that the general East Anglian area, where most 8th Air Force bases were situated, has an average rainfall varying from 18 inches in the south-east to 24 inches in the western extreme, figures far lower than those for many parts of the United States. If the total amount of precipitation is not large, the presence of cloud is frequent, as one Atlantic low follows another in on the prevailing south-westerly winds. The temperate climate normally provides few days in winter when it rises past 50 degrees F (10°C). Yet periods of drought are a common occurrence in East Anglian summers. Changeable weather with a preponderance of damp was to leave an indelible mark on the memories of those Americans forced to live in poorly heated Nissen huts or perform difficult maintenance work in a steady drizzle. British weather can be delightful but it was the more unpleasant aspects that were remembered. However, even those who persistently 'bitched' about the English climate would concede that the United Kingdom was a good place to be stationed if one had to fight a war.

While the weather may have been slightly demoralising for personnel, its effect on the air offensive was critical. Weather conditions were a major factor influencing both the rate of combat operations and their success. Indeed, the northern European weather proved to be the biggest obstacle to accurate daylight bombing as practised by the 8th Air Force. Inclement conditions frequently caused planned operations to be cancelled, those despatched to be recalled or diverted, and were often the main reason for poor target strikes. Weather that could seriously hinder visual bombing missions prevailed on an average 250 days during a year in the general area of 8th Air Force operations. In 1943 VIII Bomber Command prescribed limiting conditions for launching a bomber mission whereby ceilings had to be no lower than 1000 feet and visibility not less than 1¼ miles at take-off. There had to be no thick layers or decks of multi-layered clouds above the base area to endanger assembly. Further, no sharp frosts, severe icing or thick cloud layers at operational levels on route to the targets, and not more than 4/10 cloud over target to permit visual attack or no clouds at flight levels if blind bombing was employed. That conditions beyond these limits were frequently encountered by aircraft despatched is evinced by over half of the abortive bomber sorties, during the first year of operations, being due to weather. Thus it will be appreciated that meteorological information and forecasting was of paramount importance in sustaining the 8th's campaign.

18TH WEATHER SQUADRON

The RAF had an extensive and comprehensive meteorological service and facilities for furnishing 8th Air Force stations with information were arranged early in 1942. However, as the planned high level daylight operations required specialised information, it was essential that the 8th Air Force develop its own reporting and forecasting service. Originally USAAF weather services consisted of establishments covering specific global regions and small weather sections assigned as integral parts of tactical and service units. By May 1942 it was decided that the regional basis was a more effective form of operating weather services, and subsequently all weather personnel in tactical and service units were, with the exception of the Staff Weather Officer, transferred to the regional weather unit. The flying unit Staff Weather Officer remained to participate in flight briefings for aircrews.

The original senior weather officer in 8th Air Force was Lt Col Anthony Mustoe who arrived in England in June 1942 to combine service as Hq Staff Weather Officer with that of Weather Regional Control Officer; later he commanded the 305th BG. Meanwhile, the 18th Weather Squadron, activated in the USA for the United Kingdom region, had its personnel despatched to England In July, settling in at Bushy Park, Teddington, on 19 August. The Squadron Hq – which moved to a building near Marble Arch, London, in February 1944, to Cheddington in May and back to Bushy Park in October that year – acted principally in an administrative capacity. The field work was performed by detachments which were eventually established at every 8th Air Force flying base and most serving the European Wing of Air Transport Command.

Creation of the first 12 detachments was ordered on 21 August 1942 and by December 1943 there were 87 involving over 1000 men. A peak was reached in April 1944 when 18th Weather Squadron had 106 detachments with 330 officers and 977 enlisted men. The number of detachments fluctuated in line with 8th Air Force operational airfield numbers. Personnel were lost to the 12th Weather Squadron in September 1942 when this unit was formed to serve the 12th Air Force then destined for North Africa. Similarly, others were transferred to the 9th Air Force's 21st Weather Squadron a year later. Movement of units from base to base saw disbandment of some detachments, although most moved with the combat group they served. Initially each detachment was identified by a letter of the alphabet but this was soon replaced by a system whereby the detachment took the number of the USAAF station it served.

Detachments at airfields established and manned weather stations, providing information for the flying units there while also collecting and transmitting data on local conditions to higher authority. The authorised strength of a combat airfield detachment was three officers and eight men (two precaster and six observers), the senior officer being termed the Station Weather Officer and usually having the rank of First Lieutenant. A three shift per 24-hours rota was normally worked so that the weather station was constantly manned. At hourly intervals – and more often in adverse conditions – local weather information would be collected by observers and consisted of total cloud amount, wind direction and speed, visibility, present and

Left: **Eighth Air Force battlefield as seen from a B-17 over Germany, October 1943. A 'solid' undercast, thunderheads on the horizon and persistent contrails above. Conditions not conducive to successful bombing operations.**

past weather, sea level pressure, temperature, cloud extents and heights, dew point temperature, barometric characteristics and tendency. These details were then sent over the teleprinter system to the Fighter Wing Hq, in the case of fighter airfields, or to Bomb Wing (later Division) Hq for bomber airfields. Subsequently the data was passed to Weather Central, the British meteorological office at Dunstable, which collected, analysed and dispensed all meteorological information.

The Bomb Wing Division obtained their weather information from Dunstable, and after preparing forecasts transmitted them direct to operational station weather detachments so that all units would have the same material to work with. In the case of fighter airfields the transmission also went via Fighter Wing Hqs. From coded data coughed out on canary yellow paper by the teletype machine the airfield weather detachment prepared maps and graphs to display actual and forecast conditions which were then made available to Flying Control and the Staff (Group) Weather Officer for his use in briefings. In the absence or in disposition of the Staff Weather Officer the Station Weather Officer (head of the 18th WS Detachment) would often perform such briefing duties. The Group Weather Officer normally held senior rank to the Station Weather Officer, being a captain or major. Detachment personnel also obtained weather information from aircrews returned from operations which was also forwarded through the teleprinter.

On all wartime-built airfields the weather detachment usually occupied a ground floor room in the control tower. This housed two teleprinters – originally British types but replaced where

Above: **An 18th Weather Squadron meteorologist preparing a weather map in the Kimbolton tower, August 1944.**

possibly by the more reliable US machines – plotting tables and various display units. Four men were usually on duty at one time, two observers and two forecaster/clerks. On airfields built pre-war as permanent RAF stations, the weather office was often already in existence on top of the headquarters building, while the observation post for gathering local weather details was adjacent or on the control tower. At some other airfields weather office and observation post were also separated, usually when insufficient room was available in the control tower. Equipment for recording local conditions was placed adjacent to the tower. It consisted of a small shelter housing a psychrometer for obtaining relative humidity readings and minimum and maximum thermometers. Near by was a theodolite position used in conjunction with the release of a small hydrogen balloon to obtain data for plotting wind velocity linked with direction. On the tower roof were a wind vane and an anemometer, a three-cup device revolved by the wind and usually linked electrically to the nine-light indicator in the weather office. A clock-like instrument, the nine-light indicator gave both wind speed and direction. Most of this equipment was of British origin.

Weather detachments at Wing and Division headquarters did not obtain local weather data, their duties being primarily concerned with analysing, forecasting and contributing to the consensus prognosis that would be used for operational briefings. On the other hand, detachments at Service Command airfields were chiefly concerned with local conditions for the despatch and reception of aircraft.

In May 1943, 18th Weather Squadron established its first detachment on an airfield used by the European Wing of Air Transport Command (which was not part of 8th Air Force) and eventually served seven of these stations. Generally, they had much larger staffs than the 8th Air Force airfield detachments as the area of weather interest was much greater. Prestwick, as the main trans-Atlantic terminal airfield had the largest complement of all – 13 officers and 39 enlisted men. In the winter of 1943–44

Above: **Standard shelter housing psychrometer and thermometers. Cpl H. Barksdale is about to release and time hydrogen balloon to obtain wind velocity data, Thorpe Abbotts, 1945.** (100 BG Memorial Museum)

detachments serving different interests were formed into separate administrative sections within 18th Weather Squadron. One specialist section was Radiosonde which covered detachments at Downham Market, Larkhill, Leuchars, Mousehole and Stornoway. Radiosonde was devoted to obtaining stratospheric data using hydrogen-filled 6 feet-diameter balloons carrying recording instruments that could be monitored by radio. Four releases were made by each site during 24 hours, with the balloon consistently reaching 60,000 feet and sometimes 100,000 feet. Pressure, humidity and temperature details could be obtained by these flights. The first 18th Weather Squadron radiosonde detachment commenced operations on 14 August 1943 at Mousehole in Cornwall. Those sites at Downham Market and Larkhill were British operated and here the US detachments were involved primarily in training.

On 21 October 1944 the 18th Weather Squadron was transferred from the 8th Air Force to HQ USSTAF, an administrative move which still left the vast proportion of its personnel serving the 8th where 84 detachments remained. In December 1944, 18th Weather Squadron joined Hq USSTAF at St Germain-en-Laye near Paris but continued to administer its 8th Air Force section from the French base until the end of hostilities.

While 18th Weather Squadron had no flight mission and no assigned aircraft, its personnel at some bomber bases were periodically called upon to fly as meteorological observers on high altitude local weather reconnaissance flights. This began in the summer of 1943 when it became practice to despatch a B-17 from a selected combat base to make a high altitude ascent about an hour prior to the launch of a mission. The purpose was to determine local clouds, turbulence and icing. These flights were later found to give the enemy early warning of an impending mission and had to be carried out on a more regular basis, with each group in a Combat Wing taking it in turn to despatch a 'weather ship'. A special flight was set up in autumn 1943 to undertake regular high altitude flights over the UK and its western approaches and it became the nucleus of the special heavy weather reconnaissance squadron later established. Volunteers from 18th Weather Squadron continued to fly as meteorology observers with this unit.

WEATHER FACTORS IN BOMBING OPERATIONS

An analysis of weather factors prepared for the US Strategic Bombing Survey shows that the 8th Air Force weather services had an overall accuracy at forecasting operational or non-operational days of 75 per cent at the daily 1600 hours Headquarters conference, and 87 per cent at the 2200 hours conference. Eighth Air Force target weather forecasts for the period June 1943 through to April 1945 had an overall accuracy of 58 per cent; 11 per cent of the time too much cloud and 31 per cent of the time too little cloud was forecast in target areas. Visual bombing conditions (less than 5/10ths) were correctly predicted 66 per cent of the time, blind conditions (8/10ths to 10/10ths) 76 per cent of the time. The intermediate 'visual – assist' category (5/10ths to less than 8/10ths) cloud was correct 38 per cent of the time.

Overall, 25 per cent of all days during the 8th Air Force's campaign were non-operational because of weather. (This compares with a figure of 37 per cent for the Italy-based 15th Air Force.) Aircraft airborne on operations that were abortive or recalled because of weather averaged over 15 per cent in the first year, decreasing to 5.8 per cent in 1945. At this later date 15th Air Force weather abortives were some 14 per cent and RAF Bomber Command 1.3 per cent. The much higher 15th Air Force figure is explained by the difficulty of forecasting route weather across the Alps plus the mountainous nature of terrain surrounding its bases. The low RAF rate can probably be attributed to aircraft flying singly and not in formation.

PART 2
ARMAMENT AND EQUIPMENT

Principal Combat Aircraft

The basic purpose of 8th Air Force was destruction. High explosives, steel and incendiary materials were the means of achieving this, conveyed and placed by aircraft. It was the aircraft that distinguished this form of warfare from others, and became the accounting term by government, military and public alike. Seemingly, an air force was its aircraft, for it was not stated in communiqués that airmen attacked, but that *aircraft* attacked and at times these were qualified by their type names – such as Fortress or Liberator.

In its operations against the Third Reich, 8th Air Force employed only a few different types of aircraft: two heavy bomber, one medium bomber, four fighter and three reconnaissance. Of these only the two heavy bombers and two fighters were used in large numbers for an extended period. No aircraft type was committed in combat operations without first receiving some modifications deemed necessary for its task. And throughout the campaign there was always a requirement for modifications, whether to meet some deficiency highlighted in operations or to include some new and advantageous piece of equipment. The following section reviews the development of each aircraft type relative to its service with 8th Air Force in the United Kingdom.

Boeing B-17 Fortress

The 'Flying Fortress' prototype first flew in 1935 and a development, the B-17C, was used in combat by the RAF as the Fortress I in the summer of 1941. That same year Boeing carried out a major redesign of the rear half of the aircraft. Popularly distinguished as the 'big tail' Fortress, the first example reaching the 8th Air Force in Britain was B-17E 41-9085, landing at Prestwick on 1 July 1942.

B-17E

Only the 97th Bomb Group arrived equipped with B-17Es. Its complement was 35 but a reserve of 14 others with crews, drawn from squadrons of 301st and 303rd Groups in the USA, was also sent to the UK. On route two B-17s crashed in the USA before departure and five made forced landings in Greenland, so that only 42 B-17Es actually reached 8th Air Force. All 97th aircraft had been through a modification centre prior to movement overseas, having enlarged gun windows sporting .50-in calibre guns either side of the nose. Many of these Fortresses also had a medium green camouflage pattern painted over their basic olive drab finish.

Further modifications, chiefly to radio equipment, were carried out in England. In the previous March, 8th Air Force officers had inspected the first B-17E to arrive in the UK for the RAF. After consulting with the RAF and Air Ministry, a list of 14 required modifications was compiled on deficiencies in radio, oxygen, bomb rack, lighting, fire extinguisher and liferaft equipment.

The B-17E model, already superseded on production before the 97th Group arrived in England, only remained on regular combat status for under two weeks. In late August the B-17Es were transferred to the newly arrived 92nd Group whose B-17Fs went to the 97th in return. The 92nd Group assumed an operational training role as the Bovingdon CCRC but its B-17Es were occasionally impressed on combat operations. The B-17E had several deficiencies as a combat aircraft, but the principal reasons for its retirement were its performance in relation to the new B-17F, making difficulties in joint operating in the same formation, and a vulnerable crew oxygen system. In January 1943 the 92nd Group moved to Alconbury leaving one squadron of 13 B-17Es at Bovingdon to provide the flying element for the CCRC. As the 92nd received new B-17Fs, its B-17Es were sent to other units. During summer 1943 each B-17 group received a B-17E for use in training, liaison, ambulance, transport or target-towing as required. For secondary duties turrets, armament, armour and bombing equipment were removed for higher speed and better handling. Several had seating installed in the forward part of the fuselage waist section. The 303rd and 379th Groups painted their secondary duty aircraft, 41-9020 and 41-9100 respectively, in bizarre bright colours to make them more conspicuous when target-towing.

At least two B-17Es were returned to the USA in 1944 and a few survived in service until the end of hostilities. By coinci-

Top right: **Main undercarriage of B-17E, 41-9017, *Heidi Ho*, tucks away after take-off from Bovingdon, September 1942. The B-17Es were the only 8th Air Force Fortresses with US ARMY painted on the undersides of wings.**

Centre right: **For 97th BG's last few missions with B-17Es it was practice to have two .30 Brownings installed in the nose ball sockets. The two .50 guns in staggered 'cheek' windows can be clearly seen on 41-9103.**

Right: **Experimental plate armour on 97th BG B-17E 'waist' gun. Found to make manipulation of the gun more difficult, as well as adding weight to the rear of the aircraft, it was soon deleted.**

Above: **Main distinguishing feature of B-17E was framed nosepiece but several of these were later replaced with the frameless B-17F type as on 41-9100, serving as 379th BG 'hack' in 1944.**

dence, the last to be broken up, at Honington in August 1945, led the 8th Air Force's first heavy bomber mission on 17 August 1942, viz 41-2578.

B-17E details
Four Wright R-1820-65 radials rated at 1200 hp each

Span 103 ft 9 in (31.62 m)
Length 73 ft 10 in (22.50 m)
Empty weight 32,250 lb (14,628 kg)
Max loaded weight 54,000 lb (24,494 kg)
Max bomb load 4000 lb (1814 kg)
Armament 8 × .50-in (12.7 mm) mg plus 1 × .30-in (7.62 mm) mg
Max speed 317 mph (510 km/h) at 25,000 ft (7620 m)
Climb 7 min 6 sec to 10,000 ft (3050 m)
Service ceiling 36,500 ft (11,120 m)
Norm range 2000 miles (3220 km) on 1730 US gallons

Tact radius 350 to 450 miles (563–724 km)
Crew 10

B-17F

The B-17F was a refined B-17E, the major difference being the introduction of wide-blade propellers to obtain more air 'bite' and give better performance. There were numerous internal changes, mostly to improve combat ability. Externally the F was distinguished by a clear moulded nosepiece, but in later months some B-17Es had their framed nosepiece replaced with one of B-17F type. This model Fortress was produced by three different plants in two different states and, thought basically similar, each manufacturer made detail changes. To identify their source, a manufacturer's suffix was introduced after the aircraft designation and block number: BO – Boeing, VE – Lockheed Vega and DL – Douglas. Block numbers identified production aircraft incorporating the same detail changes or modifications.

B-17Fs for 8th Air Force arrived in England during the first week of August 1942, making their combat debut on the 27th with 97th Group. A further 17 groups reaching 8th Air Force between August 1942 and July 1943 had B-17Fs as original combat equipment. In order of arrival they were: 301st, 92nd, 306th, 91st, 303rd, 305th, 95th, 94th, 351st, 96th, 379th, 100th, 381st, 384th, 385th, 388th and 390th. Peak strength of B-17Fs was just over 800 in early September 1943, when the Force had received approximately 1200, the balance being lost in action, scrapped or transferred. By the summer of 1944 few B-17Fs remained in operational units, being withdrawn as soon as replacements were available because of troublesome hydraulic supercharger controls. By July 1944 there were fewer than 30 F models in regular combat groups. The last known B-17F used in normal daylight missions was the 388th Group's 42-30195 *Blind Date*, destroyed in a forced landing on 7 October 1944. Last survivor in an operational special duties unit was 42-30656, *Miss Mickey Finn* of the Night Leaflet Squadron, still in service at VE-Day.

As the principal aircraft with which VIII BC developed its daylight bombing technique, the B-17 was subject to more detail changes than any other USAAF production aircraft; 'In the field' modifications too, were extensive. The environment in which the Fortress operated had a bearing on many of these changes, the high humidity and very low temperature encountered on the many missions executed by VIII BC imposed strain on equipment and systems that had been troublefree in warmer, drier climates. Many of these deficiencies were highlighted in the first few missions. The brushes in the electrical generators proved unsatisfactory at high altitude, the ball turret was beset with troubles, ice and excess oil caused guns to jam, and the rubber de-icer boots became torn by shell fragments and cartridge cases ejected from ball turret guns. Additionally two

fundamental weaknesses were recognised, the lack of forward firepower and tail heaviness. These shortcomings engendered a programme of modifications and recommendations (see the Reed Project).

Improving forward firepower became a priority when the Luftwaffe concentrated on frontal attacks in early November 1942. Most B-17Fs had ball sockets in the plexiglas nosepiece to take a .30-in machine gun, but this single rifle calibre weapon was largely ineffectual while the intention that it should be moved from one position to another as required in flight was impracticable. The first measure taken in the four combat B-17 groups was to replace or supplement the .30 guns with .50s, necessitating mountings sufficiently robust to take the recoil of the larger calibre weapons. In December and January a single .50-in nose gun installation kit, fabricated by VIII AF Service Command, was supplied to the groups. This gun was positioned off-centre of the plexiglas nosepiece, to be clear of the bombsight; in the majority of cases fitted on the right hand side. By early March 1943 the 91st and 303rd Groups had 15 of their aircraft with this fixture, the 305th 11 and the 306th 12. Additionally, 303rd had two B-17Fs with the nose gun mounted left of centre.

While the urgency of incorporating a power-operated nose gun turret on Fortress production was made plain to Washington, a twin .50-in gun arrangement was devised by 8th Air Force to project through a cutaway in the upper part of the plexiglas nosepiece, mounted on a tubular support. Three such fixtures were ordered for each group. Aircraft with these twin nose guns were usually flown flanking the group lead, to give supporting fire. With this installation it was not possible to operate a bombsight, so the bombardier served only as gunner and togglier. Accurate fire was difficult to achieve due to the recoil 'kick' of these weapons and field of fire was limited to an approximate 15

Below: **Mainstay of VIII BC's offensive until the end of 1943, the B-17F went through 27 production block changes but was externally little different.** *Cincinatti Queen*, **42-30715 was a B-17F-115-BO serving with 390th BG.**

Above right: **VIII AFSC off-set mount for .50 Browning in nosepiece ball socket of early 91st BG B-17F. When not in use the gun was secured by banjo cords to keep it clear of the bombardier.**

Right: **VIII AFSC twin .50 nose gun installations in B-17F, 42-29761, VP:W, normally flown as 'wing' aircraft to support the formation leader. Note sheet of armour plate attached to support framing under guns.**

degree cone. Yet another disadvantage was that the crouching gunner could not be afforded armour protection. Nevertheless, the twin .50 guns offered some defence against frontal assault and in late February the number of installations per group was doubled and in March raised to ten. The work, carried out at Honington at a two per day rate, could only be done when aircraft were not on standby for combat missions.

It is not clear just how many twin-gun mounts were actually completed for, in April, VIII BC standardised on a single gun .50 mount that had originated in 306th Group. This was located centrally in the upper part of the nosepiece, affording a much wider cone of fire. When not in use the gun could be swung to one side and retained with a banjo cord, so that it was clear of the bombsight. The mount was fabricated at Langford Lodge and supplied to air depots in kit form. As early as February, VIII

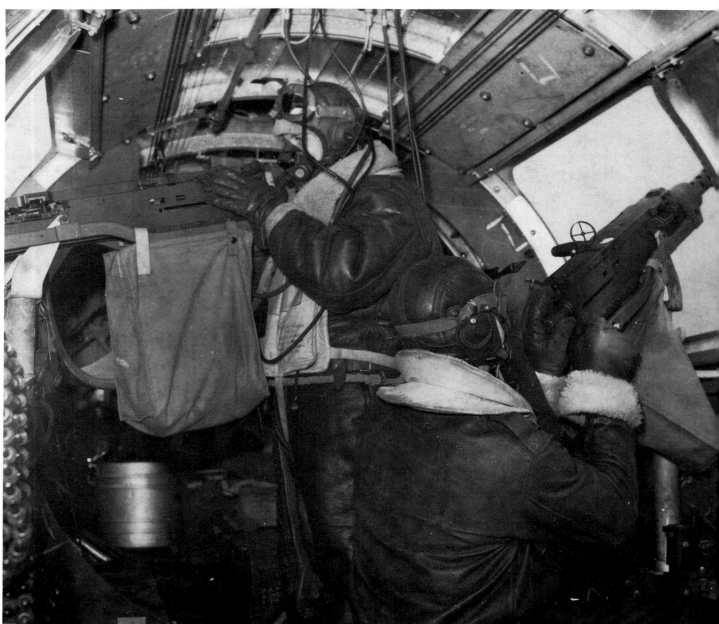

BC and VIII AFSC had discussed standardising future nose installations on a refinement of this centre-mounted arrangement, and an officer went to the USA to explain the urgency of having this modification made on new aircraft. However, it was May before a B-17F with a central nose gun mount incorporated arrived in the UK.

Difficulties with the ventral ball turret were of major concern from the early days of operations. The oxygen line, head set, throat microphone and electrically-heated suit cords, each plugged in at different places in the turret, could become tangled during gun charging, jam clearing or other activity of the gunner. Trace links frequently clogged in the ejection chutes and in the air it was often not possible to clear jams with the limited device carried.

On an average mission there was insufficient oxygen for the gunner and the necessity to watch for failing supply decreased his efficiency. Moreover, when a waist gunner recharged the turret oxygen, the valve often became frozen up and started to discharge the supply immediately the filler line was removed. Other troubles were the Vickers hydraulic unit which leaked at

Above: The open top hatch in the radio compartment allowed very restricted field of fire. On numerous occasions gunners shot off the Command radio antenna or peppered the aircraft's fin. In the latter half of 1944 this gun was eliminated. Gunner depicted is S/Sgt Russell M. Warren in 303rd BG's *Hell's Angels*.

Left: Waist gunners frequently got in each other's way during combat, an inconvenience not eliminated until staggered waist windows were introduced on B-17Gs in 1944. Canvas bags under the guns in this 305th BG B-17F were designed to catch spent cases.

altitude causing oil to get on equipment, and the turret door fracturing; additionally, escape procedure was far from satisfactory. The gunner had to hand-crank his turret into the correct position to lift the doors, climb into the fuselage, don his parachute and then bale out, a daunting task with an aircraft out of control. This, and the extremely restricted space inside the ball

turret, made it the least sought after crew position. New gaskets, reinforcement of doors, removal of the link ejector chutes and replacement with a redesigned type, solved most problems. As early as October 1942 an extensive modification of a ball turret had been performed by engineers at Bovingdon to overcome most of the shortcomings, but it appears there were problems in taking this concept further at that time.

Unless ammunition compartments were equipped with baffle plates, the rolling of the turret dislodged rounds in the trace and they would not feed into the breech. These plates, included initially on production, had been discarded in a weight saving programme. New plates were made in the UK for the majority of aircraft needing them, pending their reinstatement on future deliveries.

The upper turret also needed revisions. It was found that in one position the gunsight was covered by turret structure bracing, and the offending frame bar was removed at depots. Metal side panels obstructed the view; these blind spots were reported to Washington early in 1943 but several months elapsed before a redesigned dome was available. Meanwhile replacement clear panels were made in the UK. Additionally, use of the gun charging handles was proving difficult.

Another deficiency receiving early recognition was the need for armoured glass. Through Air Ministry arrangements a British manufacturer supplied sections for fixing to cockpit windshields, side windows and for the ball and tail gunners face panels for installation as required during the early months of 1943. An essential first attention to early B-17s, before reaching operational status, was VHF radio installation and modifications of antennas from trailing to fixed. Additionally, each aircraft was fitted with IFF from British sources, while the adoption of the Standard Beam Approach also entailed installing apparatus. All eligible Fortresses were equipped by mid-March 1943.

By May 1943 the standard modification list for B-17s joining 8th Air Force had 59 items, 19 pertaining to armament, nine to armour plate and bullet-proof glass fitment, three concerning electrical accessories and two the engines. Eight items covered radio and associated installations, seven were for structural changes or reinforcements and the remainder concerned oxygen, rescue equipment and miscellaneous items. With new B-17 groups arriving, the modification programme was beyond depot resources. Later that May VIII BC indicated 12 prime priorities concerning nose gun installations, upper turret charging handles, armour plate protection to pilot's instrument panel, increased ammunition supply for the radio room gun, an increase in the oxygen supply to top and ball turrets, replacement of radio antenna, a change from Mk II to Mk III IFF sets, fitting a remote-indicating compass, changes to the liferaft release and to other emergency equipment. In second priority, time and resources permitting, were bullet-proof glass in pilots' windows and side panels, mounting brackets for an N-3A reflector sight on all .50 guns, repositioning waist gun mounts to achieve a better field of fire, installation of *Gee*, additional changes in the oxygen system and the supercharger regulator, and collectors for links and cases ejected by guns. There were also third and fourth priorities.

This list was superseded on 19 July by a 'staging letter' to cover all tasks to be performed in stages at depots before delivery of new aircraft. Although this had 101 items, 72 of which were stage 1 priority, it did not actually represent a great workload increase as some items were only points for check and inspection. Eleven were instructions to remove various items of equipment, including bomb-bay tanks, de-icer boots, steps and extra seating. Stage 1 priority listed armament items including nose gun installation, increases in ammunition capacity and flexible feed arrangements, harmonisation of guns, reworking the charging handle in the upper turret, substituting G-4 type solenoids in the upper and ball turrets, replacing gaskets in ball turret hydraulics and checking all bolts in this turret. Two radio

Visibility restrictions were a major complaint from gunners operating the Sperry A-1 turret in early B-17s. As an improvement, the metal panels were replaced by clear perspex manufactured in the UK. S/Sgt Joe Collette of 306th BG is gunner in picture.

items concerned substituting Mk III for Mk II IFF and changing the radio antenna. Five items pertained to servicing engines and accessories. Sixteen items dealt with structure: reduction of armour plate in pilot's compartment, drilling holes in radio room door, modifying liferaft release, plus 11 removal and maintenance items and a complete wash-down of the airframe. There were also eight miscellaneous items featuring additions to oxygen system, sea rescue equipment and minor changes such as flares, safetying, stencilling, etc.

Stage 2 'desirable' modifications provided for: reinforcement of fuselage to prevent cracking due to gun blast, re-positioning waist gun mounts to pivot clear of the skin line to provide wider fields of fire, installing a distant-reading compass, introducing armour plate to protect the instrument panel and replacement of the metal panels on the upper turret with plexiglas. Stage 3 included mounting brackets for reflector gunsight Mk IIA on .50 guns, bullet-proof glass in the pilot's compartment and collectors for links and cases ejected by guns. Stage 4 provisions were for items usually installed by mobile engineering units only on special mission aircraft such as leaflet delay release mechanism, resin identification lights, special radars, etc. Stage 5 contained 15 items to be incorporated in the US and continued in the UK only until supply of kits was exhausted. These included additional armour plate, windshield frost proofing, reinforcement of ball turret doors, modifications to bomb-bay doors, bullet-proof glass for the ball turret, flexible ammunition feeds, changing the tail gunsight control cable, removal of cross bar impeding sight from upper turret and installation of 200 amp generators on outboard engines.

Many of the modifications were not required, being incorporated on new aircraft, but the list was prepared to cover all eventualities, particularly as there was considerable variance in modifications and equipment installed by manufacturers and centres in the USA. Eventually the three manufacturing plants introduced most of the required modifications on production but there was always several months delay. The weak frontal armament complaint and the initial request for some form of power

turret made during the autumn of 1942 resulted in the promise of the Bendix 'chin' turret. While this did appear on the YB-40 'escort' Fortress in May 1943, it was September before the arrival of bombers so armed. There was also promise of electrically-actuated supercharger controls to answer the most troubling feature of flying the B-17F at high altitude. The hydraulic controls required constant exercising as changes in temperature and altitude affected oil viscosity, upsetting regulator settings. This could lead to overspeeding of the turbine bucket causing either bearing failure or disintegration of the wheel. Loss of a supercharger meant lack of high altitude power, failing performance and inability to maintain formation, leading to straggling and probable loss. The extremely low temperatures at operating altitude also caused bomb-bay doors and bomb shackle releases to freeze, failures solved with a crowbar in the early days. As with guns, care taken to remove moisture while on the ground was a major preventative step, although at one point there was consideration of flying B-17s without their bomb-bay doors. The practice of operating the doors a few inches on route to ensure they would open on the bomb run allowed time to free them if they failed to respond.

A condition not easily rectified was the tail-heavy balance condition of the B-17F. When fully combat-loaded with two waist gunners in position, the aircraft had a centre of gravity rearward of the maximum safe limit. To counteract this tail heaviness it was necessary to adjust elevator trim tabs from their neutral position in sustained flight, placing stress on this component. It was estimated that this trimming robbed the B-17 of about 10 mph. The importance of rearward defence checked the move to lighten the tail end by removing one waist gunner and limiting ammunition. Nevertheless, crews were cautioned to exercise care in positioning any equipment in the rear.

In most major air battles during the first half of 1943 there were some incidents of self-inflicted damage from waist gunners running their fire into wing and tail surfaces. In some cases this was serious enough to jeopardise the safe return of the aircraft and at the least it caused skin repair work. In July 1943 1/Lt Samuel R. Sepienza and M/Sgt William L. Caldwell of 359th BS, 303rd Group, perfected an electric cut-off apparatus which automatically checked the firing mechanism of a gun when swung into line with any part of the wing or empennage. The device was later approved for manufacture at a depot for fitting on all waist guns. Another shut-off device perfected by a 385th Group officer a month later was apparently not used outside his group.

The most significant development of B-17F production was additional fuel cells providing another 1080 US gallons, increasing range by nearly a thousand miles. For VIII BC this meant almost doubling the tactical radius of action to 650 miles, allowing Fortresses to be used on much deeper penetrations. Popularly known an Tokyo tanks, through the impression that they would give the Fortress the range to reach that far off enemy capital, they took the form of nine rubber-composition self-sealing cells positioned between the ribs in each wing. New groups, the 381st and 384th, with the long-range B-17F (from factory blocks 80-BO, 25-DL and 30-VE) began arriving in May 1943. As the next Group, the 100th, arriving in early June, and two others following soon after, were all completely equipped with the new long-range versions, VIII BC decided to concentrate them all in the 4th Wing and commenced a programme of exchange with 1st Wing groups. The 94th, 95th and 96th Groups passed all their short-range Fs to 1st Wing and received long-range aircraft in return.

Although many long-range aircraft remained in 1st Wing and its groups rapidly received this version as replacements, a number of the short-range B-17Fs remained in service and had to be restricted to operations requiring only five or six hours endurance. In the winter of 1943–44 many of these early Fortresses were concentrated in the three groups of 41st Combat Wing, preparing to use glide bombs which, because of drag induced by their external carriage, were to be delivered against short-range targets. This Combat Wing was later given the GH bombing aid, also limited to shorter ranges. While Tokyo tanks gave a much needed boost to range, they also increased combat vulnerability. During the summer of 1943 crews witnessed several instances where explosions destroyed the outer wing sections of B-17s. Fuel had to be transferred from auxiliary to main tanks for engine feed, the gasses in the partly emptied Tokyo tanks and accumulating in the outer wing section being easily ignited by incendiary bullets or cannon shells. The earlier short-range B-17Fs without Tokyo tanks were definitely more battle-hardy.

Modifications also originated from ground personnel, particularly those aimed at simplifying or quickening a particular task.

On the early B-17Fs the bomb-bay cable hoist took on average 40 minutes to raise a full load by hand cranking, both up and down. By modifying the cable drum men at 97th Group devised a quick release that eliminated the need to crank down the load-free cable, halving the time taken to place a full bomb load. In October 1942 this idea was taken up by VIIIBC and arrangements were made for Langford Lodge to carry out a programme of modifications. The deep bomb-bay, small compared with those of British heavy bombers, could take six armour-piercing bombs of 1600 lb each as a maximum internal load, but in 8th Air Force where range considerations were paramount, the normal load was 4000 to 5000 lb, depending on range factors and type of bomb. The B-17F had the capability to lift much heavier loads if external wing racks were used when it was possible but not practicable to attach 4000 lb bombs. With the prospect of increasing bomb loads to short-haul targets, in August 1943 B-17 stations received kits for installing external racks on their aircraft. A few missions were flown during the next month where, in addition to a normal internal load, two 2000 lb bombs were carried externally by each Fortress. With the adverse effect on climb and high altitude performance making formation flying even more difficult and considerably reducing endurance, VIIIBC soon decided that high altitude bombing was sufficiently difficult without this added burden. Underwing racks were removed, thereafter to be used only for special tasks.

B-17F details
Four Wright R-1820-97 radials rated at 1200 hp each

Span 103 ft 9 in (31.62 m)
Length 74 ft 9 in (22.78 m)
Empty weight 34,000 lb (15,422 kg)
Max loaded weight 65,500 lb (29,712 kg)
Max speed 299 mph (481 km/h) at 25,000 ft (7620 m)
Tact operating speeds 180–215 mph (290–346 km/h) at 25,000 ft (7620 m)
Climb 25 min 42 sec to 20,000 ft (6100 m)
Tact climb rate 1 hr 20 min to 25,000 ft (7620 m)
Service ceiling 37,500 ft (11,430 m)
Norm tact altitude 21,000 to 27,000 ft (6400–8230 m)
Norm range 1300 miles (2092 km) (original), 2200 miles (3542 km) (Tokyo tanks)
Fuel consumption 160 US gallons (606 ltr) per hour at 180 mph (290 km/h)
Max bomb load 9600 lb (4355 kg) (internal)
Norm tact bomb load 4000 lb (1814 kg)
Armament 11 to 12 .50-in (12.7 mm) mg
Crew 10

Inability to feather a propeller resulted in this damage to No 4 Engine on *Round Trip Ticket III*, causing the pilots to make an emergency landing at North Weald in June 1944. This veteran 549th BS, 385th BG B-17F was retired as 'war-weary' in August after 57 missions. Stripped of battle equipment it was loaned to 17th Airborne Division, US Army and during the winter of 1944–45 made daily transport flights between Grove and Melun.

YB-40

Early in 1942 USAAF considered long-range bomber escort, based on a substantial airframe having a large number of gun positions. Before any decision was reached on a special design for this purpose, a proposal was accepted to test the practicability of modifying a B-17F for escort duties. The work was undertaken by the Vega factory and the prototype, designated XB-40, began tests in September 1942. The following month the USAAF ordered 13 similarly modified B-17Fs designated YB-40s for combat trials. A further 12 were ordered in January 1943 as replacement.

Modification work on Vega-built airframes were conducted at the Tulsa Douglas Modification Centre where the first 13 YB-40s were ready for delivery by late March. After a brief period of crew training, overseas movement was made early in May via the North Atlantic ferry route. One aircraft (the first YB-40, 42-5732) got off course and when on the point of running out of fuel was 'bellied in' on a Lewis bog; later it was removed to Stornoway for repair. The remaining 12 YB-40s and crews, arriving safely at Alconbury on 8 May, were established as the 327th BS of 92nd Group.

The YB-40's armament was impressive. Tail, under and upper turrets were as the B-17F but an additional upper two-gun power turret was located above the radio room. There were also direct-sighted twin guns at each waist window and, most notably, a remote-controlled twin gun 'chin' turret. The waist and tail guns were hydraulic power-boosted to make them easier to manipulate and steadier when firing. The tail position also had a reflector sight in place of the B-17F's ring and post type. First weeks in England were occupied with flight testing and making theatre modifications. The YB-40s had arrived without the navigator's side nose gun and it was felt these could well make a useful addition to the aircraft's firepower, as well as help to counter the aircraft's obvious tail heaviness, so installations were made, raising the gun total to 16. There was a considerable amount of armour plate at crew positions which was in large measure responsible for the 4000 lb increase in weight over the standard B-17. The mechanism and gunner in the radio room Martin turret were protected by a cylinder of armour plate which extended to within two feet of the floor. To enter the turret the gunner had to get down on all fours and squirm up through the armour plate to reach his seat. It was obvious that this

gunner would have little chance of escape in an emergency. The chin turret was hydraulic-electric actuated, the gunner using a remote reflector sight on a control arm situated in the nosepiece. Ammunition was stored throughout the aircraft but the bulk was forward to help the centre of gravity. The advised total was 11,200 rounds, but 8th Air Force considered loading substantially more. Even with the recommended ammunition load, the YB-40 grossed over 58,000 lb (26,310 kg), some 10,000 lb more than a loaded B-17F. YB-40s often took-off at 63,000 lb (28,577 kg).

Crew of the YB-40 consisted of pilot, co-pilot, navigator, chin gunner, forward upper turret gunner, rear upper turret gunner, ball gunner, right and left waist gunners and tail gunner. There was no radio-operator, VHF communications being handled by the pilots. There was consideration of allowing the navigator to operate the chin turret, thus permitting one man to act as an ammunition carrier to all gun positions. The bomb-bays were as the B-17F but bombing equipment had been deleted.

The first YB-40 mission was flown on 27 May 1943 to St Nazaire when seven participated. This initial experience dictated the necessity for modifications to the waist and tail gun feeds and ammunition supplies. It also indicated the basic defect of the YB-40, its inability to keep up with normal B-17Fs, especially after they had bombed. Following the ammunition feed modifications the YB-40s were despatched on five missions during late June, on the first of which 42-5735 was lost to flak. The YB-40s extreme tail heavy flight attitude and reduced performance made it virtually impossible to fly in formation with B-17s as position could not be maintained. After using these aircraft to flank the leaders of combat wings it was decided to try them in their own separate formation. After a ninth mission on 4 July, Col William Reid, CO of 92nd Group, reported that although the YB-40s firepower was theoretically 20 per cent greater than that of the B-17F, on operational missions it had actually been only 10 per cent more effective, chiefly through the chin turret. As at that time 75 per cent of Luftwaffe fighters were believed to attack head-on, the additional rear armament was little used. He believed that any advantage in armament

YB-40 showing the Martin turret and twin waist guns in stowed position.

was outweighed by the disadvantage of taking crew and aircraft into hostile airspace without a bomb load to deliver. He further recommended that no further YB-40s be sent to 8th Air Force. General Eaker concurred with these views and while not altogether condemning the idea of an escort bomber, asserted that it should carry bombs and have the same flight characteristics as other Fortresses.

The 327th BS obtained B-17Fs and went over to a bombing role in July 1943, six of the YB-40s being transferred to the 91st and 303rd Groups. There is no record of their being flown on further combat missions. A plan to transfer the aircraft to a Pacific war theatre for long range reconnaissance was considered but dropped. Several YB-40s were returned to the US in early 1944 and subsequently stripped of armour and armament and used for training. With the exception of one aircraft, all other YB-40s of the second batch were converted to trainers. The exception, 42-5833, had been extensively modified in the USA to meet the objections notified by 8th Air Force about the first YB-40s, and in October this aircraft was flown to England. Externally it was distinguished from the earlier aircraft by a new tail position. This featured hand-held guns in a cupola allowing an approximate 90 degree cone of fire. An N-8 reflector sight was fitted. It had a revised Bendix chin turret and increased ammunition supply to the two top turrets. There was a reduction in armour in the rear of the aircraft but additional armour around the engines. This effected a definite improvement in weight distribution and consequently improved flight characteristics, but it was still exceptionally heavy and had no bombing provisions. It was test flown by 8th Air Force and returned to the US with technical comment.

While the YB-40 concept proved unsuccessful, it did introduce a number of armament innovations adopted for later B-17s, particularly the chin turret, staggered waist windows and the lightweight tail gun positions.

YB-40 details
Four Wright R-1820-97 radials rated at 1200 hp each

Span 103 ft 9 in (31.62 m)
Length 74 ft 9 in (22.78 m)
Empty weight 38,235 lb (17,344 kg)
Max loaded weight 63,500 lb (28,804 kg)
Max speed 292 mph (470 km/h) at 25,000 ft (7620 m)
Tact operating speed 250 mph (402 km/h) at 25,000 ft (7620 m)
Climb 48 min 6 sec to 20,000 ft (6100 m)
Service ceiling 25,100 ft (7650 m)
Norm range 2260 miles (3637 km)
Tact radius 350 miles (563 km)
Bomb load nil
Armament 16 × .50-in (12.7 mm) mg
Crew 10

YB-40s of 92nd Bomb Group

Serial No	Original Nickname	Disposition
42-5732		To USA 28.3.44
42-5733	Peoria Prowler	To 91st BG 7.43. To USA 2.11.43
42-5734	Seymour Angel	To 91st BG 7.43. To USA 25.1.44
42-5735		MIA 22.6.43
42-5736	Tampa Tornado	To 303 BG 7.43. To 379 BG 9.43. To USA 28.3.44
42-5737	Dakota Demon	To 303 BG 7.43. To USA 2.11.43
42-5738	Boston Tea Party	To USA 2.11.43
42-5739	Lufkin Ruffian	To 303 BG 7.43. To 384 BG 9.43. To USA 2.11.43
42-5740	Monticello	To USA 2.11.43
42-5741	Chicago	To 91 BG 7.43. To USA 2.11.43
42-5742	Plain Dealing Express	To USA 28.3.44
42-5743	Woolaroc	To USA 2.11.43
42-5744	Dollie Madison	To USA 2.11.43
42-5833		To USA 26.5.44

THE REED PROJECT B-17

During the early months of VIII BC operations the engineering section of the Bovingdon CCRC was used in investigating technical and operational problems that arose. Weaknesses in B-17 crew organisation and armament, that became apparent after the first few missions, were of immediate concern and Major Robert J. Reed, the Engineering Officer, conducted a special study with a view to making recommendations on how best these could be overcome. A B-17E of 92nd Group was set aside for use in planning and effecting trial modifications.

By late January 1943 Major Reed was able to submit a detailed report on these investigations. The problems were defined as: lack of sufficient firepower forward, insufficient organisation of the combat crew, tail heavy balance condition, difficulties with the lower ball turret and inadequate oxygen supply for turrets. Solutions were proposed and some modifications had been carried out on the B-17E 41-9112. VIII BC was impressed with Reed's work and as many of the changes proposed involved major specialist engineering that could not readily be undertaken by the 8th Air Force at that time, it was arranged to send the aircraft to the United States to have this work performed. Major Reed was to oversee the project and while in the US make known the shortcomings of current production B-17s to Materiel Command and the manufacturers.

Reed and his B-17E returned in February 1943 to the USA where modifications were undertaken at Wright Field. The work was not completed until September and early in October the Reed project bomber, nicknamed Dreamboat, was flown back across the Atlantic. The purpose was to elicit opinion from 8th Air Force engineering staff and combat group commanders, for while USAAF Hq viewed Reed's aircraft favourably, they felt that incorporation of such extensive revisions to production line Fortresses would cause unacceptable delays.

Dreamboat featured radical armament changes. Consolidated hydraulic power turrets, similar to that used in the B-24D, were installed in nose and tail. They provided better optical conditions for sighting, armour plate and bullet-proof glass protection, and a more comfortable and efficient operating position for the gunners. The nose gunner was separated from the bombardier who was provided with a separate compartment in

the form of an under-nose blister. The duties of bombardier and navigator were combined. All the radio equipment was removed to the nose compartment and the radio operator given a position adjacent to the navigator. In addition to the benefit of having navigator and radio operator together, so that they could communicate directly if the interphone failed, moving the radio position helped considerably in improving the centre of gravity of the aircraft.

A longer radio aerial wire running from nose to fin and fin to wing provided a stronger signal. In the cockpit the pilot was provided with an armoured seat affording a high degree of protection for the occupant and, although not actually installed, it was intended that a similar protected seat should be available for the co-pilot. The Sperry upper turret was replaced by a 120 lb lighter Martin type, providing sitting position for the gunner, better armour protection and taking up less flight deck room. A set of folding panel bomb-bay doors was fitted which when fully opened extended only eight inches below the bottom of the fuselage. This eliminated the excessive drag encountered when normal B-17 bomb-doors were opened, did not obstruct vision and firing line of the ball turret gunner, and made it more difficult for the enemy to observe when the bay was open, so indicating that a bombing run was under way. A power boosted twin .50 gun mounting was made in the former radio room top hatch, providing a field of fire: 180 degrees azimuth, 78 degrees elevation and 45 degrees depression. This was an open position, protected by a windshield, designed to replace the waist guns and eliminate gunners in that position. The ball turret had an external ammunition supply, sufficient for a mission without reloading. Removing ammunition from inside the turret allowed more room for the gunner, enabling him to wear a B-8 back-pack parachute. Short, straight chutes conducted ejected links out of the side of the turret thereby eliminating the cause of many stoppages. Unlike the standard ball turret it was also possible to raise the gun covers 90 degrees to clear a blockage or make an adjustment. The tail turret provided a field of fire approximately six times greater than the original emplacement. Guns could be swung 180 degrees azimuth, 70 degrees elevation and 40 degrees depression.

The oxygen system layout was completely redesigned to make it as invulnerable as possible. Each crew member had his own independent double line so that if one line failed he could still receive a half supply. By eliminating the waist guns the crew was reduced from ten to eight. In addition to combining bombardier and navigator duties, the radio operator served as nose gunner and only one gunner was required in the waist area to operate in the former radio room position. With centre of gravity near the ideal, and over 1,000 lb saving in weight on a comparable B-17F, the handling characteristics of *Dreamboat* were better than the latest production Fortresses. Speed and

Top: *Dreamboat* was obviously not named for aesthetic qualities. Note raised twin gun mount in dorsal position which replaced waist window firepower.   (Smithsonian)

Above: **Bombardier gondola and folding bomb-bay doors show in this view of Reed Project B-17.**

power requirements were practically the same due to the less streamlined features of the Reed bomber. During October and November 1943 Major Reed and the *Dreamboat* visited each 1st and 3rd Division combat base for inspection and comment. All commended its features, particularly the folding bomb doors and double oxygen system. Criticism was levelled at cramped nose quarters and the vulnerability of crew and radio equipment to a single cannon shell strike in the nose. A second Martin turret for the radio room position was also suggested. *Dreamboat* remained in the UK for many months, usually resident at air depots. Frequently taken to be a B-40 by uninitiated spectators, its presence became known to enemy intelligence, and probably accounts for Luftwaffe reports of the mysterious B-40 described as having 25 guns! That the improvements made by Reed were not incorporated in B-17s was due principally to the oncoming production of the B-29 and B-32 which were expected eventually to replace the B-17 and B-24.

B-17G

The final production model of the Fortress – and also the most numerous – began to reach 8th Air Force in September 1943. The B-17G was basically a B-17F with a chin turret, in fact the first production chin turrets appeared on 66 Douglas built B-17Fs which were relabelled as B-17Gs. The Bendix chin turret, which had been proved on the YB-40, provided the long sought power turret defensive armament for Fortresses. The first production Gs dispensed with the navigator's guns but VIII BC, believing in their value, had installations made at English depots. Eventually the 'cheek' guns were restored on production lines.

A major step in the advancement of the B-17 design was the introduction of Minneapolis-Honeywell electric turbo-supercharger regulators, first appearing in England on the Vega-built B-17G-5-VEs and Douglas-built B-17G-15-DLs late in October 1943. Control of manifold pressure (boost) on all four engines simultaneously was obtained by a simple control knob. It eliminated the concern with turbine overspeeding through temperature and altitude changes affecting former hydraulic controls. The change was particularly popular with pilots and helped to remove some of the fatigue imposed on long missions by constantly having to manipulate power controls to prevent the oil in regulator lines becoming sluggish. The new mechanism also contributed to greater operational efficiency through reducing aborts and losses. It was this feature more than any other that sped the retirement of early B-17Gs and B-17Fs once the models with electric turbo controls became plentiful.

Other significant changes in production of the B-17G were the enclosing of waist gun positions to shield gunners from the icy air blast, and staggering their relative positions to give each gunner more room. Douglas-built B-17Gs with these changes began to be received in March 1944, Boeing-built in April and from Vega in May. In June 1944 new Fortresses arrived with what

Above: **Fortress 42-31078, WW:R on its Thurleigh dispersal in November 1943. One of the first Seattle-built B-17Gs received by 306th BG it had no cheek gun installations.**

Left: **Improvised cheek gun installation on 94th BG's B-17G 42-3537 offered very limited field of fire through shattered plexiglas window. This aircraft was one of the first batch of Douglas-built Fortresses with chin turrets, originally designated as B-17F-75-DL but redesignated as B-17G-1-DL.**

was popularly known as Cheyenne tail gun positions. Similar in design to that installed on the last YB-40, this provided better visibility for the gunner, featuring hand-held guns with a substantially widened field of fire, and a reflector sight. This revised tail gun position had previously been fitted to some B-17Gs at VIII AFSC depots when the original tail position had been damaged.

There were numerous other changes, albeit mostly minor, introduced during the 22 months production run of the B-17G identified by 22 different block numbers. While these met many of the deficiencies or requirements raised by 8th Air Force there was still need to maintain a modification programme in the UK on all Fortresses received. Apart from special theatre requirements, some changes on production presented new problems.

On the first operations with B-17Gs it was found that if chin turret guns were fired at maximum elevation the blast cracked the plexiglas nosepiece. A solution was the fitting of 18 inch long blast tubes on each barrel. Sometimes manufacturing processes were found wanting as a weakness might only be highlighted after considerable operational use. An example is a plague of B-17 oil cooler radiator failures during the winter of 1943–44. The copper core fractured and in some cases the subsequent loss of oil brought engine seizure. One station had to return over 200 defective oil radiators to its air depot in four months. Hydrostatic pressures, vibration, plus the extreme variations in temperature encountered were more than the coolers could withstand, but it took some time for this general weakness to be appreciated. By February 1944 8th Air Force was calling the situation alarming and requesting speedy development of a more robust design. During 1943 VIII BC became increasingly aware that many B-17s were placed in jeopardy by the inability to feather propellers. In the event of engine failure, feathering – angling the blades so that leading edges faced forward – was essential. Failure to do this allowed the free-running propeller to pick up excessive speed, cause dangerous vibration and threaten the safety of the aircraft.

Early B-17s were equipped with a standpipe in each oil tank designed to hold back sufficient oil to operate the feathering pump even if the tank supply became seriously depleted. In a weight reduction programme for production B-17Fs this standpipe had been deleted as a sacrificeable extra. By the winter of 1943 there had been enough incidents where, through battle damage or leaks, oil loss had been so rapid that there was insufficient left to allow feathering, to cause 8th Air Force to have a kit for an oil standpipe installation designed. Although ready for production in December 1943 other priorities and difficulty in obtaining special materials in the UK caused a postponement. In July 1944 a report covering the cause of bomber loss, prepared from interviews with badly disabled crewmen who had been returned from imprisonment in Germany, caused increased concern about the inability to feather engines. An analysis revealed that this was a direct or contributory factor in nearly half the cases under review. Urgent requests were made to Washington for the reintroduction of emergency oil standpipes on B-17 engines but aircraft with these fitted did not arrive until September 1944. Modification kits from the USA also arrived later in the year for aircraft delivered earlier. It was not a task that could be carried out quickly as it entailed replacing an oil line with one of a larger bore, and was still incomplete by VE-Day

Another victim of measures to reduce weight was the engine fire extinguisher system. Considered not very effective, it was deleted with the fitting of the Tokyo tanks on B-17F production. It took the form of CO_2 dispensing jets rigged in a ring around the rear of the engine cylinders just forward of the firewall. However, experience showed that many fires on early B-17Fs had been extinguished by this system and requests were made for its reintroduction. Deletion on the production line had been a comparatively simple task; reintroduction was another matter and it was May 1944 before engine fire extinguishers were seen on new B-17Gs in England.

Another serious failure during 1944 was in the Sperry top turret. After considerable rotation the electrical wires and oxygen lines running up the hollow turret spigot became frayed at the outlet. In several instances this led to an electrical short igniting oxygen while in the air, with the resulting fire getting beyond control. Operational Engineering's stop-gap solution to the problem was to fill the hollow lead-in with concrete to isolate and seal the wires and lines.

Several B-17s with new equipment or special changes were received in the UK for operational trials during the last year of hostilities. In June 1944 12 special aircraft were received with *Azon* transmitters for use in radio bomb release, with so-called

Above: *Cheyenne* tail gun position of 384th BG B-17G. Reflector sight is an N-6A.

Above right: **Boeing-built B-17G of 447th BG with high-profile Sperry turret, original type tail gun position and enclosed waist windows (a post-production modification).** (A. Swanson)

Right: **Later B-17G from same factory had blunter plexiglas nose, one-piece plexiglas waist window and *Cheyenne* tail gun position. A 487th BG aircraft, it has all-yellow empennage.**

'snap' bomb-bay doors which had faster movement, and armoured engines. The armour was installed on the curved section of the cowl ring to about six inches back, on propeller governors, ignition harness, oil sump, carburettor, fuel strainers, oil temperature regulator assemblies and booster pump covers. These aircraft were used by the 96th Group in trials, as were most of another 13 that followed in July. Results showed definite advantage in protection but the additional weight produced sluggish performance and suspected engine strain. The 'snap' bomb doors were not liked because the sudden opening prior to bomb release affected speed and control at a critical time.

The centre of gravity problem persisted but in May 1944 1st Combat Wing originated a policy eventually adopted by all 8th Air Force B-17 units. With increasing long-range fighter support gunners were only occasionally involved in action. Records showed that the radio room gun was the least used weapon and had little success. There was also recent evidence that both waist guns were rarely in use at the same time. As a weight saving measure, one waist gunner was dispensed with and the radio room gun removed. The quantity of ammunition carried in the rear of the aircraft was halved and storage of extra supplies for that section placed forward in the radio room. These measures moved the CG from 12 to five inches nearer the correct position.

A development to improve performance was the introduction of water injection on the R-1820 engine. Intended for short-period operation, it gave a 17 mph increase in speed at 20,000 feet. Kits to effect this modification were produced by BADA commencing in August 1944.

In the final days of the war, when enemy fighter attacks were rare and then usually a single fast pass, other armament reduction trials were carried out. In March 1945 1st Combat Wing had 91st Group fly without waist guns or gunners, 381st Group with ball turret removed, and 398th with chin turret removed. In 3rd Division the 94th Group removed chin and ball turrets. A sub-

stantial improvement in performance was reported by the 94th where a combination of better streamlining, weight reduction and improved CG resulted in an estimated 25 mph speed increase.

With flak becoming the major danger for the bombers some gunner armour plate was removed and in its place in January 1945 flak curtains, laminated steel plates held in canvas, were tried at some crew positions, both to save weight and because it was believed they would be more effective in stopping shell splinters.

An all-electric bomb release (the A-4) had been introduced in the spring of 1944 but production changes in the system brought considerable trouble in operations. There were many instances of bombs failing to release, traced to a combination of factors including moisture entering solenoids and faulty indicator lights on the bombardier's panel. Little wonder that engineers 'in the field' expressed feelings that development agencies of Materiel Command should leave well alone.

Some 6500 B-17Gs were assigned to 8th Air Force, with peak strength of around 2370 in March 1945; 1301 went missing in action.

B-17G details
Four Wright R-1820-97 radials rated at 1200 hp each

Span 103 ft 9 in (31.62 m)
Length 74 ft 9 in (22.78 m) (original), 74 ft 4 in (22.66 m) (Cheyenne)
Empty weight 36,135 lb (16,391 kg)
Max loaded weight 72,000 lb (32,659 kg)
Max speed 287 mph (462 km/h) at 25,000 ft (7620 m)
Tact operating speed 180–215 mph (290–346 km/h) at 25,000 ft (7620 m)
Climb rate 37 min to 20,000 ft (6100 m)
Tact climb 1 hr 30 min to 25,000 ft (7620 m)
Norm range 2000 miles (3220 km)
Tact radius 650–800 miles (1046–1287 km) depending on bomb load
Max bomb load 13,600 lb (6169 kg)
Norm tact bomb load 4000 lb (1814 kg)
Armament 12 × .50 in (12.7 mm) mg
Crew 9 or 10

AIRBORNE LIFEBOAT B-17

In November 1944 8th Air Force was asked to return 50 suitable B-17s to the USA for use as carriers of the new Higgins A-1 airborne lifeboat. This request was not met as no suitable second-line aircraft were available. At this time 8th Air Force's own air/sea rescue squadron was awaiting six airborne lifeboats which had been requested by Hq in August. Plans called for them to be based at Boxted where additional hard-standings were to be provided for the B-17 carriers. However, the lifeboats were not available until 1945 by which time the ASR unit had moved to Halesworth. In preparation, during January, 8th Air Force took stock of suitable war-weary B-17Gs in combat units that could be converted to carry the boats. There were several 'war-wearies' at depots but these lacked armament and were not suitable. Late in January it was learned that a project officer from Wright Field was being sent to provide technical information and oversee the modifications which, at that time, included sea-search radar 'in the chin turret'.

The six 'war-weary' B-17Gs eventually selected were 42-31706, 43-37765, and 42-38021 previously with 457th Group, and 42-38167, 42-37717 and 42-39790 released by the Night Leaflet Squadron. Modification work was carried out at Honington in March. Original intentions were to install SCR-717B sea search radar, SCR-729 *Rebecca* to home on the dinghy beacons, and an AN/APN-1 radar altimeter, but for

Ex-457th BG B-17G with Higgins A-1 lifeboat taxiing at Halesworth. (J. Archer)

expediency, only fittings to hold the 33-ft lifeboat were made to the first B-17s for conversion. Ball turrets were removed but all other armament was retained. First operational drop of the Higgins airborne lifeboat occurred on 31 March 1945 to save a bomber crew in the sea off Denmark.

On 18 April 1945 six new B-17Gs were assigned for ASR work and modified. These were 44-83451, 44-83301, 44-83474, 44-83470, 44-85548 and 43-39417, with the required radar aids, but it appears this work was not completed before they were redeployed to the USA in late May. Four of the earlier batch assigned to the ASR unit were sent to Marseilles after VE-Day.

TRANSPORT AND UTILITY B-17s

The flight stability and good handling characteristics of the Fortress made retired battle veterans popular for conversion into liaison transports. It was usual to remove all armament, turrets, armour, oxygen and bombing equipment, with additional seating installed as required. Several B-17E and B-17Fs thus lightened were used by VIII AFSC in the absence of sufficient C-47s or other basic transports. Eighth Air Force, 1st and 3rd Division Headquarters, and those of most Fortress Combat Wings had B-17 transports at one time or another. The 3rd Division's, 42-29780, usually based at Honington, had its camouflage paint removed in the late summer of 1943 to become the first B-17 in 8th Air Force to appear in bare metal. This aircraft was said to have a top speed of 25–30 mph above that of a combat configured B-17G. Over 50 different B-17s are known to have been converted to transport or utility duties by 8th Air Force.

Above right: *Silver Queen* was the VIP transport often used by Generals LeMay and Partridge. Stylised Z-in-a-square on tail fin was identification marking of 3rd Division Hq. (via G. Fry)

Right: The 303rd BG painted its tow-target B-17E, 41-9020, in red and white stripes. It also received a new nickname – *Tugboat Annie*. (Rex Lacewell)

Assignment of B-17Es to VIII Bomber Command Groups for Target Towing and Liaison Use, August 1943

91BG	41–9023 *Yankee Doodle*	381BG	41–9043 *Peggy D*
92BG	41–9154	384BG	41–9022 *Alabama Exterminator II*
94BG	41–9017 *Heidi Ho*	385BG	41–9103 *Dixie Demo*
95BG	41–9013	388BG	41–9129
96BG	41–9089 *Johnny Reb*	390BG	41–9021 *Hunger Queen*
100BG	41–2629	482BG	41–9017
303BG	41–9020 *Phyllis*	482BG	41–9019 *Lil Skunkface*
305BG	41–2628	11CCRC	41–9025 *Little John*
306BG	41–9148 *Boomerang*	11CCRC	41–9085 *Jarrin Jenny*
351BG	41–9121 *The Big Bitch*	11CCRC	41–9119
379BG	41–9100 *Birmingham Blitzkrieg*	11CCRC	41–2578

SPECIAL RADAR B-17s

Special installations of radar for bombing and navigational aids were made in many Fortresses. *Oboe* B-17s required no major modifications and these aircraft were only distinguished externally by additional antennas. Eighteen *Oboe* Mk 1 B-17s were originally planned for 813rd BS and 12 are known to have entered service with that unit in the second half of 1943. Two B-17s with *Album Leaf* (*Oboe* Mk II derivatives) were also used by the squadron.

Identities were:

Oboe Mk I		*Oboe* Mk II	
42–30328	PC:B	42–3525	PC:D
42–3385	PC:C	42–31166	PC:K/Z
42–3527	PC:G		
42–3382	PC:I		
42–30613	PC:J		
42–3521	PC:L		
42–37753	PC:O		
42–37733	PC:W		
42–37735	PC:X		
42–3536			
42–3521			
42–5745			
41–24359			
42–3358			

A total of eight H2S conversions were made, all to B-17Fs, during the second half of 1943. The H2S scanner was located in a plastic blister-shape container beneath the nose of the aircraft, with internal instrumentation in the nose and radio room. When these aircraft were withdrawn from operational service in March 1944 the radar equipment was removed. Identities were:

42–5793	PC:M	Cr 10.11.43	42–3357	PC:S	MIA 8.2.44
42–5909	PC:N	MIA 4.2.44	42–5970	PC:T	
42–3398	PC:Q		42–30731	PC:U	
42–5819	PC:R		42–30729	PC:V	

The original 12 H2X-equipped B-17s that arrived in the UK for 812th BS in October 1943 had the radar scanner placed under the nose. Unlike that on the H2S aircraft it was semi-retractable with its plastic radome. Radar instrumentation was located in the nose and radio room. Eleven of the aircraft were B-17Gs with chin turrets, the twelfth, the prototype, was a B-17F. These aircraft were taken off regular operations in late March 1944, the radars eventually being removed as the scanners were required for Mosquitoes. Identities were:

42–3483	MI:A		42–3491	MI:G	MIA 6.3.44
42–3484	MI:B		42–3492	MI:H	
42–3485	MI:C		42–3500	MI:J	MIA 4.2.44
42–3486	MI:D	MIA 11.1.44	42–3511	MI:K	
42–3487	MI:E		42–30280	MI:L	MIA 22.2.44
42–3490	MI:F	MIA 21.6.44	42–37745	MI:M	

Above: **In common with other survivors of 812th BS's original 12 H2X B-17s, *Chopstick A-Able* (R/T call-sign) was retired in April 1944 and subsequently became a VHF radio relay aircraft. The crude 'X' on the rear fuselage is a 'marking of the day' intended for exposing suspected enemy-operated B-17s that might join a formation. It is believed that 'markings of the day' were only used on one occasion.** (L. Redman)

Left: **H2X nose radome on B-17G 42-34511.**

B-17Gs with production H2X sets began to arrive in the UK in February 1944. These featured a scanner in a semi-retractable radome in what was the ball turret well with instrumentation in the radio room. These aircraft were initially used by the 1st and 3rd Division pathfinder squadrons. By the end of 1944 every group had its own H2X B-17s and at the end of hostilities there were some 260 H2X B-17Gs on hand in the Force. Those H2X B-17s equipping the first divisional PFF units as at 18 March 1944 were:

422nd BS, 305th BG		413th BS, 96th BG	
42–31801	JJ:R	42–97534	MZ:A
42–39766		42–97542	MZ:B
42–40018	JJ:U	42–97545	MZ:D
42–97514	JJ:H	42–97554	MZ:E
42–97523		42–97555	MZ:F
42–97532	JJ:V	42–97556	MZ:G
42–97533	JJ:E	42–97560	MZ:H
42–97543		42–97564	MZ:J
42–97557	JJ:S	42–97565	MZ:K
42–97574	JJ:A	42–97569	MZ:M
42–97578		42–97577	MZ:N
42–97592	JJ:T		

The first B-17G with *Eagle* (AN/APQ-7) arrived at Alconbury in October 1944. Aircraft with this ground-search radar could be distinguished by the wing-like airfoil housing the scanner suspended on two pylons below the aircraft's nose. Considerable technical problems were encountered with this radar and the first experimental combat operation was not flown until the night of 2 April 1945. At this date 482nd Group had received 11 B-17Gs with *Eagle*. Only two *Eagle* B-17s, 44-6252 PC:A and 44–6990 PC:O were used in the 13 experimental combat sorties flown. In May 1945 all 13 *Eagle* B-17s were transferred to 96th Group scheduled for the occupational air force. However, continued difficulties with this radar caused the aircraft to be withdrawn by the autumn of 1945.

RADIO COUNTERMEASURES B-17s
The B-17Fs withdrawn from regular combat units early in 1944 and used to equip the 803rd Bomb Squadron (P) at Oulton were 42–30177, 42–30039 and 42–30066 with four, later six, *Mandrel* and nine *Carpet* sets each; 42–31078, 42–6080, 42–30353, 42–3438 and 42–30363 with six *Mandrel* sets each; 42–30114 with a *Jackal* set; 42–3518 with ELINT apparatus (S 27 and SCR 587); 42–37743 with ELINT and *Mandrel*. Two new B-17Gs were assigned early June 1944, one being 42–97691 with *Jackal* and *Rug*.

Externally all these aircraft were as normal day bomber B-17s apart from additional antenna. Most of the original 11 aircraft were made available to the *Aphrodite* project following their withdrawal from the 803rd BS(P) during July–August 1944.

Aphrodite B-17s

DOUBLE-AZON APHRODITE B-17
This radio-controlled explosive-laden expendable missile was devised by OES at the instigation of *Aphrodite* Project on 22 June 1944. One B-17 robot and one B-17 controller were prepared in two days, radio control being installed by the Signal Maintenance Section at Burtonwood, then flight tested on 24 June and transferred to Bovingdon. Initially ten war-weary B-17Fs and B-17Gs were stripped of unrequired items at Honington as follows: bombsight and associated panel, all guns, ammunition, ammunition boxes, turrets, gun mounts, armour plate, seats other than the pilot's, oxygen fitments, bottles, regulators and tubing, radio compass loop, driftmeters, navigation equipment but not navigator's table, radio equipment except VHF set, all heating equipment, fire extinguishers except one set in cockpit, liferafts, bomb racks, bomb-bay door motors and worm gear, all brackets and attachments in radio room, de-icer boots, and aerials other than those for VHF. After stripping, the Tokyo tanks were drained and sealed. Bomb-bay doors were bolted shut and the navigator's stool positioned in the co-pilot's seat location. The nose hatch was enlarged to facilitate bale-out and a wind deflector fitted. The AFCE (bombsight stabilisation unit and C-1 autopilot) was retained. At Burtonwood two *Azon* radio-control units were installed and linked to the flight controls to over-ride the auto-pilot, a radar altimeter (AN/APN-1) was fitted to maintain altitude at 250 feet. Loading of *Double-Azon* varied and was performed at the operational base. The approximate 20,000 lb load was boxed in 55 lb units and positioned between flight deck, radio room and bomb-bay. The ten B-17s originally assigned for use were: 42–30342, 42–37760, 42–30595, 42–3461, 41–24639, 42–31394, 42–3440, 42–39835, 42–6080 and 42–3493; another eight with *Double-Azon* followed. When *Double-Azon* was discontinued in August 1944 remaining aircraft were withdrawn and not used for *Castor* control. The two B-17G *Azon* controlling 'mothers' were 43–37637 and 43–37793.

CASTOR APHRODITE B-17
For this radio-controlled, explosive-laden expendable missile war-weary B-17s were stripped and modified as with *Double-Azon* conversions. Radio-control sets, developed in the US, arrived in the UK in July 1944. The AN/ARW-1 receiver was linked to the flight controls and the AN/APN-1 radio altimeter was retained. Additional equipment on the *Castor* robots was a television transmitter RC-489 placed in the nose of the aircraft and trained forward down to scan through the plexiglas. A repeat-back magnesium compass was supported in front of the television camera so that the operator in the mother aircraft could see the heading. An AN/TPN-1 *Eureka* radio beacon was installed as an aid to locating the robot if lost from sight by the operator. A smoke dispensing tank, fitted under the fuselage, held 75 gallons of chemical which could be dispensed at a rate of 1.5 gallons per minute when a solenoid actuated a valve by radio control.

The general loading of a *Castor* – at the operational station – was Torpex, a British explosive composed of 41.8 per cent RDX, 40.2 per cent TNT and 18 per cent aluminium powder. Packed in boxes 6 × 12 × 17½ in, each grossed 63 lb, the net weight being 55.5 lb. The total load of 21,105 lb (net 18,425 lb) was positioned in 25 boxes on the flight deck, 210 in the bomb-bay and 100 in the radio room, secured with cable and wood to the floor or sides of the aircraft. A series of fuses and linking primacord was armed manually by the pilot before leaving the

aircraft. A conversion batch of 20 B-17s was acquired for *Castor* of which 11 were deployed operationally.

The five B-17 control aircraft, 43–37946, 43–37953, 43–37962, 43–38006 and 43–38081 had AN/ARW-18 control units and SCR-550 television receivers. *Rebecca* AN/APN-2 was used in conjunction with the *Eureka* beacon. The television screen was mounted in the nose in front of the controller who sat on a modified bombardier's seat. Control signals were sent via control box BC-756. The transmitting carrier was frequency modulated by an audio tone originating in the modulator of the transmitter, unit BC-925, situated in the radio room. In an adjacent location was an amplifier to boost power if enemy jamming was experienced. Signals were transmitted via a whip aerial centrally mounted on the fuselage just aft of the radio room top hatch.

Above: **Stripped B-17F 42-30066 ready for *Castor* installations photographed on a Fersfield hardstanding. This aircraft, nicknamed *Mugwump* while in use on regular bombing operations with 100th and 96th BGs, was aimed at Heligoland on 30 October 1944.**

Below: **Servo-motor and linkage to B-17 *Castor* throttle controls.**

Below: **Upper and lower receiving aerials on *Castor* B-17.**

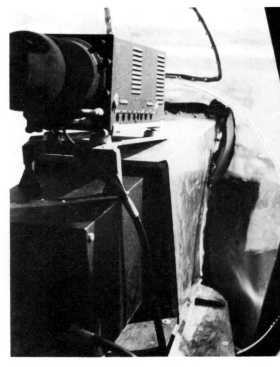

WEATHER RECONNAISSANCE B-17

B-17F and G of the provisional weather units were aircraft which for some reason – such as missing war equipment – were not suitable for combat operations. Weather recording equipment was from British sources. When new B-17Gs were assigned following the withdrawal of B-24s, these had their top and bottom turrets removed together with all armament except the tail guns. A psychrometer was installed on the side of the nose. These Fortresses were prepared for 652nd Bomb Squadron by 1st SAD.

Left: *Rebecca* antenna on *Castor* Mother, 43-37953.

Right: **TV camera installation (which had the cover name 'Block') in a *Castor* baby (Viewed forward through the right side of nosepiece).**

Distinctive aerial array of VHF relay B-17G. This aircraft, formerly of 303rd BG, served 67th FW units and was based at Honington during last months of war. Equipment included sets for automatic voice relay.

Consolidated B-24 Liberator

The Liberator prototype first flew in 1939 and early production versions went into action with RAF Coastal Command in 1941. Some five years newer than the B-17 design, the B-24 was scheduled for mass production in its refined B-24D form as the major heavy bomber type for the USAAF; ultimately Liberators became the most numerous of all American warplanes.

B-24D

The 93rd Group was the first bomb group to reach the 8th Air Force with Liberators, their B-24Ds arriving in England during September 1942. The following month the 44th Group arrived similarly equipped. These were the only operational Liberator bomb groups of the Force until June 1943 when the 389th Group arrived, the last to bring B-24Ds to join the 8th Air Force. The contribution of this comparatively small force during the first

Above: *Mr 5 by 5*, **B-24D 41-24234, of 506th BS, 44th BG with .50 'tunnel' gun in position aft of fuselage under-skid.** (via M. Bailey)

Left: **B-24D, 40-2354's special ventral gun position. This aircraft, *SNAFU*, was MIA with 44th BG on 16 February 1943.**

Below: **Nose armament as on early B-24D – two .50 cheek guns and a single .50 at floor level.**

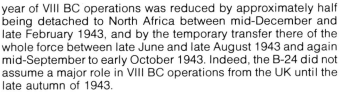

year of VIII BC operations was reduced by approximately half being detached to North Africa between mid-December and late February 1943, and by the temporary transfer there of the whole force between late June and late August 1943 and again mid-September to early October 1943. Indeed, the B-24 did not assume a major role in VIII BC operations from the UK until the late autumn of 1943.

In July 1943 the 479th Antisubmarine Group had formed at St Eval with B-24Ds for maritime patrol, but while it used 8th Air Force maintenance facilities the Group was not assigned to this force.

As with the B-17, the initial theatre modifications made to B-24Ds during the first winter in England mainly involved radio, armament and armour. On arrival B-24Ds received a VHF command radio installation, the replacement of their trailing antenna by a fixed type and an IFF update. Armament weaknesses in the nose and undersides were apparent. A remote control ventral turret fitted in early production aircraft had proved impracticable and had been deleted from the production aircraft equipping the 93rd Group. There was provision for a single

.50 gun to be fired through the opened rear fuselage under-hatch, but the field of vision and fire were too restricted for this defence point to be effective. In September a 44th Group B-24D, 40-2354, incorporating armament modifications made at Wright Field, arrived at Bovingdon for evaluation. Its most notable feature was a revised ventral gun position incorporating a .50 gun and scanning windows for the gunner. A review of this and other armament ideas resulted in 93rd Group B-24D 41-23721 being sent to Langford Lodge for prototype armament changes to be made. Work included an improved arrangement for a ventral gun position occupying the well of the deleted remote control turret. Scanning windows were placed in the fuselage sides just above this position and the floor was lowered. Other modifications included scanning windows on each side of the rear hatch 'tunnel' gunner position, adding armour plate shields on the waist guns – which gave better balance as well as gunner protection, lowering nose section flooring and raising the .50 gun mount six inches to allow easier operation and an increased field of fire.

The modifications, plus extra ammunition carried in the rear section, caused pronounced tail heaviness. It appears that 41-23721 was retained for experimental purposes, but on similarly modified 44th Group B-24Ds boilerplate was fixed in the nose section to protect the occupants and act as a counterbalance. On one aircraft at Shipdham, 12 mm boilerplate was fitted behind the instrument panel, on the fuselage sides to protect the pilots, and another section was bolted to the floor of the bombardier's compartment. Larger ammunition boxes to increase the tail and waist gun supply to 750 rounds each were requested at this time.

Although the B-24D received a flexible .50 gun installation on either side of the nose at modification centres in the USA, a blind spot remained in the upper part. During December 1942 work was put in hand at Langford Lodge to develop superior nose armament. The twin-gun installation eventually accepted was fitted higher in the nosepiece than the single gun. It was limited in azimuth movement to about 30 degrees but had 60 degree elevation and depression.

A standard list of modifications developed for B-24s, to be performed at depots before delivery, grew to 56 items in May 1943. The list included 14 armament items, ten covering armour plate and bullet-proof glass, six radio apparatus, two engine accessories, nine structural modifications and the remainder miscellaneous items such as identification lights, windshield wipers, oxygen, camera and emergency equipment. In general modifications paralleled the theatre installations and changes applicable to the B-17, but the B-24D appeared to have fewer weaknesses at that stage. An exception was the bomb hoist beam and support brackets which, found to buckle under the weight of 2000 lb bombs, had to be strengthened.

In contrast to the B-17, the priority modifications for the B-24D, issued on 28 May 1943 comprised of only ten items. These provided for twin .50s in the nose, a remote-indicating compass, replacement of IFF Mk II by Mk III, modifications to command and liaison radio antenna, three changes in the oxygen system, armour plate to protect the instrument panel, 500 rounds supply of ammunition to each waist gun and changes to emergency equipment. In second priority were 12 items, the most notable being additional armour plate and bullet-proof glass round the cockpit, windshield wipers, *Gee* installation, mountings for Mk IIIA reflector gunsights on all flexible .50 guns. and moving the waist guns closer to the fuselage sides. Strengthening the bomb hoist beam and reinforcement of the fuselage to prevent skin cracking from gun blast were relegated to third priority. As it was, some of the essential modifications had to be by-passed at depots because parts or kits were not available or the aircraft would be too long delayed.

In an effort to bring more conformity to the modification pro-

gramme, VIII AFSC on 23 August 1943, issued a letter of B-24D priority stages. This listed 17 Stage 1 items, eight Stage 2, 11 Stage 3, seven Stage 4 and six Stage 5. Of the Stage 1 items, some were only for checking and inspection or the changing of lubricants for low temperature operation. Significant changes were installation of first aid kits and bale-out oxygen bottles, and replacement of blister glass in the pilot's and co-pilot's windows with plain plexiglas or bullet-proof glass if available. Stage 2 items, required if kits were available, included moving the waist gun mounts closer to the skin line of the fuselage, armour plate for instrument panel and bombardier's floor, a ditching belt in the rear fuselage, emergency equipment and flexible ammunition feeds. Stage 3 included the Mk IIIA reflector gunsight mounting, two minor changes in the Martin upper turret and to the bulkhead forward of the tail turret, and the fuselage bomb hoist beam reinforcement. Stage 4, to be performed on certain aircraft only, was similar to the B-17 list providing for special radio and radar installations, distant-reading compass, flame dampers and strike camera to meet the requirements of lead aircraft or those engaged in special duties. Stage 5 was for twin waist guns, but as these were still in the experimental stage they could not be mounted – and in fact never were.

Overall the B-24D required fewer theatre modifications than the B-17F, albeit that VIII BC experience with the Liberator was more limited. Nevertheless there were troubling operational problems inherent in the design, poor high altitude performance being the most serious. Over 20,000 ft instability made it dangerous to fly in really close formation because of the risk of collisions; but in loose formation defensive fire could not be massed against attacking fighters. Because of handling difficulties, B-24Ds were usually flown at 20,000 to 23,000 ft, some three to five thousand feet below the B-17 optimum altitude. This exposed the B-24s to greater danger from anti-aircraft fire and tended to make their detached force more inviting to enemy fighter attack. Like the B-17, the B-24D also suffered from a centre of gravity displaced to the rear, due chiefly to added armament. Difficulties experienced at high altitude in trimming

Below: **Martin upper turret of B-24D provided far better visibility for the gunner than the B-17's Sperry. Guns have been removed from the cooling barrels of 'top turret' on 93rd BG's** Liberty Lad, **here demonstrated for the photographer by T/Sgt Al Lee.**

Above left: **Handling forward-firing gun was improved by repositioning it directly under the clear bombsight panel. Pfc James Wisniewski of 93rd BG 'rods' barrel watched by Constable A. Morton of local police at Alconbury.**

Left: **VIII AFSC further improved field of fire of the bombardier's gun by placing it at the bottom of the sighting panel and lowering the floor.**

Below: **A twin .50 installation eventually superseded the single forward-firing gun. Unlike the B-17F with twin nose guns, the bombsight could still be used in B-24Ds having this armament modification.**

out the nose-up flight attitude were so prevalent that in training pilots were taught a procedure whereby the aircraft was climbed above the desired flight level and then dived back to the former altitude to bring the nose down.

Poor ditching qualities, a matter investigated by the British prior to arrival of 8th Air Force B-24s, was another concern. The high wing configuration was not conducive to successful water landings as the fuselage took all the initial impact. The weak bomb-bay doors collapsed and the inrush of water tended to break the fuselage, causing the front section to nose under. Only the lucky escaped. In January 1943 a ditching drill for B-24 crews advised that six members gather on the flight deck close to the upper hatch and that the four gunners in the rear of the aircraft brace themselves against a wide ditching belt strung between the waist gun posts. The ditching belts, manufactured by VIII AFSC, were based on an experimental model fabricated at Burtonwood in December 1942. Although these belts were eventually made available in all 8th Air Force B-24s there was little improvement in the survival figures for ditching B-24 crews.

Of B-24D production changes, that most important to operational use was the addition of 'Tokyo tank' fuel cells in the outer wings giving an extra 450 US gallons, increasing the endurance and radius of action by some two hours and 200 miles. These were introduced on the B-24D-20-CO and B-24D-1-CF blocks, the first arriving in the UK in March 1943.

B-24Ds, with a retractable Sperry-designed ball turret for ventral defence, did not reach the UK as replacements until the late summer of 1943, by which time B-24Hs were arriving. The weight and drag of the ball turret had such a detrimental effect on stability and performance at high altitude that in January 1944 2nd Division received permission to remove these turrets from 26 B-24Ds.

B-24Ds continued to be received in England as replacements until November, their last known use in regular 8th Air Force daylight combat missions being early May 1944. At this time there was an urgent requirement for B-24Ds for the 801st Group and all suitable Ds remaining with the 44th, 93rd and 389th Groups were transferred for that unit. The reason was the need for good forward visibility from the nose to aid low level navigation at night (see Carpetbagger B-24 for description). Thirteen B-24Ds of the Carpetbagger programme were retired in November 1944, and one of these, 41-23682 Blasted Event, an original aircraft of 329th BS, 93rd Group, amassed 1075 hours flying time since reaching Britain in September 1942. The oldest, 41-11916, previously served with the 15th Air Force.

B-24D details
Four Pratt & Whitney R-1830-43 radials rated at 1200 hp each
Span 110 ft (33.53 m)
Length 66 ft 4 in (20.12 m)
Empty weight 34,000 lb (15,422 kg)
Max loaded weight 65,500 lb (22,711 kg)
Max speed 303 mph (488 km/h) at 25,000 ft (7620 m)
Tact operating speed 216 mph (348 km/h) at 25,000 ft (7620 m)
Initial climb rate 22 min to 20,000 ft (6100 m)
Tact climb rate 1 hr 15 min to 20,000 ft (6100 m)
Service ceiling 28,000 ft (8530 m)

Norm tact altitude 19,000–23,000 ft (5790–7010 m)
Norm range 2000 miles (3220 km) (original), 2300 miles (3703 km) (Tokyo tanks)
Tact radius 605 miles (974 km) (original), 800 miles (1287 km) (Tokyo tanks)
Fuel consumption 200 US gallons (1136 ltr) per hour at 220 mph (354 km/h)
Max bomb load 12,800 lb (5806 kg) (internal)
Norm tact bomb load 5000 lb (2268 kg)
Armament 10 or 11 × .50-in (12.7 mm) mg
Crew 10
(Tactical figures refer to normal high altitude operations)

B-24H

This version introduced the long sought nose-mounted power turret, an Emerson electrically-powered twin-gun design. While the turret added weight to the nose to help bring the CG back to balance, this was partly negated by additional provisions in the aircraft. All told, 2500 lb had been added compounding the high altitude instability. In consequence, this and following Liberator models were much more demanding of pilots than the original B-24D, particularly in the winter weather conditions of north-west Europe. This apart, the B-24H had a generally high degree of reliability and a lower requirement for theatre modification than the Fortress.

Some of the first B-24Hs from the Ford production line equipped the 392nd Group which arrived in England in August 1943. Thereafter the 445th, 446th, 448th, 453rd, 458th, 466th, 467th, 486th, 487th, 34th, 489th and 490th Groups arriving in succession November 1943 to May 1944 had B-24H models from Ford, Douglas Tulsa and Consolidated Fort Worth plants as original combat equipment.

Notable improvements introduced during B-24H production had been electrically-operated turbo-supercharger regulators and enclosed waist gun windows, both first seen on Liberators arriving in England from November 1943. Many earlier aircraft were retro-fitted later at depots. The last H models from Ford reached 8th Air Force in June 1944. Many B-24Hs endured until the end of hostilities with extensive operational records.

The B-24H was superseded in production by the B-24J which became the standard model from all five sources of production. While Liberator production differed considerably in detail changes after the B-24H, these had little effect on performance figures.

B-24H details
Four Pratt & Whitney R-1830-65 radials rated at 1200 hp each

Span 110 ft (33.53 m)
Length 67 ft 2 in (20.47 m)
Empty weight 36,500 lb (16,556 kg) (B-24L & M with lightweight tail turret 36,000 lb (16,330 kg))
Max loaded weight 67,800 lb (30,754 kg)
Max speed 290 mph (437 km/h) at 25,000 ft (7620 m)
Tact operating speed 205 mph (330 km/h) at 25,000 ft (7620 m)
Climb 25 min to 20,000 ft (6100 m) at 56,000 lb (25,402 kg) gross
Tact climb rate 1 hr to 20,000 ft (6100 m)
Service ceiling 28,000 ft (8530 m)
Norm tact altitude 18,000–22,000 ft (5490–6700 m)
Norm range 2100 miles (3380 km)
Tact radius 700 miles (1126 km)
Max bomb load 12,800 lb (5806 kg) (internal)
Norm tact bomb load 5000 lb (2268 kg)
Armament 10 × .50-in (12.7 mm) mg
Crew 10

Early B-24H of 705th BS, 446th BG with ball turret lowered.

B-24J

Basically similar to the B-24H, the J originated at the Consolidated San Diego factory and initially could be distinguished from the B-24H by the different type of nose turret. This was of Consolidated's own design and hydraulically operated, whereas the Emerson model in the B-24H was a more responsive electrically-powered type. The first B-24Js reached 8th Air Force in November 1943 as replacements, and it was not until May 1944 that a new group arrived with this model as original equipment. In fact, the last three bomber groups sent to the UK, 491st, 492nd and 493rd, were all B-24J-equipped. Most were B-24J-150-CO block aircraft featuring thermal wing de-icers – ducting hot air from the engines – that replaced the familiar rubber boot de-icers along the leading edges of the wing. After a month of combat use, 8th Air Force approved the new

Hairless Joe, an 'original' B-24J of 860th BS, 493rd BG. Note raised slipstream deflector at waist window.

arrangement as satisfactory, but noted that it made battle damage repairs more difficult.

The San Diego production line continued to turn out B-24Js without waist gun window protection and some were fitted with waist window glazing at Warton. By April 1944 all Liberator plants were producing the J model and there was much detail variation. There was a reversion to the Emerson nose turret on production and some changes were made in tail turret type. The last B-24Js reached 8th Air Force in late November 1944.

B-24L

By the summer of 1944 the output of Liberators by Ford Willow Run and Consolidated San Diego became sufficient to meet the needs of all US and Allied air forces and the other three plants were put to producing other aircraft types. At this time Ford and Consolidated went over to the B-24L designed to facilitate a joint production standard. For Consolidated this meant the overdue inclusion of enclosed gun positions, but basically the L was a refined J. Production of this model was short-lived, for by the time B-24Ls reached England in November 1944, produc-

Almost all B-24Ls reaching 8th AF units were fitted with AN/APS-15A as was 446th BG's 44–49355. This aircraft also had 'hand-held' power-boost tail guns in lightweight turret. Circle on tail distinguished aircraft as a pathfinder.   (via M. Bailey)

tion had given way to the B-24M the previous month. Less than 50 B-24Ls went to 8th Air Force, all Ford built; having AN/APS-15A radar, they were generally used as lead aircraft.

B-24M

First examples of the B-24M were received by 8th Air Force in January 1945. This model was another redesignation acknowledging production refinements but with no radical changes apart from the B-24M-20-CO featuring a revised cockpit cover to give pilots improved visibility. A few examples of this block arrived in England in April 1945.

In the spring of 1944 B-24 production was reaching a point where it was in excess of requirements and 8th Air Force had a reserve by July of almost 400 new B-24H and B-24Js. Although the despatch of new B-24s from the US was slowed, the decision to convert the five 3rd Division B-24 groups to B-17s kept the reserve high. From a peak of 1609 in July 1944, the numbers of B-24s in the UK gradually reduced. In November, 8th Air Force was ordered by USSTAF to transfer 100 B-24s to the 15th Air Force in Italy. The first 47 were despatched in December, followed by 38 in January 1945. These were all H and J models, mostly those withdrawn from 3rd Division and the 489th Group redeployed to the USA. The final 40 sent in February, including 12 brand-new B-24Ms, made the total 125. Another 19 B-24Hs were transferred to the 15th Air Force when the *Carpetbagger* 859th BS was transferred to Italy in January 1945. In September and October 1944 the RAF had received 20 H and J models for use in RCM work, plus five others early in 1945. Other Liberators were made available for conversion to transports for IX Troop Carrier Command and USSTAF's 302nd Air Transport Wing.

Some 3800 Liberators of all models were received by 8th Air Force between September 1942 and May 1945. A total 1099 were officially listed Missing in Action and 36 as missing to unknown causes. A total 551 were written off in operational crashes or through battle damage, 221 were destroyed in non-operational crashes or damaged beyond economical repair and 213 were scrapped because of age.

Above: **B-24M had larger observation windows for navigator and revised cockpit glazing to improve pilots' visibility. WV:E, 44-50732 served 445th BG.** (via M. Bailey)

Below: **Large bulged co-pilot and navigator windows on B-24M 44-50548 of 466th BG.** (M. Bailey)

MODIFICATIONS TO H, J, L AND M MODELS

One of the first complaints from crews flying the B-24H was about the sealing around the nose turret. Continued turret movement caused the felt to become worn and displaced, resulting in draughts bringing considerable discomfort to the occupants of the nose area. A new nose turret seal held against turret sides by air pressure was designed by BADA. This became a priority modification on all new Emerson turret B-24s reaching the 8th Air Force and was still being effected in the last months of the war.

Another problem with the Emerson turret was that the original gun-charging handles could be broken by fouling part of the structure. A modification to prevent this was introduced in March 1944.

Having agitated for a nose turret, 8th Air Force now found that the type fitted in the B-24H severely restricted the frontal view of both bombardier and navigator. An analysis of mission failures by B-24 units attributed poor navigation as a major cause, to which the interference with forward vision was considered a contributory factor. The turret also reduced the space in the nose for bombardier and navigator. An immediate solution was to provide large blister windows at the navigator's position on either side of the nose, and to have a pilotage navigator ride in the nose turret of lead B-24s to assist the regular navigator. Dissatisfaction with crew restrictions posed by this nose armament led 8th Air Force to experiment with a Bell power turret taken from a B-26 tail position. This turret was installed in the

lower part of a B-24H's nose, with the bombsight and clear sight panel positioned above. A seat was provided for the bombardier who could operate both sight and guns from the same position. Highly favoured by 2nd Bomb Division crews who inspected it, the aircraft was sent to the US with the intention of having a similar installation included on production. In the summer of 1944 another installation featuring a Bell turret was made on a B-24H. The original Emerson turret was replaced with a special 'glass house' cover, with the Bell turret positioned in the centre of the nose above the bombardier's position. This was generally considered an improvement on the standard nose turret arrangement, but more restrictive in both outlook and movement than the earlier Bell modification. In the winter of 1944–45 B-24J, 44-10508, was modified in a similar way to the first Bell nose turret arrangement and was used operationally as a lead aircraft by 93rd Bomb Group.

In April 1944 B-24Hs were received with an armoured pilot's seat which, while giving excellent protection to the occupant, restricted arm movement, interfered with view, made flight control adjustments difficult and hindered egress. Dubbed 'Coffin Seats', they were so disliked that in May Warton commenced a programme of replacing them with the original type seat. Although 'Coffin Seats' were eventually dropped from production, 8th Air Force felt that the manufacturers still did not appreciate the difficulty of hasty exit from the cockpit, for it was still necessary to remove seat arm rests and, later, a vertical brace for attaching flak curtains from all new B-24s received.

The external steel sheet armour (now 14 mm) introduced on the B-24D continued to be bolted below the pilot and co-pilot side windows.

Dissatisfaction with the handling characteristics of the B-24 led to measures to reduce weight. Armour was removed from the rear flight deck bulkhead until this was eventually eliminated from production late in 1944. Top turret armour was almost completely removed. Ammunition supply to each gun in the rear fuselage was limited to 500 rounds. When in the spring of 1944 sufficient fighters were available to provide continuous escort, it was decided that the ball turret might be removed. This weighed approximately 1100 lb and, with ammunition and gunner included, some 1500 lb could be saved by its deletion. Additionally when in the lowered position the turret reduced airspeed and added to the handling difficulties. The noticeable improvement obtained without the ball turret was such that in June 1944 Hq 8th Air Force gave permission for its general removal from B-24s. It was, however, initially left to each group to decide on this matter and a few groups continued to retain ball turrets believing that they made a substantial contribution to defence.

Problems with the bomb-bay roll-up doors creeping from the fully open position, causing an electrical fault and engaging a safety lock to prevent bombs being released and damaging the doors, brought a number of failures to bomb. A simple device developed in 389th Group allowed a degree of safe creep without the locking device coming into play, and from August 1944 this was fitted to all B-24s reaching BADA.

Continued concern over the poor ditching qualities of the Liberator led to further investigation during the winter of 1943–44 when it was decided that more lives could be saved if a special ditching deck was fashioned immediately above the rear bomb-bay, with the escape hatch built in the fuselage skin above. A B-24 incorporating this modification was flown back to the US in the spring of 1944 with the intention of getting this change made in production. As this entailed re-positioning oxygen bottles and the construction of a hatch, it was deemed too costly in man-hours for BADA to undertake. While slated for production, a revised version was not actually effected until the B-24L-15-FO and B-24M-20-CO, of which only a few examples were received late in the war. Another modification which BADA carried out on all new B-24s was adding an external release lever for the liferaft. Additionally the internal release was reworked to provide a more substantial lever and give a more positive release. From January 1944 the liferaft compartment was enlarged to enable more equipment to be accommodated.

The Liberator nosewheel assembly was not the most robust of components. Several production changes were introduced to make the nose gear more dependable, but trouble with this part remained throughout the war. As late as March 1945 VIII AFSC

Above: **Operational Engineering's Bell turret modification on** *Hap Hazard*, **B-24H 42-7580. This aircraft flew 27 missions in combat with 445th BG before being declared war-weary in August 1944. Following the nose turret modification, in early November the aircraft was flown by Col Al Key back to Wright Field where it was hoped it would influence changes in production. However, the B-24K with Emerson ball turret in the nose was supposedly about to enter production (it did not) and no action was taken.**
(via Al Blue)

Below: **B-24 groups of 3rd Division had G-H pathfinders, at first concentrated in 486th BG and later when this group converted to B-17s, with 34th BG at Mendlesham. Here the G-H leadships were distinguished by all-red fin and rudders. B-24H 41-29605,** *Leo*, **still carries the code marking of its former operators on the rear fuselage.**

were reporting cases of B-24H and B-24J nose wheel fork axles breaking. Inspection of other Liberators found that the fork axles in a large percentage of these models were cracked. As no satisfactory repair was possible there was a sudden demand for new axle replacements.

Manufacturing changes often produced weaknesses that did not show up until aircraft had been in service for some time. B-24Ls reaching 100 hours began to have engine cowl retaining supports break, a weakness found common to all and requiring replacement or strengthening action.

H2S B-24

The prototype installation of H2S in a B-24 was made in co-operation with the British radar research unit at Defford during 1943. Considerable difficulty was experienced in design and engineering and in obtaining a satisfactory performance with the equipment. As installed in B-24D 42-40987, tested at Alconbury late in 1943, the radar scanner was housed in a retractable plastic cover – shaped like a trash bin – positioned in the ball turret well. A batch of eight B-24H-1 aircraft were used for operational installations, made at Burtonwood during November 1943 to January 1944. As with the prototype, the scanners were housed in retractable 'trash bin' radomes in the ball turret well. Radar scope and operator were positioned on the flight deck. They operated from 11 January 1944, continuing in service until the 482nd Group was withdrawn from regular operations in late March. The H2S equipment was eventually removed from these aircraft. The original operational H2S B-24s of 814th Bomb Squadron were:

B-24H 41-29120 with H2S 'trashbin' lowered on target approach. Some 814th BS aircraft carried 44th BG tail symbols.

41-29120	SI:A	
41-29163	SI:B	
41-29177	SI:C	
42-7644	SI:D	
42-7645	SI:E	Missing 2/3/44
42-7646	SI:F	
42-7669	SI:G	Collided 29/1/44 Gissing
42-7672	SI:H	Crashed 23/1/44 Shingay

H2X B-24

The first B-24Hs fitted with H2X radar were received by 482nd Group in February 1944. Positioning of equipment was similar to that in H2S B-24s, but the scanner cover had more pronounced dome-shaping. With the decentralisation of radar aircraft, a pathfinder squadron was formed in 389th Group during March 1944 and received most of the H2X Liberators then available. Subsequently all 2nd Division groups received their own H2X aircraft and by March 1945 there were approximately 100 in

H2X radome in ball turret well was fully retractable but in lowered position reduced a Liberator's speed by an estimated 10 to 15 mph. This pathfinder is B-24J 42-50587 of 712th BS, 448th BG. (via M. Bailey)

the Division. The 2nd Division required some changes to H2X aircraft as received from the US and from the summer of 1944 these were subject to a modification programme. The operator's position was changed from rearward-facing to forward-facing on the left side of the flight deck directly behind the pilot. A table and other navigation facilities were provided at this position and a K-24 camera remote scope installation mounted against the bulkhead behind the operator. Original H2X B-24H-DTs assigned to 564th Bomb Squadron on 18 March 1944 were:

41-28673	41-28715	41-28653
41-28690	41-28767	41-28700
41-28713	41-28763	41-28696
41-28714	41-28789	41-28676

MOLING B-24

The aircraft of 329th Bomb Squadron used for this abortive experiment in daylight nuisance raids were equipped with British *Gee* (TR1335) sets and DR compasses at a navigator position on the flight deck opposite to the radio operator. Although at first only eight aircraft were given these instruments it appears that two additional B-24Ds of the squadron were eventually so equipped. *Moling* B-24Ds of the 329th Bomb Squadron in February 1943 were:

N	41–23809	*Hells a Droppin'*	Sal	19/1/45
O	41–23667	*Ball of Fire*	Sal	5/5/45
P	41–23717	*Exterminator*	MIA	1/8/43
Q	41–23682	*Blasted Event*	Sal	24/11/44
R	41–23658	*Tha She Blows*	Cr	8/3/43
S̄	41–23810	*Tarfu*	MIA	4/1/44
I	41–23934			
V	41–23683	*Jo Jo's Special Delivery*	Sal Trans 9AF	27/7/44 8/43
W	41–23982	*Jack Frost*		
Y	41–23847			

EAGLE B-24

Six B-24Ms with AN/APQ-7 *Eagle* radar were received by 482nd Group at Alconbury during February and March 1945. These aircraft were quite distinctive as the scanner, housed in an airfoil-shaped cover, was suspended beneath their noses. Eight operations using two *Eagle* B-24Ms, 44–42189 and 44–42283, were flown from the night of 12/13 April by the 482nd Group to test this equipment. The other *Eagle* B-24Ms were 44–42282, 44–42291, 44–42315 and 44–42324.

AZON B-24

To drop and direct *Azon* controllable bombs, ten B-24J-I55-CO were modified in the USA and assigned to 753rd Bomb Squadron in May 1944. Nine additional B-24H and J aircraft of the squadron were eventually modified in England. The *Azon* transmitter unit AN/ARW-9 was installed on the flight deck and linked to the three-mast aerials under the rear fuselage, with control unit situated at the bombardier's position operated by a simple left-right toggle. An observation port was made in the fuselage floor aft of the bombsight to aid the bombardier in observing the missile during its descent. Between the two operational periods for *Azon*, 31 May to 22 June and 17 August to 13 September, three aircraft – 44–40066, 44–40277 and 44–40283 – were detached to work with the *Aphrodite Double-Azon* guided drones. The aircraft returned to the 753rd in August but the crews transferred to the *Aphrodite* project. Following the cancellation of *Azon* operations in September, the equipment was removed from all aircraft which were then used on normal daylight bombing operations. The original *Azon* B-24Js assigned to the 753rd Bomb Squadron were:

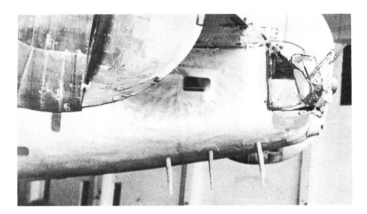

Three aerial masts under the rear fuselage of B-24J 44-40273 identify it as an Azon director.

44–40264	J4:K	*Kiss Me Baby*	Written off 8/9/44
44–40273	J4:T	*Bowen's Banshee*	
44–40275	J4:L	*Shack Time*	Written off 14/11/44
44–40277	J4:P	*Miss Used*	
44–40281	J4:Q	*A Dog's Life*	Cr Norwich 13/2/45
44–40283	J4:I	*Lassie Come Home*	Cr Norwich 14/1/45
44–40285	J4:H	*Table Stuff*	
44–40287	J4:J	*Bachelor's Bedlam*	
44–40288	J4:S	*Bad Girl*	Written off 3/10/44
44–40291	J4:O	*Royal Flush*	Cr take-off 31/5/44

RADIO COUNTERMEASURES B-24

In the latter part of June 1944 the 803rd BS(P) commenced conversion from B-17s, in line with an 8th Air Force directive that all special units should use B-24s in order to conserve the limited supply of Fortresses. By a gradual transfer it was mid-August before the unit received its full complement of ten operational and two training Liberators. These aircraft were fitted with jamming equipment which in August 1944 consisted mainly of varying numbers of *Mandrel III* jammers. A B-24J 42–51308, received later in the month, was fitted out for electronic intelligence gathering (ELINT) with S-27, SCR-587, *Bagful* and *Blinker* devices and one B-24H was used for dual *Carpet-blinker* training.

Modifications for RCM included the installation of a floor in the right rear bomb-bay cell to support a *Mandrel* set and a seat, lighting, electric heating and oxygen supply points for an operator were also provided in this compartment. *Mandrel* aerials were fitted under each wing and in the tail. Another jamming device, *Dina* (AN/APT-1), was fitted in nine aircraft during October. Later in the year the aircraft strength was increased to 18 and six were fitted with the device *Jackal*. Most aircraft were subject to changes in the type and position of antennas, which was the only visible external difference between these RCM aircraft and conventional day bomber Liberators. In August 1944, B-24J 44–40380 was used as a prototype for *Big Ben*, the project to jam V-2 rockets in the mistaken belief that they were

B-24H *Ready N' Able* displaying *Dina* antenna on the wing, three Carpet jammer 'blisters' beneath the nose with one receiver below the nose turret, and the short SCS-51 beam approach aerials under the bomb-bay. (via L. Hendricksom)

electronically controlled. The prototype aircraft had a formid-able collection of equipment: *Jostle IV, Carpet III, Dina-Dinamite* jammers, plus direction finding equipment and analysers. Following completion of the prototype by BAD 1 in early September, work started on 12 aircraft but these were

eventually turned over to the RAF as *Big Ben* became its pre-rogative.

A total of 32 different B-24s are known to have been used by the special RCM Squadron. The 21 on strength on 1 January 1945 were as follows:

Codes	Serial	Nickname	RCM Equipment
R4:A	42–95221	*Ready N'Able*	*Mandrel, Dina,* & *Orvils*
R4:B	42–51304		Radio Bomb Release
R4:C	42–51239	*Uninvited*	*Mandrel I & III, Dina* & Low Frequency *Dina*
R4:D	42–95507		Radio Bomb Release
R4:E	42–51230	*Lil' Pudge*	*Mandrel I & III, Dina* & *Jackal*
R4:F	42–50671	*Ramp Roster*	*Mandrel I & III, Dina* & Search Receiver
R4:G	42–51576		None
R4:H	42–50385	*Beast of Bourbon*	*Mandrel I & III, Dina* and *Jackal*
R4:I	42–50844	*Miss B Havin*	*Mandrel,* & *Dina*
R4:J	42–50476		None
R4:K	42–50665	*Lady in the Dark*	*Mandrel, Dina* & *Jackal*
R4:L	42–51546	*I Walk Alone*	*Mandrel* & *Dina*
R4:M	42–51308	*Modest Maid*	*Mandrel, Dina* & tunable *Carpet*
R4:N	42–50622	*This Is It Men!*	Search Receiver, VHF spoof & tunable *Carpet*
R4:O	42–51188	*Lady Jane*	*Mandrel I & III, Dina* & *Jackal*
R4:P	42–50750		1 × *Mandrel I & III, Dina*
R4:Q	42–51307		None
R4:R	42–51685		None
R4:S	44–10609		None
R4:T	42–51311		Visual *Monica, Carpet* & *Jostle*
R4:U	42–51315		Visual *Monica, Carpet* & *Jostle*

CARPETBAGGER B-24

In October 1943 32 B-24Ds were scheduled for special modi-fications at Burtonwood to meet the requirements of the *Carpet-bagger* programme. With only one or two exceptions the aircraft actually involved were in blocks B-24D-1-CF and B-24-70-CO to 125-CO which had previously served with the disbanded 479th Antisubmarine Group at Dunkeswell. Work on the first 12 aircraft began in November. The modification list covered nine removal and 23 installation items. Items removed were sea-search radar and associated equipment, waist guns and mounts, all nose

guns, the ball turret and all oxygen equipment. Notable provi-sions were flame dampers, *Gee*, gun flash eliminators, a DR compass in the bombardier's position, blister windows for the cockpit, a plywood floor from station 6.0 to 7.2 for stacking packages around the ball turret well, blackout curtains in the rear of the navigator's compartment and between the radio operator and the upper turret, *Rebecca* and S-phone beacon and radio sets (if available) and a Mk V drift-meter for the navigator. Finally, the aircraft were painted overall matt black.

Because an unobstructed outlook from the nose was essential

for the *Carpetbagger* mission, initially the B-24D was the only acceptable model. However, by early February 1944 few remained in the UK so those still with the 44th, 93rd and 389th Groups were used as replacements and to expand the complement of the two *Carpetbagger* squadrons. By April 1944 almost all acceptable B-24Ds had been drawn from 2nd Division, the exceptions being those in use as Assembly Ships, which in most cases had no tail turrets. With the decision to double the *Carpetbagger* force the position became critical and endeavours were made, without success, to obtain B-24Ds from the US or the 15th Air Force. It was then decided to modify B-24Hs for the mission by removing the nose turret and fashioning a 'glass house' structure to replace it; work initially undertaken at Burtonwood.

By late May the modification list had grown to 20 items for removal and 48 for installation. These were mostly detail changes, including additional blackout curtains and instrumentation while, in an effort to improve handling, all rear armour and superfluous fittings were eliminated. The *Rebecca* and S-phone sets were still in short supply and not all aircraft could be fitted with them. Strong points were fitted near the 'Joe Hole' for attaching parachute static lines, and a plywood floor was installed on the deck above the rear bomb-bay as a handy location for

Top: **All-matt black *Carpetbagger* B-24D (42-63775) of 856th BS, 801st Bomb Group. *Rebecca* antenna can be seen just forward of white protective canvas hanging from pitot head.** (Al Habeny)

Above: **B-24H with faired nose and overall gloss-black finish modified by BAD 2 after over-running the Warton runway for a first test flight.** (via H. Holmes)

stacking supplies. The bomb shackles in the bay were replaced by British conversion shackles to allow parachuted canisters to be carried. Gloss black replaced the former matt finish.

By mid-June 1944 the 801st BG had 54 *Carpetbagger* B-24D and H; five more were being modified at Burtonwood and another ten were awaiting modification. All told some 80 B-24s were modified for *Carpetbagger* work. In November 1944 the 13 remaining B-24Ds were declared obsolescent, primarily because they did not have electronic supercharger controls and could not be easily adapted for the night bombing role which had been given the *Carpetbagger* squadrons at that date. Three of these aircraft then had over a thousand flying hours each.

FUEL TANKER B-24

On 15 September 1944 8th Air Force received a directive to haul 345,000 US gallons (1,305,825 ltr) of 80 octane vehicle fuel per day for the 12th Army Group on the Continent. The immediate plan called for five B-24 groups to be released for this work and only second-line aircraft were to be used. Each B-24 would have four 400 gallon bomb-bay tanks and the Tokyo wing tanks would be isolated and used to give a total load of 2000 US gallons (7570 ltr) transported on each flight. In the event, as there were insufficient bomb-bay tanks available, the usual load for each aircraft was two 400 gallon tanks in the forward bay, four 108 gallon fighter drop tanks placed in the aft bomb-bay and two more secured in the rear fuselage over the ball turret well, plus the Tokyo tanks for a maximum 1800 gallons. The

groups actually given the fuel 'Truckin' assignment were the 458th, 466th, 467th and 492nd, using mostly reserve crews. 'War-weary' B-24s from other units were also used. Fuel loading took place at home bases and air depots. Additionally, some first line B-24s were used to carry fuel in 5 gallon cans. These were hand-loaded and mostly stacked on a makeshift bomb-bay floor, the usual total being 218 cans. A crew of five was usually carried for these duties. Total weight of fuel transported during the two week period of this requirement was 8225.9 US tons.

The second-line aircraft used for this work could not be returned to combat operations as their Tokyo tanks were contaminated with 80 octane fuel. Replacement or purging of the tanks was necessary.

FORMATION ASSEMBLY B-24

In February 1944 the 2nd Division authorised the use of 'war-weary' aircraft specially fitted out to aid assembly of individual group formations. Known as Assembly or Formation Ships, they featured distinctive paint schemes, signal lighting and provision for quantity discharge of pyrotechnics. The aircraft used in the first allocation were B-24Ds retired by 44th, 93rd and 389th Groups; replacements were mostly B-24Hs. Arrangements for signal lighting varied from group to group, but generally consisted of white flashing lamps on both sides of the fuselage arranged to form the identification letter of the group. All armament and armour was removed, and in some cases the tail turret. In the B-24Hs used for this purpose the nose turret was removed and replaced by a *Carpetbagger* type nose. Following incidents when flare guns were accidentally discharged inside the rear fuselage, some Formation Ships had pyrotechnic guns fixed through the fuselage sides. As these aircraft normally returned to base once a formation had been established, a skeleton crew of two pilots, navigator, radio operator and one or two flare discharge men was carried. In some groups an observer officer flew in the tail position to monitor the formation. The original Formation Ships were:

Red and white striped 'Formation Ship' 5Z:Z of 492nd BG. B-24D 42-40743 previously flew combat with 389th BG.

Group	Serial	Original Nickname
44BG	41–23699	*Lemon Drop*
93BG	41–23667	*Ball of Fire*
389BG	41–23683·	*Jo Jo's Special Delivery*
392BG	41–23689	*Minerva*
445BG	41–24215	*Lucky Gordon*
446BG	41–23737	*Eager Beaver*
448BG	41–23809	*Hell's a Droppin'*

Group	Serial	Original Nickname
453BG	41–23738	*Wham Bam*
458BG	42–40127	*Tha She Blows*
466BG	41–24109	*Ready and Willing*
467BG	42–40370	
489BG	42–7552	*Lil' Cookie*
491BG	42–40722	*Little Gramper*
492BG	42–40743	

TRANSPORT B-24

The general shortage of aircraft suitable for use in transporting men and materials between depots and operational stations was a considerable handicap to VIII AFSC during 1942 and 1943. Despite the scarcity of Liberators, on 27 October 1943 VIII AFSC was assigned ten B-24Ds withdrawn from 479th Antisubmarine Group. These, to be converted to cargo transports by BADA, were: 42–40499, 42–40543, 42–40551, 42–40552,

Right: Retired from combat with the 44th BG, B-24H 42-7535, *Peep Sight* had all turrets removed and was used as a transport for 3rd SAD. A special clear transparent fairing replaced the nose turret. (via M. Bailey)

42–63779, 42–63780, 42–63783, 42–63785, 42–63787 and 42–63790. It appears that another ex-479th B-24D, 42–63781, was substituted for '551' at a later date. When BADA was taken over by USSTAF, four of these aircraft were used by 3rd SAD at Watton (three identified as CB-24s and the fourth as a C-87). Surviving aircraft of the whole batch were turned over to ATC in the summer of 1944 and returned to the US.

During the last year of hostilities a few B-24Hs were converted at Watton for transport use as CB-24Hs. Most had the nose and tail turrets removed and replaced by fairings. Bomb-bays were sealed and a wood floor installed. Loading of freight took place through the rear under-hatch.

B.T.O, a 489th BG B-24J (44-40072) lands at Bricy with foodstuffs, September 1944. VIII AFSC made temporary wooden bomb-bay floors for this purpose. (P. Gandillet)

Martin B-26 Marauder

Early 8th Air Force plans scheduled B-25 Mitchells and B-26 Marauders for the 3rd and 4th Bomb Wings respectively. By the late summer of 1942, when heavy bombers had taken preference over medium bombers, both B-25 and B-26 units were planned for concentration in a single wing, the 3rd. The total number of medium bomber groups to be established in England varied between eight and 12 in the monthly planning schedules issued by USAAF during the winter of 1942–43, but by the following spring it became clear that the 8th's medium bomber force would, for the time being, be composed only of B-26 units.

With the movement of 3rd Wing Hq into the UK, its commander designate, Col Charles T. Phillips, flew B-26B 41-17550 via the north Atlantic ferry route, reaching Honington on 15 September 1942. This short-wing-span Marauder, the first of its type to reach 8th Air Force in England, was used for type evaluation in preparing an operational plan for the employment of B-26s in the ETO. Nicknamed *Hornet's Nest*, it remained the only Marauder in 8th Air Force for nearly six months.

However, other USAAF Marauders reached the UK in October 1942 for assignment to 12th Air Force and movement to North Africa from November. While based at Attlebridge, Norfolk, these short wing-span B-26Bs were given logistical support by 8th Air Force and received some radio and minor midifications at Honington Advanced Air Depot. In March and April 1943 advance elements of 322nd Group brought more Marauders to 8th Air Force. Some of these short-wing B-26Bs were used in two unsuccessful low-level operations in May, the remaining aircraft being withdrawn for use in the B-26 Combat Crew Replacement Centre at Toome, Northern Ireland, later that year. The first big-wing B-26B and B-26C models arrived in April and May 1943 with the other squadrons of 322nd Group and 323rd Group. The latter had 60 B-26C-6 variants for single pilot low-level operations. When low-level operations were abandoned in favour of medium altitude attacks both groups received retraining and aircraft internal equipment changes before operating in mid-July. The 386th and 387th Groups arriving in June and July respectively had a mixture of big wing B-26B and C aircraft, the basic difference between the models being their source of manufacture, Baltimore or Omaha plants.

All four B-26 medium bomber groups were transferred to 9th Air Force in October 1943, leaving Toome the 8th Air Force's sole Marauder station which continued to operate in a training role until CCRCs were dissolved in September 1944. A few Marauders remained in 8th Air Force for other uses, chiefly non-operational, during the last year of the war.

In July 1944 an urgent requirement for a night photographic aircraft to operate over V-weapon sites was met by converting four B-26Gs. These were used by 25th Group, first on combat operations and then for training purposes. A number of tow-target AT-23B Marauders served at Toome and later at various 8th Air Force bomber and fighter stations until the summer of 1945.

177

Small-Wing Marauders

B-26B-2 AND B-26B-3

In March 1943 the 450th Bomb Squadron of 322nd Group arrived at Bury St Edmunds with nine B-26B-2 and five B-26B-3 small-wing Marauders. As these aircraft lacked the .50-calibre side package guns, deemed essential for low-level attack, they were only used for training. A few had package guns installed in the UK. Subsequently these models were withdrawn from 322nd Group and sent to depots and in September 1943 used for the flying element of the B-26 CCRC formed at Toome.

B-26B-4

Apart from being the first Marauder with production fuselage side package guns for strafing, this variant had a longer nose-wheel leg increasing the angle of attack (wing to ground) which helped to shorten take-off runs. The 452nd Bomb Squadron reached Bury St Edmunds with 13 B-26B-4s in April 1943; a further 32 arriving during the next two months were used to re-equip 450th BS and expand 452nd BS.

For the low-level concept of operations, aircraft in service with 452nd BS and a few new B-26B-4s assigned to 450th BS received hasty modifications in April and May 1943. An N-6 or N-6A reflector gunsight was fitted as an improvised bombsight fixed to the decking behind the right windshield for use by the co-pilot. The nose-mounted D-8 bombsight was removed, being found unsatisfactory for 'zero' altitude attack. A cable cord terminating in a release button was run from the bomb release apparatus to the co-pilot's position. A compass was installed in the nose, where the navigator was re-positioned to pin-point course at low-level and report over the interphone to the pilots. Most of these changes were made at the 322nd's base and flight crews assisted ground crews in expediting this work. The necessary VHF radio installation and other theatre radio and IFF modifications were made at Honington. Following the abandonment of low-level attack most of these aircraft were eventually employed at medium altitude with the bomb release point re-established in the nose. However, 322nd Group maintained training for low-level attack for two months after its initial combat missions and modifications for this role continued to be made in both this and later models.

On 18 May 3rd Wing proposed sending a B-26 to the Base Air Depot at Langford Lodge with a view to its use in developing modifications then in the experimental stage. Twelve items were listed, mostly pertaining to armament or structure and predominantly low-level requirements. They included additional nose and tail gun ammunition capacity, improved feed to the nose gun and converting this from a flexible weapon operated by the navigator to a fixed weapon fired – like the package guns – by the pilot. A British Mk IIA reflector sight was proposed for the hand-held tail guns. A control for operating the bomb-bay doors was required in the cockpit for pilot operation since the bombs were to be dropped by the co-pilot and not the bombardier/navigator in the nose. An improved cockpit compass replaced the existing one found unreliable when the aircraft practised evasive action; the same was required for the navigator whether positioned behind the pilots or in the nose. There was need for more armour plate at crew positions to protect against small arms fire. Finally, some emergency system to lower the undercarriage and close the bomb-bay doors if the hydraulic system was damaged was most desirable. Information received from B-26 units operating in North Africa had warned of the consequences of not being able to close the bomb-bay doors, with drag taking 25 to 30 mph off speed and making it impossible to maintain altitude if only one engine was functioning.

B-26B-4 *Jezabelle* at Bury St Edmunds, May 1943. This 'small-wing' Marauder served in combat with 452nd BS at Andrewsfield during the summer of 1943 and was later transferred to Toome as a training aircraft. It remained with the 3rd Replacement & Training Squadron until that unit ceased to function in September 1944. Stored by BADA it was finally broken up at Stanstead in February 1945.

While these modifications were under consideration, two weaknesses came to light in small-wing Marauders. On 29 May one crashed on Bury St Edmunds airfield while practising violent evasive action. The cause was loss of the tail fin, traced to fracturing due to the securing bolts having worked loose. This led to a modification at air depots when a strengthening plate was added to the fin attachment point on short-span B-26Bs. Less serious was the discovery that evasive action flying put such strain on bomb shackles that the locks bent. A strengthened shackle was eventually forthcoming, although the change to medium altitude operations removed the need for violent manoeuvring.

B-26B-4s remained in 322nd Group until spring 1944 although many were withdrawn from service earlier and sent to 3 CCRC as trainers. Some endured until May 1945, to be scrapped at depots in the UK.

B-26B-4-MA details
Two Pratt & Whitney R-2800-43 radials rated at 2000 hp each

Span 65 ft (19.81 m)
Length 58 ft 3 in (17.75 m)
Empty weight 22,380 lb (10,152 kg)
Max loaded weight 34,000 lb (15,422 kg)
Max speed 317 mph (510 km/h) at 14,500 ft (4420 m)
Norm cruise speed 200 mph (322 km/h)
Initial rate of climb 1250 ft (380 m) per min
Service ceiling 23,500 ft (7160 m)
Norm range 1150 miles (1850 km)
Norm combat range at 10,000 ft (3050 m) 800 miles (1287 km) on 962 US gallons (3641 ltr)
Fuel consumption 155 US gallons (587 ltr) per hour cruising
Max bomb load 4000 lb (1814 kg)
Armament 9 or 11 × .50-in (12.7 mm) mg
Crew 6

Big-Wing Marauders

B-26B-10-MA AND B-26C-5-MO AND FOLLOWING PRODUCTION BLOCKS

In its original configuration the B-26 had a comparatively high wing loading demanding high take-off speed and long landing run. Coupled with poor directional stability and slow control response, the aircraft needed experienced pilots. To reduce wing loading and improve handling, the designers increased the span by 6 feet and enlarged the tail surfaces. But by the time these changes had been incorporated on production, the advantage of increased wing area had been negated by increased weight through additional war equipment. Despite its vices, experienced pilots preferred the old short-span Marauder to the redesign for unrestricted flying as it was more manoeuvrable, more responsive and faster. The wide-span Marauder, however, proved a more stable aircraft for close formation flying.

Big-wing B-26s arrived in the UK from late April 1943. They incorporated more equipment to aid low-level attack, including an additional fixed machine gun (firing through the lower nose) to boost the ground strafing gun total to five. In addition to the turret and tail mounted guns the flexible .50 remained in the centre of the nosepiece and two other hand-held guns could be swung out of the lower rear fuselage side hatches. The bombsight was still the D-8; when the decision was taken to fly medium altitude operations it was necessary to replace these by the M-7 Norden. However, these sights were in short supply and not until July were 40 made available to 3rd Wing. This shortage was partly responsible for the delay in starting medium level attacks.

The 449th and 451st Bomb Squadrons of 322nd Group arrived mainly with B-26-B-10 and a few B-26C-5 models. The 323rd Group came in May with a complement of B-26C-6s, a special single-pilot variant for ground attack (described later). A mixture of B-26B-15, B-26C-10 and C-15 versions made up 386th Group arriving in June. The B-15 was as the B-10, apart from dispensing with the fixed oxygen system which was not necessary in an aircraft normally operating below 12,000 feet. The C-10 introduced the Bell M-6 hydraulic tail turret which replaced the hand-held gun installation on earlier models. The B-26C-15 was similar, differing chiefly in upper turret specification. The 387th Group, last Marauder unit to join 8th Air Force, brought an exclusively B-26B-20 complement when it arrived in late June. The B-20 had a simplified nose-wheel hydraulic system and also introduced the Bell tail turret to the B series. Replacement aircraft received by the four groups during their time with the 8th Air Force included all these model blocks plus B-28B-30 and C-20 introducing steel armour plate to protect the pilot, and B-35 and C-25 dispensing with the troublesome alcohol carburettor de-icer system.

While there was still some uncertainty as to how the B-26 force would be employed, 3rd Wing required both low and medium level equipment and modifications. By 13 July, three days before the first medium altitude mission, the modifications list had grown to 14 necessary and eight desirable items for B-26s coming in from the States. Most essential were installation of a VHF SCR-522 command radio and crystal changes in other radios. The trailing aerial for the SCR-287 liaison radio had to be replaced with a fixed antenna. A B-16 pilot's type compass was to be fitted in the nose section for navigator/bombardier, although this was soon found to be unsatisfactory and another type was substituted. The interior release mechanism for the liferaft had to be changed. Any bomb-bay tanks had to be removed. Fixtures had to be provided for the Norden sight, and the cockpit bomb release and low-level sights arrangements made. There was also a carburettor modification to carry out which consisted of replacing two dural bolts in an air valve. Desirable modifications were: a mechanism to extend nose-wheel gear and close bomb-bay doors, resin wingtip lights, a stabilised compass, strike camera fitment, additional armour, relocation of the drift-meter in the nose and removal of de-icer boots and equipment. Most of this was performed at Aldermaston, which had become the B-26 holding airfield, albeit that the list was far too ambitious and only essentials were actually performed.

By mid-August, when medium level bombing was the confirmed method of employment for Marauders, a realistic modification list of six 'musts' and six 'desirables' was introduced. The 'musts' covered the previous radio and antenna requirements and nose mounted compass, plus the removal of all factory installed low-level equipment and the torpedo dropping release mechanism in the bomb-bay. The torpedo carrying requirement had originated in the Pacific during the previous year but, as often happened, by the time this had been incorporated on production lines, the requirement no longer existed. The torpedo release mechanism obstructed part of the bomb racks limiting carriage of 100 lb bombs to 18. After removal 28 such bombs could be shackled to the racks. A final 'must' was an automatic camera switch for use with a K-21, K-24 or F-24 strike camera when carried.

Desirable changes, but rarely added at this date were: a means to extend the landing gear and raise the bomb-bay doors if hydraulics failed, provisions for the navigator in the nose (in medium level operations he was re-positioned behind the pilots but it was still desirable to have a navigator in the nose of lead aircraft), armour plate on the fuselage sides to protect the pilots (and on B-30s a sheet on the co-pilot's side similar to that on the pilot's side), re-instalment of engine fire extinguisher system (deleted on the early B model blocks to save weight), provision of a lower entrance and escape hatch in the right-hand side of the navigator's compartment (as on the special B-26C-6s), and changing the interior liferaft release mechanism. At this time there were also 14 undeveloped modifications, six of these pertaining to hydraulics and three to controls.

Various technical problems arose as operations progressed; one early and frequent fault was electrical generator failure causing several turnbacks. This was finally traced to short circuiting of the leads on the generator housing. The occurrences were reduced by the issue of new inspection and maintenance procedures. Before the first Marauder with the new Bell tail turret had seen action there were several instances of gun barrels breaking the plexiglas at maximum depression. To prevent this a modification order was issued on 19 July to be carried out at combat bases. It consisted of a simple wood stop on the gun mount restricting the down movement of the guns. However, the Bell turret was prone to trouble throughout the period of 8th Air Force B-26 use. A persistent problem was spent links blocking gun discharge chutes. Various modifications were largely unsuccessful and many tail gunners preferred to remove the chutes altogether and let the spent cases and links heap up under their guns. Jamming of guns was also common due to varying feed rate of the traced rounds. The cause was improper adjustment of the switches on the electric motors that boosted the trace along, but the correct setting was difficult to maintain. A number of nose-wheel collapses on touch-down led to a modification, ordered at the beginning of September, to make a sight hole through the nose floor so that the leg lock could be checked for correct position. A regular annoying occurrence was oil overflowing from the propeller de-icer pump and tank onto the fuselage floor. The pumps did not effectively separate oil from air and a procedure for preventing this spillage had to be advised in mid-September.

Top: **Big-wing B-26B 41-31718, KS:O *El Capitan* of 557th BS, 387th BG off on its 15th mission. The Marauder proved a very durable medium bomber and B-26s with over 100 missions were almost commonplace by the war's end.** (AFM)

Above: **Fixed and flexible nose guns show well in this view of cleaning operations on a 322nd BG B-26B.**

Right: **Gunner knelt on a cushion to manipulate .50 guns in rear side hatches (viewed from just forward of tail gunner's position).**

The principal cause of most B-26 bombing failures was the intervalometer which either worked erratically or did not release the bombs at all. There were electrical weaknesses in the system and it was more than two months before the problem was overcome satisfactorily. The B-26's hydraulic system proved vulnerable to battle damage as had been already experienced in North Africa. Nevertheless, priority on other modifications prevented much work on the highly desirable windlass in the radio operator's compartment for emergency winching up of the bomb doors. These were being installed in increasing numbers when the Marauders passed to 9th Air Force. At that time, October 1943, 8th Air Force had some 480 B-26s on hand of which 260 were with the four combat groups, 30 in the CCRC and the rest at depots.

Despite a bad reputation through a high accident rate at US training establishments and some early combat disasters, the Marauder proved a reliable and highly effective medium altitude bomber in 8th Air Force service. Its sortie loss rate during this period was only 3 per cent as against 10 per cent for B-17s.

Right: **Bell power-assisted tail gun position on B-26C** *Lady Luck*. **Gunner decorating his position is S/Sgt Robert Dall, 386th BG.**

B-26B-10 and B-26C-5 details
Two R-2800-43 radials rated at 2000 hp each

Wing span 71 ft (21.64 m)
Length 58 ft 3 in (17.75 m)
Empty weight 24,000 lb (10,886 kg)
Max loaded weight 38,200 lb (17,327 kg)
Max speed 282 mph (454 km/h) at 15,000 ft (4570 m)

Combat cruising speed 195 mph (314 km/h) at 10,000 ft (3050 m)
Climb 24 min 30 sec to 15,000 ft (4570 m)
Norm range 1150 miles (1850 km)
Combat range 550 miles (885 km) on 962 US gallons (3641 ltr)
Norm bomb load 4000 lb (1814 kg)
Armament 12 × .50-in (12.7 mm) mg
Crew 7

B-26C-6

Sixty B-26C-5 bombers were modified to a special ground attack configuration before delivery. The co-pilot's seat and control column were omitted and a lightweight seat substituted so that the navigator could operate flaps and undercarriage controls during take-off and landing. Navigational equipment was re-positioned in the nose leaving only the command radio, liferaft and the auxiliary starting engine in the original navigation area behind the pilot. An escape and entrance hatch was built into the bottom of the right-hand side of this compartment. These aircraft were assigned to the 323rd Group as original overseas equipment. Single pilot operation was based on the pretext that as the Marauder was to be used for low-level attack it could be classified as an 'attack' aircraft, a category for which USAAF required only one pilot. Dispensing with the co-pilot was also an experiment in aircrew economy. As these aircraft were never used for ground attack they were usually flown in formations led by orthodox Marauders. Some B-26C-5s were converted to dual controls but most were replaced in 323rd Group when other model Marauders became available. In all other respects the B-26C-6 was as the B-26C-5.

Single-pilot B-26C-6 of 456th BS, 323rd BG showing access door peculiar to this model open, aft of nose wheel doors.

NIGHT PHOTOGRAPH B-26G

In July 1944 an urgent requirement arose for night photographic coverage of enemy V-1 site activity in France, a project code named *Dilly*. The 25th Group's 654th Bomb Squadron, having the night photographic mission, was then still awaiting its first Mosquito XVI modified for this role. As only shallow penetration of enemy airspace was involved, it was decided that until the Mosquitoes were available less speedy but more quickly adaptable aircraft could be used. Four new B-26Gs assigned for this purpose were sent to Mount Farm for camera installations. Two K-19B night cameras were fitted in the aft bomb-bay following removal of ferry fuel tanks. Some auxiliary equipment was also removed at this time. Painted gloss black the first aircraft, 43-34205 (Y), completed on 30 July, flew its first sortie on the night of 10/11 August and was despatched on a total of 14 before Allied ground forces overran the V-site areas at the end of August. The next two Marauders 43-34193 (W) and 43-34195 (X) arrived at Watton only in time to be despatched on four and three sorties respectively. The last aircraft, 43-34226 (Z), did not arrive before the *Dilly* project was terminated. The B-26Gs were retained by 25th Group until March 1945, being used for training, experimental and non-combat activities. The B-26G had a

Black B-26G, 43-34205, used for *Dilly* operations.

similar performance to the late B and C models. A 3½ degree increase in wing incidence angle greatly improved take-off lift, shortening the required run as well as eliminating the Marauder's nose-up flight angle thus improving visibility from the cockpit.

AT-23

This was the designation of B-26B and C blocks built for a target towing role. Devoid of armament, armour and bombing equipment, they had an electric cable winch for sleeve towing positioned in the fuselage aft of the wing. No 3 CCRC at Toome received 12 AT-23s in May 1944 for use in gunnery training. On the closing of the station the following September, some of these aircraft were sent to the 9th Air Force and others distributed among 8th Air Force units in England, chiefly fighter groups. Some 1200 lb (544 kg) lighter than the combat B-26, the AT-23 had better climb, handling characteristics and was 25 mph (40 km/h) faster. A total of 13 AT-23B and two AT-23A served 8AF.

Lockheed P-38 Lightning

At the time of the prototype's appearance in 1939 the Lockheed twin-engine fighter gave promise of a very advanced performance. The P-38's subsequent development was delayed by both technical and flight problems but it remained much favoured by the USAAF hierarchy. With good manoeuvrability and top speed the type appeared ideal for the high altitude bomber support requirements of 8th Air Force, but was to prove a disappointment. It did, however, acquit itself well in less exacting aerial environments, particularly in the Pacific war zones.

P-38F

The initial overseas flights to the 8th Air Force in England included P-38Fs of the 1st Group arriving at Prestwick on 9 July 1942. The 14th Group also flew P-38Fs via the Greenland, Iceland ferry route. By early September there were 133 Lightnings in the UK, 80 in 1st Group, 46 in 14th Group and the remainder reserves. One squadron of the 14th Group had remained in Iceland for local defence. All aircraft had carried two 150 US gallon steel drop tanks (actual capacity 165 US gallons) for their trans-Atlantic flight. Immediate modifications involved the changing of crystals in their SCR-522 VHF radio to comply with theatre usage. Initial troubles were radio masts and nose-wheel doors breaking off at high speeds and during violent manoeuvres. The masts, insufficiently robust, were replaced with Spitfire masts pending provision of a stronger American type. The loss of nose-wheel doors was diagnosed as faulty adjustment of the safety catch, allowing the door to be forced open slightly in sharp movements and air pressure doing the rest.

British opinion of the Lightning, based on an RAF test the previous year, was summed up in an Air Ministry communication as 'not likely to be of any use for anything except convoy escort and against the occasional unescorted bomber'. The aircraft tested had lacked turbo-superchargers which, at the time, were not released to the British. However, British opinion of the P-38F put through trials by their Air Fighting Development Unit in August 1942 was generally laudatory. P-38F 41-7592 flown by Major Cass Hough was found as fast as the Spitfire IX at all but very high levels and to have an equal or better rate of climb. Indeed, the report found few shortcomings in the fighter and considered that a P-38F pilot could engage the enemy with confidence except for one factor, the diving speed limitations imposed through aerodynamic compressibility, an inherent design weakness. But the unwary still got into trouble. There were two accidents through this cause in England, one near Thirsk in Yorkshire.

P-38Fs of 1st FG at Kirton-in-Lindsey, July 1942.

As the P-38F units were transferred to the 12th Air Force in mid-September 1942 and subsequently moved to North Africa, little technical experience was gained with the type in operations from England. There was some trouble with ammunition feed and gun mounts but these did not become serious until the P-38F went into action in North Africa. One, 41-7592, retained by VIII FC for experimental purposes at Bovingdon became the personal mount of Major Cass Hough, head of Air Technical Section, VIII FC. This aircraft was modified to become the first two-seat Lightning in the ETO, achieved by removing radio equipment behind the pilot.

Some P-38Fs and P-38Gs were returned to UK depots from the MTO during 1944 after retirement from first-line service. Three RAF Lightnings, AF105, AF106 and AF108 were also turned over to the USAAF in the UK.

P-38F details
Two Allison V-1710 (-49 right, -53 left) rated at 1325 hp each

Span 52 ft (15.85 m)
Length 37 ft 10 in (11.53 m)
Empty weight 12,264 lb (5563 kg)
Max loaded weight 18,000 lb (8165 kg)
Max speed 395 mph (636 km/h) at 25,000 ft (7620 m)
Tact cruise speed 250–320 mph (402–515 km/h)
Climb 8 min to 20,000 ft (6100 m)
Service ceiling 39,000 ft (11,890 m)
Norm range 425 miles (684 km) (internal fuel)
Tact radius 200 miles (322 km)
Fuel consumption 110 US gallons (416 ltr) per hour average mission; 300 US gallons (1136 ltr) per hour full power
Armament 1 × 20 mm cannon and 4 × .50 (12.7 mm) mg

P-38G

Similar to the P-38F, apart from changes to supercharging and engine giving slightly improved performance, the P-38G equipped two groups in the UK – the 78th and 82nd. Their aircraft, shipped in September 1942, were made ready at Langford Lodge and Speke. The 82nd Group was only briefly assigned to 8th Air Force before flying its 80 aircraft to North Africa in December 1942. That same month the 78th Group received P-38Gs and began training at Goxhill, with 58 on hand in late January. However, during February 1943, both aircraft and pilots were withdrawn for North Africa as replacements for the three P-38 groups of the 12th Air Force. Some 200 P-38Gs were asembled in the UK and ferried to North Africa between November 1942 and March 1943.

P-38H

Faced with increasing losses to its day bombers, 8th Air Force was given priority for new P-38 units in the late summer of 1943. With drop tanks these fighters had a greater range potential than the P-47 and it was hoped they would be able to give target support to bombers up to 450 miles from home base. In August P-38H shipments arriving were processed through Langford Lodge for the 20th Fighter Group reaching England towards the end of that month and the 55th Group three weeks later, both having been trained on Lightnings. As the experience level of the latter was higher it was the first to be made operational, from 15 October, being later joined on missions by single squadrons of the 20th Group.

The P-38H with up-rated engines and revised turbo-supercharging to give better high altitude performance, also featured automatically-operated air cooling radiator flaps designed to obviate pilot error. However, use of the H for high altitude long range escort was limited by an internal fuel capacity of only 300 gallons, the same as the P-38F, at a time when range requirements were substantially extended. On internal fuel alone, its radius of action was little better than that of the current P-47 – about 175 to 200 miles. While two 150 gallon drop tanks allowed the Lightning to reach up to 400 miles, its position was more critical should it be forced – by interception – to discard the tanks early in a mission. High altitude performance proved disappointing with persistent engine difficulties at between 25,000 and 30,000 feet, mostly diagnosed as the old problem of turbo-supercharger inter-cooler inefficiency causing overheated air to be fed to the carburettors. Another deficiency, also afflicting previous models, was poor cockpit heating. Warm air ducted from the engines into the cockpit was totally inadequate to meet the extreme sub-zero high altitude temperatures encountered over north-west Europe in winter.

P-38Hs were withdrawn as the P-38J became available in substantial numbers at the end of 1943. In January many were

Below: A P-38H, 42-67064 CG:C, and P-38J, 42-67199, CG:Y, of the 38th FS, 55th FG. Principal feature distinguishing the two models was the larger air intake under the J's engines. (P. Green)

transferred to the 554th Fighter Training Squadron at Goxhill and the following month 45 were sent to the less severe operating environment of the Mediterranean theatre.

P-38H details
Two Allison V-1710-89/91 inlines rated at 1425 hp each

Span 52 ft (15.85 m)
Length 37 ft 10 in (11.53 m)
Empty weight 12,380 lb (5616kg)
Max loaded weight 20,300 lb (9208 kg)
Max speed 402 mph (647 km/g) at 25,000 ft (7620 m)
Tact cruise speed 250–320 mph (402–515 km/h)

Climb 8 min to 20,000 ft (6100 m)
Service ceiling 40,000 ft (12,190 m)
Tact ceiling 30,000 ft (9140 m)
Norm range 300 miles (483 m)
Tact radius 200 miles (322 mm) (internal fuel)
Max tact range 2 × 150 US gallons (568 ltr)
drop tanks 350 miles (563 km)
Fuel consumption 90–120 US gallons (340–454 ltr) per hour at cruise speed; 320 US gallons (1211 ltr) per hour at max power
Armament 1 × 20 mm cannon and 4 × .50-in (12.7 mm) mg. Two 500 or 1000 lb (227–454 kg) bombs could be carried in lieu of drop tanks

P-38J

The original intercooler system in the P-38 (cooling the compressed air before it was fed to the carburettors), neatly housed in the leading edge of the wings, was not efficient at altitude. The main change between the original J models and the H was the repositioning of the inter-cooler under the engine between the oil radiators, the whole enclosed in an enlarged housing, making this the principal visible difference between the two models. The P-38J also had a revised windshield arrangement to improve vision and defrosting qualities. The space in the wings left by relocating the intercooler was utilised for an additional 110 gallons of fuel. The first Js received in the UK, during November 1943, were without these 55 gallon tanks although kits were sent the following month for installation at Langford Lodge. The first 42 leading edge tanks were fitted in the last week of the year and during the next two months 120 P-38Js were processed. The additional fuel, increasing range by 100 miles, made the P-38J much more useful for escort duties. During January 1944 both 20th and 55th Groups rapidly converted to P-38Js with the additional wing tanks. Unfortunately, the J model did not overcome engine failure or cockpit heating problems. Pilots were so numb with cold after return from some winter missions that they had to be assisted from cockpits. Additional clothing was procured, particularly gloves and boots from RAF sources, in order to prevent frostbite. In March some of the pilots received electrically-heated suits which greatly improved matters.

The engine problems were two-fold. Repositionig the intercoolers led to too much cooling at high altitude and pre-detonation. Oil temperature also could not be kept high enough above 22,000 feet, and oil consumption rose at an alarming rate, prticularly above 25,000 feet. In fact avage consumption rate of two to four pints per hour for missions when flying below 25,000 feet rose to from eight to 16 pints per hour at 25,000 to 30,000 feet. Oil throwing due to low temperatures was so bad that engine life was halved. Moreover, with the sudden increases of power necessary in combat, engines seized or threw connecting rods. Yet another problem was that common to all turbo-supercharged aircraft with hydraulic actuated regulators; low temperatures thickening the oil and allowing the turbine to go out of control and fail. In late February 1944 the two P-38 groups adopted a policy of making the penetration flight at not more than 22,000 feet to avoid the extreme cold. Additionally, every 20 minutes power settings were increased to 3000 rpm and 45" Hg for 30 seconds to raise temperatures and clear the engines. A portion of the intercooler radiator was blocked off to achieve higher temperatures, while the 20th Group tried piping hot air from the engine exhaust to the supercharger regulator. These actions eased but did not eliminate the troubles. Oil temperature regulators became the most critical replacement part for P-38Js by late March. In an effort to control

Supercharger turbine in right-hand boom of a P-38H. Raised strip on left is a guard to deflect metal if turbine disintegrated.

oil consumption wedge-type piston rings were fitted to the Allisons of a 55th Group P-38J, but one engine failed after 44 hours flight time. Another approach was use of the new 150 octane grade fuel which was tested in two 55th Group P-38Js during the same month in the hope of improving performance.

The P-38J could only operate with difficulty above 25,000 feet and with its distinctive configuration was easily distinguished by enemy fighters and frequently attacked from above. By March VIII FC had become somewhat disillusioned with the P-38 because of the high number of abortives through mechanical failures on almost every mission. That month the 364th Group commenced operations and in late May the 479th, both with P-38Js. But faced with continuing technical problems a decision was taken to convert all P-38 groups to P-51s.

The suggestion that the P-38 would be better served by fitting Packard-built Merlin engines was taken up by VIII FC and Operational Engineering. Following discussions with Rolls-Royce at Derby, P-38J 42–67488 was delivered early in May 1944 to Hucknall from Bovingdon for a test installation of Merlins to be made. Calibration tests suggested that the Merlin engined version would be 38 mph (61 km/h) faster in top speed and 1300 feet (396 m) per minute faster in climb. However, this project was stopped and in early July the Lightning was returned to Bovingdon. The reasons appear to have been political as orders to cancel this project were made by USAAF Hq in Washington.

In July 1944 a further cause of engine trouble was identified. It had previously been established that fuel was not being metered properly at high altitude, the problem varying from aircraft to aircraft. Operational Engineering found one cause was vapour lock in the fuel system, minimising it by simplifying the plumbing to eliminate or reduce sharp bends. Nevertheless, poor fuel metering at altitude, with incipient detonation providing the immediate cause of engine failire, still persisted and was recognised as a basic deficiency plaguing the operation of Lightnings during previous months.

Although the high speed compressibility problem had been investigated in 1942, a device for slowing the aircraft when the critical speed was approached was not forthcoming on production until the late P-38Js reaching the UK in summer 1944. It took the form of electrically-extended dive flaps under the wings. The 479th Group received two aircraft with such flaps in August 1944 – at which time it was the last P-38 equipped group in VIII FC. After some hours flying with them they complained that the flaps continually broke down; one aircraft had needed repair nine times. The Group arranged to exchange these aircraft for two without flaps. The 479th flew its last P-38 mission on 27 September, terminating the Lightning's service as a fighter with 8th Air Force. All first-line P-38Js, except a few retained at Bovingdon and Hitcham for experimental purposes, were turned over to the 9th and 15th Air Forces. Second-line Js used by 554th FTS for training included two modified to carry a

passenger behind the pilot – 42–68037 and 42–67655.

P-38J details

Two Allison V-1710-89/91 inlines rated at 1425 hp each

Span 52ft (15.85 m)
Length 37 ft 10 in (11.53 m)
Empty weight 12,780 lb (5797 kg)
Max loaded weight 21,600 lb (9843 kg)
Max speed 414 mph (666 km/h) at 25,000 ft (7620 m)
Tact cruise speed 250–320 mph (402–515 km/h)
Climb 13 min 30 sec to 30,000 ft (9140 m)
Service ceiling 44,000 ft (13,410 m)
Tact ceiling 30,000 ft (9140 m)
Norm range 450 miles (724 km) (leading edge tanks)
Tact radius 275 miles (442 km) (leading edge tanks)
Max tact radius with two 150 US gallon (586 ltr) drop tanks 425 miles (684 km)
Fuel consumption 100–150 US gallons (378–568 ltr) per hour cruise; 320 US gallons (1211 ltr) per hour full power
Armament 1 × 20 mm cannon and 4 × .50 in (12.77 mm) mg. Two 2000 lb (907 kg) bombs could be carried on wing racks; the normal load was two 1000 lb (454 kg) bombs

P-38L

In late July 1944 the first P-38Ls arrived in the UK. The only significant difference between this model and late P-38Js was their improved V-17110-111/113 engines, incorporating refinements to overcome the weaknesses highlighted in the previous winter. For all practical purposes, its performance was the same as the J. When this model became available for

combat units in August, only the 479th Group still retained fighter P-38s in 8th Air Force and replacements it received were mostly low-hours P-38Js turned in by the units that had recently converted to P-51s. The few P-38Ls received by 8th Air Force included one for evaluation by Operational Engineering at Bovingdon, and those fitted out for photographic or special radar work detailed below.

F-4

The P-38E converted for photographic reconnaissance was designated the F-4. All armament was removed from the nose where three or four K-17 cameras were installed. Thirteen F-4s

were provided for the 5th Photographic Squadron at Podington in September 1942, this unit being transferred to the 12th Air Force and moving into Steeple Morden on 2 November.

F-5A

The photographic version of the P-38G was designated the F-5A. In January 1943 the 13th Photographic Squadron at Podington collected 13 F-5A-3-LOs from Speke. Few replace-

F-5A-10, 42-13319 of 7th PG on its Mount Farm dispersal. The aircraft is painted overall in RAF 'PR Blue'. Note camera windows in nose. Because it caused negative distortion, over 40% of glass in F-5 camera windows had to be replaced with panels obtained from the British.

ments were available until June when F-5A-10-LOs were obtained from 7th Photo Group. There were never more than 20 F-5As on hand. The F-5A suffered the same engine problems as contemporary P-38s operating at high altitudes, cutting out and pre-detonation which sometimes prevented operation above 22,000 feet – although the minimum safe altitude for photographic reconnaissance aircraft was advised as 24,000 feet. Little could be done about this inherent problem.

In the spring of 1943 VHF radios suffered increasingly from interference, a problem British radio experts traced to ignition leaks and cured with bonding and filters. A more serious trouble became apparent in the summer of 1943. On 24 July, during comparison tests with a Mosquito and Spitfire, the tail broke off an F-5A causing a fatal crash. Subsequent investigation showed that the elevator trim tab push-pull rod had broken during a dive, leading to overstrain of the tail. On 18 August an F-5A going out on a mission, meeting severe turbulence in a thunderstorm, suffered a similar failure. F-5As were then grounded for two weeks until sufficient strengthened trim tab push-pull rods were obtained. They were withdrawn from service early in 1944 when later models became available, but 7th Group retained 42–13320 for training until March 1945.

F-5B AND F-5C

Production photographic version of the P-38J-5 was the F-5B, ten of which were first received by 7th Photo Group in December 1943. The F-5C designation applied to P-38J-5 aircraft converted for camera work at modification centres. Both versions were prone to the same engine troubles experienced with the fighter P-38Js. In March 1944 the position was critical with aircraft grounded through engine failures. There were, however, a few aircraft that led a charmed life. In July 1944, F-5C 42–67114, *Maxine* became the first 7th Group aircraft to complete 50 sorties. It had suffered no mechanical failures on operations and the only damage incurred was when a pilot performing an incautious 'buzzing' put two small holes in the Mount Farm Intelligence hut and scuffed propellar blades. This aircraft went on to fly 14 more combat missions before retirement in November 1944. For self-defence experiments, .50-cal package guns were installed on the fuselage sides of F5B 43–28577 in March 1945.

F-5C 42-67132 carrying two 150 US gallon drop tanks.

F-5E

The F-5E-2, a photographic conversion of the P-38J-15, was first seen in 8th Air Force in July 1944 and F-5E-3, a conversion of the P-38J-25 with electronic supercharger controls, reached the UK in the same month. F-5E-4, a conversion of the P-38L-1, arrived in September with first examples being sent to 7th Group the following month. Camera arrangements were two split K-22 vertical sight 24-in focal lengths and one K-22 or K-17 vertical with 6- or 12-in focal length.

F-5F AND F-5G

A few examples of these models, both conversions of P-38L-5-LOs, were on hand at 4th SAD in April and May 1945. Camera arrangements for both were two split K-22 verticals with 24-in focal lengths and a 'Tri-mat' installation, plus one forward-facing oblique K-17 in the F-5G.

DROOP SNOOT P-38

Largely the creation of Col Cass Hough of Operational Engineering, the *Droop Snoot* was a P-38 converted to carry a bombsight and bombardier in the nose. Work on a prototype commenced at Bovingdon in January 1944, the project being transferred to Lockheed at Langford Lodge for the major engineering needed. The aircraft's name was bestowed when someone, viewing the cut-off nose during modification, enquired as to the purpose of the 'droop snooted P-38'. Changes involved all armament and associated equipment being removed from the nose, an escape hatch fashioned in one side, a plexiglas moulding fitted to the front, Norden bombsight and bombing fitting installed, together with a seat for the bombardier and oxygen supply. Tactical employment was planned whereby the *Droop Snoot* would lead a tight formation of standard P-38s, all carrying bombs on the wing shackles, to make a high-speed attack on heavily defended targets such as airfields. A mass drop would be made on the *Droop Snoot* release in similar fashion to the mode of attack used by medium and heavy bombers. Design bomb load for a *Droop Snoot* was two × 1000 lb but a maximum of six × 500 lb could be carried. Successful trials were carried out from Bovingdon over the Bradwell range using 42–68184, while six other conversions were being made by Langford Lodge.

The first operational use of the *Droop Snoots* was on 10 April 1944 when 20th and 55th Groups used one each to lead formations. *Droop Snoots* were subsequently employed by all four 8th Air Force P-38 groups and by the 56th Group to lead P-47s. Other conversions were made by BADA for 9th Air Force. In July it was recommended that all but three *Droop Snoots* be transferred from 8th Air Force, those retained being 42–104075 used by Operational Engineering, 43–28490 used for the *Aphrodite* project, and the third for the *Dilly* project. Four *Droop Snoots* were later prepared for special ELINT duties, monitoring enemy radar defences. These aircraft – 43–28479, 44–23156, 44–23501 and 44–23515 – operated with RAF No100 Group. During these operations one, 44–23515, was missing in action.

Pilots were provided by 7th Group, to which the aircraft were assigned.

Operational Engineering's *Droop Snoot* 42-104075 displays bomb symbols for participation in combat missions and two stars over a wheelbarrow for transporting a Major General.   (via K. Braybrook)

H2X P-38L

In July 1944 8th Air Force was notified it was being sent 12 P-38Ls which had H2X equipment and an operator's compartment in a special bulbous nose. Of these 44-23880 was used for trials, flying ten night sorties in January and February 1945 with 654th BS, 25th Group, to take scope pictures of potential targets. The programme was discontinued on 13 February 1945

as B-17s and B-24s could more adequately perform these missions.

P-38L 44-23880, Q3:0, with H2X in nose was used for operation trials by 325th Recon. Wing. As scanner only swept through 210 degrees, scope photos produced by B-17s with scanners sweeping the full 360 degrees were preferred.   (via K. Barybrooke)

Republic P-47 Thunderbolt

Designed to utilise the most powerful turbo-supercharged radial engine available, the P-47 was originally nted as a high-altitude interceptor. Introduction to combat was with 8th Air Force in which it was successfully developed as an escort fighter and, later, for ground attack purposes. Considerably larger and about twice the weight of most of its Allied and enemy contemporaries, the Thunderbolt still proved able to acquit itself well in fighter versus fighte combat.

P-47C AND P-47D

The first of 200 P-47Cs arrived by ship in the UK on 24 December 1942, followed in April 1943 by the first P-47Ds. While the D featured detail improvements, the change of model designation was principally to establish an identification system for product standardisation as a second manufacturing source entered large scale production. Thunderbolts from the original plant, Farmingdale, were identified by an RE suffix and those from the new Evansville factory by RA. Although Thunderbolt production was subject to numerous detail changes during the period January 1943 to March 1944 the basic airframe was little altered and early aircraft received by 8th Air Force were up-dated to an acceptable combat standard by modification. It was May 1944 before VIII FC units began to receive a radically different model.

While a basically sound design, the new and untried fighter was soon found to have its problems: insufficient range for escort duties, a poor rate of climb, excessive radio noise interference, limited forward vision, engine failures, armament defects, gunsight inadequately matched to the speed of the aircraft, poor gun mountings and frequent stoppages in the ammunition feed. The 4th Group pilots to whom the first aircraft were made available in January 1943 had little confidence in their new aircraft; they complained about its two inherent weaknesses, poor climb and acceleration.

An early trouble was the radio mast on P-47C-2-RE models breaking off at the base during high speed. VIII AFSC reinforced the mast to withstand the strain while an urgent cable was sent to the US for a supply of new type masts. As with other early USAAF aircraft, P-47s received the necessary radio changes for VHF operation but pilots complained of excessive radio noise, a problem first noted in January and not satisfactorily overcome for some weeks. The ignition system of the engine, poorly designed from the standpoint of interference with radio equipment was found to have some 36 leaks and the unfiltered booster coil allowed a leak back into the battery system. After the leaks had been located, special shielding was designed as a remedy. The necessary modifications finally developed needed 40 man-hours per aircraft for installation. Liberal use of a special sealing compound was a major factor in curing this trouble. Based on information provided by VIII FC, a new ignition harness was designed in the US and incorporated in subsequent P-47s. Instances of partial or complete engine failure during the early months of P-47 operations in England were in some cases due to oil starvation of the secondary couterbalance, particularly during inverted flight. The counterbalance was redesigned in the US and pendulum oil tanks substituted for the original type to prevent the failure of supply during violent manoeuvres. All aircraft were eventually modified using the 4000 kits sent from the US for this purpose. A series of technical modification directives from the engine manufacturers received February to April 1943 in connection with the counterbalance problem were so complicated that rather than send P-47s to Burtonwood for engine re-working, VIII FC decided to keep the aircraft at combat stations and replace engines with those delivered fully modified.

The introduction of the P-47 into combat was also delayed by a serious shortage of parts. Early in February a batch of A-2 oxygen regulators in these aircraft were notified as faulty and there was much delay in obtaining replacements. As received, the first Thunderbolts had no gun cameras but urgent cables to the US finally resulted in an initial supply of 100 cameras arriving on 9 February. A lack of tail wheel tyres caused suitable British stocks to be used until the first replacement consignment arrived at the Wattisham depot in early May. Also, a shortage of replacement sparking plugs was so critical that in late April some P-47s had to be grounded for this reason. Here again supplies were obtained locally. The British also supplied the battery trolleys for engine starting at P-47 bases. Another shortage that developed in April 1943 was of propeller and blade spares.

One of the original P-47Cs received by 4th FG in January 1943, 41-6192 served with the group for over a year, for most of this time as personal aircraft of Lt 'Woody' Sooman. Photograph taken in June 1943 by its crew chief, T/Sgt Glesner Weckbacker.

Early P-47D was basically as the P-47C. Photographed while being flown by Maj Charles Hines, Chief Test Pilot of BAD 2, 42-8400 served first with 355th FG and then 352nd FG. (H. Holmes)

Improving the rate of climb was not something that could be quickly undertaken but two successful modifications were eventually introduced, wide blade propellers and engine water injection. These were developed in the US and kits were produced for the UK where it was planned to make the necessary installations as rapidly as possible. The 'paddle' blade propeller programme carried out at Wattisham from December 1943 was hindered by a shortage of blades and certain accessories. P-47's of the 56th Group, the first to be processed, were not fitted out until late April, at which time the 356th Group had only just started to have paddle blades fitted. It was another month before the programme was completed. On production, paddle blade propellers were fitted from P-47D-16-RE 42-76029 and P-47D-21-RA 43-25634.

The water injection system, designed to increase the humidity of carburettor air and allow more power to be drawn from the engine for short periods, was first available to VIII FC as a kit. It consisted of two parts: the Republic kit with water tank, pump and piping, and the Pratt & Whitney kit consisting of carburettor fittings and jet. Kit manufacture was disappointingly slow for a while. Although modification started in the autumn of 1943, it was the late spring of 1944 before all P-47s in the UK had been fitted. The installation was incorporated in production beginning with the P-47D-10-RE and P-47D-11-RA.

In general, the early armament problems of the P-47 were not difficult to overcome and in many cases the defects were corrected by ground crews or combat base service units. The P-47 was originally equipped with the N-3A reflector gunsight which was not accurate at high speed. In February 1943 it was decided to replace this sight with the Mk II sight procured from the British and to manufacture a suitable mounting at a base air depot. Subsequently a similar US-made sight, the Navy Mk VIII, was put into production but the first P-47s with this did not arrive until late in 1943. Minor modifications were made to the mounting of the new sight in order to increase vertical adjustment.

Gun stoppages in early P-47Cs were found to be caused by protrusions in and around the ammunition compartment. The head of the separator mechanism was round and the ammunition sometimes caught underneath this head. The simple expedient of crimping the head eliminated this trouble. Other stoppages were traced to round-head rivets in the compartment which were replaced with flat-head rivets.

Range could best be increased by auxiliary, disposable fuel tanks. The only type developed for the P-47 was a 'belly' tank of 200 US gallons capacity, used in the US for ferrying, which proved unsuitable for operational use. Four different types and capacities of fuel tanks were subsequently developed in the UK for use on P-47s which, together with cruise control techniques, eventually made it possible to treble their radius of action.

P-47 modifications were subject to the same attempts to establish conformity through so-called staging letters. The first, issued 7 July 1943, listed 48 items of which 15 were inspection and maintenance items for new aircraft. Stage 1 required the elimination of radio noise, the removal of IFF set with its control box and antenna (not used on fighters), pressurisation of the engine ignition harness, the wrapping of external power conduits, modification of ammunition compartment installations, the removal of engine winterisation equipment, the installation of a locally-designed mounting for the Mk II gunsight and emergency exit panels in the canopy sides. Stage 2 gave water injection (not then applicable) and installation of the pendulum oil tanks. Compliance with this letter for the first three stages required some 700 man hours per aircraft. However, all stages were never completed on any one aircraft due to the lack of facilities and supplies, particularly modification kits. The 100 hour inspections alone required between 100 and 200 man-hours and left little time for all but essential modifications. This situation existed until November 1943 when a revised staging letter relegated maintenance inspections to their proper place, combat stations.

The P-47 staging letter was revised monthly until November 1943 and then not until February 1944. The November 1943 listing had 23 Stage 1 items of which nine were inspections and had to do with identification markings, three were directions for removal of equipment including identification plates on the engine, winterisation accessories, and IFF fittings. Stage 2 comprised ten items including the pendulum oil tank, camera over-run control unit, reworking of sights, a change in a fuel line, inspection and reworking of gun mounts. Stage 3 consisted of 13 items, most being minor, with the exception of the expendable tank release mechanism. The other items included quick removable bolts for the SCR-522 VHF radio, repainting the cockpit interior dull black, pinning gun mount screws, substituting channel-tread tyres for smooth ones, painting the auxiliary bead sight on the windshield and taping a solenoid conduit.

During 1943 much attention was paid to increasing the Thunderbolt's radius of action. While the under fuselage drop tank proved most successful, there was a limit to the size and thereby capacity due to limited ground clearance; P-47s operating from rough grass airfields could not use 108 gallon tanks for this reason. To increase the P-47's external stores carrying capability, bomb shackle pylons for attachment under each wing were designed in the US and sent as kits to the UK in November 1943.

Initially fitting had to be made at Burtonwood where only ten aircraft sent by groups could be modified each week, the first in mid-December. Warton also began to fit these shackles but it took several weeks to deal with all P-47s in VIII FC. The attachments allowed two 108 or 150 gallon tanks to be carried, extending the P-47's radius of action to between 400 and 500 miles. The increasing availability of the P-51B Mustang during the early months of 1944 allowed VIII FC to convert five of its P-47 groups and exchange another two with the 9th Air Force for new

P-51 groups, the Mustang being superior for the long-range escort role. The groups converted were the 4th, 355th, 352nd, 359th and 361st while the 358th and 50th were exchanged, the latter before arrival, leaving the 56th, 78th, 353rd abd 356th with P-47s. Peak inventory for 8th Air Force P-47s was November 1943 when 1,200 were on hand in depots and flying units. 'War-weary' P-47Cs and P-47Ds were retained by P-47 groups for operational training when this became a requirement ~f combat stations in the autumn of 1944.

BUBBLE CANOPY P-47D

The most significant change in the P-47 since the early combat-worthy models appeared was an all-round vision canopy which, together with greater internal fuel and oxygen capacity, was first incorporated on the P-47D-25-RE. Surprisingly, these new features were not acknowledged by a new model letter. 'Bubble' canopy P-47s began to arrive in the UK during May 1944 and a few examples were on hand in the four Thunderbolt groups by D-Day. Performance was little changed but a marked lack of directional stability was evident through the lowered fuselage spine. Later in the year a fin fillet kit was avaialble to rectify the matter but few 8th Air Froce P-47Ds were so fitted.

To improve pilot visibility in the earlier high-backed P-47s, a British manufacturer supplied a clear 'bubble' moulding known as the Malcolm hood that could be fixed in the sliding canopy frame. However, few VIII FC combat P-47s received this fitment as P-51s had first priority.

In September the P-47D-30 introduced an electrically operated release for wing stores in place of the manual type, and conversion kits were made available for older models. Again, few conversions were made in 8th Air Force. During the last quarter of 1944 the 353rd, 356th and 78th Groups converted to P-51s leaving the 56th as the sole Thunderbolt fighter group in the Force. Although it was planned that this group would convert to the new P-47M in January 1945, troubles with the new model caused the 56th to retain P-47Ds until late March. Most of its replacement Ds during this period were low-hours aircraft withdrawn from the other groups. The majority of old type canopy P-47Ds were retired from first-line service by the end of 1944. The oldest P-47 Thunderbolt in first-line service was the 56th's P-47D-4-RA, 42-22763, LM:B *Virginia*.

'Bubble' canopy Thunderbolts suffered from poor directional stability until a tail fillet was added. Originally received in bare metal finish, P-47D-25 42-26459 displaying the colourful yellow and black checkerboard of 353rd FG, had a pattern of green and grey camouflage painted on the upper surfaces. This was advised by VIII FC in anticipation that 8th AF fighter groups would be moved to the Continent where enemy air attack on airfields was to be expected. (via K. Rust)

P-47D details

One Pratt & Whitney R-2800-59 radial rated at 2000 hp (P-47C and early P-47D models had the -21 and -63 models which signified lack of water injection and modified for water injection, respectively. Power rating for water injection was 2300 hp).

Span 40 ft 9½ in (12.43 m)
Length 36 ft 1 in (11.00 m)
Empty weight 9900 lb (4490 kg)
Max loaded weight 15,000 lb (6804 kg)
Max speed 433 mph (697 km/h) at 30,000 ft (9140 m)
Tact cruise speed 210 to 275 mph (338–442 km/h)
Climb rate 20 minutes to 30,000 ft (9140 m)
Norm range, internal supply 400 miles (644 km) (early) 590 miles (945 km) (late) at 25,000 ft (7620 m)
Tact radius 200 miles (322 km) (early), 250 miles (402 km) (late) on internal fuel
Max tact radius with two 108 US gallon (408 ltr) wing drop tanks 475 miles (764 km)
Fuel consumption 100 US gallons (378 ltr) per hour cruising to 300 US gallons (1135 ltr) per hour at full power
Armament 8 × .50-in (12.7 mm) mg

P-47M

This was basically a late P-47D airframe with the more powerful 'C' series version of the R-2800 engine (P-47Ds had the 'B' series). The power was obtained without increases in piston displacement by redesigning components for greater strength so as to withstand higher manifold pressures. The result was a much improved performance and when water injection was used the P-47M could attain more than 460 mph for short periods. All P-47Ms produced were sent to the UK and used to re-equip the 56th Group. The first aircraft reached the Group's base at Boxted on 3 January 1945 and was used operationally on the 14th. However, the new model was plagued with snags. The first problems were engines cutting out at high altitude, low cylinder head temperatures at cruise speeds and difficulty in climbing above 28,000 ft. Technical Services at Bovingdon suspected a repetition of troubles experienced with the P-47C two years before; cracked insulation on ignition leads, lack of lagging on the push-rod covers and incorrect correlation of throttle setting to turbo-supercharger regulation. The diagnoses were largely correct. Many leads on the ignition harness of P-47Ms were found to be cracked and were replaced with more durable neoprene covered leads. Lagging the push-rod covers did not help, but a metal baffle positioned to restrict airflow through the cowling outlet flaps did raise temperatures. This also helped in equalising individual cylinder temperatures – a problem encountered before and caused by the streamlined shape of the cowling affecting air currents over different parts of the engine. Readjusting the control cam setting for the throttle-turbo linkage solved the P-47M's lack of enthusiasm to gain high altitude. Additionally, propeller feathering mechanisms failed on some aircraft, a trouble quickly traced to broken springs.

By early February it was hoped the problems had been mastered but this was not to be. A series of take-off crashes following engine cut-out caused the grounding of all 67 P-47Ms on hand at Boxted on 26 February 1945. The cause was attributed to the rupture of carburettor diaphrams. Representatives of Bendix, the carburettor manufacturers, were able to obtain suitable replacement diaphragm material from the Zenith Company in London and all P-47Ms had replacements fitted within 48 hours. But engine failures still continued. This time burned pistons were diagnosed. Suspicion that the 150 octane fuel was the culprit caused comparison tests to be carried out with 130 grade fuel, but engines still failed using lower octane. On 16

Externally the P-47M was indistinguishable from late P-47Ds. This example, seen at Glatton, was on a delivery flight to Stansted in January 1945 when forced to divert due to bad weather. The aircraft was later assigned to the 61st FS as HV:W with upper surfaces painted matt black. A fin fillet was also added.

March 8th Air Force decided to ground all P-47Ms until the mystery could be solved. It was noticed that practically all the engines that had failed did so during the first 25 hours, but after reaching 50 hours they appeared to be trouble-free. Examination of low-hours engines showed burned pistons and scuffed cylinder barrels leading to the conclusion that the engines had not been properly treated against corrosion before shipment, a diagnosis later confirmed. All P-47M engines with less than 50 hours were changed and slow time put on the replacements as rapidly as possible to allow the group to return to operations. In the final days of hostilities the 56th Group did some excellent work with the P-47M which was held in great esteem by its pilots. All 130 P-47Ms built were at one time or another in service with 56th Group, but some not until the immediate post-war days.

P-47M details

One Pratt & Whitney R-2800-57 radial rated at 2100 hp (2800 hp with water injection)

Span 40 ft 9½ in (12.43 m)
Length 36 ft 1¾ in (11.02 m)
Empty weight 10,340 lb (4690 kg)
Max loaded weight 18,000 lb (8165 kg)
Max speed 473 mph (762 km/h) at 32,000 ft (4750 m)
Tact cruise speed 220 to 290 mph (354–437 km/h)
Climb rate 13 min 24 sec to 32,000 ft (9750 m)
Service ceiling 41,000 ft (12,500 m)
Norm range, internal supply 530 miles (848 km) at 26,000 ft (7920 m)
Tact radius 250 miles (402 km) on internal fuel
Max tact radius with 200 US gallon (757 ltr) belly tank 475 miles (764 km)
Fuel consumption 100 US gallons (378 ltr) per hour at cruising speed to 330 US gallons (1250 ltr) per hour at full power
Armament 8 × .50-in (12.7 mm) mg

P-47N

The P-47N featured a redesigned wing with distinctive square-cut tips. The wing root section incorporated fuel cells to substantially increase the Thunderbolt's endurance. A small shipment arrived in the UK in April 1945 but were never issued to units. Five returned to the US from Speke in May 1945 were: 44-88343, 44-88344, 44-88352, 44-88353 and 44-88420.

ASR SPOTTER P-47s

In May 1944 25 'war-weary' P-47Ds were drawn from every P-47 group in VIII FC to equip the air/sea rescue spotter squadron at Boxted. For spotter duties a prototype equipment configuration was carried out on 42-75855, consisting of a British M-type dinghy pack carried on the belly shackles, a rack for two marker smoke bombs under each wing and two 108 gallon drop tanks on the wing racks. This produced too great a loading and was revised so that an M-type dinghy pack was carried on each rack and a 150 gallon drop tank on the fuselage belly shackles. The four smoke bombs were positioned on a single rack aft of the belly tank where they caused less drag. This arrangement was eventually made on all other ASR P-47s. To further reduce wing loadings only three .50 guns were installed in each wing and this was subsequently reduced to two. All aircraft were also given yellow markings on flight surfaces and a red, white and blue ringed cowling. Three replacement aircraft were received in August 1944 and six others early in 1945. The squadron complement was reduced to ten P-47s by the end of hostilities, seven being those originally assigned to the unit. Original P-47D Spotters of Detachment B, Flight Section, Hq, 65th Fighter Wing – later 5th Emergency Rescue Squadron were:

Red, white and blue-nosed P-47D, 42-75228, of ASR Squadron, in D-Day markings June 1944. Note smoke flare rack aft of 108 gallon drop tank.

Serial	Code	Name	Notes
42-75855	5F:A	Tony	
43-25534	5F:B	Invincible Faye	
42-8375	5F:C		
42-25711	5F:D	Bubbles	MIA 1/8/44
42-8693	5F:E	Miss Margaret	
42-8402	5F:F		Collided 5F:U landing 8/8/44
42-75228	5F:G	Harriet	
42-75528	5F:H	Deane III	
42-75154	5F:I		
42-74690	5F:J		
43-25565	5F:K	Katie	Cr Westleton 15/12/44
42-8410	5F:L		Retired 1/8/44
42-7899	5F:M		
42-22784	5F:N		
42-74705	5F:O	Lady Loralie	Cr Fritton 8/4/45; air collision with 42-76175 5F:D
42-74744	5F:P	Blind Date	
42-7910	5F:Q		
42-74622	5F:R	Terry	
42-8586	5F:S		
42-8485	5F:T		
42-74664	5F:U		Collided 5F:F landing 8/8/44
42-22476	5F:V		
42-8554	5F:W		
42-8496	5F:X	Galloping Catastrophe	Cr 14/3/45
42-8646	5F:Y	Primrose Peggy	

FORMATION MARSHALLING P-47

In November 1944 8th Air Force authorised the assignment of one P-47 to each bomb group, two to each combat wing headquarters and two to each division headquarters for the purpose of marshalling and observing bomber formations. This allowed radio directions to be given to bomber leaders to ensure individual formations were positioned as planned. These aircraft were all 'war-weary' P-47C or P-47D models, from which armament and most combat equipment was usually removed. Paint schemes reflected the unit markings of the organisation to which they were assigned. Prior to this order many bomber headquarters already had a P-47 assigned for liaison duties.

TWO-SEAT P-47

By removing the radio equipment and repositioning it further back in the fuselage it was possible to make room for a second occupant in a P-47. Prior to the end of hostilities three such conversions were known to have been made by 8th Air Force units. P-47C 41-6259, used by the Hq 65th Fighter Wing and flown from Debden had such additional accommodation and was used for liaison work. P-47D, 42-27606, served 78th Fighter Group for training. P-47D, 42-75276, of 56th Group, was more carefully appointed with additional oxygen supplies. It was used unsuccessfully in an operational experiment on 10 April 1945 and three subsequent missions with Perfectos intercept radar. This aircraft had a lengthened canopy, which when slid fully back allowed the rear cockpit to be entered through a hinged section.

The 78th FG 'piggy-back' P-47 embodied a Malcolm hood over the rear cockpit. The aircraft was painted bright red overall. (F. Oiler)

NORTH AMERICAN P-51A MUSTANG

The Mustang was designed in 1940 to meet a British order for an advanced fighter. While the Allison engine used gave the Mustang an excellent low and medium level performance, its power output fell off rapidly above 15,000 ft (4570 m), causing the RAF to employ the aircraft in tactical fighter and reconnaissance duties. This was also the mode of employment for most of the Allison-engined Mustangs with the USAAF as the P-51 and P-51A. To realise the full potential of the airframe a Packard-built Merlin was substituted for the Allison on production during 1943, resulting in a much improved performance. For the 8th Air Force this Mustang version proved an excellent escort fighter, allowing the day bomber campaign to continue and achieving a high measure of air superiority over the enemy homeland.

P-51A

This Allison-engined model was scheduled as re-equipment for three squadrons of the 67th Observation Group at Membury in the spring of 1943, but in the event these units did not receive the P-51A until October, when the Group had been transferred to the 9th Air Force.

MUSTANG X

Reports of the excellent performance obtained from the Merlin 61 series engine Mustang conversion, performed by Rolls-Royce, led VIII FC to request one for evaluation. These aircraft were officially designated as Mustang Mk X, although usually referred to as Merlin Mustangs. The Merlin 61 series featured a two-stage supercharger and gave excellent high altitude performance. At the end of February 1943 the second Mustang X, AM203, was delivered to Bovingdon for trials by the Air Technical Section. This aircraft, however, was returned to Rolls-Royce after a short stay and replaced by AM121, which arrived at Bovingdon from AFDU Duxford on 18 April. Trial flights did not produce great acclaim from ATS, for while the speed performance was acknowledged, directional stability, particularly on take-off and landing, was considered poor. Compared with the smooth flying and comparatively easily-handled P-38, the Merlin Mustang was a wayward mount. However, range was good as the 184 US gallons internal fuel gave over three hours endur-

Mustang X AM 121 taxiing out at Duxford. Deep nose air intake distinguished this experimental model from the P-51B. (via G. Fry)

ance. At the time, VIII FC was still hopeful that the improved P-38, when available, would meet its requirements and thus, initially, there was only limited enthusiasm for the Merlin Mustang. Mustang X AM121 coded VQ:R remained at Bovingdon until August 1944 when it was broken down to spares.

P-51B

In USAAF planning, the production model of the Merlin Mustang, the P-51B, was scheduled as a tactical fighter unit for similar duties to those of the P-51A. Four new groups sent to 8th Air Force in the winter of 1943–44 were to be equipped with P-51Bs, but by the time these arrived the tactical role had been passed to the 9th Air Force. Thus, although VIII AFSC handled the preparation of P-51Bs, early deliveries from 11 November 1943 were to 9th Air Force units. But by that time a crisis in the day bomber campaign, highlighting the urgent need for more long-range fighters, gained 8th Air Force some priority for P-51s with temporary operational control of the first group, the 354th. At the end of January 1944 the P-51B-equipped 357th Group joined VIII FC, for which the 8th had exchanged their P-47-equipped 358th Group. Another exchange was made with the 50th and 339th Groups arriving in the following April. A programme to convert P-47 groups to P-51s got under way in late February when the 4th Group received P-51Bs, and during the next three months the 352nd, 355th, 359th and 361st also converted. A few P-51Bs were also received by the 20th and 55th Groups when they changed from P-38s in July.

A month after delivery of P-51Bs began, a consignment of 85 US gallon fuel tanks arrived from the US for installation in the fuselage aft of the radio equipment. When fitting started at Warton in December, there were 253 P-51Bs in the UK. Following P-51B shipments had this tank incorporated during production. While the additional tank added considerably to the P-51B's radius of action, when full it made the aircraft tail-heavy, adversely affecting handling. Longitudinally unstable and easily stalled, the manufacturers advised restrictions calling for avoidance of violent manoeuvres until this tank had been emptied. It then became standing operational procedure to use at least 60 gallons from the fuselage tank on the route out to escort.

In February 1944, P-51Bs were grounded for a short period pending clarification of the correct method of securing the empennage. Attachment bolts were found to be too long and not being properly tightened.

A fault in the engine design led to sparking plug fouling on the left block front cylinder. It became policy to change this plug regularly after every long flight and for pilots to periodically apply high power to 'clean out' the engine when prolonged cruising was involved. British RC5/5 plugs were found much superior to the original type and were used almost exclusively from late March 1944. A more serious development was a number of incidents when engines were reported breaking away from airframes, usually in pulling out of a dive or in tight turns. Following a spate of such losses in early March 1944, all P-51Bs were grounded until engine bolts had been inspected.

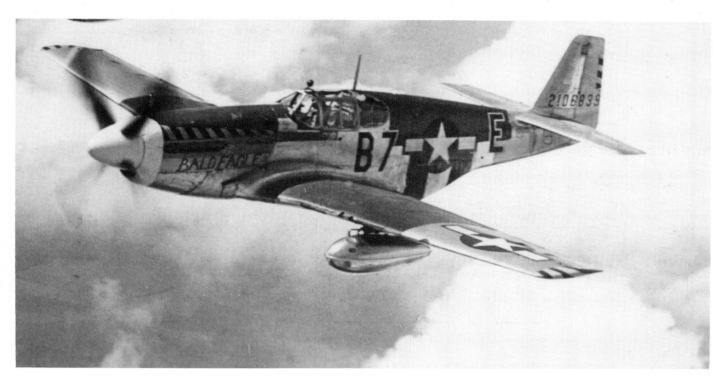

Above: **P-51B of 374th FS, 361st FG carrying 110 US gallon drop tanks. Armament and restricted visibility from cockpit were weakest points of this model Mustang.**

Left: **Malcolm Hood, the bulged perspex sliding canopy installed on 359th FG P-51B 43-6491, CV:E. Aerial mast had to be repositioned further back on fuselage.** (R. Bowers)

Examination of wreckage had revealed that the mounting bolts were cracking and breaking, being insufficiently robust to hold the heavy Merlin; thereafter they were regularly inspected.

Perhaps the most critical situation with the P-51B arose over persistent gun stoppages. The armament layout was different from that in earlier Mustangs, the feed to the four .50 guns – two per wing – proving highly unsatisfactory. The failures were chiefly through jammed or displaced rounds; in some instances aircraft returned from combat with only one gun operative. In early March 1944 the 354th Group at Boxted (9th Air Force) had successfully overcome the feeding stoppages by the addition to the gun feed chute of a Martin electric ammunition booster from the B-26. It had been discovered that the traced rounds passing from the ammunition compartment to the feedway of the gun were improperly aligned in that they were slightly cocked in relation to the axis of the breech bore. This happened when the pull on the trace exceeded 17 lb (7.7 kg). With the booster motor set to come in automatically when the pull exceeded 15 lb (6.8 kg), feeding stoppages were largely eliminated. It took two mechanics four hours to assemble and install this modification, which was advised for VIII FC groups early in April. Gun failures were also attributed to the freezing of mechanisms, for which minimum lubrication was the only remedy; and to links jamming in the discharge chutes, avoided by modifying the chutes.

Outlook from the cockpit was poor, with a blind spot to the rear that could only be covered by mirrors. The British had improved visibility from the cockpit of their Mustang IIIs (P-51B & C) by replacing the hinged hood with a one-piece bulged clear moulding in a sliding canopy frame. Known as the Malcolm Hood, examples were secured for the 8th Air Force P-51s in March 1944, with priority for formation leaders, as demand was more than the manufacturer could meet. Only a small proportion of the total P-51B force received this canopy.

The P-51B remained in first-line service until February 1945,

although numbers were few after the late autumn of 1944. B models were used by all Mustang groups for OTU purposes and examples were on hand in most squadrons well past VE-Day. The P-51B also predominated in the 555th Fighter Training Squadron.

P-51B details
One Packard Merlin V-1650-3 or -7 inline rated at 1380 hp (the -7 having better power output at lower altitudes)

Span 37 ft (11.28 m)
Length 32 ft 3 in (9.83 m)
Empty weight 6985 lb (3168 kg)
Max loaded weight 11,800 lb (5353 kg)
Max speed 440 mph (708 km/h) at 30,000 ft (9140 m)
Tact cruise speed 210 to 320 mph (338–515 km/h)
Climb rate 12 min 30 sec to 30,000 ft (9140 m)
Service ceiling 41,800 ft (12,740 m)
Usual tact ceiling 35,000 ft (10,670 m)
Norm range, internal fuel 700 miles (1126 km)
Tact radius 325 miles (523 km) on internal fuel; 750 miles (1207 km) with two 108 US gallon (409 ltr) drop tanks
Fuel consumption 64 US gallons (242 ltr) per hour for average mission, 120 US gallons (454 ltr) per hour at full power
Armament 4 × .50-in (12.7 mm) mg 2 × 500 lb (227 kg) bombs could be carried in place of drop tanks

P-51C

When a second source of Merlin Mustang production commenced at Dallas, Texas, these aircraft were identified as P-51Cs. Apart from detail changes they were equivalent to the Inglewood, California production P-51B. The first P-51Cs arrived in the UK in February 1944, when they were also the first with unpainted finish. They were used with P-51Bs to equip or re-equip the 352nd, 339th, 359th and 361st Groups. A few C models endured in first-line service until early in 1945 and in Group OTUs and other training units until the late summer of 1945. Performance figures were as for the P-51B.

VIII FC groups received only a small number of P-51Cs. This example was the personal aircraft of 487th FS 'ace' Lt Glennon Moran. (G. Murphey)

P-51D

The D was used in larger numbers by 8th Air Force than any other P-51 model, there being nearly 1000 on hand at peak inventory in December 1944. Built by both plants, it was notable for increasing the number of guns from four to six, as well as providing an all-round vision 'bubble' hood. There were a number of other refinements. First P-51D-5-NAs from Inglewood arrived in late May 1944, but the first P-51D-5-NTs from Dallas were not seen until September.

A change, not for the better, was highlighted by the loss of two Warton test pilots in June 1944 shortly after the first D models arrived. Assembled at Speke or Renfrew, the Mustangs were flown to Warton for inspection, modification and checkout. In both fatal test flights a wing had been seen to break off. Examination of the wreckage revealed the cause. To simplify landing gear operation for the pilot, a change had been made. In the P-51B and C lowering the landing gear was a two-stage operation, first moving a lever to release the safety up-locks, followed

by placing the selector in the down position for the hydraulic system to lower the undercarriage. In the P-51D it was only necessary to move the undercarriage selector, the whole operation being hydraulically sequenced and the up-locks releasing automatically. It was discovered that when the selector lever was returned to the neutral position there was insufficient hydraulic pressure in the system to hold the undercarriage fairing doors flush in the wing. At high speed airflow forced open the doors, pushing the undercarriage out and so over-stressing the wing. Until a modification could be effected to ensure that the up-locks did not release when hydraulic pressure was neutralised, pilots were advised to keep the selector level in the 'up' position.

Instances of wing and empennage failures occurred throughout the Mustang's operational use, the causes of which were difficult to identify. Reinforcement plates were added externally to both wing and tailplane in the late summer of 1944 after persistent skin wrinkling had been reported on P-51Ds. At this

To simplify maintenance and supply, General Doolittle expressed a desire to standardise on a single bomber and fighter type – the B-17 and P-51. By January 1945 14 of the 15 fighter groups were flying Mustangs, primarily the P-51D, and the remaining group, the 56th, was scheduled to convert to the P-51H in the following May. The P-51D proved a very versatile combat aircraft. *Pauline* 'belonged' to Major Joe Thury and was credited with destroying 25 enemy aircraft by ground strafing.

time Technical Services estimated that Mustang losses through structural failure might be averaging two per week.

The reduced height of the rear fuselage with the all-round vision bubble canopy brought a marked increase in the Mustang's directional instability. This was particularly noticeable in take-off when many an incautious pilot veered off the runway to the right. A dorsal fin, together with reversed rudder boost tab were incorporated in production from P-51D-10-NA, 44-14254, the first examples of which were received by VIII FC units in August 1944. For retroactively fitting earlier Mustangs a dorsal fin kit was available during the same month.

Another serious problem was inoperable radiator shutters causing engine overheating. The shutter, at the rear of the radiator scoop, functioned automatically to maintain correct temperatures. If it failed it could be controlled from the cockpit. All this worked electrically but there were an increasing number of instances of the whole system failing as winter approached and the atmosphere became damper and colder. In December it was recommended that the winterisation doors added to the scoop be removed in order to prevent overheating if the shutter control failed. However, a spate of failures led many units to improvise mechanical methods to force the shutter open. Technical Services eventually developed a manually operated, telescopic, spring-loaded arm between cockpit and shutter. This enabled the pilot to force five inches of scoop opening in an emergency.

The most vulnerable part of the P-51 was its cooling system, never more so than when the aircraft was engaged in ground attack. A single rifle bullet through the radiator cores could start a leak that would quickly lead to engine overheating. As so many Mustangs were lost to this cause, USAAF introduced quarter inch thick metal plate for the scoop and despatched enough in January 1945 for all P-51s in England. When it was

discovered that each sheet weighed 105 lb (47.6 kg), 8th Air Force declined to fit them.

The P-51D was the principal model involved in the conversion to the Mustang of 20th, 55th, 353rd, 356th, 479th and 78th Groups, in that sequence, during the second half of 1944. The D continued as a replacement to the end of hostilities at which time 25-NA and 25-NT block production were being received. Numerous detail changes were made during this period, of which the most significant was the introduction of the K-14 gunsight with the 20-NT and 25-NA. The K-14 was the USAAF designation for the American-produced version of the British Mk IID gyro gunsight affording extremely accurate deflection shooting. Given operational trials during July and August 1944, it was then eagerly adopted by most units. Installation in the Mustang was difficult owing to the size of the instrument and required positioning relative to the pilot. The 357th Group produced a successful fixture, devised by two mechanics. It entailed cutting away part of the fuselage decking just inside the windshield to allow the sight to be recessed. In November this arrangement was approved for all 8th Air Force P-51s as it placed the sight so it would not be a hazard to a pilot's head in a crash-landing. K-14s were fitted progressively in all P-51s during the autumn and winter of 1944.

P-51D details
One Packard V-1650-7 rated at 1490 hp

Span 37 ft (11.28 m)
Length 32 ft 3 in (9.83 m)
Empty weight 7125 lb (3232 kg)
Max loaded weight 11,600 lb (5262 kg)
Max speed 437 mph (704 km/h) at 25,000 ft (7620 m)
Tact cruising speed 210–320 mph (338–515 km/h)
Climb rate 13 min to 30,000 ft (9140 m)
Service ceiling 41,900 ft (12,770 m)
Usual tact ceiling 35,000 ft (10,670 m)
Norm range, internal fuel 700 miles (1126 km)
Tact radius 325 miles (523 km) on internal fuel; 750 miles (1207 km) with two 108 US gallon (409 ltr) drop tanks
Fuel consumption 64 US gallons (242 ltr) per hour for average mission; 120 US gallons (454 ltr) per hour at full power
Armament 6 × .50-in (12.7 mm) mg; 2 × 500 lb (227 kg) bombs could be carried in place of drop tanks

P-51K

In September 1944 the Dallas production line changed from using a Hamilton standard propeller to the Aeroproducts A-5A-2A-1 type. The Mustang then received a new designation; otherwise the P-51K was as a P-51D. Later in the year the Hamilton propeller was reintroduced and Dallas Mustangs again became P-51D. P-51Ks reached 8th Air Force squadrons in November 1944. The model was not generally popular as the electrical feathering mechanism proved less reliable than the hydraulically-operated Hamilton on the D. Performance figures were as for the P-51D.

P-51K Beautiful Dope of 353rd FG, pilot 1/Lt Hakonen.

TWO-SEAT MUSTANGS

With the formation of an OTU flight in all fighter groups in January 1945 permission was given for each group to modify a war-weary P-51B or C as a two-seater. The purpose was to allow an instructor to demonstrate proper techniques to replacement pilots.

By removing the 85 gallon fuselage tank and repositioning battery, dynamotor and radio equipment, it was possible to fashion a compartment large enough to hold a passenger directly behind the pilot's seat. Interphone, compass, altimeter, air speed indicator and oxygen installations were made. Such conversion work was generally carried out by base engineering units with VIII AFSC instructions. The canopy arrangement to cover each cockpit varied as individual units had their own ideas on the best way to provide easy access and egress for pilot and passenger. No stunting was allowed with two-seat Mustangs. The 339th Group provided passenger accommodation in a P-51D and used this on at least one occasion to convey a medical officer on a combat mission so that he could obtain first-hand knowledge of pilot stress factors.

In May 1945 the 4th Group had P-51D 44-72210 modified to take a passenger and also fitted with airborne intercept radar for experimental trials. During the spring of 1945 four two-seaters appeared in bright colours. The 4th and 78th Groups both had a two-seater painted red overall, the 4th also had one painted all blue, while 479th Group's was all yellow.

Known two-seaters were: 43–12195 (4FG), 44–72210 (4FG), 44–13649 (355FG), 43–6991 (355FG), 43–6787 (357FG), 44–14055 (361FG), 44–63218 (55FG), 42–106751 (353FG), 42–106826 (78FG), 43–6528 (55FG), 43–6593 (78FG), 44–13341 (479FG) and 44–13965 (339FG – prototype)

One of 4th FG's two-seat P-51Bs used for teaching combat techniques to new pilots. Front and rear canopies could be opened separately. (P. Betz)

Left: **One 78th FG two-seat conversion was effected on P-51B 42-106826. Note crash pad to protect rear passenger's face. Aircraft was finished red overall.**   (Emil Meink)

de Havilland Mosquito

USAAF interest in this British twin-engine high-performance aircraft was evinced in several quarters during 1942–43. Colonel Elliott Roosevelt, the President's son, commanding photographic reconnaissance organisations in North Africa was much impressed with the capabilities of RAF Mosquitoes used on long-range sorties in that theatre. In February 1943 USAAF indicated to the British an interest in acquiring Mosquitoes for long-range photographic reconnaissance as they considered the type better for this work than their F-5 Lightning which lacked range, ceiling, and could not be modified to take the desirable 36-inch focal length camera. The following June, General Arnold made a formal request for an allocation of PR Mosquitoes, and although current RAF needs could not be met, it was agreed that USAAF should receive 120, including 90 from Canadian production. US production was considered, but American aeronautical establishments found little merit in the type, notably its wooden airframe.

The first 8th Air Force request for Mosquitoes was made by General Eaker to the Air Ministry in September 1943. He outlined his desire to acquire 30 to establish a target weather reconnaissance unit at Mount Farm, to reach target areas ahead of bombing formations and radio weather conditions to the leaders. By the end of the month the British had agreed to supply 30 Mosquito FB VI fighter bombers, the only model readily available, and to cover replacement the offer was raised to 43. After inspection by US test pilots, it was decided that the required modifications would take too long to effect and that, even then, performance would not be on a par with a true PR model. USAAF then indicated it would prefer to wait for a true PR version and, on 1 December, Eaker was promised 20 PR XVIs with deliveries planned from February 1944. At this time, total USAAF allocation from British production for 1944 was set at 102.

In January 1944, 8th Air Force planned to use its Mosquitoes for night photographic reconnaissance and H2X radar-scope photography in addition to target weather scouting. On 18 February three units to conduct the three types of activity were proposed. Subsequently two Mosquito-equipped squadrons were formed, operating from Watton, Norfolk, under a provisional headquarters, 802nd Reconnaissance Group, until 9 August and then as the 25th Bomb Group.

By August 1944 the 802nd Group had a full complement of PR XVIs, but the specialised conversion caused delays. On 1 September, the Mosquito strength of 8th Air Force was 61 PR XVI plus two T III dual control trainers. By that date 16 PR XVIs had already been lost by enemy action or crashes since operations

with the type began. Plans for the supply of eight Mk XVI per month were approved for 1945, but by early March that year low attrition brought a request to suspend new deliveries until July unless special contingencies arose. Production of the PR XVI was due to be superseded by the PR XXXIV which USAAF officers inspected and found fully acceptable without modifications. At VE-Day 8th Air Force had 76 Mosquito XVIs of which 62 were airworthy at Watton and the rest under repair or overhaul. There were also three T IIIs (and two Oxfords) for conversion training. Time limit between major overhauls had been 320 hours, with the RAF carrying out repairs and maintenance outside the 25th Group's capacity at Nos 54 or 71 Maintenance Units. All Mosquitoes were returned to the RAF in June 1945.

The Mosquito had a high degree of reliability and was pleasant to fly, but take-off required particular caution due to the torque of the powerful engines causing a veer to the left. The most troublesome maintenance aspect was faulty parts or components accountable to the numerous small production units over which it was extremely difficult to maintain effective quality control. Repair of the wooden construction was in most instances not difficult and allowed many wrecked aircraft to be returned to flying status. In wheels-up landings the airframe frequently suffered little damage. In many heavy crash-landings crew survival chances were good as frequently the cockpit area remained intact.

Near the end of hostilities there was a recommendation that the British free-flow oxygen system in the Mosquito be replaced by the US demand type system. This was the outcome of intensive survey by US medical staff who found that the British system produced greater fatigue on long flights. Hostilities ceased before any action was taken on this recommendation. In all, 145 Mosquitoes are known to have served with the 8th Air Force.

Mosquito PR XVI details
Two Rolls-Royce Merlin 72 or 73 inlines rated at 1710 hp each

Span 54 ft 2 in (16.51 m)
Length 41 ft 6 in (12.65 m)
Empty weight 14,635 lb (6638 kg)
All-up weight 25,917 lb (11,756 kg)
Max speed 408 mph (657 km/h) at 30,000 ft (9140 m)
Cruising speed 245 mph (394 km/h)
Initial climb rate 2850 ft (870 m) per min
Ceiling 37,000 ft (11,280 m)
Max range with two 100 Imp gallon (455 ltr) external tanks 3340 miles (5375 km) (light weather version), 1500 miles (2414 km) without external tanks

LIGHT WEATHER MOSQUITO PR XVI

A total of 20 Mosquito PR XVIs were planned for weather reconnaissance flights from 15 April 1944, the first (MM338) being sent to Burtonwood to be modified for this duty. Here, it was fitted with SCR-287 liaison radio and *Gee* in the nose, SCR-522 VHF and SCR-297N command radio in the forward bomb-bay, American RC-36 interphone system, a gyro fluxgate compass, American turn-and-bank indicator and RC-24 radio altimeter. It was planned to fit *Monica* and *Boozer* radar tail-warning

devices but this did not transpire. While the prototype installation was made other Mosquito XVIs intended for weather scouting were delivered to Cheddington where flight training was carried out. These aircraft were later flown to Burtonwood for the same radio and instrument modifications, as facilities permitted. Throughout the period of operational use, May 1944 to May 1945, the light weather squadron, 653rd BS, used some 60 different Mosquito PR XVIs.

H2X MOSQUITO PR XVI

A need to obtain photographs of radar screen images of target locations deep in Germany led to the selection of the Mosquito as the most suitable aircraft for use in this project. Paramount in this choice was the Mosquito's high performance, affording a higher degree of survival in hostile airspace than any other available type. In January 1944 arrangements were made with de Havilland for two Mk XVI from the USAAF allocation to be

Below: **NS538, H2X-equipped Mosquito XVI at Watton. This aircraft was used extensively for radar scope photograph sorties by 654th BS during the summer of 1944. Bulbous nose was the distinctive feature. H2X scanner moved through 180 degrees.** (P. Frost)

Bottom: **Typical H2X instrument installation in a Mosquito XVI in the fuselage aft of the cockpit.** (via J. Archer)

specially modified to receive a nose radar installation. The prototype, MM308/G, was ready to be flown from Hatfield to the 8th Air Force radar centre at Alconbury on 11 February 1944, where H2X ground scanning radar APS-15 installation took 65, 72 and 200 man-hours for cable shop, machine shop and radar mechanics respectively. Only the pre-production H2X scanner could be fitted into the Mosquito's nose space as the production type was too large. As pre-production scanners were only fitted to the original 12 B-17s received at Alconbury, it was necessary to utilise these to make further H2X conversions in Mosquitoes. Radar scope and 16 mm camera were located with the navigator behind the scanner. Flight trials carried out in late March proved the equipment satisfactory. The scanner view was a full 180 degrees forward and the range at 10,000 ft some 25 miles (40 km). Flight instrumentation and radio installations were the same as for light weather conversions. The original camera set-up was later replaced by a modified K-24 attached to the scope.

The second H2X Mosquito, MM311, arriving at Alconbury in March, was duly fitted with radar. On 13 May the two Mosquitoes

were allotted to the 802nd Reconnaissance Group, although on the previous day the prototype crashed overshooting Alconbury. It was sent for repair, but later reduced to spares. As the 802nd Group's base at Watton had rough grass runways, unsuitable for the sensitive radar equipment, operations were conducted from Alconbury until 25 July when a new concrete runway was ready at Watton. Operational sorties beginning in May were restricted due to lack of aircraft, further H2X conversions not being available until June; from July three new aircraft a month were delivered. In early September, however, there was some concern following an incident when fuel fumes collecting in the rear fuselage of an H2X Mosquito caused an explosion; on the 24th operations were suspended. H2X scope-photo operations were to be left to H2X-equipped P-38 Lightnings, expected to arrive at this time. Of four H2X Mosquitoes with 654th BS, the operating unit, two were to have their radar removed, but the order was apparently rescinded. The P-38s did not materialise for some weeks and as by mid-October the fume problem had been satisfactorily resolved, H2X Mosquito missions were resumed. In the course of operations, flown mostly at night, three of the 11 H2X Mosquitoes were lost in action. The 12 H2X Mosquito conversions used by 654th BS and 802nd/25th Groups were: MM308/G (cr 12/5/44) MM311 (MIA 8/8/44), MM364, NS538, NS583 (MIA 8/2/45), NS584, NS625 (MIA 20/8/44), NS638, NS676, NS677 (MIA 2/11/44), NS686 and NS709.

NIGHT PHOTOGRAPHIC MOSQUITO PR XVI

Planned modifications for Mosquito Mk XVIs, as listed in March 1944, included flight instrumentation and radio equipment as for the weather reconnaissance version, plus camera and flash-bomb facilities. This involved removal of the 58 gallon tank from the forward bomb-bay and the installation of seven shackles to carry M-46 flashlight bombs. A K-19B night camera was to be installed in the bay forward of the flashbombs, to be adjustable to provide a 5 degree tilt forward and 10 degree tilt aft. By May the long-range specification had been changed to include two K-19Bs in the forward bomb-bay and one in the rear fuselage, to be known as Model B. A short-range version was also proposed which would have the same camera arrangement but would have the 63 gallon rear bomb-bay tank removed to allow fittings to carry 14 flashbombs. The plan called for four short-range and eight long-range models. Two 100 gallon external wing tanks were required to extend range.

After basic modifications at Burtonwood the aircraft were to receive camera and bomb-bay installations at Langford Lodge. The prototype H2X and weather scouting Mosquitoes had priority but work on the prototype night photographic aircraft was protracted and although the operating squadron at Watton had received its original complement of 12 aircraft by mid-July, ten of these were still at Watton waiting to go to Langford Lodge. The first fully converted aircraft, NS544, was not received at Watton until the end of July and for more than a month was the only one of its type available for operations. Two were received in September and another six before the end of the year. The 11 Night PR XVIs that actually saw service with 654th BS were: NS551, NS552, NS553, NS554, NS556, NS557 (cr 5/8/44), NS559, NS568 (cr 6/11/44), NS581, NS582 (cr 28/11/44) and NS583 (MIA 8/2/45).

CHAFF MOSQUITO PR XVI

On 6 October 1944, 8th Air Force decided to combine in a single Mosquito the functions of weather scouting and *Chaff* dispensing for heavy bombers. At the request of 3rd Division an experimental installation was made in the bomb-bay of a light weather aircraft by removing the lower rear fuel tanks and fitting two 8 ft (2.44 m) wooden magazines to dispense *Chaff* through metal chutes in the bomb-bay doors. Between 1400 and 1800 bundles of *Chaff* type CHA-28 could be carried and discharged through automatic stripper heads at 200 units per minute, the total load being something under 600 lb (272 kg). On 28 October 12 653rd BS Mosquitoes were sent to Abbots Ripton Depot (Alconbury) for modification but as many fittings had to be pre-fabricated and the A-1 *Chaff* dispensing heads were in short supply, the first aircraft was not delivered until December. A further four aircraft were allocated to the project, but by mid-February only five *Chaff* converted aircraft were on hand and only 12 had been delivered by the end of hostilities. Although assigned to 25th Group these aircraft were available as required to each Air Division Headquarters.

NS519 was used by Colonel 'Bud' Peaslee to pioneer Chaff dispensing with the Mosquito. Difficulty in obtaining dispenser parts delayed conversion of the 12 Mosquitoes assigned for this task.

RED STOCKING MOSQUITO PR XVI

In September 1944 there was a requirement for high-performance aircraft to receive signals transmitted by agents on the ground in enemy held territory. The Mosquito was the obvious choice and initially two were made available on call for the OSS. Five different aircraft were used on these sorties flown by 654th BS. They carried an operative in the converted bomb-bay with S-phone and recording apparatus which would pick up UHF transmissions from the ground set. A former H2X aircraft, NS676, and a night photographic aircraft, NS559, were used for

Black-painted special operations Mosquito XVI at Denain/Prouvy, France in the spring of 1945. (R. Hiatt)

these duties together with NS707, NS725 and NS740. The latter three were transferred to 492nd Group on 18 March 1945 when 492nd Group commenced using its own experienced crews for this duty. Following complaints as to the condition of the inherited aircraft, 492nd Group received on 1 April two new Mk XVIs, RG157 and TA614.

F-8 MOSQUITO

In 1943 the USAAF had ordered 90 Mosquitoes from Canadian production. From July 1944 16 of these, with the USAAF designation F-8, arrived in the UK and were sent to Watton. The F-8, equivalent to the Mosquito B IV bomber, did not match up to the performance of the PR XVI of which the 25th Group currently had sufficient. In particular, the F-8's performance was not satisfactory at 25,000 ft and above. It also required extensive instrument and radio changes to meet the Group's requirements, added to which the standard of construction was generally considered inferior to the Mk XVI. Nonetheless, there was some pressure for the Group to operate US-funded aircraft and the F-8's use as a *Chaff* dispensing aircraft was proposed but rejected because of its inferior high altitude performance. Stored at Watton for a few

weeks, ten were transferred to the RAF and the remainder returned to the USA. The 16 F-8s known to have reached the UK were: 43-34934, 34936, 34938, 34940, 34942, 34950, 34951, 34952, 34953, 34954, 34955, 34956, 34958, 34959, 34962 and 34963.

Specification: Two Packard Merlin 31 inlines rated 1460 hp each
Span 54 ft 2 in (16.51 m)
Length 40 ft 9½ in (12.43 m)
Weight empty 13,400 lb (6078 kg)
Max speed 380 mph (612 km/h) at 20,000 ft (6100 m)
Cruising speed 265 mph (426 km/h)
Ceiling 30,000 ft (9140 m)

MOSQUITO T III

For pilot conversion 8th Air Force acquired dual control trainer Mosquitoes on loan from the RAF which retained their British roundels. It was usual for 802nd/25th Group to have two available at any one time. A third T III was on hand in 492nd Group at

May 1945. A shortage of Mk IIIs at the end of 1944 led 25th Group to request Oxfords for use in transition training. Mosquito T IIIs known to have been used by 8th Air Force were LR516, LR530, LR534, LR553 and LR584.

Vickers Supermarine Spitfire

In a reverse Lease-Lend arrangement 350 Spitfire fighters were allocated to USAAF in the United Kingdom during 1942, some 150 of these going to 8th Air Force units. These Spitfire Mk Vs were considered a stop-gap by 8th Air Force until US types, more suited to their mode of operations, arrived from America.

After March 1943, only non-operational units continued to use this model Spitfire in the UK. A requirement for high-performance long-range photographic reconnaissance aircraft led 8th Air Force to obtain sufficient Spitfire Mk XIs to equip a squadron late in 1943 and the type was employed operationally until mid-March 1945, at which time all remaining Spitfires were returned to the RAF.

SPITFIRE V

On 2 May 1942, Maj Gen J. E. Chaney, Commander USAAF in the British Isles, wrote to Air Chief Marshal Portal, requesting Spitfires to equip the 52nd Fighter Group whose personnel were shortly to arrive in the UK. It transpired that the reason given for this approach was an acute shortage of fighter aircraft in the USA. At this time there was also concern at USAAF Hq over the inferior performance of both the Bell P-39 and Curtiss P-40 compared to their Luftwaffe adversaries, and it seemed sensible to equip the first units with a proven fighter. A preliminary agreement to supply 8th Air Force with 80 Spitfire Vs per month was made on 6 May. However, in many respects the performance of the Spitfire V did not match that of the latest Me 109 and FW 190 models.

Both 31st and 52nd Fighter Groups received Spitfire Vs when they arrived in the UK, becoming operational during July–October 1942. Additionally, at the end of September 1942, the three RAF 'Eagle Squadrons' were transferred to VIII FC at Debden to become 4th Fighter Group, retaining their Spitfire complement. This brought a peak of Spitfire strength in 8th Air Force service with 55 in the 4th Group, 42 in 31st Group and 37 with 52nd Group. In mid-October the 31st and 52nd Groups were switched to the North African invasion force, picking up new Spitfires shipped to Gibraltar, their discarded aircraft going to the 67th Observation Group at Membury, the Atcham training base and a few to the newly-formed 350th Fighter Group at Duxford. At the end of January 1943 the Spitfire V inventory stood at 51 in 4th Group, two with 350th Group, 29 with 67th Group, 40 at Atcham and seven with VIII FC Hq at Bovingdon.

Spitfire VB EN 759 operated by 307th FS, 31st FG at Westhampnett, August 1942. Spitfires were passed to other 8th AF units when the 31st Group personnel sailed for North America late in October.

The 4th Group began converting to P-47s in January 1943, the last of their Spitfires being withdrawn in April. During the spring of 1943 three squadrons of 67th Group were built up to a unit establishment of 18 Spitfire Vs each and were still so equipped when transferred to the 9th Air Force the following October. Also, during that spring, the Spitfire complement at Atcham were reduced to three as training requirements for the type diminished. When the 7th Photographic Group acquired Spitfire XIs in November 1943, two Mk Vs were used for conversion training at Mount Farm. A few Spitfire Vs were used by 496th Fighter Training Group at Goxhill during early 1944, and odd examples were to be found elsewhere but by 1945 Mount Farm was believed to have the sole remaining Mk V in 8th Air Force service – EN904, finally returned to the RAF on 23 March that year.

Spitfire Vs used by 8th Air Force were mostly the VB variant, with 2 × 20 mm cannon and 4 × .303 machine guns. However, records indicate that four Mk VA with 8 × .303 machine guns were used by 67th Group squadrons for training during the spring of 1943. A few clipped wing low-level versions of the VB, designated LF VBs, were also in 8th Air Force service. Most Spitfire Vs allocated to the 8th Air Force were sent from store or repair units rather than from production.

Spitfire VB details
One Merlin 45 inline rated at 1470 hp

Span 36 ft 10 in (11.23 m) (LF version, 32 ft 2 in (9.80 m))
Length 29 ft 11 in (9.12 m)
Empty weight 5065 lb (2297 kg)
Max speed 369 mph (594 km/h) at 19,500 ft (5940 m)
Norm cruising speed 270 mph (435 km/h) at 5000 ft (1520 m)
Initial climb 4750 ft (1450 m) per min
Ceiling 36 200 ft (11,030 m)
General range 395 miles (636 km)
Fuel capacity 102 US gallons (386 ltr)

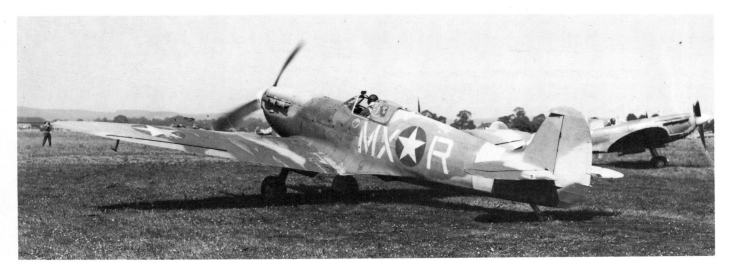

SPITFIRE IX

The Spitfire IX was introduced into service in RAF Fighter Command in 1942 and No 133 (Eagle) Squadron was equipped with this mark late that summer. Three days before this unit was transferred to the USAAF on 29 September, 11 of its aircraft were lost, and one crash-landed in England, mainly as the result of fuel exhaustion after operating over the Brest peninsula. When No 133 Squadron RAF became 336th Fighter Squadron USAAF

it received Mk Vs to make up the recent losses. Three Mk IXs, however, were retained by 4th Group until the end of the year. There was no allocation of Mk IXs to 8th Air Force, but pilots of 67th Group flew them in RAF squadrons on combat experience flights, a pilot of the Group's 12th Recon Squadron, Capt John R. Walker, being lost in EN564 on 14 July 1943.

Basically, the Mk IX was a refined Mk V airframe with the Merlin 61 engine and four-blade propeller.

Spitfire IX details
One Merlin 61 inline rated at 1565 hp

Span 36 ft 10 in (11.23 m)
Length 31 ft (9.45 m)
Empty weight 5634 lb (2556 kg)

Loaded weight 7900 lb (3583 kg)
Max speed 408 mph (657 km/h) at 25,000 ft (7620 m)
Norm cruising speed 325 mph (523 km/h) at 20,000 ft (6100 m)
Initial climb rate 4100 ft (1250 m) per min
Ceiling 43,000 ft (13,100 m)
Norm range 235 miles (378 km)

SPITFIRE XI

On 14 December 1943 General Eaker informed the RAF that the current model P-38 used for photographic reconnaissance by 7th Group was not to the standard required. As improved models would not be available for a few months, he enquired if it would be possible to obtain the use of 12 Spitfire Xs to tide them over. They were in short supply, as only one production line handled the Mk XI. To meet Eaker's request the RAF took three aircraft awaiting delivery to its own units and another nine from production. Some delay was anticipated as the aircraft had to go through a modification programme at Benson. First deliveries reached Mount Farm in mid-November and operations began almost immediately. Initially the Spitfires were distributed in three squadrons but on 7 January 1944 they were all concentrated in the 14th Photographic Squadron.

The Spitfires were used almost exclusively for the deepest penetrations of enemy airspace or to areas where the risk of interception was greatest. Pilots with F-5 experience found the Spitfire cockpit cramped and noisy by comparison, plus a degree of vibration not so evident with the smoother-running Allisons. Performance was another matter for the Spitfire provided speed, range and altitude that could not be achieved with the Lightning models on hand in the winter of 1943–44. Few technical problems arose with the Spitfire XI in 7th Group service, although there was some trouble with the fuel system vapour lock during July/August 1944 caused by hot weather at ground level. The Group's Spitfires had only a 5 per cent

mechanical failure rate over their operational period. It was estimated that the Spitfire took but one third of the maintenance time required for the F-5 and had a 70 per cent availabilitiy, which 7th Group stated would have been even higher if the supply of spare parts had been simplified. There was standard British camera installation of a split 36-inch (914 mm) F-52 camera, positioned in the fuselage aft of the wing, although MB946 operated with a special US camera installation for a period. A prototype installation of APS-13 tail warning radar was made on PA892 in February 1945.

In March 1945 a USAAF policy decision that operational units should, where possible, be equipped with American-built aircraft was acted upon and 7th Group was ordered to return its Spitfires to the RAF and re-equip 14th PS with F-5s and F-6s. Shortly before the move from Mount Farm to Chalgrove the 12 Spitfires were turned over to the RAF, the last on 3 April. A total of 21 Spitfire XIs were used by 7th Group between November 1943 and April 1945. Seven went missing in action and two were wrecked in accidents. Serial numbers were: MB945 (MIA 1/3/44),MB946, MB948, MB950, MB952 (MIA 8/9/44), MB955 (MIA 19/9/44), MB956, PA841, PA842, PA851 (MIA 23/12/43), PA892, PA914, PA944, PL767 (Cr 28/6/44), PL782 (MIA 5/9/44), PL790 (MIA 5/6/44), PL866 (MIA 14/2/45), PL959, PL962 (Cr 20/1/45), PL972 and PM153.

Spitfire XI details
One Merlin 63 or 70 inline rated at 1640 hp

Span 36 ft 10 in (11.23 m)
Length 31 ft (9.45 m) or 31 ft 4½ in (9.56 m)
Max speed 422 mph (680 km/h) at 27,500 ft (8380 m)
Norm cruise speed 340 mph (547 km/h) at 20,000 ft (6100 m)
Initial climb rate 4350 ft (1325 m) per min
Ceiling 44,000 ft (13,410 m)
Range 1360 miles (2190 km)
Total fuel capacity 218 Imp gallons (991 ltr)

Operational with 14th PS from December 1943, MB955, nicknamed *Lease Fleece*, did not return from a sortie over Germany on 19 September 1944. Pilot was 2/Lt Paul Balogh. The Spitfire IX proved a reliable photographic aircraft. Most troublesome problem was tyre blow-outs, only solved by fitting new design split wheels. (R. Besecker)

Other American Combat and Support Aircraft

Bomber Types

NORTH AMERICAN B-25 MITCHELL

Although 8th Air Force was originally scheduled to have a whole bombardment wing equipped with B-25s it transpired that only a single aircraft was actually assigned.

From September to November 1942 some 50 B-25Cs of the 310th Group used 8th Air Force airfields at Hardwick and Bungay, being maintained by Honington depot. Assigned to 12th Air Force these bombers departed for North Africa in November although stragglers remained at 8th Air Force bases until February. That spring the Eighth's own 3rd Wing was expecting at least three B-25 groups, but the 345th scheduled to arrive in April were sent instead to the south Pacific and the rest of the Mitchell complement never materialised.

While 3rd Wing still expected Mitchells a single B-25C was

Miss Nashville, 8th AF's lone B-25, in her final 'dress' – bare metal. (7PG Association)

acquired via North Africa for evaluation and tractical planning. This aircraft, 42-53357, arrived at Honington in March, but with no B-25 units in view, the aircraft was passed to other depots and used for communications work. However, in September 1943 the 7th Photo Group by devious means 'acquired' 42-53357 from Burtonwood. Thereafter the Mitchell, nicknamed *Miss Nashville* resided at Mount Farm as general 'hack'. In late July 1944 there was an urgent requirement for night photography of V-weapon sites and until B-26s could be equipped for the task the B-25 was loaned to the 25th Group for these missions. *Miss Nashville* did 13 combat sorties between 4 and 18 August. Originally finished in olive drab and neutral grey, then painted overall pathfinder blue, the B-25 received a black finish for its night assignment. Following this, all paint was removed and the aircraft in bare metal was used for courier work. On 26 October 1944, while on such work over France, the aircraft strayed over the front lines, was damaged by anti-aircraft fire and crashed near Chalons-sur-Saône.

B-25C details

Two Wright R-2600-13 radials rated at 1700 hp each

Span 67 ft 7 in (20.60 m)
Length 52 ft 11 in (16.13 m)
Empty weight 20,300 lb (9208 kg)
Max loaded weight 34,000 lb (15,422 kg)
Max speed 284 mph (457 km/h) at 15,000 ft (4570 m)
Cruise speed 170–230 mph (273–370 km/h)
Range 1500 miles (2414 km)
Tact radius 350 miles (563 km)
Fuel consumption 120 US gallons (454 ltr) per hour at cruise speeds

BOEING B-29 SUPERFORTRESS

Had the war in Europe continued into the summer and autumn of 1945, it was planned that nine B-29 groups would be based in the UK. This was to be achieved by converting groups in the 2nd Division from the B-24. At the close of 1944 it was expected that this would take place between June and September, although lengthening of runways at suitable bases had yet to be put in hand. Boscombe Down was proposed as the location of a conversion and training establishment. The plan was apparently abandoned in February 1945.

In March 1944, when B-29s were being sent to India, 41-36963 was diverted to the UK where it remained until returning to the USA on 10 May. The purpose of this visit was for evaluation by 8th Air Force tactical and technical staff, and to mislead German intelligence into believing that deployment of the B-29 in Britain was imminent. The aircraft visited the operational stations at Glatton and Knettishall during its stay in the UK.

B-29 41-36963 at Glatton on 11 March 1944. (via J. Wilson)

DOUGLAS DB-7B BOSTON

The first flying unit of 8th Air Force, the 15th Bomb Squadron, flew its early combat sorties using Boston III light bombers of No 226 Squadron, RAF. On 29 June 1942 Capt Charles Kegelman and crew flew an operational sortie in AL743 coded MQ:L. On both 4 and 12 July six crews in 226 Squadron Bostons took part in operations over occupied territories. As suitable USAAF aircraft were unlikely to be available for some time, the squadron received 23 Boston IIIs from the British: AL372, 381, 397, 409, 429, 436, 441, 445, 451, 452, 455, 486, 490–9 and 672. They were repainted USAAF style with olive drab upper and neutral grey lower surfaces, with US national insignia. Operations were conducted in September using 17 of these Bostons. In November 1942 the Squadron moved to North Africa, leaving ten Bostons with the 8th Air Force: AL381, 397, 409, 441, 451, 452, 490, 491, 496 and 672. Nine of these aircraft were used for target-towing work by VIII BC groups up to September 1943, and

then for communications by Wing headquarters. Three, AL672, 452 and 381, survived until after VE-Day, having been operated by several units. In 8th Air Force service the Boston was usually referred to by the maker's designation DB-7B. For target-towing and communications use all war equipment was taken out and in a few cases, during 1944, camouflage paint was removed.

DB-7B details
Two Wright R-2600-A5B0 radials rated at 1500 hp each

Span 61 ft 4 in (18.69 m)
Length 47 ft 3 in (14.40 m)
Empty weight 15,051 lb (6827 kg)
Max loaded weight 21,580 lb (9788 kg)
Max speed 321 mph (517 km/h) at 12,800 ft (4000 m)
Tact cruise speed 200–260 mph (322–418 km/h)
Climb 5 min to 10,000 ft (3050 m)
Range 525 miles (840 km)
Tact radius 200 miles (322 km)
Fuel consumption 120 US gallons (454 ltr) per hour at 216 mph (348 km/h)
Max bomb load 2400 lb (1088 kg)
Armament 5 × .303-in (7.7 mm) mg

Boston III AL381 when assigned to the 67th Observation Group at Membury in March 1943.

DOUGLAS DB-7 & 7A HAVOC

Earlier models of the DB-7 supplied to the British were adapted for night fighting as their Havoc I and II. Rated as obsolete in this role by 1943, the RAF agreed to supply a number to 8th Air Force for use by the 67th Observation Group then awaiting A-20Bs. Commencing in February, 13 Havoc I and six Havoc II were transferred and in May were concentrated in the 153rd Observation Squadron at Keevil. Most were withdrawn after the arrival of A-20Bs and given to VIII ASC B-26 groups for target-towing duties. Later in the year some Havocs were sent to Northern Ireland and used by 3 CCRC and, later still, 4th Gunnery and Tow Target Flight which still had five on strength in May 1944. Condition of the tow-target Havocs was poor and they were out of commission 50 per cent of the time. Surviving Havocs were gradually returned to the RAF during 1944. At least three of the aircraft sported cut-off noses, having at one time been fitted with Turbinlite searchlights for night fighting. Performance and dimensions were similar to the DB-7B.

Although correctly a Boston I, in common with all other DB-7 and DB-7A aircraft obtained from the RAF for target towing, AX922 was known as a Havoc in 8th AF service. Nicknamed 'Lil Jeanne, this aircraft was photographed while serving with 387th BG at Chipping Ongar. Later it was transferred to 3 CCRC at Toome. (Bob Allen)

DOUGLAS A-20B HAVOC

Scheduled for 8th Air Force in early plans, the three A-20 bomb groups eventually sent for operations from England did not arrive until 1944 and then became part of the 9th Air Force. In September 1942 the 47th Group had left the US with 58 A-20Bs flying the North Atlantic ferry route. These aircraft were first stationed at Bury St Edmunds and then Horham, before departing for North Africa with the 12th Air Force during November and December. While in England the 47th Group A-20Bs were sustained by the Honington depot. The 67th Observation Group, which arrived at Membury in the autumn of 1942, was scheduled to receive 18 A-20Bs to equip one squadron but these were not available until April. Concentrated in the 153rd Observation Squadron at Keevil, a lack of spare parts and special servicing tools was the cause of only a few aircraft being serviceable at any one time. Fitted out with different camera arrangements, the A-20s were used for a number of photographic sorties over northern France in August and early September. However, in that month the discovery that the 153rd was using the wrong Table of Organisation led to the A-20 unit being redesignated the 2911th Bomb Squadron (P) on 1 October, and subsequently disbanded. A-20B were then converted for target towing, most going to Composite Command bases. In February 1944 the 2nd Gunnery and Tow Target Flight at Goxhill acquired six A-20Bs for this purpose: 41-3367, 41-3370 (D), 41-3379 (B), 41-3383 (F),

41-3388 and 41-3439 (C). When the unit was assigned to 3rd Division and moved to Leiston in late 1944, two of the remaining three A-20Bs were given – one each – to the two other tow-target flights in England. These aircraft survived to the end of hostilities.

A-20B details

Two Wright R-2600-3 radials rated at 1600 hp each

Span 61 ft 4 in (18.69 m)
Length 48 ft (14.63 m)
Empty weight 14,830 lb (6727 kg)
Max loaded weight 23,800 lb (10,796 kg)
Max speed 350 mph (563 km/h) at 12,000 ft (3660 m)
Tact cruise speed 200–260 mph (322–418 km/h)
Climb 5 min to 10,000 ft (3050 m)
Range 825 miles (1327 km)
Tact radius 200 miles (322 km)
Fuel consumption 125 US gallons (473 ltr) per hour at 216 mph (348 km/h)
Armament 3 × .50-in mg

DOUGLAS A-20G & J HAVOC

Used operationally by 9th Air Force. At least one example of each model was acquired 8th Air Force. A-20G 43-9944 served with 8th AF Hq Flight in the summer of 1944 and was later passed to 361FG as a tow-target aircraft. A-20J 43-22021 was assigned to 491BG for similar purposes near the end of hostilities.

DOUGLAS A-26 INVADER

Commencing summer 1944, the A-26 was sent to the ETO as a replacement for the A-20 and B-26 in 9th Bomber Command. Late that year the OSS had a requirement for a fast multi-place aircraft for use in dropping agents over Germany and occupied territory. Mosquitoes were employed for many missions, but they did not have sufficient space to carry more than one agent. Two A-26Cs were obtained by 8th Air Force for use when the Mosquito was not suitable. They operated with two navigators to pinpoint the course from the nose and were painted black overall.

Flown by a 25th Group crew, A-26C 43-22500 flew a first sortie over northern Holland on the night of 3 January 1945, followed by another on the 7th to northern Germany when hydraulic failure on return caused it to crash-land at Watton. Another sortie from Watton was made early on 2 March by 43-22524 to deliver two agents close to Berlin. Thereafter, A-26 operations were carried out from Harrington under 492nd Group, five aircraft being available. On the night of 20 March, 43-22524 failed to return. The last A-26C operation by 492nd Group took place on 9/10 May. The other A-26Cs were 43-22513, 43-22610 (cr Rackheath 3/4/45) and 43-22626.

A-26C details

Two Pratt & Whitney R-2800-79 radials rated at 2000 hp each

Span 70 ft (21.34 m)
Length 51 ft 3 in (15.62 m)
Empty weight 22,850 lb (10,365 kg)
Max loaded weight 35,000 lb (15,876 kg)
Max speed 373 mph (600 km/h) at 10,000 ft (3050 m)
Tact cruise speed 200–280 mph (322–450 km/h)
Climb 8 min to 10,000 ft (3050 m)
Range 1800 miles (2896 km)
Tact radius 400 miles (644 km) (800 miles/1287 km with
  bomb-bay fuel tanks)
Armament 4 × .50 mg

Gloss black-painted A-26C used for 'agent dropping' operations from Watton and later Harrington.   (via D. Mayor)

VULTEE A-35 VENGEANCE

Originally accepted by the British as a dive-bomber, many Vengeances were eventually converted for target-towing. From April 1944 a number of Vengeance Mk IV Series Is were made available to the 8th Air Force and assigned to tow-target flights and CCRC stations. All armament was removed and a light cable winch fitted in the rear fuselage for sleeve towing. Some of these aircraft continued to be flown with British national markings and serial numbers, most notably by the 3rd G&TT Flight at East Wretham. Others were repainted in USAAF colours with that service's serial number applied to the fin. A few aircraft exhibited both US and British serials. By late June 1944 there were seven A-35Bs at Cluntoe, seven at Greencastle, ten at Sutton Bridge and six at East Wretham. When the CCRCs were dissolved in the autumn the A-35Bs were transferred to combat groups, most fighter and several bomber groups having one on charge at some time during 1945. A-35Bs did not show a high state of serviceability and were generally considered troublesome to maintain. Also designated as RA-35B (R for Restricted).

Right: **Vultee A-35B 41-31367 operated by 1st G & TT Flt at Halesworth. Cable attachment can be seen directly below fuselage national insignia.**

A-35B details

One Wright R-2600-13 radial rated at 1700 hp

Span 48 ft (14.63 m)
Length 39 ft 9 in (12.12 m)
Empty weight 10,300 lb (4672 kg)
Max loaded weight 17,100 lb (7756 kg)
Max speed 279 mph (450 km/h) at 13,500 ft (4110 m)
Norm cruise speed 170–220 mph (273–354 km/h)
Climb 11 min 18 sec to 15,000 ft (4570 m)
Range 550 miles (885 km)
Crew 2 (pilot and winch operator)

Amphibian Aircraft

CONSOLIDATED OA-10 CATALINA

Although the USAAF acquired US Navy PBY type amphibians for rescue work and had them operating in the Mediterranean by the summer of 1943, it was only in the closing weeks of the war that the type was used from the UK. RAF amphibians gave rescue service to 8th Air Force from the outset of its operations but by the summer of 1944 the Americans wished to make their own contribution to the work. On 15 August, General Spaatz cabled a request for OA-10s (amphibian version of the Catalina known as Canso) for the 8th's air/sea rescue squadron. Although Washington gave approval, considerable delay was experienced before six of these aircraft arrived in England via the south Atlantic ferry route. The first four landed at Bovingdon on 17 January 1945 and were joined a few days later by the other two. These were Canadian built Vickers OA-10As; 44-33915, 44-33916, 44-33917, 44-33920, 44-33922 and 44-33923. In late

January, after evaluation by Technical Services, they were transferred to the Halesworth ASR base where it was planned that the recommended theatre modifications would be carried out by mobile units. As a high degree of specialised engineering was entailed the aircraft were sent to Neaton in mid-February. This work involved removal of their Canadian radio equipment for replacement by SCR-274N (Command radio) and SCR-287 (Liaison), installation of SCR-269 Radio Compass and AN/AIC-2 interphone equipment in place of the original, removal of SCR-521 radar and installation of AN/APS-3 sea search radar and SCR-729 *Rebecca*. In addition, the driftmeter and all armour plate had to be removed; the sloping floor at the waist windows had to be replaced with a flat floor; two left hand glass panels above the navigator's position had to be replaced with metal to prevent glare. A Stewart-Warner heater was fixed in the cabin to warm rescued men; a streamlined prow was fitted over the bombardier's window in the nose, and the sea anchor was modified and locks fabricated for the controls for use when

at rest on water. As a result of these time consuming modifications, operational ASR flights were unable to start until the end of March.

Nine further OA-10As were received in March and April, the 5th Emergency Rescue Squadron complement being increased to nine with the rest held in reserve. Eleven OA-10s were returned to the US at the end of May and the remaining two a month later. Two OA-10s, 44-33917 and 44-33915, had been lost – the former to enemy action. Serials of aircraft not already mentioned were: 44-33987, 44-33991, 44-33995, 44-34003, 44-34005, 44-34013, 44-34017, 44-34028, 44-34067.

OA-10A details
Two Pratt & Whitney R-1830-92 radials rated at 1200 hp each

Span 104 ft (31.70 m)
Length 63 ft 10 in (19.46 m)
Empty weight 21,910 lb (9938 kg)
Max loaded weight 33,975 lb (15,411 kg)
Max speed 179 mph (288 km/h) at 7000 ft (2130 m)
Cruise speed 100 to 125 mph (161–200 km/h)
Climb 20 min to 10,000 ft (3050 m)
Range 2500 miles (4023 km)
Armament Nil but received with 4 × .30-in mg
Crew 6 (pilot, co-pilot, navigator, engineer, two radio operators)

OA-10A *Sophisticat* of 5th ERS undergoing maintenance at Halesworth, April 1945.

Other Fighter Types

BELL P-39 AIRACOBRA
Unorthodox, in that the engine was positioned aft of the cockpit and the propeller driven by an extended shaft, the P-39 was considered only suitable for a ground attack role by the time the first USAAF units arrived in the UK. Both 31st and 52nd Groups had been trained on the type but because of its poor performance in comparison with contemporary enemy fighters, these groups received Spitfires. In October 1942 the first shipment of P-39s arrived in the UK and in the following month 250 were on hand. These were P-39L models plus P-400Es, USAAF designation for the version of the Airacobra rejected by the RAF. Later P-39Ms were similar to the L except for a different propeller gear ratio. The P-400E was equivalent to the earlier P-39D, having a 20 mm cannon firing through the propeller boss instead of the 37 mm type in other Airacobras.

The 81st Group arriving in October for 12th Air Force received Airacobras at Goxhill and, later, Atcham. A new group, the 350th, was formed by 8th Air Force at Duxford in October to absorb a large reserve of P-39 pilots that had reached the UK. Its squadrons received mostly P-400s, as did two of the 68th Observation Group at Wattisham. Both 350th and 68th Groups

were to be part of the 12th Air Force. Movement of Airacobras to North Africa involved 36 of 68th Group, 78 of 81st Group and 80 of 350th Group and was spread over several weeks, the last aircraft not leaving England until March 1943. For a few weeks five were retained at the Atcham training base until the last pilots destined for North Africa had passed through. After April there were only three USAAF P-39s in the UK and from September only a solitary example remained. This was P-39M, 42–4746, retained for experimental work and finally salvaged by BAD 2 in December 1944.

P-39M details
One Allison V-1710-83 inline rated at 1200 hp

Span 34 ft (10.36 m)
Length 30 ft 2 in (9.19 m)
Empty weight 5610 lb (2545 kg)
Max loaded weight 8400 lb (3810 kg)
Max speed 386 mph (621 km/h) at 8500 ft (2590 m)
Climb 4 min 24 sec to 15,000 ft (4570 m)
Range 700 miles (1126 km)
Tact radius 200 miles (322 km)
Armament 1 × 37 mm cannon and 4 × .50-in mg

CURTISS P-40 WARHAWK

No USAAF units sent to the UK were equipped with P-40s. Fifteen arrived in March 1943 for transfer elsewhere, but no other batches were received. Two P-40Es were acquired by VIII BC and used for fast liaison by the Hq Flight. One, 41–36028, crashed near Berkhamsted on 23 Sep 1942 killing the pilot. The other, 41–35934, remained with VII BC during 1943.

NORTHROP P-61 BLACK WIDOW

In the summer of 1944 a conversion of the P-61 was considered for use in night radar scope reconnaissance. Hitherto the P-61 had been employed exclusively as a night fighter in 9th Air Force squadrons. On 26 July 1944 approval was given for four P-61s to be made available to 8th Reconnaissance Wing. One, 42–5556, was sent to Langford Lodge to have the turret removed while the others were retained at BADA, where one had extra tanks installed. Subsequently all four P-61s were transferred to Mount Farm and then to Watton. The project was cancelled after evaluation trials revealed that the type was not as acceptable as the Mosquito or the expected H2X version of the P-38.

Transport and Liaison Aircraft

DOUGLAS C-47 SKYTRAIN AND C-53 SKYTROOPER

Versions of the DC-3 commercial airliner were produced as C-47 general military transports and C-53 troop transports and supplied to the RAF as their Dakota. On 7 July 1942 the C-47s of 60th Troop Carrier Group started to arrive at Chelveston and a month later the Group moved its full complement of 58 aircraft to Aldermaston. A second C-47 troop carrier group, the 64th, arrived at Membury in August and a third, the 62nd, at Keevil late in October when the total of USAAF Douglas transports present in the UK stood at 157. The three troop carrier groups were re-assigned from the 8th to the 12th Air Force in September, when only the ground echelon of 62nd Group was present, the peak inventory for C-47s in 8th Air Force being at the time of transfer 119. The C-47 force was used to carry British and American paratroopers from airfields in south-west England to North Africa during the TORCH operation in early November. At the end of that month only a solitary DC-3 type remained in USAAF service in the UK. During the following month the 315th Troop Carrier Group arrived at Aldermaston with 24 aircraft, half C-47s and half C-53s.

The C-53 was built at the Douglas Santa Monica, California, factory and did not have the large cargo doors of the C-47. The C-53 saw only limited production (under 400), whereas over 9000 C-47s were built by two plants. The aircraft complement of 315th Group was small because two squadrons had been re-assigned to other war theatres prior to leaving the US. On joining 8th Air Force, the aircraft were impressed as transports for VIII AFSC; about half were regularly employed in these duties. In May 1943 16 aircraft were sent on detachment to North Africa, the remaining eight and VIII AFSC's own C-53 continuing to shoulder 8th Air Force transport requirements. The 434th, first of several new C-47 troop carrier groups, arrived in the UK early in October but was soon transferred to 9th Air Force, together with 315th Group. Thereafter the only 8th Air Force C-47s and C-53s were those which 27th Transport Group of VIII AFSC managed to obtain, but these too were transferred when USAAF was formed early in 1944. A few C-47s were later obtained by VIII AFSC for inter-depot flights. VIII FC Hq also had six when it moved to France – four C-47A and two C-47B. During October 1944 the 325th Recon Wing received one C-47 and five C-53s, chiefly for transport flights to its units on the Continent, the C-53s 42–6484 and 42–15546 being retained until March 1945.

To enable clandestine landings to be made in occupied France during darkness the *Carpetbagger* 801st Group procured four C-47s in July 1944. These made 35 sorties carrying mostly weapons and ammunition to resistance forces. Assigned 856th Bomb Sqdn, the aircraft were: 42-92840 (Q), 42-93728 (Z), 43-15177 (V) (cr France 9/3/45) and 43-47981 (M).

C-47-DL details
Two Pratt & Whitney R-1830-92 radials rated at 1200 hp each

Span 95 ft (28.96 m)
Length 63 ft 9 in (19.43 m)
Empty weight 16,970 lb (7698 kg)
Max loaded weight 29,300 lb (13,290 kg)
Max speed 220 mph (364 km/h) at 7500 ft (2290 m)
Cruise speed 150–185 mph (240–298 km/h)
Range 1500 miles (2414 km)
Crew 3 or 4
Norm load limits 7000 lb (3175 kg) cargo or 24 passengers

LOCKHEED HUDSON V (CA-29)

In the summer of 1943 25 Hudsons were made available by the British for the use of VIII AFSC, who were at that time desperately short of air transports for light cargo deliveries. These aircraft were carried on 8th Air Force records as CA-29s. As used by VIII AFSC they were stripped of all war equipment including their turret and some were repainted in USAAF colours. All were transferred by BADA early in 1944. As more suitable transports became available the CA-29s were gradually returned to the RAF, the first in May 1944 and the last, AM653, in February 1945.

CA-29 details
Two Pratt & Whitney R-1839-S3C4-G radials rated at 1200 hp each

Span 65 ft 6 in (19.96 m)
Length 44 ft 4 in (13.51 m)
Empty weight approx 11,600 lb (5262 kg)
Max loaded weight 20,000 lb (9072 kg)
Max speed 260 mph (420 km/h) at 12,500 ft (3810 m)
Cruise speed 170 to 210 mph (274–338 km/h)
Climb 8 min to 10,000 ft (3050 m)
Range 1500 miles (2414 km)
Crew 2 or 3
Norm load limit 2000 lb (907 kg)

One of the fleet of converted Hudson Vs obtained from the British and operated by VIII AFSC and BADA to ferry supplies.

BEECH UC-45 EXPEDITOR

A small number of Beech light transports were received by 8th Air Force during the winter of 1943–44 and mostly assigned to headquarters flights for staff officer use. Two C-45Fs assigned to 8th Air Force Hq Squadron in 1944 were 44-47492 (A) and 43-35928 (D).

A UC-45F, photographed in May 1944, the preferred liaison transport in 8th AF.

C-45F details
Two Pratt & Whitney R-985-AN-1 radials rated at 450 hp each

Span 47 ft 8 in (14.53 m)
Length 34 ft 8 in (10.57 m)
Empty weight 5785 lb (2624 kg)
Max loaded weight 9000 lb (4082 kg)
Max speed 206 mph (332 km/h)
Cruise speed 160 mph (258 km/h)
Range 1200 miles (1930 km)
Crew Pilot and 6 passengers

FAIRCHILD UC-61 FORWARDER

Twelve UC-61s were received by 8th Air Force in April and May of 1943 and a few others at a later date. These were initially used as headquarters communications aircraft, but when liaison types became more plentiful during the latter part of 1944, UC-61s were distributed among combat groups, there being 27 of this type on hand by September. UC-61As assigned to VIII BC

Right: **UC-61A 43-14500 of 8th Air Force Hq Flt at Bovingdon early in 1944.**   (via C. W. Cain)

(later 8th Air Force) Headquarters Squadron at Bovingdon in 1943 were 43-14483, 43-14484, 43-14485 (K), 43-14500 (E) and 43-14603 (T). Additionally, the 27th Air Transport Group was loaned an Argus (British name for the UC-61), serial HM172, which was returned to the RAF in May 1944.

UC-61A details
One Warner R-500-1 radial rated at 165 hp

Span 36 ft 4 in (11.07 m)
Length 23 ft 9 in (7.24 m)
Empty weight 1613 lb (732 kg)
Max loaded weight 2500 lb (1134 kg)
Max speed 132 mph (212 km/h)
Cruise speed 100–120 mph (161–193 km/h)
Range 640 miles (1030 km)
Crew Pilot and 3 passengers

NOORDUYN UC-64 NORSEMAN

Eventually the most numerous USAAF utility transport in Europe, the Canadian-built UC-64s were shipped to the UK early in 1944. They were used extensively by VIII AFSC for visiting combat bases and inter-depot journeys. The UC-64 was also made available to both bomber and fighter groups later in 1944, most having either a UC-64 or UC-78 on strength by the end of hostilities when some 60 UC-64As were serving with the 8th Air Force. It was considered a noisy aircraft, but useful, with good cabin space.

UC-64A details
One Pratt & Whitney R-1340-AN-1 radial rated at 600 hp

Span 51 ft 6 in (15.70 m)
Length 32 ft 4 in (9.85 m)
Empty weight 4250 lb (1928 kg)
Max loaded weight 7400 lb (3357 kg)
Max speed 162 mph (260 km/h) at 5000 ft (1520 m)
Cruise speed 120–145 mph (193–233 km/h)

UC-64A 44-70382 taking off from Snetterton Heath.

Climb 7 min to 5000 ft (1520 m)
Range 450 miles (724 km)
Crew Pilot and 9 passengers

CESSNA UC-78 BOBCAT

In April 1943 8th Air Force received eight UC-78 liaison transports assigning one to each wing and two to command headquarters flights. In September that year VIII BC Hq operated 42-58438 and 42-58439 from Bovingdon, 1st Wing had 42-58434 at Bassingbourn, 2nd Wing 42-58436 at Hethel and 4th Wing 42-58559 at Honington.

By the following summer the 8th Air Force Hq Squadron (originally VIII BC Hq Flight) had two later UC-78s; 43-32091 (B) and 43-32102 (H). At this time a few UC-78Bs with wooden propellers were received. Bobcats were subsequently made available to groups and other units and by August 1944 there

were 36 assigned to the 8th Air Force. Some structural problems were encountered with the UC-78. They were grounded for a short period in November 1943 when fuselage distortions were found, and also in December 1944 because of coring leading edge failures. In the latter instance a wing strengthening modification had to be performed on UC-78s from 43-7555 and on UC-78Bs from 43-32191, but 16 aircraft in these ranges were eventually salvaged.

One of the first eight UC-78 Bobcats received by 8AF in April 1943, 42-58439 served as a headquarters transport. (via C. W. Cain)

UC-78 details
Two Jacobs R-755-9 radials rated at 225 hp each

Span 41 ft 11 in (12.78 m)
Length 32 ft 9 in (9.98 m)
Empty weight 3500 lb (1588 kg)

Max loaded weight 5000 lb (2268 kg)
Max speed 175 mph (282 km/h)
Cruise speed 140 mph (225 km/h)
Range 750 miles (1207 km)
Crew Pilot and 4 passengers

LOCKHEED C-57 LODESTAR
A lone example of this 17-seat airliner, 41-23169, was used for passenger flights by VIII AFSC. The aircraft was salvaged in January 1944.

NORTH AMERICAN AT-6 TEXAN
A small number of AT-6Ds were obtained by 8th Air Force from a shipment arriving in the UK in April 1944. All these aircraft were in 'silver' finish. Allocations were made chiefly to fighter groups where the aircraft were used for dual instrument training. A total of 23 AT-6s were assigned by November 1944. A few AT-6F were received late that year.

AT-6D details
One Pratt & Whitney R-1340-AN-1 radial rated at 600 hp

Span 42 ft (12.08 m)
Length 29 ft (8.84 m)
Empty weight 4271 lb (1937 kg)
Max loaded weight 5620 lb (2549 kg)
Max speed 208 mph (335 km/h) at 5000 ft (1520 m)
Cruise speed 140–170 mph (225–274 km/h)
Range 850 miles (1368 km)
Crew 2

AT-6D serving 2nd Combat Wing at Hethel in the summer of 1944.

NORTH AMERICAN HARVARD
During 1942 and 1943 the RAF made available a number of Harvard trainers for 8th Air Force use in communications flights. BD135 was flown by VIII FC and BD136 and BD137 by VIII BC during 1942. These were identified as AT-6s by 8th Air Force.

Later Harvard IIBs FT140, FT147, FT227, FT236, FT241, FT243, FT253 and FT307 were obtained from the RAF and returned in June 1944. These Noorduyn-built aircraft were identified as AT-16s by the USAAF. Details as AT-6D.

BEECH AT-7
Basically the advanced trainer version of the UC-45, two AT-7s were utilised for VIP transport when other, more suitable, types were unavailable in 1942. These were 42-2428 and 42-2429, both often used to transport visiting dignitaries to combat bases. At-7 42-2429 was assigned to VIII BC during 1943 and later 8th AF Hq Flight at Bovingdon. The 2nd Bomb Division Hq operated 42-2428 from Hethel during 1944.

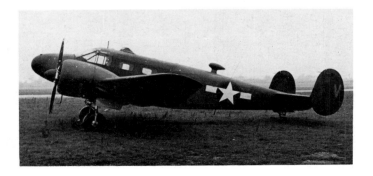

Right: **AT-7 42-2429 was frequently used by General Eaker to visit VIII BC bases during 1943.** (via C. W. Cain)

PIPER L-4 GRASSHOPPER

The military version of the popular Cub sportsplane was, despite its official name, commonly referred to as 'Cub' by 8th Air Force personnel. First L-4Bs were received in October 1942 and three months later 11 were held by VIII BC and six by VIII FC. These aircraft were eventually distributed to combat groups for liaison purposes. Further assignments were to 315th Troop Carrier Group, which had three in May 1943, and the 67th Observation Group which had 32 in the same month. Some of these aircraft were detached to serve VIII ASC bomb groups later in the year. Later shipments of L-4s reaching the UK went to the US Army. By August 1944 there were 26 L-4Bs in 8th Air Force.

'Cub' 43-686 assigned to VIII FC and photographed at Kingscliffe in February/March 1943.

L-4B details

One Continental O-170-3 engine rated at 65 hp

Span 35 ft 3 in (10.74 m)
Length 22 ft 5 in (6.83 m)
Empty weight 730 lb (331 kg)
Max loaded weight 1220 lb (553 kg)
Max speed 90 mph (145 km/h)
Range 300 miles (483 km)
Crew Pilot and 1 passenger

VULTEE L-5 SENTINEL

This light aircraft was mainly used by 9th Air Force in Europe but a few examples, probably less than ten, reached 8th Air Force units during 1944–45. First three, 42–98996, 42–989997 and 42–98998 went to the courier unit at Cheddington in April 1944.

L-5 details

One Lycoming O-435-1 engine rated at 185 hp

Span 34 ft (10.36 m)
Length 24 ft 1 in (7.34 m)
Empty weight 1477 lb (670 kg)
Max loaded weight 2000 lb (907 kg)
Max speed 115 mph (185 km/h)
Range 275 miles (443 km)
Crew Pilot and 1 passenger

An L-5 photographed at Goxhill in the summer of 1944.   (P. Green)

WACO CG-4A

A number of CG-4A assault gliders were shipped to the UK in late 1942, some being assembled and assigned to the 315th Group at Aldermaston. A total of 30 were on hand in May 1943, but they were rarely used for training.

CG-4A details
Span 83 ft 8 in (25.5 m)
Length 48 ft 8 in (14.83 m)
Normal towed speed 125 mph (200 km/h)

British Communications and Training Aircraft

When 8th Air Force arrived in the UK in the spring of 1942 little provision had been made for USAAF liaison aircraft essential to fast communications. This situation was not radically changed until early in 1944 when substantial numbers of UC-78 Bobcats, UC-64 Norsemen and other American types became available.

To meet the original deficiency, 8th Air Force arranged for the loan of suitable British types which by late 1943 totalled some hundred aircraft. Thereafter numbers declined, but an order that all types except Oxfords were to be returned to the RAF by 1 July 1944 was not fully complied with for various reasons. A few British aircraft were retained until the end of the war. In 8th Air Force service many were given US national insignia but the majority continued to be flown with British roundels.

AIRSPEED OXFORD

The Oxford was the most numerous British-made aircraft used for communications in USAAF service. Between June 1942 and May 1945 132 different Oxfords are known to have seen service with 8th Air Force units, some for only very short periods. Principal use was for personnel transportation at wing and group level. When the British Blind Approach landing system was adopted by VIII BC in February 1943, four Oxfords – DF299, DF331, DF335 and DF399 – were provided for 8th Air Force's 1st BAT Flight (Prov) at Bassingbourn. The 2nd Wing's BAT Flight at Shipdham received Oxfords DF507, DF514 and DF528, while a fourth, DF364, went to Bungay. In August 1944 the 8th Air Force had 25 Oxfords on strength. Almost all Oxfords were returned to the RAF by the end of 1944 but in December that year two were obtained by 25th Group for use in transition training in lieu of Mosquito Mk IIIs. These two aircraft were still on strength at the end of May 1945.

Oxfords were spartan and noisy in comparison with US-made liaison types but not unpopular. They were also fairly reliable, although in February 1944, after a series of failures, it was necessary for a revised elevator hinge to be fitted to most Oxfords in US service.

Oxford II details

Two Armstrong Siddeley Cheetah X radials rated at 395 hp each

Span 53 ft 4 in (16.26 m)
Length 34 ft 6 in (10.52 m)
Empty weight 5380 lb (2440 kg)
Max loaded weight 8250 lb (3742 kg)
Max speed 190 mph (306 km/h)
Cruise speed 120–155 mph (193–250 km/h)
Range 900 miles (1448 km)
Crew Pilot and five passengers

Oxford AS728 in USAAF colours served 4th FG and later 495th FG before being handed back to the RAF in October 1944.   (via G. Fry)

AVRO ANSON

Very few Ansons were turned over to 8th Air Force for communications use. Eight are known to have been provided by the RAF against requisition requests during the year from August 1943. Two, W2656 and AX358, were involved in accidents and the others returned to the RAF during the spring and summer of 1944. These, with their last operators, were: DJ188 – 447 BG, DJ577 and N9610 – 3 SAD, DG763 – 87 ATS, AW911 and NK654 – 1 CCRC.

Anson details

Two Armstrong Siddeley Cheetah IX radials rated at 350 hp each

Span 56 ft 6 in (17.22 m)
Length 42 ft 6 in (12.95 m)
Empty weight 5375 lb (2438 kg)
Max loaded weight 9540 lb (4327 kg)
Max speed 188 mph (303 km/h)
Cruise speed 130–160 mph (210–258 km/h)
Range 800 miles (1287 km)
Crew Pilot and seven passengers

PERCIVAL PROCTOR

Derived from the Vega.Gull sports plane of the immediate pre-war years, the Proctor was operated in small numbers by various 8th Air Force units from the summer of 1942 until December 1944. Forty different Proctors are known to have been involved, of which six were written off in accidents. Only three remained in service by August 1944 and were relinquished by 2nd Division units by the end of the year.

Proctor details

One de Havilland Gipsy Queen II air-cooled inline rated at 210 hp

Span 39 ft 6 in (12.04 m)
Length 28 ft 2 in (8.58 m)
Empty weight 2450 lb (1111 kg)
Max loaded weight 3500 lb (1588 kg)
Max speed 157 mph (252 km/h)
Cruise speed 135–145 mph (217–233 km/h)
Range 500 miles (800 km)
Crew Pilot and three passengers

DE HAVILLAND DOMINIE

Military version of the pre-war D.H.89 Dragon Rapide biplane transport, four Dominies are known to have been loaned to 8th Air Force for communications use in December 1942. V4724 was relinquished in October 1943, while X7403, X7522 and X7523 were used by 27th Transport Group and returned to the RAF in May 1944. In April 1944 X7454 and X7346 were made available to 27th ATG at 2nd SAD and returned to the RAF by August.

Dominie details

Two de Havilland Gipsy Six or Queen air-cooled inline rated at 200 hp each

Span 48 ft (14.63 m)
Length 34 ft 6 in (10.52 m)
Empty weight 3230 lb (1465 kg)
Max loaded weight 5500 lb (2495 kg)
Max speed 157 mph (252 km/h)

Dominie Mk II X7523 resplendent in USAAF camouflage and insignia.   (de Havilland)

Cruise speed 120–140 mph (193–225 km/h)
Range 550 miles (885 km/h)
Crew Pilot and eight passengers

MILES MASTER

An advanced trainer which was supplied to 8th Air Force in 1942 for fast communications work. A total of 22 Mk IIs and IIIs are known to have been loaned by the RAF. The majority were returned by August 1944 but the last, DL830, was turned in by 3rd G & TT Flight in December that year.

Master III details

One Pratt & Whitney R-1535-SB4-G radial rated at 750 hp

Span 39 ft (11.88 m)
Length 30 ft 5 in (9.27 m)
Empty weight 4200 lb (1905 kg)
Max loaded weight 5500 lb (2495 kg)
Max speed 232 mph (373 km/h)
Cruise speed 150–185 mph (241–298 km/h)
Range 320 miles (515 km)
Crew 2

HAWKER HURRICANE

Only three Hurricane fighters are known to have been loaned to 8th Air Force, one of which was based at Bovingdon for a time and used for fast liaison work. Z4631 was salvaged in October and P3757 in December 1943, while V6844 was returned to the RAF in January 1944.

Hurricane I details

One Rolls-Royce Merlin III liquid-cooled inline rated at 1030 hp

Span 40 ft (12.19 m)
Length 31 ft 5 in (9.58 m)
Empty weight 4670 lb (2118 kg)
Max loaded weight 6600 lb (2994 kg)
Max speed 316 mph (508 km/h)
Cruise speed 212 mph (342 km/h)
Range 750 miles (1207 km/h)

DE HAVILLAND TIGER MOTH

The RAF's basic trainer, this small biplane was supplied as a light liaison aircraft to a few VIII FC fighter groups in 1943. Eleven aircraft are known to have been loaned by the RAF, one of which was wrecked in a crash. A popular aircraft, many were retained until late in 1944, the last two being surrendered by 4th and 356th Groups in early December.

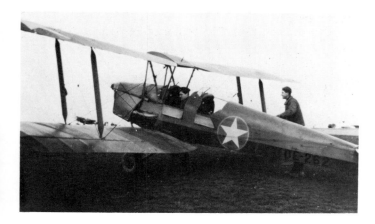

Tiger Moth details
One de Havilland Gipsy Major air-cooled inline rated at 130 hp

Span 29 ft 4 in (8.94 m)
Length 23 ft 11 in (7.29 m)
Empty weight 1100 lb (499 kg)
Loaded weight 1825 lb (828 kg)
Max speed 100 mph (161 km/h)
Cruise speed 85–93 mph (137–150 km/h)
Range 300 miles (483 km)
Crew 2

Left: **Tiger Moth DE262 delighted the pilots of 4th FG during 1943 and 1944. It was one of the last of its type returned to the RAF.** (J. Gibson)

WESTLAND LYSANDER

Originally designed as a ground forces support aircraft, most Lysanders had been modified for target-towing when 8th Air Force arrived in the UK. As early as July 1942 a few were made available for use by newly arrived bomber and fighter groups. Lysanders were also supplied for the Gunnery and Tow Target Flights when they were formed in 1943, remaining the principal type for sleeve towing in these units until replaced by A-35s in

the spring of 1944. Most were returned to the RAF by August that year but V9302 was held at the Snettisham gunnery school until the end of the year. Twenty-five Lysanders are known to have served with 8th Air Force – there were 15 on strength in March 1944.

Lysander V9817 photographed while assigned to the 3rd Gunnery and Tow Target Flight in March 1944. Serviceability of the ageing Lysander was a constant problem for US operating units as much repair was of a specialised nature and could only be carried out by hard-pressed RAF Maintenance Units. The situation became so critical by January 1944 and that 8th Air Force requested other suitable tow-target types from the British. (L. Redman)

Lysander II details
One Bristol Perseus XII radial rated at 905 hp

Span 50 ft (15.24 m)
Length 30 ft 6 in (9.3 m)
Empty weight 4065 lb (1844 kg)
Max loaded weight 6000 lb (2722 kg)
Max speed 220 mph (354 km/h)
Cruise speed 150–200 mph (241–322 km/h)
Range 600 miles (966 km)
Crew 2

BOULTON PAUL DEFIANT

Two Defiant Mk III target-towers were supplied for use by the 11 CCRC at Bovingdon in September 1942 and operated over the Snettisham range in the following year. One, DR944, remained at Bovingdon until returned to the RAF on 5 July 1944. The other aircraft, DR945, was used by 94th Bomb Group at Bury St Edmunds for some months before being turned over to the RAF in August 1944.

Defiant III details
One Rolls-Royce Merlin XX liquid-cooled inline rated at 1280 hp

Span 39 ft 4 in (12.00 m)
Length 35 ft 4 in (10.77 m)
Empty weight 6078 lb (2757 kg)
Loaded weight 8000 lb (3629 kg)
Max speed 260 mph (418 km/h)
Range 200 miles (322 km)
Crew 2

Aircraft Fuels

All 8th Air Force tactical aircraft operated on special high octane fuel rated on a performance number scale as 100/130. They use of an inferior anti-knock value fuel in high performance engines would have resulted in overheating, detonation and pre-ignition, all causing engine damage. The 100/130 fuel was also used by the RAF and all aviation fuel supplies in the UK were the responsibility of the British. While 8th Air Force bombers were fuelled with 100/130 throughout hostilities, early in 1944 there was interest in the possible use of grade 100/150 fuel which would permit the use of higher war emergency power in fighters. In March, selected fighter squadrons tested this new grade, the results indicating that while the fuel permitted more power to be drawn from engines, it caused increased maintenance, primarily through persistent sparking plug fouling. Despite reservations in some quarters, all 8th Air Force fighter groups went over to 100/150 fuel between July and late September 1944. Attempts to reduce plug fouling by decreasing valve settings and adjustment of carburettor enrichment valves did not appear to help matters. During the autumn there was an alarming increase in the number of P-51 take-off crashes due to engine failure, mostly attributed to use of the 'Purple Passion' fuel.

Wright Field recommended the addition of ethylene dibromide fluid with 100/150 to prevent fouling problems and in December 1944 the 355th Group was given the task of testing this grade, known as 'Pep'. By mid-January the trial was satisfactorily completed but British agencies were not so enthusiastic, their tests indicating that the additive in the fuel caused engine damage. On 8 February 1945 Technical Services reviewed the 355th Group experience, noting that no chamber corrosion or valve distortion had been found and that no field maintenance on valves had been necessary. Further, the use of 'Pep' had appreciably reduced engine maintenance time because plug fouling was practically eliminated. Other gains noticed were: reduction to a minimum of abortive sorties due to engine roughness, increased range, and less brake wear as the P-51s were able to taxi at lower rpm. It was felt that any extra wear on the valves or other engine parts was due to the use of higher power and not the 'Pep' fuel. As a result, 'Pep' 100/150 was being supplied to all fighter groups by March. However, contrary to Technical Services findings, fighter groups reported that while sparking plug life was prolonged, valve adjustment had simultaneously become a problem, checks having to be made every third or fourth mission instead of the usual 50 hours. Opinions differed but the most likely reason was thought to be valve seat inserts burning out, leading to diminishing valve clearance and loss of power. Enthusiasm for the new fuel waned quickly and in the same month some units requested a return to 100/130. As the old grade had been largely replaced by 100/150, supply was difficult. By April the position with 'Pep' was so critical that a valve check was advised after every 25 hours flight. In the middle of the month a message to Wright Field requested valve seat inserts on V-1650 engines be made of stelite or other suitable material with corrosion resistant properties. It was found that there was additive separation when fed to the engine, forming hydrobromic acid which attacked the valve seats. In May the British had made a decision to supply 100/150 containing less ethylene dibromide as additional sparking plug maintenance was preferred to short engine life, a decision with which 8th Air Force concurred.

At this time the British were experimenting with 130/170 grade containing acetylene tetrabromide which they believed would make a more homogeneous mixture.

Auxiliary Fuel Tanks

BOMBERS

To extend the range of bomber aircraft during ferry flights, provision was made in production for the installation of auxiliary fuel tanks in bomb-bays. These tanks of metal did not have self-sealing properties. The capacity of those used in B-17s and B-24s was 400 US gallons, the maximum load being two per aircraft. For the B-26 two 250 US gallon tanks were available. Bomb-bay tanks were occasionally used by 8th Air Force for combat operations.

FIGHTERS

The development and provision of jettisonable auxiliary fuel tanks for 8th Air Force fighters were among of the most significant technical developments affecting operations. Known as 'belly' or 'drop' tanks, they allowed sufficient range for fighters to give continuous protection to bomber formations and carry out offensive missions deep in enemy territory.

First 8th Air Force enquiry about the availability of jettisonable fuel tanks was signalled to Materiel Command on 3 October 1942. P-38s and P-39s reaching the UK in the second half of 1942 were equipped with 150 and 75 gallon rated metal tanks for ferrying purposes. The P-38's two 150 gallon tanks with an actual capacity of 165 US gallons each later came to be identified as such. The single P-39 tank had a true capacity of 84 US gallons but continued to be called a 75 gallon tank.

In January 1942, when it became clear that for the time being VIII FC would only be concerned with the P-47, arrangements were made for a consignment of Republic Aviation 200 gallon ferry tanks. Following a small number arriving in February the type was evaluated at Langford Lodge and 8th VIII FC's Air Technical Section at Bovingdon. Major Cass Hough, conducting flight trials with this bath-tub shaped tank, found that it had poor aerodynamics and that fuel could not be satisfactorily drawn above 22,000 feet due to lack of atmospheric pressure. Further, when released the tank banged along the underside of the aircraft; if fuel was left in it for more than a few hours it began to leak, and its paper plastic construction made it insufficiently strong to withstand pressurisation.

In the meantime VIII AFSC at Langford Lodge had been requested to design a steel 100 gallon tank suitable for attachment under a P-47.

The prototype tank was successfully tested in late March and arrangements were made for British firms to manufacture 43,200, supplied at the rate of 1000 per month commencing 1 June 1943. However, sheet steel shortages delayed production. In May the 100 gallon tank was successfully pressurised by ATS using the vacuum exhaust from the P-47 instrument vacuum pump; tests proved that adequate fuel could be drawn flying as

Above: **200 US gallon flush-fitting 'paper' tank in place on a 78th FG P-47C. The triangular wooden wedge attached to the front of the tank allowed the slipstream to force the front of the tank down and away from the aircraft on release.**

Top: **Sheet steel 75 gallon tank on Thunderbolt 'belly' shackles and with sway braces in place.**

Above: **Sheet steel 150/165 gallon tanks for P-38s being moved by 55th FG personnel at Nuthampstead. These were US-made and not modified for pressurisation.**

Left: **Grey painted steel 108 US gallon tank installed on P-47D wing shackles. Spring-loaded fork strut pressing against rear end ensured tank did not strike wing flaps when released. This tank was used by both P-47 and P-51 units.**

high as 35,000 feet. Control valves, to ensure a constant pressure as altitude changed, were obtained from the British Thermostat Company and by early June the inclusion of glass connections in the tank-to-fuselage plumbing gave a clean breakaway when the tank was jettisoned.

Continuing delay in getting the 100 gallon steel tank into production caused Hough and the ATS team to turn to the RAF's paper composition tank, originally designed for ferrying Hurricanes. This 108 US gallon tank, considered earlier in the year, had been found to be insufficiently strong. Arrangements were made with Bowater Lloyd, the manufacturers, to reinforce the paper tank to withstand 17 pounds per square inch working pressure. Satisfactorily flight tested, the tank was approved for production on 7 July 1943.

The urgency of extending fighter escort for the bombers led to the use of the 200 gallon paper tanks by 4th, 56th and 78th Groups from 24 July 1943, at a time when there were some 1150 on hand. Only 100 gallons of fuel was actually carried in each tank and they were released at 23,000 feet. In July 4000 P-39 type 75 gallon metal tanks arrived from the US and, as insufficient numbers of the 108 gallon paper tanks were yet available (the first was delivered on 12 July), it was decided to modify the 75 gallon tanks for the P-47's two-point belly shackles. Tested and approved by ATS on 17 August, these tanks were first used operationally by 56th Group later that month.

At the beginning of September 1943 the first locally-made steel 108 gallon tanks, the production version of VIII AFSC's 100 gallon tank, were received. That same month 108 gallon paper

tanks arrived in significant numbers and P-47s used them on their 27 September mission to Emden. There was only 4 inches ground clearance under these tanks and they could not be used on 'rough' airfields. A design for a 'flat' 150 gallon belly tank was accepted for additional production in the UK in mid-August, replacing the steel 108 gallon tanks in the spring of 1944.

Further large consignments of 75 gallon tanks arrived during the final months of 1943 but VIII FC cancelled all further shipments in December, by which time 7500 locally-made 108 gallon tanks had been received. The 75 gallon tanks became the standard tank for use on P-51 wing shackles, Mustangs using this type until stocks were depleted in the spring of 1944. In March 1944 all 75 gallon tanks were withdrawn from P-47 groups and sent to the P-51 stations. With the fitting of wing shackles to P-47s in early 1944, two 180 gallon tanks were a usual load. However, their use was delayed through the need for suitable sway braces. In February a consignment of US made 150 gallon 'flat' steel tanks was received for use by P-47s and

Right: A 108 US gallon Bowater paper composition tank in place on a P-51D. Glass connecting tubes were used so that plumbing broke away cleanly when tank was released. The 4th FG was the first P-51 unit to receive these; the 355th FG the second.

Below: *Flying Jeanie III* 42-106944 of 376th FS, 361st FG carrying two US-made 110 gallon steel tanks. Of similar tear-drop shape to the 75 gallon tanks but longer, they were painted silver.

introduced to operations by 56th Group that month. The first British-made 'flat' 150 gallon steel belly tanks for P-47s were received in March. The 150 gallon tanks became the favoured type for P-47s during the spring of 1944 and allowed the use of the wing shackles for bombs. While it was possible to carry two 150s under each wing, the load made handling difficult.

No special tanks were produced for P-38s during operations with 8th Air Force. P-38s used their standard 165 gallon tanks for which pressurisation was not provided, the tanks usually being released at 20,000 feet. The same tank could be fitted to P-47 wing shackles, but they were too large and ungainly for operational use.

With the depletion of the 75 gallon stock, P-51 groups went over to using the 108 gallon paper tank in May 1944. As this tank had originally been designed as a P-47 belly tank the fuel standpipes were at the rear. This necessitated a large amount of undesirable external plumbing – which had also been the case with the 75 gallon tank. A new design was prepared with the

Above: **Steel 150 gallon 'flat' tank on P-47M wing shackle.**

Left: **M-10 smoke dispenser tank on 62nd FS P-47M, 44-21228, April 1945. The 56th FG was to undertake ground attack operations using smoke dispensers for flak cover but the collapse of Nazi Germany occurred before such an operation could be mounted. Airfield in background is Raydon.**

standpipes in the front of the tank, thus eliminating the external plumbing and adding an extra 5 mph to performance. The new model became available in December 1944.

From May 1944 to the end of the war the paper 108 gallon tank was the standard Mustang fitment and allowed ample capacity for all types of mission. Nevertheless, in the summer of 1944 a large consignment of metal 110 gallon tanks was received from the US. Intended for use on P-47 belly shackles this tank was adapted for use on the P-51. Selected units used these tanks which, being heavier than the paper 108, were not popular with pilots or ground crews. The supply was mostly exhausted by the end of the year and standardisation on 108s continued from there on. Materiel Command at Wright Field had requested two

of these tanks for trials in August 1943, reporting back to 8th Air Force several months later that the tank was unsuitable for operational use! As wing tanks considerably reduced the performance of the P-47, in October 1944 Technical Services were asked to produce a belly tank of 200 gallons so that the wings could be left 'clean' (shackle pylons were removable). In two weeks a new tank had been designed and a prototype made. Production followed, and the first tanks were received by 56th Group exactly 34 days after the project was initiated. Actually of 215 US gallons capacity, the tank was a wider version of the flat 150 gallon tank.

Jettisonable fuel tanks built in the UK comprised 159 different items involved 43 companies in their manufacture.

Classification US gallons	(ltr)	Actual Capacity US gallons	(ltr)	Basic Material	Source of Supply	Aircraft Type Usage	Radius of Action miles	(km)
75	(284)	84	(318)	Steel	US	P-47	280	(451)
						P-51	650 (2 × 75)	(1046)
108	(409)	108	(409)	Steel	UK	P-47	325	(523)
108	(409)	108	(409)	Paper	UK	P-47	325	(523)
						P-51	750 (2 × 108)	(1207)
110	(378)	110	(378)	Steel	US	P-51	750 (2 × 110)	(1207)
150	(568)	165	(625)	Steel	US	P-47	375	(504)
150	(568)	165	(625)	Steel	UK	P-47	550 (2 × 150)	(885)
165	(625)	165	(625)	Steel	US	P-38	600 (2 × 165)	(966)
200	(757)	205	(776)	Paper	US	P-47	275	(443)
200	(757)	215	(814)	Steel	UK	P-47	480	(773)

Note: Actual capacity varied particularly with the large locally made tanks. Some 200 gallon P-47 tanks held 220 gallons (833 ltr).

Munitions and Associated Equipment

Bombs

GENERAL PURPOSE (GP)/HIGH EXPLOSIVE (HE) BOMBS

VIII BC began operations with old type bombs of 100, 300, 600 and 1100 lb size ratings. Supplies of these were mostly exhausted by late September 1942 when the new standard AN (Army/Navy) bombs were reaching stores. There were five GP types, the M30 classified as 100 lb, M31 as 300 lb, M43 as

500 lb, M44 as 1000 lb and M34 as 2000 lb. In general 500, 1000 and 2000 lb bombs were used against industrial targets and the smaller sizes against airfields, although little use was made of the 100 lb M30s. In the campaign against the submarine pens the 1000 and 2000 lb GP bombs used had little

A load of 500 lb GP M-43s for a 303rd BG leadship, *Satan's Workshop.* **Bombs were painted red and white to make their release easier to see by bombardiers in following aircraft.**

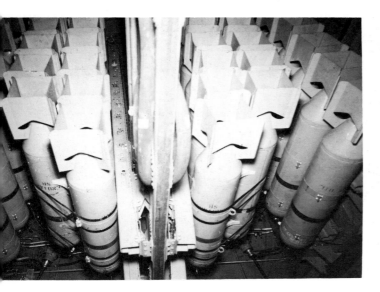

Top left: **The 100-pounder was considered an uneconomic bomb for heavy bombers to carry. Its use was generally confined to communications targets or for 'pot-holing' airfields. The M-30s stacked in the Bury St Edmunds bomb dump in December 1943 are having their nose plugs inspected by Lt J. B. Campbell, an ordnance officer.**

Top right: **Largest bomb normally carried by B-17s and B-24s was the 2000-pounder which tended to tumble when released due to an inherent design fault. The M-34 had to be handled by mobile crane (here operated by Pfc Charles Shanefelt, while Pfc D. Clyde Seitz guides the bomb into position). This revetment at Bury St Edmunds is covered by camouflage netting.**

Above: **M-44 1000 lb GP slung on a 303rd BG B-17F's wing racks, 18 September 1943, ready for a mission to France. Single yellow band round rear and front of bomb casing indicated TNT or Auratol filling.**

Left: **To obtain an economical load of 100 lb M-47 incendiaries, cables were used to lash additional bombs to those shackled to the central racks as in this B-17 photographed at Bovingdon in June 1943. Incendiary bombs were painted light grey with purple distinguishing bands. The M-47 case used for poison gas had green bands and for smoke, yellow.**

Above: Special bombs fitted to a salvaged B-17 bomb rack used by 487th BG to instruct armament crews. Top to bottom: The M-81 fragmentation bomb. Scored casing was designed to give multiple fragments (note double yellow bands indicating RDX filling); 20 lb M-41 frag bombs clustered on an 8-unit frame; the 100 lb M-47A2 napalm-filled incendiary with M-126 nose fuse, and the 500 lb M-17A1 aimable cluster. Considered the most effective incendiary device the M-17 used an M-127 or M-138 clockwork fuse to burst cluster 5 to 92 seconds after release.

harmful effect on the massive concrete structures protecting the U-boats; significant damage was usually only done to surrounding port facilities. At one time it was planned to attack in two waves, the first dropping 1600 lb US Navy Mk 1 armour-piercing bombs which were expected to crack the concrete, and then to follow up with a second wave dropping 2000 lb GPs to blast through. Two attempts to achieve this were made at Lorient but the only successful drop, on 30 December 1942, gave disappointing results, basically because it was not possible to obtain successive strikes with the two types of bombs. The GP bombs used in early missions were fitted with .025-second delay tail fuses as the actuating force plus a .1-second insurance fuse in the nose. In September 1943, however, VIII BC became interested in fuses of .01 second delay in the hope that these would bring a detonation just after penetration of building roofs to cause maximum fragmentation damage.

An intelligence report on the December 1942 Lille raid showed that 30 per cent of bombs dropped were duds. There were indications that the mechanical arming mechanisms of the fuses had frozen. Trials indicated that the situation could be improved if the bombs were not fused until shortly before take-off, thus reducing the time the fuses were exposed to damp. Nevertheless, a high percentage of duds persisted, even in warmer weather. British fuses were adapted for American bombs and in the spring of 1943 US chemical action long delay fuses were received for service tests. The chemical fuses had an anti-withdrawal trap device to prevent defusing by the enemy. Fortunately a method was devised in the UK for removing these fuses safely, sometimes necessary with aircraft that crashed on take-off. Following an incident in autumn 1943 when bombs on four B-26s had to be defused following failed take-offs, a modification was developed to allow the arming of anti-withdrawal fuses when bombers were airborne. Several other fusing changes were introduced during the 8th's campaign to improve destruction at different types of target.

A new range of GP bombs became available late in 1943, the M57, classified at 250 lb replacing the M31, and the M64, M65 and M66 of 500, 1000 and 2000 lb respectively. These made up the greater part of the tonnage delivered by 8th Air Force during the final year of operations. A small number of 4000 lb M56 were received in 1944 but these could not be carried internally by either B-17 or B-24. Experiments to use them on under-wing racks of B-17s were not successful and there is no record of M56s being delivered on combat missions. While the large 1000 and 2000 lb bombs continued to be preferred for industrial targets, in January 1945 analysts were recommending 250 lb GP for use against synthetic oil plants, refineries and storage as well as against ammunition supply and dump targets. The 100 lb GP bomb was advised for attacking marshalling yards and 'pot holing' airfields.

The individual weights of GP bombs varied slightly, and the average type weights differed from the classification by as much as 40 lb in the case of the M31. In most GP bombs between 50 and 60 per cent was explosive and the rest steel. On the shuttle missions using Russian bases, Soviet 225 kg (496 lb) bombs were used by B-17s to attack targets on the leg to Italy.

There were a number of serious accidents with bombs during loading operations. On 27 May 1943 twelve 500 lb bombs exploded during bombing up a 95th Group B-17 at Alconbury, causing the deaths of two officers and 17 men. On 23 June a similar accident occurred at Ridgewell with the explosion of eleven 300 lb bombs under a 381st Group Fortress which killed 23 men. Investigations of both accidents indicated that handling methods were to blame since both explosions had been caused by the dropping of fused bombs. A revision of handling procedures was made throughout VIII BC, notably that fuses were not to be inserted until the bombs were securely located in the aircraft. In a concentrated safety campaign a modification was made to the fuse arming mechanism and to the D-6 shackles that fixed to the bomb lugs and secured the bomb to the racks. On 9 July 1943 the 95th Group again accidentally dropped a bomb during loading, this time an M34, but no harm or damage was done. In fact, there were no further serious bomb handling incidents until the following April. On the 21st, during fusing of a load of M30s on a 447th Group B-17 at Rattlesden, an explosion killed 14 men and injured two. Five lives were lost in a catastrophic accident at Metfield on 15 July 1944. Members of a Negro unit were unloading bombs they had transported by rolling them out of trucks and letting them fall to the ground. An apparently unstable bomb detonated and in the ensuing chain reaction 1200 tons of bombs in the dump exploded.

INCENDIARY BOMBS

The first incendiary bombs were British – mostly 250 lb (used on VIII BC's second mission) but 500 lb were also available. Both were filled with a rubber/gasoline mixture. In November 1942 the American M50A1 4 lb magnesium incendiary arrived in 100 lb clusters. That winter the M50A1 arrived in 500 lb clusters and 100 lb M47 types, which were rubber/gasoline filled, were also received. However, the first mission with US incendiaries was not flown until 14 May 1943 when clusters containing M50A1s were used. On this and later missions these clusters proved unsatisfactory as they opened quickly causing excessive dispersion, with some aircraft in the formation being damaged by clustering material. Use of this cluster, the M11, was eventually suspended. Thereafter, VIII BC began trial missions with the M47, the principal problem being that a full load only amounted to 24 due to the limited number of shackle points in a B-17 bomb-bay. In July 1943 a successful method of clustering M47s together was achieved. Wire cables with snap hooks were used to hold three or four bombs together, but in such a way that after release there was separation, the cables being carried down with one bomb. This not only allowed three or four M47s to be shackled to one station in the bomb-bay, increasing the total load to 42, but also avoided damage to other aircraft. The device was later standardised for use with various other small bombs. The first large-scale attack by 8th Air Force with M47s took place on 4 October 1943. The supply of M47s barely kept ahead of requirements during the autumn and winter of 1943.

Other incendiary types that arrived in 1943 were a small number of M52, a 2 lb magnesium type, and the M69 which weighed 6 lb and was filled with petroleum gel. The M69 was tested in the UK in June 1943 and later packed in the M12 cluster. In January 1944 8th Air Force started to use the 500 lb M17 aimable cluster containing 110 M50A1s with better ballistics than the earlier M11 cluster; it had a primecord release that could be set to give the desired scatter. This became the favoured incendiary during the spring of 1944 and after D-Day few M47s were used. A larger petroleum gel filled bomb, the M76 of 500 lb, was introduced in 1944 and used with some effect during the rest of the 8th's campaign.

The M50A1 which made up magnesium incendiary clusters, had a hexagonal, cored magnesium alloy body with hollow steel sheet fins containing thermite with an igniting charge and fuse. On ignition, the M50 burned for six to eight minutes at a temperature of 2300 degrees F. The preferred jellied-oil incendiary, the M47A2, had a thin-walled steel cylindrical body weighing 26 lb empty and on impact gave a 120 feet fire spread.

Developed from the M47, classified as 70 lb, it contained a petroleum mix of greater calefaction but was not used by 8th Air Force. The M47A1 had a filling containing 93 lb of white phosphorus. The composition in the M76 was jellied-oil, heavy oil, petrol, magnesium powder and sodium nitrate. The mix had particularly good adhering qualities and was difficult to extinguish.

As high explosive and incendiary bombs had different trajectories there was difficulty in accurate attack if carrying mixed loads in one aircraft. This was overcome by preparing time lag tables indicating the interval in release of different bomb types in order to hit the same target. Ultimately these were developed to cover all contingencies, including wind strength at various altitudes.

NAPALM BOMBS

A refined petroleum jelly known as napalm became available during the second half of 1944. Handled in bulk it was intended for filling as required. Tested in various containers, the preferred type was the paper composition fighter fuel tank of 108 US gallon capacity. Known as Class C-Fire Bombs, napalm tanks were used on a few special missions where blanket fire cover was required, notably against German strong-points on the French coast in April 1945. Usually six napalm tanks were carried in a B-24 and four in a B-17; small incendiary igniter units were fixed to each tank.

Right: **Armourers of the 390th BG filling 108 gallon 'paper' drop tanks with napalm mixture pumped from 50 gallon drums. April 1945**

FRAGMENTATION BOMBS

Fragmentation bombs, basically anti-personnel, were used mostly in tactical attacks supporting ground forces. The 20 lb M41 was common to both the M1 and M1A1 (differing in attachment arrangement) clusters of 120 lb and the M26 clusters of

500 lb. The M1A1 was employed extensively in heavy bomber loads. To enable fragmentation bombs to be used in conjunction with the Norden sight it was necessary for special computation tables to be provided as the maximum trail angle of the sight was not great enough for the light bombs.

POISON GAS BOMBS

Stored at bomb depots as a deterrent stock during hostilities, the original poison gas bombs were of British origin. There were two types: the 400 lb mustard gas bomb, known as the 'Flying Cow', and a 500 lb phosgene bomb. Early in 1943 several

thousand M47A2 HS unfilled incendiary bombs for jellied-oil were set aside for use with mustard gas and held ready in stores. Storage levels were 40,000 M47 100 lb mustard gas bombs, 50,000 'Flying Cows', and 5000 phosgene bombs.

VB-1 *AZON* BOMB

A standard 1000 lb bomb, type AN/M44, fitted with special tail unit, enabling the bomb to be controlled in azimuth by over 200 feet on either side of the normal point of impact when dropped from 20,000 feet. Control was effected by an AN/ARW-9 transmitter installed in the dropping aircraft. Because of the size of the bomb when fitted with the 164 lb *Azon* tail, it could only be suspended from a 2000 lb bomb shackle in a B-24 bay. This tail assembly contained an AN/ARW-10 receiver operating two rudder control motors powered by a 24-volt battery. Two gyros linked to the control surfaces operated continuously during descent to prevent roll.

Right: *Azon* tail assembly fitted to 1000 lb M-44. Each fin has movable section controlled by radio signals to electric motors. Note flare installation centred at rear of *Azon* unit and arming fuse with label attached. (Smithsonian)

GB-1 GLIDE BOMB

An M34 2000 lb bomb with 12 feet span glider wings and tail unit making it 11 ft 7 in long constituted the GB-1 glide bomb. The GB-1 was carried on a B-17 underwing shackle, two per aircraft. Although it was free-fall, an automatic stabilising device assisted directional control. Three groups of 41st Combat Wing were trained to deliver GB-1s, code named *Grapefruit*, during the winter of 1943–44. This stand-off weapon proved highly inaccurate on the one occasion it was used operationally – against Cologne – in April 1944 and was thereafter abandoned. Principal obstacle to accuracy was the veering winds encountered at high altitudes.

Above: **GB-1 glide bombs slung under a 303rd BG Fortress.**

Right: **A GB-1 released against Cologne by a 384th BG Fortress on 26 April 1944.**

GB-4 and GB-8

A development of the GB-1 glide bomb with radio control of flight surfaces and a TV camera installed under the nose became the GB-4. Three B-17Gs, 42-97518, 42-40042 and 42-40043, fitted with directional radio equipment and wing racks for these bombs arrived in the UK in early 1944. Trials were made under the 8th Air Force code name *Batty*, but only

42-40043 was actually used for the combat sorties. GB-4 weighed approximately 2600 lb, had a 12 ft span and was 12 ft 2 in long. Five magnesium flares were attached to the rear of the warhead. TV range was 15 miles and transmission time to target from 15,000 ft averaged 6 minues. GB-8 was a similar weapon without the TV installation which was available to the *Batty* unit but never employed.

DISNEY ROCKET BOMB

Developed by the Royal Navy for use in penetration and destruction of U-boat and E-boat shelters. Weighing 4500 lb, the *Disney* bomb was free-fall after release until the rocket motor ignited at 5,000 feet, propelling the missile to a speed of 2400 feet per second at impact. A penetration of 20 feet was recorded before detonation.

As the bomb was 14 feet long there was no suitable British aircraft to deliver them. The USSTAF was approached for help in this matter, and in the autumn of 1944 trials were conducted by Operational Engineering from Bovingdon using a B-17G carrying *Disney* bombs on wing racks. With this 9000 lb load the B-17 grossed 66,000 lb at take-off, requiring a 1400 yard run. Climb to 20,000 feet took 40 minutes at 150 mph IAS. To prevent oscillation of the bombs on their racks it was necessary to make gentle manoeuvres. Only main fuel tanks were filled when carrying *Disney* bombs. First used operationally by 92nd Group on 14 March 1945 and in later missions by 305th and 306th Groups as well. The 94th Group was also preparing to carry *Disney* bombs during the final weeks of the war.

A *Disney* bomb slung on a 94th BG B-17. ('Blisters' on wing contain *Carpet* aerials.)

Principal Bomb Types used by 8th Air Force

Model	Classification	Approx weight	Principal content	Dimensions	Remarks
M1	120 lb FRAG		6 × M41		See M41
M6	150 lb IB Cluster		34 × M50A1		See M50A1
M7	550 lb IB Cluster		128 × M50A1		See M50A1
M11	500 lb IB Cluster		110 × M50A1		See M50A1
M12	100 lb IB Cluster		14 × M69		See M69
M17A1	500 lb IB Cluster		110 × M50A1-A3		Aimable; see M50A1
M19	500 lb IB Cluster		38 × M69		Aimable; see M69
M26	500 lb FRAG Cluster		20 × M41		See M41
M30	100 lb GP	100 lb (45 kg)	HE	38½ × 8¼ in (96.5 × 20.3 cm)	—
M31	300 lb GP	260 lb (118 kg)	HE	48 × 11 in (122 × 28 cm	—
M34	2000 lb GP	2050 lb (930 kg)	HE	93 × 23½ in (236 × 58.4 cm)	—
M38A1	100 lb Practice	100 lb (45 kg)	Inert	47½ × 8 in (119.3 × 20.3 cm)	—
M41	20 lb FRAG	20 lb (9 kg)	HE	22½ × 3½ in (56 × 7.6 cm)	See M1 & M26
M43	500 lb GP	510 lb (131 kg)	HE	59¼ × 14¼ in (150 × 35.5 cm)	—
M44	1000 lb GP	965 lb (438 kg)	HE	69½ × 19 in (175 × 48.2 cm)	—
M47A1	100 lb IB	120 lb (54 kg)	White phosphorus	49 × 8 in (124.5 × 20.3 cm)	—
M47A2	100 lb IB	100 lb (45 kg)	Petroleum gel	49 × 8 in (124.5 × 20.3 cm)	—
M50A1	4 lb IB	3¾ lb (1.7 kg)	Magnesium	21¼ × 3 in (53.3 × 7.6 cm)	See M6, M7, M11 & M17
M52	2 lb IB	2 lb (0.9 kg)	Magnesium	18 × 3 in (45.7 × 7.6 cm)	—
M56	4000 lb GP	4201 lb (1906 kg)	HE	117¼ × 34¼ in (297 × 86.3 cm)	—
M57	250 lb GP	260 lb (118 kg)	HE	48 × 11 in (122 × 28 cm)	Developed M31
M58	500 lb SAP	500 lb (227 kg)		57¾ × 11¾ in (146.7 × 29.8 cm)	—
M59	1000 lb SAP	990 lb (449 kg)		70½ × 15 in (179 × 38 cm)	—
M64	500 lb GP	520 lb (236 kg)	RDX	62½ × 14¼ in (157.5 × 35.3 cm)	Improved M43
M65	1000 lb GP	995 lb (451 kg)	RDX	69½ × 19 in (175.3 × 48.3 cm)	Improved M44
M66	2000 lb GP	2050 lb (930 kg)	RDX	93 × 23½ in (236 × 58.4 cm)	Improved M34
M69	6 lb IB	6 lb (2.7 kg)	Petroleum gel	19½ × 3 in (48 × 7.6 cm)	See M12 & M19
M76	500 lb IB	475 lb (215 kg)	Petroleum gel	59¼ × 14¼ in (150 × 35.5 cm)	M43 case
M81	260 lb FRAG	260 lb (118 kg)	HE	43¾ × 18 in (109 × 45.7 cm)	—
MK1	1600 lb AP	1590 lb (721 kg)	HE	83½ × 14 in (210.8 × 25.5 cm)	USN development
Mk12	500 lb GP	HE			USN development
Mk13	1000 lb SAP	HE			USN development

(*Abbreviations:* AP = Armour Piercing; SAP = Semi-Armour Piercing; FRAG = Fragmentation; GP = General Purpose)
IB = Incendiary Bomb)

Above: **Painted light blue for identification purposes, the content of M-38A2 practice bomb was sand with 3 lb of black powder for a spotting charge. At approximately 100 lb they could be manhandled − Pfc Thomas Planguach, 303rd BG is the man flexing his muscles in this picture.**

Right: **Filling Sky Marker smoke bomb cases with FM mixture at Molesworth in February 1945. These were yet another use of the M-47 incendiary case. On contact with the air the FM mixture formed titanium hydroxide smoke and a small amount of hydrochloric acid vapour.**

Below: **Assembling an M-26 parachute flare at Kimbolton in December 1943. This long-burning device was used on occasions for assembly and route point marking purposes.**

Below right: **The bomb-bay of a 25th BG(R) Mosquito filled with 12 M-46 Photoflash bombs for target illumination in darkness.**

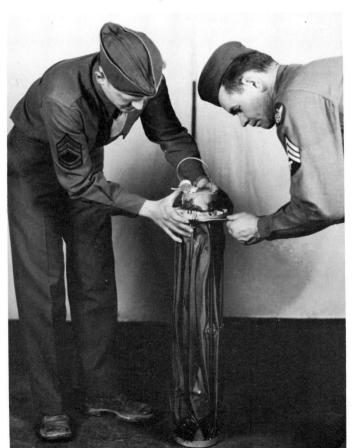

Guns and Ammunition

The USAAF's standard weapon for both offensive and defensive purposes was the .50-calibre machine gun. While a .50-in round lacked the destructive force of a 20 mm cannon shell, the mass fire from batteries of .50s in US fighters proved very successful in both air fighting and ground attack. In bomber defence it was less effective, particularly where .50s were used individually on flexible mounts. The gunner was handicapped by inferior firepower, lack of a simple and accurate sighting procedure, and also needed to be alerted to the presence of an enemy to open fire before it approached to within 1200 feet of his bomber. Ammunition was at first available in armour piercing, incendiary and tracer rounds. Tracer was soon found to be of questionable value as it caused gunners to disregard their sights when using it. Tracer also offered a serious optical illusion, particularly with beam shooting. On the other hand, it had advantages in alerting other gunners in a formation and was also of value as a deterrent to attacking enemy pilots. It became general practice to only use tracer rounds in front and rear turrets where optical illusion was negligible. A brighter tracer round, known as 'headlight', was introduced during 1944 and used in these positions in a one tracer to four AP incendiary rounds ratio supply – at this time the combined armour piercing incendiary had replaced the separate AP and incendiary rounds in general usage.

There was no major development in aircraft armament on the Allied side during 8th Air Force's operational period. In contrast to Luftwaffe guns which were in most cases specifically designed for aircraft, the US weapons were adaptions of ground warfare guns.

0.50-CALIBRE M2 BROWNING MACHINE GUN

The 'point fifty' weighed 64 lb (30.4 kg) and was 57 inches (1.45 m) long. Muzzle velocity was 2850 feet (870 m) per second and rate of fire 750 rounds per minute. Extreme range, the point at which forward travel terminated, was 21,500 feet (6550 m) and effective range, that at which penetration of an airframe or engine had destructive force, was 3,500 feet (1070 m). These figures were USAAF specimen stated figures, there being considerable variation in battle performance through factors such as the condition of individual weapons, temperature and ammunition feed. In one test as much as 200 rounds per minute difference was recorded between guns in the same fighter. A static test carried out in March 1944 by 4th Group on a P-51B with flash hider and muzzle booster attachments gave a wider variation. Without any attachments the gun fired 694 rounds per minute. With a flash hider this was reduced to 677 rpm. When the booster was fitted 857 rpm was obtained but after firing 600 rounds in short bursts the rate rose to 949 rpm. During the 8th Air Force's campaign several production refinements were introduced on both fixed and flexible versions of the .50 although basically the gun was unchanged.

'Point fifty' rounds were 5.47 inches (13.9 cm) long and weighed 1.71 ounces (48.5 g). They were available as armour piercing (identified by black painted tip), tracer (red), incendiary (blue), and armour piercing incendiary (silver). There were combat tests of experimental ammunition, the most notable was identified as T-48, a concentrated incendiary round intended for use against the low-grade fuel in jet aircraft. Muzzle velocity was 3400 feet (1036 m) per second and fighter aircraft required a new harmonisation pattern to use it effectively. The 56th Group tested T-48 successfully in strafing attacks on airfields in April 1945.

Standard gun in both USAAF bombers and fighters was the .50-inch calibre M2 Browning. Accurate fire was difficult to obtain with hand-held models due to sighting and handling problems. Note ring and post sight and charging handle on right side of breech mechanism on the right waist gun manned by S/Sgt Louis Skinner of 306th BG.

0.30-CALIBRE M2 BROWNING MACHINE GUN

Fitted as nose defensive armament in the early 8th Air Force B-17s and B-26s, the 0.30-in (7.62 mm) M2 Browning was rarely used after the spring of 1943. Both B-17E and B-17F models reaching the UK in 1942 had four sockets in the nose plexiglas for use with the .30 guns. At 23 lb (10.4 kg) basic weight and 40 inches (1.02 m) long, the .30 was supposedly easy for the bombardier to move from socket to socket as required. In practice it was quite a feat to do this at 25,000 feet and these guns usually remained in one location throughout a mission. Although most of the early B-17Fs were eventually modified to take a .50 gun through a nose socket, some retained a .30 in one of the other sockets. The .30 had a muzzle velocity of 2600 feet (792 m) per second and an extreme range of 5400 feet (1650 m). Although the rate of fire was 1,200 rounds per minute, for bomber defence the .30 was considered to be largely ineffective, lacking range and destructive power. Rounds, which weighed 2.1 ounces (59.5 g) each, were armour piercing and tracer for 8th Air Force use. A similar rifle-calibre weapon, the .303 Browning, was part of the armament in the Spitfire VBs used by 8th VIII FC squadrons.

20 mm M2 HISPANO CANNON

The only American combat aircraft in 8th Air Force with the 20 mm cannon were the P-38 and P-400. This weapon was also used experimentally in wing rack mounted pods on a P-47D and in the nose of a B-17F. The 20 mm cannon, 94 inches (2.39 m) long and weighing 102 lb (46.3 kg) had a 600 rounds per minute rate of fire, muzzle velocity of 2850 feet (870 m) per second and an extreme range of 15,000 feet (4570 m). An explosive round weighed 4.82 ounces (136.6 g). This gun was similar to the 20 mm cannon used in the Spitfire VB.

The 20 mm cannon was centrally mounted in the nose of the P-38 under the four .50 weapons. Rear magazine fed the shells to this gun.

37 mm M4 AMERICAN ARMAMENT CORPORATION CANNON

Fitted to P-39L and M aircraft transferred to the 12th Air Force, the M4 weighed 215 lb (97.5 kg) and was 89 inches (2.26 m) long. It had a 150 rounds per minute rate of fire, muzzle velocity of 2000 feet (610 m) per second and an extreme range of 12,000 feet (3660 m). The weight of each round was 21.44 ounces (607.8 g).

4.5-inch M10 ROCKET LAUNCHER

Only limited use was made of rockets by 8th Air Force fighters in ground attack, amounting to no more than an operational trials period. Although the weapon had good destructive power, it was difficult to aim owing to the uncertain trajectory due to the delay in reaching maximum velocity after release. The 4.5-inch (114 mm) rocket was an adaption of the US Army infantry rocket and used 10 feet (3 m) long tubes. The assembly fitted to P-47s consisted of three clustered tubes under each wing. Four sets of rocket installations with 60 projectiles were provided for each of the four P-47 groups in August 1944. The 56th and 353rd Groups immediately fitted trial installations but the 78th and 356th were delayed through lack of special tools. All these groups made a

M-10 rocket tubes installed on a 353rd FG P-47D. The assembly could not be jettisoned on these trial installations. The tubes were made from a flameproof plastic.

number of ground attack sorties with rockets during August and September 1944. The installation points were later removed from most P-47s. The 4.5-inch M8 projectile was 34 inches (86.4 cm) long, weighed 38.4 lb (17.4 kg), of which the high explosive content was 5.3 lb (2.4 kg). Ignited electrically, maximum velocity was 860 feet (262 m) per second.

In October 1944 experiments were initiated with the use of rearward-firing rockets on bombers as a defence against mass formation attacks by enemy fighters. A 4.5-inch tube cluster was fitted beneath the rear fuselage of 389th Group B-24H 42-50290, in such a way that the tubes could be raised and recharged with projectiles through the under hatch. The rockets were fired electrically from the tail turret. The preferred fuse was the proximity type T-5, which armed one second after launching and detonated automatically when passing within 50 to 70 feet of the target. Although successful trials were conducted with this prototype, there was no opportunity to test the device operationally before the end of hostilities.

GUNSIGHTS

In contrast to guns, several different types of gunsight were used in 8th Air Force bombers and fighters. On early B-17s and B-24s all the hand-manipulated guns had so-called iron sights, mostly simple ring-and-post, necessitating a gunner maintaining a constant eye base. Four different iron sights were pro-

duced for .50 guns and there were also several others developed by individual units seeking improvements. Accuracy of fire with the iron sight depended very much on the skill of individual gunners in estimating deflections. In an effort to improve the general standard of gunnery, VIII BC devised a method of estimation based on an RAF practice, known as the Zone System of firing.

REFLECTOR SIGHTS

These optical sights allowed a gunner to change his distance from the sight without introducing error in deflection. The gunner had only the target to watch as the reticule in the optical viewer appeared superimposed upon it, permitting accurate estimation of deflection allowances. However, the one-ring reticule of the N-3 and early N-6 models caused errors as high as 25 per cent on beam shots. The three-ring reticule N-8 gave much more accurate indications of deflections. N-series reflector sights were used in some positions in B-17s, B-24s and B-26s. In fighters the N-3 reflector sight was originally standard in the P-38, P-47 and P-51. P-38s retained the N-3 series in production until the P-38J-10. The N-3 could not be installed behind the redesigned windshield of this model so the Lynn Instrument Company's independently developed L-3 sight was used on this and subsequent P-38s. Dissatisfaction with the operation of the N-3 in P-47s caused VIII FC groups to replace it with the British Mk II sight until Republic installed the similar US Navy developed Mk VIII late in 1943. The P-51B was fitted with the N-3B which was replaced in some groups by Mk II sights and in others by Mk VIIIs. The P-51D featured an improved reflector sight, the N-9.

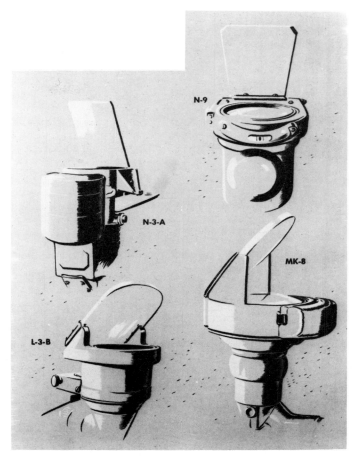

Above: **Reflector gunsights.**

Left: **Mk II gunsight in a 4th FG Spitfire V.**   (R. Wehrman)

COMPUTING SIGHTS

Fully computing rate-by-time sights were used in the dorsal and ventral power turrets of B-17s and B-24s. Providing an aircraft was in range, whether attacking or not, they measured angular velocities of the target with respect to bomber motion. However, they were only accurate if level flight was maintained, producing error in rough air or if the bomber engaged in evasive action. The only sights of this type used in 8th Air Force bombers were the mechanically-functioning Sperry K-3 and K-4 in B-17s, and the Fairchild K-8 in B-24s which was electrical.

COMPENSATING SIGHTS

Used only in bombers and compensating for the forward speed of the bomber plus the trail and motion of the attacking fighter, were the Sperry K-10 and K-11 sights tested by 8th Air Force during 1944 in tail and nose turrets respectively, and the K-13 tried that summer on waist guns. There were conflicting views on their value, although from November 1944 the K-13 was fitted extensively to waist guns.

A simple but ingenious compensating sight was designed by the gunnery officer of 389th Group, Capt John Driscoll, and later adopted for flexible guns by the 2nd Division. Although less accurate than the optical Sperry models, it was available and used operationally during the early part of 1944 when Luftwaffe fighters were still making curving beam attacks. It consisted of a post sight on a hinged arm, to the other end of which a small wind-vane was attached. Slipstream manoeuvred this attachment into giving deflection sighting.

Right: **Capt John Driscoll demonstrating his compensating sight for flexible guns.**

GYRO COMPUTING SIGHTS

Based on the British gyroscopic Mk IIC and Mk IID giving very accurate deflection shooting within range, regardless of the relative positioning of target and gun, the K-15 was received in limited numbers during the final months of the war and several were used operationally. The British Mk IIC on which it was based was first tried in the tail turret of a B-24 in October 1944. The K-14 was the fighter version, first received for trial installations in July 1944 and progressively installed in as many fighter aircraft as possible after August, replacing all other types of sight. It was fitted on production P-47s from January and on P-51s from March 1945.

Gunsights in 8th Air Force Aircraft

Model	Aircraft Types and Station
N-3	P-38F-1 cockpit, B-24D top and tail turrets.
N-3A	P-47C & D to D-15 cockpit.
N-3B	P-51B & C. P-38F-5 to P-38J-5 cockpits.
N-6	Late B-24D top and tail turret. B-24H & J tail turret. B-17G chin turret.
N-6A	B-17G chin and tail turret. B-24H & J nose, top and tail turrets.
N-8	B-17G from 43-38473, 44-6251 & 44-8287 in tail. Some B-24 waist.
N-9	P-51D & K cockpits.
K-3	B-17F & G top turret.
K-4	B-17F & G ball turret. B-24D, H & J ball turret.
K-8	B-24H & J top turret from 4/44.
K-10	Some B-17G and B-24H, J, L & M tail turrets.
K-11	Some B-17G and B-24J, L & M nose turrets.
K-13	B-17G & B-24L & M waist guns from 11/44.
K-14	P-47D & P-51B, C & D & K conversions for cockpits.
K-14A	From P-47D-35-RA & P-47M, P-51D-20-NT & P-51D-25-NA cockpits.
K-15	B-17G & B-24J, L & M conversions tail turrets.
Mk II	P-47 & P-51 conversions. Spitfire V cockpits.
Mk IIIA	B-17G nose, some B-17F tail and some B-24D waist and nose.
Mk VIII	P-47D-15 onwards. P-47D and P-51 conversions. Cockpits.
L-3	P-38J-10 onwards. Cockpits.

Top right: A target was viewed between the gunner's spread legs in a ball turret. Using the K-4 computing sight is Sgt S/Sgt Norman Sampson, 303rd BG.

Right: K-14 'gyro' sight.

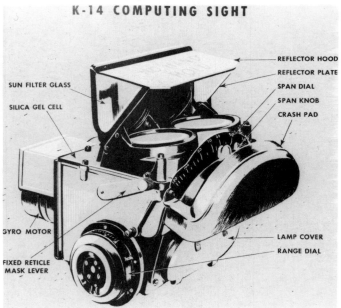

K-14 COMPUTING SIGHT

SUN FILTER GLASS
SILICA GEL CELL
GYRO MOTOR
FIXED RETICLE MASK LEVER
REFLECTOR HOOD
REFLECTOR PLATE
SPAN DIAL
SPAN KNOB
CRASH PAD
LAMP COVER
RANGE DIAL

Bombsights

D-8

The low-altitude sight installed as original equipment in B-26B and B-26C Marauders reaching 8th Air Force in 1943 was the D-8, a sight unsuitable for very low level attack or bombing at medium levels as required by VIII ASC. D-8s were therefore replaced by M-7s in the summer of 1943 and were never used operationally.

S-1

A Sperry designed sight suitable for use in radar-guided bombing, the S-1 was used by 492nd Group in medium level night operations during the winter of 1944–45.

M-7 AND M-9

The famous M-7 Norden sight remained the standard bombsight for 8th Air Force high altitude and medium level bombing throughout hostilities. A very advanced and, for its time, highly sophisticated instrument, the Norden computed information on bomb ballistics, ground speed, drift and trail, fed in by the bombardier. With a telescopic attachment on the sight the bombardier established and compensated for deflection to synchronise the instrument. The bombs then released automatically when the bomber reached the point computed by the sight. In B-17s and B-24s the Norden system was in two parts, the sight proper and a base unit holding electronics and incorporating the Automatic Flight Control Equipment (AFCE). The AFCE was linked to the A-5 or C-1 autopilot and enabled the bombardier to control lateral movement of the bomber through his adjustments of the sight. Early VIII BC bombers had the M-7 model installed; the refined M-9 was introduced in late 1943.

Right: **M-7 bombsight in position in a B-17. Lower part contained gyroscopic instrumentation to maintain horizontal stability and usually remained in the bomber. The detachable upper half contained a gyroscope for vertical stabilisation of the instrument. Telescope eyepiece is at top right, window for levelling devices on left and control knobs on extreme right.**

Below: **Lt Edward Weathers of 97th BG carrying the optical part of a Norden bombsight to his aircraft under armed guard, July 1942. Although such precautions to keep details of the bombsight secret were soon relaxed, photographs and technical details of the instrument were not released for many months. Unbeknown to the USAAF the Germans already had full information on the Norden.**

Radio and Electronic Equipment

USAAF radios and radars were originally identified by a number designation with the prefix SCR – Signal Corps Radio. In 1942 a joint service system for designating apparatus was introduced. A prefix, AN for Army-Navy, was followed by three classification letters and a number for each different design within that class, in the form AN/APN-3. In this series, the first letter related to where the equipment was installed with A the appropriate letter for aircraft and P for portable or pack equipment. The second letter denoted the type of equipment, for example: I – interphone, P – radar, R – radio and S – special including security projects. The third letter gave the purpose of the equipment in a range including: A – assemblies or auxiliary equipment, B –

bombing, C – communications, D – direction finding, G – fire control, N – navigational aid, Q – special, S – detecting, ranging or bearing indicating, T – transmitting, W – controlling and X – identification.

Equipment of earlier design retained their original Army designation and sometimes with the new Army-Navy prefix. Although much American radio and radar equipment was based on British developments, the US equipment was generally held to be more compact, easier to operate and of a much higher standard of reliability due to better manufacturing techniques and quality materials unobtainable in wartime Britain.

Aircraft Communications Sets

COMMAND RADIO SCR-274-N

Provided for short range voice communication with nearby aircraft or ground stations, the SCR-274 was employed in 8th Air Force for contact with airfield control towers within a maximum 30 miles (48 km). B-17, B-24 and B-26 bombers usually had three receivers each and two transmitters per set. Transmitters were any two of types BC-457-A, BC-458-A and BC-459-A with frequency ranges 4.0–5.3 Mcs, 5.3–7.0 Mcs and 7.0–9.1 Mcs, respectively. The receivers were BC-453-A, BC-454-A and BC-455-A covering frequency ranges 100–650 Kcs, 3.0–6.0 Mcs and 6.0–9.1 Mcs, respectively. Morse transmission facilities were available to the pilots of the B-17 and B-24. The SCR-274-N was fitted in some early fighters received by VIII FC, but this was replaced with SCR-522. In addition to local airfield and to bomber-to-bomber contact, SCR-274 was also used for *Darky* and balloon squeaker monitoring.

Right: **Sgt Robert Siavage, 306th BG tuning SCR-274N transmitters in a B-17F, January 1943. Receiver sets are on lower shelf.**

LIAISON RADIO SCR-287-A

The SCR-287-A provided for long-range, two-way voice and morse code communication between aircraft and a ground station but in VIII BC was normally utilised solely for coded signals by W/T (wireless telegraphy). The set was used to send mission progress signals or distress calls when at long range. It consisted of a BC-348 receiver, BC-375 transmitter and two tuning

units at the radio operator's position in B-17, B-24 and B-26 aircraft operating on frequency ranges of 200–500 Kcs and 1.5–18 Mcs. Up to five spare transmitter tuning units were carried at an adjacent position. Early B-17s and B-24s reaching the UK were fitted with both a fixed and trailing aerial for SCR-287, but the latter was removed at a modification centre.

VHF COMMAND RADIO SCR-522-A

A Very High Frequency set, based on the British TR1143 and interchangeable with it, the SCR-522-A was the principal operational set for verbal communication with both 8th Air Force bombers and fighters. Four push-button operated, crystal-controlled channels were provided with frequency ranges of 100–156 Mcs. The only radio set in fighters, it provided for communication with other pilots in the same group, fighter wing control, rescue and homing services. Where very long distances were involved, radio-relay aircraft were provided to re-transmit messages from a suitable point within range of the source aircraft. Relay was also necessary when low-level operations were conducted. VHF transmissions were attenuated when travelling near the surface of the earth as they were not reflected by ionised layers of the upper atmosphere. It was necessary for transmitter and receiver to be in line for signals to be received. Range of VHF was approximately 150 miles (240 km) for an aircraft at 20,000 feet (6100 m). In contrast to the other aircraft radios, VHF was not subject to any appreciable fading at height but it did suffer from interference if ignition and other electrical systems on an aircraft were not efficiently suppressed. During the second half of 1943 SCR-522 sets were installed in lead bombers, and later all bombers, to enable

SCR-522 VHF radio positioned behind the pilot's seat in a P-38H.

fighter-to-bomber contact to be made during missions. The set was eventually fitted to production B-17s and B-24s.

RC-36 AND AN/AIC-2 INTERPHONE

Providing intercommunication between crew members of multi-place aircraft and reception of command, liaison and radio compass signals at crew stations, the interphones used consisted of a dynamotor and amplifier with a jackbox at each crew station which had a throat microphone, headset and the necessary extension cords. In addition, the pilot and co-pilot on bombers each had a radio compass signal filter and switchbox, and a microphone push-button on the control wheel. RC-36 was common to B-17, B-24 and B-26 with type refinements and the RC-36B version was re-designated AN/AIC-2 in 1944.

Direction Finding, Beacon and Warning Sets

EMERGENCY DINGHY TRANSMITTER SCR-578

A portable unit with accessories for use in case of forced landings on water, the SCR-578 was contained in a yellow water-proof bag which had buoyant qualities. Originally it was carried on the flight deck of B-17s and B-24s, to be either released on the small tethered parachute provided just before impacting the water or thrown out by a crew member after ditching. In 8th Air Force the SCR-578 pack was soon repositioned in the dinghy escape hatch and made accessible from outside the aircraft. Operating on the international distress frequency of 500 Kcs, the set automatically transmitted a coded signal. The aerial wire was carried aloft by either a kite or balloon provided.

SCR-269-G RADIO COMPASS

For use in direction finding with radio beacons, the SCR-269-G in 8th Air Force service was employed in conjunction with the 'buncher' and 'splasher' systems for assembly and undercast conditions. The instrument, tuned and controlled by the radio operator, presented visual display indicators on the pilots' instrument panel and over the navigator's table, or aural reception in modulated code. Both a rotating loop (in a streamlined housing) and whip aerials were normally provided on B-17s and B-24s, although operational policy sometimes required one or the other removed. A few 356th Fighter Group P-47s ferried to the UK via the north Atlantic ferry route had SCR-269-G installed but this was removed on reaching the UK. In the summer of 1944 SCR-269-G was redesignated AN/ARN-7 on production.

RC-43 MARKER BEACON

A production fit on B-17s, B-24s and B-26s for receiving high frequency signals transmitted by ground navigational beacons, the RC-43 was not normally used by 8th Air Force. It was, however, adapted for use in both beam approach and radio bomb release systems devised in the UK.

SBA – STANDARD BEAM APPROACH

The RAF's Lorenz radio beam landing aid system, which became known as SBA, was adopted by 8th Air Force in August 1942 and installed in B-17s. A radio beam, transmitted along a runway approach track by a ground station, was received in an aircraft and presented visually and aurally to the pilot. As the aircraft descended along the beam a directional indicator, synchronised with the magnetic compass, indicated any deviation from the track. Two low-power marker beacons, one on the airfield boundary and the other about two miles out, gave the pilot indication of his distance from the head of the runway. These signals were also received both visually and aurally. The aerial replaced the unused RC-43 marker beacon aerial on the underside of the B-17 nose. To aid pilot training in SBA, a provisional Blind Approach Training flight with eight Oxfords was organised and started its first class on 1 March 1943. Because of supply difficulties, use of this British airborne equipment was later abandoned in favour of modifying the SCR-274 and RC-43 receivers to operate in the SBA frequency range.

SCS-51 INSTRUMENT LANDING SYSTEM

A US development similar to SBA, but giving an alternative glide approach angle, the SCS-51 initial programme announced on 20 June 1944 concerned installations at 16 airfields: Bovingdon, Harrington, Chelveston, Cluntoe, Seething, Deopham Green, Wendling, Framlingham, Bassingbourn, Thurleigh, Ridgewell, Deenethorpe, Thorpe Abbotts, Bury St Edmunds, Burtonwood and Warton. Later Cluntoe was eliminated and Attlebridge scheduled in place of Deopham Green. It was intended that eventually all bomber stations would have this system but by the end of 1944 only ten ground installations were in place and the original schedule was not met until the following March. The aircraft glide path receiver, for use with SCS-51, was RC-103 and, later AN/ARN-5A. From early December 1944 8th Air Force maintained a detachment on the Continent equipped with the ground element of SCS-51 for the purpose of marking the front line to ensure positive identification of friendly troop positions.

DARKY

A British system to aid aircraft over the UK requiring an approximate position check, coded *Darky*, could in an emergency be called repeatedly to home to a station. In 8th Air Force one transmitter in each bomber SCR-274-N command radio was modified to use the system within limited R/T range to prevent enemy monitoring on the *Darky* frequency of 6,400 Kcs. Modification was made on all US bombers arriving in the UK from February 1943.

AN/APN-1 RADAR ALTIMETER

Used in *Carpetbagger* and other special duties aircraft engaged in low altitude operations, AN/APN-1 gave an approximate indication of an aircraft's height above ground surface through measuring pulsed and returned radar signals.

SCR-729 AND AN/APN-2 *REBECCA*

Rebecca was a self-contained airborne interrogator which worked with beacons as an aid to navigation. A set comprised a transmitter/receiver, two reception antennas (left and right) and a quarter-wave transmission aerial. The transmitter part of the equipment was used to broadcast a trigger impulse which activated a transmission from the nearest suitable ground beacon. The beacon signal was picked up by the two reception aerials and the pilot given indication of his bearing relative to the beacon. Principal use by 8th Air Force was in *Carpetbagger* operations to locate dropping zones where an AN/PPN-2 *Eureka* was available. Near the end of hostilities *Rebecca* was installed in ASR B-17s and OA-10s for use in locating dinghy beacons.

SCR-729 was similar to British *Rebecca* Mk I. AN/APN-2 was the US version of *Rebecca* Mk II. The device, of which there were several variants, could also be employed as an IFF set.

AN/APS-13

A tail warning search radar for fighter and reconnaissance aircraft, AN/APS-13 gave visual and audible warning to a pilot of the approach of another aircraft from the rear within some four miles. Trial installations were made in autumn 1944 on reconnaissance aircraft. A fighter installation programme entailing antennas placed each side of the fin, commenced in March 1945 with the 355th, 4th and 361st Groups in that order. It was also installed in night flying B-17s and B-24s of 482nd Group. Incorporated on production P-51Ds from blocks 20-NT and 25-NA, the first of these were received in March 1945. AN/APS-13 was similar to the British tail warning device called *Monica* and in RAF use was known as *Monica* Mk VII.

Right: Left antenna of AN/AP-13 tail warning radar on the fin of a 357th FG P-51D.

BOOZER

The British radar warning installation ARI 5538 *Boozer*, giving bomber crews notice of detection by enemy radar transmissions was installed experimentally in a B-17F during the summer of 1943. This was followed by an operational trials installation in B-17G 42-31032 of 422nd Bomb Squadron which crash-landed on 13 May 1944, only three days after completion of the installation.

AN/APN-19 *ROSEBUD*

An airborne 'S' band radar beacon for fighters, *Rosebud* worked in conjunction with the Microwave Early Warning (MEW) ground control radar. *Rosebud* transmissions could be identified on MEW reception, allowing positive identification of friendly formations over long range and increasing the ability of MEW control to vector aircraft towards enemy formations. First tested at Wattisham in December 1944, it was subsequently allotted to six fighter groups, but installation was delayed through unavailability of beacons.

SCR-535, SCR-595 AND SCR-695

IFF – Identification of Friend or Foe consisted of a receiver/transmitter, dynamotor-coder and antenna, triggered by friendly investigative radars, and automatically pulsed a signal which identified the aircraft as friendly. IFF was switched on while flying over the UK and for specified distances departing and approaching the UK coast. British sets were made available to 8th Air Force and later a copy of a British IFF, produced as SCR-535 USAAF Mk II, was fitted on production B-17F, B-24D and B-26H bombers. From April 1943 this was being replaced at UK modification centres with British IFF Mk III or IIIG, until the equivalents from US production, SCR-595 and SCR-695, were available. IFF was not normally fitted in 8th Air Force fighters.

Navigational, Search and Bombing Radars

GEE

A British navigational aid, *Gee* enabled an aircraft to fix its position by measuring the relative time required for pulses of radio energy to travel from three ground stations to the aircraft. The ground stations were identified as Type 7000 and comprised a master and two slave stations with about 100 miles between master and slaves. Transmissions from the ground stations were displayed as blips relative to grid lines on an indicator set (radar scope). These gave *Gee* co-ordinates and by reference to data charts the navigator could fix the aircraft's position. Accuracy decreased with range but a competent navigator could usually place the aircraft within five miles of true position at 250 miles (400 km). Maximum *Gee* range was about 350 miles (560 km), but depended on atmospheric conditions.

In 8th Air Force it was first used in B-24Ds of 93rd Group assigned to Moling operations in the winter of 1942–43. Thereafter it was adopted as a general navigation aid for all VIII BC bombers. Commencing April 1943, 12 aircraft in each group were to receive *Gee* in the initial programme, the 92nd, 305th and 306th having been equipped by early June. By the end of the year 515 B-17s and B-24s had *Gee*, about half the total on hand. All 8th Air Force bombers were not equipped until the following spring. The *Gee* Mk II set used was identified as ARI 5083, comprising receiver R1355 and the indicator as Type 62. VIII BC navigators mostly used the Eastern *Gee* Chain which had stations at Daventry (7111), Stenigot (7122), Gibbet Hill (7123) and Clee Hill (7124).

Right: *Loran* box fixed over the navigator's desk in the nose of a B-17

SCR-622 AND AN/APN-4 *LORAN*

This Long-Range navigational system developed by the NDRC was similar to *Gee*, but could be used over a much greater distance permitting fixes of within five to ten miles accuracy at over 1,000 miles range. Originally known as SCR-622, *Loran* was expected to be available for installation in 8th Air Force Mosquitoes early in 1944. Due to delays in supply of equipment, it was not until the autumn that the first Mosquito sorties for *Loran* calibration purposes (preparation of charts) commenced, and then not on a significant scale until the new year.

AN/APN-3 *SHORAN*

A very accurate Short-Range navigational system for similar employment to *Oboe* in blind bombing, *Shoran* had a maximum range of 280 miles (400 km) at 30,000 feet (9140 m). The 8th Air Force initiated a programme of installation and trial for *Shoran* on 25 March 1945, but little progress was made during the weeks before VE-Day. During April the first two installations were carried out at Alconbury on B-17s of 305th Group.

OBOE

A British blind bombing system, *Oboe* contrasted to *Gee* in that an aircraft's position was established by two Type 9000 ground stations measuring distance by re-radiation of signals directed at an aircraft. Range was limited to 280 miles (450 km) at 28,000 feet (8530 m), although by using repeater aircraft it could be extended. After a brief operational period in 482nd Group B-17Fs *Oboe* Mk I equipment (ARI 5148) was transferred to the 9th Air Force for use in B-26s. A version of *Oboe* Mk II, using a higher frequency, was given operational trials under the code names *Album Leaf* and *Aspen* which covered its use with components of a US Navy sea search radar (ASG-3). The *Oboe* ground stations were known as Type 9000 and those for the Mk I Eastern chain were at Swingate, Trimingham, Hawkeshill Down (Oldstairs) and Winterton.

H2S

An airborne ground-scanning 'S' band (10 cm) radar, H2S had a revolving antenna beneath the aircraft feeding signals to the indicator unit which presented images of ground terrain. It was used operationally in 482nd Group B-17Fs and B-24s in the autumn and winter of 1943–44 and was popularly known as *Stinkey* in 8th Air Force. British designation of installation was ARI 5153.

H2X – AN/APS-15

An airborne ground-scanning 'X' band (3 cm) radar, H2X was a US development of H2S. Popularly known as *Mickey* in 8th Air Force, it was the major blind bombing and navigational device used in 8th Air Force bombers during the final 18 months of hostilities. A refined model, APS-15A, was introduced in the autumn of 1944.

Right: *Mickey* scope. AN/APS-15 receiver, display and control unit in the radio room of a 401st BG B-17. Range displayed could be switched to four positions, 90, 50, 5 and 2 miles.

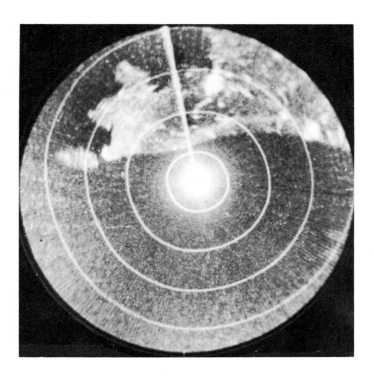

Left: **H2X radar scope photo (with range circles) of Dutch coast. Built-up areas show white.** (V. Maslen)

Below: **B-17G, 42-39880, MI:O, was the first B-17 in 8th Air Force to have an H2X scanner in the ball turret well positioned. The conversion was made at Alconbury and the radome was not retractable.**

AN/APQ-7 *EAGLE*

An airborne ground-scanning 'X' band radar, *Eagle* was housed in a 16 feet (4.8 m) wide airfoil-shaped section under the forward fuselage of B-17s and B-24s, the search beam being formed in the forward path of the aircraft. The antenna was fixed, the side to side sweep through 60 degrees being obtained electronically. While of little use for navigation, it gave better target delineation than H2X. Synchronisation with the optical bombsight was part of the system for employing this radar. A B-17 with *Eagle* was received by 482nd Group in the autumn of 1944 but considerable difficulty was experienced in both operating and maintaining APQ-7. It was only in the last few weeks of the war that operational trials were conducted.

NOSMO

Apparatus providing a high degree of co-ordination between Norden bombsight and H2X was dubbed *Nosmo*. The H2X circuits and bombsight telescope could be synchronised with the bombsight controls, allowing both radar and visual information to be fed into the bombsight computations and giving more completely co-ordinated bombing results. AN/APA-46 *Nosmo* Modification I, a production version of the original *Nosmo* produced in the UK, was installed experimentally in a 482nd Group B-17 in January 1945. Several aircraft were fitted with *Nosmo* in March and April for operational trials.

GEE-H

A British developed beam radar for navigation or blind bombing, *Gee-H* (or G-H) was in effect *Oboe* in reverse with an airborne transmitter interrogating two ground beacons to obtain a fix. *Gee-H* had good accuracy and was used by 1st and 2nd Divisions during 1944; its range was around 300 miles (480 km) at 20,000 feet (6100 m), but it was susceptible to jamming. Both Mk I (ARI 5525) and Mk II (ARI 5597) versions were used, the latter having extended frequency range.

MICRO-H

Beam radar combined with H2X used as *Micro-H* bombing system was exclusive to 3rd Division from December 1944. A *Micro-H* Mk II (AN/APA-40) production version allotted in January 1945 to 482nd Group for service testing was installed in B-17G 42-97702 MI:D and given operational trials in March 1945.

SCR-717 AND AN/APS-2 & 3

Sea-search 'S' band radar, used by the US Navy as ASG-3, was adapted by the USAAF for special purposes as SCR-717 or AN/APS-2. The APS-3 was an 'X' band sea-search radar fitted to OA-10s for locating airborne lifeboats and aircraft dinghies equipped with *Corner*, an umbrella device that reflected radar emissions.

Radio Countermeasures Sets

APT-2 *CARPET I* & APQ-9 *CARPET III*

A jamming transmitter for use against *Würzburg* ground radars, *Carpet I* radiated noise over the 430–700 Mcs band and was first used operationally by 96th and 388th Group B-17s in October 1943. To fully mask a bomber formation it was necessary to have a number of aircraft with *Carpet* barrage to saturate the whole *Würzburg* frequency range. A programme of making 40–50 installations in each of two groups of each combat wing was delayed through the slow supply of APT-2 sets. For selective 'spot' jamming in a selected band with APT-2, an APR-1 receiver set was used to identify and place *Würzburg* signals. Power output of APT-2 was between five and ten watts.

APQ-9 *Carpet III* was an improved jammer, with a power output of between 15 and 80 watts, for use against *Würzburg* and gun laying radars. It could be used as a barrage jammer or, in conjunction with an AN/APR-4 receiver, as a spot jammer. *Carpet III* spot jamming installations were made in 2nd Division aircraft during the summer of 1944, the usual B-24 installation comprising one AN/APR-4 search receiver and three AN/APQ-9 transmitters. Each set had a distinctive fish-hook like aerial which, on the B-24, was enclosed in a clear plastic dome to protect it from damage. AN/APR-4 had a semi-automatic sweep through the 300–1000 Mcs band, monitored by an operator. APQ-9 was also used for barrage jamming, with either a single or double installation in an aircraft.

Left: **B-24 *Carpet* spot-jammer fish hook aerials in standard position aft of nose-wheel door. Aircraft is 392nd BG's *The Chiefton*, 42-51169.**

Above: **Two AN/APT-2s** (at bottom) **and one AN/APQ-9 spot jammer sets positioned aft of the pilot in a B-24** (looking to the rear).

AN/APQ-2 *RUG*

A similar noise modulated jammer to *Carpet* covering the 200–500 Mcs frequency band with an output of 20 watts. Only used experimentally in 8th Air Force.

RC-183 AND AN/APT-3 *MANDREL*

US development of a British device designed to jam early warning radars of the *Freya*, *Mammut* and *Wassermann* types in the 85–135 Mcs band, *Mandrel* consisted of a transmitter with modulator and power source built into a single unit and providing a two watt power output. Identified as RC-183 when first received in December 1943, initial plans required 14 installations to be made in 96th Group B-17s. Aircraft fitted were transferred to the 8th Air Force's provisional RCM unit at Oulton. The transmitter produced a noise jamming effect and up to ten sets were carried in each RCM aircraft employed in *Mandrel* screening.

AN/APT-1 *DINA*

A development of *Mandrel* with a greater frequency range, *Dina* operated against early warning radars working in the 95–210 Mcs band, being first used by the RCM squadron in the autumn of 1944 to replace *Mandrel* sets.

AN/ARQ-8 *DINAMITE*

A special embellishment of *Dina* as *Dinamite* was introduced in RCM squadron aircraft at the end of 1944.

AN/ART-7 *JACKAL*

A device for jamming the VHF radio transmissions of enemy armoured fighting vehicles operating in the 27.2–33.4 Mcs band, *Jackal* was a modification of a standard VHF SCR-522 radio and was often referred to as an SCR-522 jammer.

JOSTLE

A powerful British device for jamming radio transmissions over a wide range of frequencies. *Jostle* was included in a formidable array of jamming equipment installed in a few B-24s prepared during the autumn of 1944 for the *Big Ben* project. The purpose was V2 rocket detection under the erroneous assumption that the latter were radio controlled. *Big Ben* and associated aircraft became the RAF's prerogative in October 1944. In December that year two 36th Bomb Squadron B-24Js, 42-51311 and 42-51315, had *Jostle* Mk V installed as a high power alternative to *Jackal* for use against AFV communications. *Jostle* was a cylindrical unit, weighing 600 lb (272 kg) and 51 inches (1.29 m) long, carried in the bomb-bay of a B-24.

PERFECTOS

A British device designed to interrogate enemy aircraft VHF communications pulse and provide a bearing for interception. Installed in a 56th Group 2-seat P-47D and used operationally during March and April 1945. *Curtain*, a basically similar installation but having a 100 mile (160 km) range as against 50 miles (80 km) with *Perfectos*, was given experimental trials in a 353rd Group two-seat P-51B.

Crew Attire and Equipment

Flight Clothing

The rigours of high altitude flight in Fortresses and Liberators were considerable. For periods of up to ten hours aircrew could be subjected to continuous loud noise, vibration, glare, cramped and bitterly cold quarters, heavy flying clothing and equipment as well as adherence to oxygen; all contributed to extreme fatigue even without the stress of combat. When involved in intensive periods of operations, most bomber men did little else but eat and sleep between missions.

Minus temperatures of between 30 and 50 degrees F (−34 to −46°C) were quite normal over northern Europe at 25,000 feet,

the optimum altitude for 8th Air Force heavy bombers. Frostbite, a constant hazard, made the provision of suitable crew flight clothing essential. The USAAF had developed electrically heated flying suits in the early 1940s, available for gunner use during the winter of 1942–43, only to find them completely unreliable when used operationally. The F-1, 24-volt one-piece under-suit in light blue made by General Electric, supplied to B-17 and B-24 crews had an inherent weakness. Being wired in series, any element wire fractured would cause electrical failure throughout the whole with serious consequences for the wearer if flying in sub-zero temperatures. The frequency of failure was so great that most men chose either not to use them or, if they

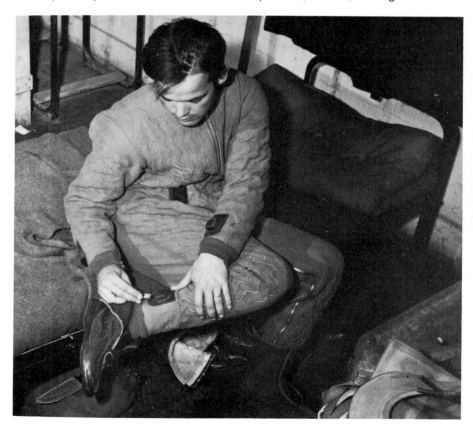

Above: **S/Sgt William W. Fleming, 303rd BG wearing an F-1 electric suit and D-1 electric boots. July 1943.**

Right: **Lt James Smith, 379th BG pilot in Shearling suit (A-5 and B-6), B-5 helmet and harness for the chest pack parachute held in his left hand with infantry type steel helmet. January 1944.**

did, to wear heavy clothing over the electric suit. Electrically heated accessories to be worn with the F-1 suit were D-1 boots and E-1 gloves; both were in short supply and British types were modified to use with the F-1 suit. During the first winter of operations 8th Air Force devised electrically heated muffs for warming hands and feet if gloves or boots failed, and electric blankets were acquired to protect wounded crewmen.

In lieu of effective and reliable electrically heated garments, bomber crews used a variety of protective clothing, dependent on an individual's choice and his crew station, including A-5 trousers and B-6 sheepskin jacket two-part flying suit. Cockpit heating was provided in both the B-17 and B-24 so the pilot's requirement was different from that of gunners exposed to the icy blast from open hatches.

In the spring of 1943 a typical combat dress for a B-17 or B-24 gunner consisted of heavy woollen underwear, two pairs of lined wool socks, a modified F-1 electric suit, RAF Taylor electric gloves and socks, standard A-6 boots and A-4 coveralls (summer flying suit) with a B-5 shearling helmet. Additionally some men wore a leather A-2 jacket over the coveralls. If an electric suit was not worn the standard protective garb was the heavy fleece-lined B-6 jacket and A-5 trousers. Also known as the shearling suit, these thickpile sheepskin garments with brown leather-paint finish, were also taken on missions for use if electric suits failed. Alternative helmets were the chamois-lined A-7 and unlined gabardine A-9 or the RAF type 'C'. Also available was a flameproof fabric protective hood to lessen the risk of face and neck frostbite. Later in 1943 a new lined helmet, the A-11, replaced most of the earlier types.

New flight garments available to bomber crews in the following winter to replace the combersome sheepskins were alpaca and wool intermediate B-10 jacket and A-9 trousers, followed soon after by the similar but improved B-15 jacket and A-11 trousers. Heavier garments in this material were the B-11 and

Top: **Members of Capt Harlod Beasley's crew, 91st BG, wearing assorted flight garb. Man nearest camera has RAF boots and C-type helmet, USAAF leather A-2 jacket and AN6530 goggles. May 1943.**

Above: **By the spring of 1944 carrying bags were provided so that bomber crews could put on and remove cumbersome protective flight clothing at their aircraft. Here a 384th BG gunner, returned from Berlin in B-17 42-31740, removes modified F-1 electric suit. (Note machine guns on ground ready to convey to armament store for cleaning).**

1/Lt Ray Shewfelt, a 2nd Scouting Force pilot wearing the M1944 goggles with a single plastic lens. Secured by press studs, the lens could be easily changed if it became scratched or damaged. The very similar B-8 goggles had more pronounced rubber framing. These two models superseded most other types during the final months of hostilities. Shewfelt is also wearing a B-15 jacket with fur collar and a C-type helmet.   (Shewfelt)

A-10. Early in 1944 a new electric two-piece suit in olive drab, the F-3, was received for use under or without an intermediate suit. It had two parallel circuits in the jacket and three in the trousers, so that if one circuit failed partial heating would be maintained. A further improvement was mask-type elements, similar to that in RAF heated suits. Enhanced reliability led to all crew members using electric suits during the final winter of the war, over-garments continuing to be an individual's choice. The A-11 and B-15 intermediate flying suit was standard issue during the last year of 8th Air Force operations, although in March 1945 a small number of a new one-piece version of this suit were received for operational testing.

Fighter pilots, with the exception of those in P-38s, had better cockpit heating and did not normally require heavy clothing or electric suits. A-4 coveralls with an A-2 leather jacket were popular and, in the last year of the war, the A-11/B-15 intermediate flying suit. Helmets were a matter of choice although the A-11 was standard issue from 1943. RAF helmets, gloves and boots were popular with fighter pilots before more efficient American items were available. It was learned that the A-6 boot had a tendency to jerk off the foot when a parachute canopy opened, and for this reason many pilots preferred to use the long-legged and more secure RAF boots. RAF silk under-gloves were another item available to US airmen.

The P-38 had poor cockpit heating and during the winter of 1943–44 pilots were forced to wear shearling garments to keep warm. In the spring some electric suits became available for their use, but heavy clothing continued to be worn for fear of electrical failure. F-5 and Spitfire pilots also relied on heavy sheepskin clothing on high altitude reconnaissance flights to avoid the risk of dependence on electric suits.

Oxygen Equipment

Of crucial importance to successful operations in the sub-stratosphere was an adequate supply of oxygen. The system in the B-17E and early B-24D was continuous flow, fitted with A-8A regulators which crew members adjusted to control the amount of oxygen reaching their face masks. The mask used was the moulded rubber A-8, with a distinctive bladder and constructed to allow some air to be drawn and mixed with the oxygen. VIII BC had considerable trouble with this mask in preventing breath moisture freezing and obstructing. The problem became so acute that extra masks were always carried on missions. From the beginning of 1943 B-17Fs and B-24Ds had four independent low-pressure systems to reduce the possibility of complete oxygen supply failure in combat. This was a continuous flow system and was fitted with an improved regulator, the A-9, but still made use of the troublesome A-8 mask.

By the spring of 1943 B-17s and B-24s were being fitted with the new A-12 demand-type regulator at each crew station. Developed from a German type by Dr R. Lovelace and the Aero

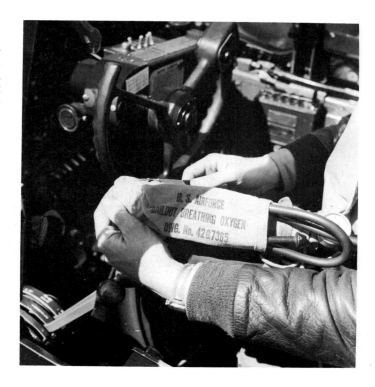

Right: A portable oxygen unit was available for photographic reconnaissance pilots who might have to bale out at very high altitude. The unit was strapped to a leg and a pilot could draw oxygen through a mouth tube during his descent.

Medical Laboratory, Wright Field, it was fully automatic and increased the oxygen content of the air supply as an aircraft gained altitude, maintaining ground level value. It also only functioned when a man was inhaling and automatically adjusted to individual speeds of breathing. The A-9 and A-10 masks were issued for use with the new regulators, but initially they had freezing problems and needed to be modified. A microphone could be fitted in the nose section. The A-12 demand regulator was fitted retrospectively in earlier B-17s and B-24s during the summer of 1943. To minimise the effect of battle damage both B-17 and B-24 had 18 lightweight G-1 oxygen storage bottles, each holding approximately five hours supply for one man. A single independent F-1 bottle was fitted in the ball turret. Walk-around bottles were carried in both heavy bombers for use when crew members had to move from their usual stations. The A-4 bottle had sufficient oxygen for a maximum 15 minutes but VIII BC found this insufficient and bottles giving an hour's supply were requested from the US in the summer of 1943. B-26 crews did not normally require oxygen and a simple portable supply system was installed in these aircraft.

P-38s, P-47s and P-51s were all fitted with the demand-type system and the A-12 regulator. During 1944 a refined A-14 regulator was introduced for fighter aircraft but initially proved troublesome.

A-9 and A-10 masks, and later A-12 and A-14 types, could all be used with the bomber and fighter demand systems. In operation they were basically the same: an expiratory flapper valve closed when the user inhaled, permitting oxygen to be drawn into the mask, and opening when the user exhaled, allowing discharge into the atmosphere.

All oxygen was obtained from British sources and supplied in standard steel cylinders. These were loaded onto special carts and towed out to dispersals to replenish aircraft oxygen storage bottles.

Safety and Life Saving Equipment

PARACHUTES

VIII BC groups were equipped with five different types of parachute during the early days of operations. These were seat-pack types, S-1 and S-2, back-pack types B-7 and P3-E-24 and a few US chest packs AN 6513-1, a new design. A study carried out in January 1943 showed that most B-17 and B-24 pilots and co-pilots wore seat type parachutes; bombardiers, navigators, waist and radio gunners used seat and back types. Very few turret gunners found they could wear a parachute while at their stations. B-17 tail gunners used back types. Because of the fatigue caused by the additional weight and interference with movement, half the men who could wear parachutes did not.

Below: **Lt Vernon Burroughs, 355th FG, with S-type seat parachute and dinghy back pack. He is wearing RAF Mk VII goggles and a G-1 jacket.**

Below left: **Capt Ben Klose, 93rd BG bombardier wearing a B-7 back pack, April 1943.**

The parachutes were therefore placed at the nearest handy spot, crew members trusting that they would have enough time to retrieve them and get into the harness, although pilots and ball turret gunners took a very fatalistic view of their chances if forced to bale out. With the exception of the chest type, all these parachutes had attached harness requiring three or four separate actions to attach and detach, without any provision for attaching individual life-saving dinghies.

Pilots wearing seat packs found that they could not get out of their seats without first unbuckling leg straps. Even the quick-attachment AN 6513-1 chest pack parachute was found far from satisfactory, chiefly because its fixings were not sufficiently strong. To improve the situation, in June 1943 the 8th Air Force Central Medical Establishment recommended that all bomber crews wear the RAF quick-release harness and Observer chest-pack parachute until better types were forthcoming from the USA. The advantages were that the harness could be worn at all times and in one operation could be completely and quickly removed; both parachute and dinghy packs were quickly attached to it by simple snap hooks. Some back-pack parachutes were retained for special purposes and the US chest pack, AN 6513-1, continued to be used until sufficient Observer packs were available. Also the harness for the AN-6513-1 was modified for quick attachment and many canopies from back and seat parachutes were repacked in the British chest packs.

RAF Observer chest packs were supplied to all 8th Air Force bomber groups until a new US chest pack with nylon canopies was received in 1944. Despite successful projects to modify ball turrets to enable gunners to wear a back-pack, no similar move was made in production and escape from this crew station remained the most precarious.

In fighter aircraft back or seat type parachutes were worn. On

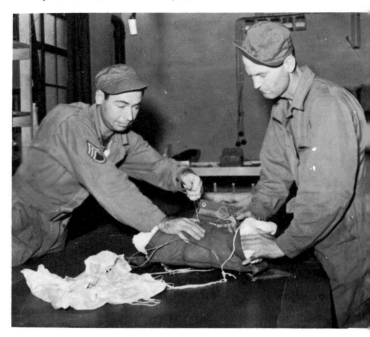

Parachutes were inspected after every mission and repacked if necessary. Pfc Otis Starnes and S/Sgt Lester Sade working on a chest pack at Great Ashfield, September 1943.

P-47s an S type seat-pack parachute was worn with a C type dinghy back-pack. With the P-51 the dinghy pack was the seat cushion and a B-8 back-pack parachute was worn.

LIFE PRESERVERS
Commonly known as a Mae West, an RAF originated term likening the wearer of an inflated life preserver to a well-endowed Hollywood actress. Made from rubber and covered in bright yellow canvas, the B-3 or B-4 Mae West was worn over all flight clothing. Two small CO_2 cylinders were attached for inflation and a mouth tube was provided for the same purpose. Some were supplied from British sources.

INFLATABLE LIFERAFTS AND DINGHIES
Liferafts carried in B-17s and B-24s, types A-2, A-3, B-3 or B-4, were multi-place provided with drinking water, chocolate rations, flashlight, sea anchor, mast and sail, pyrotechnic signals, first aid kit and inflation equipment. Release was from either inside or outside the aircraft but with B-17s in particular, much trouble was experienced in the first year of operations with rafts being released in flight due to malfunction of the securing mechanism.

The British one-man dinghy, identified as a K type dinghy in a C type pack, was provided for all VIII FC fighters. This was either worn as a back-pack by the pilot (in P-47s) or as a seat-pack (in P-51s). It was attached to the pilot's harness by two snap rings. The pack contained a telescopic mast, sail, CO_2 and bellows inflators, collapsible canvas bucket for baling, a drogue sea anchor, leak plugs, six distress flares, sea marker dye cake and paddles. Because of the lack of suitable US-made dinghies, 8th Air Force made the C pack dinghy pack available for bomber crewmen. A US-made model, the similar C-6, became available early in 1945. However, the C type pack continued in common use until the end of hostilities.

BATTLE ARMOUR
Aware that a large proportion of wounds sustained by bomber crewmen were made by low-velocity missiles, in the autumn of 1942 Brig Gen Malcolm Grow, 8th Air Force Chief Surgeon, became interested in the provision of lightweight body armour. Using information from British experiments, which showed that magnesium steel plates of 20 gauge would stop a .303 bullet when the muzzle velocity was reduced to 1300 feet (396 m) per second, the Wilkinson Sword Company were asked to make one bullet proof vest. The plates were 1¾ inches (44 mm) wide, of varying length and arranged with a ⅜-inch (9.5 mm) overlap. This body armour, which came to be known as a 'flak vest' or 'flak suit', weighed 20 lb (9 kg). The plates were held in heavy canvas and the whole, designed to be worn over the parachute harness, was quickly removed by a pull cord. Production of an experimental batch was authorised on 15 October 1942 and the first operational use occurred on 12 December when worn by two crews of 322nd Bomb Squadron, 91st Group. No tangible evidence of their value was acquired on this mission but on 20 December at least one crew member would have been seriously

wounded if he had not been wearing a flak suit. Thereafter combat crews showed much more interest. An investigation carried out early in 1943 established that of combat wound causes 40 per cent were flak shrapnel, 40 per cent 20 mm shrapnel, 10 per cent machine gun bullets and 10 per cent fragments of aircraft structure blasted by shell hits. Later the value of body armour was established by the fact that two-thirds of men hit by missiles or fragments while wearing flak jackets escaped injury, and only 8.2 per cent of the remainder were killed.

Wilkinson's production was supplemented by US made flak suits late in 1943. Four models were available: M-1, a vest with armoured front and back panels, similar to the original Wilkinson vest, weighing 18 lb 2 oz (8.7 kg); the M-2 vest weighing 9 lb (4 kg), armoured in the front only and intended for use by men in armoured seats; M-3 weighing 4¾ lb (2.1 kg), a tapered apron for men in a sitting position where the lower part of the body required protection and the M-4 weighing 7½ lb (3.4 kg), protecting the full frontal body area, usually worn by standing gunners. The M-5 covered legs and groin and was produced for pilots.

At the same time that body armour was introduced, the ordinary steel helmet was used for head protection at crew stations except top turret, radio, ball and tail gunner positions where it was too bulky. The helmet was modified for use with earphones, the approved method being to make up each individually to suit its wearer. A ⅝-inch (15 mm) hole was punched through each side to be adjacent to the wearer's ears and canvas pockets affixed to hold earphones. A winter flying helmet was worn inside the steel helmet. Thus modified, the helmet was known as the M-1. Many bomb groups, using their own ingenuity and machine shop equipment, modified steel helmets in a variety of ways to suit the same purpose. While these were most satisfactory in affording protection, the infantry steel helmet was still cumbersome, so special protective helmets were designed in the USA. These became available during the summer of 1944 as the M-3 and M-4. Made from magnesium steel, the M-3 was shaped like a conventional helmet and had ear flaps, while the exterior of the M-4 was covered with leather and the interior lined with chamois. Body armour and helmets were not usually worn until penetration of enemy territory or on the run-up to the target area.

B-26 crewman of 32nd
emonstrating
nson battle armour
dard vest and attached
n) with unmodified
try steel helmets.

e: Lt Lawrence Johnson
8th BG wearing an M-3
elmet. February 1945.

: Maj Pierce McKennon,
G, wearing a Berger
it over overalls.
collared jacket is a B-15,
lar with fighter
s.   (D. Morris)

G-SUITS

Pre-war work had been carried out in the US to perfect some form of pressure suit that would prevent pilot 'blackout' in aircraft performing sharp manoeuvres at speed. The benefit in fighter combat was clear, for prevention of blackout would allow a pilot to make tighter turns. The 8th Air Force became interested in the American Berger anti-G suits in September 1943 and in early 1944 acquired sufficient to conduct tests. Comparative trials were run with the RAF water pressure anti-G device, the Frank suit. The results showed both equally effective, and as 9th Air Force had a priority on the Berger suit, VIII FC decided for the time being to use the Frank suit as this was more readily available. During April 1944 the 4th Group gave the suit an extended trial but pilots took a dislike to it because of bulk, weight, heat and discomfort, to say nothing of the difficulties if it sprang a leak. Faced with this disapproval, VIII FC decided to abandon the Frank and wait for the Berger. By 3 June sufficient Berger G-3 suits had been obtained from 9th Air Force to equip the 339th Group, who quickly appreciated the benefits and wore the suits on every mission. A larger supply of G-3s was not available until October, but all groups were equipped by November.

Ground Support Equipment

Aircraft Servicing and Other Vehicles

Top: **Flying Control runway-head trailer in the standard black and white checkerboard finish. Mostly built on individual stations, they varied considerably in size and appointments. The 385th BG example had a windsock and plexiglas nosepiece from B-17 over controller's position. Parked next to the trailer is the Chance mobile floodlight beacon. February 1945.**

Above: **Chevrolet truck was utilised by 78th FG for a checkered runway control vehicle. It had a B-26 nosepiece as an observation dome.**

Right: **Standard US bomb trailer carrying 4 x 1000 lb GPs at Andrewsfield, September 1943. Maximum load was 3 tons. Tricycle arrangement featured dual front wheels.**

Top and above right: **'Gas wagon' servicing B-17s of 92nd BG (l.) and 384th BG (r.). The fuel servicing tankers had a capacity of 4000 US gallons (a B-17 or B-24 held 2500). The 6 x 7½-ton F-1 tractor units were built by Biederman, Federal and Reo companies.**

Right: **Before US-made refuelling vehicles were available in the UK, 8th AF used RAF bowsers. Largest was the AEC which had 2500 Imperial gallon capacity. This example is seen refuelling *Yankee Doodle* at Grafton Underwood after the first 8AF mission heavy bomber mission. August 1942.**

Top: **Smaller bowser had a capacity of 1000 Imperial gallons. This one is being used to replenish a 31st FG Spitfire V at Westhamptnett. August 1942.**

Above: **Cletracs were to be found at all 8th AF bases serving as tractors to move aircraft and heavy trailers. They were particularly useful for extracting vehicles that had become bogged down with mud. Track had rubber-faced cleats. This example photographed in August 1944 at Hethel.**

Left: **Best known of all US military vehicles, the ¼-ton 4 x 4 Jeep served a variety of purposes and was frequently overloaded. This one was transport for 4th FG pilots, February 1943. Built by Willys (as model MB) and Ford (as model GPW) there was little visible difference between makes and parts were interchangeable. Rated at 54 bhp, the Jeep was 132 inches long and had an 80 inch wheelbase.**

Above: **A Command Car had seating for six but frequently carried pilots for a whole fighter squadron — to say nothing of their equipment — from briefing to aircraft. Passengers are men of (left) 78th FG, Duxford and (right) 353rd FG Metfield, October 1943. Built by Dodge it had a 92 bhp engine and was 175 inches long with a wheelbase of 98 inches. Also produced in a truck body version as a Weapons Carrier.**

Right: **Dodge ambulance at Molesworth. These 4-wheel drive vehicles had replaced most British-made ambulances by 1944. Based on the Command Car chassis it was 194½ inches long.**

Below: **Workhorse of the US Army, many hundreds of GMC 6 x 6 2½-ton trucks were used by 8th Air Force units. These vehicles were employed for general haulage including aircrew transportation on airfields. The 852nd Engineering Battalion (Av) mounted water-cooled .50 guns when parading its '6 x 6s' on completion of construction of Harrington airfield in November 1943. Produced in long (270 in x 164 in) and short (244 in x 145 in) wheelbases and different cab configurations, power was provided by a 91.5 bhp GM engine. Studebaker also made 6 x 6s which could be identified by lack of hood louvres.**

Left: GMC 6 x 6 with crane fixture used by 33rd Service Group at Boxted, December 1944. GMC identification was model CCKW 353 (long) and CCKW 352 (short).

Below left: A 4—5 ton, 4 x 4, Autocar Model U 7144T tractor unit with 10 ton gross Fruehauf semitrailer. The tractor was powered by a 112 bhp Hercules engine. The trailer was fitted out with a 110 volt generator for power tools, storage bins, plus heating and ventilation. This particular outfit was operated as a mobile repair unit by Little Staughton, September 1943.

Right: Many RAF vehicles were used, especially during 1942 and 1943 before adequate numbers of US made vehicles trucks were available. A British-built 3-ton Dodge lorry was used as a round-the-base bus at Molesworth. Pfc Monroe Klein waves it down, April 1943.

Below: A line-up of British-made fire-fighting and ambulance vehicles with crews awaiting the return of a mission to Great Ashfield, summer 1943. The fire fighting tenders are Fordson WOT1, 3-ton 6 x 4, with combined 400 Imperial gallon water and saponine tanks. Ambulances are Austin K2/Y 3-ton 4 x 2s. (via John Archer)

PART 3
INSTALLATIONS

Airfields and Air Depots

The work involved in construction of an airfield took several months and the ultimate size of the force to be based in the UK, together with regular up-dates on the expected flow of units, was essential information to the British agencies primarily responsible for provision of installations for US forces. Inevitably, the rate of aircraft production, training of crews, diversions to other theatres and altered strategy brought reassessments and changes in both deployment and flow rates. Thus the USAAF in the UK as projected in January 1942 was much different from the eventual strength and composition of the 8th Air Force at full strength in June 1944.

Prior to America entering hostilities plans were in the making for US forces to take over the defence of Northern Ireland from the British and for US fighters to provide air defence of ports and shipping lanes in that and the Clyde areas. In January 1942 the British Air Ministry allocated Eglinton and St Angelo in Northern Ireland for housing two day and one night USAAF fighter squadrons and Ayr for the same number and types of unit in Scotland. The Ayr units, it was intended, would also make use of Turnberry, West Freugh and Machrihanish as required. This deployment was for the protection of ports and shipping.

A month later the Air Ministry listed airfields for an Air Support Command the US Army proposed to establish in Northern Ireland, composed of one medium and one light bomb group, one transport group, two pursuit (fighter) groups (additional to those already planned) and four observation squadrons (tactical reconnaissance). Ballyhalbert, Kirkistown, Eglinton, St Angelo, Greencastle and Maydown were to house the fighters, Long Kesh and Bishop's Court the light bombers, Nutts Corner and Cluntoe the mediums, Toome and Langford Lodge transports, while observation squadrons would go to Maghaberry (2), Long Kesh and Toome. Both plans, however, were soon passed over in favour of others that were deemed better to meet the deployment of the forces scheduled.

What came to be accepted as the first reliable plan for the USAAF deployment in the UK was received by General Eaker on 24 March 1942 and subsequently became the basis for airfield and support installation requirements. Totalling 115 groups to be in place by the end of June 1944, it was made up of 45 heavy, 10 medium, 12 light and five dive bomber groups, 26 fighter groups, seven observation (tactical reconnaissance groups), eight troop carrier (transport) groups and seven light and one heavy photographic reconnaissance squadrons. Although the flow rate forecast for arrival of units in the UK would be regularly revised in following months, the eventual totals of types of unit were little changed until late spring 1943. There was, however, some fluctuation in the number of light and dive bomber groups

forecast due to uncertainty about the development and value of the latter class of aircraft. However, the projected combined total of light and dive bomber groups remained around 15.

The first consideration was bases for the large heavy bomber force. As the major maintenance and supply installations were to be in north-west England and Northern Ireland, near to sea ports, VIII Bomber Command staff were attracted to the idea of establishing the heavy bombers in the York area rather than East Anglia, as proposed by the British. While York offered advantages in communications, RAF Bomber Command already had its main combat organisations in this or adjacent areas and their movement would cause disruption to operations. East Anglia, however, did offer room for expansion as RAF heavy bomber presence was limited, being largely contained in an area between Cambridge and The Wash.

In January 1942 the British Air Ministry was notified that four heavy bomb groups would leave the USA for the UK between mid-March and the end of May. In consequence, the Air Ministry made plans for distributing these groups among parent and satellite stations in the area already earmarked for USAAF bomber use. These groups were the 29th which was expected to arrive in late March and would go to Molesworth and Kimbolton, the 30th, expected early April, to go to Polebrook and Grafton Underwood, the 34th expected late May allocated to Thurleigh and Little Staughton, and the 39th expected early June going to Chelveston and Podington. The schedule was over-optimistic and the first heavy bomber did not reach the UK until July 1942. In fact, only one of the designated units in this early plan ever reached the UK, and then not until nearly two years later.

By May 1942 East Anglia had been accepted as the general area for US bomber bases and on 4 June the Air Ministry issued a list of airfields to be transferred to VIII Bomber Command by November that year. These included eight already accepted in the Huntingdon area plus another 20, chiefly in counties to the east. They were, in order of the temporary USAAF station numbers allotted, B-1 to B-28: Molesworth, Grafton Underwood, Polebrook, Thurleigh, Chelveston, Podington, Kimbolton, Little Staughton, Stradishall, Honington, East Wretham, Wattisham, Foulsham, Wendling, Hardwick, Hethel, Tibenham, Rattlesden, Horsham St Faith, Bungay, Chedburgh, Shipdham, Earls Colne, Knettishall, Thorpe Abbotts, Ridgewell, Market Harborough and Desborough. For bomber crew operational training Bovingdon and Cheddington were proposed. On the same date arrangements for accommodating the first five pursuit groups were notified, with a parent and one or two satellite stations for each. These were Atcham and High Ercall, Goxhill, Kirton and Hibaldstow, Eglinton and Maydown, St Angelo and Kirkistown, Digby, Wellingore and Kings Cliffe. No definite provision was made for observation and transport groups at this time other

USAAF COMBAT GROUPS SCHEDULED FOR THE ETO

Source and Date	Heavy Bomb Group	Medium Bomb Group	Light Bomb Group	Dive Bomb Group	Fighter Group	Observation Group	Transport Group	Photo Group	Night Fighter Group	Total
Jan 42 AWPD/1	54	10	–16–		10	2	8	2½	2½	105
Mar 42 AAF Hq	45	10	12	5	26	7	8	2	–	115
Sep 42 Peabody	45	11	4	10	25	8	12	–	–	115
Mar 43 Bradley	46	9	–15–		24	8	9	1	¾	112¾
May 43 Trident	51	9	–15–		25	8	9	2	½	119½
Aug 43 Quadrant	56	8	3	0	36	4	10	2	½	119½
Dec 43 Sextant	41½	8	3	0	36	1	10	2	½	102
Aug 44 Actual	40½	8	3	0	33	2	14	2	½	103

May 1943 figures reflect uncertainty over dive bombers. In August 1943 these units have been eliminated and converted to a fighter-bomber role. The December 1943 schedule shows the diversion of 15 heavy bomber groups from 8th AF to 15th AF. The smaller number of fighter groups actually in the theatre on 1 August 1944 was due to the decision to leave 3 P-38 groups in the MTO, but four C-47 groups were moved from that theatre.

than a statement that at least two airfields would be provided in Northern Ireland and, if possible, 11 would be found in the Salisbury Plain area of England where these units would be able to train with British and US ground forces. The 4 June allocation was tentative and ten of the named airfields were never occupied by US flying units. Neither was the allocation adequate to meet the requirements of the various 8th Air Force Commands who had independently conducted their own negotiations with the Air Ministry and RAF.

In July 1942 the programme of airfield procurement was consolidated and after a series of meetings plans to provide for the total 8th Air Force deployment were drawn up. It was calculated that 127 airfields would be required of which 98 must have hard surfaced runways and parking areas to support bombers and transports; the remainder for fighters and reconnaissance units could be grass surfaced. Of the total, 81 existed or were at some stage in construction and the remainder were still to be built, 29 by British agencies and 17 by US engineer troops.

The standard British airfield for the operation of heavy multi-engine aircraft had a flying field with three converging runways, a perimeter track and 36 aircraft dispersal points all of concrete construction. It was current RAF practice to base two heavy squadrons on each airfield and to group airfields in clutches of three, one being a base station with more extensive operational and technical facilities than its satellites. As the aircraft establishment of a US heavy bomb group was currently 35, one airfield would be allotted to each group. But as the establishments of light and medium groups were 57 aircraft, and that of transport 55, it would be necessary to allocate two such groups the use of three airfields. Fighter groups with 80 aircraft posed a similar problem and would have to be split between two airfields. Although this policy would have to be pursued, initially consideration was given to expanding the facilities at each airfield so that eventually a whole group would occupy one airfield. In the spring of 1942 the USAAF informed the British that ultimately the unit establishment of a heavy bomb group would be raised to 48. As a result of this, plans were made to increase the number of aircraft standings on each airfield to 50.

VIII BOMBER COMMAND

The major part of the 8th Air Force would be the bomber contingent which, based on the March 1942 plans, called for 72 groups. As the British had designed their airfield system and its communications on the base and satellite basis with a number of such clutches controlled by an area headquarters, General Eaker considered it wise to set up VIII Bomber Command within a similar framework. Particularly, he saw the need for intermediary headquarters between the bomber command and the huge number of combat groups it was to control.

The following principles were therefore adopted: each group would occupy a single airfield and the three groups in a clutch would form an operational organisation eventually to be known as a combat wing. Five of these would comprise a bombardment wing (eventually to be termed a bombardment or air division). VIII Bomber Command would have five such bombardment wings. This meant that planning would centre around an anticipated 75 bomber groups. To control them five numbered bombardment wing headquarters were being formed in the US for despatch to the UK. The 1st Bomb Wing would control B-17 units, 2nd Bomb Wing B-24s, 3rd and 4th Bomb Wings B-25s, B-26s and A-20s, and the 5th Bomb Wing B-17s or B-24s.

In July 1942 the Air Ministry produced a list of 75 airfields in five areas for consideration by VIII Bomber Command. After some amendments and approval by 8th Air Force headquarters this plan, superseding that of 4 June, was issued on 10 August a week prior to the first 8th AF heavy bomber operation, as part of a document covering all 8th AF airfield requirements. The VIII BC plan listing proved of major significance in that all but one of the bases eventually used by USAAF bomber groups in England were included. Of the 75 airfields, eight were already occupied by VIII Bomber Command, ten occupied by the RAF were to be transferred, nine in the final stages of construction would become available in a matter of weeks and 12 more were due to be completed by the end of the year, 28 others were in the early stages of construction or awaiting construction and eight were at this date still to be selected from 12 surveyed sites. These latter were Finedon, Buckden, Maldon, Southminster, Cold Norton, High Roding, Burnham, Bulphan, Beaumont, Weeley, Crowfield and Ingatestone. Other sites for US bomber bases recently eliminated were Assington and Fressingfield in Suffolk and Little Clacton in Essex. The required eight had been finalised by October. Seven of the airfields to be transferred from the RAF were currently grass surfaced and would have hard runways laid.

To aid the already over-burdened British airfield construction programme, arrangements had been made early in 1942 for US Army Engineer Battalions to help in the construction at some airfields. In September that year ten airfields were allocated to these troops: Glatton in Huntingdonshire, Eye and Debach in Suffolk, Chipping Ongar, Gosfield, Great Dunmow, Great Saling, Matching and Stansted in Essex, and Nuthampstead in Hertfordshire. The first of these to be completed was Great Saling (Andrewsfield) opened in April 1943.

THE DEFINITIVE MAP OF VIII BOMBER COMMAND BASES

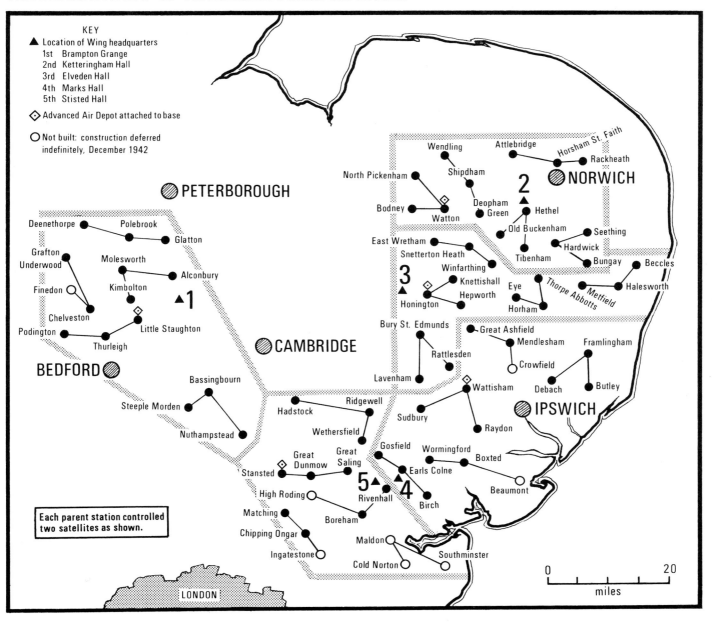

VIII FIGHTER COMMAND

The 10 August 1942 document allocated 23 airfields to VIII FC of which seven it already occupied. Fifteen of the 23 were located in south-west England, two in the West Midlands, two near the east coast and four in Northern Ireland. Of the total only two would eventually come to be 8th Air Force fighter bases of long duration due primarily to changes in policy affecting the operational employment of the American fighter units. An initial airfield allocation in June had been based on the consideration that units would require to undergo extensive operational training before being committed to bases within range of enemy territory.

Operation *Round Up*, the Allied plan for an early invasion of the Continent, required provision of fighter airfields in south-west England as close as possible to the contemplated targets along the French coast. In early July RAF Fighter Command

agreed to make eight airfields in this area available for US fighters. Unlike the bomber airfields, the majority were complete and available as needed. However, the decision to abandon *Round Up* in favour of the North African landing, *Torch*, resulted in the transfer of most US fighter units to the new 12th Air Force, formed to support this invasion. Prior to this, only two VIII FC groups became established in south-west England using Westhampnett and Merston, Ibsley and Colerne. General Spaatz wished to rebuild VIII FC in the general vicinity of the bomber airfields where the mission of new fighter units would be defence and escort. Consultation with the Air Ministry and RAF Fighter Command during early September resulted in a revised allocation issued on the 22nd of that month in which 25 airfields were allocated, six being already occupied by VIII FC. These were as follows and were planned to provide accommodation for 14 Groups:

Parent	Satellites	Deployment
Goxhill	Kirton-in-Lindsey	Group Hq and two
Atcham	High Ercall	squadrons on parent
Eglinton	Maydown	and one squadron on
Debden	Gt Sampford	satellite
Duxford	Fowlmere	
Ballyhalbert	Kirkistown	Group Hq and one
Coltishall	Matlask, Ludham	squadron on parent, other
Wittering	Collyweston, Kings Cliffe	squadrons on satellites
Martlesham	—	Group Hq and all
Leiston	—	squadrons
Horsham St Faith	—	
Rackheath	—	
Attlebridge	—	
Metfield	—	

VIII GROUND AIR SUPPORT COMMAND

The 10 August 1942 airfields allocation document was the first to name those to be assigned to VIII Ground Air Support Command (redesignated Air Support Command on 18 September 1942), charged with army support. Of the total of nine airfields, seven were in the Salisbury Plain area and the remaining two in Northern Ireland, which were only intended for temporary use. They were Aldermaston, Greenham Common, Ramsbury, Hampstead Norris, Keevil, Welford, Membury, Maghaberry and Newtownards. With the exception of Welford, in the early stages of construction, these airfields could be made available for occupation within weeks; in fact, two troop carrier groups had already moved into Aldermaston and Ramsbury.

Over the next few months there were several changes to the allocation. In late August Earls Colne and Wattisham were substituted for Welford and Newtownards and Bury St Edmunds and Rattlesden were added, all on a temporary basis. A month later Tarrant Rushton and Isle Abbotts – both under construction – were also added and in early October Grove was substituted for Hampstead Norris. During this period five of these stations

(Aldermaston, Ramsbury, Keevil, Wattisham and Bury St Edmunds) were briefly occupied by groups assigned to the 12th Air Force but with the departure of that force the only flying tactical group in VIII ASC was 67th Observation Group at Membury. In December 1942 a new troop carrier group arrived at Aldermaston and for six months the two groups remained the only two major tactical flying units in the Command. In consequence, the four East Anglian bomber airfields temporarily assigned were relinquished in December 1942. Meanwhile, on 11 November 1942, the Air Ministry had issued a revised list of the 'permanent' airfields allocated to VIII ASC for use by observation and transports, all built to bomber standard. In existence were Membury, Aldermaston, Keevil, Ramsbury, Greenham Common, Grove and Chilbolton, of which the first three served the Command's purposes during the first half of 1943 and the others were used temporarily by the RAF. Under construction were Tarrant Rushton, Welford and Isle Abbotts and awaiting construction were Fairford, Cricklade, Chalgrove, Upottery, Down Ampney and Broadwell.

VIII COMPOSITE COMMAND

Operational training airfields were ultimately to be the responsibility of VIII Composite Command and the 10 August 1942 plan listed seven airfields in Northern Ireland and two in England as bomber combat crew replacement centres, plus two

fighter CCRC in each area. However, at this date the establishments in England, the fighter training airfields of Atcham and Goxhill and their satellites as listed above, were controlled by VIII BC and VIII FC.

Bomber CCRC airfields were already established at Bovingdon and Cheddington. A third site, Maidenhead, was added to the Bovingdon CCRC clutch, but was never built. The new bomber CCRCs proposed for Northern Ireland were to be at Nutts Corner, Long Kesh, Toome, Cluntoe, Greencastle, Bishop's Court and Mullaghmore. As the flow of units to the 8th Air Force failed to come anywhere near the promises made

early in the year, there was no immediate requirement for additional CCRCs and in consequence Bishop's Court, Long Kesh and Nutts Corner were used by the RAF and remained with them. The two fighter airfields earmarked as CCRC, St Angelo and Maydown, were also returned to the British, being surplus to immediate requirements.

VIII AIR FORCE SERVICE COMMAND

The three airfields originally selected for use as major supply and repair depots – Burtonwood, Warton and Langford Lodge – were confirmed in the 10 August document. There had been various plans for Advanced Repair and Supply Depots to serve operational airfields culminating in that announced on 12 October 1942, proposing one for each bombardment wing area situated on the following airfields: 1st Bomb Wing – Little

Staughton, 2nd Bomb Wing – Watton, 3rd Bomb Wing – Honington, 4th Bomb Wing – Wattisham, and 5th Bomb Wing – Boreham or Ridgewell. The first three of these were to be set up immediately. In the event Honington was the first to be established and Thurleigh was used as a temporary depot while Little Staughton airfield site was completed. The 5th Bomb Wing depot site was eventually established at Stansted.

REVISION OF BOMBER AIRFIELD PLANS

While VIII BC based its planning on an ultimate 75 groups, after the depredations caused by the 12th Air Force and continuing diversions of several bomber groups originally earmarked for the 8th Air Force to other war theatres, there was doubt about the total number of airfields that would be required. On the other hand there was growing concern over the rate of progress in construction of many new airfields. Wet autumn conditions had restricted work, and there were shortages in labour, equipment and materials. The building programme for the USAAF – which was expected to cost £115,000,000 – was planned with an anticipated 190,000 construction workers but by November 1942 only 51,000 were employed plus the 1200 men of the US engineer battalions.

In December the Air Ministry, in consultation with the RAF and USAAF, reviewed the whole airfield building programme. A decision was taken to postpone all planned airfields where work had not actually started. As a result eight VIII Bomber Command stations, that at the time had not progressed beyond surveying, planning and notice of land requisition, were indefinitely postponed. They were Finedon in 1st Division area, Crowfield in 3rd Division area, Beaumont in 4th Division area, and High Roding, Ingatestone, Maldon, Cold Norton and Southminster in the 5th Division area. Some of these planned airfields, having been given USAAF Station Numbers persisted in 8th Air Force directories until the end of hostilities, making Beaumont and Cold Norton a mystery to the uninitiated as only farmland was to be found at these Essex villages.

Although the concept of Air Divisions and Combat Wings had yet to be approved by Washington, 8th Air Force was now using these terms in planning. Indeed, reference to the 5th Bomb Wing area could lead to confusion for although that organisation was readied to come to the UK from the USA it was finally despatched to North Africa in the autumn of 1942 to act as a bomber headquarters.

The reduction in the overall number of bomber bases under construction was not of immediate concern to VIII BC as the first flow chart received from Washington in the New Year indicated that a maximum 61 such airfields would be required by the end of 1943, and that the major influx of new units would not occur until the latter part of that year. In fact, it appeared that VIII BC might have a surplus of airfields during the months immediately ahead. At that time – January 1943 – RAF Bomber Command was seeking to acquire extra airfields in East Anglia and it was proposed that ten airfields in the 5th Division area be released to the RAF, to be returned if required or an alternative area

substituted. As few of these airfields were ready for use and Bomber Command considered the 140 foot wide runways of the US built fields unsuitable for night operations, it was next proposed to exchange the 2nd Division airfields in Norfolk for those RAF airfields in the Grantham area. Although at first approved, this exchange was abandoned early in March because of progress already made in tailoring 2nd Division bases to special USAAF requirements.

The 75 airfields plan of August 1942 had been further modified by the forced temporary allocation of five airfields to VIII Air Force Service Command for use as Advanced Air Depots. In view of all these changes VIII BC considered a regrouping of airfields was imperative in order that permanent arrangements could be made for the most efficient and workable operational scheme. Thus in March 1943 new recommendations were made to the Air Ministry which resulted in VIII BC issuing a revised plan on 9 April 1943 providing for 67 bomber airfields instead of 75. The five already being developed as advanced air depots were to be temporarily disregarded as bomber group bases until such time as the special depot facilities being constructed adjacent to each of these airfields would allow a dual function. It was expected that Little Staughton and Stansted would not be available for bomber units until early in 1944. The 5th Air Division was eliminated and its allotted airfields regrouped, the Ridgewell clutch going to 1st Division and the Chipping Ongar and Great Dunmow clutches to the 4th Air Division. Sudbury and North Pickenham were to have Combat Wing Hq facilities while similar plans for Chelveston and Boreham were dropped. Lavenham was to be transferred from the 3rd Division to the 4th Air Division and Mendlesham and Great Ashfield moved from the 4th to the 3rd. Additionally, Steeple Morden was now considered unsuitable for enlargement into a heavy bomber base due to the surrounding terrain and it was proposed to exchange this airfield for VIII FC's Fowlmere which was satisfactory for bomber development.

This plan was short-lived chiefly due to the continuing lag in the completion of airfields in the 4th Air Division area. Originally it was planned that medium or light bombers would use this area but the flow charts received during the early part of 1943 revealed that the majority of new groups scheduled to arrive in the spring would be equipped with B-17s. The 4th Bomb Wing in the 4th Air Division area was then prepared to receive B-17 groups but in April some concern arose over the availability of suitable airfields, for while there was no shortage of completed flying fields, essential support facilities on many stations were still lacking. The position was only little better in the 3rd Air

Division area which shortly expected a number of B-25 and B-26 groups. In an effort to improve the situation, work was suspended on Winfarthing, Hepworth and Butley during April in order to switch manpower and equipment to complete other bases in the 3rd and 4th Air Division areas.

The failure of the first two B-26 low-altitude combat missions, and suspension of this type from operation in May, led to a change of policy whereby the medium bombers were transferred to the control of Air Support Command. At the same time it was decided to transfer the three Marauder groups on hand to the 4th Air Division area in Essex, where they would be better placed for attacking suitable targets in occupied territory, while the Fortresses of 4th Bomb Wing moved to 3rd Air Division area

where airfields were generally in a more advanced state of development. This plan was issued on 7 June 1943 and apart from the switch in location of the 3rd and 4th Bomb Wings the only other changes were the transfer of the Halesworth clutch from the 3rd Air Division area to the 2nd Air Division area – these airfields were on temporary loan to VIII FC – and the Framlingham clutch from 3rd to 4th Air Division areas.

Despite the date of issue for this new plan its contents were apparently not made known to the 4th Bomb Wing in time to prevent the movement of the 95th Bomb Group at Framlingham ten miles to Horham in the Wing's new area. However, at this date Horham was a completed base whereas Framlingham was not.

REVISION OF FIGHTER AIRFIELD PLANS

A new plan for VIII FC was also issued in June 1943. In the previous February higher authority had confirmed that US fighter units in the UK should be employed primarily in offensive roles in support of bombers, with the proviso that they could be used for defence if a critical situation developed. Absolved from participation in the air defence of Northern Ireland and East Anglia, VIII FC then relinquished the four airfields in Ulster which were considered too remote from its general area of operations. Proposals followed for an organisation in which the

promised influx of fighter groups would be placed under three fighter wings with functions paralleling those performed by the bombardment wings in VIII BC. After several conferences to evaluate this proposal and other matters pertaining to the deployment of the fighter force, an interim plan was prepared whereby wing headquarters were to be established at Debden, Duxford and Wittering. At the same time a policy of basing a complete fighter group on one airfield was established, increasing where necessary accommodation and technical facilities to meet this requirement. As a result the satellite bases Kirton-in-

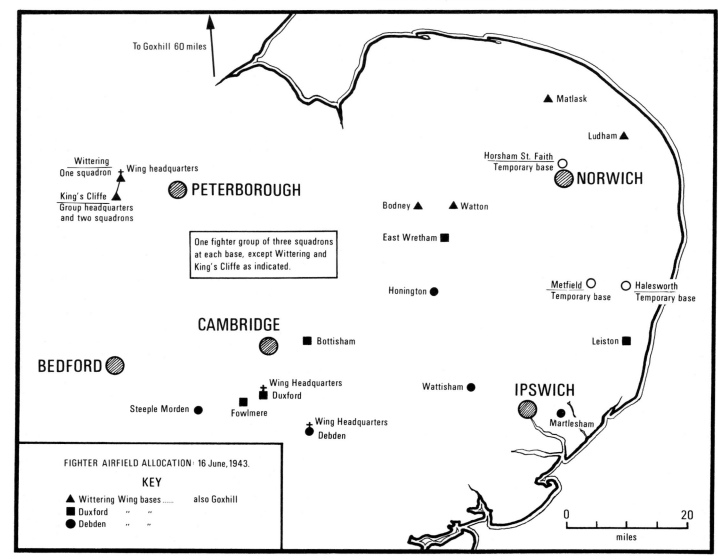

Lindsey, Great Sampford and Collyweston were removed from the list, while Bottisham was added. The temporary use of bomber airfields was still proposed, with Horsham St Faith, Halesworth and Metfield allocated. However, the plan was subject to amendments in April and again in June when the construction of concrete runways at the grass airfields assigned to VIII BC were, with one exception, abandoned and these airfields made available to VIII FC. This resulted from renewed attempts to concentrate on existing bomber field construction, the probability that sufficient bomber airfields were already under construction, and a shortage of airfields in the East Anglian area for VIII FC. The airfields now available were Wattisham, Watton, Honington, Bodney, Fowlmere and East Wretham. The exception was Horsham St Faith where work on laying concrete runways for bomber use was about to start.

The many changes in the plan for VIII FC fighter deployment culminated in the 16 June 1943 issue providing for 16 fighter groups scheduled for basing in East Anglia. The other nine groups scheduled to complete the VIII FC total were ground support fighters and accommodation for these had yet to be found. Of the 16 airfields, Wittering was an RAF Fighter Command station and the US units would be lodgers. Bottisham, Ludham and Matlask still in RAF use, would require extra accommodation and technical facilities before they could house a complete group. East Wretham and Bodney were also still under development in this respect and were unlikely to be ready until September unless tented accommodation was used. King's Cliffe and Fowlmere were available but would have to be enlarged to take a whole fighter group, while Watton, Wattisham and Honington could not be occupied until the new air depots were completed, allowing release of the existing camps and technical sites.

The flying field at Martlesham had to be enlarged in order to make operations by P-47s safe and would not be ready until October. Leiston was a completely new airfield and would have bomber type concrete runways, although it was not expected to be completed until October. Only four airfields in the list were immediately available and of these Debden, Duxford and Goxhill were already occupied. Of the loaned bomber stations, Horsham St Faith was shortly to be vacated and Metfield and Halesworth would have to serve the immediate needs of the Command. An additional bomber airfield had to be utilised in September 1943 with the arrival of a much needed P-38 group. This was Nuthampstead, which was made available by VIII BC until the following spring.

DEPLOYMENTS

The transfer to VIII FC of the existing grass airfields originally scheduled for development as bomber bases, brought a further regrouping of VIII BC clutches. Deopham Green replaced East Wretham in the Snetterton Heath clutch so, with the loss of Bodney and Watton, the North Pickenham clutch was dissolved with North Pickenham becoming the third station in the Shipdham clutch. Further changes were brought about in June and July 1943 by the incomplete state of some new airfields. When the 385th BG arrived it was placed on Great Ashfield and brought into the Bury St Edmunds clutch to replace Hepworth where work had been temporarily halted. As a similar situation existed with regard to Winfarthing, the third station of the Horham clutch, the newly arrived 390th BG was placed at Framlingham. As the other two stations of the Framlingham clutch were only in the early stages of construction, Framlingham remained as the third station of the Horham clutch. To give the 4th Bomb Wing additional stations, the Boxted clutch was to be transferred from the 3rd Bomb Wing by 31 October 1943. Only Boxted itself was in use and the B-26 group there moved to Great Dunmow in late September.

Concern over the availability of sufficient airfields for the 8th Air Force arose again when in August 1943 USAAF flow charts scheduled an ultimate 56 heavy bomb groups in addition to the tactical flying units that would support the planned cross-Channel invasion in 1944. In consequence 8th Air Force Hq reviewed the possibility of establishing a fourth air division for heavy bombers in the north Essex/south Suffolk area and an Air Ministry plan for placing the tactical fighter groups in southwest England, north Yorkshire and lowland Scotland. That this never went beyond the tentative planning stage was due to Allied successes in Italy. Capture of the Foggia plain was followed by the decision in October 1943 to divert 15 heavy bomb groups, scheduled for the 8th Air Force to airfields in this area, to establish a new strategic bombing force.

Another decision taken during the late summer of 1943 was the formation of a separate US tactical air force in the UK charged with supporting the forthcoming cross-Channel invasion of continental Europe. In mid October VIII Air Support Command became the foundation for this organisation, the 9th Air Force, – originally operating in the Mediterranean war zone but now redundant – and stations assigned to VIII ASC passed to the Ninth. VIII BC requirements were now re-scheduled as 42 airfields by June 1944 and it appeared there would be a definite surplus of bomber stations. In consequence when large numbers of new units for both 8th and 9th Air Forces arrived during the winter of 1943–44 five bomber airfields in the Colchester area were made available for 9th Air Force fighters, notably the new long-range P-51s. These stations were Boxted, Raydon, Wormingford, Gosfield and Rivenhall. Other 9th AF fighter groups – there were ultimately 18 in all – were placed on airfields along the south coast. Some of these were Advanced Landing Groups (ALGs) with single steel mesh or planked runways and basic services. The staggered construction programme on 27 ALGs was begun in the winter of 1942–43.

By April 1944 the imminent arrival of the remaining heavy bomb groups for 8th AF and the light bomb groups (A-20s) for the 9th AF resulted in the five 9th AF fighter units around Colchester moving to ALGs in Kent. The VIII FC groups on the bomber airfields at Nuthampstead, Metfield and Halesworth were then moved to Wormingford, Raydon and Boxted respectively where they remained until the end of hostilities. The designated fighter airfields at Matlask and Ludham were available but apparently lacked the communication links with VIII FC which were already in place for Boxted, Wormingford and Raydon. Both Matlask and Ludham remained allocated to VIII FC until the late summer of 1944 but were never occupied by flying units. It should be noted that in April 1944 a few 8th AF bomber bases had still to be completed, namely Winfarthing, Butley and Hepworth which, when work resumed on these sites, were renamed Fersfield, Bentwaters and Shepherd's Grove.

The fortieth and last heavy bomb group sent to the 8th Air Force arrived in England in May 1944. Although another was scheduled in the SEXTANT plan this (a B-24 group) eventually went to the Pacific war theatre. At this time, of the 61 Class A airfields actually built or developed for USAAF bombers in the UK, 41 were occupied by the three bomb divisions of 8th Air Force, 11 by medium and light bombers of the 9th AF, three were occupied by VIII FC fighters, one had been returned to the RAF and five – Beccles, Bentwaters, Birch, Fersfield and Shepherd's Grove – were unoccupied. Fersfield was later used as a base for the secret *Aphrodite* project but the others had all reverted to RAF control and use by November 1944. From May 1944 until the end of hostilities 8th AF bomber deployment was stabilised, with the exception of the vacation of Metfield when the group there moved to North Pickenham following the disbandment of the original Pickenham B-24 group. Thereafter Metfield was utilised by the European Division of Air Transport Command, hiding a unit engaged in clandestine transport flights to Sweden via Scottish staging bases.

However, in January 1945, USSTAF decided that the six B-17 groups of the 15th AF could be more usefully employed from English bases and approached the Air Ministry on this matter. The possibility of bringing nine B-24 groups up from Italy was also mentioned. Surprisingly, weather had proved a greater limiting factor to operations from Italy than in Britain. As a result of this request the Air Ministry allocated the bases in south Lincolnshire then being vacated by the C-47 and C-46 troop

carrier group of the 9th Air Force. Once again the 8th AF appeared about to gain a fourth air division, but yet again this was never realised as the plan was never implemented.

With the exception of the temporary deployment of two Mustang groups to Belgium during the Ardennes crisis, plans to move all fighters to the Continent never materialised. The only change of fighter group location in England after D-Day was the movement of the 361st in September 1944 from overcrowded, soft-surface Bottisham to hard-surface Little Walden. During January 1945, when this group was on the Continent, Little Walden was loaned to 3rd Division for use by 490th and 493rd Groups while their home bases, Eye and Debach, had runway repairs. It transpired that only the 493rd made this move.

TRAINING BASES

Although Northern Ireland had been selected as the main area for operational training units, and the controlling headquarters, VIII Composite Command, was established there in September 1942, it was to be December 1943 before all planned installations were functioning. CCRCs were established at Toome, Cluntoe, Greencastle and Mullaghmore, while Maghaberry saw some training activity but became the home of ferry and transport squadrons of VIII AFSC. A further development at these

bases was their use as aircraft storage parks when the flow of replacements from the US began to exceed immediate requirements of the combat stations in England. The largest parks were at Greencastle and Langford Lodge where work commenced on providing an additional 102 standings at each. Toome, Cluntoe, Mullaghmore and Maghaberry were scheduled to get 50 each. However, the operational training and storage requirements were not as great as first envisaged and US activities at Maghaberry were gradually run down with

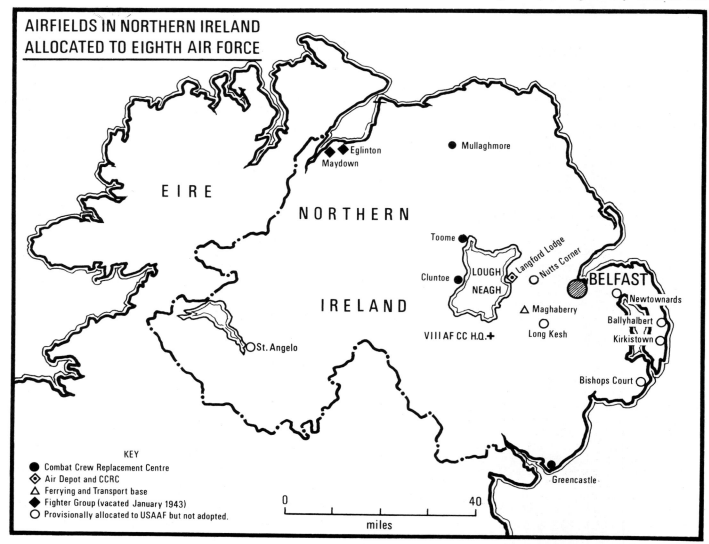

AIRFIELDS IN NORTHERN IRELAND
ALLOCATED TO EIGHTH AIR FORCE

EIRE

NORTHERN

IRELAND

Eglinton
Maydown

Mullaghmore

Toome

LOUGH
NEAGH

Cluntoe

Langford Lodge

Nutts Corner

BELFAST

Newtownards

Maghaberry

Ballyhalbert

VIII AF CC H.Q. ✛

Long Kesh

Kirkistown

St. Angelo

Bishops Court

KEY
● Combat Crew Replacement Centre
◆ Air Depot and CCRC
△ Ferrying and Transport base
◆ Fighter Group (vacated January 1943)
○ Provisionally allocated to USAAF but not adopted.

0   40
miles

Greencastle

the base reverting to RAF control in the following June. Mullaghmore was also vacated in the spring of 1944, being returned to the RAF in May.

The desirability of having all 8th Air Force operational flying training sited in one area brought a plan in July 1944 for the transfer of the remaining CCRCs in Ulster and the fighter units at Atcham and Goxhill to airfields near the two CCRC bomber bases in south central England. Specifically, it was proposed to the Air Ministry that four airfields vacated by the 9th AF – Aldermaston, Chalgrove, Welford and Membury – be used. This was yet another plan that never reached fruition, primarily because of the move towards operational training being performed at combat bases. Matters were brought to a head in September 1944 when USSTAF Hq decided to use VIII CC to furnish the personnel for Air Disarmament Command, an organisation directly under USSTAF. With the demise of Composite Command, Toome and Cluntoe were returned to the RAF early in November 1944 and only Greencastle and Langford Lodge continued in US occupancy until the end of the war, primarily an aircraft park and modification centre respectively. Fighter training groups survived but were moved from Atcham and Goxhill to Cheddington and Halesworth at the end of 1944.

SPECIAL DUTIES AIRFIELDS

The one Class A bomber airfield occupied by the 8th Air Force and not listed in the master list of 10 August 1942 was Harrington in Northants. Built by US engineers for the RAF, it was transferred to the USAAF in April 1944 for use by the special American unit engaged in support of continental resistance movements. Harrington, on the western edge of the general 8th AF base area, was selected as being reasonably near to the packing and storage facilities base at Holme, 35 miles away.

For tutelage in the techniques of photographic reconnaissance developed by the RAF, 8th Air Force units with this mission were placed at Mount Farm, satellite of Benson the centre of RAF PR activities. Liaison between the two services and use of the interpretation centre at Medmenham were considerations in Mount Farm becoming the 'permanent' home for 8th Air Force PR and undergoing extensive development. In the spring of 1945 the 7th Photo Group moved into nearby Chalgrove which had previously housed the 9th Air Force photographic squadrons and had more substantial facilities.

TEMPORARY STATIONS AND FORWARD STAGING POSTS

In addition to the airfields allocated as 8th Air Force bases, the Air Ministry also arranged facilities for US units to operate from stations under RAF control as lodger units, or to use them as staging posts for extending operational range. The lodger units were predominantly those that were undergoing training with the RAF or co-operating with them on special operations. Early US fighter squadrons equipped with Spitfires and P-38s spent short periods on RAF No 11 Group stations in southern England during the summer and autumn of 1942; these were Kenley, Biggin Hill, Tangmere and Ford.

USAAF night fighter squadrons formed in 1943 to operate Beaufighters with the 12th Air Force in the MTO were under 8th Air Force administrative control, while being trained by the RAF at Scorton, Coltishall, Cranfield, Ayr, Acklington and Usworth.

The special RCM squadron formed in 1944 spent its formative weeks as a lodger unit at RAF Sculthorpe and Oulton alongside RAF RCM units engaged in these duties. A special night intruder flight of P-51s and P-38s lodged at Little Snoring while experimenting in their intended function. The secret *Aphrodite* unit lodged at Woodbridge for a while in summer 1944 because that airfield's extra long runway was deemed more suited to the operations envisaged.

The provision of staging bases with refuelling facilities was first requested by VIII BC when its bombers were striking at the U-boat ports on the French Atlantic seaboard in the autumn of 1942. In response the Air Ministry made available five airfields in south-west England as advanced or emergency airfields: Davidstow Moor, Dunkeswell, Lasham, Hurn and Tarrant Rushton. As some of these were not then in a position to receive many heavy bombers Predannack and Exeter were also added. At the same time Lossiemouth, Tain and Kinloss in Scotland were proposed for use if VIII BC should have need of advanced bases in Scotland. In fact, facilities for servicing US heavy bombers at these two airfields were available to the 8th Air Force until the end of hostilities but were rarely used.

With a view to extending Marauder operations over the Brest peninsula, in August 1943, the RAF agreed to provide refuelling and other services at Portreath, Predannack, Exeter and Davidstow Moor – the same bases which were eventually prepared to receive US heavy bombers. However, the B-26 force never used these airfields as forward bases while in 8th Air Force service.

AIR DEPOTS

Of prime importance in the establishment of logistical support for the 8th Air Force combat units were airfields specialising in aircraft overhaul, repair and parts supply. Administered by VIII Air Force Service Command, the largest establishments with extensive workshops and stores were at Burtonwood and Warton in Lancashire, close to the port of Liverpool through which the bulk of seaborne supplies came. These, eventually known as Base Air Depots, were transferred to the 8th Air Force in July 1942. A third base air depot was established at Langford Lodge, Northern Ireland.

Between the base air depot and the combat station it was initially planned to establish Advanced Repair and Supply Depots to service one clutch of operational stations each and specialise in one particular aircraft type. Until these could be set up, Auxiliary Supply Depots were to serve combat airfields within particular localities, but of the seven planned – in July 1942 – only one, at Molesworth, was actually established. The location of the Advanced Repair and Supply Depot airfields announced at the same time was soon considered too ambitious and revised so that there was only one ARSD for each of the proposed bombardment wing areas. In a 12 October 1942 plan these were listed as Little Staughton for 1st Wing, Watton for 2nd Wing, Honington for 3rd Wing, Wattisham for 4th Wing, Boreham or Ridgewell for 5th Wing. Later the 5th Wing depot was finally placed at Stansted which had better road and rail communications. These airfields were only temporarily assigned to VIII AFSC and would be returned to VIII BC for bomber use once the new depot site had been built adjacent to the existing airfield. In all cases the depot site was placed on the far side of the airfield from the original technical site and consisted of a loop taxiway from the perimeter track with additional hard standings, four T2 hangars, machine shops and storage buildings. The depot living sites were dispersed in the immediate surrounding countryside. Air traffic to the depot would use the airfield runways and perimeter track but no other facilities so that depot work would not interfere with further combat operations.

Early in 1943 ARSDs became known as Advanced Air Depots and later still as Strategic Air Depots although their function remained basically the same. Although Little Staughton came into operation as an AAD, before work began on building its site depot a decision was made to use Alconbury which had better communications. Consequently, when depot construction was completed at Alconbury, Little Staughton was vacated by VIII AFSC. At this time the RAF were in need of another airfield in the locality for their expanding Pathfinder Force and arranged to take over Little Staughton. The new depot sites did not use the airfield name that served them. As a security measure the names selected were those of villages on the far side of the airfield and not those of the parish in which the depot was built. For example the depot at Wattisham airfield was built in the parish of Nedging and yet the given name for the depot was Hitcham, a village situated three miles away on the opposite side of the airfield.

Construction and Layout

The airfield construction programme for the USAAF was directed by the British Air Ministry's Directorate General of Works (AMDGW), the same Civil Service establishment which met RAF requirements for installations. In 1941 the AMDGW had conducted a survey of possible airfield sites in eastern England and produced a plan for 180 bomber type airfields divided into 12 areas each approximating to an RAF Bomber Group. The plan encompassed some airfields already in existence while the majority would have to use farm land, the sites being secretly surveyed so as not to arouse local opposition. Each Group area would be developed when and if required, as the survey far exceeded current RAF Bomber Command expansion planning. Following the United States' entry into hostilities with the intention of basing a sizeable air force in the UK, it was proposed to allot some of the planned Group areas to the American bomber forces. Initially they were to receive the area west of Huntingdon, where airfields were being currently constructed. Subsequently US bombers would be based in A, B, C and D areas

located in Essex, Essex/Suffolk, Suffolk and south Norfolk respectively. While little work had been done in A and B areas, development of a number of stations in the C and D areas was already under way when America entered the war.

The material requirements for building a single airfield suitable for heavy bombers were substantial, involving 18,000 tons of dry cement, 90,000 tons of aggregate and 50 miles of drainage pipes and cable conduit. To meet the required stress factors of 2000 pounds per square inch for runway concrete, necessitated the laid slab being a minimum of six inches thick over a consolidated hardcore base. As there was no natural rock at the East Anglian sites, imported stone for hardcore was necessary. In practice, concrete thickness varied from six to nine inches. The finished surface on the early airfields occupied by 8th Air Force was generally a thin layer of macadam or similar tar-based material for weatherproofing. Later constructions had tarred surfaces spread with wood chippings, but on others the surface was simply a concrete screed. Several airfields had a mixture of surfaces due to material not being available or the arrival of flying units before completion.

CLASS A STANDARD AIRFIELD LAYOUT
Throughout 1940 and 1941 the design criteria for airfields underwent a succession of 'stretches' in an attempt to keep pace with increases in aircraft weights and performances. The final outcome of these changes was the Class A specification promulgated in August 1942. This defined the minimum standards for the construction and layout of operational airfields considered essential for safety in operating aircraft. The intention was to provide airfields suitable for the operation of any type of aircraft in service or under development, and the specification remained the standard until the airfield building programme ended in 1945. The possibility that B-29 very heavy bombers might be based in England led to a few existing airfields being re-developed to requirements in excess of Class A, but these were uncompleted at the end of hostilities.

The main requirements were that an airfield should have three strips for landings and take-offs, ideally placed at 60 degrees to each other and with the longest, designated the main strip, aligned SW–NE wherever possible. Each strip was to be 600 ft (183 m) wide cleared, graded and surfaced with turf and with a concrete runway 150 ft wide placed centrally down its length. Minimum length for the main strip was 6000 ft (1830 m) and for subsidiaries 4200 ft (1280 m). On each side of the main strip an

additional 300 ft (90 m) was cleared of obstructions, levelled and had all holes filled. Maximum gradients for strips were defined as 1 in 80 longitudinal and 1 in 60 transverse. Flightway approaches to each strip, termed funnels, were based on an inclined plane set at a slope of 1 in 50 rising from the ends and bounded horizontally by a 15 degree angle outward from each corner. All obstructions were removed from funnels.

The ends of the runways were connected by a taxiway, or perimeter track, for movement and marshalling aircraft. The standard width was 50 ft (15 m) with 30 ft (9 m) on either side levelled and cleared of obstructions. Minimum centre line radius for curves was to be 150 ft (46 m) for angles of 60 degrees or more, and 200 ft (61 m) for those less. Gradients, either longitudinal or transverse were not to exceed 1 in 40 and all buildings were to be positioned at least 150 ft from the edges of taxiways. Concrete hardstandings for aircraft, where provided, were to be positioned clear of the strips and funnels. Minimum separation edge to edge for single standings was to be 150 ft and their centres were to be the same minimum from the edge of the taxiways.

All these provisions were presented as the ideal standard and in practice variations in the alignment of the main strip and in the angle between the strips were dictated by the local topography. Small reductions in the ideal lengths of strips were also permitted for topographical reasons but clearances and gradients, more easily achieved, were strictly observed.

Bad weather and night flying aids when provided consisted of Standard Beam Approach equipment for the main runway and Drem Mk II lighting for the airfield circuit and funnels.

BOMBER AIRFIELDS

Most of the airfields provided for 8th Air Force bomber groups were Class A but nine bases occupied by early arrivals in 1942 – all in 1st Division area – had been completed in 1941 and had runways shorter than the 1942 standard. Extensions and new taxiway connections were constructed between the autumn of 1942 and the spring of 1943 to bring these as far as possible into line with Class A requirements. Limitations imposed by existing constructions produced awkward layouts at some stations and affected ease of marshalling for take-off on the runways concerned. Additional hardstandings were also built at these and all other bases intended for 8th Air Force bomber groups so that the full group strength of 48 aircraft could be accommodated. On earlier airfields hardstandings took the form of a 125 ft (38 m) circular pad joined by a taxiway to the perimeter track, often laid out in well dispersed branched clusters of three or more.

A later and more economical design placed the pad closer to the perimeter with a short connecting lead-in. From their appearance, this type was named 'frying pan', soon shortened to 'pan' and applied indiscriminately to any type of single hard-standing. The diameter of a pan was increased to 150 ft. In August 1942 the Air Ministry introduced the 'loop' type hard-standing requiring less material in construction and allowing easier manoeuvring of large aircraft. Loops were built in linked groups directly off the perimeter track or on short access spurs leading to it. Clusters of loop hardstandings were usually limited to a maximum of eight to effect a degree of aircraft dispersal. At some airfields an occasional large loop, set farther back from the others, was used as a dispersal measure. The majority of the increased number of hardstandings at 8th Air Force bases were the loop type and loops became the norm at all airfields built from late 1942 onwards. Only a single B-17 or B-24 could be comfortably parked on a pan, but two could be accommodated on a loop, which aided the parking problem when the number of heavy bombers per group was increased to as many as 72.

Beside one pan hardstanding a Shooting-In butt was provided. A large earth mound, it was used for test firing aircraft guns in position.

FIGHTER AIRFIELDS

The construction and layout of the airfields on which the VIII Fighter Command units eventually became established varied considerably. The original intention was that fighters would operate from grass surface airfields and allocations to VIII Fighter Command in 1942 and 1943 were made up chiefly of such airfields already in use by the RAF. Only one Class A airfield in the building programme was allocated – Leiston, originally planned as part of the coastal chain of RAF fighter

bases. Ultimately VIII FC groups occupied nine airfields with paved runways (four being Class A bomber fields), five having steel mesh or similar supported sod runways and one with part paved and part supported sod. It was soon discovered that large American fighters such as the P-47 were too heavy to

The finger of 'Y' shaped aircraft storage standings filled and overflowing with US P-47Ds at Burtonwood, June 1945.

operate from grass surfaces in the wet winter months and that hard runways or stabilised surfaces were desirable. Although several of these grass airfields had underdraining, a programme of laying steel wire mesh – known as Sommerfeld track – was undertaken. By the end of hostilities only Bodney had unsupported grass runways and this because of its sandy, free draining soil. The runways laid down at Martlesham Heath were constructed of a special tar/sand composition.

Perimeter tracks were constructed in concrete, stabilised soil, PSP (pierced steel planking) and Sommerfeld track or combinations of these materials. There were at least six types of construction for fighter hardstandings and at least seven shapes and sizes. All fighter airfield surfacing was done on an individual basis as conditions dictated, thus no two of the true fighter airfields occupied by 8th Air Force were alike. A feature of some fighter airfields was the provision of a number of blast wall protected dispersal points known as 'pens' with soil retained by bricking.

Airfield Buildings

CONTROL TOWER

Although in some instances trees, deserted farm buildings and hedges were left in those areas between the landing strip clearance zones and the perimeter track, the only high structure within the perimeter track was the control tower (US terminology) or watch office (British). This was sited so that the staff had an unobstructed view of the whole flying field. The standard control tower design from 1942 was a square brick, cement rendered, two-storey building with balcony and flat roof. The flat roof often supported a weather observation post and the weather recording instruments. The control tower housed flying control, signals and weather offices. Adjacent to the tower was the Fire Tender shelter, a 24 by 30 ft Nissen or other type with large end doors to house the fire truck or crash ambulance.

Right: **Standard control tower building at Framlingham with 'glass house' built on top to serve as a watch office. Masted weather instruments on roof are a wind vane and anemometer. Flying control occupied second storey room fronting balcony.**

Below: **Control towers on airfields built prior to 1942 were usually smaller structures. That at Attlebridge was a typical example.**

Above: **Standard design control tower building at Martlesham Heath with weather office on roof utilised to display the bearing of the runway in use. Signal square displays dumbell symbol to indicate landing on runways only, and landing directional 'T'. Letters MH identify the airfield.**

Right: **Flying control at Shipdham, February 1943. Both visual and radio contact was maintained with station's own aircraft and visitors. Shipdham, in common with most standard flying control towers built in 1941 and early 1942, had large wall-high windows fronting the airfield.**

HANGARS

In May 1942 the Air Ministry reaffirmed the intention of providing four T2 type hangars on each heavy bomber airfield, only two of which were to be erected initially. Of the wartime built 8th Air Force bases, Thurleigh was unique in having four hangars and while a few early bases had three T2s, from late 1942 provision was only made for two of this type on new airfields. The T2/23, 239½ × 115 ft and 29 ft high, could accommodate three B-17s for sheltered maintenance and repair. The steel girder portal frame was clad with corrugated sheets. Double sliding doors

Below: **Sliding doors on T2 hangar allowed just under 5 inches clearance between a B-17's wing tips and the open doors, but for a B-24 this was just an inch and a half! Aircraft about to be sheltered from the January cold at Eye is B-17G 43-37907.**

Above: **Curved roof J-type hangar at Polebrook. T2 in background and tower on right.** (J. Greenwood)

Left: **Pre-war 8-bay fighter station C-type hangar and typical flat roofed brick buildings of technical site at Debden.** (L. Nitschke)

Below: **Large blister hangar to house fighters.**

Bottom: **Canvas hangar provided shelter at 5 SAD at Merville, France where a 78th FG P-51D was being cannibalised.**

were installed at each end. T2s erected in 1942 were mostly painted in a disruptive camouflage pattern of green, black and brown. Later constructions were finished in black overall. Prior to the standardisation on the T2 type the Air Ministry had an alternative specification for bomber bases of two T2 hangars and one of the larger J type. Airfields built in 1941 – Chelveston, Molesworth and Polebrook – had this arrangement. Unlike the T2 the J hangar, 300 ft long, spanning 151 ft and featuring bricked lower walls with an arched steel frame roof clad with steel sheeting, was considered a permanent structure.

Stations occupied that had been built in the late 1930s – Bassingbourn, Debden, Horsham St Faith, Wattisham and Watton – had C type hangars spanning 152 ft and were 300 ft long with hipped ends. Built in brick and steel, they were topped by a series of gable roof sections. The still older stations like Duxford and Martlesham Heath had hangars dating from the First World War. At most fighter airfields there were a number of blister hangars, a simple steel curved frame or ribbed wooden arch, clad with corrugated sheet, placed over a hardstanding. Canvas drapes were available for the open end but at some stations additional weather protection was obtained by cladding one end with steel sheet. There were several types of Over Blister, as they were officially called, varying from 60 ft to 90 ft overall width.

AIRCRAFT DISPERSAL SITE HUTS

Ten general purpose huts, normally 36 × 10 ft Nissens, were dispersed around the Class A airfield, usually in the ratio of one to every five hardstandings. Their purpose was to provide ground crew with cover for minor repairs plus storage of parts and equipment needed at aircraft dispersals. A latrine block was placed near each of these huts.

Right: **Inadequate protection from the weather out on aircraft dispersals led many ground crews to construct their own shelters from packing cases and other handy material. This shack at Nuthampstead has oil-fired heating using old engine sump oil.** (via M. Osborn)

TECHNICAL SITE

Adjacent to the hangar line, the technical site comprised general and special purpose buildings for repair, maintenance and storage of aircraft and crew equipment. The buildings, used for briefing and crew rooms, as well as administration were also on or closet to the technical site. At pre-war build stations the technical administration site was flanked by the living sites, but on wartime fields it was usually isolated. When hangars were some distance apart, a section of the repair and maintenance facilities was positioned with the second hangar. A standard wartime bomber airfield had buildings and facilities in the technical site area as follows:

One or two bulk oil storage tanks for 3500 Imperial gallons, usually underground but at some stations mounted on a concrete base above ground.

Lubricant and Inflammable Materials Store, an 18 × 54 ft Nissen or brick building for holding 1500 gallons capacity tanks for kerosene, lubricants and other fluids.

Petrol Installation, a 5000 Imperial gallon underground tank for motor vehicle fuel with pump and metering.

Main Stores of two 96 × 35 ft Romney huts, brick buildings or

30 ft-span Nissen, plus one 16 × 48 ft Nissen for quartermaster supplies. One large building for clothing, personnel equipment and salvage, the other for technical equipment, motor and aircraft supplies, and the smaller building for offices.

Main Workshops of two 96 × 35 ft Romney huts, brick buildings or 30 ft-span Nissens, for major repairs to engines and aircraft components, equipped with machine, welding and carpenters' shops, plus a fabric room.

Maintenance Unit building of 127 × 24 ft Nissen type with rooms for instrument, radio and other aircraft systems repair, associated equipment storage and battery charging.

A second maintenance unit building was usually placed near hangar No 2.

Technical site at Steeple Morden, looking east, July 1945. Control tower fronts taxiway (near parked P-51 and AT-6). Tall building on road leading from the tower is the bombing training building erected when the RAF used the airfield as a bomber station. (Romack)

Ordnance Maintenance Unit of two 90 × 24 ft Nissens for turret repair, general ordnance repairs, with gun cleaning room, weapon oil store and camera store. An attached shed housed an oil bowser. A second set of ordnance maintenance buildings was located near hangar No 2.

Armoury of brick or a Nissen building 60 × 18 ft used as station ordnance office and for repair of guns and storage of small arms ammunition.

Guard House and Fire Party Station, an 85 × 24 ft Nissen or half brick construction building used for guard room, detention cells, warders' room, lavatory, shower and prophylactic store. Another part of the building was the fire party barracks and store for fire fighting equipment.

Parachute Store of brick 50 × 20 × 16 ft high, used for hanging, drying and folding parachutes.

Fire Tender House, a 24 × 30 ft Nissen with large doors, positioned close to the perimeter track and used to house spare fire tender or ambulance.

Link Trainer Block, normally a brick building 18 × 75 ft housing three units.

Floodlight Trailer housing, a shed positioned near perimeter track for the floodlight beacon trolley.

Maintenance Staff Block, a 42 × 24 ft Nissen office for the engineering officer and his staff. A second building for this purpose was located near hangar No 2.

Motor Transport Bays and Office comprising brick garage sheds, despatchers' office, workshop, greasing pit, vehicle washing yard and loading ramp, all grouped together, usually near MT fuel store.

Turret Instruction Block or Free Gunnery Trainer housed in a 75 × 24 ft or 60 × 82 ft blister hangar for demonstration and training in turret operations.

Bombing Teacher, a two-storied 20 × 20 ft brick building for indoor practice bombing on simulated targets.

Dinghy Stores, a 28 × 35 ft brick building for rubber dinghies.

Fabric Stores, an 18 × 45 ft brick building for extra parachutes and all types of clothing.

Work Services Hut and Yards providing office and storage facilities for the resident British engineer and his staff.

Squadron Offices of two 45 × 18 ft brick or Nissen buildings usually shared by two squadrons for CO's office and staff.

Gas Defense Center, a brick building without windows intended for decontamination and having an air-lock, showers, cleansing equipment and dressing rooms.

Gas Clothing and Respirator Store, a 28 × 120 ft brick building divided into two sections, one with clothing racks for gas defence crews and the other a store.

Gas Chamber, brick 18 × 10 ft, used for testing gas masks.

Photographic block, a 72 × 24 ft Nissen or brick building

Briefing room at Alconbury was a large 'Nissen' structure. Black areas on map indicated latest known flak zones. Wood benches did not encourage long briefing sessions. Note in centre of roof projector used for displaying target photos on portable screen. January 1944.

used for laboratories, stores and offices.

Locker, Rest and Drying rooms requiring two large Nissen buildings utilised for briefing and interrogation, heated in order to dry flight clothing.

Flight Offices of brick or Nissen, 30 × 18 ft, for various staff or operational purposes. Four on the technical site and two more on the secondary site near No 2 hangar.

Squadron Armoury buildings comprising two 24 × 121 ft Nissens used for the repair and storage of machine guns; each building used by two squadrons.

Bombsight Building of brick for repair and storage of bombsights.

Fuel Compound for storage of coal, coke and wood.

An HF/DF transmitting station with aerial mast was housed in a brick and wood building usually situated on a small site on the far side of the technical site from the airfield.

At Bassingbourn, Debden, Duxford, Honington, Wattisham and Watton, all pre-war RAF stations, camp buildings were mostly constructed in brick and tile.

HEADQUARTERS SITE

Situated about a quarter mile from the technical site, the central building of the headquarters complex was the Operations Block, a brick, concrete rendered and windowless construction with air-lock entrances. It contained the intelligence and opera-

Right: Station Headquarters site at Ridgewell, typical of such layouts on Class A bomber airfields. Large, windowless flat roof building in brick, concrete and steel housed Group Operations and Intelligence sections. It was proofed against poison gas and bomb blast. Smaller flat-roof building was the bombsight store. The two small slant-roof buildings in rendered brick and asbestos are standard type latrines. Large Nissen-type structures housed Hq administration offices. Note air raid shelter in foreground.

Station Headquarters building at Thurleigh was built in brick (rendered) with asbestos roofing. Early wartime stations had many buildings of this type whereas later constructions were predominantly Nissen type. As with most hangars erectd before spring 1942, the T2s at Thurleigh were shadow-shaded in black, green and tan. Photograph was taken on the occasion of official transfer ceremony in December 1942. Col C. B. Overacker receives the station fro Sqdn Ldr D. A. Batwell.

tions rooms. Adjoining Operations and connected by a corridor was Station Headquarters, consisting of two Nissen or brick buildings, 72 × 24 ft and 60 × 24 ft. These included quarters for

senior staff officers. Adjacent was a 72 × 24 ft Nissen or brick structure built as a crew briefing room, but not always used for that purpose.

COMMUNAL SITE

Situated not less than 500 yards from the technical site, the communal site or sites, for there were often two, formed the centre of personnel welfare. Large brick or Nissen buildings connected by a centrally placed kitchen formed a mess hall catering for 200 men. Three such mess halls were found on a communal site. Also present were a number of smaller buildings for meat and grocery stores, a ration breakdown hut for distribution of rations, a Post Exchange (PX) for personal purchases, barber, tailor and shoemaker shops, gymnasium and squash courts, library, and also officers' and enlisted mens' clubs, heated ablutions, showers and sewered latrines.

Standing in line, 386th BG ground men wait at the mess site for chow. Rendered building at the end is a projection room, the mess hall also serving as a cinema, at Boxted.

SICK QUARTERS SITE

The main sick quarters building was 24 × 30 ft Nissen or brick construction to house a 22-bed ward. Connected to it by a covered corridor was a smaller building for use as an isolation or special ward. Other buildings on the site, which was not less

than 500 yards from the other sites, were an 18 × 30 ft Nissen for medical staff quarters, a similar building for medical orderlies, and a 24 ft-span Nissen used as part ambulance garage and part mortuary.

LIVING SITES

Dispersed in the local countryside with at least 200 yards separation from the communal site, each living or sleeping site had from ten to 25 Nissen or prefabricated huts. Accommodation, depending on the type of hut, varied from four to 42 persons, and on any one site the maximum figure of total accommodation was

250, although in practice on some bomber stations there were over 300. There were six main makes of prefabricated hut – Hall, Janes, Laing, Orlit, Seco and Thorne – 13 types and four sizes. The majority, either Nissen or pre-fabricated, were either 576 or 1110 square feet ground area. On bomber stations there were seven living sites, one of which was designated for WAAF use.

As the only billeted women on USAAF combat airfields were the few representatives of the Red Cross Clubs, the WAAF site was used for males.

Additionally, latrine blocks and semi-submerged air raid shelters were situated on all camp sites. A loud-speaker 'Tannoy' system covered the whole base, the microphone being located in the Speech Broadcast building adjacent to the Operations block. Water and electricity were obtained from local civilian sources with emergency supplies available from high level water tower tank storage and stand-by generators, respectively. A sewage works and filter beds were provided for the main camp. Concrete roads linked all sites to communal or technical areas.

Above: **Living site at Thorpe Abbotts, Nissen huts dispersed in green meadows. In foreground is standard open type air-raid shelter, brick with earth banking.** (J. Miller)

Left: **Typical Nissen, home for men of an engineering battalion. Roof was double corrugated steel sheet held on steel frame. Ends were brick or wood. Tortoise coke stove gave inadequate heat and required much skill in tending.**

Below: **Picket post building on living site utilised as Hq for 837th BS office at Lavenham. Rendered brick walls, steel window frames and asbestos roof. All huts were supplied by overhead electricity lines.** (R. Snell)

BOMB STORE

Situated adjacent to the airfield but removed from all other sites, the bomb dump consisted of a series of narrow concrete roads running between bomb and ammunition storage points. Four open revetments each with four bays separated by earth and brick blast walls were designed to hold 50 ton of high explosive in each bay. While the actual tonnage of bombs in store varied considerably from day to day during intensive operational periods, 2000 to 3000 tons was quite normal. Buildings located in or adjoining the bomb dump were normally Nissen types of which six were used for incendiary cluster storage, six for pyrotechnics, and two for fuses and arming wires. Two fusing buildings, not wide enough to take US bomb trailers, were in some cases also used to store incendiaries. Four Nissens held .50 ammunition and another grenades and station defence ammunition.

AVIATION FUEL INSTALLATION

The original planned fuel installation for bomber airfields comprised six 12,000 Imperial gallon tanks giving a total of 72,000 gallons. As most of this quantity could be consumed in a single mission it was necessary to construct another fuel dump at each airfield to double the quantity of fuel held. A third 72,000 gallon site was added at some stations during 1944. All fuel tanks were normally buried and had both electric and hand pumping facilities. Fuel sites were normally situated outside the perimeter track but often quite close to aircraft dispersals.

GENERAL

It should be appreciated that references to Nissen type structures imply either Nissen, Romney, Iris or other designs. Other types of sheds and huts, such as Everite, Handcraft, Marston, Maycrete or other makes were erected, depending on the locality and the contractor concerned.

Fortress fortress. Base defence at Framlingham, early April 1944. Gun emplacement under camouflage net houses 40 mm anti-aircraft weapons. Hedge bordering public road to Little Glemham has been cut down to afford better field of fire to the south. White rudder bar on B-17F 42-3312 *Sequatchiee* identified aircraft as flying with 390th BG's 'B' group when double-group formations were despatched. Peculiar to 13th Combat Wing, this distinguishing marking was soon discontinued when such separation of aircraft within the Group was found impractical.

8th Air Force Combat Airfields

The following 62 plates show operational airfields exactly as they were laid out during occupation by 8th Air Force units.

Scale is 3 inches to 1 mile. CT is an abbreviation of Control Tower. In some instances the numbering of camp sites and hardstandings was changed. The given runway heading numbers were also varied by one degree from the original in a few cases.

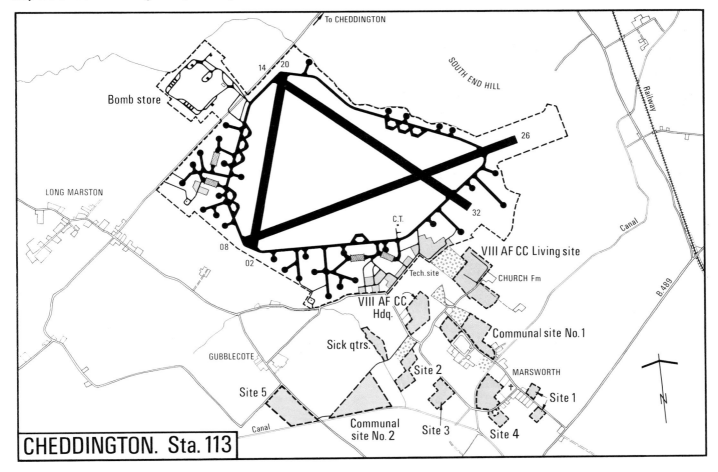

CHEDDINGTON. Sta. 113

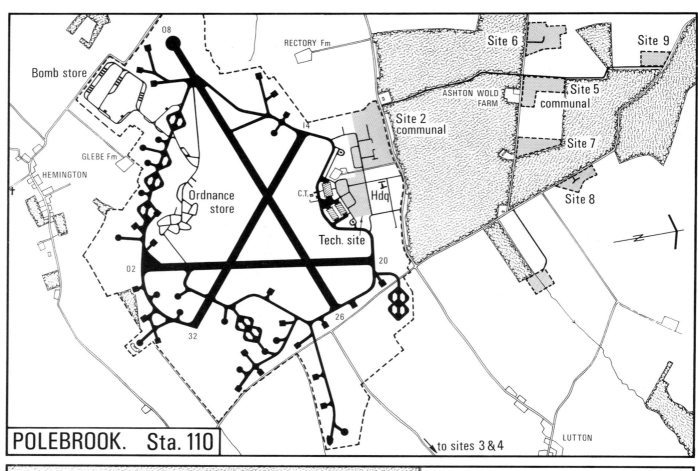

POLEBROOK. Sta. 110

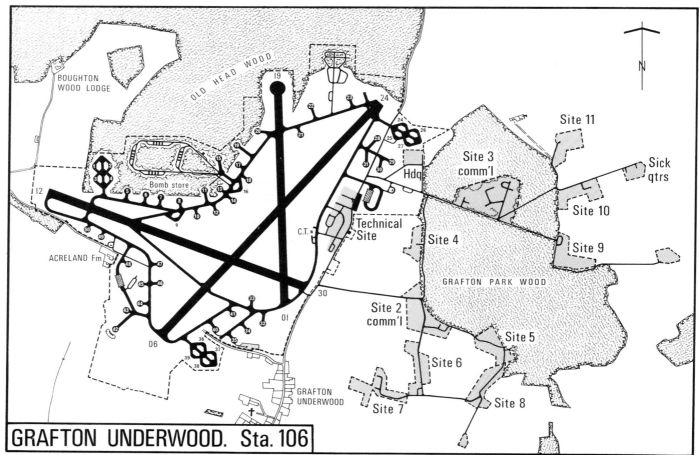

GRAFTON UNDERWOOD. Sta. 106

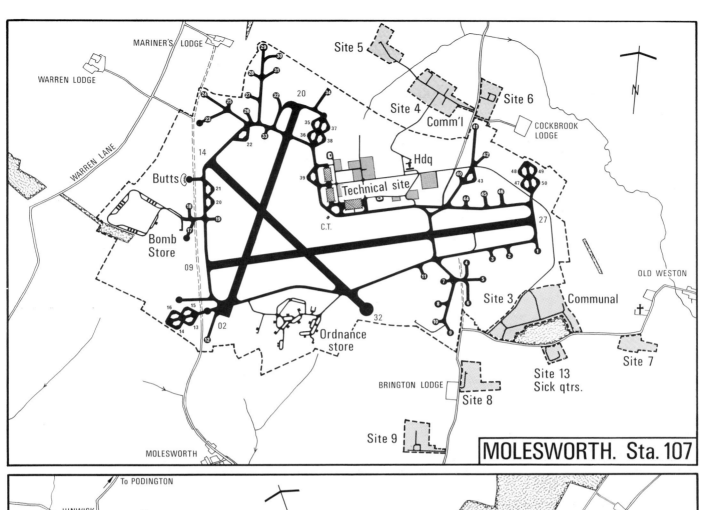

MARINER'S LODGE

WARREN LODGE

Site 5

Site 4
Comm'l

Site 6

COCKBROOK
LODGE

WARREN LANE

14

Butts

09

Bomb
Store

16

02

12

Ordnance
store

32

C.T.

Hdq

Technical site

27

Site 3

Communal

OLD WESTON

Site 7

Site 13
Sick qtrs.

BRINGTON LODGE

Site 8

Site 9

MOLESWORTH. Sta. 107

MOLESWORTH

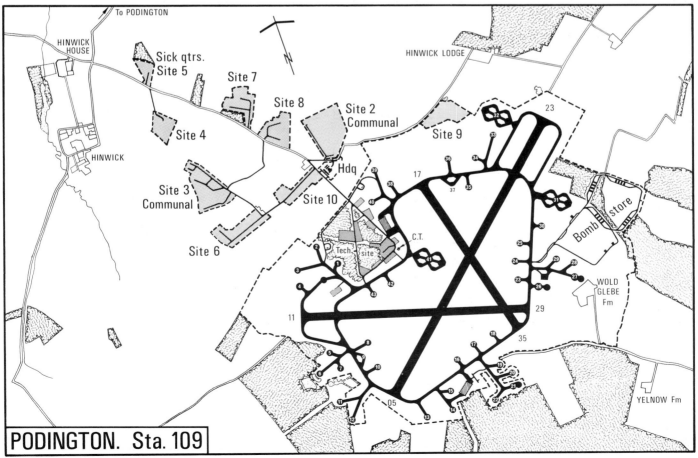

To PODINGTON

HINWICK
HOUSE

Sick qtrs.
Site 5

Site 7

HINWICK LODGE

Site 8

Site 2
Communal

Site 4

Site 9

23

HINWICK

Hdq

Site 3
Communal

Site 10

17

Bomb store

C.T.

Tech. site

29

WOLD
GLEBE
Fm

Site 6

11

35

YELNOW Fm

05

PODINGTON. Sta. 109

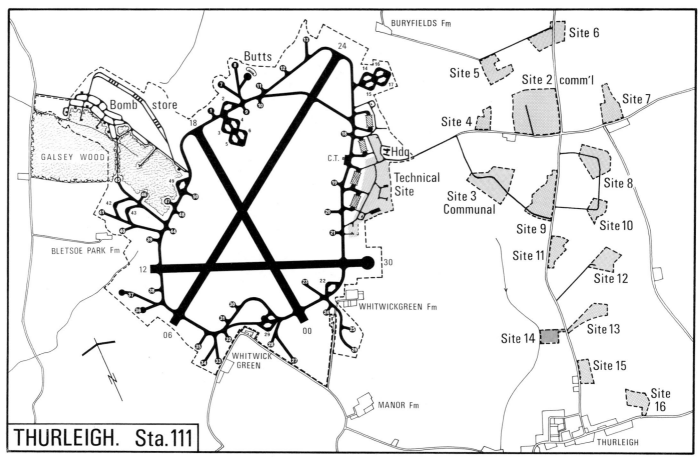

Thurleigh labels: BURYFIELDS Fm, Site 6, Site 5, Site 2 comm'l, Site 7, Site 4, Butts, Bomb store, Site 3 Communal, Site 8, Site 10, C.T., Hdg, Technical Site, Site 9, Site 11, Site 12, GALSEY WOOD, Site 14, Site 13, Site 15, BLETSOE PARK Fm, WHITWICKGREEN Fm, Site 16, WHITWICK GREEN, MANOR Fm, THURLEIGH

THURLEIGH. Sta.111

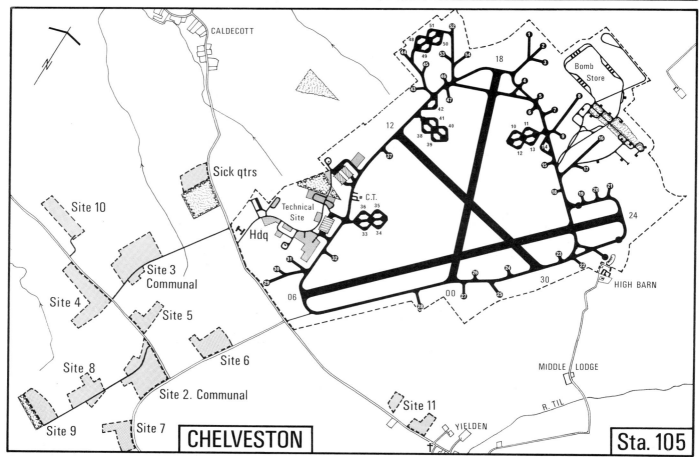

Chelveston labels: CALDECOTT, Bomb Store, Sick qtrs, Site 10, Technical Site, C.T., Hdq, Site 3 Communal, Site 4, HIGH BARN, Site 5, MIDDLE LODGE, Site 6, Site 2. Communal, R. TIL, Site 8, Site 11, YIELDEN, Site 9, Site 7, **CHELVESTON**, **Sta. 105**

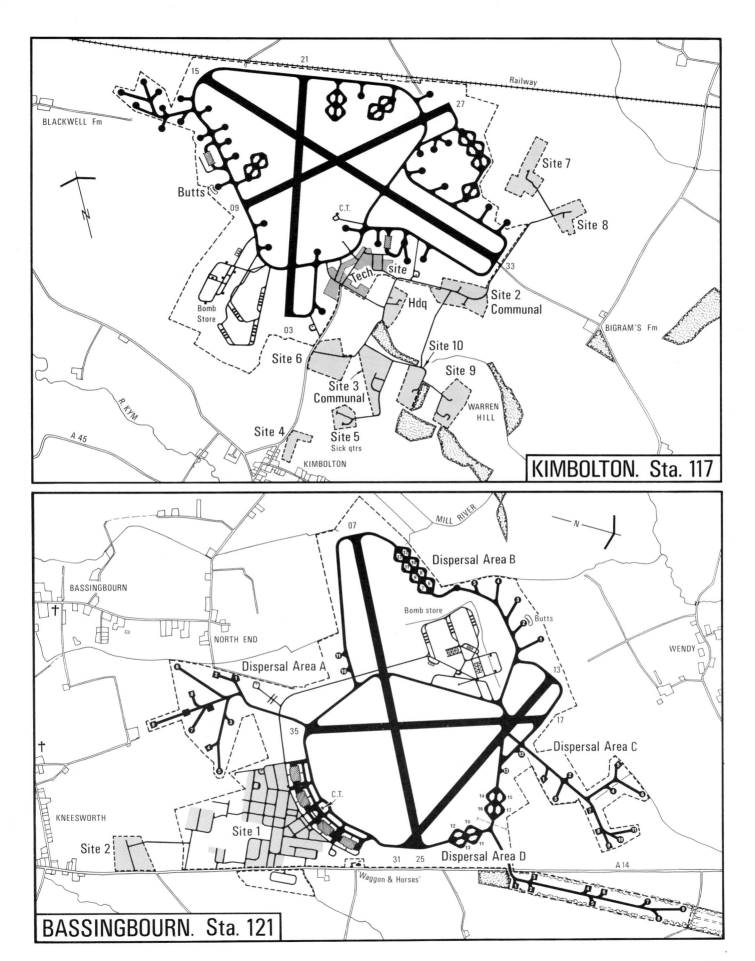

KIMBOLTON. Sta. 117

BLACKWELL Fm
21
15
Railway
27
Site 7
Butts
09
Site 8
C.T.
33
Tech. site
Site 2
Hdq
Communal
Bomb
Store
03
Site 10
Site 6
Site 9
Site 3
Communal
WARREN
HILL
R. KYM
Site 4
Site 5
A 45
Sick qtrs
KIMBOLTON
BIGRAM'S Fm

BASSINGBOURN. Sta. 121

MILL RIVER
07
N
Dispersal Area B
BASSINGBOURN
Bomb store
Butts
NORTH END
WENDY
Dispersal Area A
Dispersal Area C
35
Dispersal Area D
C.T.
KNEESWORTH
Site 1
Site 2
A 14
31   25
'Waggon & Horses'

277

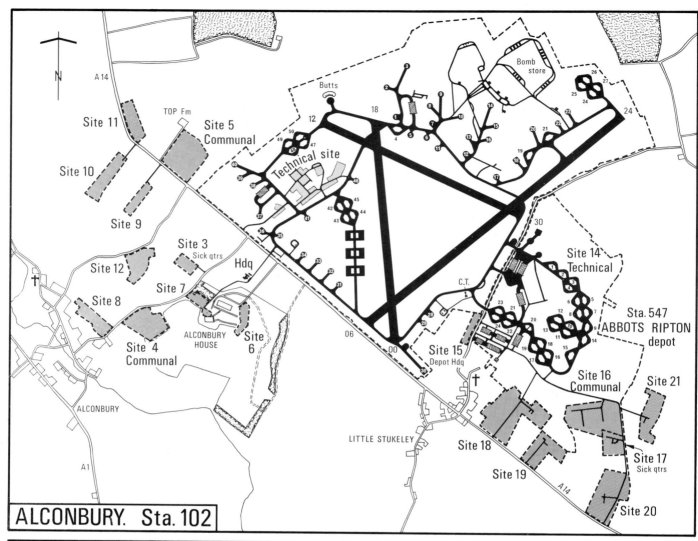

ALCONBURY. Sta. 102

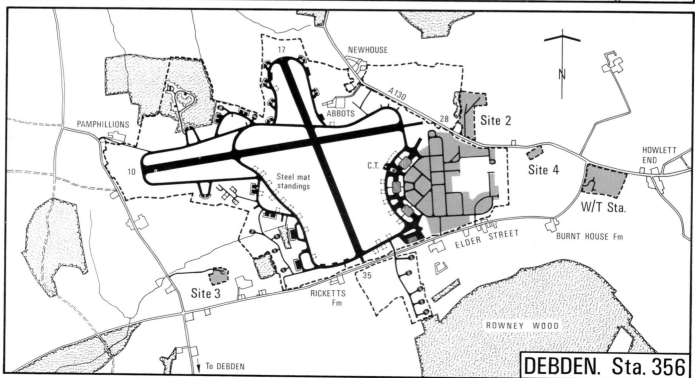

DEBDEN. Sta. 356

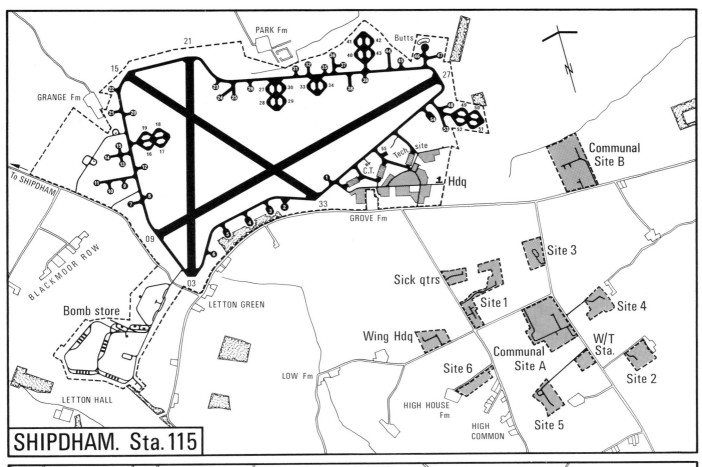

SHIPDHAM. Sta. 115

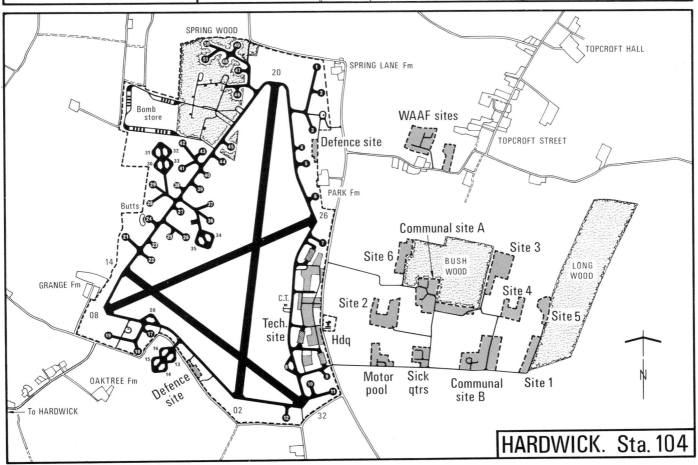

HARDWICK. Sta. 104

279

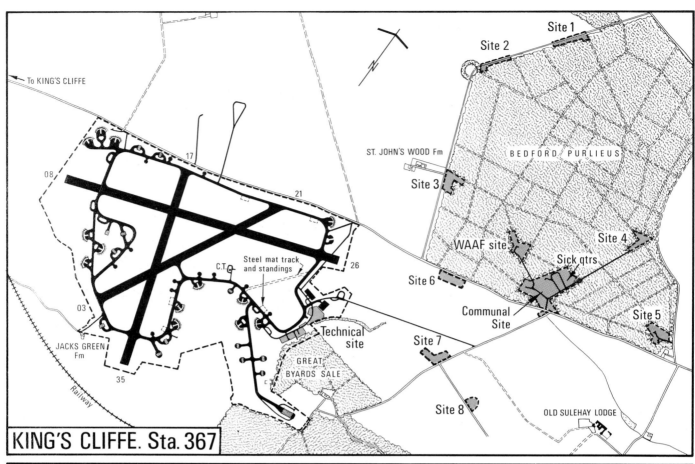

KING'S CLIFFE. Sta. 367

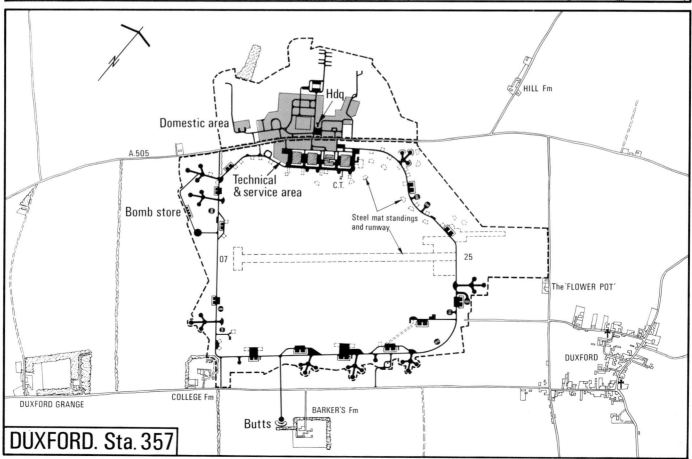

DUXFORD. Sta. 357

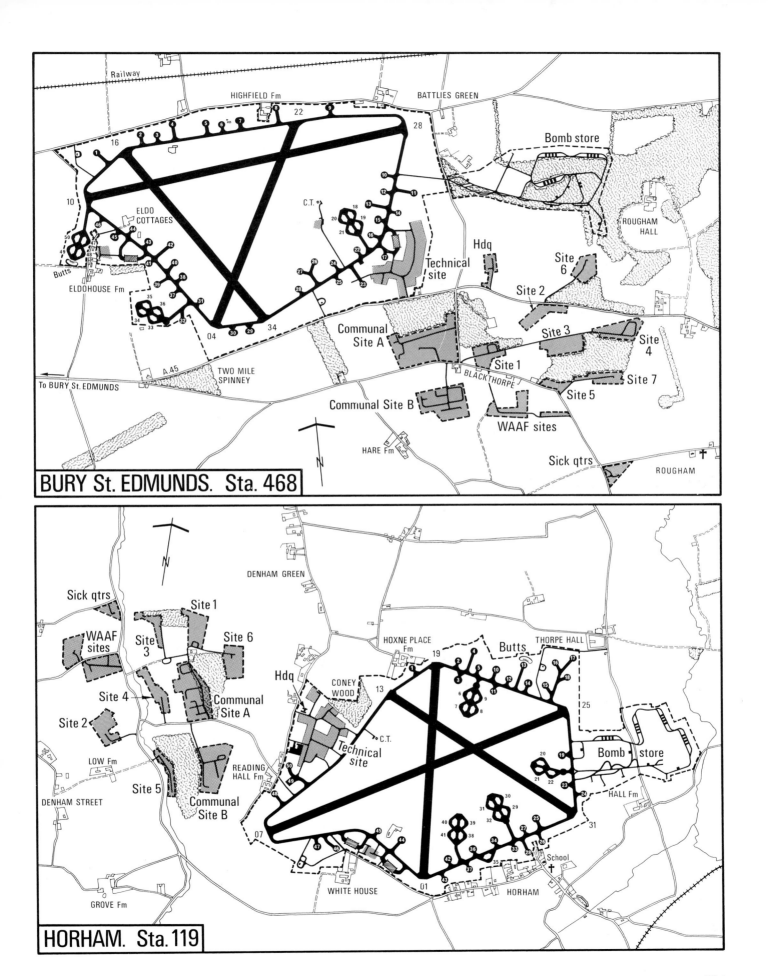

BURY St. EDMUNDS. Sta. 468

HORHAM. Sta. 119

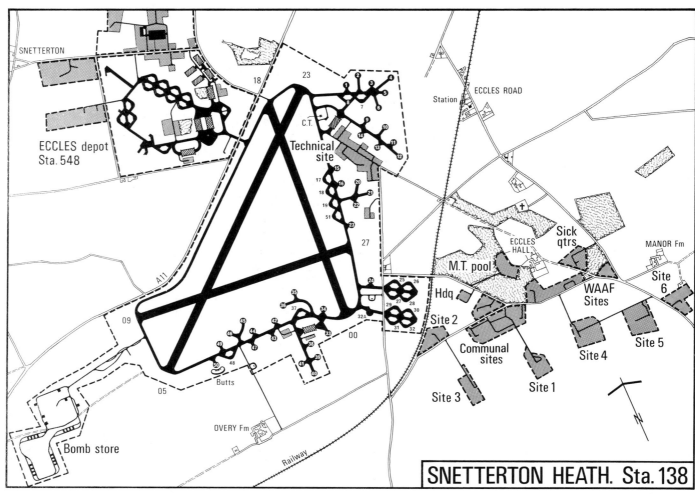

SNETTERTON HEATH. Sta.138

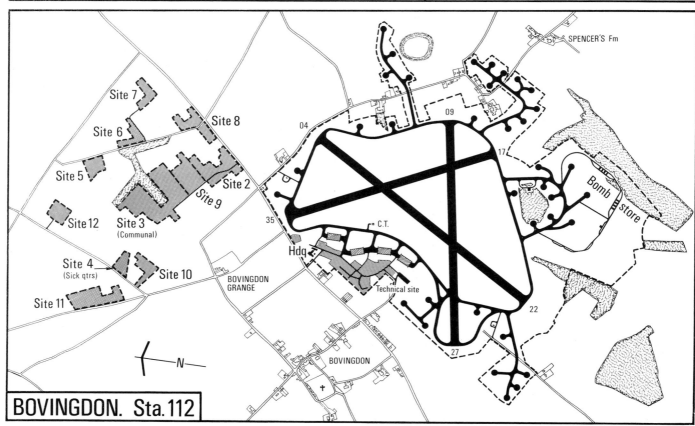

BOVINGDON. Sta.112

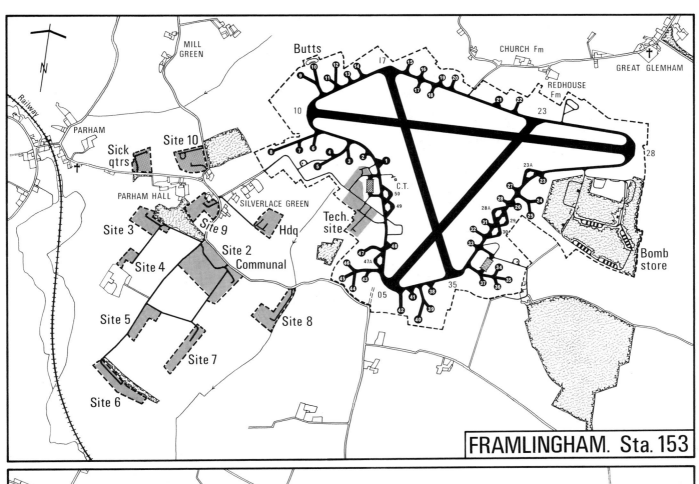

FRAMLINGHAM. Sta. 153

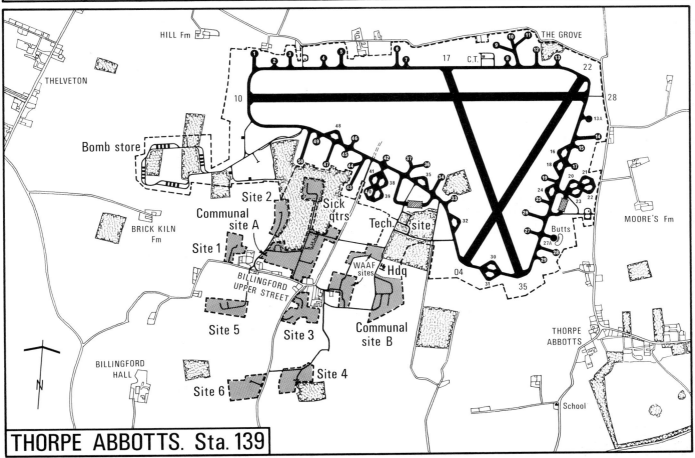

THORPE ABBOTTS. Sta. 139

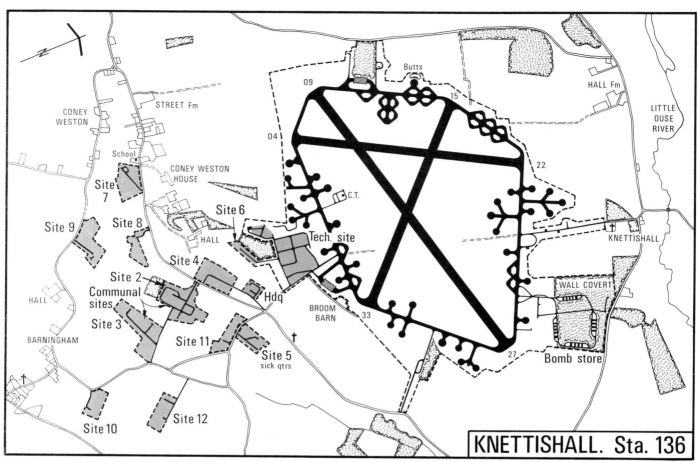

KNETTISHALL. Sta. 136

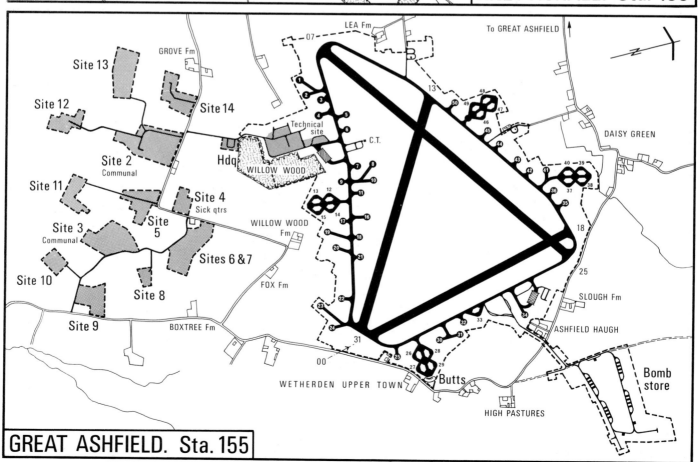

GREAT ASHFIELD. Sta. 155

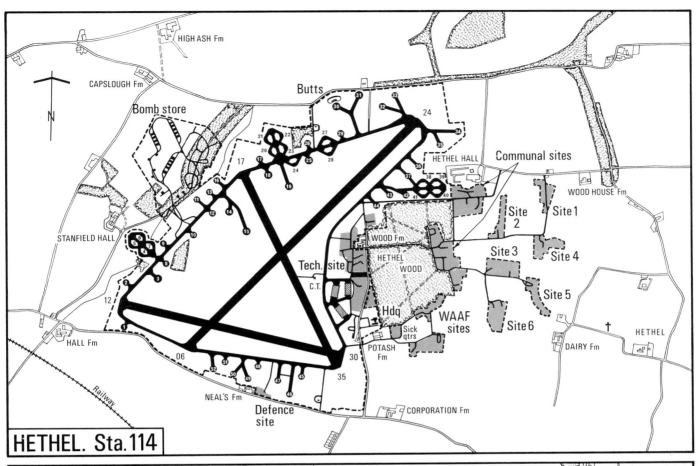

HETHEL. Sta. 114

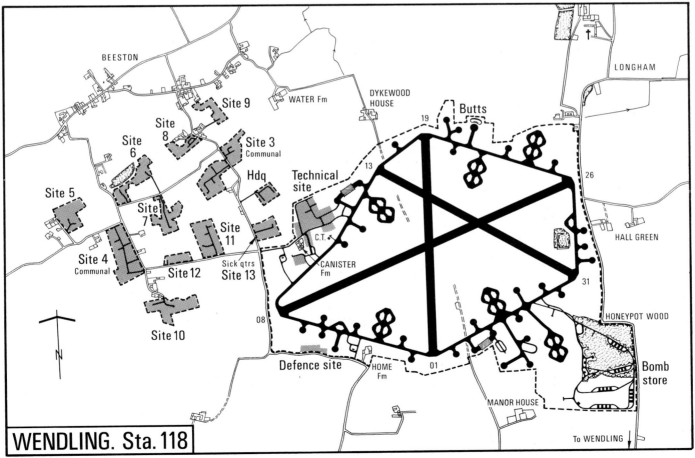

WENDLING. Sta. 118

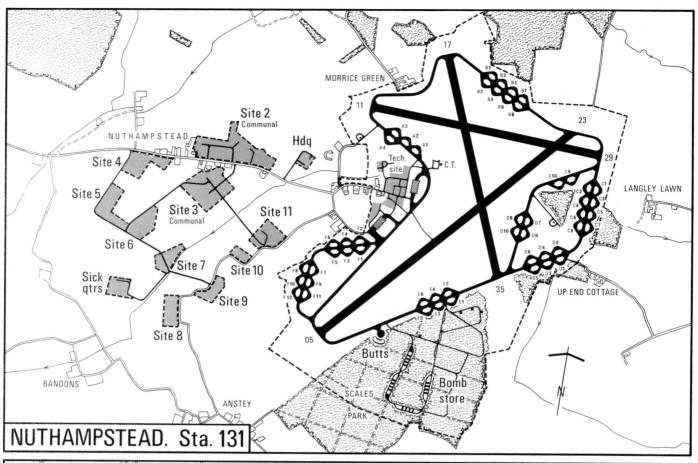

NUTHAMPSTEAD. Sta. 131

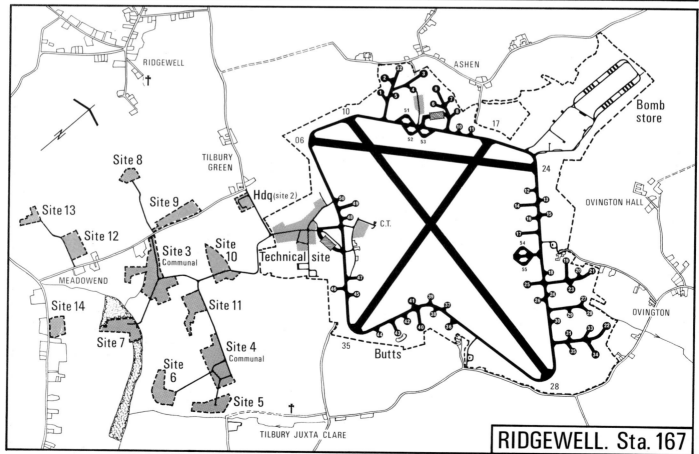

RIDGEWELL. Sta. 167

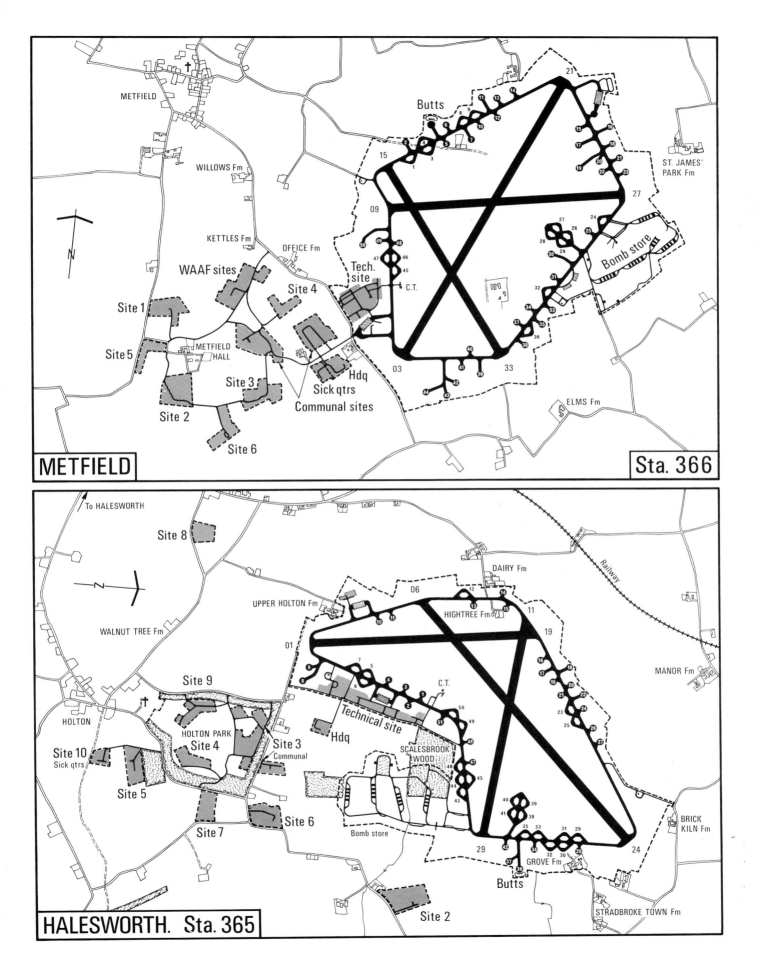

METFIELD — Sta. 366

METFIELD
WILLOWS Fm
KETTLES Fm
OFFICE Fm
WAAF sites
Site 4
Site 1
Site 5
METFIELD HALL
Site 3
Site 2
Site 6
Tech. site
C.T.
Hdq
Sick qtrs
Communal sites
Butts
Bomb store
ST. JAMES' PARK Fm
ELMS Fm

HALESWORTH. Sta. 365

To HALESWORTH
Site 8
WALNUT TREE Fm
UPPER HOLTON Fm
DAIRY Fm
HIGHTREE Fm
Railway
MANOR Fm
HOLTON
Site 9
HOLTON PARK
Site 4
Site 3
Communal
Hdq
Technical site
Site 10
Sick qtrs
Site 5
SCALESBROOK WOOD
Site 6
Site 7
Bomb store
Butts
GROVE Fm
BRICK KILN Fm
STRADBROKE TOWN Fm
Site 2

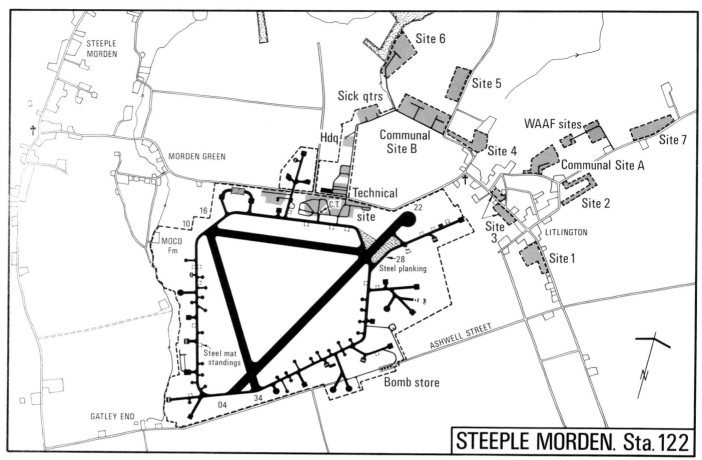

STEEPLE MORDEN. Sta. 122

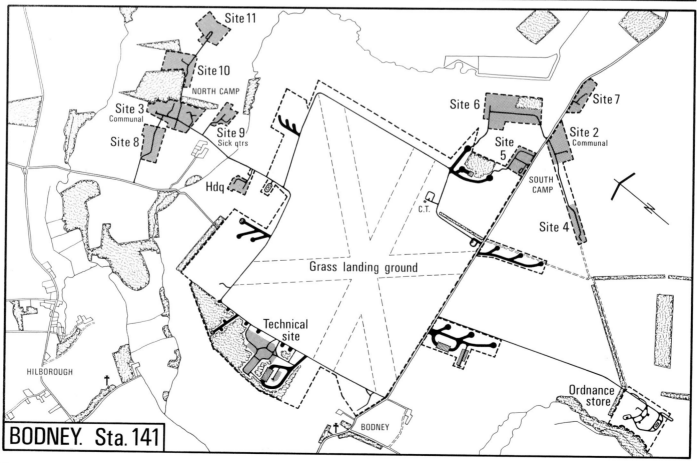

BODNEY. Sta. 141

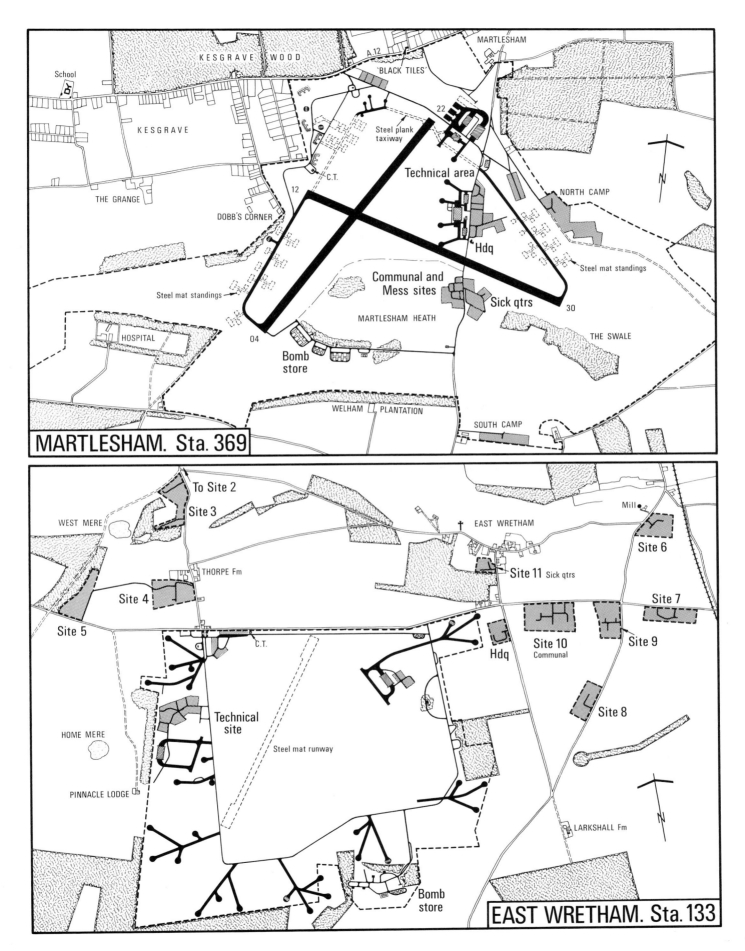

MARTLESHAM. Sta. 369

School

KESGRAVE WOOD

'BLACK TILES'

MARTLESHAM

A.12

KESGRAVE

Steel plank taxiway

22

Technical area

C.T.

12

THE GRANGE

NORTH CAMP

DOBB'S CORNER

Hdq

Steel mat standings

Steel mat standings

Communal and Mess sites

Sick qtrs

30

HOSPITAL

MARTLESHAM HEATH

THE SWALE

04

Bomb store

WELHAM PLANTATION

SOUTH CAMP

EAST WRETHAM. Sta. 133

To Site 2

Site 3

WEST MERE

Mill

EAST WRETHAM

Site 6

THORPE Fm

Site 11 Sick qtrs

Site 4

Site 7

Site 5

C.T.

Hdq

Site 10
Communal

Site 9

HOME MERE

Technical site

Steel mat runway

Site 8

PINNACLE LODGE

LARKSHALL Fm

Bomb store

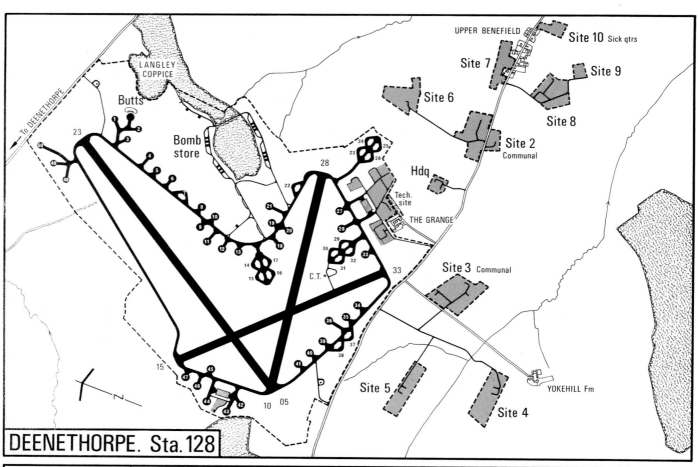

DEENETHORPE. Sta.128

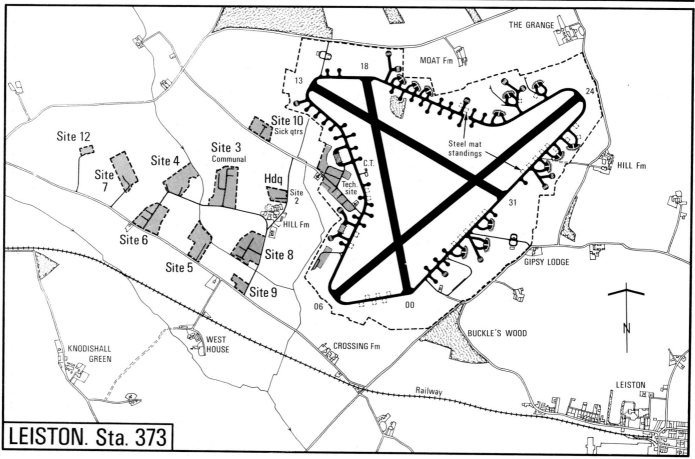

LEISTON. Sta. 373

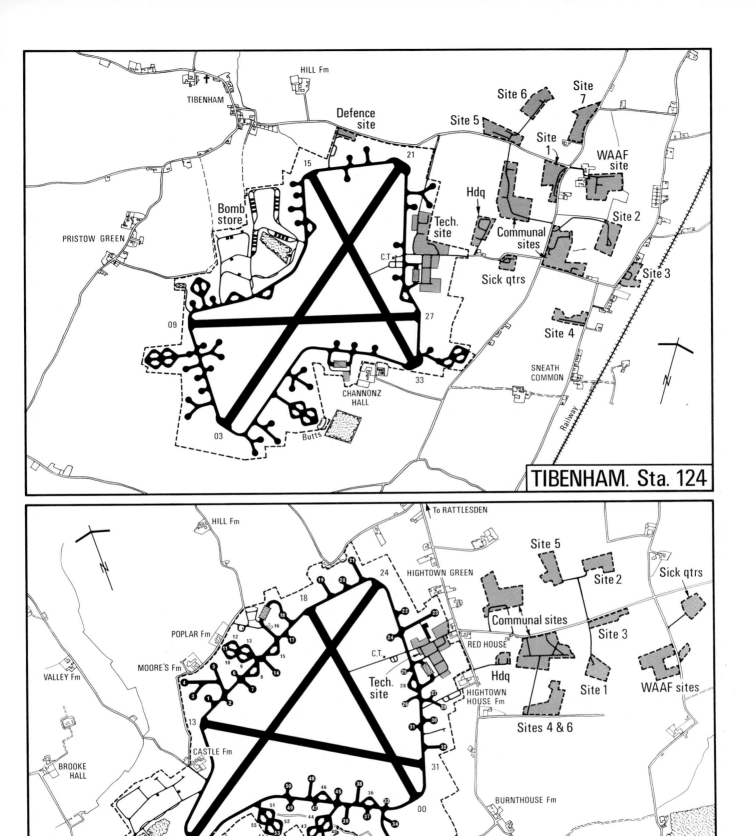

TIBENHAM. Sta. 124

RATTLESDEN. Sta. 126

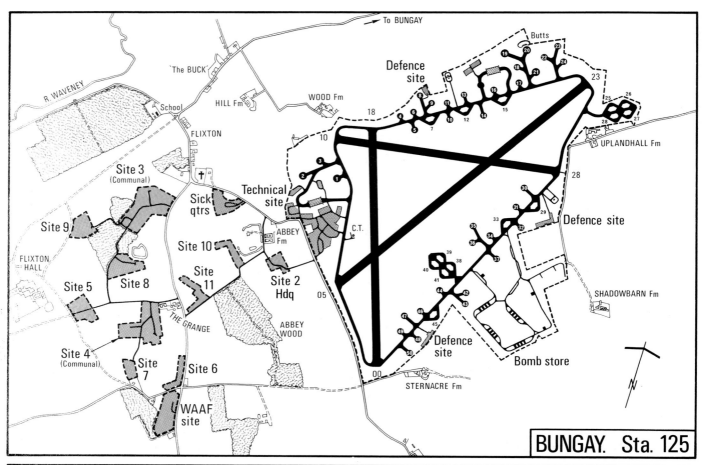

BUNGAY. Sta. 125

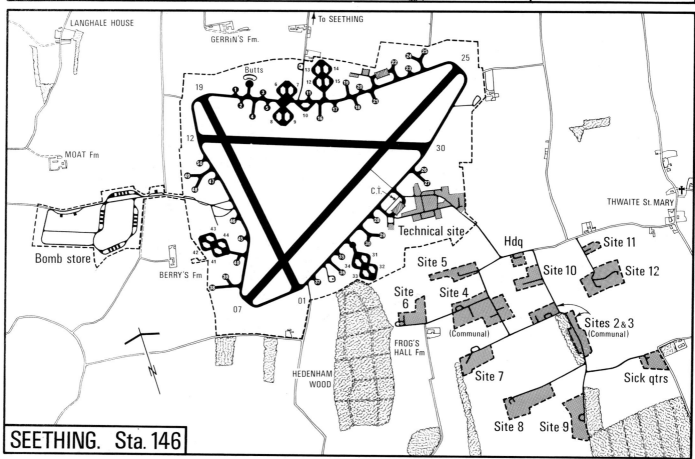

SEETHING. Sta. 146

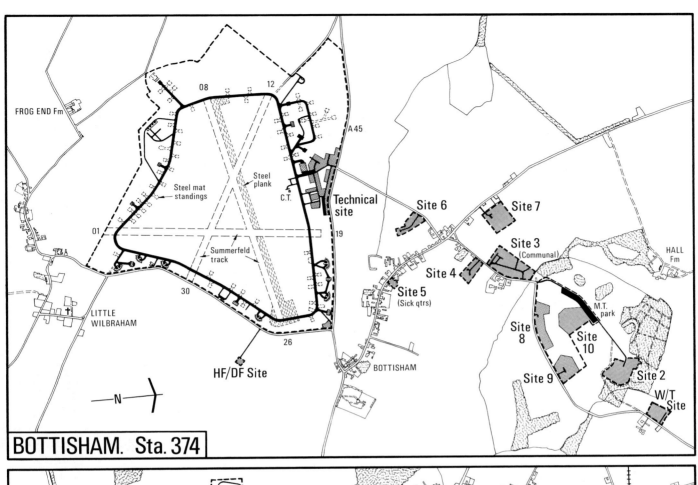

FROG END Fm

Steel mat standings

Steel plank

08 12

A 45

C.T.

Technical site

Site 6

Site 7

Site 3 (Communal)

Site 4

01 19

Summerfeld track

Site 5 (Sick qtrs)

HALL Fm

Site 8

M.T. park

Site 10

30

LITTLE WILBRAHAM

26

Site 9

Site 2

W/T Site

HF/DF Site

N

BOTTISHAM

BOTTISHAM. Sta. 374

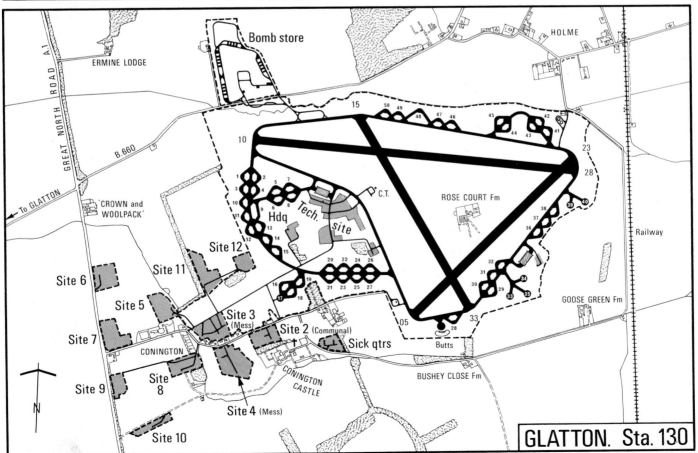

Bomb store

HOLME

GREAT NORTH ROAD A.1

ERMINE LODGE

15

50 49 48 47 46

45

44 43

42 41

10

23

28

B.660

To GLATTON

'CROWN and WOOLPACK'

C.T.

ROSE COURT Fm

Railway

1 2 5 7
3 4 6
10 9
8
11
Hdq
Tech. site

13
14
15

38
37
36

Site 12

12

39 40

Site 11

20 22 24 26
21 23 25 27

32
31
30 29 34
33 35

Site 6

16 19
17 18

05

GOOSE GREEN Fm

Site 5

Site 3 (Mess)

Site 2 (Communal)

Site 7

Sick qtrs

33

CONINGTON

Butts

Site 9

Site 8

CONINGTON CASTLE

BUSHEY CLOSE Fm

N

Site 4 (Mess)

Site 10

GLATTON. Sta. 130

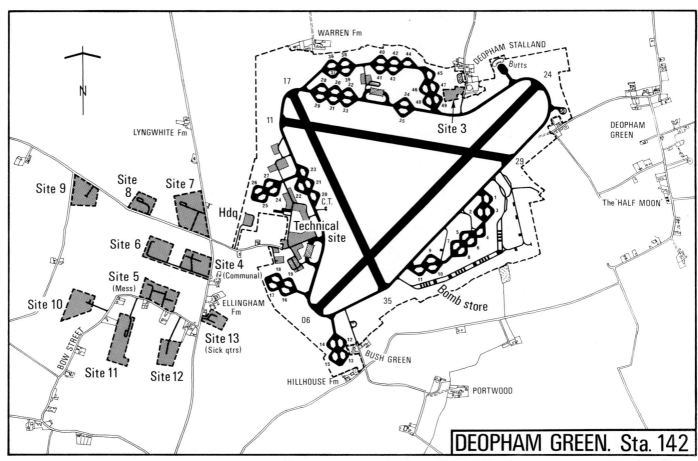

DEOPHAM GREEN. Sta. 142

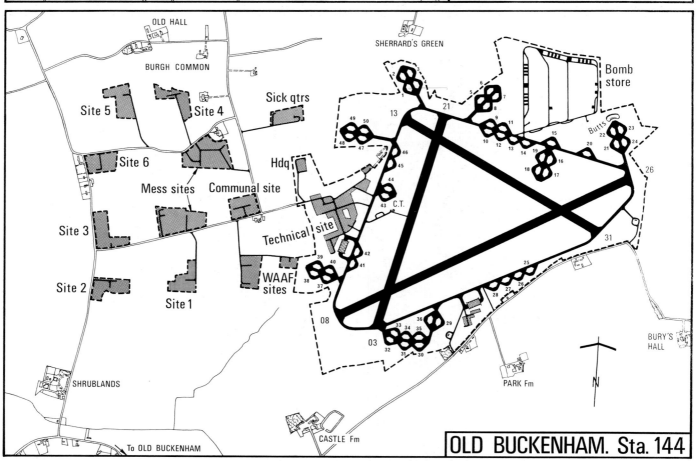

OLD BUCKENHAM. Sta. 144

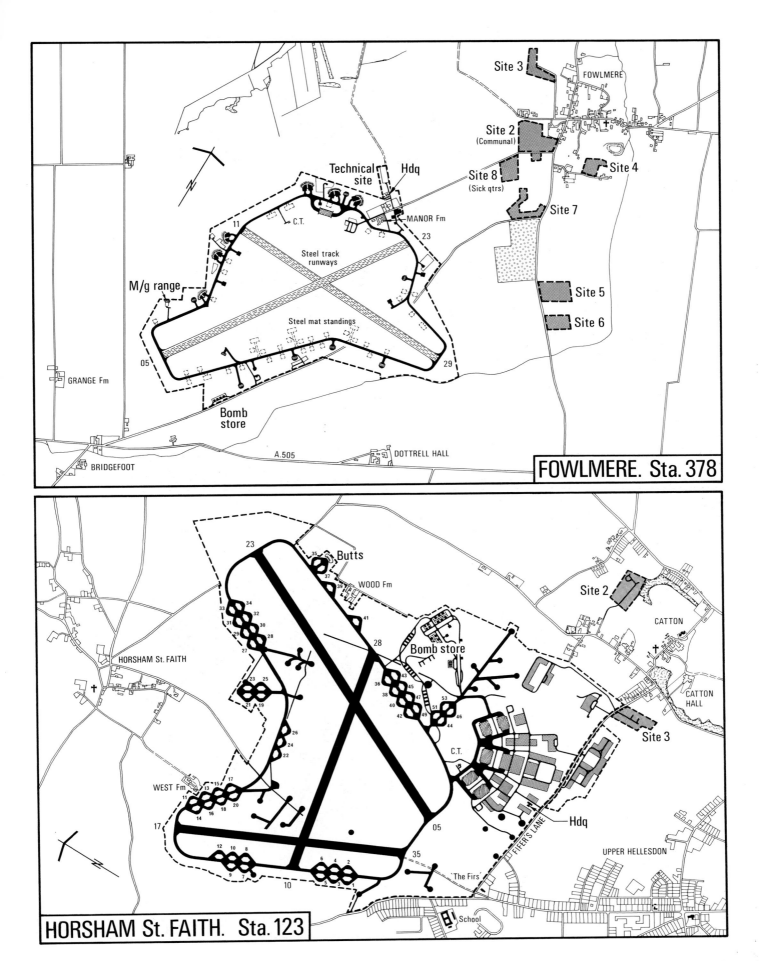

FOWLMERE. Sta. 378

Site 3

FOWLMERE

Site 2
(Communal)

Site 4

Technical
site

Hdq

Site 8
(Sick qtrs)

Site 7

MANOR Fm

11

C.T.

23

Steel track
runways

M/g range

Site 5

Site 6

Steel mat standings

05

29

GRANGE Fm

Bomb
store

A.505

DOTTRELL HALL

BRIDGEFOOT

HORSHAM St. FAITH. Sta. 123

23

Butts

35

37

39

WOOD Fm

34

33
32

41

Site 2

CATTON

31
30

29
28

27

28

HORSHAM St. FAITH

Bomb store

23 25

21 19

36
38

43
45
47

53
51

40

49

46

42

44

CATTON
HALL

26

24
22

C.T.

Site 3

15 17

WEST Fm

11 13
18 20

16

14

Hdq

FIFER'S LANE

05

17

12 10 8

UPPER HELLESDON

9 7

35

6 4 2

10

5 3 1

`The Firs'

School

295

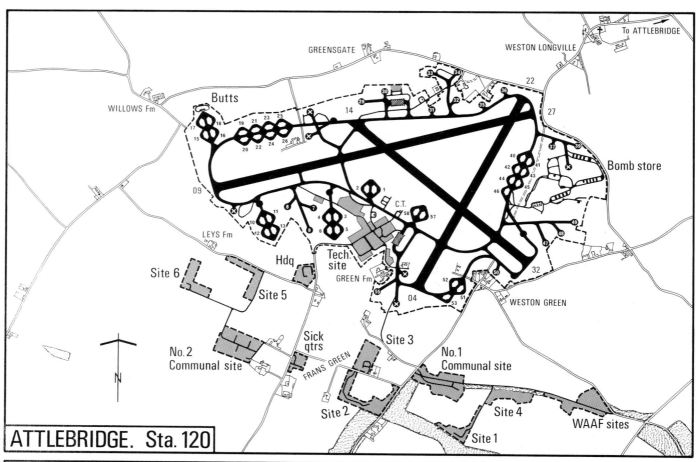

ATTLEBRIDGE. Sta. 120

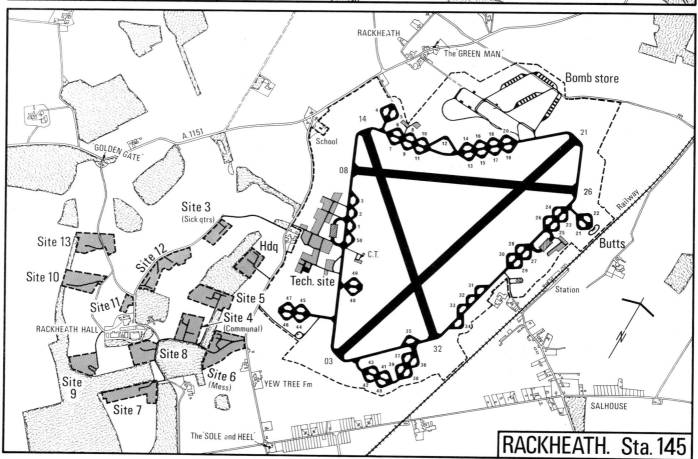

RACKHEATH. Sta. 145

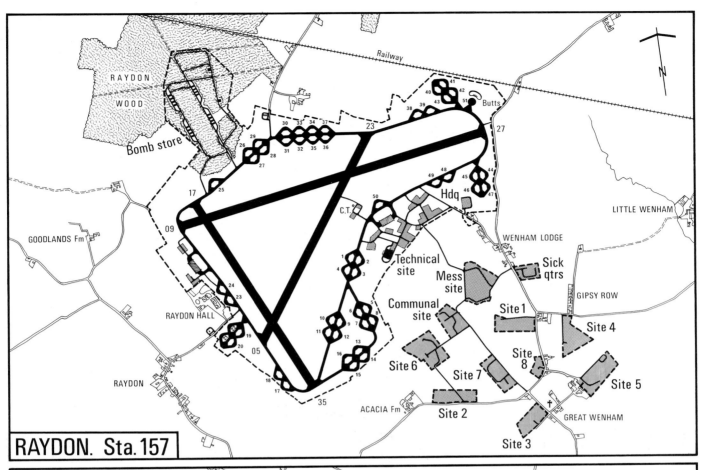

RAYDON. Sta. 157

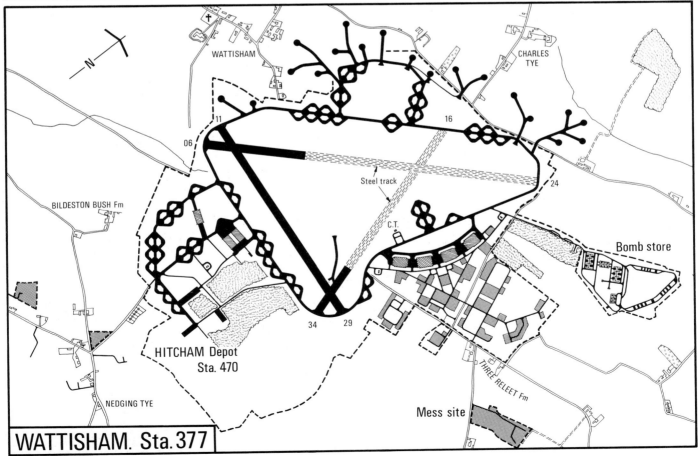

WATTISHAM. Sta. 377

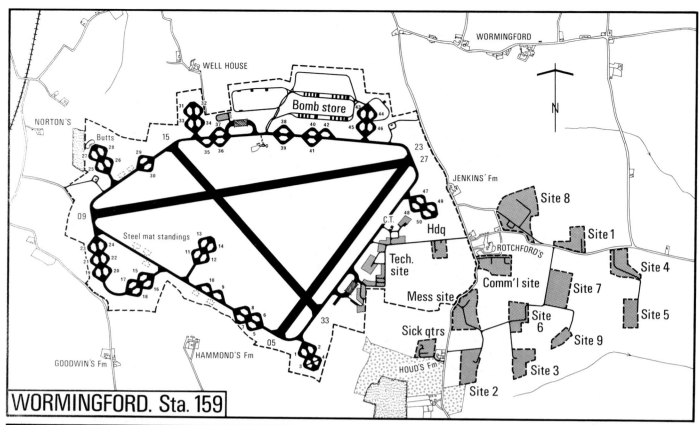

WORMINGFORD. Sta. 159

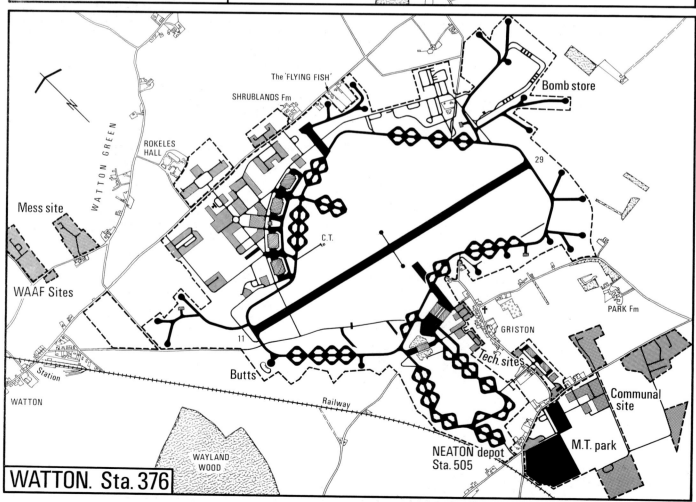

WATTON. Sta. 376

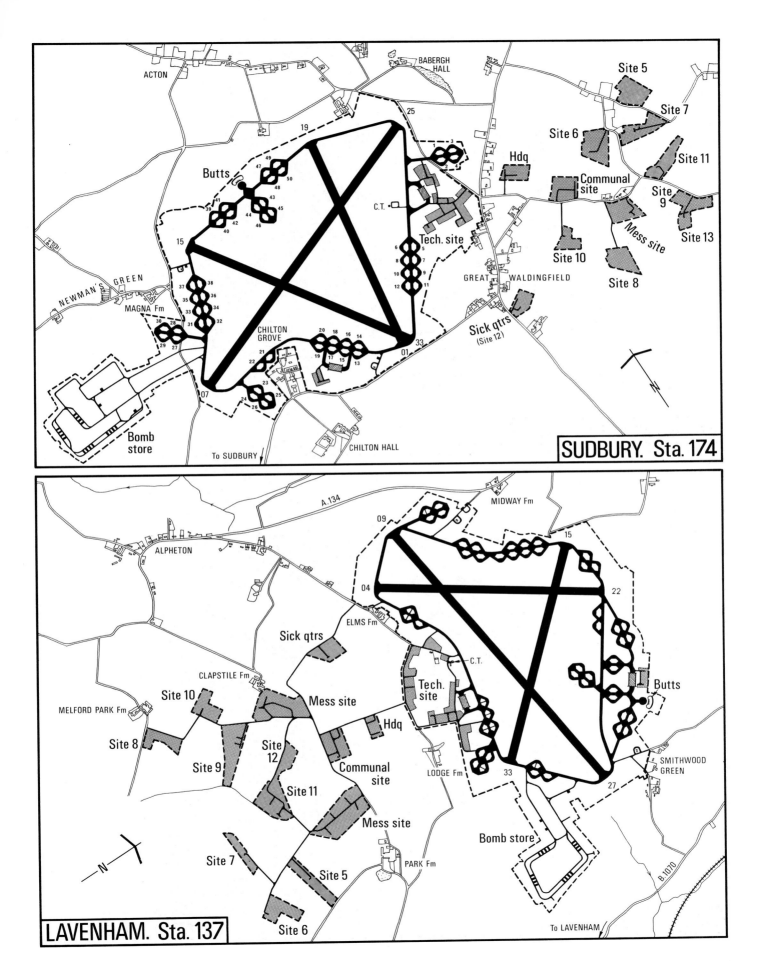

ACTON

BABERGH
HALL

Site 5

25

Site 7

19

Site 6

Hdq

Communal
site

Butts

47 49
48 50
43
45
11 41
39
44
42
46
40

C.T.

Tech. site

Site 11

Site 9

Site 13

15

6   5
8   7
10 9
12 11

Mess site

NEWMAN'S GREEN

37 38
35 36
33 34
31 32

Site 10

Site 8

MAGNA Fm

30 28
29 27

CHILTON
GROVE

20 18 16 14
19 17 15 13

33

GREAT WALDINGFIELD

Sick qtrs
(Site 12)

21
22

N

07

23 25
24 26

01

Bomb
store

To SUDBURY

CHILTON HALL

SUDBURY. Sta. 174

A.134

MIDWAY Fm

09

ALPHETON

04

15

ELMS Fm

22

Sick qtrs

C.T.

CLAPSTILE Fm

Mess site

Tech.
site

Butts

MELFORD PARK Fm

Site 10

Hdq

Site 8

Site 12

Communal
site

LODGE Fm

SMITHWOOD
GREEN

Site 9

33

27

Site 11

N

Mess site

Site 7

Bomb store

Site 5

PARK Fm

B.1070

Site 6

To LAVENHAM

LAVENHAM. Sta. 137

299

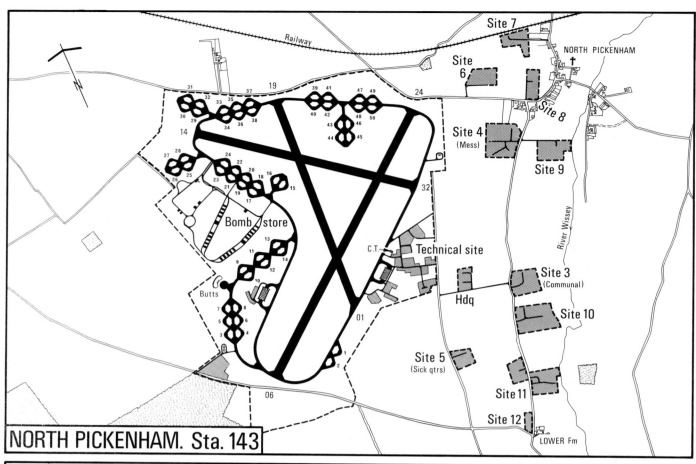

NORTH PICKENHAM. Sta. 143

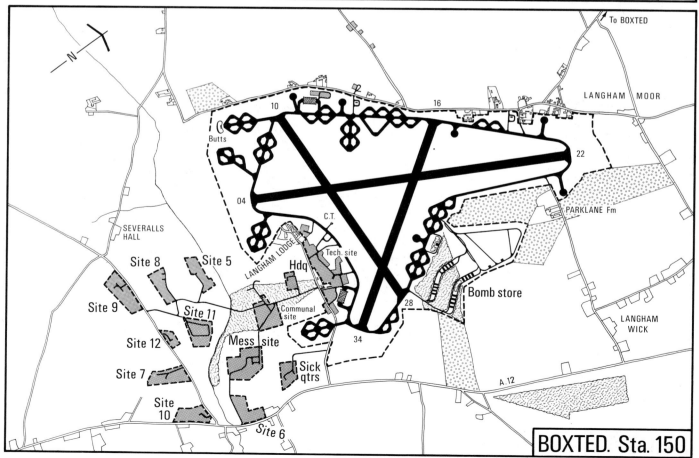

BOXTED. Sta. 150

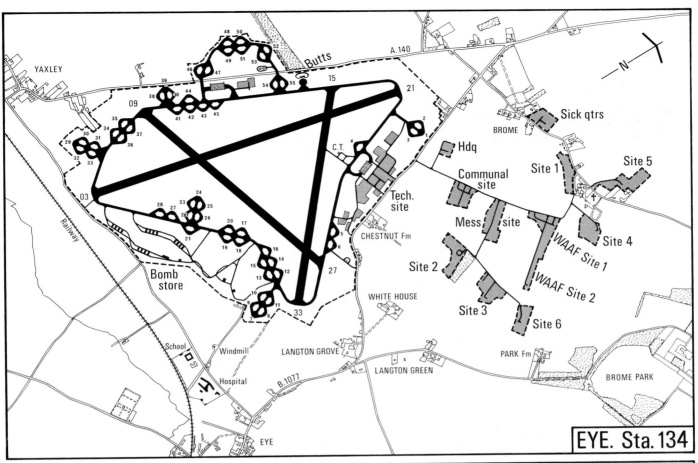

EYE. Sta. 134

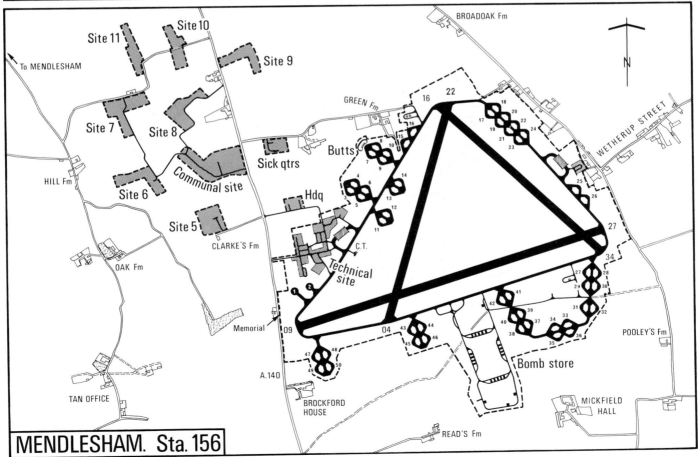

MENDLESHAM. Sta. 156

301

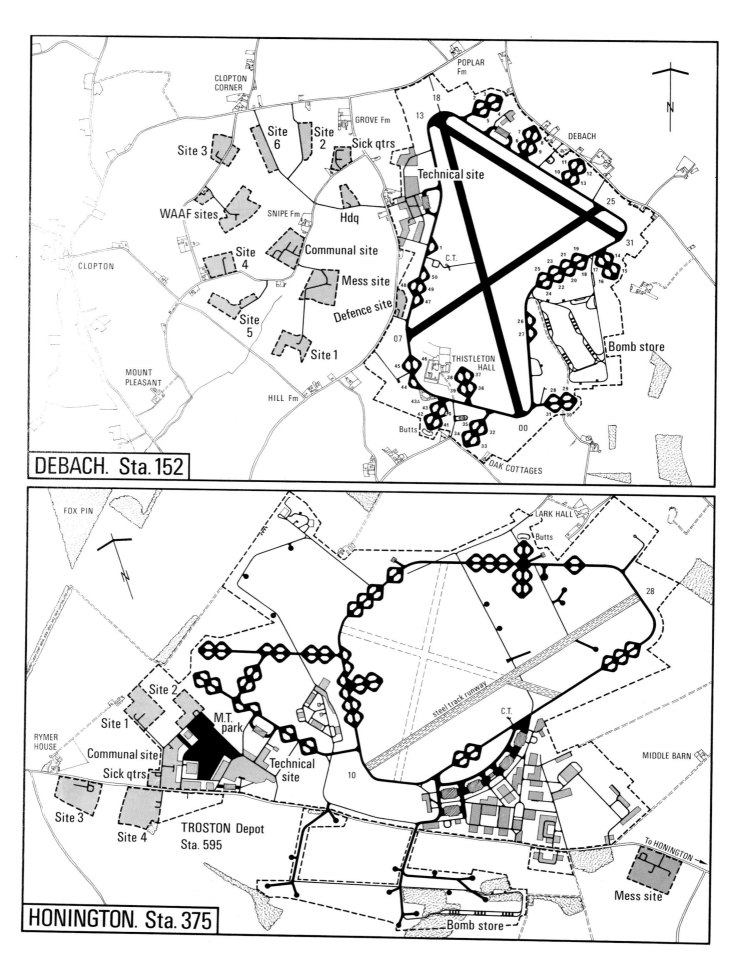

DEBACH. Sta. 152

Site 3
Site 6
Site 2
Sick qtrs
GROVE Fm
CLOPTON CORNER
POPLAR Fm
DEBACH
Technical site
WAAF sites
SNIPE Fm
Hdq
Communal site
CLOPTON
Site 4
Mess site
Defence site
Site 5
Site 1
MOUNT PLEASANT
HILL Fm
C.T.
Butts
THISTLETON HALL
Bomb store
OAK COTTAGES

18
13
25
31
07
00

N

HONINGTON. Sta. 375

FOX PIN
LARK HALL
Butts
N
28
Site 2
Site 1
M.T. park
RYMER HOUSE
Communal site
Technical site
Sick qtrs
steel track runway
C.T.
MIDDLE BARN
Site 3
10
Site 4
TROSTON Depot
Sta. 595
To HONINGTON
Mess site
Bomb store

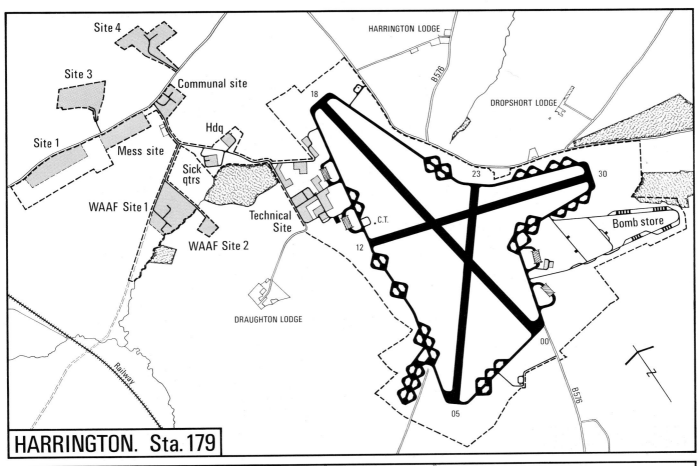

HARRINGTON. Sta.179

Site 4
Site 3
Communal site
Site 1
Mess site
Hdq
Sick qtrs
WAAF Site 1
WAAF Site 2
Technical Site
Draughton Lodge
Railway
Harrington Lodge
Dropshort Lodge
Bomb store
C.T.
18
23
30
12
00
05
B576

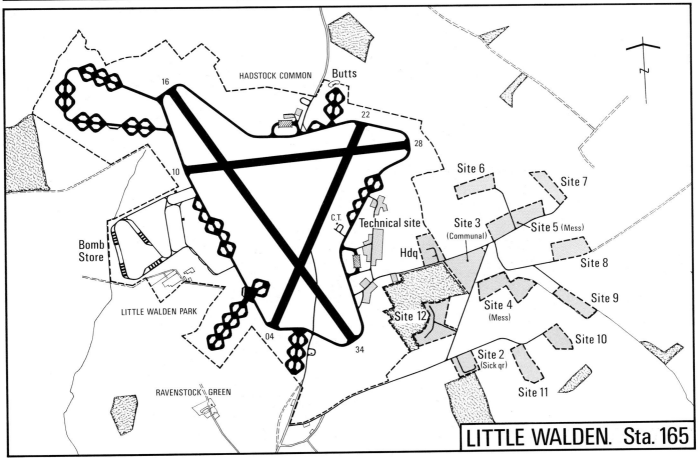

LITTLE WALDEN. Sta.165

Hadstock Common
Butts
Site 6
Site 7
Site 3 (Communal)
Site 5 (Mess)
Technical site
Hdq
Site 8
Bomb Store
Site 12
Site 4 (Mess)
Site 9
Little Walden Park
Site 10
Site 2 (Sick qr)
Ravenstock Green
Site 11
C.T.
16
22
28
10
04
34

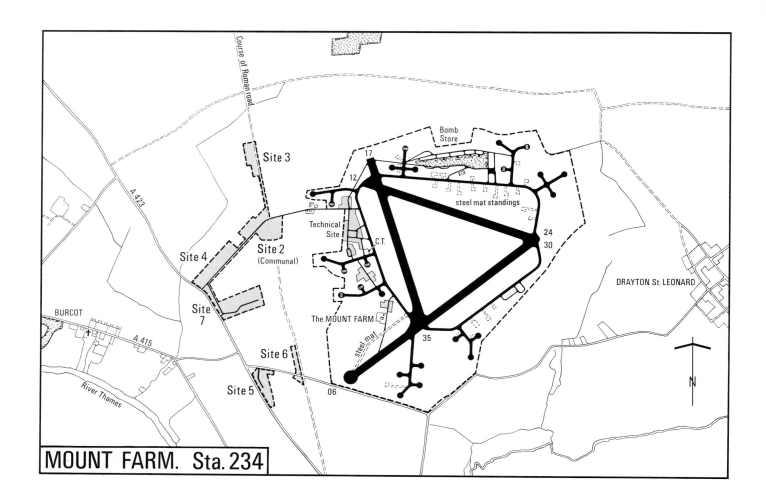

MOUNT FARM. Sta. 234

Stations Listing

Official station names were bestowed by the Air Ministry and in the case of airfields care was taken to see that names were distinctive enough to avoid confusion. The name given was not necessarily that of the site. Many airfields, constructed on land taking in two or three parishes, might be known locally by the name of one, while the name officially bestowed could be that of the nearest village or town of some size. An example is Framlingham, built in the parishes of Parham and Glemham. In the district the airfield was known by either parish name whereas the official tag came from the small town three miles north-west of the site. A few airfields were located in parishes with the same name but in different counties. For this reason the airfield at Langham, Essex was named Boxted – a neighbouring village – because a Langham airfield already existed in Norfolk.

To promote a more distinctive name, some airfields were renamed during construction. Little Walden was originally known as Hadstock and Bury St Edmunds as Rougham. In the case of Andrews Field, this name was given to Great Saling, the first airfield in England completed by US engineers, to commemorate Lt Gen Frank Andrews, killed in a flying accident. Less obvious is the reason for renaming Butley, Winfarthing and Hepworth, airfields on which work was temporarily suspended in 1943, as Bentwaters, Fersfield and Shepherd's Grove. This may have been to avoid confusion with new contractual agreements for completion of these sites. Confusion did, however,

arise through the apparent official neglect of avoidance of name duplication and similarity at other stations. Examples are the depot at Sudbury, Derbyshire which was often confused with Sudbury airfield, Suffolk, and the headquarters at Bushy Park and Bushey Hall.

In addition to the British official names, a few 8th Air Force headquarters were given camp names in the tradition of the US Army. Code names were also used for some headquarters and other special bases.

In accordance with military practice, USAAF stations in the UK were given station numbers. In June 1942 a tentative system utilised a B prefix for bomber bases, P for pursuit, O for observation, D for rear supply depots and R for repair depots. This was replaced in August that year by a system of three digit numbers. At its introduction, numbers in the 100 range were allotted to VIII BC stations, VIII AFCC stations received numbers in the 200 range commencing at 231, VIII FC had the 300 range commencing at 341, VIII GASC had the 400 range commencing at 466, and VIII AFSC the 500 range starting with 586. Eventually the majority of numbers in the whole 400 and 500 ranges were used as 9th Air Force succeeded VIII ASC and Air Service Command facilities increased. Numbers for new stations were then extended into the 800 and 900 ranges.

A few stations had numbers identifying them with other commands, for example, Bury St Edmunds, Station 486 and Halesworth, Station 365. Both were built as bomber bases but received their respective numbers when one was temporarily loaned to VIII GASC and the other to VIII FC. There were also cases of re-issued numbers; Station 173, originally allotted for Southminster bomber base that was never constructed, later became Dunkeswell's number.

USAAF station numbers should not be confused with APO (Army Post Office) numbers allotted to stations. These were purely for postal purposes and a single APO number usually embraced a number of stations.

United Kingdom Airfields Allocated for 8th Air Force Use 1942–1945

Note: Runway compass bearings in brackets after their length. Unless otherwise stated. Mk II Lightning.

Acklington
Location: 8 miles SE Alnwick, Northumberland. Allocated 8AF for tactical fighter use 12 July 1943. Never occupied by 8AF.

Alconbury Station 102
Locations: Alconbury Hill, Huntingdonshire. (4 miles NW Huntingdon.) Allocated 8AF 10 Aug 42 as bomber base. First occupied by USAAF Sep 42. Officially transferred to 8AF 19 June 43. Allocated as airfield serving 2 SAD in July 43. Transferred RAF 26 Nov 45. Built: 1938. Main contractor: W & C French Ltd. Runways: concrete, laid 1941, originally 4125 ft, 3720 ft and 3300 ft extended to 6000 ft (240), 4200 ft (180) and 4200 ft (300) respectively in late 1942. A/c dispersals: concrete, 30 pan with 15 loops added later. Hangars: two dispersed T2. Camp: utility buildings for 2894 persons. Served Abbots Ripton depot (Sta. 547) which had additional dispersals and 4 T2 hangars.

Aldermaston Station 467
Location: 10 miles SW Reading, Berkshire. Allocated 8AF as an air transport base 11 June 42. First occupied USAAF June 42. Officially transferred 8AF 30 June 43. Transferred 9AF Oct 43. Built: 1942 as Class A airfield. Runways: concrete, 6000 ft (060), 4200 ft (170) and 4200 ft (350). A/c dispersals: 49 pans and 2 loops. Hangars: 4 T2 grouped on Tech' site.

Andrews Field (Great Saling) Station 485
Location: Great Saling, 3 miles W Braintree, Essex. Allocated 8AF as bomber base 10 Aug 42. Renamed Andrews Field on 21 May 43 in honour of Lt Gen Frank Andrews, CG US Army in ETO who was killed in a B-24 crash in Iceland. Officially transferred to USAAF 15 June 43. Transferred 9AF Oct 43. Transferred RAF 1 Oct 44. Built: 1942 – Apr 43, first airfield completed by US forces in UK. Main constructor: 819th Engineer Btn, US Army. Runways: concrete with tar and wood chip surface, 6000 ft (270), 4200 ft (020) and 4200 ft (330). A/c dispersals: 46 loops, 4 large loops and 1 pan. Hangars: 2 dispersed T2. Camp: utility buildings for 2800 persons.

Appledram
Location: 1 mile S Chichester, Sussex. Proposed as site of 8AF fighter base 10 Aug 42 but not proceeded with.

Atcham Station 342
Location: 5 miles E Shrewsbury, Shropshire. Allocated 8AF 4 June 42 as fighter base. First occupied USAAF 10 June 42. Officially transferred 8AF 2 May 43. Returned to RAF 14 Mar 45. Built 1940 – 41 as sector fighter station for RAF. Runways: concrete, 4440 ft (235), 4050 ft (187) and 3700 ft (297). A/c dispersals: 12 twin pens and 22 fighter pans. Hangars: 3 Callender & Hamilton, 4 over blisters and 4 extra over blisters. Camp: utility buildings for 1652 persons.

Attlebridge Station 120
Location: 1 mile SW Weston Longville, Norfolk. Allocated to 8AF 10 Aug 42 as bomber base. Allocated as temporary fighter base 22 Sep 42 but removed from this status early in 1943. First occupied USAAF Oct 42. Temporarily loaned RAF No 2 Group Mar 43 to Jan 44. Officially transferred to 8AF 10 Apr 44. Returned to RAF 15 July 45. Built: 1941 – 1942. Main contractor: Richard Costain Ltd. Enlarged Jan – Oct 43. Runways: concrete, originally 3660 ft, 3360 ft and 3240 ft; extended to 6000 ft (270), 4200 ft (220) and 4200 ft (140) respectively. A/c dispersals: originally 30 pans with 34 loops added. Many of the pans were lost or sterilised during reconstruction. Hangars: 2 dispersed T2. Camp: utility buildings for 2894 persons.

Ayr
Location: 2 miles NE Ayr, Scotland. Allocated 8AF as tactical fighter base 12 July 43. Never occupied by 8AF units.

Ballyhalbert
Location: 11 miles SE Newtownards, Down, Northern Ireland. Allocated tentatively for Air Support Command 28 Feb 42. Allocated 22 Sep 42 as fighter base but cancelled Apr 43. Allocated 8AF for tactical fighters as lodger units 12 July 43. Never occupied by USAAF. Runways: 3 hard surface.

Bassingbourn Station 121
Location: Parishes of Bassingbourn and Wendy, Cambridgeshire (3½ miles NNW Royston). Allocated 8AF 10 Aug 42 as a bomber base. First occupied USAAF Oct 42. Officially transferred 8AF 21 Apr 43. Returned to RAF 10 July 45. Built: 1937–38. Main contractor: John Laing & Son Ltd. Grass flying field. Reconstructed 1941–Apr 42. by W & C French Ltd. Runways: concrete with asphalt surface; originally 2850 ft, 3300 ft and 3600 ft, extended in 1942 to 4170 ft (308), 4300 ft (350) and 6000 ft (254). A/c dispersals: 35 pans and 16 loops. Hangars: 4 C type. Camp: permanent buildings for 2972 persons.

Beaumont Station 148
Location: Immediately north of Beaumont village, Essex. Tentatively allocated 8AF as bomber base to Class A standard 10 Aug 42. Confirmed Sep 42. Indefinitely postponed 16 Dec 42.

Beccles Station 132
Location: Ellough, Suffolk. (2 miles SE Beccles.) Allocated 8AF 10 Aug 42 as bomber base. Returned to the RAF 14 Aug 44. Never occupied by 8AF flying unit. Built: 1943–44. Runways: concrete, 6000 ft (090), 4200 ft (172) and 4200 ft (226). A/c dispersals: 50 loops. Hangars: two dispersed T2. Camp: utility buildings for 2894 persons.

Bentwaters (Butley) Station 151
Location: Between Rendlesham and Butley, Suffolk. Originally named Butley. Allocated 8AF 10 Aug 42 as bomber base. Renamed Bentwaters winter 1943–44. Transferred RAF Oct 44. Never occupied by 8AF units. Built 1942–Apr 44. Work ceased Mar 43 to hasten work on other sites. Runways: concrete, 6000 ft (254), 4200 ft (018) and 4200 ft (315). A/c dispersals: 50 loops. Hangars: 2 dispersed T2. Camp: utility buildings for 2894.

Birch Station 149
Location: Between Birch and Messing, Essex. (5 miles SW Colchester.) Allocated 8AF as bomber base 10 Aug 42. Transferred 9AF Oct 43. Returned to 8AF Apr 44. Reserve airfield for 3rd Division early 1945. Never used by 8AF flying units. Built: 1943–Mar 44. Last airfield completed by US Army for 8AF. Main constructor: 846th Engineer Btn. Runways: concrete, 6000 ft (260), 4200 ft (200) and 4200 ft (310). A/c dispersals: 50 loops. Hangars: 2 dispersed T2. Camp: utility buildings for 2894.

Bishops Court
Locaton: 7 miles E Downpatrick, Down, Northern Ireland. Tentatively allocated 28 Feb 42 and bomber training airfield. Confirmed Sep 42. Surplus to requirements and transferred RAF for an air gunners' school 1 Apr 43. Never occupied by 8AF. Built 1942–Mar 43. Class A airfield with hard runways.

Bodney Station 141
Location: Immediately E of Bodney village, Norfolk. (4½ miles W Watton.) Allocated 8AF 10 Aug 42 to be developed as bomber base, Class A standard. Only technical site and camp enlarged to meet these

requirements. Reallocated as fighter station 16 June 43. First occupied by 8AF July 43. Officially transferred 8AF 17 Aug 43. Returned to RAF 8 Nov 45. Opened 1940 as grass airfield. Runways: sod; 3000 ft NE–SW, 2700 ft NW–SE and 2700 ft E–W. Mk I lighting. A/c dispersals: 12 small asphalt and 15 large asphalt. Hangars; 2 dispersed T2 and 5 blisters. Camp: utility buildings for 1709.

Boreham Station 161
Location: Between Boreham and Little Waltham, Essex. (3½ miles NE Chelmsford.) Allocated 8AF 10 Aug 42 as bomber base. Transferred 9AF Oct 43. Built: 1943–Mar 44. Main constructors: 861st Engineer Btn., US Army. Runways: concrete, 6000 ft (340), 4200 ft (210) and 4200 ft (270). A/c dispersals: 50 loops. Hangars: 2 dispersed T2. Camp: utility buildings for 2658 persons. Never occupied by 8AF.

Bottisham Station 374
Location: Between Bottisham and Little Wilbraham, Cambridgeshire. Allocated 8AF as fighter base 16 June 43. Officially transferred 8AF 3 Jan 44. Transferred RAF 10 Nov 44. Prepared 1940. Runways: originally sod. US engineers laid 4400 ft PSP main runway Jan 44. Other runways Sommerfeld track, 3600 ft (020) and 4305 ft (090). A/c dispersals: 15 concrete pens and 68 PSP. Hangars: 1 T2 and 7 blister. Camp: temporary buildings for 1709 persons. (Enlarged for USAAF use during second half 1943.)

Bovingdon Station 112
Location: 2 miles SW Hemel Hempstead, Hertfordshire. Allocated 8AF 16 May 42 as bomber training base. Officially transferred USAAF on 28 Apr 42. First occupied 8AF July 42. Transferred Air Transport Command 15 Sep 44. Returned to RAF Dec 45. Built 1941–42. Main contractor: John Laing & Son Ltd. Runways concrete, 4800 ft (220), 4200 ft (210) and 3900 ft (350). A/c dispersals: originally 36 pans, 14 loops added. Hangars: four grouped T2. Camp: utility buildings for 2849 persons.

Boxted Station 150
Location: Langham, Essex. (3 miles N Colchester.) Allocated 8AF 10 Aug 42 as bomber base. First occupied USAAF June 43. Officially transferred 8AF 26 Aug 43. Loaned 9AF Oct 43 and returned to 8AF Apr 44. Transferred RAF 23 Oct 45. Built 1942–May 43. Main contractor: W & C French Ltd. Runways: concrete, 6000 ft (220), 4200 ft (280) and 4200 ft (340). A/c dispersals: 43 loops, 1 large loop and 6 pans. Hangars: 2 dispersed T2 and 1 blister (added May 44). Camp: utility buildings for 2894 persons.

Bungay Station 125
Location: Flixton, Suffolk. (2 miles SW Bungay.) Allocated 8AF 4 June 42 as bomber base. First occupied USAAF Oct 42. Officially transferred 8AF 5 Jan 43. Returned to RAF 20 July 45. Built 1942. Main contractor: Kirk & Kirk Ltd. Runways: concrete, 6000 ft (050), 4440 ft (000) and 4200 ft (100). A/c dispersals: originally 30 small pans with 6 large pans and 14 loops added later. Hangars: two dispersed T2. Camp: utility buildings for 2894 persons. (Enlarged during 1943.)

Burtonwood Station 590
Location: 3 miles NW Warrington, Lancashire. Allocated 8AF Apr 42 for joint-US and British operation as aircraft depot. First occupied by USAAF June 42. Officially transferred USAAF 15 July 42. Returned to RAF July 46. Built: 1939–40 and enlarged during period 1941–44. Runways: concrete, 5250 ft (270), 4350 ft (220) and 4350 ft (150). A/c dispersals: 10 concrete pans, 24 tarmac 40 ft Ys, 17 tarmac 30 ft Ys and 2 20 ft Ys. Hangars: 1 J, 1 K, 6 L, 8 AD, 22 Robin and 6 T2. Station had a total 513,695 sq ft storage and 1,074 291 sq ft workshops. Camp: utility buildings and 19,986 persons.

Bury St Edmunds Station 468
Location: Rougham, Suffolk. (3 miles E Bury St Edmunds.) Allocated 8AF 10 Aug 42 as bomber base. First occupied USAAF Sep 42. Officially transferred 8AF 27 Apr 43. Transferred RAF 20 Dec 45. Built 1942. Main contractor: Richard Costain Ltd. Runways: concrete, 6000 ft (275), 4200 ft (160) and 4200 ft (220). A/c dispersals: originally 30 pans with 8 large pans and 12 loops added early 1943. Hangars: 2 dispersed T2. Camp: utility buildings for 2972 persons.

Catterick
Location: Immediately SE Catterick, Yorkshire. Allocated 8AF 12 July 43 as tactical fighter station. Never occupied by USAAF.

Chalgrove Station 465
Location: 4½ miles NE Dorchester, Oxfordshire. Allocated 8AF 11 Nov 42 as transport or observation unit base. First occupied USAAF Jan 44. Used by 9AF and USSTAF until Mar 45. Occupied by 8AF units Mar to 1 Oct 45. Returned to RAF 1 Dec 45. Runways: 6000 ft, 4200 ft and 4200 ft. A/c dispersals: 50 loops. Hangars: 2 dispersed T2. Camp: utility buildings for 2368 persons.

Chedburgh Station B-21
Location: immediately south of Chedburgh, Suffolk. Allocated 8AF 4 June 42 as bomber base. Allocation cancelled Aug 42. Never occupied by 8AF. Class A airfield.

Cheddington Station 113
Location: 6¾ miles NE Aylesbury, Buckinghamshire. Allocated 8AF 16 May 42 as bomber training base. First occupied USAAF Sep 42. Officially transferred 8AF 16 Aug 43. Returned to RAF 21 Jun 45. Built 1941–42. Main contractor: George Wimpey & Co. Runways: 5340 ft (260), 4380 ft (200) and 3480 ft (140). Dispersals: 32 pans and 9 loops. Hangars: 4 T2 in dispersed groups of two. Camp: utility buildings for 2551 persons.

Chelveston Station 105
Location: 6½ miles S Thrapston, Northamptonshire. Tentatively allocated as a bomber base in Nov 41. Confirmed May 42. First occupied by 8AF June 42. Officially transferred 8AF 19 Apr 43. Returned to RAF 9 Oct 45. Built 1941. Main contractor: Taylor-Woodrow Ltd. Runways: concrete, originally 4100 ft, 3700 ft and 3700 ft (120). In 1942 two lengthened to 6000 ft (060) and 4167 ft (180). A/c dispersals: originally 30 pans with 6 pans and 14 loops added during enlargement of airfield. Hangars: 2 T2 and 1 J type, grouped. Camp: utility buildings for 2894.

Chilbolton Station 404
Location: 4½ miles SE Andover, Hampshire. Allocated 8AF as fighter station 10 Aug 42. Allocation rescinded Sep 42. Used by 9AF units in 1944.

Chipping Ongar Station 162
Location: Willingale, Essex. (2 miles NE Chipping Ongar.) Allocated 8AF 10 Aug 42 as bomber base. First occupied by USAAF July 43. Officially transferred 8AF 25 Aug 43. Transferred 9AF Oct 43. Returned to RAF 18 Apr 45. Built Aug 42–July 43. Main constructor: 831st Engineer Btn US Army. Runways: concrete, 6000 ft (030), 4200 ft (090) and 4200 ft (150). A/c dispersals: 48 loops, 2 large loops and 1 pan. Hangars: 2 dispersed T2. Camp: utility buildings for 2770.

Church Fenton
Location: 4 miles SE Tadcaster, Yorkshire. Allocated 8AF 12 July 43 as tactical fighter station on lodger basis. Never occupied by USAAF.

Church Stanton Station 461
Location: Between Church Stanton and Widcombe, Somerset. (6 miles S Taunton.) Allocated 8AF 10 Aug 42 as fighter base. Allocation rescinded Sep 42. Used by 9AF in 1944. Renamed Culmhead in 1945.

Cluntoe Station 238
Location: 10 miles SE Cookstown, Tyrone, Northern Ireland. (West shore of Lough Neagh.) Tentatively allocated 28 Feb 42 for use by an Air Support Command. Allocated 8AF 10 Aug 42 as bomber training base. First occupied 8AF Aug 43. Officially transferred 8AF 30 Aug 43. Returned to RAF 8 Nov 44. Built 1942–May 43. Runways: concrete, 6000 ft (240), 4200 ft (100) and 4200 ft (360). A/c dispersals: 30 125 ft pans and 50 fighter pads. Hangars: 4 grouped T2. Camp: utility buildings for 2512 persons.

Cold Norton Station 163
Location: 1½ miles W Cold Norton village, Essex. Tentatively allocated 8AF 10 Aug 42 as bomber base. Confirmed Sep 42. Construction indefinitely postponed 14 Dec 42. Took in WWI Stow Maries airfield site.

Collyweston
Location: 1 mile SE Collyweston village, Northamptonshire. (3 miles SSW Stamford.) Allocated 8AF 22 Sep 42 as fighter station – satellite for Wittering. Eliminated by Apr 43 as unsuitable for operation of P-38 and P-47. Never occupied by USAAF. Grass.

Coltishall Station 355
Location: Between Sco Ruston and Little Hobbis (Houtbois), Norfolk. (8 miles NNE Norwich.) Allocated 8AF 7 Sep 42 as fighter base. Confirmed 22 Sep 42. Allocation rescinded 13 Apr 43 as RAF wished to retain station for night fighter operation. Never occupied by 8AF flying units. Pre-war RAF station with supported sod runways.

Crowfield
Location: Immediately NE Crowfield village, Suffolk. Tentatively allocated 8AF as bomber base 10 Aug 42. Confirmed Oct 42. Construction indefinitely postponed 14 Dec 42.

Debach Station 152
Location: Between Debach and Burgh, Suffolk. (3 miles NW Woodbridge.) Allocated 8AF as bomber base 10 Aug 42. First occupied USAAF May 44. Officially transferred 8AF 9 May 44. Transferred RAF 10 Oct 45. Built 1943–Apr 44. Main constructor: 820 Engineer Btn US Army. Runways: concrete, 6000 ft (180), 4200 ft (250) and 4200 ft (310). A/c dispersals: 50 loops. Hangars: 2 dispersed T2. Camp: utility buildings for 2894 persons. (Runways resurfaced Mar 45 due to subsidence.)

Debden Station 356
Location: 1 mile N Debden village, Essex, (2 miles SSE Saffron Walden.) Allocated 8AF as fighter station 7 Sep 42. First occupied USAAF Sep 42. Officially transferred 8AF 3 May 43. Returned to RAF 5 Sep 45. Built 1935–37. Main contractors: W & C French Ltd. Runways: laid 1940–41, concrete, 4800 ft (280) and 3950 ft (350). Hangars: 3 C type and 1 Bellman grouped on technical site and 11 blisters at dispersals. A/c dispersals: 14 twin blast pens and 64 temporary standings of PSP or steel mat. Camp: permanent buildings for 2000 persons.

Deenethorpe Station 128
Location: Between Deenethorpe and Upper Benefield, Northamptonshire. (9 miles NNE Kettering.) Allocated 8AF as bomber base 10 Aug 42. First occupied 8AF Nov 43. Officially transferred 8AF 20 Dec 43. Transferred RAF 9 Oct 45. Built 1943: Main contractor: John Laing & Son Ltd. Runways: concrete, 6000 ft (240), 4200 ft (110) and 4200 ft (350). Dispersals: 49 loops and 2 pans. Hangars: 2 dispersed T2. Camp: utility buildings for 2894 persons.

Deopham Green Station 142
Location: Between Deopham and Little Ellingham, Norfolk. (1¾ miles N. Attleborough.) Allocated 8AF as bomber base 10 Aug 42. First occupied USAAF Jan 44. Officially transferred USAAF 14 Feb 44. Transferred RAF 9 Oct 45. Built 1943. Main contractor: John Laing & Son Ltd. Runways: concrete, 6000 ft (240), 4200 ft (110) and 4200 ft (350). A/c dispersals: 49 loops and 2 pans. Hangars: 2 dispersed T2. Camp: utility buildings for 2894 persons.

Desborough Station B-28
Location: 2 miles NE Desborough, Northamptonshire. Allocated 8AF as bomber base 4 June 42. Allocation rescinded Aug 42. Never occupied by USAAF units. Class A field.

Digby Station P-7
Location: 10 miles SSE Lincoln, Lincolnshire. Tentatively allocated 8AF as fighter base 4 June 42. Allocation rescinded Aug 42. Never occupied by USAAF. Regular RAF fighter station. Grass surface.

Drem Station 430
Location: 4 miles NNW Haddington, East Lothian, Scotland. Allocated 8AF for tactical fighter units on lodger basis 12 July 43. Never occupied by 8AF units. Grass airfield.

Duxford Station 357
Location: Immediately WSW Duxford, Cambridgeshire. (8 miles S Cambridge.) Tentatively allocated 8AF 7 Sep 42. Confirmed 22 Sep 42. First occupied USAAF Oct 42. Officially transferred 8AF 15 June 43. Returned to RAF 1 Dec 45. Opened 1919. Permanent RAF fighter station with drained grass surface flying field. In Nov-Dec 44 a 4100 ft PSP runway laid. PSP marshalling areas laid 1943 at both ends of grass runway. A/c dispersals: 26 tarmac pads and 47 steel mesh mats. Hangars: 3 Belfast, 1 special, and 8 blister. Camp: permanent buildings and some utility for 1700 persons.

Earls Colne Station 358
Location: Between Coggeshall and Earls Colne, Essex. Allocated 8AF 4 June 42 as bomber base. First occupied USAAF May 43. Officially transferred 8AF 14 July 43. Transferred 9AF Oct 43. Built Jan 42–Dec 42. Runways: concrete, 6000 ft (192), 4200 ft (252) and 4200 ft (302). A/c dispersals: originally 36 pans with 16 loops added in late stages of construction with 1 pan eliminated. Hangars: 2 dispersed T2. Camp: utility buildings for 2298 persons.

East Wretham Station 133
Location: 6 miles NE Thetford, Norfolk. Allocated 8AF 4 June 42 as bomber base to be developed to Class A standard. Reallocated as fighter base 16 June 43. Officially transferred 8AF 27 Sep 43. Returned to RAF 1 Nov 45. Opened 1940. Flying field grass surfaced over free-draining sand. Work on enlargement of camp and technical installations commenced in 1943 but discontinued in June 43. Runways: grass, 5740 ft NE–SW and 4200 ft NNW–SSE. A/c dispersals: 24 macadam pads, 12 PSP, and several lengths steel mesh aprons. Hangars: 2 dispersed Bellman and 7 blisters. Camp: utility buildings for 1709 persons.

Eglinton Station 344
Location: 8 miles NE Londonderry. Tentative allocation to an Air Support Command 28 Feb 42. Allocated 8AF as fighter base 4 June 42. First occupied by USAAF July 42. USAAF departed Jan 43. Allocation to 8AF rescinded June 43. Never officially transferred to USAAF. Built 1941–42. Main contractor: Stewart Partners Ltd. Runways: tarmac, built by Royal Engineers; 4800 ft (090), 3300 ft (030) and 3200 ft (150). A/c dispersals: 10 macadam pads and 12 twin pens. Hangars: 2 Bellman and 12 blisters. Camp: utility buildings.

Eye Station 134
Location: Immediately south of Brome village, Suffolk. (1 mile NW Eye.) Allocated 8AF as bomber base 10 Aug 42. First occupied USAAF Apr 44. Officially transferred 8AF 8 May 44. Transferred RAF 1 Nov 45. Built: Sept 42–Feb 44. Main constructors: 827th and 859th Engineer Btns US Army. Runways: concrete, 6000 ft (212), 4200 ft (270) and 4200 ft (328). A/c dispersals: 49 loops and 1 pan. Hangars: 2 dispersed T2. Camp: utility buildings for 2894 persons.

Exeter Station 463
Location: Clyst Honiton, Devon. (4 miles E Exeter.) Allocated 8AF as fighter base 10 Aug 42. Allocation rescinded early Sep 42. Never occupied by 8AF. Used by 9AF in 1944.

Fersfield Station 554 (**Winfarthing** Station 140)
Location: Between Fersfield and Winfarthing, Norfolk. (16 miles SW Norwich.) Originally named Winfarthing and allocated to 8AF as bomber base 10 Aug 42. Renamed Fersfield in winter 1943–44. First occupied by 8AF Apr 44. Transferred RAF 18 Jan 45. Built 1943–44. Work suspended Apr 43 while men and equipment used to speed completion of other airfields. Runways: 6000 ft (066), 4200 ft (186) and 4200 ft (304). A/c dispersals: 50 loops. Hangars: 2 dispersed T2. Camp: utility buildings for 2894 persons.

Finedon
Location: Immediately NW of Finedon village, Northamptonshire. Tentatively allocated 8AF as bomber base 10 Aug 42. Confirmed Oct 42. Construction indefinitely postponed 16 Dec 42.

Ford Station 362
Location: 1 mile WNW Littlehampton, Sussex. Allocated 8AF as fighter base 10 Aug 42. Allocation rescinded early Sep 42. Allocated 8AF for tactical fighter units on lodger basis 12 July 43. Only used by 8AF as forward base for fighters. RAF fighter station. Runways: concrete, 6000 ft and 4800 ft. A/c dispersals: 35 pads and 14 double pens. Hangars: 5 Bellman, 1 special and 20 blisters.

Foulsham Station B-13
Location: Immediately N Foulsham village, Norfolk. Allocated 8AF as bomber base 4 June 42. Allocation rescinded early Aug 42. Never occupied by 8AF. RAF RCM base at which 8AF detachments served. Built 1941–42. Runways: 5700 ft, 4200 ft and 4050 ft.

Fowlmere Station 378

Location: 1 mile SW Fowlmere village. (3½ miles NE Royston.) Allocated 8AF as fighter base – satellite Duxford – 22 Sep 42. Reallocated as bomber base for development to Class A 9 Apr 43. Reallocated as fighter base 16 June 43 when existing grass airfields dropped from bomber plan. First occupied USAAF Mar 44. Officially transferred 8AF 20 Apr 44. Returned to RAF 1 Nov 45. Opened 1940. Camp enlargement and technical facilities for US fighter station carried out by W & C French Ltd in 1943. Two steel track runways – 4200 ft (110) and 4800 ft (050) – laid winter 1943–44 together with perimeter track. No lighting. A/c dispersals: 80 concrete pads. Additional PSP laid Dec 44 to overcome mud problem. Hangars: 1 T2 and 7 blisters. Camp: utility buildings for 1709 persons.

Framlingham Station 153

Location: Between Parham and Gt. Glemham, Suffolk. (3 miles SE Framlingham.) Allocated 8AF as bomber base 10 Aug 42. First occupied USAAF May 43. Officially transferred to 8AF 15 Aug 43. Transferred to RAF 1 Nov 45. Built: 1942–43 by Haymills Ltd. Runways: 6000 ft (282), 4200 ft (173) and 4200 ft (234). A/c dispersals: 46 pans and 4 loops. Hangars: 2 dispersed T2. Camp: utility buildings for 2894 persons.

Glatton Station 130

Location: Between Holme and Conington, Huntingdonshire. (10 miles N Huntingdon.) Allocated 8AF as bomber base 10 Aug 42. First occupied USAAF Dec 43. Officially transferred 8AF 20 Mar 44. Transferred RAF 12 July 45. Built 1943. Main constructor: 809th Engineer Btn US Army. Runways: concrete, 6000 ft (140), 4200 ft (160) and 4200 ft (230). A/c dispersals: 42 loops, 2 large loops and 6 pans. Hangars: 2 dispersed T2. Camp: utility buildings for 2894 persons.

Gosfield Station 154

Location: 2 miles NW Gosfield village, Essex. (2 miles W Halstead.) Allocated 8AF as bomber base 10 Aug 42. Transferred 9AF Oct 43. Never occupied by 8AF flying unit. Built 1943. Runways: concrete; 6000 ft (317), 4200 ft (019) and 4200 ft (084). A/c dispersals: 50 loops. Hangars: 2 dispersed T2. Camp: utility buildings for 2894.

Goxhill Station 345

Location: Immediately E Goxhill village, Lincolnshire. (5 miles E Barrow on Humber.) Allocated 8AF as fighter base 4 June 42. Reallocated as fighter training base 10 Aug 42. First occupied USAAF Aug 42. Officially transferred 8AF 3 July 43. Returned RAF 20 Jan 45. Built 1940–41. Runways: Tarmacadam; 4880 ft (070), 3500 ft (010) and 3300 ft (130). No lighting. A/c dispersals: 24 pans, 6 fighter pads and 20 steel mesh standings. Hangars: 1 J, 2 T2 grouped, and 4 blister. Camp: utility buildings for 1709 persons.

Grafton Underwood Station 106

Location: Immediately NW Grafton Underwood village, Northamptonshire. (3¾ miles ENE Kettering.) Tentatively allocated USAAF as bomber base Nov 41. Confirmed May 42. First occupied USAAF May 42. Officially transferred 8AF 5 July 43. Transferred RAF 9 Oct 45. Built 1941–42. Main contractor: George Wimpey & Co Ltd. Runways: concrete, originally 4700 ft, 3300 ft and 3300 ft, increased to 5950 ft (045), 4200 ft (238) and 4950 ft (293) in winter 1942–43. A/c dispersals: originally 30 pans with 6 pans and 14 loops added in late stages of reconstruction. Hangars: 2 dispersed T2. Camp: utility buildings for 2894 persons.

Great Ashfield Station 155

Location: 1½ miles S Gt Ashfield village, Suffolk. (10 miles E Bury St Edmunds.) Allocated 8AF as bomber base 10 Aug 42. First occupied USAAF June 43. Officially transferred 8AF 17 Aug 43. Transferred RAF 9 Oct 45. Built 1942–Feb 43. Main contractor: John Laing & Son Ltd. Runways: 6000 ft (068), 4680 ft (360) and 4500 ft (132). Dispersals: 33 pans and 17 loops added late in construction programme. Hangars: 2 dispersed T2. Camp: utility buildings for 2894 persons.

Great Dunmow Station 164

Location: 1 mile W Little Easton, Essex. (2 miles WNW Dunmow.) Allocated 8AF as bomber base 10 Aug 42. First occupied 8AF Sep 43. Transferred 9AF Oct 43. Transferred RAF Oct 44. Built 1942–June 43. Main constructors: 818th Engineer Btn US Army. Runways: concrete, 6000 ft (150), 4200 ft (110) and 4200 ft (040). A/c dispersals: 50 loops. Hangars: 2 dispersed T2. Camp: utility buildings for 2553 persons.

Great Sampford Station 359

Location: 2 miles SW Gt Sampford village, Essex. (7 miles SE Saffron Walden.) Allocated 8AF as fighter base 22 Sep 42 – satellite of Debden. Eliminated Apr 43 being unsuitable for development for P-38 and P-47 use. First occupied 8AF Sep 42. Returned to RAF 28 Feb 43. Opened Apr 42. Grass flying field 4800 ft × 3150 ft with Sommerfeld track runway. Hangars: 4 blister. Camp: limited number utility buildings.

Greencastle Station 237

Location: 2 miles SW Kilkeel, Down, Northern Ireland. Tentatively allocated as bomber base for an Air Support Command 28 Feb 42. Allocated as bomber training base 10 Aug 42. First occupied USAAF July 43. Officially transferred 8AF 3 Sep 43. Transferred BADA 11 Nov 44. Built RAF 30 May 45. Runways: concrete, 6000 ft (080), 4200 ft (030) and 4200 ft (140). A/c dispersals: 30 pans, and 50 fingers or Ys added late 43. Hangars: 4 T2. Camp: 8 sites with utility buildings for 2512 persons.

Greenham Common Station 486

Location: 2 miles SE Newbury, Berkshire. Allocated 8AF as transport base 11 June 42. First occupied USAAF Aug 42. Temporarily loaned RAF for advanced pilot training Nov 42. Transferred 9AF Oct 43. Built 1941–42. Runways: concrete, 5988 ft (110), 4053 ft (140) and 3300 ft (030). A/c dispersals: 26 pans and 25 loops. Hangars: 2 T2 grouped. Camp: utility buildings for 2368 persons.

Grove Station 519

Location: 1½ miles NW Wantage, Berkshire. Allocated 8AF as transport base 4 June 42. Temporarily loaned RAF for advanced pilot training Nov 42. Transferred 9AF Oct 43. Never occupied by 8AF flying units. Built 1941–Oct 42. Runways: concrete, 6000 ft (220), 4200 ft (340) and 3600 ft (270). A/c dispersals: 24 pans and 26 loops. Hangars: 6 T2. Camp: utility buildings for 3402.

Halesworth Station 365

Location: Between Holton and Westhall, Suffolk. (2 miles NE Halesworth.) Allocated 8AF as bomber base 10 Aug 42. Temporarily allocated for fighter use Apr 43 to Apr 44. Officially transferred 8AF 20 Aug 43. Transferred RAF 25 June 45. Built 1942–June 43. Main contractors: Richard Costain Ltd and John Laing & Son. Runways: concrete; 6000 ft (240), 4200 ft (190) and 4200 ft (290). A/c dispersals: 29 pans and 22 loops. Hangars: 2 dispersed T2. Camp: utility buildings for 2972 persons.

Hamstead Norris

Location: 11 miles WNW Reading, Berkshire. Allocated 8AF as transport base 10 Aug 42. Allocation rescinded 4 Oct 42 in favour of another site. Never occupied by 8AF. Built 1943.

Hardwick Station 104

Location: 3 miles S Hempnall, Norfolk. (5½ miles W Bungay.) Allocated 8AF as bomber base 4 June 42. First occupied USAAF Sep 42. Officially transferred 8AF 12 May 43. Transferred RAF 25 June 45. Built 1941–42. Main contractor: John Laing & Son Ltd. Runways: concrete; 6000 ft (020), 4200 ft (080) and 4200 ft (140). A/c dispersals: 30 pans with 6 larger pans and 11 loops added during 1943. Later 3 PSP loops added. Hangars: 3 grouped T2. Camp: utility buildings for 2972 persons.

Harrington Station 179

Location: 5 miles W Kettering, Northamptonshire. Allocated 8AF 21 Mar 44. Transferred from RAF to 8AF 1 Apr 44. Returned to RAF 9 Oct 45. Built 1943. Main constructors: 826th and 852nd Engineer Btn US Army. Class A airfield built for RAF. Runways: concrete, 6000 ft (184), 4200 ft (230) and 4200 ft (298). Mk I lighting. A/c dispersals: 36 loops. Hangars: 4 T2 grouped in twos. Camp: utility buildings for 1782 persons.

Hethel Station 114

Location: 3 miles E Wymondham, Norfolk. Allocated 8AF as bomber base 4 June 42. First occupied USAAF Sep 42. Officially transferred 8AF 23 Aug 43. Returned to RAF 25 June 45. Built 1941–Oct 42. Main contractor: W & C French Ltd. Runways: concrete, 6000 ft (240), 4200 ft (300) and 4200 ft (350). A/c dispersal: originally 30 pans with 6 more pans and 15 loops added during enlargement of base Feb–July 43. Hangars: 3 grouped T2. Camp: utility buildings for 2972 persons.

Hibaldstow Station P-4
Location: 1 mile S Hibaldstow village, Lincolnshire. (3 miles SW Brigg.) Allocated 8AF as fighter base 4 June 42 – satellite Goxhill. Allocation rescinded July 42 as considered unsuitable. Never occupied by USAAF units. Runways: 3 asphalt.

High Ercall Station 346
Location: 2 miles E High Ercall, Shropshire. (5½ miles NNW Wellington.) Allocated 8AF as fighter base 4 June 42. – satellite Atcham. Reallocated as fighter training base 10 Aug 42. Occupied USAAF Aug 42–Feb 43. Returned RAF Apr 43 as surplus to fighter training requirements. Built 1939–40. Main contractor: Walker and Slater Ltd. Runways: tarmac; 4770 ft (110), 4230 ft (050) and 3850 ft (170). A/c dispersals: 23 hardstandings. Hangars: 2 T2, 1 J, 3K, 8 L and 12 blister. Camp: part permanent, part utility buildings for 2000 persons. Also housed RAF MU during USAAF tenure.

High Roding Station 177
Location: 1 mile NE High Roding village, Essex. Tentatively allocated 8AF as bomber base 10 Aug 42. Confirmed Sep 42. Warning of land requisition served. Construction indefinitely postponed 6 Dec 42.

Honington Station 375
Location: 2 miles NW Honington village, Suffolk. (7 miles NNE Bury St Edmunds.) Allocated 8AF as bomber base 4 June 42 for development to Class A standard. Temporarily allocated as advanced air depot Sep 42. First occupied 8AF Sep 42. Officially transferred 8AF 29 Apr 43. Reallocated as fighter base when plan to develop grass airfields for bomber use abandoned 16 June 43. Transferred RAF 26 Feb 46 – last 8AF base in UK. Served Troston air depot, Station 595. Built 1935 – 37 as permanent RAF bomber station. Runways: sod; 4200 ft NE–SW and 4200 ft SE–NW with Mk I lighting. Steel mat runway 6000 ft (280) laid by US engineers winter 1943–44. A/c dispersals: 48 loops and 1 pan constructed with perimeter track in concrete during 1943. Troston depot had 21 loops. Hangars: 4 grouped C and 9 blister. Troston depot had 1 T2 and made use of 3 C types on main field. Camp: permanent and utility buildings for 5500 persons.

Horham Station 119
Location: Between Horham and Denham, Suffolk. (4 miles ESE Eye.) Allocated 8AF as bomber base 10 Aug 42. First occupied USAAF Sep 42. Officially transferred to 8AF 12 July 43. Transferred to RAF 9 Oct 45. Built 1941–Sept 42. Runways: concrete, 6000 ft (074), 4200 ft (190) and 4200 ft (310). A/c dispersals: originally 36 pans with 16 loops added late in construction. Hangars: 2 grouped T2. Camp: utility buildings for 2972 persons.

Horsham St Faith Station 123
Location: 2 miles S Horsham St Faith, Norfolk. (4 miles N Norwich.) Allocated 8AF as bomber base 4 June 42 for development to Class A standard. Allocated as temporary fighter base 22 Sep 42. First occupied USAAF Sep 42. Officially transferred to 8AF 1 May 44. Returned to RAF 20 July 45. Built 1939–40 as regular RAF station. Originally grass surfaced approx 5000 ft × 4500 ft. Only grass airfield scheduled for development to Class A standard on which work completed. Runways: concrete; 6000 ft (230), 4200 ft (280) and 4200 ft (350) laid late summer 43. A/c dispersals: 50 loops plus 6 fighter pads from earlier works. Hangars: 5 grouped C. Camp: permanent with utility buildings on new sites for total 2972 persons.

Hutton Cranswick
Location: Immediately SW Hutton Cranswick village, Yorkshire. (8½ miles N Beverley.) Allocated 8AF for tactical fighter use on lodger basis 12 July 43. Never occupied by 8AF units. RAF fighter station with 3 concrete runways.

Ibsley Station 347
Location: 1½ miles SE Ibsley village, Hampshire. (2 miles N Ringwood.) Allocated 8AF as fighter station 4 June 42. First occupied USAAF Aug 42. Returned to RAF Oct 42 on departure of US units. Reallocated for 8AF tactical fighter use 12 July 43. Transferred 9AF Oct 43. Built 1940–41. Main contractor: John Mowlem & Co. Runways: concrete, 4800 ft, 4200 ft and 4050 ft. A/c dispersals: 18 hardstandings and 18 double pens. Hangars: 2 Bellman and 12 blister. Camp: utility buildings for 2000 persons.

Ingatestone
Location: 1 mile WSW Ingatestone village, Essex. Tentatively allocated 8AF as bomber base 10 Aug 42. Confirmed Sep 42. Warning of land requisition served. Construction indefinitely postponed 16 Dec 42.

Ipswich
Locaton: ½ mile E of town centre Ipswich, Suffolk. Allocated 8AF as fighter base 22 Sep 42 – satellite Martlesham. Allocation rescinded 9 Oct 42 as airfield considered unsuitable for operation of P-38 and P-47. Topography and proximity of built-up area precluded enlargement. Grass surface with pre-war airport buildings.

Isle Abbotts (Merryfield) Station 464
Location: 4 miles NW Ilminster, Somerset. (8 miles SE Taunton.) Allocated 8AF as transport or observation base 27 Aug 42. Allocation rescinded June 43. Later allocated to 9AF as Merryfield. Never used by 8AF units. Built 1943–Feb 44 to Class A standard.

Keevil Station 471
Location: 1 mile SW Keevil village, Wiltshire. (4½ miles E Trowbridge.) Allocated 8AF as transport or observation base 10 Aug 42. First occupied USAAF Sep 42. Officially transferred 8AF Aug 43. Transferred 9AF Oct 43. Built 1942. Runways: concrete; 6000 ft (075), 4200 ft (132) and 4200 ft (204). A/c dispersals: 9 large pans, 41 small pans and one 75 ft pan. Hangars: 2 T2 grouped and 9 blister. Camp: temporary buildings for 2000 persons.

Kimbolton Station 117
Location: 1½ miles N Kimbolton, Huntingdonshire. (8 miles W Huntingdon.) Tentatively allocated USAAF as bomber base Nov 41. Confirmed May 42. First occupied USAAF Sep 42. Officially transferred 8AF 29 June 43. Transferred RAF 4 July 45. Built 1941. Main contractor: W & C French Ltd. Runways: concrete; originally 3970 ft, 3620 ft and 3730 ft, lengthened autumn 1942 to 6000 ft (330), 4200 ft (210) and 4200 ft (270). A/c dispersals: 31 pans and 20 loops. Hangars: 2 dispersed T2. Camp: utility buildings for 2894 persons.

Kings Cliffe Station 367
Location: 1½ miles E Kings Cliffe village, Northamptonshire. (12 miles W Peterborough.) Allocated 8AF as fighter base 4 June 42 – satellite Wittering. First occupied USAAF Dec 42. Officially transferred 25 Sep 43. Only fighter airfield in first allocation to 8AF to become a combat fighter base and remain so until end of hostilities. Transferred RAF 1 Nov 45. Built 1941. Main contractor: W & C French Ltd. Runways: macadam/consolidated soil laid early 1943, 3690 ft (350), 5490 ft (260) and 3900 ft (210). A/c dispersals: 11 concrete pans, 14 PSP standings and 13 twin pens. Hangars: 1 T2, 4 blister and 8 special 55 ft blister. Camp: utility buildings for 1709.

Kirkistown
Location: 2 miles S Ballyhalbert, Down, Northern Ireland. Tentatively allocated to an Air Support Command 28 Feb 42. Allocated 8AF as fighter base 4 June 42 – satellite Ballyhalbert. Allocation rescinded Apr 43. Allocated as tactical fighter base 12 July 43. Never occupied by 8AF units. RAF fighter station with 3 hard runways.

Kirton-in-Lindsey Station 349
Location: 1½ miles SE Kirton village, Lincolnshire. (16 miles N Lincoln.) Allocated 8AF as fighter base 4 June 42 – satellite Goxhill. Allocated as fighter training base 10 Aug 42. First occupied USAAF July 42. Last US flying units departed Dec 42. Returned to RAF Apr 43 as surplus to US training requirements. Built: 1938–40. Main contractor: John Laing & Son Ltd. Grass airfield: runways, 3300 ft N–S and 3300 ft E–W. No lighting. A/c dispersals: 10 hardstandings. Hangars: 3 grouped C and 4 over-blisters. Camp: utility buildings for 1868 persons.

Knettishall Station 136
Location: Between Knettishall and Coney Weston, Suffolk. (6 miles SE Thetford.) Allocated 8AF as bomber base 4 June 42. First occupied USAAF June 43. Officially transferred USAAF 12 Aug 43. Transferred RAF 1 Nov 45. Built 1942–43. Main contractor: W & C French Ltd. Runways: concrete; 6000 ft (220), 4200 ft (270) and 4200 ft (330). A/c dispersals: 32 pans with 19 loops added early 1943. Hangars: 2 dispersed T2. Camp: utility buildings for 2894 persons.

Langford Lodge Station 597
Location: 4 miles W Crumlin, Antrim, Northern Ireland. Selected for USAAF air depot Oct 41. Tentatively allocated as temporary transport base for an Air Support Command 28 Feb 42. Confirmed as temporary transport base for 8AF 10 Aug 42 but never used for this purpose. First occupied by USAAF June 42. Officially transferred 8AF 1 Dec 42. Transferred RAF 12 Mar 46. Built Jan 42–Oct 42. Main contractor: Sir Lindsey Parkinson & Co. Runways: concrete; 6000 ft (022) and 4590 ft (066). A/c dispersals: 26 pans with 100 fingers for aircraft storage added winter 1943–44. Hangars: 9 T2 grouped. Total storage facilities: 232,328 sq ft. Camp: utility buildings for 5000.

Lavenham Station 137
Location: Alpheton, Suffolk. (3 miles NW Lavenham.) Allocated 8AF as bomber base 10 Aug 42. First occupied USAAF Mar 44. Officially transferred 8AF 21 Mar 44. Transferred RAF 12 Oct 45. Built 1943. Main contractor: John Laing & Son Ltd. Runways: concrete; 6000 ft (270), 4200 ft (220) and 4200 ft (330). A/c dispersals: 50 loops and 1 pan. Hangars: 2 dispersed T2. Camp: utility buildings for 2894 persons.

Leiston Station 373
Location: Theberton, Suffolk. (2 miles NW Leiston.) Allocated 8AF as fighter base 22 Sep 42. First occupied USAAF Oct 43. Officially transferred 8AF 14 Jan 44. Transferred RAF 10 Oct 45. Built Sep 42–Sep 43. Main contractor: John Mowlem & Co Ltd. Runways: concrete; 6000 ft (060), 4200 ft (130) and 4200 ft (180). A/c dispersals: 38 concrete pans, 17 PSP squares and 12 twin pens with blast walls. Hangars: 2 dispersed T2 and 12 blisters. Camp: utility buildings for 1709 persons. Class A airfield originally for RAF FC.

Little Staughton Station 127
Location: 2 miles SE Little Staughton village, Huntingdonshire. (8½ miles NNE Bedford.) Tentatively allocated USAAF as bomber base Nov 41. Confirmed May 42. Temporarily allocated as advanced air depot Sep 42. First occupied 8AF Jan 43. Officially transferred 8AF 1 May 43. Transferred RAF BC 1 Mar 44. Built 1941–Dec 42. Runways: concrete; originally 4850 ft (250) and 3470 ft (310) extended to 5940 ft and 4160 ft respectively, and 3060 ft (010) unchanged. A/c dispersals: 37 pans and 17 loops. Hangars: 3 dispersed T2 and 8 Robin. Camp: utility buildings for 2500 persons.

Little Walden (Hadstock) Station 165
Location: 2 miles south Hadstock village, Essex. (3½ miles NNE Saffron Walden.) Allocated 8AF as bomber base 10 Aug 42. Original name Hadstock. Renamed Little Walden May 43. Transferred 9AF Oct 43. Transferred 8AF Sep 44. Transferred RAF 30 Jan 46. Built 1943–Feb 44. Runways: concrete; 5700 ft (160), 4200 ft (100) and 4200 ft (040). A/c dispersals: 51 loops. Hangars: 2 dispersed T2. Camp: utility buildings for 2894.

Long Kesh Station 232
Location: 2½ miles SW Lisburn, Down, Northern Ireland. Tentatively allocated USAAF for an Air Support Command 28 Feb 42. Allocated 8AF as bomber training base 10 Aug 42. Temporarily loaned RAF 22 Nov 42 as Coastal Command training base and subsequently permanently transferred. Never occupied by 8AF. Built 1941–42, with 3 hard runways.

Ludham Station 177
Location: 1 mile NE Ludham village, Norfolk. (12½ miles NE Norwich.) Allocated 8AF as fighter base 22 Sep 42, but continued in use by RAF until Aug 43. Transferred RAF July 44. Never used by 8AF flying units. Built 1940–42. Main contractor: Richard Costain Ltd. Runways: concrete; 4200 ft (078), 3300 ft (198) and 3300 ft (322). No lighting. A/c dispersals: 9 concrete pans, 12 fighter pens and 50 PSP squares. Hangars: 1 T2 and 4 blisters. Camp: enlarged for USAAF use and not completed until Jan 44; utility buildings for 1709 persons.

Macmerry
Location: Between Tranent and Gladsmuir, Lothian. (14 miles E Edinburgh.) Allocated 8AF as tactical fighter base on lodger basis 12 July 43. Never occupied by 8AF units. Pre-war grass surfaced civil airport.

Maghaberry Station 239
Location: 6 miles W Lisburn, Antrim, Northern Ireland. Tentatively allocated USAAF 28 Feb 42 for an Air Support Command. Allocated 8AF as Transport or Observation base 10 Aug 42. First occupied USAAF Oct 43. Officially transferred 8AF 15 Nov 43. Transferred BADA Mar 44. Transferred RAF 6 June 44. Built 1942. Main contractor: Sunley & Co Ltd. Runways: concrete; 4500 ft (106), 3300 ft (032) and 3210 ft (156). A/c dispersals: 17 pans and 14 loops. Hangars: 2 T2. Camp: utility buildings for 2500 persons.

Maldon
Location: NE Mundon, Essex. (3 miles SE of Maldon.) Allocated 8AF 10 Aug 42 as bomber base. Confirmed Sep 42. Warning of land requisition served Oct 42. Construction indefinitely postponed 16 Dec 42.

Market Harborough Station B-27
Location: Foxton, Leicestershire. (2 miles NW Market Harborough.) Allocated 8AF as bomber base 4 June 42. Allocation rescinded early Aug 42. Never occupied by USAAF. Built 1942–43 to Class A standard with 3 concrete runways.

Matching Station 166
Location: 1½ miles NE Matching Green, Essex. (5 miles E Harlow.) Allocated 8AF as bomber base 10 Aug 42. Transferred 9AF Oct 43. Never used by 8AF units. Built 1943. Main constructors: 834th and 840th Engineer Btns US Army. Runways: concrete; 6000 ft (200), 4200 ft (270) and 4200 ft (140). A/c dispersals: 50 loops. Hangars: 2 dispersed T2. Camp: utility buildings for 2658 persons.

Matlask Station 178
Location: Immediately S Matlask village, Norfolk. (5½ miles SE Holt.) Allocated 8AF as fighter base 22 Sep 42. Used by 9AF Mar–Apr 44. Transferred RAF Oct 44. Never occupied by 8AF flying units. Opened 1940. Grass runways; 4800 ft SE–NW and 3900 ft SW–NE. No lighting. A/c dispersal: 21 concrete pads. Hangars: 1 T2 and 5 blisters. Camp: scheduled for expansion for USAAF to be completed by Jan 44, but never carried out. Never occupied by 8AF flying unit.

Maydown
Location: 4 miles NE Londonderry, Northern Ireland. Tentatively allocated USAAF for an Air Support Command 28 Feb 42. Allocated 8AF as fighter base 4 June 42. – satellite Eglinton. Allocation rescinded Apr 43 when Ulster fighter stations no longer required by VIII FC. Built 1941 by Messrs Cryer & Co. Runways: concrete; 4950 ft (180) and 4050 ft (070). No lighting. A/c dispersals: 37 pans and 6 twin pens. Hangars: 4 over-blisters. Camp: utility building.

Martlesham Heath Station 369
Location: Immediately SSW Martlesham village, Suffolk. (1½ miles SW Woodbridge.) Allocated 8AF as fighter base 22 Sep 42. First occupied by 8AF Oct 43. Officially transferred 8AF 1 Nov 43. Transferred RAF 1 Nov 45. Opened 1917. Runways: consolidated soil/tar mix laid 1943; 4900 ft (220) and 5100 ft (040). A/c dispersals: 20 steel mesh mat and 50 PSP squares. Hangars: 1 A, 1 G, 1 GS and 3 blister. Camp: mostly permanent for 1709 persons.

Membury Station 466
Location: 3 miles S Lambourn, Berkshire. Allocated 8AF 11 June 42 as transport base. First occupied USAAF Dec 42. Officially transferred 8AF 1 July 43. Transferred 9AF Oct 43. Built 1942. Runways: concrete; 4580 ft (220), 6000 ft (110) and 3350 ft (270). Runway 110 was originally 3430 ft. A/c dispersals: 24 pans and 26 loops. Hangars: 4 T2 dispersed in pairs. Camp: utility buildings for 2368 persons.

Mendlesham Station 156
Location: Immediately W Wetherup Street, Suffolk. (2½ miles SE Mendlesham.) Allocated 8AF as bomber base 10 Aug 42. First occupied USAAF Dec 43. Temporary loan to RAF FC Feb–Apr 44. Officially transferred 8AF 15 Apr 44. Transferred RAF 9 Oct 45. Built 1942–Oct 43. Runways: concrete; 6000 ft (010), 4100 ft (160) and 4400 ft (220). A/c dispersal: 48 loops and 2 pans. Hangars: 2 dispersed T2. Camp: utility buildings for 2972 persons.

Merston Station 351

Location: 2½ miles SE Chichester, Sussex. Allocated 8AF as fighter base 4 June 42 – satellite Westhamptnett. First occupied 8AF July 42. Reverted to RAF use after US units departed Oct 42. Allocation rescinded Sep 42. Allocated 8AF as tactical fighter base 12 July 43. Transferred 9AF Oct 43. Opened 1940. Grass flying field. 4200 ft × 4500 ft area. A/c dispersals: 17 hardstandings and 12 double pens. Hangars: 6 blister. Camp: utility buildings for 1200 persons.

Metfield Station 366

Location: 1½ miles SE Metfield village, Suffolk. (5 miles SE Harleston.) Allocated 8AF as bomber base 10 Aug 42. Allocated as temporary fighter base 22 Sep 42 and retained by VIII FC until Apr 44. First occupied 8AF July 43. Officially transferred 8AF 20 Sep 43. Transferred ATC Oct 44. Returned to RAF 10 Oct 45. Built 1942–43. Main contractor: John Laing & Son Ltd. Runways: concrete; 6000 ft (210), 4200 ft (270) and 4200 ft (330). A/c dispersals: 39 pans with 15 loops added late in construction. Hangars: 2 dispersed T2. Camp: utility buildings for 2894 persons.

Middle Wallop Station 449

Location: 6 miles SW Andover, Hampshire. Allocated 8AF as fighter base 10 Aug 42. Allocation rescinded early Sep 42. Allocated 9AF late 43. Never used by 8AF. Grass field with Sommerfeld track. Permanent buildings.

Molesworth Station 107

Location: 2 miles north Molesworth village, Huntingdonshire. (10½ miles WNW Huntingdon.) Tentatively allocated USAAF as bomber base Nov 41. Confirmed May 42. First occupied 8AF June 42. Officially transferred 20 Apr 43. Transferred RAF 1 July 45. Built 1940. Enlarged for 8AF use summer 1942. Runways: concrete; originally 3670 ft, 4180 ft and 3590 ft extended to 6090 ft (191), 4270 ft (255) and 4270 ft (309). A/c dispersals: originally 30 pans with 17 loops and 7 pans added 1942. Hangars: 2 T2 and 1 J grouped. Camp: utility buildings for 2972 persons.

Mount Farm Station 234

Location: Between Berinsfield and Drayton St Leonard, Oxfordshire. (8 miles SE Oxford.) Allocated 8AF as reconnaissance base Dec 42. First occupied 8AF Jan 43. Officially transferred 8AF 15 May 43. Transferred RAF 1 May 45. Built 1941 as satellite for Benson. Runways: asphalt; 3300 ft (170), 3300 ft (120) and 4800 ft (240). A/c dispersals: 24 pans and 25 PSP squares. Hangars: 4 69 ft blisters and 4 65 ft blisters. Camp: utility buildings for 1823 persons.

Mullaghmore Station 240

Location: 4 miles SW Ballymoney, Londonderry, Northern Ireland. Allocated 8AF as bomber training base 10 Aug 42. First occupied USAAF Nov 43. Officially transferred 8AF 20 Dec 43. Transferred SOS Mar 44. Transferred RAF 1 May 44. Built 1942–43. Runways: concrete; 6000 ft (190) and 4263 ft (270). A/c dispersals: 3 large and 27 small pans with 25 Ys added late 43. Hangars: 4 T2. Camp: utility buildings.

Newtownards

Location: 10 miles E Belfast, Down, Northern Ireland. Allocated 8AF for observation units 10 Aug 42. Allocation rescinded 27 Aug 42 as location too far removed from other VIII GASC bases. Never occupied by USAAF. Pre-war civil airfield.

North Pickenham Station 143

Location: 1 mile W North Pickenham village, Norfolk. (2½ miles SE Swaffham.) Allocated 8AF as bomber base 10 Aug 42. First occupied 8AF Apr 44. Officially transferred 22 May 44 – last of 66 airfields to 8AF. Transferred RAF 10 July 45. Built 1943–44. Runways: concrete; 5700 ft (240), 4200 ft (190) and 4200 ft (320). A/c dispersals: 50 loops and 1 pan. Hangars: 2 dispersed T2. Camp: utility buildings for 2894 persons.

Nuthampstead Station 131

Location: Immediately E of Nuthampstead village, Hertfordshire. (5½ miles miles SE Royston.) Allocated 8AF as bomber base 10 Aug 42. First occupied USAAF Aug 43. Allocated for temporary use as fighter base Aug 43 and retained until Apr 44. Officially transferred 8AF 1 Nov 43. Transferred RAF 10 July 45. Built 1942–43. Main constructors: 814th and 830th Engineer Btns US Army. Runways: concrete; 6000 ft (230), 4200 ft (350) and 4200 ft (290). A/c dispersals: 50 loops and 1 pan. Hangars: 2 dispersed T2. Camp: utility buildings for 2894.

Nutts Corner Station 235

Location: 2½ miles ENE Crumlin, Antrim, Northern Ireland. Tentatively allocated USAAF for an Air Support Command 28 Feb 42. Allocated 8AF as bomber training base 10 Aug 42. Transferred RAF 12 Jan 43 for use by RAF Ferry Command. Used by ATC but not 8AF. Built 1940. Runways: concrete; 6000 ft (280), 4800 ft (222) and 3600 ft (158). A/c dispersals: 50 large pans. Hangars: 2 T1 and 2 T2. Camp: 16 sites utility buildings.

Old Buckenham Station 144

Location: 2 miles NE Old Buckenham village, Norfolk. (2 miles SE Attleborough.) Allocated 8AF as bomber base 10 Aug 42. First occupied USAAF Jan 44. Officially transferred 8AF 13 Feb 44. Transferred RAF 28 May 45. Built 1942–43. Main contractor: Taylor-Woodrow Ltd. Runways: concrete; 6000 ft (075), 4200 ft (027) and 4200 ft (130). A/c dispersals: 50 loops. Hangars: 2 dispersed T2. Camp: utility buildings for 2894.

Perranporth

Location: 7 miles NW Truro, Cornwall. Allocated 8AF as fighter base 10 Aug 42. Allocation rescinded early Sep 42. Never occupied by USAAF. Grass field.

Podington Station 109

Location: 2 miles SE Podington village, Bedfordshire. (6 miles SE Wellingborough.) Tentatively allocated USAAF as bomber base Nov 41. Confirmed May 42. First occupied 8AF Aug 42. Officially transferred 8AF 20 June 43. Transferred RAF 24 Sep 45. Built 1941. Runways: originally 4900 ft and 3600 ft lengthened to 6000 ft (050) and 4200 ft (350) respectively, and 3300 ft (290) unchanged. A/c dispersals: 38 pans with 14 loops and 1 pan added early 1943. Hangars: 2 dispersed T2. Camp: utility buildings for 2894.

Polebrook Station 110

Location: Between Polebrook and Hemington, Northamptonshire. (3½ miles ESE Oundle.) Tentatively allocated USAAF as bomber base Nov 41. Confirmed May 42. First occupied USAAF June 42. Officially transferred 8AF 28 June 43. Transferred RAF 10 July 45. Built: 1940–41. Main contractor: George Wimpey & Co Ltd. Runways: originally 3840 ft, 3600 ft and 3350 ft, extended to 5850 ft (250), 4200 ft (190) and 4200 ft (310) in spring 1942. A/c dispersals: 30 pans of which 24 remained after rebuilding when 15 new pans and 14 loops added. Hangars: 2 T2 and 1 J grouped. Camp: utility buildings for 2792 persons.

Portreath Station 504

Location: 9 miles W Truro, Cornwall. Allocated 8AF as fighter base 10 Aug 42. Allocation rescinded early Sep 42. Lodger detachments with RAF during 1943–44. RAF station with 4 hard runways.

Rackheath Station 145

Location: 1 mile S Rackheath village, Norfolk. (5 miles NE Norwich.) Allocated 8AF as bomber base 10 Aug 42. Allocated as temporary fighter base 22 Sep 42 but because of delay in construction replaced by Halesworth Apr 43. First occupied 8AF Mar 44. Officially transferred 8AF 12 Apr 44. Transferred RAF 20 July 45. Built 1943. Main contractor: John Laing & Son Ltd. Runways: 6000 ft (210), 4300 ft (320) abd 4200 ft (260). A/c dispersals: 50 loops. Hangars: 2 dispersed T2. Camp: utility buildings for 2894.

Ramsbury Station 469

Location: 1 mile S Ramsbury, Wiltshire. (4½ miles E Marlborough.) Allocated 8AF as transport base 11 June 42. First occupied 8AF June 42. Temporarily loaned RAF for advanced pilot training Nov 42. Transferred 9AF Oct 43. Built 1941–42. Runways: concrete; 6000 ft (260), 3300 ft (200) and 3170 ft (320). A/c dispersals: 36 pans and 18 loops. Hangars: 2 T2. Camp: utility buildings for 2368 persons.

Rattlesden Station 126

Location: Between Felsham and Rattlesden, Suffolk. (9 miles SE Bury St Edmunds.) Allocated 8AF as bomber base 4 June 42. First occupied 8AF Dec 42. Officially transferred 8AF 26 Apr 43. Transferred RAF 10 Oct 45. Built 1942. Main contractor: George Wimpey & Co Ltd. Runways: concrete; 6000 ft (243), 4200 ft (171) and 4200 ft (310). A/c dispersals: 35 pans with 16 loops added late in construction. Hangars: 2 dispersed T2. Camp: utility buildings for 2894 persons.

Raydon Station 157
Location: Between Raydon and Gt Wenham, Suffolk. (3 miles SE Hadleigh.) Allocated 8AF as bomber base 10 Aug 42. First occupied USAAF Dec 1943. Allocated 9AF as temporary fighter base Dec 43–Apr 44. Officially transferred 8AF 10 May 44. Transferred RAF 20 Dec 45. Built 1942–43. Main constructors: 833rd and 862nd Engineer Btn US Army. Runways: concrete; 6000 ft (270), 4200 ft (170) and 4200 ft (230). A/c dispersals: 50 loops and 1 pan. Hangars: 2 dispersed T2. Camp: utility buildings for 2842 persons.

Ridgewell Station 167
Location: Between Ridgewell and Tilbury-juxta-Clare, Essex. (7½ miles NNW Halstead.) Allocated 8AF as bomber base 4 June 42. Loaned RAF BC Dec 42–May 43. First occupied 8AF June 43. Officially transferred 8AF 2 Aug 43. Transferred RAF 15 July 45. Built 1941–42. Runways: concrete; 6000 ft (100), 4200 ft (060) and 4200 ft (170). A/c dispersals: 50 pans and 5 loops. Hangars: 2 dispersed T2. Camp: utility buildings for 2894 persons.

Rivenhall Station 168
Location: Silver End, Essex. (1¾ miles N Witham.) Allocated 8AF as bomber base 10 Aug 42. Transferred 9AF Oct 43. Never occupied by 8AF units. Built 1943–44. Runways: concrete; 6000 ft (280), 4200 ft (220) and 4200 ft (340). A/c dispersals: 50 loops. Hangars: 2 dispersed T2. Camp: utility buildings for 2894 persons.

St Angelo
Location: 4 miles S Enniskillen, Fermanagh, Northern Ireland. Allocated for an Air Support Command 28 Feb 42. Allocated 8AF as a fighter training base 10 Aug 42. Allocation rescinded Apr 43 as surplus to 8AF requirements. RAF fighter airfield with 2 hard runways. Never occupied by 8AF.

Scorton Station 425
Location: 9 miles SSW Darlington, Yorkshire. Allocated 8AF for tactical fighter base 12 July 43. Used by USAAF night fighter squadrons training with RAF. Never occupied by 8AF. RAF night fighter base with 3 hard runways.

Seething Station 146
Location: 1½ miles S Seething village, Norfolk. (9½ miles SE Norwich.) Allocated 8AF as bomber base 10 Aug 42. First occupied USAAF Nov 43. Officially transferred 8AF 15 Feb 44. Transferred RAF 6 July 45. Built 1942–43. Main contractor: John Laing & Son Ltd. Runways: 6000 ft (070), 4200 ft (010) and 4200 ft (300). A/c dispersals: 34 pans and 17 loops. Hangars: 2 dispersed T2. Camp: utility buildings for 2894 persons.

Selsey
Location: 6 miles S Chichester, Sussex. Tentatively allocated 8AF as fighter base 10 Aug 42. Allocation rescinded early Sep 42. Never occupied 8AF.

Shepherd's Grove Station 555 (**Hepworth** Station 135)
Location: ¾ mile S Hepworth village, Suffolk. (9 miles NE Bury St Edmunds.) Allocated 8AF as bomber base 10 Aug 42. Original name Hepworth. Renamed winter 1943–44. Loaned RAF BC 15 Apr 44 and subsequently permanently transferred. Never occupied by 8AF. Built 1943–Mar 44. Main contractor: W & C French Ltd. Work halted Apr 43 to expedite construction at other airfields. Runways: concrete; 6000 ft (010), 4200 ft (080) and 4200 ft (140). A/c dispersals: 49 loops and 1 pan. Hangars: 2 dispersed T2. Camp: utility buildings for 2894 persons.

Shipdham Station 115
Location: 2 miles E Shipdham village, Norfolk. (3½ miles SE Dereham.) Allocated 8AF as bomber base 4 June 42. First occupied USAAF Sep 42. Officially transferred 8AF 11 May 43. Transferred RAF 25 June 45. Built 1941–42. Runways: concrete; 6000 ft (090), 4200 ft (030) and 4200 ft (210). A/c dispersals: 36 pans with 18 loops added. Hangars: 3 grouped T2. Camp: utility buildings for 2972 persons.

Snailwell Station 361
Location: 2 miles N Newmarket, Suffolk. Allocated on a temporary basis as satellite for Duxford 2 Oct 42. Returned to RAF use Feb 43. Allocated 8AF as temporary base for tactical fighter units 12 July 43. Transferred 9AF Oct 43. Not used by 8AF after Feb 43. Opened 1940. Grass surfaced with runways 4290 ft NNE–SSW, 5040 ft ENE–WSW and 4260 ft ESE–WNW. A/c dispersals: 12 hardstandings and 2 single pens. Hangars: 1 Bellman and 10 blister. Camp: utility buildings.

Snetterton Heath Station 138
Location: 2½ miles NE East Harling, Norfolk. Allocated 8AF as bomber base 10 Aug 42. First occupied USAAF June 43. Officially transferred 8AF 19 July 43. Transferred RAF 20 Dec 45. Built 1942–43. Main contractor: Taylor-Woodrow Ltd. Runways: concrete; 6000 ft (230), 4200 ft (180) and 4200 ft (270). A/c dispersals: 36 pans with 16 loops added. Of 26 planned loops on the adjoining Eccles depot site, 14 were completed and 4 partially completed. Hangars: 2 dispersed T2 and 3 T2 grouped on Eccles site. Camp: utility buildings for 2972. Eccles depot was Station 548.

Southminster Station 173
Location: Between Southminster and Steeple, Essex. (1¼ miles NW Southminster.) Tentatively allocated 8AF as bomber base 10 Aug 42. Confirmed Sep 42. Construction indefinitely postponed 16 Dec 42.

Stansted Mountfitchet Station 169
Location: 2½ miles SE Stansted Mountfitchet, Essex. (3 miles N Bishops Stortford.) Allocated 8AF as bomber base 10 Aug 42. Additionally allocated to serve as an advanced air depot Oct 42. Officially transferred USAAF Oct 43. Transferred BADA Oct 44. Built 1942–43. Main constructors: 825th and 850th Engineer Btn US Army. Runways: concrete; 6000 ft (243), 4200 ft (190) and 4200 ft (134). A/c dispersals: 47 loops and 2 pans. Hangars: 4 T2, 2 grouped and the other dispersed. Camp: utility buildings for 2658 persons. Depot site on eastern side of airfield had 24 loop standings and 2 T2 hangars.

Steeple Morden Station 122
Location: Between Steeple Morden and Litlington, Cambridgeshire. (3½ miles W Royston.) Allocated 8AF as bomber base 10 Aug 42. Later found unsuitable for development to Class A standard and reallocated 9 Apr 43 as fighter base in exchange for Fowlmere. First occupied USAAF Sep 42. Officially transferred 8AF 6 Sep 43. Returned RAF 1 Nov 45. Built 1941. Originally grass surfaced. Developed 1942. Main contractor: John Laing & Son Ltd. Runways: concrete; 4800 ft (220), 3300 ft (160) and 3225 ft (280). A/c dispersals: 21 square pads, 4 large pans, 30 small pans and 16 steel mat. Hangars: 1 T2 and 9 blister. Camp: utility buildings for 1959 persons.

Stradishall Station B-9
Location: 10 miles NW Sudbury, Suffolk. Allocated 8AF as bomber base 4 June 42. Allocation rescinded early Aug 42. Never occupied by USAAF. Permanent RAF station with 3 hard runways.

Sudbury Station 174
Location: Between Acton and Gt Waldingfield, Suffolk. (2 miles N Sudbury.) Allocated 8AF as bomber base 10 Aug 42. First occupied USAAF Mar 44. Officially transferred 8AF 23 Mar 44. Transferred RAF 10 Oct 45. Built 1943. Runways: concrete; 6000 ft (250), 4200 ft (190) and 4980 ft 150). A/c dispersals: 50 loops and 1 pan. Hangars: 2 dispersed T2. Camp: utility buildings for 2972.

Tangmere Station 363
Location: 2½ miles E Chichester, Sussex. Allocated 8AF as fighter base 10 Aug 42. Allocation rescinded early Sep 42. Allocated as tactical fighter base 12 July 43 on lodger basis. Never occupied by 8AF. Permanent RAF fighter station with 2 hard runways.

Tarrant Rushton Station 453
Location: 4 miles E Blandford, Dorset. Allocated 8AF as transport or observation base 27 Aug 42. Transferred 9AF Oct 43. Never occupied by 8AF units. Built 1942–43. Runways: concrete; 6000 ft, 4200 ft and 4200 ft: 50 hardstandings; 4 T2 hangars and utility buildings for 3000 persons.

Thorpe Abbotts Station 139
Location: 1 mile NW Thorpe Abbotts village, Norfolk. (4½ miles E Diss.) Allocated 8AF as bomber base 4 June 42. First occupied 8AF June 43. Officially transferred 8AF 20 July 43. Transferred RAF 20 Dec 45. Built 1942. Main contractor: John Laing & Son. Runways: concrete; 6300 ft (099), 4200 ft (350) and 4200 ft (043). A/c dispersals: 36 pans with 15 loops added late in construction. Hangars: 2 dispersed T2. Camp: utility buildings for 2894 persons.

Thurleigh Station 111
Location: 2 miles NW Thurleigh, Bedfordshire. (6½ miles N Bedford.) Tentatively allocated USAAF as bomber base Nov 41. Confirmed May 42. First occupied USAAF Aug 42. Officially transferred 8AF 9 Dec 42 – first combat station transferred from RAF. Returned RAF 8 Dec 45. Built 1941. Main contractor: W & C French Ltd. Runways: concrete; originally 4800 ft, 3800 ft and 3300 ft, extended in 1942 to 6000 ft (054), 4200 ft (172) and 4200 ft (288). A/c dispersals: 36 pans with 14 loops, 2 large loops and 2 pans added during field extension. Hangars: 4 grouped T2. Camp: uility buildings for 2972.

Tibenham Station 124
Location: Between Tibenham and Tivitshall, Norfolk. (13½ miles SSW Norwich.) Allocated 8AF as bomber base 4 June 42. First occupied USAAF Nov 42. Officially transferred 8AF 4 Jan 44. Transferred RAF 25 June 45. Built 1942. Main contractor: W & C French Ltd. Runways: concrete; 6000 ft (211), 4200 ft (268) and 4200 ft (332). A/c dispersals: 36 pans with 17 loops added. Hangars: 2 dispersed T2. Camp: utility buildings for 2894.

Toome Station 236
Location: 1½ miles NW Toomebridge, Antrim, Northern Ireland. Tentatively allocated USAAF for an Air Support Command 28 Feb 42. Allocated 8AF as bomber training base 10 Aug 42. First occupied USAAF June 43. Officially transferred 8AF 26 July 43. Transferred RAF 7 Nov 44. Built 1942–43. Main contractor: Farrans Ltd. Runways: concrete; 5690 ft (270), 4170 ft (330) and 4150 ft (220). A/c dispersals: 30 pans and 50 fingers added for aircraft storage winter 1943–44. Hangars: 4 T2 in pairs. Camp: utility buildings for 2512 persons.

Turnhouse
Location: 5 miles W Edinburgh, Midlothian. Allocated 8AF as tactical fighter base for lodger units 12 July 43. Never occupied by 8AF units. Permanent RAF station with 3 hard runways.

Warmwell Station 454
Location: 4 miles E Dorchester, Dorset. Allocated 8AF as fighter base 10 Aug 42. Allocation rescinded early Sep 42. Allocated 9AF late 43. Never occupied by 8AF units. Grass airfield opened 1941.

Warton Station 582
Location: 7½ miles W Preston, Lancashire. Selected for USAAF depot Oct 41. Allocated as temporary transport base 11 June 42. First Occupied USAAF June 42. Officially transferred 8AF 17 July 43. Returned to RAF Nov 45. Built 1941–42. Runways: concrete; 5631 ft (080), 4182 ft (200) and 3960 ft (330). A/c dispersals: 50 loops. Hangars: 7 grouped specials with 2 more erected autumn 1944. Storage space 137,363 sq ft and 623,005 sq ft repair shops. Utility buildings for 15,902 persons. Much of construction by MacAlpine Co Ltd.

Wattisham Station 377
Location: Between Wattisham and Gt Bricett, Suffolk. (9 miles NW Ipswich.) Allocated 8AF as bomber base 4 June 42. Additionally allocated as airfield serving an advanced air depot 12 Oct 42. First occupied USAAF Sep 42. Officially transferred 8AF 8 May 43. Reallocated as fighter base 16 June 43. Transferred RAF 15 Dec 45. Built 1938. Main contractor: John Laing & Son Ltd. Work on bringing airfield to Class A standard halted June 43. Runways: 4200 ft (110) concrete, 6000 ft (060) with 4300 ft steel mat and rest concrete, 4200 ft (350) with 1050 ft concrete and rest sod. A/c dispersals: concrete, 39 loops and 19 pans. Hangars: 4 grouped C. Camp: permanent buildings for 2000. Additional sites with utility buildings. Hitcham depot Station 470 built on south side airfield 1943 with 17 loop standings and 4 T2 hangars.

Watton Station 376
Location: 2 miles E Watton, Norfolk. (11½ miles NE Thetford.) Allocated 8AF for development as bomber base 10 Aug 42. Additionally allocated to serve an air depot 12 Oct 42. Loaned to RAF winter 1942–43. Reallocated as fighter base 16 June 43 when development of grass airfields for bomber use abandoned. First occupied USAAF Aug 43. Officially transferred 8AF 4 Oct 43. Transferred RAF 15 Aug 45. Built 1939. Main contractor: John Laing & Son Ltd. Opened as grass airfield. Runway: single steel mat until July 44 when 899th Engineer Btn US Army laid 6000 ft (110) concrete. A/c dispersals: concrete; 12 pans and 41 loops laid 1943. Hangars: 4 grouped C. Camp: permanent buildings. Neaton air depot, Station 505, built on east side of airfield with 24 loop standings and 3 grouped T2 hangars. Additionally, 3 blister and 2 B1 hangars added on airfield. Additional camp sites to serve depot had utility buildings.

Welford Station 474
Location: 7 miles NW Newbury, Berkshire. Allocated 8AF as transport or observation base 10 Aug 42. Allocation rescined 27 Aug 42. Allocated summer 43 as transport base. Transferred 9AF. Never used by 8AF. Built: 1942–43. Runways: concrete; 6000 ft, 4200 ft and 4200 ft: 50 hardstandings and 2 T2 hangars.

Wellingore Station P-8
Location: 1½ miles S Wellingore village, Lincolnshire. (10½ miles S Lincoln.) Allocated 8AF as fighter station 4 June 42 – satellite Digby. Allocation rescinded Aug 42. Never occupied by 8AF. Grass airfield with blister hangars.

Wendling Station 118
Location: 2 miles N Wendling village, Norfolk. (4 miles WNW East Dereham.) Allocated 8AF as bomber base 4 June 42. First occupied USAAF Sep 43. Officially transferred 8AF 16 Sep 43. Transferred RAF 25 June 45. Built 1942. Main contractor: Taylor Woodrow Ltd. Runways: concrete; 6000 ft (010), 4200 ft (260) and 4200 ft (130). A/c dispersals: 25 pans with 26 loops added late in construction. Hangars: 2 dispersed T2. Camp: utility buildings for 2894 persons.

Westhampnett Station 352
Location: 1 mile NW Westhampnett, Sussex. (1½ miles NNE Chichester.) Allocated 8AF as fighter base 4 June 42. First occupied USAAF July 42. Reverted to RAF when US units departed Nov 42. Allocated 8AF for tactical fighter base 12 July 43. Transferred 9AF Oct 43. Opened 1940. Runways: sod; 3300 ft WNW–ESE, 3000 ft NE–SW and 4200 ft NW–SE. No lighting. A/c dispersals: 19 large pans and 32 small pens. Hangars: 1 T1 and 8 blister. Camp: utility buildings for 1700 persons.

Wittering Station 368
Location: Immediately NW Wittering, Northamptonshire. (3 miles SSE Stamford.) Allocated 8AF as fighter base 7 Sept 42. Confirmed 22 Sep 42 for joint RAF/8AF use. First occupied by 8AF units Aug 43 on lodger basis. Reverted to sole RAF usage Feb 44. Opened 1916. Runways: sod; 4350 ft NE–SW and 1350 ft E–W. A/c dispersals: 16 fighter pens. Hangars: 2 C, 1 GS and 1 over blister. Camp: permanent buildings for 3000 persons.

Wethersfield Station 170
Location: 2 miles NE Wethersfield village, Essex. (7 miles NNW Braintree.) Allocated 8AF as bomber base 10 Aug 42. Loaned RAF BC Dec 42–May 43. Transferred 9AF Oct 43. Never occupied by 8AF units. Built 1943–44. Main contractor: McDonald & Gibb. Runways: 6000 ft (290), 4200 ft (330) and 4200 ft (040). A/c dispersals: 49 loops and 1 pan. Hangars: 2 dispersed T2. Camp: utility buildings for 2894 persons.

Wormingford Station 159
Location: 1 mile SW Wormingford, Essex. (6 miles NW Colchester.) Allocated 8AF as bomber base 10 Aug 42. Loaned 9AF as fighter base Oct 43–Apr 44. Officially transferred USAAF 9 May 44. Transferred RAF 10 Oct 45. Built 1943. Main contractor: Richard Costain Ltd. Runways: concrete; 6000 ft (270), 4200 ft (230) and 4200 ft (330). A/c dispersals: 50 loops. Hangars: 2 dispersed T2. Camp: utility buildings for 2894.

Zeals Station 450
Location: 4 miles NNW Gillingham, Wiltshire. Allocated 8AF as fighter base 10 Aug 42. Allocation rescinded early Sep 42. Allocated 9AF late 1943. Never occupied by 8AF. Grass airfield.

Other Stations

8th Air Force stations other than airfields or air depots, excluding those of Services of Supply, Air Service Command, USSTAF, 9th Air Force or RAF which lodged 8th Air Force units.

Order of details: official name, station number, assignments and use.
Abbreviations: Btn – Battalions, Chem – Chemical, CSW – Combat Support Wing (truck transport), Ord – Ordnance, Qm – Quartermaster, RD – Replacement Depot (personnel)

Aldermaston Court, Berks. (476) VIII AFSC 1943, Qm and Transport depot
Bamber Bridge, Lancs. (569) VIII AFSC 8/42–1/44 to USSTAF. Ord, Qm depot
Barnham (Little Heath Side), Suffolk (517) VIII AFSC/BADA 1943 Chemical/bomb store
Barnhman (Warren Wood), Suffolk (587) VIII AFSC/BADA 12/42–1/44 to USSTAF. Ord depot – bombs
Belfast (Victoria Barracks), N.I. (232) VIII AFSC 1943. Engineer Btn
Brampton Grange, Hunts. (103) HQ 1BW/1AD 8/42–9/45
Braybrooke, Northants. (521) VIII AFSC/BADA 8/43–1/44. Ord. depot – bombs
Bristol, Glos. (473) VIII AFSC/BADA 1943 to USSTAF. CSW transport depot.
Chorley, Lancs. (591) VIII AFSC 8/42–1/44 to USSTAF. Qm depot and officer RD
Earsham, Norfolk (545) VIII AFSC/BADA 1943 to USSTAF. Ord depot – bombs
Egginton, Derby (564) VIII AFSC/BADA 1943 to USSTAF. CSW transport depot
Elveden Hall (Camp Blainey) Suffolk (116) Hq. 3BW/4BW/3AD 9/42–10/45
Groveley Wood, Wilts. (592) VIII AFSC 9/42–1/44 to USSTAF. Ord depot and 70 RD
High Wycombe (Camp Lynn), Bucks. (101) Hq VIII BC/8AF 2/42–6/45
Hurst Park, Surrey (508) VIII AFSC 1943 to USSTAF. Vehicle maintenance depot
Huyton, Lancs. (552) VIII AFSC/BADA 1943 to USSTAF. CSW transport depot
Kettering, Northants. (596) VIII AFSC 9/42–1/44 to USSTAF. Qm depot
Ketteringham Hall, Norfolk (147) Hq 2BD/2AD 12/43–6/45
Kircassock House, Lurgan, N.I. (231) Hq VIII AFCC 3/43–2/44
Leicester, Leicestershire (527) VIII AFSC/BADA 1943 to USSTAF. Qm stores
Lichfield Barracks, Staffs. (598) VIII AFSC 7/42–1/44 to USSTAF. Engineer Btn
Liverpool, Lancs. (513) BADA 1943 to USSTAF. Port Intransit Depot 1
Lords Bridge, Cambs. (599) VIII AFSC 8/42–1/44 to USSTAF. Chem depot – munitions
Lurgan, N.I. (350) VIII AFCC 1943. Support units

Maghull, Lancs. (577) VIII AFSC 1943 to USSTAF. Truck transport depot
Marks Hall, Essex (160) VIII BC/VIII ASC Wing Hq. 1/43–10/43 to 9AF
Melchbourne, Beds. (572) VIII AFSC/BADA 8/42–1/44 to USSTAF. Ord maintenance – bombs
Melton Mowbray, Leics. (520) VIII AFSC/BADA 7/43–1/44 to USSTAF. Ord and CSW transport
Milton Ernest, Beds. (506) VIII AFSC 2/43–6/45 Hq and support units
Old Catton (Camp Thomas) Norfolk (108) Hq 2BW/2BD 9/42–10/43
Poynton, Cheshire (571) VIII AFSC/BADA 7/42–1/44 to USSTAF. Qm supply depot
Riseley, Beds. (541) VIII AFSC/BADA 1943 to USSTAF. Qm depot
Romsey (Stanbridge Earls), Hants. (503) VIII AFSC 9/42–1/44 to USSTAF 70 RD Rest Home
Saffron Walden, Essex (370) Hq 65 FW 6/43–8/45
Sawston, Cambs. (371) Hq 66 FW 8/43–10/45
Shaftesbury (Combe House), Dorset (523) VIII AFSC 8/43–1/44 to USSTAF. 70 RD Rest Home
Sharnbrook, Beds. (583) VIII AFSC/BADA 8/42–1/44. Ord and chem depot – bombs
Smethwick, Staffs. (522) VIII AFSC/BADA 1943. Qm stores
Southport, Lancs. (524) VIII AFSC 1/43–1/44 to USSTAF. 70 RD Rest Home
St Mellons, Mon. (516) VIII AFSC/BADA 1943. Port Intransit Depot 4
Stone (Beatty Hall), Staffs. (518) VIII AFSC 9/42–1/44 to USSTAF. 70 RD repl. personnel
Stone (Duncan Hall), Staffs. (509) VIII AFSC 9/42–1/44 to USSTAF. 70 RD repl. personnel
Stone (Jefferson Hall), Staffs. (594) VIII AFSC 8/42–1/44 to USSTAF. 70 RD repl. personnel
Stowmarket, Suffolk (501) VIII AFSC 11/42–10/45. Truck transport depot
Sudbury (Constitution Hill), Suffolk (382) VIII AFSC/BADA 1943 to USSTAF. Qm support
Sudbury, Derbyshire. (158) VIII AFSC/BADA 1942–1/44 to USSTAF. Ord and Chem maintenance
Sunninghill Park, Ascot, Berks. (472) VIII ASC Hq 10/42–10/43 to 9AF
Teddington (Camp Griffiss), Middx. (586) VIII AFSC Hq. 2/43–1/44 to USSTAF
Thrapston, Northants. (584) VIII AFSC 12/42–10/45. Medical and Truck transport depot
Tostock, Suffolk (502) VIII AFSC/BADA 1943 to USSTAF, CSW transport
Walcot Hall, Northants. (372) Hq 67 FW 8/43–10/45
Wapley Common, Glos. (515) VIII AFSC/BADA 1943 to USSTAF. Port Intransit Depot 3
Wellingborough, Northants. (580) VIII AFSC/1BD 8/42–45. Qm support units
Williamstrip Park, Glos. (555) VIII AFSC/BADA 1943– to USSTAF. CSW transport
Wortley, Yorks. (581) VIII AFSC/BADA 7/43–1/44 to USSTAF. Ammun. depot and CSW trucks

Index

Eighth Air Force Personnel

Other Persons, Military and Civilian

Flying Groups

1FG 76, 116, 183
3PG 84
4FG 61, 71, 72, 76, 82, 83, 130, 132, 189, 191, 198, 203, 215–17, 220, 230, 233, 238, 249, 252
7FG 84, 85, 90, 99, 122, 187, 203, 204, 263
14FG 76, 183
20FG 75, 82, 83, 130, 184, 185, 187, 195, 197
25BG(R) 85, 88, 177, 182, 188, 199, 201, 202, 207, 215, 229
27ATG 139, 140, 210, 212, 216
29BG 255
30BG 255
31FG 75, 203, 209, 252
34BG 26, 36, 51, 130, 168, 171, 255
39BG 255
44BG 36, 47, 49, 118, 130, 164–7, 172, 175, 176
47BG 207
50FG 191, 195
52FG 75, 203, 209
55FG 63, 64, 75, 82, 83, 91, 92, 130, 184, 185, 187, 195, 197, 198, 218
56FG 71, 74, 77, 82, 83, 117, 130, 187, 190–3, 197, 220, 221, 230, 232, 243
60TCG 210
62TCG 210
64TCG 210
67RG 88, 122, 125, 126, 194, 203, 206, 207, 214, 258
68OG 209
78FG 72, 77, 82, 83, 130, 184, 191,

193, 197–9, 219, 232, 250, 253
81FG 209
82FG 184
91BG 28, 31, 36, 40, 49, 97, 130, 148, 155, 158, 160, 245, 248
92BG 25, 26, 36, 47, 48, 93, 118, 119, 130, 146, 148, 154, 155, 160, 228, 239, 251
93BG 11, 36, 37, 51, 119, 130, 157, 164–7, 170, 175, 176, 239, 247
94BG 9, 10, 15, 28, 36, 37, 93, 130, 148, 153, 158–60, 217, 218
95BG 36, 98, 130, 148, 153, 160, 225, 260
96BG 14, 36, 46, 49, 93, 97, 98, 109, 130, 148, 150, 153, 158, 160, 162, 163, 242
97BG 37, 38, 40, 118, 146, 148, 235
100BG 25, 36, 130, 148, 160, 163
301BG 146, 148
303BG 10, 20, 36, 130, 137, 146, 148, 151, 152, 155, 160, 164, 222, 223, 227, 244
305BG 23, 26, 36, 38, 40, 47–9, 93, 95, 130, 131, 148, 151, 160, 228, 239, 240
306BG 36, 93, 97, 130, 150, 152, 157, 160, 230, 228, 236, 239
310BG 205
315TCG 140, 210, 214
322BG 53, 55, 120, 177–80
323BG 55, 177, 179, 182, 249
339BG 83, 130, 195, 196, 198, 249
345BG 205
350FG 203, 209

351BG 30, 36, 40, 50, 130, 148, 160
352FG 72, 82, 83, 130, 190, 191, 195, 196
353FG 63, 64, 72–4, 78, 82, 83, 130, 191, 197, 198, 232, 243, 253
354FG 82, 195, 196
355FG 61, 72, 78, 82, 83, 91, 130, 190, 191, 195, 198, 218, 220, 238, 247
356FG 81, 82, 83, 130, 190, 191, 197, 216, 232, 237
357FG 82, 83, 130, 195, 197, 198, 238
358FG 82, 191, 195
359FG 82, 83, 130, 191, 195, 196
361FG 82, 83, 130, 191, 195, 196, 198, 207, 220, 238, 262
364FG 83, 91, 130, 185
379BG 16, 29, 31, 36, 120, 130, 147, 148, 155, 160, 244
381BG 36, 130, 148, 153, 158, 160, 225
384BG 36, 90, 130, 136, 148, 153, 155, 158, 160, 227, 245, 251
385BG 8, 12, 15, 29, 36, 91, 93, 130, 148, 152, 153, 160, 261
386BG 55, 177, 179, 181, 270
387BG 177, 179, 180, 206
388BG 36, 97, 102, 103, 130, 148, 160, 242
389BG 14, 36, 49, 130, 164, 167, 171, 172, 175, 176, 232
390BG 36, 130, 136, 148, 160, 226, 261, 273
392BG 12, 36, 46, 130, 168, 176
398BG 36, 130, 158, 249

401BG 30, 31, 36, 38, 91, 130, 240
434TCG 210
445BG 17, 28, 36, 97, 130, 168, 170, 171, 176
446BG 36, 51, 130, 168, 169, 176
447BG 36, 97, 130, 159, 215, 225
448BG 36, 40, 130, 168, 172, 176
452BG 14, 23, 36, 130
453BG 25, 36, 130, 168, 176
457BG 9, 23, 36, 130, 160
458BG 36, 100, 101, 130, 168, 176
466BG 36, 130, 168, 176
467BG 36, 100, 130, 168, 176
479ASG 47, 107, 165, 174, 176
479FG 75, 130, 185, 186, 197, 198
482BG 47, 48, 51, 52, 94, 114, 115, 130, 160, 162, 172, 173, 238, 241
486BG 26, 36, 51, 130, 168, 171
487BG 36, 97, 130, 159, 168, 224
489BG 36, 130, 168, 170, 176, 177
490BG 36, 130, 168, 262
491BG 36, 97, 130, 169, 176, 207
492BG 94, 106, 130, 169, 176, 202, 207, 235
493BG 36, 92, 130, 169, 262
495FTG 122, 123, 215
496FTG 122, 123
801BG(P) 106, 167, 175, 210
802RG(P) 85, 90, 115, 199, 201
2008TG(P) 140
2900CCRCG(B)(P) 120, 124
2901CCRCG(B)(P) 120, 124
2902CCRCG(B)(P) 120, 124
2906OTG(F)(P) 124
2915CCRCG(B)(P) 124

Flying Squadrons: Bomber

4BS 34
7BS 34
15BS 53, 56, 206
18BS 26, 34
36BS 34, 99, 106, 243
66BS 34, 39
67BS 34
68BS 34
322BS 34, 248
323BS 34
324BS 34, 39
325BS 34, 47
326BS 34, 119
327BS 34, 154, 155
328BS 34
329BS 34, 51, 167, 173
330BS 34
331BS 34
332BS 34
333BS 15, 34, 49
334BS 34
335BS 34
336BS 34
337BS 34
338BS 34
339BS 34
349BS 34
350BS 34
351BS 34
358BS 34
359BS 34, 152
360BS 34
364BS 34
365BS 34
366BS 34
367BS 34
368BS 34
369BS 34
391BS 34
401BS 34
406BS 34, 106, 160
407BS 25, 34
409BS 34
410BS 34
412BS 34

413BS 34, 46, 49, 162
418BS 34
422BS 34, 49, 93–5, 162, 239
427BS 34
449BS 179
450BS 178
451BS 179
452BS 178
455BS 55
456BS 182
506BS 34
508BS 34
509BS 34
510BS 34
511BS 34, 50
524BS 34
525BS 34
526BS 34
527BS 34
532BS 34
533BS 34
534BS 34
535BS 34
544BS 34
545BS 34
546BS 34
547BS 34
548BS 34
549BS 34, 153
550BS 34
551BS 34
557BS 180
560BS 34, 102
561BS 34
562BS 34
563BS 34
564BS 34, 49, 172
565BS 34
566BS 34
567BS 34
568BS 34
569BS 34
570BS 34
571BS 34
576BS 34

577BS 34
578BS 34
579BS 34
600BS 34
601BS 34
602BS 34
603BS 34
612BS 34
613BS 34
614BS 34
615BS 34
652BS(R) 34, 90, 164
653BS(R) 34, 91, 200, 201
654BS(R) 34, 88, 182, 188, 200–2
700BS 34
701BS 34
702BS 34
703BS 34
704BS 34
705BS 34, 168
706BS 34
707BS 34
708BS 34
709BS 34
710BS 34
711BS 34
712BS 34, 172
713BS 34
714BS 34
715BS 34
728BS 34
729BS 34
730BS 34
731BS 34
732BS 34
733BS 34
734BS 34
735BS 34
748BS 34
749BS 23, 34
750BS 34
751BS 34
752BS 34
753BS 34, 100, 101, 173
754BS 34

755BS 34
784BS 34
785BS 34
786BS 34
787BS 34
788BS 34, 106
789BS 34
790BS 34
791BS 34
803BS(P) 98, 99, 162, 173
812BS 34, 47, 48, 161
813BS 34, 47, 48, 161
814BS 34, 47, 48, 114, 172
819BS 47
832BS 34
833BS 34
834BS 34
835BS 34
836BS 34
837BS 34, 272
838BS 34
839BS 34
844BS 34
845BS 34
846BS 34
847BS 34
848BS 34
849BS 34
850BS 34, 106
851BS 34
852BS 34
853BS 34
854BS 34
855BS 34
856BS 34, 94, 106, 175, 210
857BS 34, 93, 94, 106
858BS 34, 94, 106
859BS 34, 106, 170
860BS 34, 169
861BS 34
862BS 34, 92
863BS 34
2911BS(P) 207

Flying Squadrons: Fighter

38FS 82, 83, 185
50FS 90
55FS 82, 83
61FS 60, 82, 83
62FS 82, 83, 221
63FS 67, 82, 83
77FS 82, 83
79FS 65, 82, 83
82FS 82, 83
83FS 82, 83
84FS 76, 82, 83
307FS 203
328FS 82, 83
334FS 82, 83
335FS 82, 83

336FS 82, 83, 203
338FS 82, 83
343FS 82, 83
350FS 65, 82, 83
351FS 69, 82, 83
352FS 60, 82, 83
353FS 82
354FS 82, 83
355FS 82
356FS 82
357FS 82, 83
358FS 82, 83
359FS 82, 83
360FS 82, 83
361FS 82, 83

362FS 65, 82, 83
363FS 82, 83
364FS 82, 83
365FS 82
366FS 82
367FS 82
368FS 82, 83
369FS 82, 83
370FS 82, 83
374FS 82, 83, 195
375FS 82, 83
376FS 82, 83
383FS 83
384FS 83
385FS 83

434FS 75, 83
435FS 65, 83
436FS 83
486FS 82
487FS 82, 196
503FS 83
504FS 83
505FS 83
551FTS 122, 124
552FTS 122, 124
554FTS 122, 124, 185, 186
555FTS 122–4, 196
2908SEFTS 122–4
2909SEFTS 122–4

Other Flying Squadrons

1R&TS 124
2R&TS 124
3R&TS 124, 178
4R&TS 121, 124
4ASS 106
5ERS 112, 193, 209
5PS 84, 186
8AF Hqs 211, 212
8RCS(P) 90

8RWS(H)(P) 89
8RWS(L)(P) 90
12RS 203
13PS 84, 186
14PS 85, 204
19RS 89
19ASS 48, 119
22ASS 106
86ATS 140

87ATS 140
109OS 122, 124
No.133 RAF 203
153OS/RS 88, 206, 207
No.214 RAF 98
No.226 RAF 206
310 Ferry S 140
311 Ferry S 140
312 Ferry S 140

320ATS 140
321ATS 140
325 Ferry S 140
No.517RAF 89
2903R&TS 124
2904R&TS 124
2905R&TS 120, 124

Special Flights

1BAT Flt (P) 215
1G&TT Flt 126, 128, 208

2G&TT Flt 126, 128, 207
3G&TT Flt 126, 128, 208, 216, 217

4G&TT Flt 126, 128, 206
2025G Flt 126, 128

2031G Flt 126, 128

Other Flying Units

1CCRC 121, 123, 215
1SF 91, 93
2CERC 121, 123
2SF 91, 93, 247
3CCRC 121, 123, 179, 182, 206

3SF 91, 93
4CCRC 121, 124
5CCRC 121, 124
6CCRC 121, 124
7CCRC 121, 123, 124

8CCRC 121, 123, 124
11CCRC 118, 124, 160
12CCRC 118, 120, 124
AFDU 116, 183, 194
Air Tech Section 116, 117, 194, 218,

220, 221
Op Eng Section 101, 117, 158, 162, 171, 186, 188, 228
MTS 117
8 Tech Ops 192, 197, 217

Support Groups

1SG 130
2ADG 132
5ADG 134
9ADG 134
10ADG 134
21ADG 134

31ADG 134
33SG 130, 131, 254
35ADG 134
40ADG 134
44ADG 134
46ADG 134

50SG 130
79SG 130
85SG 130
97SG 130
304SG 131
314SG 130

325SG 131
328SG 106
331SG 130
333SG 130
1030SCSG 132
1121QmSG 131

Support Squadrons

5MRRS 135
5SS 130
12WS 143
17SS 130
18WS 131, 143
21WS 143

41SS 130
45SS 130, 132
50FCS 81
52FCS 81
57FCS 82
84SS 130

315SS 130
332SS 129, 130
343SS 131
356SS 130
364SS 130
378SS 130

384SS 130
394SS 130
395SS 130
464SS 130
468SS 130
469SS 130

Depots

BAD 1 137, 174
1AAD 132
1SAD 101, 133, 134, 164
BAD 2 137, 139, 190, 209
2AAD 133

2SAD 133, 216
BAD 3 137
3AAD 133
3SAD 133, 134, 176, 177, 215
BAD 4 138

4SAD 187
5AAD 133
5SAD 135, 268
12RCD 142
14RCD 142

16RCD 142
70RD 142
440SD–480SD inclusive 130

Wings

1BW 46, 94, 118, 132, 133, 153, 212, 254, 255
1CBW 158
2BW 118, 132, 133, 212, 216, 255, 259
2CBW 213
3BW 119, 125, 132, 133, 177–9, 205,

255, 259–61
4BW 132, 133, 153, 177, 212, 255, 259–61
5BW 132, 255, 259
6FW 122
8RW(P) 85, 210
13CBW 273

14CBW 46, 98
20CBW 126
40CBW 98
41CBW 51, 153, 227
45CBW 20, 98
65FW 80–3, 111, 112, 193
66FW 82, 83

67FW 82, 83
96CBW 44
302ATW 170
325RW 85, 188, 210

Divisions

1BD/AD 25, 26, 37, 43, 49, 51, 91,
120, 123, 125, 156, 158, 162, 259

2BD/AD 36, 37, 43, 44, 48, 49, 51, 91,
109, 123, 125, 167, 170, 172, 175,

213, 216, 259

3BD/AD 37, 44, 46, 51, 52, 91, 98,

109, 123, 125, 156, 158, 160, 162,
170, 260, 262

Other Units

USN Sp Air Unit No 1 102
1 Photo Int Dr 84
1 Combat Camera Unit 89
8 Sta Defense Dt 131
No 43 Group RAF 136
54 MU RAF 199
71 MU RAF 199
No 100 Group RAF 94, 98, 188
102 Sta Defense Dt 132

410 Signal Co 82
809 Eng Bt 308
814 Eng Bt 311
818 Eng Bt 308
819 Eng Bt 305
820 Eng Bt 306
825 Eng Bt 312
826 Eng Bt 308
827 Eng Bt 307

830 Eng Bt 311
831 Eng Bt 306
833 Eng Bt 312
846 Eng Bt 305
850 Eng Bt 312
852 Eng Bt 253, 303
859 Eng Bt 307
861 Eng Bt 306
862 Eng Bt 312

876 Chem Co 131
983 MP Co 131
1085 Ord Co 132
1148 Qm Co 132
1631 Ord Co 132
1632 Ord Co 131
2016 Qm Truck Co 140

Airfields and Airfield Sites: United Kingdom
(County locations given for those not allocated to 8AF. Maps indicated by bold figures.)

Acklington 263, 305
Alconbury 47, 48, 49, 51, 92, 99, 107,
114, 115, 134, 139, 146, 154, 162,
167, 173, 200, 201, 225, 241, 257,
264, 270, **278**, 305
Aldermaston 123, 133, 210, 214, 258,
263, 305
Andrews Field 178, 250, 257, 304,
305
Appledram 305
Assington, Suffolk 257
Atcham 121, 122, 123, 124, 126, 128,
203, 209, 255, 258, 263, 305
Attlebridge 119, 177, 238, 257, 258,
266, **297**, 305
Ayr 255, 263, 305
Ballyhalbert 255, 258, 262, 305
Bassingbourn 35, 49, 92, 141, 145,
212, 215, 238, 257, 268, **277**, 305
Beaumont 257, 259, 305
Beccles 257, 261, 305
Benson, Oxon 84, 204
Bentwaters 261, 304, 305
Biggin Hill, Kent 263
Birch 257, 261, 305
Bircham Newton, Norfolk 111
Bishops Court 255, 259, 262, 305
Bodney 63, 82, 83, 257, 260, 261,
266, **288**, 305
Booker, Bucks 90
Boreham 123, 132, 257, 259, 263, 306
Boscombe Down, Wilts. 205
Bottisham 82, 83, 260, 261, 262, **293**,
306
Bovingdon 89, 101, 116, 117, 118,
119, 120, 121, 124, 146, 162, 166,
183, 185, 187, 192, 194, 203, 208,
211, 212, 213, 216, 217, 218, 223,
238, 255, 259, **282**, 306
Boxted 55, 56, 63, 66, 71, 82, 83, 112,
113, 160, 192, 193, 196, 254, 257,
261, 270, **300**, 306
Bradwell Bay, Essex 111
Broadwell, Glos. 258
Buckden, Hunts 257
Bulphan, Essex 257
Bungay 47, 205, 255, 257, 292, 306
Burnam, Essex 257
Burtonwood 90, 101, 106, 110, 116,
135, 137, 139, 140, 162, 167, 172,
175, 189, 200, 205, 238, 259, 263,
306
Bury St. Edmunds 9, 12, 15, 28, 35,
49, 132, 133, 178, 179, 207, 217,
223, 238, 257, 258, 261, **281**, 304,
306
Butley 257, 260, 261, 304, 306
Catterick 306
Chalgrove 123, 204, 258, 263, 306
Chedburgh 255, 306
Cheddington 90, 91, 99, 106, 118,
120, 121, 122, 124, 143, 200, 214,
255, 263, **273**, 306

Chelveston 26, 93, 95, 210, 238, 255,
257, 259, 268, **276**, 306
Chilbolton 258, 306
Chipping Ongar 123, 126, 206, 257,
259, 306
Church Fenton 306
Church Stanton 306
Cluntoe 121, 123, 124, 208, 238, 255,
259, 262, 263, 306
Cold Norton 257, 259, 306
Collyweston 258, 261, 306
Coltishall 258, 263, 306
Cranfield, Beds 263
Cricklade, Wilts 258
Crowfield 257, 259, 306
Davidstow Moor, Cornwall 263
Debach 92, 257, 262, **302**, 307
Debden 64, 80, 82, 83, 111, 203, 258,
260, 261, 268, **278**, 307
Deenethorpe 238, 257, **290**, 307
Defford, Worcs 48, 172
Deopham Green 238, 257, 261, **294**,
307
Desborough 255, 307
Digby 255, 307
Docking, Norfolk 126
Downham Market, Norfolk 145
Down Ampney, Glos 258
Drem 307
Dunkeswell, Devon 102, 107, 174,
263, 305
Duxford 63, 82, 83, 116, 130, 194,
203, 209, 253, 258, 260, 261, 268,
280, 307
Earls Colne 55, 255, 257, 258, 307
East Wretham 82, 83, 126, 128, 255,
257, 261, **289**, 307
Eglinton 121, 255, 262, 307
Exeter 112, 263, 307
Fairford, Glos 258
Fersfield 102, 103, 163, 261, 304, 307
Finedon 257, 259, 307
Ford 263, 307
Foulsham 99, 255, 307
Fowlmere 83, 258, 259, 260, 261,
295, 308
Framlingham 35, 238, 257, 260, 261,
266, 273, **283**, 308
Fressingfield, Suffolk 257
Glatton 9, 192, 205, 257, **293**, 308
Gosfield 257, 261, 308
Goxhill 91, 121, 122, 123, 124, 126,
128, 130, 184, 203, 207, 209, 214,
255, 258, 260, 261, 263, 308
Grafton Underwood 51, 251, 255,
257, **274**, 308
Great Ashfield 12, 248, 254, 257, 259,
261, **284**, 308
Great Dunmow 257, 259, 261, 308
Great Saling 257, 304, 308
Great Sampford 258, 261, 308
Greencastle 121, 123, 124, 126, 128,
139, 208, 255, 259, 262, 263, 308

Greenham Common 133, 258, 308
Grove 153, 258, 308
Hadstock 257, 304, 310
Halesworth 82, 92, 113, 115, 126,
128, 160, 208, 209, 257, 260, 261,
263, **287**, 304, 308
Hamstead Norris 258, 308
Hardwick 33, 35, 37, 51, 205, 255,
257, **279**, 308
Harrington 96, 106, 207, 208, 238,
253, 263, **303**, 308
Hatfield, Herts 200
Hendon, Middx 140
Hepworth 257, 260, 261, 304, 312
Heston, Middx 140
Hethel 11, 14, 35, 119, 212, 213, 255,
257, **285**, 308
Hibaldstow 255, 309
High Ercall 121, 255, 258, 309
High Roding 257, 259, 309
Honington 83, 91, 99, 101, 116, 132,
133, 134, 140, 147, 160, 162, 177,
178, 205, 207, 212, 255, 257, 259,
260, 261, 263, **302**, 309
Horham 207, 257, 260, 261, **281**, 309
Hornchurch, Essex 111
Horsham St Faith 100, 101, 255, 257,
258, 261, 268, **295**, 309
Hurn, Hants 263
Hutton Cranswick 309
Ibsley 309
Ingatestone 257, 259, 309
Ipswich 309
Isle Abbotts 258, 309
Keevil 206, 210, 258, 309
Kenley, Surrey 263
Kimbolton 51, 120, 133, 144, 225,
255, 257, **277**, 309
King's Cliffe 65, 82, 83, 214, 255, 258,
261, **280**, 309
Kinloss, Moray 263
Kirkistown 255, 258, 262, 309
Kirton-in-Lindsey 121, 183, 255, 258,
260, 309
Knettishall 102, 105, 205, 255, 257,
284, 309
Langford Lodge 74, 116, 121, 135,
137, 139, 140, 150, 166, 178, 184,
185, 186, 187, 210, 218, 255, 259,
262, 263, 310
Langham, Norfolk 304
Larkhill, Wilts 145
Lasham, Hants 263
Lavenham 95, 257, 259, 272, **299**,
310
Leiston 65, 82, 83, 111, 126, 207, 258,
260, 261, 265, **290**, 310
Leuchars, Fife 145
Little Clacton, Essex 257
Little Snoring, Norfolk 263
Little Staughton 116, 132, 133, 134,
140, 254, 255, 257, 259, 263, 264,
310

Little Walden 83, 126, 257, 262, **303**,
304, 310
Llanbedr, Merioneth 73, 122, 125,
126
Long Kesh 118, 255, 259, 262, 310
Lossiemouth, Moray 263
Ludham 258, 260, 261, 310
Machrihanish, Kintyre 255
Macmerry 310
Maghaberry 121, 124, 140, 255, 258,
262, 310
Maidenhead, Berks 259
Maldon 257, 259, 310
Market Harborough 310
Matching 257, 310
Matlask 258, 260, 261, 310
Maydown 255, 258, 259, 262, 310
Market Harborough 255, 310
Martlesham Heath 71, 82, 83, 111,
258, 261, 265, 266, 267, 268, **289**,
310
Membury 122, 123, 194, 203, 206,
207, 210, 258, 263, 310
Mendlesham 171, 257, 259, **301**, 310
Merryfield 309
Merston 310
Metfield 60, 63, 64, 69, 72, 74, 82,
225, 253, 257, 258, 260, 261, 262,
287, 311
Middle Wallop 311
Molesworth 17, 35, 51, 225, 253, 255,
257, 263, 268, **275**, 311
Mount Farm 84, 85, 86, 87, 88, 90, 99,
122, 182, 199, 203, 204, 205, 210,
304, 311
Mullaghmore 121, 124, 139, 259, 262,
311
Newmarket 51
Newtownards 258, 262, 311
North Pickenham 257, 259, 261, 262,
300, 311
North Weald, Essex 153
Nuthampstead 15, 63, 64, 82, 90,
219, 257, 261, 269, **286**, 311
Nutts Corner 255, 259, 262, 311
Oakley, Oxon 118
Old Buckenham 257, **294**, 311
Oulton, Norfolk 98, 162, 242, 263
Perranporth 311
Podington 47, 84, 186, 255, 257, **275**,
311
Polebrook 255, 257, 268, **274**, 311
Portreath 263, 311
Predannack, Cornwall 263
Prestwick, Ayrshire 138, 145, 146
Rackheath 100, 257, 258, **296**, 311
Ramsbury 258, 311
Rattlesden 119, 225, 255, 257, 258,
291, 311
Raydon 65, 83, 221, 257, 261, **297**, 312
Renfrew, Renfrewshire 140, 196
Ridgewell 132, 225, 238, 255, 257,
259, 264, 270, **286**, 312

Place Names, UK

(Excluding location names in airfields listing, pages 305–13)

Place Names: Continental Europe and USA

Individual Aircraft Names
Nickname, serial number, code letters, squadron and group. Identities in Tables are not included

Annie Freeze, B-17F 41-24500, 2CCRC 120

Beast of Bourbon, B-24H 42-50385, R4:H, 36BS 99
Beautiful Dope, P-51K 44-11193, KH:Y, 350FS/353FG 198
Birmingham Blitzkrieg, B-17E 41-9100, 525BS/379BG 147
Blind Date, B-17F 42-30195, E, 560BS/388BG 148
Blood N'Guts, B-17G 42-107078, N7:U, 603BS/308BG 33
Boomerang, B-17E 41-9148, 92BG 251
BTO, B-24J 44-40072, 8R:B, 846BS/489BG 177
Butch II, P-47D 42-26459, SX:B, 352FS/353FG 191

Cincinatti Queen, B-17F 42-30715, CC:Y, 569BS/390BG 148

Daisy June IV, B-17F 42-30369, 339BS/96BG 150
Dixie Demo, B-17E 41-9103, 414BS/97BG 147

Eileen, P-47, 56FG 71
El Capitan, B-26B 41-31718, KS:O, 557BS/387BG 180
El Lobo, B-17G 42-32101, F, 749BS/457BG 23
Evelyn, the Duchess, B-24D 41-24147, A, 330BS/93BG 33

Fighting Cock, B-17F 42-3397, H, 548BS/385BG 93
Flak Alley Lil', B-17F 42-3181, JJ:L, 422BS 122
Flying Jeanie III, P-51B 42-106944, E9:A, 376FS/361FG 220
Friday the 13th, B-17G 42-3537, XM:B, 332BS/94BG 157

Green Hornet, B-17F 41-24608, BN:S, 359BS/303BG 10

Hairless Joe, B-24J 44-40437, E, 860BS/493BG 169
Hap Hazard, B-24H 42-7580, OES 171
Hard To Get, B-17G 42-39788, QE:O, 331BS/94BG 28
Heidi Ho, B-17E 41-9017, 92BG 146
Hell's Angels, B-17F 41-24577, VK:D, 359BS/303BG 151
Hell's A Poppin', B-26B 41-31614, YA:X, 555BS/386BG 55
Hellza Poppin', P-47C 41-6361, HL:C, 83FS/78FG 129

Lady Luck, B-26C 41-34947, RU:K, 554BS/386BG 181
Lady Susie II, B-17F 42-5912, 385BG 29
Let 'Er Rip, B-24M 44-50548, 2U:J, 785BS/466BG 170
Liberty Lad, B-24D, 41-23754, U, 409BS/93BG 167
Lil' Jeanne, DB-7 AX922 206

Martha II, B-17F 42-29761, VP:W, 533BS/381BG 149
Mary V, B-24B 41-17921, ER:C, 450BS/322BG 53
Miss Mickey Finn, B-17F 42-30656, J6:W, 406BS 96, 148
Monty, B-24H 41-29461, H8:B, 835BS/486BG 131
Mr 5 by 5, B-24D 41-24234, U, 506BS/44BG 165
Mugwump, B-17F 42-30066, X, 388BG 163

Nancy V, P-51D 62
Naughty Nordie, P-51D 44-72377, PI:V, 360FS/356FG 71

Pauline, P-51D 44-72437, 6N:C, 505FS/339FG 197
Peep Sight, B-24H 42-7535, 3SAD 176
Pistol Packin' Mama, B-17G 42-39782, LF:M, 526BS/379BG 16
Prowler, B-24J 42-110171, Q2:X, 790BS/467BG 134

Ragin Red II, B-17F 42-30298, FR:M, 525BS/379BG 31
Ready N'Able, B-24H 42-95221, R4:A, 36BS 174
Round Trip Ticket III, B-17F 42-30827, O. 549BS/385BG 153

Satan's Workshop, B-17F 42-29931, PU:L, 360BS/303BG 222

Sea Swoose, B-24C 41-34723, YU:B, 455BS/323BG 55
Shack Bunny, B-17F 42-5913, Q, 551BS/385BG 93
Shack Time, B-24J 44-0275, J4:L, 753BS/458BG 100
Silver Queen, B-17F 42-29780, 3BD Hq 160
Sis, P-47D 42-8602, YJ:E, 351FS/353FG 74
Six Knights In a Bar Room, B-17F 42-30353, 388BG 102
SNAFU, B-24D 40-2354, 44BG 165
Stella, B-17F 42-29651 136
Stump Jumper, B-17F 42-30237, WA:V, 524BS/379BG 29, 131

The Berlin Sleeper, B-17E 41-9042, 342BS/97BG 235
The Chiefton, B-24H 42-51169, 577BS/392BG 242
Thundermug, B-17G 42-38205, WF:K, 364BS/305BG 26
Tugboat Annie, B-17E 41-9020, 303BG 160

Virginia, P-47D 42-22763, LM:B, 62FS/56FG 191

Wiskey Jingles, B-24J 42-51114, F8:J, 733BS/453BG 25

Yankee Doodle, B-17E 41-9023, 414BS/97BG 251